CONTINENTALIZING CANADA:
THE POLITICS AND LEGACY
OF THE MACDONALD ROYAL COMMISSION

Studies in Comparative Political Economy and Public Policy

Editors: MICHAEL HOWLETT, DAVID LAYCOCK, STEPHEN McBRIDE, Simon Fraser University

Studies in Comparative Political Economy and Public Policy is designed to showcase innovative approaches to political economy and public policy from a comparative perspective. While originating in Canada, the series will provide attractive offerings to a wide international audience, featuring studies with local, subnational, cross-national, and international empirical bases and theoretical frameworks.

Editorial Advisory Board

For a list of books published in the series, see p. 473.

Continentalizing Canada

The Politics and Legacy of the
Macdonald Royal Commission

GREGORY J. INWOOD

UNIVERSITY OF TORONTO PRESS
Toronto Buffalo London

© University of Toronto Press Incorporated 2005
Toronto Buffalo London
Printed in Canada

ISBN 0-8020-8729-9

Printed on acid-free paper

Library and Archives Canada Cataloguing in Publication

Inwood, Gregory J.
    Continentalizing Canada : the politics and legacy of the
Macdonald Royal Commission / Gregory J. Inwood.

    (Studies in comparative political economy and public policy)
    Includes bibliographical references and index.
    ISBN 0-8020-8729-9

    1. Royal Commission on the Economic Union and Development
Prospects for Canada.   2. Canada – Economic conditions – 1971–1991.
3. Canada – Economic policy – 1971–1991.   I. Title.   II. Series.

HF1766.I59 2005   354.' 0971   C2004-904176-2

This work has been supported in part by a grant from Ryerson University.

This book has been published with the help of a grant from the Canadian
Federation for the Humanities and Social Sciences, through the Aid to
Scholarly Publications Programme, using funds provided by the Social
Sciences and Humanities Research Council of Canada.

University of Toronto Press acknowledges the financial assistance to its
publishing program of the Canada Council and the Ontario Arts Council.

University of Toronto Press acknowledges the financial support for its
publishing activities of the Government of Canada through the Book
Publishing Industry Development Program (BPIDP).

To Tish, Alison, and Matthew

Contents

Tables and Figures

Figures

Acknowledgments

Writing a book is a collective act, notwithstanding the appearance of a single name on the cover. While I readily acknowledge responsibility for any and all of the deficiencies of this study, it has nonetheless benefited from the advice, guidance, and support of a number of people who have assisted in various ways in its development and writing. To all of them, I owe a deep debt of gratitude.

As the only full-length, in-depth examination of politics within the Macdonald Royal Commission (and indeed one of the only full-length studies of the politics of *any* royal commission in Canada), this book benefitted from the wisdom and insights of Stephen Clarkson, who deserves special commendation for a number of reasons. His writing and teaching on Canadian nationalism and political economy ignited a spark of intellectual interest in me. And it was his suggestion that someone really ought to undertake a study of the Macdonald Royal Commission and its recommendation for free trade that got me started on this path in the first place. His pragmatic advice and intellectual contributions to my underdeveloped ideas, always delivered with a combination of good humour and common sense, have been invaluable. Sylvia Bashevkin and David Wolfe were most generous with their comments on and suggestions for an earlier incarnation of this study, and the resultant book is much the better for their input. Thanks as well are due to Mel Watkins, Evert Linquist, and Jean Kirk Laux for their insights, questions, and comments, and to the editors of Studies in Comparative Political Economy, Stephen McBride, Michael Howlett, and David Laycock, for agreeing that this topic deserved a full-length scholarly treatment. I also thank the anonymous referees who reviewed the manuscript and provided several useful suggestions.

In addition, I would especially like to acknowledge the many individuals from both within and outside the Macdonald Royal Commission who gave so generously of their time in interviews for this book. Their revelations about the internal workings of this important inquiry provide the real story here, and the book would simply be deficient without their input.

The editorial team at University of Toronto Press has been most helpful and accommodating. Special thanks are due to Virgil Duff and Anne Laughlin. Allyson May did a wonderful job copy-editing the manuscript.

I am grateful for financial assistance for the publication of this book in the form of a grant from the Humanities and Social Sciences Federation of Canada, using funds provided by the Social Sciences and Humanities Research Council of Canada.

Finally, I would like to thank my partner, Tish O'Reilly, who renewed my enthusiasm for this project when it was waning, and who carefully and conscientiously read the manuscript from beginning to end. Apart from her intellectual contributions to this book in its final stages, which vastly improved it, she has been an incredible source of strength and love throughout the entire journey.

CONTINENTALIZING CANADA

Introduction

The Canadian journey down the road to free trade ... began with one Macdonald, Conservative Prime Minister Sir John A. and his 1879 National Policy when tariffs became the chief instrument of economic policy. The end of the road was marked by another Macdonald, a might-have-been Liberal prime minister whose royal commission set the stage for the final dismantling of the National Policy.[1]

Royal commissions are as Canadian an institution as one can imagine. Over 450 of these inquiries have been struck since Confederation on virtually every subject imaginable. Many commission reports languish in obscurity, collecting dust on the shelves of the Parliamentary Library, but every once in a while, broad-based programmatic royal commissions have profoundly influenced the political landscape and set the parameters of the policy agenda for generations of Canadians.[2] Yet the politics and legacy of these important idea-generating bodies are vastly understudied. Few detailed analyses exist of the internal machinations of royal commissions and their impact on Canadian society.

This book partly remedies this shortcoming by critically exploring the politics and legacy of one of the most influential and important royal commissions in Canadian history, the Royal Commission on the Economic Union and Development Prospects for Canada (the Macdonald Commission, 1985).[3] At the time of its inception, the Macdonald Commission was the largest, most expensive, most far-reaching inquiry in Canadian history. Though saddled with an impossible title and an absurdly broad mandate, launched ignominiously and prematurely by a leak to the media, and greeted with scepticism as a hobby horse for its chairperson's political ambitions, it nonetheless provided an institutional forum for contending ideas and interests. This book critically assesses the ideas, interests, and institutions reflected in the 'mirror' of the commission, and in particular those which influenced its signature recommendation that Canada enter into a free trade agreement with the United States. Such an examination allows a greater understanding of the genesis of continental free trade while providing a unique glimpse into the mysteries of how a major royal commission operates and the way in which it can contribute to a significant change in public policy. The period immediately preceding Canada's move to free trade with the United States is thus scrutinized, rather than the details of the 1988 Free Trade Agreement (FTA), or the great national political debate leading to the adoption of that deal[4] and its successor, the North American Free Trade Agreement.[5] The book examines the key programmatic role of the Macdonald Commission in Canada's momentous change of course,[6] facilitating as it did a transformative moment in the trajectory of Canadian economic development policy. The written submissions made to the commission by organized interests, its research program, its internal bureaucratic dynamic, and its final Report supplanted for a time the larger set of regular or traditional institutions of the Canadian political economy through which ideas and interests are normally reflected.

Embracing free trade represented a historical change of direction for Canada. How such a fundamental reorientation in policy came about, – that is, how periods of policy upheaval are transformed into broad consensus around new policies – is a central question of this book. The proposed answer is that change can be at least partly accounted for by examining the interplay of ideas, institutions, and interests in the Canadian political economy in relation to the main contending economic development strategies that have long vied for primacy in this country.[7] One strategy, *nationalist* in outlook, seeks to use state intervention to foster Canada's development as an autonomous nation state, and has been based since the Second World War on left-Keynesian theoretical assumptions. These ideas found their state-administrative manifestation in the Ottawa mandarinate which dominated the construction of the Keynesian welfare state. Academically, this approach has found a home in the field of political economy. The other strategy, *continentalist* in orientation, seeks greater economic integration with the United States and is based on a free market, non-interventionist strategy. These ideas found their bureaucratic home primarily within the halls of the finance department and functional ministries whose mandates largely revolved around industrial-business interests in Canada. Academically, this perspective is closely associated with mainstream liberal economics. Representatives of these two strategies engaged in a struggle to impose their views and ideological prescriptions through the Macdonald Commission and thereby influence the Canadian state to adopt a particular set of economic development strategies.

The two views, in turn, are linked to two broader ideologies, *democratic socialism* and *neoconservatism*. This book draws an explicit link between nationalism and democratic socialism; it also reveals a connection between continentalism and neoconservatism, and argues that the adoption of free trade following from the recommendation of the Macdonald Commission marks the start of a new era in national policy and economic development strategies for Canada. As Bradford argues, 'our knowledge is limited of the when, who, how and why of "era-defining" breakthroughs in policy discourse that redefine the terms for national policy practice.'[8] An examination of the politics and legacy of the Macdonald Commission, the role of key actors therein, the interests and institutions which sought to influence it, and the ideas both reflected in it and refracted from it makes it clear that this important inquiry brought the intellectual rationales for contending paradigmatic views into sharp relief. The commission is thus an invaluable source for shedding light on the content and discourses of nationalism and continentalism, and for explaining the fundamental reorientation in national economic policy making represented by continental free trade. It also allows for a greater understanding of the contribution of the commission to that transformative moment which intensified the process of 'continentalizing Canada.'

The underlying assumptions of this book are threefold: first, 'political ideology is a fundamental of politics; it is a guiding, supporting and restraining factor in the political behaviour of individuals, groups and nations,'[9] and therefore deserves careful scrutiny and analysis; second, detailed analysis of some royal commissions, as sites of policy development, can increase our understanding of the contours of Canadian public policy,[10] particularly in transformative moments, when other, 'standard' institutions are seen to be inadequate; and third, the role of interests – both state and societal – in policy formulation needs to be elucidated more clearly.[11] To this end, my analysis of the politics and legacy of the Macdonald Commission centres on an examination of nationalism and continentalism as the main ideologies supported by particular sets of institutions and interests competing over economic development strategies for the Canadian political economy.

The traditional liberal basis of Canadian ideology was effectively transformed in the period under review. Ideological positions increasingly
polarized between social democratic nationalism and neoconservative
continentalism. The Macdonald Commission reflected these developments in action, as an examination of its four major components through
a combination of content analysis, a survey of relevant literature, interviews with key commission actors, and archival research reveals. Ideological attitudes and beliefs of key societal and state institutions and interests
are explored through five economic development strategies: government
intervention; regional economic development; foreign direct investment;
industrial policy; and trade policy.

The analysis of the first component of the commission, its public consultations, is undertaken by constructing a content analysis of public submissions to the commission. This discloses a polarization within Canadian
society, with organized labour and the popular sector adopting a state-
centred nationalist social democratic position, and a significant (though
not unanimous) segment of the business community adopting a market-
oriented, continentalist, neoconservative one. It also reveals that, notwithstanding a majority of public submissions supporting nationalist social
democratic positions, the commission adopted the opposite ideological
stance.

The second component of the inquiry, the largest social science
research program ever launched in Canada, is critically examined in light
of the literature on social science knowledge utilization and through a
series of interviews with key commission researchers.[12] Surprisingly, the
seventy-two-volume output of the research program was largely ignored
by the commission, mainly due to its sheer volume, but owing in part to
a certain anti-intellectualism among many of the commissioners. This is
true except in one vital area – free trade. The domination of mainstream
economics within the research tilted the findings of the commission in
the direction of neoconservative continentalism. Virtually no nationalists
or dissentient social scientists were among the nearly three hundred
researchers hired for the commission, although a pair of 'reluctant
nationalists' were conscripted to provide counterarguments to the dominant view emerging from the economics research. The potential wealth
of ideas in this segment of the commission was severely compromised by
watered-down nationalist arguments.

The third component of the commission, the oligarchical 'policy
group,' is assessed through interviews and archival research. It played a
vital role in ensuring that a particular ideological position was privileged

within the commission's deliberations. This group essentially took control of the commission in the period leading up to the writing of the final *Report* and steered it in a neoconservative continentalist direction over the objections of several commissioners and some researchers, ignoring as well the majority of the written public submissions.

Finally, this book examines the roles and actions of the thirteen commissioners, again through interviews. The chairperson, an avowed Walter Gordon Liberal in his early political career and Cabinet minister during the Trudeau government's most nationalist turn in office, is shown to have played a key role as the drama unfolded. The other commissioners remained relatively insignificant actors. Donald Macdonald's conversion to neoconservative continentalism was vital to the commission's outcome, as he pre-empted the findings of the commission by advocating a 'leap of faith' into free trade well before all the evidence had been heard.

In surveying these components of the commission, this book provides a unique examination of internal royal commission politics. Overall, it reveals that the Macdonald Commission reflected the disharmony in Canadian political discourse. The post-war Keynesian consensus, shattered after a series of successive crises in the 1970s, had not been reconstructed and was in a state of disarray in the early 1980s. Evidence from the commission indicates that the social democratic nationalist economic development strategies which shaped that consensus had not been entirely abandoned or discredited. Nonetheless, a contrary view was emerging based in mainstream economic theorizing in search of a new set of neoconservative continentalist strategies. The post-war breakdown in consensus concerning Canadian economic development strategies had not been replaced by a new conventional wisdom, despite the Macdonald Commission's attempt to claim otherwise. Rather, Canadian society was marked by sharp ideological polarization around the concepts of nationalism coupled with social democracy, and continentalism coupled with neoconservatism. Thus, the Macdonald Commission served as the site of a struggle between advocates of the crumbling nationalist mode of politics and proponents of a more continentalist economic regime.

Explaining Transformative Moments: A Framework for Analysis

How do we explain those transformative moments when new ideas seek to supplant old ones in promoting innovative public policy choices? Historically, conflicts within Canadian society over strategies for economic development reveal that there are periods when a new policy approach emerges and comes to constitute a dominant paradigm or a widely recognized theory that defines a problem and its solutions. Certain problems that the community acknowledges will receive attention, while others, including many that had previously been addressed, are rejected.[13] The new approach spawns a series of policy choices and changes, some of which may be profound and far-reaching in their impact and represent a radical departure from 'conventional' practice. The new approach reigns for a time – sometimes for generations – but eventually its limitations are revealed at which time another alternative conceptual framework begins to emerge, and the process repeats itself.

Ideas, though they exist in a dynamic relationship with institutions and interests, are seen here as the driving force behind many transformative moments in public policy. Hall argues: 'ideas are generally acknowledged to have an influence over policy making. Even those who seek to expose the bare conflicts of interests hidden behind political rhetoric or historical nostalgia admit that ideas play an important role in affairs of state. But that role is not easily described. Any attempt to specify the conditions under which ideas acquire political influence inevitably teeters on the brink of reductionism, while the failure to make such an attempt leaves a large lacuna at the centre of our understanding of public policy.'[14] Change occurs – sometimes referred to as a paradigm shift – when significant social and economic disruption reveals the inadequacy of existing policy. It is in these moments that ideational challenges can most successfully be mounted to the roles of governments and major ideas supporting their policies. As Hall suggests also, 'it generally takes a theory to kill a theory ...'[15]

Keynesianism became the dominant theory in the post-war years as the earlier brand of economic orthodoxy had no acceptable answers to the Great Depression. But it was discredited during the crises in capitalism which arose in the 1970s: 'When explosive inflation, massive and growing unemployment and chilling world indebtedness burst open the postwar prosperity bubble, Keynesianism itself fell into rapid disrepute. In the mid-1970s, many economists and business commentators blamed the economic crisis on erroneous government policy, which to them meant Keynesian economic policy. New doctrines like monetarism and supply-side economics and post-Keynesian economics began to surface and captured the attention of government policy makers.'[16] If a hegemonic set of ideas exists, competing meaning systems make little headway. But as contradictions intensify, the previously hegemonic ideas are no longer able to account for prevailing conditions or emerging crises.

Social actors then adopt competing meaning systems that make better sense of the new situation. Changes in material conditions in Canada (the ongoing crises in capitalism since the 1970s, and particularly the depression of 1981–2), raised serious doubts about the Keynesian formula – but how did a new set of ideas arise to replace it?

Changing conditions, particularly in periods of crisis, provoke conflict between social actors who mount arguments in the interest of preserving and promoting, or challenging and replacing, the prevailing political and economic reality. Ideological conflict is the motor of change in this process, as arguments swirl around within the political discourse. As Thompson argues, a society cannot exist without a representation of its unity, but this unity is constantly under threat. Discourse is used to stave off these threats while maintaining the illusion of an essence of society.[17] In this process, conflict between social actors takes many forms and occurs in many sites. Such conflict was clearly evident in the Macdonald Commission.

An examination of the mode of ideological struggle helps us to make sense of the radical transformation in Canada from the pro-state, interventionist, Keynesian position of most of the post-war years to the anti–state, pro-free market, deregulationist, neoclassical liberal economics position of the Mulroney years, the climax and consolidation of which was the Free Trade Agreement (FTA). This transformation was rooted in, among other things: the depression of 1981–2 and the general crisis of capitalism; the emergence of the deficit and debt and ensuing fiscal crisis; the liberalization of world trade and the pressures of globalization; the related acceleration of technological change; the rise of the new right in Britain and the United States; the decline of American hegemony and the rise of a protectionist regime in the United States; the emergence of new social actors within Canada, such as women's groups, seniors, and environmentalists, accompanied by a new discourse of rights-based entitlements arising out of the politics of the Charter of Rights and Freedoms; the persistence of regional disparities in Atlantic Canada coupled with the continuing alienation of the 'new West'; and the general constitutional crisis concerning Quebec's place in Confederation.

In contemporary discourse, the neoconservative continentalist paradigm in Canada includes a commitment to free trade and concepts such as minimal state intervention, privatization, deregulation, and an aversion to the idea of an industrial strategy. This is the language of neoclassical liberal economics and its political bedfellow, neoconservative politics. The antithesis of this position can be found in social democratic nationalism in Canada, whose advocates promote a positive, interventionist state up to and including nationalization of the economy, an industrial strategy, and regulation coupled with state-sponsored social services. They also promote a multilateral trading strategy and a role for Canada in international institutions like the United Nations as counterbalancing forces to bilateral relations with the United States. They employ the discourse of Keynesianism and its political bedfellow, moderate democratic socialism.[18] These are, of course, short-hand categorizations of positions which often demonstrate a complexity and richness which belie such simplifications. But taken as *ideal types*, these definitions are useful tools with which to capture the dynamic of ideology as it developed, and its contribution to an official embrace of integration between Canada and the United States which reversed the formal stance taken by Canadian political leadership for most of the previous one hundred years of Canadian history.

Ideological Struggle and the Role of Royal Commissions

Transformative moments arising out of ideological struggle arguably have certain *requisites* which can sometimes be found in royal commissions. These requisites are: *political viability, economic viability,* and *political and bureaucratic leadership*.[19] Political viability requires support of significant actors who can help deliver electoral success to the policy's political supporters. Economic viability refers to the ability to address serious economic problems better than existing policies, often with the imprimatur of the research community. Political and bureaucratic leadership refers to the legal and political authority of state officials and their resulting institutional capacity to sway decision makers to accept their preferred course of action.

Looking into the mirror of the Macdonald Commission, the struggle to attain political viability could be seen to a large extent through the public consultations, which are the hallmark of the inquiry process. The public consultations which accompany an inquiry are tied up in the delineation of legitimate identities and ideas.[20] When people talk about political and economic issues and problems, they draw on symbols and concepts that provide shared definitions of reality. For example, 'reduce the deficit,' 'free trade,' and 'less government' are terms that took on popular meaning only after political struggle and after the once-hegemonic Keynesianism had been challenged by the world-views propounded by neoclassical economics and elsewhere.[21] Generally, at a given point in time, one set of

definitions is privileged over others. Thus a dominant discourse is established that typically favours the interests of particular actors and allows
institutions that support the status quo to articulate the dominant discourse. Those who seek to achieve significant reform or radical change
are forced to challenge the dominant discourse and attempt to gain legitimacy for an alternative.[22] Success in these endeavours requires that
actors 'go to bat' for the proposed change. While it is generally assumed
that some measure of broad-based popular acceptance of a policy proposal is necessary for its adoption, this is not always the case. Not all collective identities can gain attention, because actors are not equally
powerful. *Who* says something is sometimes more important than *how
many* say it,[23] and this analysis of the Macdonald Commission reveals that
certain business groups lent political viability to the idea of free trade
which they later translated into electoral support for the pro–free trade
Mulroney Conservatives despite the absence of widespread popular support for the policy.[24] But in any event, the acquiescence of important societal actors is a requisite for policy change. Gourevitch notes that policies
must mobilize support from coalitions of actors upon whose support,
electoral and financial, elected politicians depend.[25]

Ideological struggle leading to transformative change is also reflected
in the research program undertaken by royal commissions. In theory, it
is here that competing visions are offered in the guise of 'learned' academic discourse. Notably, it is also here that the economic viability of a
policy proposal is conferred. Although social science knowledge utilization is presented ostensibly as disinterested, neutral, and scientific
within the context of royal commissions, it may well be biased, devoted
to agenda promotion, and profoundly ideological in nature. This is
revealed in the manner in which knowledge utilization is employed to
buttress (or attack) a dominant discourse. This aspect of the transformative moment can be enhanced if new ideas (like monetarism) energize
intellectual movements to challenge the theoretical premises of existing
dominant models (like Keynesianism). In this realm, the role of the professional research community is significant, as is the receptivity of state
administrative personnel. A new paradigm can gain considerable credence under these conditions. The Macdonald Commission research
program, as we will see, privileged the economists and allowed their
ideas to dominate. It then became possible to argue that any critics of
the newly dominant discourse of the economists were outside the
bounds of reasoned and accepted debate. Proponents of free trade
could dismiss the objections of those concerned about the political and

cultural consequences of economic integration by arguing that since economics cannot quantify or empirically measure such objections, they have no validity.[26] Opponents of the dominant discourse could also be dismissed as little more than self-interested whiners, radicals, or crackpots. Thus the ideology of the dominant discourse is persuasively imposed, but not by virtue of its strength of argument.[27] In the broader struggle for the turf of social science dominance, neoclassical economics emerged triumphant not only in university economics departments, but in the halls of government and journalism as well.[28] These developments were clearly reflected in the Macdonald Commission, where a battle of the paradigms between different collective identities took place to interpret and reshape the face of the Canadian political economy.

Transformative change generally requires a champion or champions in leadership positions who can influence the direction of change and make viable ideas which otherwise remain marginalized. Political and bureaucratic leadership during a royal commission can generally be found in the persons of the commission chairperson and senior staff. The chairperson is typically a former politician, judge, or other state official of some reputation who can command a certain degree of respect and who can bestow legitimacy on the commission, and the senior staff are often career public servants seconded from government for the duration of the inquiry.[29] As Weir notes, 'patterns of recruitment to administrative posts and procedures governing advancement are both critical factors in determining whether innovative ideas will emerge within national bureaucracies.'[30] The Macdonald Commission, as an institution extraordinarily well endowed with resources (money and personnel), carried the imprimatur of a legislatively sanctioned body empowered to draft a blueprint for the long-term future for Canadian development. This meant that the commission enjoyed the legal/political authority to translate ideas into action. Donald Macdonald's leadership of the commission, ably supported by the senior bureaucrats in the policy group, facilitated change, implanting a new lexicon into political discourse in the process (the 'leap of faith,' discussed in chapter 10).

The Plan of the Book

Chapter 1 sets the stage for my analysis of the Macdonald Commission by reviewing the major trends in the development of the Canadian political economy in the post-war years. It argues that the ideology of liberal continentalism reached its zenith in the shadow of a hegemonic neighbour, and examines the decline of that hegemon in the 1970s and 1980s. It does this as a backdrop to explaining the set of nationalist policy initiatives of the Trudeau government. Finally, it examines some of the processes within the Canadian state contributing to the political discourse of free trade, while also introducing the role of the Macdonald Commission in these developments.

Chapter 2 briefly explores the legal and political bases of royal commissions as temporary institutions with particular features, as well as their historical role in Canada. It then reviews the origin of the idea in the late 1970s and early 1980s to launch a major royal commission on the Canadian economic union, the terms of reference of the Macdonald Commission, the recruitment of a chairperson and executive director, and the embarrassing incident that brought the commission into existence.

Chapter 3 reveals the process by which the Macdonald commission carried out its work. The Commission was established amid a firestorm of controversy which is detailed in this chapter. Recruitment to the senior echelons of the commission staff is explored, as is the process by which the twelve commissioners were selected. In addition, this chapter introduces the three-pronged process and structure of the commission, which was composed of a public consultation exercise, a huge social science research program, and a small oligarchy known as the policy group, which was responsible for the contents of the final commission *Report*. Finally, the chapter assesses the free trade recommendation in that report.

Chapters 4 to 6 point out the several paradoxes of the Macdonald commission. They explore the central mystery of how this Commission, rooted as it was in a Keynesian nationalist outlook, created by a government which consciously rejected continental integration, and headed by an ex–Walter Gordon Liberal nationalist, ended up adopting a neoconservative continentalist policy prescription as its signature recommendation. Chapters 4 and 5 cast light on this mystery by examining the public consultation process in detail. These chapters point to a 'battle of the paradigms,' the struggle between the proponents of social democratic nationalist and neoconservative continentalist policy ideas described above. Although the evidence shows the former group to have been a clear majority among those who submitted written briefs to the commission, the commission decision to recommend free trade reflects the views of the latter minority group.

Chapters 6, 7, and 8 tell the story of how the research program was established and run. They reveal that the question of who was picked to do research for the commission, and how they were picked, had a significant bearing on the outcome of the massive research program. These chapters also reveal that most of the research had little impact on the sections of the final report dealing with economic development strategies for Canada. Commission officials argued that the sheer volume of research proved overwhelming; that there was some resistance to the research from certain anti-intellectual commissioners; and there was a lack of integration between the research and the other parts of the commission. The exception was the economics studies, which were afforded privileged place in the pantheon of research within the commission. The economists appeared to be the only academics with concrete policy prescriptions at the ready and were able to sway Macdonald by virtue of the nature of their discipline, favoured status within the social sciences, and ideological homogeneity. Thus, mainstream liberal economists were able to impose their ideological vision of economic development strategies for Canada.

Chapter 9 analyses the role of the oligarchy known as the policy group as well as the part played by the commission chairperson, Donald Macdonald, in facilitating the free trade recommendation. It reveals how the 'iron law of oligarchy' imposed itself on the process as the small but influential policy group took control of the final stages of the commission.

Chapter 10 looks specifically at the role played by commission chairperson Donald Macdonald and assesses his leadership. It examines his transformation from Liberal nationalist to neoconservative continentalist, and the process that led him to advocate a 'leap of faith' into the arms of the United States. It points out the important part played in his conversion by his perception of the failures of Trudeau-era government nationalist interventions, and the influence of his post-political life in the world of continental corporate power.

Chapter 11 assesses the role and influence of the remaining commissioners and reveals that they were largely bystanders in the process. It shows that there were two tiers of commissioners – those who attempted to be vitally engaged in the commission's work, and those who were less engaged. And it explains why no credible or sustained opposition to the free trade juggernaught would emerge from this group, despite the fact that nearly half wrote dissenting reports on the commission's final recommendations.

Finally, Chapter 12 focuses on the legacy of the commission by assessing its influence in 'continentalizing Canada.' It looks to the role of ideas, interests, and institutions as reflected in the work of the Macdonald Commission, as well as explaining some of the profound economic and political changes in the Canadian political economy in the post–Macdonald Commission world. In other words, the legacy of the commission is established and assessed.

The approach taken throughout is a critical one. The Macdonald Commission represented an opportunity to crystallize a loose amalgam of policy ideas rooted in Keynesian social democratic theory into a newly articulated vision of a new National Policy. Indeed, the record from the commission shows that is precisely what a majority of the interested public advocated. Paradoxically the commission may have helped to sow the seeds of organized opposition to the free trade project, since its signature recommendation actually defied popular opinion. As Ayres notes, the release of the Macdonald Commission *Report* in 1985 'was perhaps the single most dramatic event in forging the consolidation of the first major anti-free trade coalition.'[31] As Bleyer puts it, 'with free trade clearly hitched to the corporate wagon, the "popular sector" had an issue it could rally around.'[32] Arguably, then, the anti-globalization movement which later killed the Multilateral Agreement on Investment and sparked massive street protests in Seattle, Genoa, Quebec City, and elsewhere is reflective of the disjuncture between policy and the preferences of important segments of civil society revealed by the Macdonald Commission.

The commission also represented an opportunity to develop policy on the basis of an unprecedented quantity and quality of social science research. Yet the research was largely marginalized, and policy was instead developed according to the ideological predispositions of a handful of key commission staffers and the commission chairperson. The result was an embrace of neoconservative continentalism[33] and the birth of a new National Policy rooted in a political discourse articulated by a small but influential minority.

'National policies are not the inevitable product of economic or social conditions,' according to Bradford. 'They are formulated through intellectual debate, adopted through political struggle, and consolidated through administrative planning.'[34] The Macdonald Commission became the site of adoption of a powerful new set of ideas which enjoyed political and economic viability backed by strong political and bureaucratic leadership. It was not the first large, programmatic commission of inquiry used to float ideas about policy innovation. Governments have appointed royal commissions to act as intellectual catalysts on several occasions, including the Rowell-Sirois Commission, the Gordon Commission, and others.[35] But the legacy of the Macdonald Commission is especially noteworthy because it facilitated one of those rare transformative moments in public policy. As a temporary institution, for a brief period of time it supplanted the usual institutions responsible for policy change. In this case, it provided the set of requisites for the political and economic elite to forge ahead with a new continental economic constitution with which present generations of Canadians are now living. Thus the significance of the Macdonald Royal Commission – this most Canadian of policy instruments – cannot be overstated.

CHAPTER 1

Setting the Stage: Canadian Economic Development in the Post-War Years

> If the free traders cannot understand how one nation can grow rich at the expense of another, we need not wonder, since these same gentlemen also refuse to understand how within one country one class can enrich itself at the expense of another.[1]

This chapter examines the historical development of the Canadian political economy in the post-war years, when the ideology of liberal continentalism reached its zenith. It maps the development of the Canadian economy in the shadow of a hegemonic neighbour, and examines the impact of the decline of that hegemon. It then looks at subsequent attempts to reorder policy making in light of the difficulty the last Trudeau government experienced in establishing a national mode of regulation in the framework of an increasingly continentalist regime of accumulation.[2] Finally, it briefly examines some of the processes within the Canadian state leading to a political discourse favouring free trade, while introducing the role of the Macdonald Commission in these developments. But it begins with a note about the role of the ideologies of nationalism and continentalism in Canadian political economy.

This chapter reveals that a period of crisis had evolved in the Canadian political economy, in which an old paradigm was waiting to die while a new one was waiting to be born. While *some* of the requisites of transformative change were emerging in the form of political viability, economic viability, and political and bureaucratic leadership, until the facilitation provided by the Macdonald Commission, they still lacked that catalyzing element that would allow them to move beyond conception to life.

Nationalism and Continentalism

The content of nationalism, as an ideology, can assume a variety of forms, from the extremes of 'integral nationalism' to mere patriotic pride. The former is a virulent variety which postulates that 'humanity is naturally divided into nations, that nations are known by certain characteristics which can be ascertained, and that the only legitimate government is national self-government.'[3] In this limited view, the world is seen in terms of a supposed division into nations, and politics is remade in this vision regardless of the claims of history, geography, economics, art, or religion.[4] However, this ethnic or sociologically based form is not the only type of nationalism. It is an extreme position and ignores nationalistic thinking that takes a less drastic approach, according to Christian and Campbell, and which views both the notion of 'nation' and the status of the moral claims which are made on citizens in the name of the nation in a more moderate light.[5] Indeed, integral nationalism is barely applicable to the Canadian experience at all, based as it is on one language/one culture/one country. It is easy to see the difficulties of trying to promote this view in a bilingual, multicultural society,[6] and applying traditional concepts of nationalism to the Canadian case has been a frustrating pastime, according to Craig Brown: 'Debating nationalism is the great Canadian national pastime. Since Confederation, it has been the preeminent preoccupation of politicians, journalists, scholars and plain ordinary citizens. All have wrestled diligently with the problem that Canadian nationalism – if such there be – does not fit any of the classic definitions of nationalism. Common language, religion and ethnic origin must obviously be rejected ... And a common historical tradition, in the words of Mill, "the possession of a national history and consequent community of recollections, collective pride and humiliation, pleasure and regret, connected with the same incidents in the past," raises more questions about a Canadian "nationality" than it answers.'[7] Thus, nation or nationality might be defined in terms of a common political allegiance or domicile in a particular country rather than in more restrictive ethnic or linguistic terms; it can be considered more in terms of the ends which it serves. Indeed, the relatively universal propensity to love one's native land, namely patriotism, may be viewed as the moderate opposite of integral nationalism. Patriotism is neither as exclusive nor as demanding as integral nationalism; is merely one loyalty among many.[8] David Chennells defines nationalism as 'political activity seeking to create a more congruent or symbiotic relationship between the state and the the nation so as to bind the state to nation's will and to entrust the state with sustaining the nation's way of life.'[9]

The term 'nationalism' is loaded with normative content and suggestive of a broad range of definitions and interpretations. So too is continentalism. The vast literature on nationalism is not very helpful in this regard, as Sylvia Bashevkin points out. For example: 'To the extent that a literature on pan-Canadianism can be said to exist, it has been dominated by advocates and adversaries whose works present essentially normative views of the subject. Assertively pro- and anti-nationalist writers have thus competed for control of this research terrain in much the same way they have opposed each other in the public arena. Although their contributions capture the real-world flavour of many heated policy debates, from a research perspective they have built a less analytic and less systematic literature than that which exists in other areas of Canadian politics.'[10] Bashevkin also suggests that, 'where integrationist or continentalist beliefs prevail, the volume of published output has been somewhat less [than by nationalists], although, according to nationalists, it has been more politically influential.'[11]

While Canadian social science has difficulty defining and applying the term nationalism it barely recognizes continentalism as a conceptual category at all, except in a most casual usage.[12] A dictionary of Canadian political terminology defines continentalism as 'a term used pejoratively by Canadian nationalists to describe Canada–United States relations in terms of a continental region, the result of which, particularly since 1945, is for Canada to lose the capacity for independent policy-making and its distinctive identity.'[13] According to Doern and Phidd, continentalism is: 'an idea to avoid rather than support. It initially evokes a concern for Canada's stock of wealth in its natural resources and the American desire to utilize them, but it can also include American domination of the Canadian economy and of Canadian cultural life. Nonetheless, continentalist policies have been explicitly or implicitly pursued, albeit usually clothed in the positive terms of economic development and efficiency. These policies include those on encouraging foreign investment, the Autopact, defense production sharing arrangements, energy policy in the 1960s and early 1970s, and trade policy generally, including the Canada-U.S. Free Trade Agreement.'[14] Political science and political economy approaches to the concept have been used to analyse the continental relationship, and a body of literature has built up in this area.[15] Almost no one, though, posits continentalism as an ideological force. Denis Stairs, for instance, treats the topic as a contextual backdrop to Canadian politics rather than a politically advocated position in itself.[16]

The significance of nationalism and continentalism for Canadian politics is substantial. The United States has necessarily played a major role in Canadian cultural, economic, and political life, and a number of crucial turning points in Canadian history are directly traceable to the ongoing contest between the forces of nationalism and continentalism. Even a brief look at Canadian history suggests that there is good reason to analyse nationalism and continentalism in more depth than has thus far been the case. Many of the monumental struggles of Canadian nationhood have been shaped by this country's relationship to the three imperial powers – France, Great Britain, and the United States – a fact well noted in Canadian historiography. The theme of Canadian identity and nationalism infuses much of the writings of Canadian historians, all of whom have 'been nationalists of various hues.'[17] Canadian history is replete with examples of the preoccupation with imperial relationships, and while the post-war era has seen the imperial locus and the issues shift,[18] the struggle remains fundamentally the same.

The historical record suggests that the struggle between the interests expressing development ideas and the need for appropriate institutions based on nationalist ideologies versus those based on continentalist ideologies has been a far more central factor in Canadian politics than social scientists have recognized.[19] For instance, part of the impetus to Confederation in 1867 was fear of American annexationist designs, and of military invasion. But it was also rooted in cultural factors. The National Policy was formulated not just as an economic program to spur Canadian manufacturing and protect it from American competitors, but to stem the flow of emigration to the Southern republic by aggressively promoting settlement in the Canadian west. The evolution of Canadian identity before the First World War often revolved around the extent to which English Canada could sustain its 'Britishness' in the face of a rising American interloper. As it moved out of the British orbit and sought to locate a separate identity, Canada was characterized as having moved from colony to nation and, as the American presence asserted itself, back to colony again.

This concern was later heightened by the advent of new forms of telecommunications technology, which in turn spurred the concern that Canadian cultural expression would be drowned out on the airwaves. The widespread dissemination of American values through the mass media became cause for concern among nationalists. And the idea that the smaller North American partner would be overwhelmed if culture was left to the vagaries of market control began to take hold. Hence Graham Spry warned in the 1930s that the future of Canadian culture lay in 'the state or the United States.'[20] The legacy of these nationalist concerns includes the CBC, the Canadian Radio and Telecommunications Commission, and other state institutions dedicated to protecting and promoting Canadian culture.

The significance of post-war nationalist concern over Canadian culture reached a high point of sorts with the Massey Royal Commission on the Arts and Letters (1955), which advocated further state involvement in cultural life in order to protect and promote indigenous expressions of Canadiana to Canadians. This popularized an activist cultural role for the state, legitimizing later attempts to protect Canadian culture from American incursions through such instruments as the Canada Council.[21]

At the root of many cultural initiatives has been the nationalist-continentalist dispute over the proper role of the state and market. Among Canadian intellectuals, academics, artists, cultural workers, and others, the protection of Canadian culture has been an abiding concern, prompting the creation of several nationalist organizations to fight the good fight. These have included the Committee for an Independent Canada, created in 1970; the Council of Canadians, established in 1985; the Pro-Canada Network formed in 1987, and others.[22] On the continentalist side, corporate North America has countered with organizations usually rooted in economic think tanks such as the C.D. Howe Institute, the Canadian-American Committee, and the Fraser Institute.[23] These bodies have actively engaged in the dissemination of continentalist values and ideas, often in the form of economic studies advocating free market principles.

Where defining the parameters of economic life in Canada has been concerned, from the pre-Confederation period to the National Policy to the North American Free Trade Agreement, the Canadian-American relationship has been central. The abrogation of the 1854 Reciprocity Treaty in 1866, apart from acting as a stimulus to Confederation, set in motion an ongoing quest to define the trading relationship of the two countries. Confederation was largely a response to the perceived threats of a belligerent and armed America, conceived of 'as a defense strategy, as imitation, and as a general alternative,'[24] but it was also an economic palliative to the cancellation of the 1854 Reciprocity Treaty. The National Policy of 1879 was Sir John A. Macdonald's second choice after free trade with the Americans. In 1911 the free trade quest moved to the top of the Canadian political agenda, as the Liberal Party under Sir Wilfrid Laurier fought the election of that year over the issue of reciprocity with the United States. Laurier lost that battle, due in part to an anti-American campaign launched by Canadian nationalists in the business community. In 1935 and 1948, Prime Minister William Lyon Mackenzie King engaged the Americans in secret negotiations to place the trading relationship on a free trade basis, but backed off due to the fear of domestic political controversy.

The post-war years nonetheless saw the gradual loosening of restrictions on North-South trade through bilateral agreements in military procurement, agricultural machinery, and automobiles, as well as multilateral reductions of barriers to trade through the General Agreement on Tariffs and Trade, and other elements of the American-dominated post-war economic order. The Paley Report's *Resources for Freedom* revealed the significance of Canadian staple products for the United States by identifying twenty-two resources critical to American development and targeting Canada as the primary source for twelve of them. Thus, Canadian jobs, prosperity, and wealth came to be associated with the extent of Canadian-American integration. But at the same time, integration raised concerns about the economic sovereignty of a Canada fully implicated into a North American economy dominated by the other partner. Again, the debate was between nationalists who feared economic capitulation, either implicitly through the type of 'silent surrender' identified by Kari Levitt,[25] or explicitly through the overt construction of economic policy designed by and for those fractions of the business community which would benefit from economic integration.

Moreover, unilateral American initiatives revealed the fragility of the Canadian position, notwithstanding the so-called special relationship between the two nations. These actions often necessitated nationalist responses by the Canadian state, such as the creation of the Foreign Investment Review Agency, the Canada Development Corporation, and Petro-Canada. These measures, in turn, met with the scorn of the continentalist community, particularly among certain corporate interests and academic economists, who counter-attacked by advocating free trade, increased foreign investment, and a continental economic regime unencumbered by the state.

Underlying the cultural and economic debate between nationalists and continentalists has been the issue of political sovereignty. The overt political manifestations of continentalism are the most difficult to discern due to the sensitive nature of declaring preference for membership in a foreign country by those who advocate such a position. Thus economic and cultural continentalists are either loathe to openly advocate political integration or vigorously deny that cultural and economic integration will result in political integration. An early exception in Canadian history was the annexationist movement of the mid-nineteenth century.[26] More common is the propensity of continentalists to deny that economic integration leads to a loss of political sovereignty. Hence, economist Harry Johnson wrote in 1965, 'I believe that closer integration of the two economies into one continental economy would be beneficial to both countries, and would involve no loss of any Canadian nationalist objectives worth pursuing.'[27] Nonetheless, nationalists have been quick to argue that political integration is the logical and necessary outcome for a society culturally and economically integrated into a union with so powerful a partner.

This slim overview could be supplemented with many more examples.[28] But the point is that the extent of integration has had a profound effect on Canadian cultural, economic, and political life, with the strength of nationalism and continentalism waxing and waning over time. The ambiguity of Canadian attitudes towards their identity and relationship with the United States is captured in George Grant's words: 'to think of the U.S. is to think of ourselves – almost.'[29] Positions on the United States – both pro and con – are fundamental to Canadian discourse. As Alan Smith notes, 'Canada cannot be understood apart from its continental context ... the dialectic between national and continental forces is a principal structuring element in the country's history.'[30]

But the shifting ideological sands of nationalism and continentalism make it difficult to account for this variable in analyses of the Canadian political economy. For instance, the fact that these two ideologies do not neatly conform to left-right cleavages over time means that the historical record is haphazard and frustratingly dynamic. Figure 1.1 reveals the shifting allegiances of different societal actors to the ideologies of nationalism and continentalism.

The identification of nationalism with left-wing and continentalism with right-wing ideologies is historically valid for the period under consideration in this study. But left-wingers were continentalists, for instance, in the 1930s, when the government of American president Franklin Delano Roosevelt provided a progressive model with its New Deal, and trade unionism was mainly integrated across North America through the efforts of the Congress of Industrial Organizations. There were also, of course, right-wing nationalists among business groups

	Left	Right
Nationalist	national unions, 1960s–1990s Trudeau Liberals, 1970s–1980s CCF-NDP, 1930s–1990s new social movements, 1970s–1990s	business community, 1878–1930s Macdonald Conservatives, 1880s Borden Conservatives, 1911 Diefenbaker Conservatives, 1950s
Continentalist	farmers' movement 1800s–1930s Laurier Liberals, 1911 Communist Party of Canada, 1930s international unions, 1900–1970s	King, St Laurent Liberals, 1930s–1960s Mulroney Conservatives, 1980s business community, 1980s–1990s

Figure 1.1   Distribution of societal actors along left–right and nationalist–continentalist divisions

whose interests were rooted in Sir John A. Macdonald's National Policy of 1879, and who later wanted to protect capitalism from the insidious influence of American-style socialism (in the form of the New Deal). By the 1970s and 1980s there were ideological clusterings in the left-nationalist and right-continentalist camps, but these identifications were neither logically necessary nor historically consistent.

Still, given the clear significance of nationalism and continentalism as dynamic factors in Canadian history, the traditional ways of looking at them are inadequate to describe the development of Canadian society in the post-war era, and must therefore be reconceptualized. Both need to be seriously considered, particularly in light of the overt integration of Canadian into American society resulting from the FTA and NAFTA. For over thirty years after the Second World War, Canadian economic development was guided by what may be termed an ideology of mild 'liberal continentalism.'[31] But in the past thirty years this ideology has been challenged. A state-centred social democratic nationalism arose in the 1970s, though it was only partially successful in its project, and a more vigorous neoconservative continentalism supplanted it in the 1980s. Both of these contending ideologies were reflected in the Mac-

donald Commission. Social democratic nationalism and neoconservative continentalism can thus be seen as the organizing concepts which
were at odds in the conflicting economic development strategies various
social actors articulated to the Macdonald Commission. According to
Doern and Phidd, 'in many respects, the foreign policy of the Mulroney
Conservative government was forged out of opposition to the early
1980s nationalist binge by the Trudeau Liberals.'[32]

As if these terms were not fraught with sufficient ambiguity, continentalists frequently claim to be nationalists. They argue that their economic
prescriptions will actually enhance Canadian sovereignty by creating
prosperity and wealth for Canadians. As Doern and Phidd note:

> In the decisive battle over free trade, the ideas of sovereignty, nationalism
> and continentalism took on a somewhat different character than they had
> in earlier debates on Canada's foreign policy. The Mulroney Conservatives
> began to articulate a form of 'entrepreneurial nationalism,' in short, an
> inbred confidence in the Canadian business community's capacity to com-
> pete. The pro-free trade coalition portrayed the anti-free traders as being
> defenders of a 'little Canada' with narrow notions of sovereignty and pro-
> tection. The antidote to negative continentalism was not state-led sover-·
> eignty and intervention, but rather a new desire to show that Canadians
> could compete with the best and need not fear the larger global world.[33]

This reveals the malleability of ideology, a characteristic which makes it
maddeningly difficult to study.

Canadian Development in the Post-War Years

The post-war development of Canada can be analysed in relation to the
rise and decline of American hegemony.[34] Philip Resnick points out that
the decline of the American empire is a key independent variable in
explaining the rise of nationalism in Canada after 1965.[35] Under U.S.
hegemony, particularly since the Second World War, Canadian development was predicated on Keynesian macro-economic management and a
social welfare system based on an implicit accord between labour and
capital, in which both agreed to share the new post-war economic prosperity.[36] The Keynesian welfare state emerged in the advanced capitalist
countries based on the assumption that 'the state could intervene to
influence levels of investment and domestic income and thereby partially
regulate unemployment through national "demand management" poli-

cies,' as Gary Teeple suggests: 'Such intervention represented a certain socialization of the costs of production (with state credits, guarantees, grants and concessions) and of working-class reproduction (through public works and forms of income support), as part of a political compromise with the working classes in an attempt to moderate the business cycle (to prevent a repeat of the unrest of the 1930s), to help rebuild the war-destroyed economies of Europe (to ensure the reconstruction of capitalism) and to contain or diminish a growing interest in socialism ...[37] Thus, Keynesianism was seen as a middle ground adopted by Canadian liberals to prevent a return to old-style capitalism and to forestall the advances of communism.

Moreover, the Canadian version of Keynesianism was unique in that its adoption was premised on the notion that Canada was an open trading economy specializing in the export of resource staples. 'Consequently, Canada could only hope to apply Keynesian policies in a liberalized post-war trading environment that would stimulate the export of its resource products,' according to David Wolfe. 'Thus, in adopting Keynes to the Canadian context, government leaders and their economic policy-advisors fashioned a uniquely Canadian synthesis of the more general Keynesian theory with the traditional staples approach to Canadian economic development.'[38]

In this context, a Fordist system of mass production characterized economic development.[39] But the Canadian variation of Fordism, like its Keynesianism, was unique. The Canadian state increasingly became involved in developing a continental regime of accumulation due in large part to the post-war collapse of Canada's main trading partner, Great Britain, which could no longer afford to carry on its traditional role as the main market for Canadian staple goods.[40] As a result, increased emphasis was put on attracting American direct investment to replace the falling levels of British portfolio investment in Canadian natural resource development, and on import substitution in the tariff-protected manufacturing sector.[41]

Politically, the system of representation in Canada was constructed less around class-based collective identities organized within the party system (as was characteristic of the Western European experience), and more around collective identities constructed within a discourse of nation building and the institutions of federalism.[42] But Canada's universe of political discourse came under strain from at least four sources.[43] In the first place a substantial section of Canadian society looked longingly to the British Empire. Politically, this group found expression in the conservatism of John Diefenbaker's Progressive Conservative Party, and intellectual solace in the writings of George Grant and historians such as W.L. Morton and Donald Creighton.[44] In the second place were the continentalists who looked to the south and found inspiration in the rising hegemon. Politically this group found a home in the liberalism of the Liberal Party of Mackenzie King (whose continentalist development strategy was 'personified' in C.D. Howe),[45] and of Louis St Laurent and Lester Pearson. Finally, in the third place, were those who sought autonomy for Canada, free from the control of any empire. The Liberal Party also housed several of the leading proponents of this view, including Walter Gordon.[46] Gordon inspired many on the left in Canadian politics, including the socialist-nationalist Waffle movement in the New Democratic Party.[47] Kari Levitt, Mel Watkins, Jim Laxer, and others advanced this position, which often coupled anti-Americanism with anti-Liberalism.[48] In addition to these conflicting views, in French Canada the new nationalism of the Quiet Revolution further strained the country's political system.[49]

The strongest of these forces, as history shows, has been the liberal continentalist one. Canada essentially developed as a dependent American satellite state, voluntarily surrendering much of its economic, military, diplomatic, and cultural control to the United States under the aegis of mild liberal continentalism.[50] Canada's accumulation strategy became explicitly oriented towards increasing its integration with the American economy. This represented the acceleration and intensification of a process which had actually started at the turn of the century, when Canadian business and political elites began to encourage American foreign direct investment (FDI) to exploit Canadian natural resources needed by American industry. But the process intensified after the Second World War as Canada's development was modified to the new reality of American domination. Canadian nationalism after the Second World War followed the dominant liberal ideology (linked to the construction of the Keynesian welfare state), which rejected political independence as being the defining characteristic of nationalism, largely on the basis of the European experience with Fascism.[51]

In some sectors, formal continental integration was pursued as official policy.[52] For example agricultural machinery crossed the border tariff free. Defence production was integrated through the 1959 Defence Production Sharing Agreement (DPSA), which created a managed trade zone in military procurement with the Canadian sector made up largely of branch plants of the American military-industrial complex. And the

1965 Auto Pact continentalized the production of automobiles. On the diplomatic front, Canada generally acquiesced to the larger partner, choosing a strategy of 'quiet diplomacy' that suggested a non-conflictual relationship based on deference to American world leadership. Overall, in return for privileged access for American investors to Canadian resources, Ottawa received conditional exemptions from American economic measures that might otherwise threaten the Canadian economy.

However, to counter the overwhelming position enjoyed by the post-war hegemon, Canada took an active role in the construction of a multilateral global system, including the creation of the United Nations, the North Atlantic Treaty Organization, the General Agreement on Tariffs and Trade, and other international organizations. Thus, multilateralism became a cornerstone of the Canadian approach to counterbalancing the preponderant weight of its key partner to the South.

Admittedly, this continental economic framework, coupled with a Keynesian policy outlook, prevailed during a period of relative prosperity, but it brought with it a strained and conflict-riven political discourse. With the advent of the post-Fordist era and the latest crisis in the capitalist system, when the American hegemon started to go into decline in the early 1970s,[53] severe cracks surfaced in the Canadian political economy. These led to attempts to alter economic policy and ultimately further strained the Canadian discourse.

The decline of the American hegemon was marked by a number of developments, beginning in the early 1970s, whose cumulative impact was felt globally and certainly within Canada. The roots of the American crisis were widespread. As Joel Krieger notes, 'for the United States a policy package of international liberalism inaugurated as Bretton Woods and mild Keynesian-welfarism at home was jeopardized by the budgetary excesses of the Vietnam war – and effectively killed by declining U.S. competitiveness since the oil shock of 1973–1974.'[54] Civil strife on the domestic front, as well as high inflation, high unemployment, and a decline in growth in productivity all contributed to an economic and moral crisis in America. For instance, as William Berman reports:

By 1971, American global economic power was visibly declining, which was part of a process that had been under way for some time ... The American share of the world GNP dropped from 40 percent in 1950 to 23 percent in 1970. Its share of world trade stood at 20 percent in 1950; by 1970 it had declined to 11 percent. In the meantime, the United States was being integrated into a global economy to such an extent that imports now pouring into the home market began to compete effectively with American firms in a once exclusive and privileged domain. In addition, inflation was now averaging over 4 percent a year; productivity rates, having peaked in 1966, had dropped significantly; and corporate profits had slipped from 13.7 percent in 1965 to about 8 percent a year during the Nixon years.[55]

Analyses of the root causes of the decline generally split into two camps. The May 1975 report of the Trilateral Commission on governability of democracies spelled out the rightist interpretation – that political socialization was falling apart, values were changing, people were no longer as deferential to authority figures, rising expectations were revolutionizing political life, and increased demands on the state were making societies 'ungovernable.' The result was an overload of inputs with which the state could no longer cope. Analysis on the left suggested that a 'fiscal crisis of the state' and a 'legitimation crisis' was the basis of America's declining fortunes.[56] As Joel Krieger pointed out:

> Prominent right and left thinkers accepted common themes despite basic political disagreements: in the sixties, the decline of ideological commitment, and, then, in the seventies, the erosion of belief structures which motivated participation in capitalism's economic hierarchies. The message was clear: the state is no longer able to accommodate the increased demands made on it. In some sense there was a dead heat between the Trilateralists and the progressive intellectuals, as the *crisis of democracy* trumpeted by the right and the *legitimation crisis* heralded by the left equally inspired each set of academic rivals. Moreover, both – although here, very much unequally – contributed to a generalized media-hyped spirit of fragmentation, malaise, and anxiety for what was to come.[57]

The Nixon government signalled that it accepted the former interpretation of the crisis in a manner which had profound consequences for Canada. On 15 August 1971 Nixon instituted a program of devaluation of the American dollar and increased protectionism. What was most troubling about this broadside for Canadian policy makers was that Canada failed to get the exemptions it had come to expect under the terms of the 'special relationship.' As Clarkson put it, 'The United States was declaring Canada to be independent, a statement the President made in so many words in the Canadian House of Commons in 1972.' Nixon had said 'the fact of our mutual interdependence and our mutual desire for independence need not be inconsistent traits. No self-respecting nation can or should accept the proposition that it should always be economically dependent upon any other nation.'[58]

Moreover, the existing levels of integration between the Canadian and American economies compounded these developments, since the vast majority of Canadian staples exports headed south to the United States while Canada's main sources of manufactured imports and foreign investment also originated there. Thus America's decline had special implications for a country characterized by 'permeable Fordism.'[59]

The crisis in capitalist systems, which came to be characterized by the phenomenon of 'stagflation,' was a global one, and so affected Canada as well as the United States. But it had specific consequences for a Canada linked so closely to the American hegemon. According to Wolfe, the emphasis on staples exports as the cornerstone of the Canadian economy contributed a note of instability and distorted the successful application of Keynes to Canada, particularly in relation to the goals of full employment and high growth. The demands by labour for full employment and rising real wages as against the need for increasing profit levels by business people led to increasing conflicts. The failure of the state to mediate these growing conflicts was graphically symbolized by growing levels of unemployment and simultaneous spiralling rates of inflation in advanced capitalist countries, or stagflation: 'Canada's stagflation problem was compounded by the instability introduced by its continued reliance on a high level of staple exports and steadily rising levels of manufactured imports and foreign investment. This pattern of growth resulted in a steadily worsening balance-of-payments problem that seriously constrained the goals of the Keynesian welfare state. In the years after 1975, the commitment to the Keynesian welfare state was gradually eroded and the political compromise between business and labour abandoned.'[60]

In attempting to cope with these new constraints on policy making, the Trudeau government was pushed into adopting a more nationalist package of economic policies. Canada's position as a dependent continental partner of what it had assumed would be an ever more prosperous United States was now in jeopardy, as the United States itself embarked upon a more national and less continental position.

Canada responded with a number of measures: in 1973 it created a state-owned oil company, Petro-Canada, to 'open a window' for the state on this volatile key sector of the economy; it created a state-financed holding company, the Canadian Development Corporation, to funnel national capital into indigenously owned enterprises and increase domestic ownership of the economy; it created the Foreign Investment Review Agency to screen foreign direct investment; and it initiated the Third Option policy of diversifying trade away from the United States. As well, the Canadian government floated the idea of a comprehensive national industrial strategy, a proposal implying a much more interventionist role for the government in the economy, especially in the manufacturing and high technology sectors.[61] On the cultural front, a new nationalist spirit swept the arts, buttressed by government-sponsored institutions, funding, and legislation that promoted Canadianization in film, literature, television, and radio.

But the Canadian economy showed many of the signs of trouble that characterized the American one, including high inflation, high unemployment, increasing trade deficits, and low growth in productivity.[62] As well, the implicit accord between labour and capital, underpinned by negotiated collective bargaining, began to come apart. And the social welfare state began to come under attack.

By the late 1970s and early 1980s, the Trudeau government had established the broad framework of a nationalist set of policy responses to the new realities. But Canadian capital had become increasingly continental. This underscored the problem that a satellite or dependent economy cannot so easily extract itself from the tentacles of a continental regime of accumulation that had built up over many years between Canada and the United States. And so the problems of a dependent economy inextricably linked to a declining hegemon confounded the Canadian government's attempts to chart a new course.

Perhaps the most graphic symbol of the conundrums faced by the last Trudeau government was the National Energy Program (NEP) of 1980. Among the many forces pulling the Canadian state in different directions, the failure of the NEP imposed an unbearable strain on the Trudeau government's nationalist mode.[63] The goal of the NEP was to redistribute rents from oil-rich Alberta to the federal government, which wanted the windfall profits resulting from the second OPEC-induced oil crisis to establish a national industrial strategy based on massive resource development megaprojects. But this strategy laid bare the differences between the oil-producing western provinces, who found a new chapter to add to the historical book of grievances against central Canada, and the consuming provinces.[64] Reflective of the lack of Liberal Party representation in western Canada, this episode served to exacerbate regional tensions while fuelling anti-statist neoconservative views. But the unsustainability of the high cost of oil brought declining revenues in the wake of massive spending commitments, and thus led to the failure of the NEP. The premise of the government's industrial strategy – that high world prices for oil would finance megaproject development in other staples and in turn generate backward and forward linkages in the economy to enhance the Canadian manufacturing sector – proved to be unfounded. That the NEP proved to be unworkable in light of declining oil prices did not lessen the perception that its failure was traceable to government intervention according to a growing chorus of anti-state forces in both Canada and the United States.[65]

As the NEP drama was unfolding, the Trudeau government was also moving towards the other major pillar of its administration – the patriation of the constitution with a Charter of Rights and Freedoms in 1982. But the lack of Quebec's signature on the Constitution called into question the success of patriation, notwithstanding the legitimacy conferred on the government by the popularity of the Charter. The constitutional politics of the late 1970s and early 1980s underlined the elitist nature of the political process, giving rise to serious criticisms of 'executive federalism.'[66] The result was increased demands for citizen representation and recognition.[67] Ironically, the process of executive federalism itself gave rise to this by producing the Charter, through which a variety of heretofore marginalized groups could make legitimate claims to recognition and rights on the state.[68]

The rise of new social movements created further stresses as women, Aboriginals, environmentalists, seniors, gays and lesbians, visible minorities, the disabled, and others arose to challenge and redefine the prevailing mode of politics in the country. Duncan Cameron argues that 'reflecting the increased ideological conflict engendered in Canada by the economic crisis, groups unhappy with reliance on market and state rationality for the resolution of social problems began to use a new language in public debate.'[69] The politics of coalition building was one result, the increased use of the courts to redress grievances was another. A third was an erosion of the fragile left-right ideological dichotomy in Canada, as these groups coalesced along cleavages other than traditional left-right ones.[70] Overall, the rise of new social movements compounded the problems of a state under siege from the growing demands of a culture of increased expectations in a context of economic crisis.

The Trudeau government thus received two serious body blows from which it proved unable to recover. Trudeau's pan-Canadian constitutional approach left a bitter aftertaste among many Québécois while providing the constitutional mechanism (the Charter) for increased numbers of dispossessed and marginalized groups to challenge the state. And on the economic front, liberal and social democratic approaches to governing lost credibility in the face of the failed NEP and the grinding depression of 1981–2. All of this was underscored by the declining hegemony of Canada's main economic partner in the face of the global crisis of capitalism.

What emerged was the disjunctive position of the early 1980s. The attempts to impose a more nationalist, social democratic style of governing involving state intervention in the economy ran up against an increasingly continentally oriented business community and economy. To compound this problem, a new, more assertive American administration took over in 1980 under Ronald Reagan.[71] It was dedicated to erasing any trace of government intervention in the economy, to reasserting American hegemony, and to reimposing a continental regime of accumulation based on neoconservative principles.[72] Reagan and his advisers were intuitively unsympathetic to the state-centred economic development strategies often employed by Canadian governments. They were convinced by their right-wing supporters that the Canadian government represented a dangerous socialist menace to the accumulation of capital, and that the NEP represented the nationalization of the oil industry in Canada and a threat to their property rights, since it involved confiscation of American assets.[73] The Reagan administration preached liberalization abroad and protectionism at home, and it targeted the Canadian government with a vengeance.

In addition, Canadian business underwent changes in this period which led it to a position diametrically opposed to the Trudeau government's nationalist thrust. Significant fractions of the capitalist class had, in the words of some political economists, 'matured.'[74] That is, they had become consequential multinational enterprises, and had begun to export more aggressively both to the United States and beyond as a result of the gradual lessening of tariffs brought on by successive GATT rounds. The Canadian Manufacturers' Association (CMA), for example, reversed its stand on free trade in light of this new reality, and the Business Council on National Issues (BCNI) took up the cause too.[75] As well, Canadian foreign direct investment abroad increased tremendously throughout the 1970s and into the 1980s. By 1975, Canada became a net exporter of capital for direct investment, with most going to the United States.[76] At the same time, a worldwide decline in exports prompted business interests to press the Canadian government for measures guaranteeing enhanced and secure access to the American market. While Canadian companies required more capital to take advantage of new technologies and equipment to sustain their competitiveness, foreign MNCs were unsure of the advisability of investing in a country without guaranteed access to a large market. Thus the perception of a capital shortage developed within Canada. As well, the GATT timetable for trade liberalization was proceeding too slowly and was fraught with uncertainty. Finally, the depression of 1981–2 reinforced the integrationist tendencies of many firms as the search for new solutions proceeded.

Sensing the shifting winds of change, elements within the Progressive Conservative Party, inspired by Alberta Premier Peter Loughheed's struggles with Ottawa, began to openly advocate closer ties with the United States through greater economic integration, thus reversing the traditional position of the party of arch-nationalists Macdonald and Diefenbaker. Indeed, the liberal centre in Canadian politics could no longer hold. As the Keynesian underpinnings of the post-war order unravelled, an ideological polarization began to take place in Canada. Neoconservatism emerged on the right, consisting of some traditional elements of Canadian conservatism plus the right-wing of traditional Canadian liberalism (frequently referred to as business liberalism), which is dominated by a free market orientation towards economic life, and which desires less government intervention in the economy. Democratic socialism retrenched on the left, encompassing the traditional elements of Canadian socialism, as well as left-wing liberalism (often referred to as welfare liberalism), advocating a greater degree of government intervention in the economy.[77] Thus, as the 1980s unfolded, two main ideological camps emerged, effectively squeezing out the liberal centre by the end of the decade.[78]

The economic dislocations of 1981–2 made the need for a palliative to this disjunctive position painfully obvious and inspired the search for new public policy prescriptions. Typically, the search for solutions manifested itself in the time-honoured Canadian tradition of a royal commission. 'An important policy response of the Trudeau Liberals to international economic disorder and the depressed Canadian economy was to set up the ... Macdonald Commission,' Cameron suggests. 'With welfare liberalism and Keynesian doctrine in disgrace, it is little wonder that a party which believed in both and had used both to electoral advantage, should now look for a new direction for Liberals and perhaps a new definition of liberalism itself.'[79] An inquiry of this type permits the airing of a broad cross-section of ideological positions with regard to economic development strategies. It lays bare the positions of various social actors struggling to impose their perspectives regarding appropriate policy approaches by the Canadian state. It creates the possibility (but only the possibility) for the coalescence of political viability, economic viability, and political and bureaucratic leadership to engender a transformative moment.

Before exploring the phenomenon of the Macdonald Commission, however, more of the story leading to the transformative change facilitated by the commission needs to be elucidated. One proposal for a solution to the conundrums facing the Canadian political economy was free trade with the United States. But the idea in general lacked the necessary requisites for viability. Only a small handful of politicians, bureaucrats, academics, and societal interests stepped forward as advocates of free trade through the period under consideration. But their numbers and influence gradually increased as the economic crisis proceeded. It is useful to look at the machinations within the state and among certain business groups regarding the concept of free trade before examining the specific struggle between nationalism and continentalism through the Macdonald Commission.

The Free Trade Path: The Debate within the State

How significant was the issue of free trade in the Canadian political consciousness before the Macdonald Commission? To establish its significance, and hence viability, the prominence of the idea in the 1970s and early 1980s needs to be traced. Throughout the 1970s free trade was undoubtedly 101st out of the top 100 items on the Trudeau government's agenda. It was virtually nowhere to be seen on the policy horizon. Indeed, as noted above, the Trudeau government was heading away from greater integration with the United States and towards a more nationalist stance with policies such as the CDC, FIRA, Petro-Canada, the Third Option, the NEP, and cultural Canadianization programs. The free trade debate had been settled in 1911, after all![80]

In 1983, the Conservative Party underwent a leadership contest in which one of the principal contenders, John Crosbie of Newfoundland, announced that he was in favour of free trade with the United States. The winner of that contest, Brian Mulroney, responded viscerally and negatively to Crosbie's idea: 'The country could not survive with a policy of unfettered free trade. I'm all in favour of eliminating unfair protectionism, where it exists. [But] this is a separate country. We'd be swamped. We have in many ways a branch plant economy, in many ways, in certain important sectors. All that would happen with that kind of concept would be the boys cranking up their plants throughout the United States in bad times and shutting their entire branch plants in Canada. It's bad enough as it is.'[81] On another occasion Mulroney proclaimed, 'Don't talk to me about free trade, that issue was decided in 1911. Free trade is a danger to Canadian sovereignty, and you'll hear none of it from me now during this leadership campaign or at any other time in the future.'[82] Of course Mulroney later changed his mind, citing three main reasons for his about-face: 'First of all, the terrible swing to protectionism in the United States, which threatened to pick off Canadian industries one by one. [Secondly] the move in Europe to 1992, to a much greater trading bloc. Thirdly, *the excellent and thoughtful Macdonald Royal Commission Report* with its exhaustive examination of Canada's economy and its future prospects.'[83] Still, as the Macdonald Commission initiated its work in November 1982, there was little indication that free trade would become its signature recommendation. Of all the economic development strategies under consideration by Canadian governments in the post–Second World War era, free trade with the United States seemed like one of the most remote possibilities in the early 1980s: 'Free trade with the United States would have looked like a very long shot at the beginning of the 1980s. Few would have predicted that within four years Canada would propose sectoral free trade, and fewer still would have believed that two years later Canada would go the whole way and offer to negotiate a comprehensive free trade agreement with the Americans.'[84] Indeed, Under-Secretary of State for External Affairs Alan Gotlieb, who played a key role as Ambassador to the United States during the free trade negotiations, wrote in 1981 that it was 'axiomatic' that the benefits of economic development for Canada 'will not fall out of a free trade, free investment, free-for-all continental economy. This is not an option for Canadian development.'[85] Thus, none of the three major political parties endorsed free trade as a goal and influential senior civil servants regarded it as outside the pale of policy considerations. In short, it lacked the requisites of political viability, economic viability, and political and bureaucratic leadership.

Part of the reason why free trade nonetheless emerged comes from the machinations of bureaucratic politics within the federal government in the early 1980s. Michael Hart, a career bureaucrat who wrote most of the Macdonald Commission's recommendation for free trade, has suggested that while the issue may not have been explicitly on the public policy agenda in the early 1980s, it certainly was an idea that was 'in the air:' 'In terms of the intellectual background to it, there's a whole history – and I put that in the commission report. I mean, the work of Jack Young at the Gordon commission; the work of the Economic Council; work by the Wonnacotts and so on. So there was a long, kind of professional economic view on free trade. Then the Economic Council had done their "Looking Outward" report in 1975 which covered a lot of research done by them. Then the Van Roggen committee in the Senate did hearings on it and that resulted in things.'[86] Hart also argued that Canadian business had begun to rethink its position on free trade by the early 1980s. Until that time, the Canadian business establishment was about 80 per cent against the idea. The resource sector largely had free trade, and was quite happy with it, and the manufacturing sector in Canada was a 'miniature replica' branch plant manufacturing sector. Both sectors of the Canadian business establishment really had very little reason to push for it, according to Hart. But by the late 1970s and early 1980s, with the onset of globalization, it became clear that the level of protection Canadian business enjoyed was no longer significant. Moreover, it began to be hit by American contingency protection. 'All of these things created a very uneasy business sector in Canada,' Hart maintained. 'And you see that in various reports they put out and discussions they had with the government, and discussion they had with themselves.'[87] The Canadian Exporter's Association moved first, then the Chamber of Commerce, and finally by 1981–2, the Canadian Manufacturers' Association: 'They did not know where they wanted to go, but they knew the status quo was not satisfactory. This is all taking place in the recession of 1981–1982. But the status quo would not hold. I mean, they were experimenting with world product mandates and all that stuff, so that was a worry to them. And so you see the first kinds of requests coming out of the Business Council on National Issues and so on, looking for some kind of an agreement with the U.S. They did not know what, but one that would resolve disputes and that kind of stuff.'[88] Hart also put the growing interest in the free trade issue in the context of the apparent failure of the GATT negotiations to progress satisfactorily. In short, free trade was a notion contained within the political discourse of certain groups within Canadian society. But it clearly was not yet a part of the dominant discourse.

The origin of the impetus to engage the United States in negotiations for free trade can be found in the climate of crisis engulfing relations between the two countries in the early 1980s: 'The majority Liberal government elected in 1980 had adopted an ambitious national policy agenda designed to enhance the resources and visibility of the federal government. The Liberal aim was to redress what was viewed as a serious imbalance within Canadian federalism. Central to the Liberal strategy were initiatives such as patriation of the constitution, renegotiation of social programs and equalization payments to the provinces, and the creation of a Western Development Fund.'[89] Symbols of the government's national mode, such as the NEP and FIRA, alienated many business people, particularly in resource-dependent western Canada,[90] and aggravated relations with the United States.[91] The response of American business people was to exert pressure on the Reagan administration to counter vigorously what they perceived as an assault on their freedom to do business in Canada. As a result, 'U.S. plans for retaliatory measures targeted the Canadian Achilles' heel of trade dependence on the United States.'[92] The bogeyman of American protectionism raised its ugly head and scared many Canadian business people: 'The acute conflict, and the fears it aroused in Canadians and their government, represented a turning point for Canada in its relations with the United States. The U.S. had openly threatened the security of Canadian access to a market on which Canada was overwhelmingly dependent. The implications for employment and investment for Canada were profound. Both business and government were forced to reassess the value to Canada of secure and enhanced access to the U.S. market, especially in the context of the severe economic recession then developing.'[93]

In response, a review of overall government policy by the Priorities and Planning Committee of Cabinet was undertaken in 1981. Within this review, the Department of Industry, Trade and Commerce (ITC) looked at trade policy, while the Department of External Affairs (DEA) reviewed Canada-U.S. relations. Coincidentally, departmental reorganization in early 1982 brought the trade elements of ITC into a reorganized DEA as a new trade and economic wing reporting to its own minister for international trade. Denis Stairs regarded this departmental reorganization as important to the eventual outcome of the Macdonald Commission:

If you look at what was happening in Ottawa, the department that would presumably stand for representing the country writ whole, would have been External Affairs. But what had happened, of course, was that the department had become dominated by the trade side. Those were the guys that were in the ascendency in the department, and they were supported by Finance and a variety of other places, and ultimately, of course, by the prime minister. But there is an irony in that, of course, because that change in External Affairs was initiated by the Trudeau government. I think very largely by accident. The effects of that bureaucratic change were quite accidental. The department got left with the trade division because they didn't know what else to do with it. But in so doing, they changed the character of the department very fundamentally. So, there were very powerful forces in External Affairs and elsewhere that were making similar kinds of [free trade] arguments.[94]

Part of the reorganization included moving the trade policy review to a DEA task force. 'This shift was important,' according to Doern and Tomlin, 'since the free trade option had less chance of emerging from ITC with its mandate to protect and nurture Canadian industry.'[95]

The project director of the task force was the ardent pro-free trader Hart, who organized a series of consultations with representatives of the Canadian business community and provincial governments. The primary concern expressed at these meetings was to 'get the Canada-U.S. relationship right': threats to Canadian exporters by protectionist American policies had to be overcome.[96] Herein we begin to see the requisite bureaucratic leadership emerging, which combined with a nascent political viability developing among leading segments of the business class in Canada. Leading the Canadian business position was the BCNI and the CMA: 'During 1982 and 1983, the president of the BCNI, Thomas d'Aquino, was active in advocating negotiations for a comprehensive trade agreement as a means to guarantee access to the U.S. market. Equally important, however, was the reversal by the influential CMA of its long-standing opposition to free trade with the United States. It was the crisis in the economy that the task force examination of Canada's trade policy would centre on securing access to the U.S. market. And the Canadian business lobby saw to it that the negotiation of some form of trade liberalization was put forward as an option for consideration by the task force.[97] As the depression was deepening, 'the emerging economic crisis guaranteed that the threat to secure access to the American market for Canada's exports would be defined as the central problem for Canadian trade policy.'[98]

The DEA released its report, *Canadian Trade Policy for the 1980s*, in 1983.[99] It reasserted the centrality of GATT and multilateral trade for Canada, but it also raised the option of *sectoral* free trade with the United States. The sectoral free trade proposal had an eager champion in the person of Gerald Regan, the minister of international trade, representing the emerging requisite political leadership. He persuaded his more cautious Cabinet colleagues to go along with the sectoral free trade suggestion 'despite the suspicions of the "nationalist" group in the Liberal Cabinet.'[100] Regan emphasized sectoral free trade even though it was not the centrepiece of the report: 'Seizing on its most controversial element, the minister announced the demise of the Third Option and proclaimed the government's intention to pursue a limited free trade agreement with the United States. Regan's proclamation did not, by any means, reflect mainstream thinking in External Affairs. The concurrent review of the Canada-U.S. relationship that had been prepared for the deputy minister for foreign relations had reaffirmed the basic tenets of the Third Option. That report was overtaken by events, however. It was the trade policy review that provided the opening for fundamental change in Canadian-American relations, as sectoral free trade negotiations became the preferred option of the Liberal government of Pierre Trudeau.'[101] While some preliminary discussions were held in Washington between Canadian embassy officials and the Americans, the former ITC, reorganized as the Department of Regional Industrial Expansion (DRIE) in January 1982, was still leery about the idea.[102] So too were the Americans, and as few areas of mutual compatibility could be found, the talks went nowhere.[103]

This might have been the end of the story but for a change in government in Ottawa which contributed greatly to the political leadership that helped to engender the transformative moment facilitated later by the Macdonald Commission. During the 1984 election campaign, the Tories made no secret of their desire for closer relations with the United States. 'Unlike some other matters of economic policy on the Mulroney agenda,' notes David Leyton-Brown, 'free trade with the United States was not clearly foreshadowed in the election campaign, though closer relations with the United States were.'[104] Because of a lack of progress by the outgoing Liberals on the sectoral free trade front, several leading Conservatives favoured, if only tentatively, a broader approach to free trade: 'Although it would appear that the signals were somewhat mixed, when examined closely the new government was anything but equivocal on this issue. [Finance Minister] Michael Wilson spoke strongly in favour of a free trade agreement on a number of occasions. Joe Clark, who seemed less sure than the Finance Minister, [was] quoted as saying 'Canadian nationalists must take account of international economic situations ... the country has matured dramatically and if we were vulnerable to American influences in the 1950s and 1960s, we are much less vulnerable now.'[105] Rank-and-file Conservative Party members also revealed a more continentalist attitude. Questioned at the 1983 Tory leadership convention, over 80 per cent favoured closer economic integration with the United States.[106]

After several years of thinly veiled animosity between the Reagan and Trudeau administrations, the arrival of the Mulroney Conservatives heralded a new era even more intimate than the old 'special relationship' between the two countries. Mulroney's speech, shortly after taking office, to New York investment brokers and bankers, in which he pronounced Canada 'open for business'[107] signalled that a new ideological attitude had taken hold in Ottawa. Most significant, though, was the document *Agenda for Renewal*, released by Finance Minister Michael Wilson on 5 November 1984.[108] It became the ideological blueprint for the new government, 'the bible of Mulroney's Ministers,'[109] and clearly signalled a confluence of world-views between the new Canadian administration and the Reagan Republicans. Still, the new Canadian government approached the free trade issue with caution. The Minister for International Trade, James Kelleher, said in a September 1984 speech that 'Canada was prepared to continue discussions with the United States to identify potential areas for action on trade relations between the two countries, but not "to create fortress North America."'[110]

Two more studies of the trade issue were commissioned. One, by the DEA, focused on the sectoral approach, found it wanting, and decided to study a comprehensive approach. This review was headed by Derek Burney, assistant deputy minister for U.S. affairs in the DEA, an ardent proponent of comprehensive free trade, and another important actor in the marshalling of bureaucratic leadership for the changes to come.[111] Still, the Conservative government was unsure about whether to fully support free trade, although as Doern and Tomlin point out: 'the Autumn of 1984 saw pressures mount for the government to pick up the free trade agenda. Canadian business organizations engaged in a vigorous lobbying effort to shore up support for a comprehensive free trade arrangement, and their position was given serious attention by a government committed to making Canada a better place to do business.'[112] In fact, this statement needs to be amended; it was but a small, well-organized portion of the business community that had adopted this attitude, as the evidence below will reveal.

The Mulroney government needed a final push to be convinced of the merits of embarking on comprehensive free trade negotiations:

The negotiation option probably received its most substantial boost in November 1984 from Donald Macdonald ... Although [his] Commission had neither completed its studies nor framed its conclusions, Macdonald nevertheless announced that he favoured free trade between Canada and the United States as the principal long-term solution to Canada's economic problems ...

Macdonald's call for a 'leap of faith' was a big news item in Canada. And because the Commission was bipartisan and seemingly authoritative, Macdonald's support provided important momentum to the free trade option at a critical juncture, as the new government was considering its options.[113]

Around that time, Burney in the DEA presented free trade arguments to the government in a review of trade options entitled *How to Secure and Enhance Access to Export Markets*.[114] It was not warmly endorsed, and it initiated a struggle among pro- and anti-free traders in the DEA and DRIE: 'The conflict resulted from Burney's determination to put the comprehensive free trade option before the government. From a DRIE perspective, trade liberalization would threaten Canadian industries supported by an average tariff that was roughly double that of their American competition. In External, the opposition centred on traditional concerns over political autonomy. In the end, Burney was forced to override opposition from the most senior administrative levels of his own department, which wanted to suppress the free trade discussion.'[115]

As 1984 drew to a close, the Canadian government inched closer toward its historic decision to seek a free trade agreement with the United States: 'Prime Minister Brian Mulroney had the support of his principal ministers, the party faithful, much of the Canadian electorate, virtually all professional economists, and would soon have the endorsement of the Macdonald Royal Commission. Moreover, the opponents of free trade were not mounting any appreciable counter offensive.'[116]

The newly improved Canadian-American relationship was symbolized by the 'Shamrock Summit' between Reagan and Mulroney in Quebec City in March 1985. Largely orchestrated by Burney, the event was highlighted by an announcement by the president and prime minister that they would instruct their respective governments to examine ways in which barriers to trade could be eliminated between the two countries. The U.S. Trade Representative and the Canadian minister for trade were instructed to report within six months on mechanisms to achieve this goal.

Kelleher met with numerous organized interests over the next half year on the various proposals for trade in the Burney report: the status quo; sectoral free trade; or comprehensive free trade:

In a series of public forums, Kelleher and his people heard from a variety of business and labour groups. What they heard from business indicated substantial, though not unanimous, support for a comprehensive bilateral trade deal that would secure access to the American market for Canadian companies. Labour was not similarly disposed, however. Kelleher's public forums were followed in May, 1985 by a series of private consultations with Canadian firms and business organizations conducted by Tom Burns, former president of the Canadian Exporter's Association. Burns's mission also centred on the trade options discussion paper, and provided further evidence of widespread support for some kind of comprehensive approach to bilateral trade.[117]

Meanwhile, a right-wing think-tank, the C.D. Howe Institute, began providing some of the economic viability needed to bring about the transformative moment by promoting a study co-authored by economist Richard Lipsey on the benefits of comprehensive free trade.[118] The institute aggressively lobbied government members and senior civil servants to convince them of its benefits. And several pro–free trade economic research studies published by the Macdonald Commission began appearing.[119] The institute's efforts, 'along with the trade policy studies prepared by the Macdonald Commission, helped to shatter many of the prevailing myths about free trade.'[120] While the Mulroney Cabinet was still cautious in its approach to the issue, the Kelleher and Burns consultations helped ease any reservations which reluctant ministers still held.

Two more incremental steps were then taken in the direction of a full-blown free trade initiative before the Macdonald Commission *Report* was released. The first was the May 1985 government green paper on foreign policy.[121] 'This paper reaffirmed the goal of enhanced and secure access to the U.S. market, set out the same options that had been presented in the [Kelleher] January discussion paper, and again made the case for a comprehensive agreement by raising doubts about the other options.'[122] External Affairs Minister Joe Clark used this green paper as the basis of a joint Senate–House of Commons review of foreign policy. This permitted the three political parties to stake out their positions and open up the debate to a wider audience: 'In its interim report of August, 1985, the committee recommended a fairly cautious approach to the trade issue in a recommendation drafted with the concurrence of both Conservative and Liberal members of the committee, but not the New Democratic Party members, who issued a dissent. The report proposed that the government begin preliminary trade discussions with the U.S., but not move immediately to formal bilateral negotiations. Instead the committee urged the government to centre the discussions on the resolution of existing trade irritants and the exploration of issues involved in further trade liberalization.'[123] However, just two weeks after this joint government committee report came out, the Macdonald Commission *Report* was released: 'The royal commission report was in the hands of the prime minister earlier in the summer, even as the special joint committee was conducting its hearings. He saw immediately the opportunity it presented for a bold policy initiative with ready-made bipartisan support. And Mulroney relished the prospect of using a former Liberal cabinet minister to give bipartisan legitimacy to the initiative. The volumes of the report arranged on his desk, Mulroney spread his hands over them and told officials present in his office that summer day that he would use the report to beat John Turner in the next election.'[124] The importance of the Macdonald Commission *Report* cannot be overestimated. It is cited by most observers as the key influence on Mulroney, convincing him to take the leap of faith. 'Prime Minister Brian Mulroney was politically shrewd enough to see that a comprehensive and authoritative pro-business program articulated by a highly regarded former Liberal cabinet minister could meet his government's desperate need for a coherent policy agenda.'[125] As Michael Hawes noted, the *Report* 'was surprisingly consistent with Tory rhetoric – especially with regard to the necessity of negotiating a trade deal with the United States and the need to move the Canadian economy into the twenty-first century.'[126]

Conclusion

This account of activities within the Canadian state only partially explains the move to free trade. Set within the context of a declining American hegemon, and an emerging crisis within the Canadian political economy, it marks the beginnings of an identifiable moment wherein some of the requisites for transformative change were clearly in evidence. Some business groups, like the BCNI and CMA, were nudging towards free trade and laying the groundwork for the political viability needed to raise support for so radical a measure as continental free trade. A small but influential group of economists were weighing in in various universities and think-tanks like the C.D. Howe Institute, providing a measure of economic viability, although no new dominant discourse had supplanted the Keynesian paradigm as of yet. And political and bureaucratic leadership was beginning to emerge as well, facilitated by institutional restructuring within the Canadian state. This restructuring allowed the emergence of new champions to promote ideas heretofore regarded as marginal. With Trudeau and his national mode more or less discredited, the conditions were developing for change. The election of the Mulroney Conservatives further consolidated the new political and bureaucratic leadership which would assist in the process of evolution towards a new economic development strategy for Canada.

In retrospect, 1985 was the turning point leading to the FTA and Canada's new continentalization, and the key event was the release of the Macdonald *Report.* But it remains to be seen exactly *why* the Macdonald Commission recommended free trade, and why the discourse of neoconservative continentalism emerged so forcefully in the commission's *Report.*

CHAPTER 2

The Macdonald Commission:
The Struggle Engaged

I saw an old man in the park;
I asked the old man why,
He watched the couples after dark;
He made this strange reply: –

I am the Royal Commission on Kissing,
Appointed by Gladstone in '74;
The rest of my colleagues are buried or missing;
Our minutes were lost in the last Great War.

But still I'm a Royal Commission
Which never has made a report,
And acutely I feel my position
For it must be a crime (or a tort)
To be such a Royal Commission.
My task I intend to see through,
Though I know as an old politician
Not a thing will be done if I do.[1]

This book argues that the transformative change in public policy resulting in the embracing of free trade was the consequence of a coalescence of certain requisites which found a temporary institutional site in the Macdonald Commission. To appreciate the role played by the commission an elaboration of the nature of this type of inquiry is required, thus the present chapter briefly examines the legal basis of royal commissions in Canadian politics and the historical and political roles these inquiries have traditionally played. It also examines the origin of the idea to stage a Royal Commission on the Economic Union and Development Prospects for Canada, the drafting of its terms of reference over the late 1970s and early 1980s, the recruitment of a chairperson and executive director, and the embarrassing incident that brought the commission to life.

This brief overview of royal commissions generally, and the Macdonald Commission specifically, establishes *why* these bodies *may* become the site of transformative change. As Thomas Berger comments, royal commissions 'supplement the traditional machinery of government, by bringing to bear the resources of time, objectivity, expertise, and by offering a forum for the expression of public opinion.'[2] In essence, they represent temporary institutional structures wherein ideas and interests are given a scope and leeway they might not typically realize in other, more common institutional sites (the executive, legislative, and judicial branches of government, say, or political parties, interest groups, and social movements).

The Legal Basis of Commissions of Inquiry[3]

The institution of royal commissions, like other types of public inquiries, are governed by the Inquiries Act, which is divided into two parts. Part I provides for 'public inquiries,' which are described as inquiries 'made into and concerning any matter connected with the good government of Canada or the conduct of any part of the public business thereof.' Part II authorizes 'departmental investigations,' which investigate and report upon the business of government departments and personnel.

The Inquiries Act, formally entitled 'An Act respecting inquiries concerning Public Matters,' was given royal assent on 22 May 1868; it was based on an earlier Act passed in 1846. The Inquiries Act itself, in Part I, proclaimed that the governor general, whenever he or she 'deems it expedient to cause inquiry to be made into and concerning any matter connected with the good government of Canada, or the conduct of any part of the public business thereof' may give commissioners the power to summon witnesses who must testify under oath and produce whatever documents or things are requested by the commissioners. The second section gives a commissioner the same power to enforce the attendance of witnesses and to compel them to testify. It also provides that any 'wilfully false statement' made by a witness shall be punished in the same manner as perjury and states that no witness 'shall be compelled to answer any question, by his answer to which he might render himself liable to a criminal prosecution.'

These provisions were reformed when, on 7 May 1880, royal assent was given to 'An Act to authorize making certain investigations under oath.' This Act provided for a minister, with the authority of the governor-in-council, to appoint a commissioner or commissioners to investigate and report upon the business of a government department and personnel of that department. The commissioner(s) were given the power of access to any public office or institution and its records, and the power to issue subpoenas for witnesses who would have to testify under oath, and who could be compelled to bring with them 'any document, book, paper or thing' in their possession relevant to the inquiry. The Act of 1880 required that a person who failed to attend when required, or to produce evidence required, or who refused to be sworn or answer any proper question, was liable to a fine not exceeding four hundred dollars.

In 1889, the Act of 1868 was amended to provide that witnesses shall not be excused from answering a question on the grounds that their answer might self-incriminate. Any such evidence, though, would not be admissible in a criminal proceeding, except in the case of a witness charged with having given false evidence.

In 1906, the Acts of 1868 and 1880 were joined in the Revised Statutes of Canada as 'An Act Respecting Public and Departmental Inquiries.' The Act of 1868 became Part I, and the Act of 1880 Part II, of the new statute. In 1912, important sections were added to what was now the modern Inquiries Act, and the final part of the Act was put into place in 1934 by an amendment dealing with international commissions and tribunals.

Although no exact accounting exists, it is estimated that from 1867 to 1977, over 450 commissions had been appointed by the federal government under Part I of the Inquiries Act, while about 1,500 had been appointed since 1880 under Part II. But as the Law Reform Commission of Canada points out: 'Sometimes it is uncertain under what authority a commission of inquiry has been appointed. On some occasions, a royal warrant was issued, but no order-in-council can be discovered; some commissions appear to have been established without either a royal warrant or an order-in-council. There is no way to estimate what must be the very many times that the powers bestowed upon a commissioner by the Act have been exercised pursuant to another statute which makes explicit reference to the Act.'[4]

The Macdonald Commission was created under Part I of the Inquiries Act by Privy Council Order 1982-3438 in order to: 'inquire into and report upon the long-term economic potential, prospects and challenges facing the Canadian federation and its respective regions, as well as the implications that such prospects and challenges have for Canada's economic and governmental institutions and for the management of Canada's economic affairs.'[5] But the dry, legalistic description of royal commissions belies the essentially political nature of these bodies, and the way they reflect the greater struggles within society. So, before considering the Macdonald Commission itself in some detail, we will examine the political role of these types of inquiries.

Royal Commissions in Canadian Politics

Many volumes of study have been produced *for* royal commissions over the years, yet few have been produced *about* them, despite their significance in sustaining and legitimizing, or challenging and undermining, political ideas and discourse.[6] An intrepid reporter once determined that 'royal commission reports and the transcripts of their hearings occupy an entire alcove in the parliamentary library, or about the same amount of space as the bound volumes of Hansard.'[7] Another noted the centrality of royal commissions to the Canadian identity. Talking about the 1955 Massey Commission on the Arts, Letters and Sciences, he observed that 'some nations develop a culture through centuries of accumulated custom and achievement; others forge an identity through revolution or war. Canada established a royal commission. Could there be a more eloquent comment on our national character?'[8]

The historical significance of royal commissions in the Canadian experience is profound. Many have produced recommendations later adopted by governments which have resulted in fundamental alterations in Canadian public policy; which have contributed substantively, in other words, to transformative moments. These include the Rowell-Sirois Commission, the Massey Commission, the Gordon Commission, the Commission on the Status of Women, and the Berger Commission. Others, like the Commission on Aboriginal Peoples, have held great promise, but have not delivered according to their advance billing. There are also commissions whose impact is more nebulous. For instance, 'the Trudeau government dealt with the Pepin-Robarts Report [from the Task Force on Canadian Unity] by ignoring it.'[9] Nonetheless, this inquiry is often cited as having an important impact on the great constitutional debates of the 1970s and beyond.

Despite their influence on the course of Canadian history in the literature of the social sciences there are few detailed analyses of the role, processes, and outcomes of royal commissions, although there are several short essays on particular aspects of this phenomenon.[10] Because of their unusual nature and the wide range of forms which take, royal commissions exist somewhere between the various disciplines which might logically seek to analyse them, such as political science, political economy, law, history, sociology, or economics.[11] According to one observer, the academic literature on policy-oriented commissions tends to focus on three characteristics: '(a) analyzing a commission's report for themes and recommendations; (b) assessing the impact of a commission's report on the policy development and implementation processes; and (c) on the basis of 1 and 2 [sic] trying to answer the question of whether a commission's benefits outweigh its costs.'[12] Another participant-observer of royal commissions claims 'a commission is chiefly remembered for its final report. The untold story, normally, is how the commission produced the thing for which it is remembered.'[13]

Royal commissions have usually dealt with the most pressing issues of their times and the range of topics covered is quite wide. As Trebilcock et al. have suggested, royal commissions 'have studied a vast range of subjects, ranging from the very narrow (the sex life of the oyster, the sex life of a cabinet minister, the fall of a bridge) to the very broad (bilingualism and biculturalism), and including virtually all the major social, economic and political issues facing the country.'[14] For example. in the early years after Confederation transportation policy and alleged lapses in the accepted standards of public administration were investigated. During the first decades of the 1900s, commissions considered such topics as the ownership of natural resources, industry and banking, immigration, and defence policy. As a consequence of growth in the concerns, size, and scope of government after the 1930s, several more comprehensive and significant commissions of inquiry have been struck to deal with broad social and economic issues.[15] Indeed, there have been over 450 federal commissions of inquiry since Confederation, with and without the title 'royal.'[16] While taxonomies of royal commissions have been created, these bodies defy easy categorization due to their flexible nature.[17] Analyses of the decennial frequency of royal commissions reveals that a low of twenty-three such inquiries were held between 1870 and 1879, and a high of eighty-three between 1910 and 1919. More recently, the 1960s witnessed twenty-nine such inquiries. Twenty-eight were held in the 1970s, while twenty-one were convened in the 1980s.[18]

Given the frequency of royal commissions, the range of topics covered by them, and their pivotal role in the delineation of public issues and public debate, it is surprising that little comprehensive analysis has been done on them. Nonetheless a benign conventional wisdom has devel-

oped in that area of political science concerned largely with constitutional law: 'The inquiry is a particularly complex and interesting
phenomenon in the political life of western democracies. It offers the
public an unlimited opportunity for experiencing direct democracy,
that is, widespread political participation in the formation of specific policies. It offers an opportunity to define specific public issues, in the public view, with the participation of the clients of those policies. It provides
an avenue for a public investigation of public and private conduct, far in
excess of that conducted by the Ombudsmen. At the same time of
course, inquiries provide governments with the opportunity to delay,
obfuscate, and defuse political controversy, and with advice that they are
free to ignore.'[19] A sanguine view of their utility, presented by a former
commissioner, is that 'the work of commissions of inquiry, both through
their hearings and in their reports, has brought new thinking into the
public consciousness; expanded the vocabulary of politics, education,
and social science; and added to the furniture that we now expect to find
in Canada's storefront of ideas.'[20]

But the nature of royal commissions contains a fundamental internal
tension with regard to their role and their potential for contributing to
transformative moments in public policy. This is the potential of inquiries to incorporate radical discourse while maintaining an orientation to
limited and pragmatic policy goals.[21] An inquiry operates with a mandate,
but often its scope is so broad that there are almost no practical limits to
the information it can receive, or the proposals it can consider. But at the
same time, inquiries must report to government, and more than any
other advisory body, their members are focused on the task of persuasion
and the need to create recommendations that are agreeable, or at least
feasible, to those who receive them.[22] Liora Salter identifies this as a contradiction within the royal commission process. 'The first contradiction
of this inquiry process lies in the capacity of inquiries to incorporate quite
radical debate,' Salter says, 'while oriented to the quite limited, highly
pragmatic and, indeed, reformist goal of producing specific recommendations for policy.'[23] Richard Simeon, a research coordinator with the
Macdonald Commission, put it this way: 'Royal commissions are
appointed by governments in power. By their very nature they can be no
more than meliorative and reformist, rather than revolutionary. Members are representatives of established elites. Commissions are also crea-
tures of their times; perhaps the best that can be expected is that they
collect, and then express, a shifting conventional wisdom, tilting it in one
or other way, but working well within the bounds of the existing order.'[24]
In other words, commissioners must find a balance between acceptable

reformist prescriptions for the problems they are studying and the more radical suggestions they receive. Inherently, if the commission adopts the radical agenda presented to it, it calls into question the very legitimacy of the government and system as a whole. But if it does not pay heed to the more glaring criticisms offered, it undermines the legitimating role it was intended to serve. Alternately, it can frame its recommendations in such a way as to foreclose the more radical options it receives. In this regard, royal commissions play a significant role regarding the maintenance of existing dominant societal paradigms or the construction and emergence of new ones.

Salter compares the Macdonald Commission to the Berger Commission[25] to underline this point. In the Macdonald Commission, the description of a 'crisis' in the economy served to limit the range of proposals that would be taken seriously. In Berger's case a new description of the problem, generated through the inquiry itself, permitted it to go beyond the limitations of the original mandate. Salter sees the two as a contrast between radical and reformist models, and claims the primary struggle in both inquiries was over how to define and understand the problem to be addressed: 'It was a struggle over *language* because the description of the "crisis" in each case would predetermine the acceptability of proposals to respond to it. This is an important insight ... We would do better if we understood that recommendations are important primarily because the pressure to produce them exerts a powerful control upon the commissioners and forces even the most radically inclined inquiries to be pragmatic and reformist in the final analysis.'[26] Salter identifies an important problem inherent in royal commissions, but concedes that further analysis is needed to explain this lack of radicalism and why inquiries seldom reach beyond the narrow limits of pragmatic politics.

Other political economists provide an alternative explanation for this apparent contradiction within royal commissions. They argue that in theory a royal commission is a useful device for shaping public debate and creating a consensus on divisive issues, and that such a model existed in the Berger Commission. But ultimately, 'royal commissions are rarely an exercise to get to the bottom of things. Nor are they established primarily to educate the public, as many political scientists suggest.' In fact, Daniel Drache and Duncan Cameron argue that royal commissions serve an explicitly political purpose:

Governments need to defuse explosive issues. Since royal commissions are perceived to operate impartially, they are the ideal instrument of brokerage politics. In contrast to the theoretical purpose of *producing* a consensus through a formal process of fact-finding, the job of a royal commission is to *appear* to have produced a consensus.

A royal commission can change not only the focus of public discourse but also conventional wisdom, by generating an 'expert' body of knowledge. For this reason the commission must be headed by a high-profile, supposedly neutral person, often an ex-politician or judge, who is seen to be acting in the national interest ...

This legitimization is completed by the hiring of learned academics to research and write background studies and the final report.[27]

The so-called contradiction identified by Salter is readily understandable as commission politics which outweigh concerns about giving a fair hearing to radical propositions from social actors.[28] As the evidence provided below reveals, this contradiction lies at the heart of the debate about the legitimating role the Macdonald Commission played in forwarding the neoconservative continentalist position. When seen through the lens of a transformative change model, royal commissions can readily be identified as sites where considerable potential exists to marshal the requisites of viability and leadership to fundamentally alter the ideational landscape and foster the emergence of new paradigms.

Establishing the Macdonald Royal Commission

Faced with a seemingly intractable contradiction between the national mode of its major policy initiatives and an emerging continentally oriented economy in the early 1980s, the Canadian government responded by creating the Macdonald Commission. Its mandate was immediately criticized as absurdly broad and unwieldy.[29] The whole story of the Macdonald Commission has not yet been told. So far, all we have are snapshots of the process leading up to the decision to create the commission, speculation as to the motivations of the players involved, and reviews of the final *Report*.[30] The following sections summarize the key events in the creation of the commission and conclude with an examination of its multifaceted mandate.

The Origin of the Idea

According to one observer of public inquiries, 'the important moments in the life of a public inquiry occur right at the beginning with the decision to establish an inquiry, the selection of its members and the drafting of its terms of reference. Once these executive acts have taken place,

there is no going back ...'[31] It is unclear who was primarily responsible
for the idea of staging this royal commission. The notion was bandied
about in the Prime Minister's Office and Privy Council Office for many
years before the decision was actually taken to proceed. In the late
spring and summer of 1982, discussions were ongoing between the
prime minister and two of his key advisers: Michael Pitfield, clerk of the
Privy Council; and Michael Kirby, deputy clerk. They were assisted by
Robert Rabinovitch, secretary to the Cabinet Committee on Priorities
and Planning, and Ian Stewart, senior economic adviser to the prime
minister.[32] Originally, they contemplated a royal commission specifically
on the economy. According to Kirby, the idea was not initially his, but
probably Pitfield's, or possibly Stewart's. 'It was sort of born, and then I
don't remember when the first meeting was where we would have talked
about it. But basically Michael and I took charge of it using Ian's brilliant pen, and input from Bob.'[33]

Whoever fostered the idea initially, the circumstances giving rise to the
need for a commission were fairly clear. Kirby suggested that:'Michael
and Ian and Bob and I had concluded that, look, the country was about
to go through a major transformation. There was a clear need to restructure the economy, there was a clear need to reform all the social programs we were doing. And what we really needed was the best kind of
creative thinking that we could get, free from the constraints of the government, and free from the narrow ideology of either the right or the left.
And so, we would go ahead and create the commission.'[34] Macdonald
recalled that the origin of the commission could be found in the unfin-
ished constitutional project of the last Trudeau government: 'As the
name indicates, the first inspiration for it came out of dealing with the
aftermath of the constitutional changes of 1982. There was a strong feeling at that time that insufficient progress had been made on the question
of inter-provincial barriers to trade, and on the struggle within the economic union generally. So that one of the thoughts that originated, I suspect in the PCO, perhaps even among the prime minister's own staff, was
that a lot of work had been done, they felt some progress had been made,
but it didn't gel into anything, so that they wanted to continue on that.[35]
But by the time Macdonald was recruited to the commission in the summer of 1982, 'it was quite a fully fleshed out proposition.'[36]

Drafting the Terms of Reference

The development of the terms of reference for this inquiry was in the
hands of this small coterie of officials closely linked with the Trudeau

nationalist policies of the 1970s and early 1980s. While Pitfield, Kirby, Stewart, and Rabinovitch guided the commission to life, the person who 'held the pen' drafting the terms of reference for them was Alan Nymark, a PCO functionary who later became a key player in the writing of the commission's *Report* and in the emergence of free trade as a key recommendation.

The terms of reference went through many drafts, dating back to the late 1970s. Macdonald recalled that 'the general description of it had been worked on for some time.'[37] While it did start out as a commission on the economy, the prime minister, Pitfield, and Kirby were quick to agree that a proper economic study could not be conducted without broadening its terms; that they could not look at market institutions without dealing with government institutions. And they could not examine government institutions without dealing with certain legal and constitutional issues.

As the terms of reference were developed, Nymark played an important role. Kirby had known both Nymark and lawyer Gerry Godsoe (who became the Macdonald Commission's executive director) when they worked for him on the constitution in 1980–2 in the Federal-Provincial Relations Office. Godsoe recalled that Nymark 'was the guy who was kind of keeping the manuscript. For example, we would mark it up and say "we want to do this or we want to do that." And he would come back with the next draft.'[38]

Nymark recalled that the terms of reference evolved over a number of years, with many hands contributing to them. He also suggested that it reads as though there were many hands. He personally 'held the pen,' but noted there were a lot of inputs. Nymark reported to Kirby and Pitfield, who had a determining influence on what the terms of reference would look like at the end of the day. The prime minister had his own hand in it as well. Nymark sent drafts of the document up the line through Kirby and Pitfield to the prime minister on many occasions, each draft reflecting Nymark's perception of the changing views of the prime minister and his senior advisers.[39]

The idea of staging a broad royal commission was bound up in the view that the government needed to step back from the day-to-day affairs of governing to look at the bigger picture. According to Nymark, in many respects Canada, and much of the world, was beginning to lose its way in terms of policies and institutions. People were losing faith in the traditional tools of economic analysis, and there were strong ideological and methodological debates within the economics profession reflecting this among supply-siders, monetarists, Keynesians, neo-Keynesians, and so forth.[40] This reassessment of traditional academic nostrums, according to Nymark, was partly the result of the rapid changes confronting Canada and the world, both of which had been buffeted by a series of shocks as revealed in the government's emerging fiscal crisis. While great leaps forward were taken in the social services areas in the 1950s, 1960s, and early 1970s, that era appeared to be drawing to a close, and it looked in Nymark's view increasingly impossible to sustain traditional Canadian programs. As well, the problems of federalism appeared to be irreconcilable, and there was a sense that even if there was a constitutional settlement, it would not really resolve the fundamental underlying economic problems facing Confederation. The post-war era of development appeared to be drawing to a close, and Canada was entering a new, largely undefined, era.[41]

Nymark also contended that globalization was beginning to make itself felt at this time. Canada was going to have to be increasingly concerned about dealing with global issues and competitiveness. The basis of Canada's competitiveness, the natural resource sector, had been a cushion and Canadians were overly confident that it could continue to generate wealth that would allow an ever-increasing rise in standards of living. But the basis of wealth, the management of the economy, the social benefits Canada traditionally enjoyed, and Canada's role in the world all appeared to need redefinition. Nymark claimed that Canada needed to look forward and redesign the country, in essence, in a number of fundamental areas. The idea of a royal commission according to Nymark, was to take hold of these ideas and articulate future directions.[42]

Discussions of these matters continued during the brief Conservative interlude of the Clark primeministership in 1979–80, and when Trudeau returned to power, the notion of a royal commission continued to be mooted. It was felt that even though Trudeau had a strong agenda, including patriation and the NEP, his government still needed to look forward to the latter half of the 1980s and beyond, and to do some fundamental rethinking about a new Canada. But creating a royal commission too early in the government's life would be admitting the government was incapable of coming to terms with the rapid changes buffeting the Canadian state. So while Trudeau returned to power with a fairly clear set of goals in 1980, he also kept the idea of a broad royal commission alive for launching towards the end of his mandate.[43]

The idea of staging a royal commission was intellectually appealing to the prime minister and his key advisers. 'If you look at the three of them, the prime minister, Pitfield and Kirby, all of them have an interest in this kind of thing,' Macdonald recalled.[44] While Trudeau did not play a proactive role in the development of the commission, he had some input according to Kirby:

> He reviewed the terms of reference when we gave them to him, and he talked about names. He had views on certain names. I don't remember the names of all the people beyond Don. But he had views on the pros and cons of certain individuals. But it was not an issue that galvanized him the way certain other issues did, but that was natural. I mean, we were in the midst of the constitutional thing which had just blown through town for a year and a half, and we had economic problems coming out our ears. So it was intellectually important to him, but he also knew that the commission would not be reporting until after the next election. It was intellectually appealing in that he wanted to be comfortable with the terms of reference, but he was not going to devote a lot of his effort to it. You send other people out to develop the terms of reference for you.[45]

Macdonald recalled that he dealt primarily with Kirby in the early stages of planning the commission. 'Michael Kirby, for example, was the principal interlocutor, although I did talk to the prime minister from time to time,' Macdonald remembered. 'I talked to the prime minister more after I accepted the position, and got some feel of how he saw it, what the government's purpose was in doing it, and what he thought about it.'[46]

Indeed, in February 1983, Trudeau met with all the commissioners over dinner at 24 Sussex Drive. He opened the meeting in an informal manner, suggesting that Macdonald chair. Trudeau stressed the autonomy of the commission, and also pointed out that he had originally expected it to be a small one composed of very bright Canadians who, independently of the political process, could look at the larger issues confronting Canada. While the discussion proceeded informally, each commissioner was offered the opportunity to suggest what they thought was the most pressing issue confronting the commission. Many, like Angela Peters, Daryl Seaman, Jack Messer, and Clarence Barber, stressed the economic issues in the mandate. The prime minister responded by indicating that he did not see the main role of the commission as economic forecasting and proceeded to make a lengthy intervention on federal-provincial relations from Confederation to the present.[47] The focus for the prime minister was clearly federalism rather than the economy generally or free trade specifically.

But Macdonald also noted the purview of the project kept growing beyond its original intent. The prime minister, Kirby, Pitfield, and the other senior advisers 'felt that there was a clearer definition required on the inter-provincial relations question. But inevitably, it kept getting joined to questions of where, in a broader sense, is the economy going? And also are there some failures systemically in the political system that we can try and do something about? So it is like a continuous web, and the more you looked, the broader it got.'[48] Significantly, when presented with the terms of reference, and in helping to develop them in discussion with the prime minister and his top advisers, Macdonald recalled that free trade was never mooted and did not even come up as a potential topic of investigation for the commission.[49] That the development of the terms of reference was in the hands of a small coterie of officials closely linked with the developing Trudeau nationalist mode is an important point, revealing the ideological distance the commission travelled to reach the neoconservative continentalist prescriptions eventually arrived at.

Selecting a Chairperson

According to Doern and Tomlin, 'Donald Macdonald's role in the free trade story provides the irony that makes politics interesting and unpredictable.' Macdonald was Alberta Premier Peter Lougheed's nemesis as federal energy minister from 1972 to 1975, when he introduced many of Ottawa's interventionist policies. But later, in 1988, they co-chaired the pro-free trade coalition: 'Throughout his political career, Macdonald was known as a strongly partisan Liberal and a member of the nationalist wing of his party. Yet he and the Commission he headed provided nonpartisan legitimacy for free trade and a reduction in the role of government as a policy for Canada's economic salvation.'[50]

Kirby was made personally responsible for recruiting Macdonald. As to why Macdonald agreed to serve, Kirby insisted that there is an inherent appeal to working on a project like a royal commission for certain kinds of civic-minded individuals. He counted Macdonald among those who are so inclined, and claimed that Macdonald put his finger on why these individuals will even sacrifice their careers and potentially higher earnings in order to be part of such endeavours. Kirby personally visited Macdonald on behalf of the prime minister to do the 'sales pitch,' while Trudeau was expected to 'do the closing':

So we were sitting in Don's back yard, and we got talking before I made the pitch about how he liked being in the private sector, and he said something intriguing, which I now believe on the basis of my own private sector experience. He said 'the difference between the public sector and the private sector is you get paid a lot more in the private sector, you have a lot more free time, you are not hounded by the media so you can be your own person – and it is incredibly boring.' And he is right! And that is it! And his point is that it is very hard once you have played in the game here to be truly content doing other things which may make you more money and give you more free time ... And if you are intellectually engaged, it is very hard to get out of it.[51]

There was no doubt for Kirby that Macdonald was in this category. Macdonald 'could have made a fortune,' according to Kirby, and in fact lost money every single day he worked for the commission. Moreover, he took public abuse for the fact that he was being paid eight hundred dollars a day, although he could have made twice that in his law practice. Macdonald would do this apparently thankless job because it was intellectually engaging, according to Kirby.[52] But he also did it for altruistic reasons: 'And the other thing about Don, of course, the other Achilles heel about the guys around here, is that you can always appeal to them on the altruistic ground that your country needs you. And we have all been sucked in. And it is a combination of altruism and ego. You have to be egotistical to think that your country needs you and you really matter, but you also have to have the ego to think you can actually make a difference.'[53]

There were also countless rumours that the position was given to Macdonald as a sop by Trudeau. Macdonald had quietly let it be known that he was considering seeking the nomination to succeed Trudeau, and when Trudeau unexpectedly stayed on, Macdonald may have felt betrayed. Thus Trudeau, the rumour went, made him the commission chair partly in order that he might use the high-profile sinecure to position himself for a run at the leadership after Trudeau really retired. The personal reasons for accepting such a daunting assignment are complex and difficult to disentangle. But wrapped up with intellectual stimulation, altruism, political motivations and satisfying egos are much deeper ideological forces which shaped Macdonald's decision. These are explored in more detail in chapters 10 and 11.

Ottawa was rife with rumours after Macdonald's appointment was announced as to who had been considered for the plum job of heading up this commission. A number of prominent Liberal names surfaced as also-rans, including Pitfield's. Godsoe confirmed that Pitfield was considered, but noted his was but one name among many.[54] Pitfield himself admitted, 'I would have given my right arm to do [the royal commissioner's job] ... But the more I talked to people, the more I concluded I did not have the credibility.'[55] Pitfield was too closely associated with the worst excesses of Trudeau's secretive and arrogant inner circle of advisers to be credible as chair of the commission.[56] Nonetheless, Godsoe suggested that the most helpful person to him in Ottawa without question in the early days was Pitfield, for two reasons. First, he had considerable experience with royal commissions, and had obviously thought this one through while putting it together. And second, he gave generously of his time and advice to Godsoe, despite his onerous duties as clerk.

Selecting an Executive Director

While recruiting Macdonald, Kirby was also recruiting Godsoe as the commission's executive director. 'I also recruited Gerry Godsoe, because Godsoe is part of my "Maritime mafia," so I recruited him as Executive Director, with Don's approval, obviously. But it was a perfect fit. It was good for him, it was good for Don.'[57] Like most other commission staff, Godsoe did not intend to work full time on the commission. Kirby said he 'kind of sucked Gerry in, because that is the only way you ever get people to do these jobs.' He told Godsoe initially that he could do it three days a week over a year and a half, although in fact Godsoe ended up working full time for three years. 'It was something painfully ridiculous, but unless you have done those things before, you don't know it's ridiculous. Of course, once he got into it, he couldn't get out of it, which is fine. And he loved it, by the way, in spite of all the bitching you will get from him.' Kirby knew that once Godsoe became intellectually engaged, he would be hooked: 'if they have the kind of intellect you want, once you get them engaged intellectually, you can let the workload build up, and they will never quit on you.'[58]

In recruiting for the commission, however, Kirby could not expound on the exact nature of the project:

> I approached Gerry without telling him – my problem was I was trying to recruit two guys, without them getting in contact with each other, because I didn't want a leak. And in fact, I even recruited Godsoe to the job without telling him what the job was. I mean, Gerry is a long time friend of mine, right, so it was one of these obscure conversations about 'will you be interested in doing something in Ottawa if the federal government decided to do something along the following kind of vague lines?' I mean, he couldn't possibly figure out what we were trying to do. But with these jobs, you do

that all the time. What you are basically trying to find out from somebody early on is, without putting it to them bluntly, is if I come back to you with a specific proposition, do I have a deal? But you have to do it in a way that you don't tell them what the deal is, because if he says no, you don't want a leak, and you want at that point also to be able to say, frankly, you never formally offered the job to them. But Godsoe was a long time friend of mine, and he also knew Macdonald well, and he is very bright, so it was a good match.[59]

Kirby approached Godsoe in July 1982 about whether he would contemplate becoming involved at a senior level in a particular project about which he could say nothing. Godsoe, practising law in Halifax at the time, was intrigued, but initially said no. Godsoe's own background as a Liberal Party stalwart deeply involved in public issues included working with Kirby on economic and constitutional issues in the 1980–2 round of constitutional negotiations. Throughout July and August, Godsoe continued to resist Kirby's blandishments, which, cast in vague terms due to the secrecy surrounding the proposed commission, left Godsoe feeling he was involved in the dance of the seven veils. Obscure references to a challenging, historic project of immense consequence and dimensions, however, intrigued Godsoe such that his initial reticence gave way to curiosity, and he finally agreed to become the executive director of the commission.[60]

Once he joined the commission, Godsoe gave careful consideration to the task ahead of him. He was cognizant of the hierarchical bureaucratic structures that dominated Ottawa, and took steps to ensure that the commission would not find itself too far down the pecking order to be taken seriously by officialdom. For instance, there was a considerable amount of discussion about what Godsoe's title would be, and how he should be appointed. Ultimately, after consulting with some of the country's most senior bureaucrats, it was determined that Godsoe would be called 'executive director' rather than 'secretary,' and that he would be appointed by the same order-in-council that appointed the commission. As an order-in-council appointment, Godsoe carried the same rank as a deputy head, which allowed him the clout he needed to get things done in 'official' Ottawa.[61]

But before accepting, Godsoe came up with a list of conditions. One was to be involved in shaping the mandate. He also wanted the full support of the prime minister and the government, and of the commission chairperson, and to talk to the chairperson before making a final decision. As it turned out, both the prime minister and chairperson had already discussed and approved of Godsoe. That summer of 1982, Godsoe went to Toronto for a meeting with Macdonald, whom he had also known for years through the Liberal Party, and talked to him for quite some time about the challenge and the mandate of the proposed commission. One of the key points Godsoe wanted to address was the nature of the relationship between the chairperson and executive director, particularly as it was evident that the former would be working part-time and the latter full-time on the commission. Godsoe recalled, 'He looked at me and he said "Why, you would be my alter ego." And I said, "That satisfies me. I'll do it."'[62] And that, according to Godsoe, was the basis of their working relationship.

When Godsoe went to Ottawa in September 1982 to begin organizing the commission, nobody outside of a small, select circle knew anything about it. The whole enterprise was shrouded in a cloak of secrecy. He was given a pass and security clearance by the RCMP, and a small broom closet of an office on the fifth floor of the Langevin Building. He proceeded there directly each day without stopping in the PMO or anywhere else along the way because very few people knew about his activities at that point. Godsoe started working with Kirby and his secretary and Pitfield and his executive assistant on designing the mandate and membership for the commission, and on mapping the structure, budget, and how to run it.

Godsoe had not seen the actual terms of reference while he was being courted to participate in the commission by Kirby. It had been described to him, but he was not given a copy of them until after he had taken an oath and formally signed on to work for the commission, because it was a secret document. It was described to him as its mandate evolved through the summer of 1982 from an economic one to one which turned out to be considerably broader, and by the time Godsoe arrived the terms of reference were reasonably complete. Heavily weighted towards economic issues, but also dealt with political, legal, and labour issues, although there was still considerable ambiguity. One of the first tasks Godsoe embarked on in his cubby-hole office was to try to frame the terms of reference in a way that suggested all these disparate issues were interdependent and not consecutive issues. He wanted them analysed from the perspective that they were interrelated, horizontal issues which cut across each other in various ways, and thus had to be treated as such. The commission, then, would not start with the economy and then move on to government issues, but rather analytically treat both as connected, interdependent concerns.[63]

Godsoe also thought about process, and he insisted upon three provisions which had never been thought of before in a royal commission mandate, as far as he was aware.[64] One was that the commission would be subject to an automatic sunset clause. Godsoe was aware that the Privy Council, as the administrative superintendent for all statutory royal commissions, historically has had enormous problems in bringing commissions in on time and under budget. Controlling royal commission expenditures is terribly difficult because there is no easy mechanism to do so. Thus a sunset clause was inserted into the terms of reference, giving the government a whip with which to enforce the notion that either the commission would produce a report by a certain date or the whole thing would simply be shut down. Godsoe regarded this as an important imposition of discipline, and he had the full support of Macdonald, as neither wanted to make the commission a life's work. They recognized there is always a trade-off between speed and efficacy and quality. Godsoe feared his researchers constantly pleading, 'for God's sake, if you can only give us six more months or another year or even six more weeks, it can make a big difference on quality.' But they agreed that, while the thirty-six-month time frame of the commission was going to be difficult to observe, given the mountain of work ahead of them, ultimately it was desirable. If a window had not been imposed, the project might never have been completed.[65]

The second provision Godsoe insisted on was a directive to the government to provide the commission with any information it required. On achieving this Godsoe immediately wrote to all of the deputy ministers and deputy heads of government departments or agencies in which he thought the commission had an interest and asked them for a list of all pertinent studies, papers, commentaries, and analyses they had on a series of topics of potential interest to the commission. The right of access to government information and documents caused some consternation among senior bureaucrats. But Godsoe had a suspicion that there were plenty of bright ideas in various government studies which might offer the commission a shortcut, but which had perhaps been blocked by the bureaucracy or by the political process.[66]

The third condition was the right to publish the research of the commission. This is not automatic, because all the commissioners are required to do is deliver a report to the governor-in-counsel under the enabling statute. Godsoe inserted a 'right to publish' clause to ensure that even if the commission research was highly critical of the government, it could not be blocked for partisan political reasons. He was relieved to discover that this requirement went unchallenged.[67]

As Godsoe wrestled with the initial plans for the commission, and as each successive draft of the terms of reference broadened its mandate, he encountered several problems. Macdonald recalled that 'in the circumstances, the organizational problem we had as we started the project was to try and narrow it down to workable propositions because the subject matter was so broad.'[68] But ultimately, before a final acceptable draft of the terms of reference could be completed, they were forced into action by unforseen circumstances.

The Leak

The first public fact of the commission's life was that its existence was leaked to the press on 5 November 1982, before the commission's terms of reference were finalized. Nymark recalled the terms of reference were almost finished when the premature launch of the inquiry became necessary. But he thought that it could have taken another full draft before the government was formally prepared to issue it. Nonetheless, it was on the street and the decision was taken to proceed. Still, it took some scrambling to launch, and another three months or so to name all the other Commissioners after the initial announcement.[69]

Needless to say, the leak proved to be a source of embarrassment for the government. Since a great deal of secrecy surrounded the establishment of the commission, even Trudeau's Cabinet and caucus colleagues were unaware of its existence until the day it was revealed through the media.[70] Kirby explained the secretive process surrounding the creation of the commission by drawing an analogy to Senate appointments: 'Like Senate appointments, they [royal commissions] are the prerogative of the Prime Minister. And he had not wanted a leak of it, partly because it was his prerogative. Trudeau was interesting on some of these things. If it was his prerogative, he might or might not discuss it with other people. Other than that, there was no particular reason that I can recall.'[71]

Godsoe was in Ottawa staying at the Chateau Laurier when he received a call from a reporter from Standard Radio Broadcast News at two o'clock in the morning asking for a comment on the announcement of a major royal commission. The fact that the story leaked had both positive and negative consequences for Godsoe: it was a big shock to the system, since it had been kept a secret very successfully, but now Godsoe could literally come out of his closet, openly consult with people, and really start to get some work done.[72]

One of the only published accounts of the initiation of the commission is provided in the memoirs of Trudeau's former minister of state for regional and economic development. Despite being a member of Trudeau's Cabinet, as well as a close personal friend of the prime minister, Donald Johnston was excluded from the decision-making process that led to the creation of the Macdonald Commission, and cites this as evidence of the emasculation of the Trudeau Cabinet in the final years of its tenure. In his autobiography *Up the Hill,* Johnston recalled that on 5 November 1982, Liberal MP David Collenette rose during Question Period to ask the prime minister the following question: 'According to press reports, an announcement will be made of a special Royal Commission to deal with the economy. I should like to ask the Prime Minister if this is true and, if so, if he is at liberty to reveal its membership?' Trudeau's response was the following:

> Madam Speaker, I am happy that the Honourable Member has shown interest in this matter. I can assure the opposition that, as far as I know, the interest is purely spontaneous. I am glad to have an occasion to answer this in the House because it is a matter of some embarrassment to me that this leak has occurred, and I am sure it is of great embarrassment to Mr. Donald Macdonald who has been approached to be the Chairman of such a Commission.
>
> With your indulgence Madam Speaker, I am happy to give what details I can of the Royal Commission ... the purpose of which would be to inquire into the economic prospects in Canada in the middle and longer term, and to look at the institutional arrangements which might be necessary for the strengthening of that economic union ... To add to my embarrassment, I have not even consulted my colleagues in cabinet or caucus on this project, although the Deputy Prime Minister knows about it ... I think this Royal Commission will be extremely important, in terms of the change in thinking regarding the future of the country. I hope it will play a role as important as that played by the Rowell-Sirois Royal Commission in the years after that was produced ...[73]

With this rather inauspicious beginning, the largest commission of inquiry in Canadian history was launched.

Johnston recalled that 'the Prime Minister's announcement struck me with the force of a lightning bolt. As minister of State for Economic and Regional Development, it was inconceivable to me that such a Royal Commission would be named without prior consultation with the Minister of Finance, Marc Lalonde, and myself.'[74] Johnston also wrote:

Hearing that exchange on the floor of the House my feelings were better imagined than described. The Prime Minister had just told Canadians that a Royal Commission on the economy, which he judged would be of equal importance to the Rowell-Sirois Commission had been named without consulting Cabinet, and that the terms of reference had been completed and would be submitted to the Governor General that same day.

Not to have consulted me was incredible enough, but not to have consulted or informed the Minister of Finance was unbelievable ... I have often seen Lalonde annoyed, even angry, but seldom had I seen that jaw as set and those dark eyes flashing as they did that day. Even Deputy Minister Allan MacEachen confessed that he had just learned of the creation of this Commission during Question Period when he enquired about the leaked newspaper item which was in front of his seat mate, the Prime Minister. At least we all had equal treatment.[75]

Godsoe was given the thankless task of explaining this oversight to Lalonde. He was understandably anxious:

I remember a meeting in the Prime Minister's Office at the House of Commons and learning for the first time that the Minister of Finance had not been told about this major royal commission to be chaired by a former minister of finance on 'the economy and other things.' That sort of struck terror in me, and I was told 'well he knows now, and you, Godsoe, are going to go and brief him on the mandate because he hasn't seen it.' So, I dutifully did it with my head under my arms already severed to see Marc Lalonde who, you recall, was a person of very strong words and strong emotion when the case calls for it, and he was certainly justified. Anyway, he absolutely tore me to shreds. We've been very good friends since, but it was certainly not a high point in the relationship.[76]

Nymark argued that the Departments of Finance and Economic Development were in fact well informed of the ongoing intentions of having a royal commission on the future of the modern development of Canada, but there was no doubt that the leak and the announcement precluded full Cabinet discussion. But since prime ministers normally see the appointments of royal commissions as essentially their prerogative, it should not be surprising to other Cabinet members that they might not be fully consulted.[77] Nonetheless, Johnston makes the interesting point that this was the first step in undermining the credibility of the Macdonald Commission:

The handling of the whole Macdonald Royal Commission was such a high-handed affair that, at the outset, its credibility was undermined ... Initially it was widely seen as an effort by the Prime Minister's entourage to give Donald Macdonald a profile from which he could move forward into a leadership context as a strong alternative to John Turner. In other words, the creation of the Commission was seen more as a political move in the interests of the anti-Turner forces than in the interests of the economy ...

I am driven to the conclusion that, in this case as in others, Trudeau and his advisers decided to pursue certain objectives on their agenda and damn the consequences even if it meant alienating the caucus and Cabinet. His advisers scorned the views of elected representatives who might question their judgement.[78]

The 'official' explanation for the leak was contained in a document labelled 'Briefing Notes for Commissioners: Confidential.' In dealing with the embarrassment, commissioners were instructed to say 'there is no doubt that the Prime Minister would have engaged in full consultation with his ministers and advisers in the normal course of things in advance of any public announcement. It is regrettable that process was short-circuited.' It went on to suggest, 'Nonetheless, the chairman and all commissioners believe that a "false start" will not interfere with the serious nature and substantive items that we have to address.'[79]

But credibility problems would plague the commission throughout its existence and continue to cast a shadow on its work. They will be considered in more detail in the next chapter.

The Macdonald Commission Mandate

Perhaps the two most noteworthy aspects of the commission's terms of reference were its complexity and the absence of any indication that free trade was to figure prominently in its deliberations.

The complexity of the commission's mandate[80] was frequently criticized. For example, many of the groups that presented written briefs to the commission lamented the unfocused nature of the mandate, which made it difficult for them to comment intelligibly on the problems facing Canada. Indeed, several of the commissioners themselves made disparaging remarks about the definition of the task they were assigned. Macdonald recognized this problem early on, as he told a *Globe and Mail* reporter: '[Macdonald] says the subject matter is so amorphous – the broadest mandate given any royal commission, he claims – that many of the commission's recommendations or observations will probably be couched in vague terms, or carry disclaimers saying "it's very difficult to get any kind of clear shape of the future."[81] Some of the many issues considered included: trade relations; labour-management relations; unemployment insurance; profit sharing; the quality of the school system; industrial restructuring; the business culture; management techniques; entrepreneurialism; funding of the arts; tax reform; foreign ownership of the economy; the management of natural resources; and Arctic sovereignty, among others. In hindsight, Kirby admitted that the breadth of the terms of reference 'was one of the great mistakes of trying to do this. But they were broad partly because Don wanted them broad in a couple of places, and partly because our desire was to really have a truly creative look at the big problems facing the country.'[82] Furthermore, the designers of the commission did not want 'to constrain the Commission from getting into any area that it wanted to get into. So they [the terms of reference] were left as vague as possible to maximize the flexibility of the Commission.'[83]

Nymark justified the breadth of the mandate by arguing that Canadian society was undergoing such a fundamental transformation that anything less than a hugely comprehensive investigation would not be able to do justice to gaining an understanding of what palliative the country required. The essence of the genesis of the commission reflected a sea change across the broad spectrum of Canadian society and the issues that government must deal with, according to Nymark. It was not any particular set of issues that drove the framers of the mandate over the years. Rather, different sets of issues arose and the interconnectedness of those issues was the compelling reason for developing what many people described as overly comprehensive and unwieldy terms of reference. Indeed, the commission renamed itself a 'Commission on Canada's Future' because the set of issues were that broad (and because its formal title was such a mouthful). According to Nymark, that was seen as both the strength and the uniqueness of the commission.[84] 'Kirby felt that the basic motivation for the Commission was straightforward enough: The basic motivation was, look, there are a huge number of problems coming down the road, all of which were ultimately identified in the royal commission. And what we really needed to do was get a good objective look at the whole thing, where the country's going. And the only way to do that is to put it out into a third, independent, neutral party, like a royal commission. And what you wanted to do is you wanted to find people who are really bright and yet pragmatic enough to understand the real world as opposed to putting out a bunch of academic stuff.'[85] Thus, the view developed within the government that an arm's-length examination of the country's longer-term predicament was the only way to come to terms with the changes and crises confronting Canadians. A royal commission was chosen as the instrument for this because, Nymark felt, governments are not particularly known for their ability to reflect on fundamental issues, nor for their ability to see the linkages between economic, social, and institutional areas. Governments are also not particularly good fore-casters of future events and future trends, he argued. Those sets of link-ages, a comprehensive, global approach to the future, and a period of reflection were seen by Nymark to comprise the rationale for a study external to government.[86]

The principal instruction to the commission was 'to inquire into and report upon the long term economic potential, prospects and chal-lenges facing the Canadian federation and its respective regions, as well as the implications that such prospects have for Canada's economic and governmental institutions and for the management of Canada's eco-nomic affairs.' As well, the commission was to recommend 'the appro-priate national goals and policies for economic development' and 'the appropriate institutional and constitutional arrangements to promote the liberty and well being of individual Canadians and the maintenance of a strong competitive economy.'[87]

An incredibl two hundred questions were posed by the commission in just fifteen pages in its initial publication, *A Commission on Canada's Future: Be Part of It.* This document spelled out the commission's terms of reference and invited Canadians to comment on the country's future. But it posed so many theoretical questions that it was hard for either com-missioners or the public to know where to begin. Nonetheless, the dis-course of the terms of reference is striking for the way in which it reflects the dominant paradigm of the era in which it was written. That is to say, the terms reflect a faith in Keynesianism, though not an unwavering one, and a presumption of a role for government in the economy. Strikingly, there is little of the discourse which came to characterize the neoconser-vative continentalist view which would so quickly become dominant, and which found expression in the commission's *Report.* It is particularly sig-nificant that there is next to nothing in the terms of reference that sug-gest that comprehensive free trade with the United States should be considered, let alone be the key economic development strategy for Can-ada in the future. It is worth examining the discourse of the terms of ref-erence to elucidate the ideological paradigm within which this inquiry appeared to be framed. In terms of considering economic development strategies for Canada, these questions can be summarized under five general categories: government intervention; foreign direct investment; industrial strategy; regional economic development; and trade policy.

What is most striking in hindsight about the terms of reference is the emphasis placed on the presumption of a role for government in the economy. For example, the commission was instructed, in pursuing its inquiry and preparing its report, to proceed by reference to several principles, including most significantly that: 'the Government of Canada has the primary responsibility for managing the national economy, for encouraging reasonably balanced economic growth among the various regions of the country and for ensuring that fiscal disparities among the provinces are reduced, while at the same time the provincial governments also have important responsibilities in the development and carrying out of economic and social policy.'[88] Furthermore, reference was made to the principle that 'the Canadian economy is founded on the enterprise and productivity of individual Canadians supported by a unique mixture of public and private sector activity that reflects the traditional values of Canadian society.'[89] As well, the commissioners were advised that 'Canadian economic policy must be assessed in the context of its relationships to Canadian political and economic independence and to the broader aspirations of Canadians as must be reflected in the responsibilities of governments.'[90] In short, there was much to guide the commissioners along the path of traditional Canadian economic development strategies focusing on nationalist policies with a prominent role for government, and little to suggest a turning point entrenching a continentalist economic blueprint that reduced the role of government and threatened Canadian independence.

Nonetheless, there were clues that suggested an opening to the neo-conservative discourse that the commission would ultimately adapt. '*What is the role of government?* What is the "unique mixture" of public and private sector activity on which the Canadian economy is founded?' the commission asked.[91] These questions, of course, were in the minds of many not only in Canada, but in most Western industrial democracies. Some governments, like those of Thatcher and Reagan, had clearly made up their minds to minimize government involvement in the economy. The Canadian government, in true Canadian fashion, equivocated and left the question to a royal commission. It went on to explore a series of related questions:

Can we measure a precise percentage of government involvement that is the 'right' mixture, a percentage which can serve as a goal and a guide for governments and a standard by which government can be measured by individual Canadians?

... Is there a set of principles which can define the appropriate role of government given shifting economic circumstances, preferences and needs?

Does the best course into the future involve a clear separation of the public and private sectors? Or does it involve a closer partnership? Are there ways for government and the private sector to keep each other better informed? If such a partnership is undesirable in terms of the domestic economy, does intensified competition abroad require a greater concerting of public and private resources in foreign markets?

Within the questions concerning the relationships between governments and the private sector lie another set of questions related to the way the bureaucratic systems of the private sector on the one side and of government on the other side affect the capacity of our national industrial structure to adapt.[92]

Related to these kinds of questions were those about the proper level of regulation in the economy, and the place of Crown corporations. Did the answers to Canada's difficulties lie in 'regulation, in codes of economic conduct or in the encouragement of more competition so that those without power or access to power are guaranteed choices and alternatives?' the commission asked. 'Are crown corporations, as economic institutions of growing importance, sufficiently under the control of government? Or have they become rogue elephants, operating in the private economy with the impunity of the Crown? Should they be subject to the same rules as private sector companies with which they compete? Do they add to our economic adaptability or impede it because they are not subject to the rigors of market discipline?'[93]

The contentious issue of foreign direct investment also loomed large in the commission's thinking: '*What are our goals in terms of capital?* Do we want to emphasize investment in Canada by Canadians? Do we need foreign capital to create the kind of flexible industrial structure we may require in the future? If we do, how do we preserve Canadian control of the economy? *Are there ways in which we can diversify our sources of foreign capital?* Or does our best chance lie in becoming a capital exporter?'[94] Although it did not use the term 'industrial strategy' explicitly, the concept clearly concerned the commission. This was placed in the context of the broader question of how goals are set in Canada and by whom:

Is one of the sources of present economic difficulty the lack of goals or the wrong goals? Or is it that we do not have the means to establish any goals that can command the support of those who ultimately must implement them, even if they are the appropriate goals? ...

Beyond the life of the Commission, what means will be in place to adapt goals to change and altered circumstances, reassess the possibilities and to ensure that the goals – or the policies and programs to achieve them – continue to command the broad support essential to their achievement?

Is that a task for planning expertise? For governments? For organizations related to but separate from governments like the Economic Council of Canada and provincial economic councils? For Parliaments and Legislatures? For First Ministers and the bureaucratic structures that provide their advice? ...

Or does our greater problem lie in the lack of effective means to co-ordinate the economic actions of governments in order to achieve accepted goals?[95]

The commission went on to ask what goals, policies, and programs were most suitable to the Canadian condition:

Are the goals to be long-term in nature or short term, or a set of short-term targets leading toward a long-term result? ...

Are the objectives to be specific and quantifiable or general and directed to establishing an approach or strategy rather than a specific result? For example, is the goal a precise percentage increase in growth, inflation, productivity, output or employment? Or is the goal to shift from a resource-exporting to a technology-exporting, or an energy-based to an information-based, or a production-based to a service-based economy?

Are the objectives to be based on our performance relative to our past performance, on regional performance relative to other regions, or national performance relative to our competitors?

Do we need one set of goals for the national economy and a strategy to achieve them, ten sets of goals and ten strategies, or national goals incorporating regional objectives?[96]

Related to the question of an industrial strategy, the thorny issue of regional economic development was broached within the context of Canada as a trading nation:

Do we need separate goals for the export oriented regions and for those under pressure from imports? If we have separate regional economic goals and strategies, how do we integrate them into a clear set of goals for the national economy?

How do internal barriers affect our ability to improve our international perfor-
mance and meet the goals we set? How do they affect our ability to achieve balanced growth throughout the economy? Do these barriers prevent the
development of world-scale industries? Should it be a basic goal to remove
the explicit barriers that exist?

What are the hidden barriers to the effective operation of the economy implicit in
national policies, provincial polices and local policies with regard to standards of
safety, incentive grants and tax provisions? Do we need to harmonize policies
that may unintentionally prevent us from embracing economic opportunities? What is the balance to be drawn between the need to improve our
economic performance on a concerted basis and the need to preserve a
healthy diversity?

How do we overcome the barriers that are an inevitable part of Canada – the
geographical distances, the linguistic differences, and the regional differences – so as
to enhance our economic prospects? How do we better employ the creative possibilities of these same differences so as to gain greater advantage from
diversity?[97]

Not surprisingly, the commission asked a set of questions concerning
Canada's future trading relationships:

Are we to be more open to the world, in order to secure our opportunities abroad? Or
are we to be more closed to insulate ourselves from the effects of instabilities in a more interdependent world? And if we are to be more open or
closed, what are we to be more open or closed to? Goods? Services? Technology? People?

Do we concentrate our international efforts on preserving a relatively open inter-
national trading and financial system as a continuing basis for our economic poli-
cies? Or do we shift our emphasis toward the development of a major
trading bloc in order to reduce our vulnerability to the shocks transmitted
through the open international system?

If that is the approach, what are the high growth economies on which we
should concentrate?[98]

These questions, the commission stated, bore directly on the Canadian-
American relationship, especially in light of the decline of American
hegemony:

Does our best course lie in greater access to U.S. technology, ideas, capital, markets
and expertise – that is, in a harnessing of our economic interests to American eco-

nomic strengths? Or does it lie in greater distance so as to insulate ourselves from the instabilities the United States itself creates for the Canadian economy and the world, and so as to acquire greater room for manoeuvre in dealing with other economies?

Has the very openness and complexity of the Canada-U.S. relationship created too great a dependence on one market for Canada to have much room for manoeuvre toward economic performance significantly better than the U.S.? Are there ways to create, over time, more room for manoeuvre? What are the costs and are we prepared to bear them?[99]

While these latter questions were not particularly prominent in the document, there was nothing initially to suggest that the issue of trade would feature so prominently in the commission's *Report*, much less that bilateral free trade with the United States would become the signature recommendation of this commission. Peter Warrian, who acted as a special adviser to Commissioner Gerard Docquier, recalled: 'Free trade as a policy issue has been booted around, it has come and gone consistently. There is no doubt that the commission was supposed to discuss the economic union and was expected to deal somehow with the free trade debate in some fashion. That falls well short of, and if you take the terms of reference, that falls significantly short of making it the unilateral, dominant issue, which is certainly what the outcome of the *Report* and the handling of the commission's work came to be. If you read the original mandate, it is a much broader spectrum than just the free trade issue. But all anybody got out of it [the commission] was free trade, and take a whack out of the Unemployment Insurance.'[100]

Moreover, there was little that suggested a preference for neoconservative discourse, especially when the language of the terms of reference and commission mandate are compared with that of the final *Report*. Nor was there evidence to suggest that the commission would be anything less than open to ideas – even radical ones. If Drache and Cameron are right about the corporate bias of the commission and its rejection of popular sector alternative economic strategies, it is not because the commission was not initially open to hearing from these groups. Indeed, by asking the question, 'Do we need significantly greater democratization of economic decision-making, both publicly and in private organizations?,'[101] the commission implicitly invited the kinds of alternative prescriptions which Drache and Cameron assert it later ignored. This controversy will be considered in more detail in later chapters when an examination of economic development strategies presented by organized interests to the commission is undertaken.

Conclusion

The legal basis of royal commissions reveals little about the underlying political struggles engendered by such bodies. Nonetheless, the important role these inquiries have traditionally played in reinforcing or challenging societal paradigms is rooted in the legal and institutional structures within which they are organized, as well as the roles and predispositions of the key actors involved. In view of these factors, the establishment and goals of the Macdonald Commission are cast in a revealing light. Most striking, apart from its ignominious start, is the comprehensiveness of the terms of reference and their omission of free trade. But also of significance are the recruitment of key personnel and the ideological starting point they generally occupied. The next chapters elaborate on these points by assessing the process by which agents were selected to work on the commission, and by analysing the major components of the inquiry: the public consultations; the research program; and the policy group and the writing of the *Report*.

CHAPTER 3

Seeking a New Consensus

> The task of the commission could have been defined as 'the universe is in
> trouble – please advise.'[1]

This chapter examines the process by which the Macdonald Commission carried out its work. As such, it sketches the interplay of ideas, institutions, and interests. It first notes the strains engendered by a variety of
political factors at the outset of the inquiry. It then briefly outlines the
three main components of the commission before concluding with a
short review of the recommendation for free trade in the commission's
Report. In so doing, the chapter notes the manner in which the public
submissions to the commission contributed to the generation and evolution of political viability; the ways in which the research program contributed to the generation and evolution of economic viability; and the
contributions of the chairperson and policy group to the generation
and evolution of political and bureaucratic leadership.

Strains in the Universe of Political Discourse

While a royal commission is often seen as a tool to repair or reinforce
political discourse and societal paradigms, the launch of the Macdonald
Commission appeared at first to have had the opposite effect. For example, both the choice of Macdonald as chairperson and the $21 million
price tag attached to the commission were objects of criticism in the
media and among opposite parties.[2] Macdonald's per diem of $800, the
alleged partisan motives behind his appointment, and the charge that
the commission simply duplicated numerous existing economic and
public policy research bodies were frequently mentioned.[3]

Macdonald's fee in particular attracted the ire of the Opposition, especially since he continued to be involved in his law practice while chairing the commission: 'The New Democrats called the fee "obscene" and when Mr. Trudeau replied that half the fee would go to Mr. Macdonald's law firm, McCarthy and McCarthy, to cover overhead, Conservative MP Ray Hnatyshyn said it wasn't part time work for which Mr. Macdonald was being paid, but "pork time."'[4] Conservative leader Joe Clark vowed to fight the commission and to ensure that it was made accountable to Parliament, and not just the government that appointed it.[5] Macdonald's ill-considered response to this criticism only fanned the flames even higher. He argued that the commission actually represented a pay cut for him. 'The chairman, who had a billing rate of $2,000 a day in his law office, was knocked pretty hard for getting $800 on the Commission.'[6]

Comments such as these, made during the worst recession in Canadian history since the 1930s, were hardly going to endear the commission to ordinary Canadians, and provided much fodder for media headlines. 'Press reaction in general was unsympathetic, and a representative view could be seen in the Globe and Mail editorial [11 November 1984] that quoted with approval the remarks of the NDP House Leader Ian Deans: "If the government needs a Royal Commission to find out what is wrong in this country, what should be done about it, its time they got the hell out of here."'[7]

Commissioner Albert Breton recalled the initially negative reception the commission encountered: 'The climate at the time was very anti–Macdonald Commission. The media was very much against it. The media turned pro-Macdonald the day the *Report* came out. When they saw it they said you did *all* of this over such a short period! But earlier, they never referred to the commission without mentioning that Macdonald was paid $800 a day. And then Don gets irritated easily and said things which I think he would agree he should not have said, like "I should be paid a hell of a lot more." There were groups that thought that we were not [legitimate].'[8]

Macdonald recalled being stung and surprised by the initial negative response the commission received, particularly in the media, which he partly blamed for the commission's credibility problems. 'The reporting is just so incredibly superficial,' he claimed, 'it hasn't encouraged people to think that, "gee, this is worthwhile thing you're doing, an occasion to do something."'[9] He further claimed, 'they really dropped a load on us. But the newspapers in 1985 and since then have been recording it as an authoritative document, but not at the time.'[10] He felt that the public consultation process helped to dispel some of the initial negativity toward the exercise: 'Those arguments just went away. They dropped away. Perhaps it [the consultation process] did this. You would, every now and then, run into a reporter who was obviously totally unprepared to cover the Commission, who would run to the paper's files, find the $800 story, and ask questions that were asked. But on the whole that ceased to be a problem. Maybe we got a momentum of our own, or maybe the press just got bored of it and went somewhere else. Anyway, the criticism dropped of.'[11]

The choice of Macdonald as commission chairperson was, as described above, clouded by reports that the position was a consolation prize for having the leadership of the Liberal Party snatched from his grasp when Trudeau returned from his short-lived retirement in 1980. Robert Prichard, Macdonald's close friend and confidant, recalled:

> The first that I learned of the prospect of the commission was Don telling me that he was contemplating doing it, and I certainly understood it, if I wanted to put a political spin on it, that Mr Trudeau had badly disappointed Mr Macdonald in, whenever it was, December, January of 1979, after Mr Trudeau had announced his resignation, had visited Mr Macdonald, had asked Mr. Macdonald to run, urged him to run. Don had for many years decided not to, but changed his mind, not just with the urging of Mr Trudeau, but others, had agreed to do it, geared up, was on the verge of announcing, and then Mr Trudeau didn't [retire] ... I don't say it to be critical. I'm just saying, if you're trying to understand the dynamic I certainly saw the dynamic as one which this was Mr Trudeau and his colleagues giving Donald a, not a consolation prize in any sense, but a genuine opportunity to serve his country that wasn't inconsistent with the longer term prospects for his leadership. If he were to write a vision of Canada that was compelling, it would make him that much more qualified to be the leader at a later date.[12]

But Kirby dismissed reports that Macdonald's position was related to Trudeau's change of mind: 'People get all these ideas. We went to Don for two reasons. One, he is very smart. He has all of the criteria you could ask for. He is a really bright guy. The brightness is important in that Don is able to deal with concepts and big issues, as opposed to being narrowly constrained. That is number one. The second thing he had going for him was that we wanted someone who had a mixture of both governmental experience and business experience, because we did not want an abstract, theoretical result. So that is why we went to Don.'[13]

As for the notion that the commission was a consolation prize, Kirby exclaimed, 'are you kidding? He needed that like a hole in the head.' While the commission would have propelled him into a very public position, Macdonald had 'by then, for a number of personal reasons, basically the illness of his wife, decided he wasn't going to enter the [leadership] campaign anyway.'[14] Nonetheless, this speculation dogged the commission and its chairperson as they set about their work, further inhibiting the legitimacy problems.[15]

Recruitment to the Commission

Kirby and Pitfield drafted lists of potential commissioners and senior staff and presented them to the prime minister, who had some ideas on names himself. According to Kirby, 'we then put the rest of the commission together, the way these things are always done, by looking for a combination of talent and geography and sex, and all of the other stuff.' Besides Macdonald and Godsoe, Kirby also helped recruit Nymark, Senior Adviser David Ablett, and Special Adviser Michel Vastel, among others: 'Nymark was working for me at one point, early on, on the constitutional exercise. One of the guys that was in there, well down the list, but in the group. And Godsoe needed someone who knew the Ottawa bureaucracy really well, and knew the Finance Department particularly well, because in a sense they had to be able to get access to information in the government. So Nymark happened to be available. Alan wasn't chosen because of any particular ability – he was chosen for being smart, and able, and all of that, which were sort of minimum requirements – but in addition he was chosen because he really knew the Ottawa system.'[16] But Nymark was not actually hired by the commission until after it had been up and running. He recalled that he had been invited to join the commission because it appeared to be getting off to an excessively slow start, and it needed reinforcements. The combination of a large number of commissioners appointed over a short period of time and very broadly based terms of reference meant there was some difficulty in structuring the commission. Plus, staffing went more slowly than anticipated.[17]

Some of the others in the upper echelon of the commission, such as Ablett, were suggested by Rabinovitch: 'He [Ablett] was in the PCO. Ablett had been working for Bob Rabinovitch, and Rabinovitch thought this would be great, right down his line. Ablett's background was as a *Toronto Star* newspaper guy, and he was brilliant – one of the best writers I have ever, ever run into. And they were obviously going to need that talent, and what a great place to put him.'[18] Vastel was sought out by Macdonald and Godsoe, who recognized the need for a Francophone communications ability. Vastel and Macdonald had a relationship going back to the latter's incarnation as a government minister and the former's as a press gallery journalist. But as brilliant as these appointments may have seemed to Kirby, they had the effect of tainting the commission. All were well-connected Liberals, or associated in some way with the fading Trudeau regime. Hence the legitimacy of the commission was suspect for this reason too.

Godsoe decided early on that he wanted to second talent from the private sector to work on the commission. But he found corporate Canada disinterested in committing resources to this undertaking, and was disappointed by the general lack of enthusiasm. Originally, he thought that he could draw half of his senior staff from the private sector and half from the public sector. As a corporate lawyer, Godsoe was well-connected to the Canadian business world. But when he went to the major umbrella business organizations and tried to convince senior executives to join the commission, he discovered that Canadian businesses were not prepared to release anybody useful, although lots of 'dead wood' was readily available. The result was that the commission had more bureaucrats than Godsoe felt healthy. On the other hand, among those organizing the hearings were people from non-government organizations (NGOs) who knew how to organize public participation exercises. The commission ended up with the NGOs dominating the hearing process, the academics dominating the research process, and the bureaucrats dominating in the policy group and occupying most senior positions within the commission.[19]

Godsoe also picked his own administrative officer, who reported directly to him. Harry Stewart had been an administrative officer for the Privy Council and came out of retirement to work on this commission as a favour to Godsoe. Stewart only agreed to do it, though, after the direct intervention of the prime minister on Godsoe's behalf. It was Stewart's job to ensure that the commission was administratively 'squeaky clean,' and to act as the whip to ensure the project came in on time and under budget. It did, and it was.[20]

As Godsoe, Macdonald, and Kirby began to put people in place on the commission, they considered the idea of running the commission out of Toronto. Godsoe and Macdonald in particular both thought that getting away from Ottawa would permit a fresh perspective on the problems facing the country, allow for some new ideas uncoloured by the weariness of a spent government, and give them the chance to escape the constraints of officialdom found in the nation's capital. But the Toronto option proved to be impossible for two main reasons. First the administrative costs would have been substantial. By working in Ottawa, the commission received a number of 'freebies' from the government it would not have otherwise received. For example, the commission got a good deal on rent from Public Works for its offices on Sparks Street which it would not have realized in Toronto, despite the fact that the federal government has land and buildings in Toronto. In addition, the commission received tremendous support from the PCO, because it could spare people on an as-needed basis. As well, Ottawa provided the commission with a bilingual capacity which it would have been more difficult to obtain in Toronto. Also, the commission could draw administrative and clerical support from the federal government and guarantee that the people involved could return to their old jobs once the commission was finished. They could not do this if they hired staffers off the street in Toronto, and they would incur severance obligations and other complications. Godsoe and Macdonald thus concluded that the commission had to be run out of Ottawa. Nonetheless, it was agreed that Macdonald, as a part-time commissioner, would spend a considerable amount of his time working in Toronto.[21]

Selecting Commissioners

The selection of commissioners was initially in the hands of the prime minister, Pitfield, and Kirby, according to Nymark.[22] Later, Macdonald, Godsoe, and others became involved. Besides the commission chairperson, twelve other commissioners – nine men and three women – were named. They were: Clarence Barber, a University of Manitoba economics professor; Albert Breton, a University of Toronto economics professor; Gerard Docquier, Canadian director of the United Steelworkers of America; William Hamilton, president of the Employer's Council of British Columbia; John Messer, a former NDP Cabinet minister in the Saskatchewan government and Saskatoon resources expert; Angela Cantwell Peters, chairperson of Bowring Brothers Limited of St John's, Newfoundland; Laurent Picard, dean of the Faculty of Management at McGill University and former CBC president; Michel Robert, a Montreal lawyer; Daryl Seaman, chairman of Bow Valley Industries of Calgary; Tommy Shoyama, a University of Victoria professor and former federal Ministry of Finance mandarin and senior bureaucrat in the CCF-NDP governments of Tommy Douglas in Saskatchewan; Jean Wadds, former Canadian high commissioner to the United Kingdom and Conservative MP; and Catherine Wallace, a retired educator and executive from New Brunswick.[23]

The size of the commission, mockingly referred to as Christ and the disciples in some quarters, was the largest in Canadian history. When asked why so many commissioners were chosen, Macdonald suggested: 'It was a classic Canadian problem of representativeness. We were trying to represent regions, of course. You tried to represent different functions in the community, so you had Gerry Docquier, who was vice-president of the CLC, and Bill Hamilton, who was president of the B.C. Employer's Federation. Then you wanted to have someone like Catherine Wallace who had been in the education field. And on the other hand, you wanted to have a couple of business people, which Doc Seaman from western Canada, and Angela Cantwell Peters from Newfoundland were.'[24] The selection process was undertaken, according to Kirby: 'the way these things are always done, which is a very inefficient process, but there is no other way of doing it. You kind of decide what is the number you want, and then you figure out, you better have so many from each region, and then you better make sure you have a number of females, and you have got to have an Aboriginal. I mean, this is not a scientific process here. But you had to make sure that they were people Don could work with, and so in some cases, he actually interviewed some of them.'[25] Originally it was thought that six or seven commissioners would be sufficiently representative while being a small enough number to permit a consensus to emerge. But the more the government considered the composition of the commission, the more complex it became. The more commissioners the prime minister, Pitfield, and Kirby added, the more they found they had to add.

A number of criteria were applied to the selection of commissioners, including regionalism, political partisanship, representativeness, and so on. For instance, because they decided to name someone from Alberta, it was thought that there had better be commissioners from other western regions. Thus British Columbia had to be included. But you could not allow the entire prairie region to be represented by Alberta, so Saskatchewan had better be represented. And if two of three prairie provinces were going to be included, it would not look proper to omit Manitoba. The same type of approach, of course, had to be applied to the Atlantic provinces. The internal logic of regionalism imposed itself upon these considerations.

As well, the commission had a high-profile Liberal at its head but could not be seen as a partisan body. Some balance had to be struck between the major political orientations in Canada, and thus New Democrats and Conservatives were conscripted. It was also decided that the major representational groups in Canadian society should be represented, beginning with business and labour, in order to lend credibility to the commission. But wary of being charged with bias, a document entitled 'Briefing Notes for Commissioners: Confidential' instructed neophyte commissioners on how to deflect media questions about the make-up of the commission. It suggested they say, 'the Commissioners represent a broad cross-section of Canadian enterprise. It is multi-partisan, and reflects experience in federal and provincial government, in business, labour and the academic community.' It went on to suggest 'if there is any "bias" in the Commission, it reflects a commitment to the long-term economic and social future of our country, and none of us will apologize for that.'[26]

These extraordinary attempts at representativeness reflected the Trudeau government in the last gasps of its final mandate going into a tailspin and 'getting a little bit closer to the bunker.' The prime minister was increasingly unpopular, there was an ugly mood in the country, and the appointment process was seen in part as a method of defusing the potential political controversy that might erupt around the commission.

The massive size of the Macdonald Commission proved to be a liability in organizational terms. The naming of thirteen commissioners was a mistake, according to Kirby, 'because we got caught – that was stupid, number one, in retrospect. It was so large precisely because we were trying to be all things to all people. In large part that was driven by geography, in large part it was driven by the need for a whole variety of special interests to be covered off. That was not a good idea, by the way.'[27] This highlights the problem of trying to be representative in a country like Canada, and reiterates one of the initial problems confronted by the commission – its general lack of legitimacy. The chairperson was acutely aware of this problem. 'Yes, it was not perfect,' Macdonald offered, 'but I don't know that perfection is achievable.'[28]

Ironically, Drache and Cameron criticized the commission for failing to be representative of Canadian society as a whole: 'While this list covers Canada's regions and makes a token nod to ethnic diversity, its social and economic makeup is awry. The members are mostly older and well off; government, academia and business are well represented in a sort of plurality of the establishment. But farmers, churches, the voluntary sector, the arts community, social agencies, Native Peoples, the young, the poor and the unemployed are all absent. Labour is clearly under-represented, and while there are three female members, there is no representation from the women's movement.'[29] Partly on the basis of the composition of the commission, Drache and Cameron conclude that the process was biased in favour of corporate Canada from the outset. But perhaps the real futility of trying to be as representative as possible of every segment of Canadian society is best illustrated in this anecdote related by Macdonald: 'Eventually we arrived at this number, and we sat down at one of our early panels, and Tommy Shoyama, who is a Japanese-Canadian, was confronted by a man who said "I don't know if I should talk to you because you don't have any visible minorities." I was stunned, and I didn't know what to say. It was certainly true that we didn't have a wide range of them. And Tommy spoke up and he said, "sir, how visible a minority do you have to be before you get noticed?" And the fellow did a double take and sat down.'[30]

The question of representativeness was particularly acute for the lone labour representative on the commission, Gerard Docquier. Peter Warrian, director of research for the United Steelworkers of America, assisted Docquier throughout the commission.[31] Warrian recalled that the legitimacy question for Docquier was threefold. First, to have no labour representation at all on a commission of such magnitude was seen as unwise. There was much discussion within the CLC as to whether having a labour representative on the commission would co-opt the labour movement, but in the end it was decided that 'you had to have some labour person there, and he got agreement for that position from his colleagues on the executive committee of the CLC.'[32]

Second, there was a division within the house of labour between two of its most powerful unions, the Steelworkers and the Auto Workers, over economic development strategies for Canada, particularly as they related to trade issues. Warrian argued that Docquier, as a member of the Steelworkers, was only too conscious of the similarities and differences between these two labour actors, which might make it difficult for him to present a unified labour face to the commission. For instance, both Steel and Auto are major industrial unions in Canada, and they both work in industries that have huge export components. But Warrian argued that the Auto workers have for historical reasons had a major amount of institutionalized protection. They have free trade in autos, but they have employment and production guarantees which gives them 'a bit of a free ride when they oppose free trade.'[33] The Steelworkers also have a major stake in the trade issue, but without the protection afforded the Auto Workers by the Auto Pact. So Docquier had to perform a careful balancing act in presenting labour's position.

Third, as Warrian explained, the experience of labour in the tripartite experiments of the 1970s had not been a happy one. The first time there had been institutionalized participation by labour in any tripartite body occurred in 1978, with the Trudeau government's twenty-two sector task forces on the economy. According to Warrian, 'the union leadership automatically assumed they were entering a stacked deck, but there were at least some defensive political reasons why they better be there with respect to certain undertakings. They better be there to fight the good fight, being pretty skeptical about what would come out of it.'[34] This scepticism carried over to Docquier's appointment. But the decision was made to participate, and Docquier was given the blessing of the CLC executive, since there was an overriding 'legitimate concern that labour be represented, and that was accepted by the CLC executive.'[35]

Still, Docquier suggested that the make-up of the commission was a liability and failed to be reflective of the interests of Canadians. Moreover, he argued, there was an ideological as well as a political slant to the commission which was never entirely overcome. If he had been in charge of establishing this commission, Docquier would 'try to have a better balance of the interests of the people in Canada. And I would say the same thing in terms of the research. I think I would try to have a larger scope of individuals in terms of their political thinking or, I don't like the word ideology because that does not always serve the best interests of the group to base your decision on ideology, but maybe I would do it from a wider angle, let's put it that way. And try to collect the views of more different orientations.'[36] Despite his reservations about the term 'ideology,' Docquier conceded that the commission was ideologically narrow in its outlook: 'The composition of the board again, it was obvious that they were trying to do a balancing act. There was somebody from labour, there was a guy from the NDP, there were Conservatives. But all of the others were certainly Liberals, or with Liberal connections. And that could have been maybe a little less obvious – no, not obvious, a couple of other people with a more socially-oriented kind of bias would have provided a better balance.'[37] Then the outcome of the report might have been different, he suggested. 'You never know. It could have been different. Sometimes one feels lonely there.'[38]

The Process

After the controversy surrounding its establishment in November 1982, the Macdonald Commission set about its work in earnest in 1983. At the time of its creation, it was the largest, most expensive, and widest rang-

ing inquiry into the state of the Canadian nation. No other royal commission had ever ever so broad a mandate, consulted so widely, or
engaged so much research. The Macdonald Commission undertook a
three-pronged approach to consultation through public hearings, private meetings, and an all-encompassing academic review of government
policies.[39] Included in this process was the three-month journey across
Canada in the fall of 1983 to twenty-eight towns and cities, where the
commission met with more than 700 groups and individuals, and gath-
ered more than 1,000 briefs and transcripts totalling some 40,000 pages.
Coupled with the seventy-two-volume output of the policy review, this
massive amount of material served as the raw data through which the
commissioners sifted in order to arrive at their recommendations. To
assist the commissioners, a small but influential 'policy group' was created under the guidance of Nymark. A brief introduction to each component of the commission and its place in providing the requisites for
policy transformation follows.

The Consultation Process

The consultative process was the first of the three main divisions of the
commission. It incorporated innovative techniques for tracking and
recording the views of Canadians using computer technology and content analysis of the briefs submitted by commission participants. Every
individual and every group appearing before the commission was
logged onto a computer which also recorded the topics of their submissions, and which cross-referenced each submission with similar topics. It
also broke the groups down by region, sector of activity, and organization type. Transcripts of all public hearings were recorded, and the computer kept track of the huge volume of correspondence received by the
commission. Thus, it was a relatively easy task for the commissioners to
access any piece of information they required which arose out of the
hearings process, the largest public participation process ever held in
Canada to that point in time. The entire exercise was coordinated by
Michel Rochon, commission secretary, who wrote in a memorandum,
'in order to capture the hopes and desires of Canadians and to make
meaningful recommendations on how to proceed in the future, it is
essential that our Commission hear from all sectors of society.'[40]

   The commissioners embarked on an epic journey to hold public hearings in numerous communities across Canada. From these meetings
comes a rich public record of the attitudes, values, and beliefs of thou-

sands of Canadians. But perhaps equally important were the numerous private meetings and consultations for which no public record exists. Some of these latter meetings involved all the commissioners, some only some of the commissioners, and others just Macdonald. They occasionally involved commission staff, but frequently did not. For example, one senior commission officer recalled a meeting with the thirteen commissioners and Shell Canada at which the corporation shared its confidential world mandate plans. On other occasions, Macdonald met separately with the American ambassador to Canada, or with senior executives of various corporations. The National Archives, which houses the printed record of the life of the Macdonald Commission, is regrettably silent on such meetings.[41]

Nymark felt that public consultations were the only way for the commission to gain legitimacy. Dealing with a subject such as the future of Canada, he argued, one could not go away in secrecy for a couple of years with a bunch of academics and develop a vision as to what should be done in Canada in such a broad array of policy areas. Public consultations were necessary. There is, of course, always debate as to the role public consultations play in comparison to the research program and the deliberations of the commissioners. But Nymark felt quite clearly that all three streams of activity were fundamental to the kinds of recommendations that were made, and particularly free trade.[42] This subject will be examined in greater detail in subsequent chapters, involving as it does the controversial question of who actually influenced the commissioners' decision to adopt free trade as a major recommendation and lending the political viability to proceed with this policy option.

The Research Program

Royal commissions often have multiple objectives, and the Macdonald Commission was no exception. Indeed, the commission research program alone was designed to do several things, of which three are particularly important. One was to produce a state-of-the-art review of Canadian social science scholarship over the previous thirty years, rather than a body of original research. Some original research was called for, but only to fill in gaps. It was felt that this research would then be usable by policy decision makers as well as by academics and for teaching purposes. The second purpose of the research program was to leave behind a useful body of literature about Canada and the issues that it faced. A third rationale was to forge a network of the best and the brightest young scholars who would be able to work together in a constructive way and who might be called on by policy makers in the future for advice.[43]

The decision to develop a huge research component was made in the expectation that one of the commission's legacies would be a fundamental body of knowledge providing comprehensive survey work integrated across disciplines. The goal was not to engage in wild forecasts of what the world would look like by the year 2000, or to re-invent Canada. It would be a far-reaching research effort, according to Nymark, but one that would be conservative in nature rather than speculative while actually contributing to the government's agenda and connecting with political reality and policy making in Canada.[44] The research program was divided into three disciplines. The political science section was headed by Alan Cairns; the economics section was headed by David Smith; and the law section was headed by Ivan Bernier. All three were given the title of research director. But it was Smith's section that emerged as the predominant force, supplying the expert knowledge and research to sustain economic viability for the changed course of direction recommended by the Macdonald Commission.

The Policy Group

Despite the elaborate and impressive public consultation and research program, the commission staff felt that an organizing body of some sort was needed to bring the disparate elements of the commission's work together into a coherent whole. Godsoe was persuaded by Nymark of the need to create a small, expert body of bureaucrats who could perform this role. Nymark convincingly argued that, despite the elaborate organization put in place, there was still something missing. The commissioners were going to be receiving volumes of information which had been analysed and logged. The staff would be informing the commissioners of significant issues arising from the hearings, and working closely with them, helping them prepare questions for the submitters so they could tease out their real positions and what was truly significant. And then, of course, the work of the three hundred or so researchers would be ongoing. But it was a process that was really very decentralized, despite the efforts of research coordinators and an elaborate research network under the three research directors. Ultimately, Nymark felt, some mechanism was needed to pull these elements together in a coherent manner for the commissioners, and give them some focus. Some effort was needed to overcome the inherent decentralization of the process and the various voices crying in their own particular academic wildernesses which might or might not hear from one another, or from the hearings.

Organizationally, as it turned out, the two processes of the hearings and the research were almost totally divorced from one another. The mechanism designed to pull things together was the policy group that Nymark headed up. Ostensibly, its job was to forge links between what the commissioners were hearing and what they were reading in the research. As well, the policy group was to assist the researchers in gaining insights into what was going on in the world via the submissions. The group was also charged with helping the commissioners, through seminars and workshops, to get information from the research while they were still carrying on public hearings. The intention was to provide the commissioners with a richer understanding of the issues being raised and an analysis of the background to those issues. Logistically, however, this proved difficult to do because as the hearings were getting under way in the spring of 1983, most of the researchers were heavily engaged in their academic year at universities. Thus, the researchers complained, they were expected to begin work on their own research projects, for which they would receive 'a pittance' from the commission, while finishing their school year, and they were expected to follow developments in the hearing process too, while being prepared to inform the commissioners of the results of their research even as they were still conducting it. Several logistical problems ensued, and the policy group was conscripted to smooth over these bumps. In the process, it metamorphosed into the most significant player in the drafting of the commission *Report*, as control was heavily centralized in this oligarchy, and it supplied the catalyzing agency in the form of political and bureaucratic leadership which brought about the conditions for the transformative moment leading to free trade.

What to Do with the Commissioners

At the outset of the commission, before the hearings or research was under way, and before the policy group had begun to assert its control over the writing of the *Report*, there were some initial difficulties in getting the commissioners engaged. No one seemed to know for sure quite what they were expected to do. The commission was going through a period of some distress in the spring of 1983 because of media criticism. It was also a period of low activity for the commissioners, as neither the hearings nor research were under way. So really, there was nothing for the commis-

sioners to do. This was acknowledged in an internal memorandum out-
lining the purposes of the public consultation process. Apart from
providing an opportunity to have informal 'get to know you' sessions with
the public, and a forum for an exchange of opinion on the mandate, the
consultations were expected 'to provide a constructive use of Commissioner's time while the Commission itself was being organized.'[45]

Meanwhile, these thirteen disparate individuals had to be brought
together to act as a team, and mutual trust and support had to be developed among them. To this end, techniques were employed to force the
commissioners to spend time together – meeting for breakfast, meeting
socially, being stranded at airports together, waiting together in various
situations so that they would have common experiences. Thus, it was
hoped, both passion for the job and respect for each other would
develop.[46] While organizationally critical, this process certainly did not
prevent the persistence of disparate opinions and views throughout the
commission's life.

Another consideration was to develop ties of trust between the commissioners and the staff, particularly the senior players, who needed to
be well exposed to the commissioners on a personal basis so that they
had both credibility and influence with them. This would also permit
the commissioners to assess their abilities and usefulness, and to reach
the point where they felt they were not marooned on an island in the
midst of hostile Canadians, but rather had some real support that they
could count on.[47]

Godsoe and Macdonald had recognized a tremendous restiveness
among the commissioners shortly after their appointment. Many were
nonplussed by the negative public image of the commission. They
agreed to serve in the expectation that they would be doing something
for their country, not having to defend Macdonald's eight hundred dollars a day honorarium. Several began to wonder what they were doing
this for at this stage in their careers and professional lives. In addition,
the commission was also coming under fire because the country was
moving into an election period; it became a target for criticisms of the
bankruptcy of the Liberal government.[48]

To some extent, the commissioners initially got the impression that
the commission was just a big black box. They did not know what was
going on, or exactly what was expected of them, and they were getting
angry about this, Godsoe recalled. While the early spring of 1983 was a
period of furious activity for the commission staff, the commissioners
themselves more often than not had their noses pressed against the window looking in, and they did not appreciate their inactivity.

To clarify the commissioners' role, a series of meetings was devised by Godsoe and Macdonald. First, town hall–style meetings were organized in the spring at various universities so the commissioners could talk to reasonably small groups of people to hear suggestions about how the commission should be run, who should be running it, what should happen, what the issues were, where the country was going, and so on. In addition, several private meetings were held with only the commissioners and a few senior staff in attendance. These were designed to give the commissioners some insight into what Macdonald was cooking up with Godsoe, Rochon, Ablett, the research directors, and other senior members of the staff.[49]

One of the most significant of the special early meetings occurred in Victoria in early 1983. To engage the commissioner more fully, each was asked to write a few pages, some notes, or a short article on an issue that was close to their heart, spelling out what their views were, and where they thought the country should be going. This was an effort to get the group to betray their own biases and preferences, and their own thinking on the future of the country, according to Godsoe, and thus everyone's cards would be on the table. The exercise was a success and the commissioners loved it. It had an enormously important effect in that it helped them develop a feel for any 'hidden agendas' that might exist, and to get people on board. Thus, there was a bonding process involved through these meetings.[50]

But the real significance of this forced activity was that it foreshadowed the relative powerlessness of the commissioners as a group. It demonstrated quite clearly that commissioners were incidental to the running of the commission. Their role was peripheral and their guidance over the inquiry minimal. A pattern was established at the outset in which the titular heads of the commission played relatively insignificant parts in the design and execution of the commission. While several Commissioners expressed dismay at their marginalization in the writing of the *Report* (discussed in chapter 11), the precedent had been set for their non-decision-making roles very early on. Political and bureaucratic leadership would be tightly held in the hands of Macdonald and the policy group.

The Final Report and the Free Trade Recommendation

The end result of the massive exercise that was the Macdonald Commission was a three-volume, 1,911-page *Report* published in August 1985. A basic issue for all royal commissions is, simply, who writes the report, and how does it get written? The view that the commissioners write it is not self-evident, particularly on a large commission with part-time commissioners. On a small commission with full-time commissioners it is both more possible and more likely, especially if the scope of the report is finite, and the report is not too long. Another possibility is to have the executive director write the report, as was the case with certain earlier commissions. Yet a third option is to recruit somebody specifically for the task. Finally, since many commissions are driven by research, usually by either academics or non-academic experts, it is often the researchers who end up writing the report.

None of these options appeared satisfactory to the brain trust running the Macdonald Commission. First, the commissioners were too numerous, and only working part-time. Second, Godsoe rejected the option of having the executive director author the report, arguing that policy analysis, rather than writing, was his forte. Recruiting an outsider was seriously considered for a time, but this proved untenable for pragmatic reasons, including the scope and timing of the final document. Leaving it to the research team was also considered, but Macdonald and Godsoe were concerned that if the directors of research wrote the report, they would end up with too heavy a workload. As well, it would be more difficult to maintain control of the agenda, the issues raised, and ultimately the content of the report. And it would mean the bureaucrats would be largely marginalized, or, perhaps worse, the commission would end up with a huge amount of research, but no real substantive report. The research would hastily be rewritten as the report, and no one would be happy. In the end, Macdonald and Godsoe decided that there had to be some kind of parallel processes going on alongside the research which they could direct and control, and which reflected their own values. In this way, full control over the content of the report could be maintained. This is most evident in the drafting of the free trade recommendation.

The commission's recommendation for continental free trade is the single most important legacy of the MacDonald Commission. It marked the consolidation of the political discourse of continentalism, which triumphed over that of nationalism, and as such represented an exercise in the ideological legitimation of a new discourse advocating a radical shift to an even more integrated continental economy.[51] But in reading the terms of reference, and given the nationalist mode the Trudeau government had embarked upon, it is somewhat difficult to understand where the commission ended up.

The recommendation and rationale for free trade found in volume I of the commission's *Report* argue that Canada's trade options are limited for historical, geographic, and economic reasons to improving our relationship with our dominant trading partner. After exploring the notion of a common market and a customs union, the *Report* weakly concludes that, by 'process of elimination,' the only possible option is a free trade area.[52] The commission argued that a successful free trade agreement would include the following arrangements:

§ It should be a broad agreement, covering substantially all trade between the two countries, rather than a collection of sectoral agreements.
§ Some sectors could be excluded from the agreement's coverage.
§ It should be consistent with Canada's continued participation in GAAT.
§ It should apply to tariffs, contingency protection and other forms of non-tariff barriers.
§ The elimination of tariffs should be phased in over a period of several years. In recognition of the relatively greater effect on the Canadian economy, the phase-in period of the elimination of the Canadian tariff should be longer than that for the United States.
§ Non-tariff barriers should be neutralized or reduced by means of common procedures and controlled by codes of conduct; these codes should provide for decision making and implementation by a joint tribunal.
§ It should provide for agreed measures of transitional adjustment assistance and safeguards.
§ It should include effective dispute-settlement procedures whereby national politicians jointly arrive at final decisions; compulsory arbitration by a neutral panel should be stipulated as a procedure of last resort.
§ It needs to be guaranteed by national laws, and it should provide adequate room to involve provincial and state interests.[53]

Claiming to have carefully studied the evidence, the commissioners determined that Canada should continue to support the multilateral trading system that had sustained Canadian prosperity for forty years. But they argued that Canada was now sufficiently strong and independent enough to pursue bilateral initiatives with the United States.

Moreover, it was argued that Canada should minimize any new protection, reduce existing protection gradually as part of bilateral or multilateral negotiations, and accelerate adjustment processes. Echoing Mitchell Sharp's 1975 exploration of Canada's three options in international relations, the commission argued that in light of the changing nature of patterns of international trade, Canada was confronted with several options in formulating trade policy, each of which is contained within one of three options or approaches.

The *Report* argued that Canada could maintain the status quo with current levels of protection in place, but with selective efforts to improve access to foreign markets and to protect Canadian industry on a limited case-by-case basis. Second, Canada could participate in a new round of multilateral trade negotiations under the auspices of GATT in order to improve and secure Canada's access to foreign markets, to open up Canadian markets, and to strengthen the legal framework for international trade. Finally, in addition to initiating elimination of trade barriers at the multilateral level, Canada could open negotiations with the government of the United States to reach an agreement on a substantial reduction of tariff and non-tariff barriers between Canada and the United States.[54]

The commission rejected any increase in protectionism as well as a policy of import substitution, arguing that both lead in the longer term to major inefficiencies in the economy, a loss of jobs and lower incomes, and to an erosion of the multilateral trading system. While arguing for a strengthened international trade regime through GATT, the commission ultimately supported 'negotiations with the United States to reach an agreement on a substantial reduction of barriers, tariff and non-tariff, between Canada and the United States. Such an agreement would have to stand within the terms of Article XXIV of the GATT, and it would provide for a reduction of barriers between the two countries, but would leave each country with freedom of action to maintain separate trading policies with other economic partners. We do not recommend a more intensive arrangement such as a common market or an economic union, where even closer integration would take place between these two economies.'[55] For all its enthusiasm for free markets and disdain for the state, the commission was surprisingly ambivalent in some regards. For instance, it recommended that Canada negotiate a legal arrangement with the United States which incorporated strong safeguards to limit what it called 'spill-over' from the free trade arrangement in order to protect 'substantive policies.' These included culture and defence which, it was suggested, were functionally unrelated to trade in goods and services. 'Indeed,' the commission intoned, 'a policy that creates no linkage should be explicitly confirmed in order to avoid surprises if the Government of Canada, as we recommend, were to pursue a more aggressive policy of support for indigenous cultural expression as a concomitant trade initiative.'[56]

Moreover, the commission recommended that tariffs be phased down to zero over ten years and that effective rules of origin be developed. Enforcement would be placed in the hands of a new Canada-United States intergovernmental body known as the Canada-U.S. Trade Commission (CUSTC), and detailed codes of national conduct would be developed to govern resort to non-tariff measures such as discriminatory government procurement practices, product standards, and customs and administrative procedures. Arguing that the Canadian economy would bear proportionately greater adjustment costs than the United States, the commission proposed a two-track approach to phasing in tariff cuts to allow United States rates of duty to be reduced at a faster rate or earlier than Canadian tariffs.[57]

To make the transition to free trade as painless as possible, the commission also recommended that the Canadian government implement a 'framework for adjustment.' This would develop government programs that assisted workers to adjust to new 'employment possibilities' in the world of free trade. Thus, the Transitional Adjustment Assistance Program (TAAP) was formed to 'encourage the flexibility and growth orientation required by a freer-trade environment.'[58]

The *Report* also comments on the uses to which it put the hearings and research. In discussing policy choices with Canadians, it argues, the weight of the briefs and hearings favoured bilateralism over multilateralism regarding trade. And it referred favourably to the federal government's 1983 study of trade, *Canadian Trade Policy for the 1980s: A Discussion Paper*,[59] which had argued for comprehensive free trade with the United States:

> As a result of our hearings across the country and our study of the numerous briefs presented to us, we Commissioners believe there is broad consensus in Canada about the objectives of Canadian trade policy as described in the federal government's 1983 trade policy paper. We were told again and again that our government should use the instruments available to it to stimulate a stronger, more efficient, productive, competitive and growing economy, and promoting a more stable and open international trading environment. We heard too, that Canadian producers need better, more stable and more secure access to a large market. Many consider that the Canadian market is too small to achieve the economies of scale that would stimulate greater productivity and efficiency.[60]

The *Report* also claimed to have been cognizant of the counterarguments to this position. But the commissioners rejected them:

> The Commission heard, however, from Canadians who advanced a course of increasing protection and encouragement for the development of sec-

ondary manufacturing through import substitution. Such an approach would use protectionist measures such as production quotas, content requirements and high tariffs as a defensive strategy to counteract the effects both of high foreign investment in Canada and protectionism in foreign markets.

In a brief to this Commission, Professor Abraham Rotstein, a leading proponent of such a defensive strategy, called for a halt to further movement toward freer trade and argued for much greater emphasis on a more active industrial policy as a first priority. The first building block of such a strategy, in his view, would be import substitution ... We wish to state that we do not recommend the type of massive intervention proposed in this alternative approach, although we do believe that it is important to coordinate industrial policies very closely with trade policy.[61]

Thus the ideological arguments in favour of free trade emerge very forcefully in the *Report*.

How did the Macdonald Commission, rooted as it was in a Keynesian nationalist outlook, established by a government which consciously eschewed continental integration, with a commission headed by an ex-Walter Gordon Liberal nationalist, end up adopting a neoconservative continentalist ideological prescription? To discover the answer to this question, the remainder of this book focuses in more detail on the interplay of institutions, interests and ideas and the requisites for transformative change as manifest in the three major segments of the inquiry.

CHAPTER 4

The Public Submissions: Reflections in the Mirror of the Macdonald Commission

> Historians, economists and political scientists will probably spend many years debating this period of Canadian history and prepare great theories of economic, political and cultural development, probably using to great advantage the materials and documents generated by this Royal Commission.[1]

This chapter examines the ideological belief systems underlying the arguments presented in written briefs to the Macdonald Commission. The briefs, while not always wholly coherent, were sufficiently articulate to make it possible to outline the main characteristics of two broad paradigms and to ask how the commission arrived at its recommendation for free trade in light of them. The two paradigms are herein referred to as neoconservatism and democratic socialism, and this study draws explicit links between continentalism and neoconservatism, nationalism and democratic socialism. Representatives of these paradigms engaged in an ideological struggle to impose their own views on the commissioners, and thereby influence the Canadian state to adopt a particular set of economic development strategies.

This chapter presents evidence of nationalist and continentalist ideologies among business, labour, and popular sector groups and assesses the contributions of the briefs in terms of the manner in which they contributed the political viability requisite for transformative change. In so doing, it reveals some of what the Macdonald Commission saw when it held up a mirror to Canadian society.

Of the hundreds of social actors who presented written briefs to the Macdonald Commission on the subject of economic development strategies, most groups favoured the discourse of a state-centred nationalism.

Nonetheless, the commission recommended a market-oriented continentalist strategy focusing on bilateral free trade with the United States. While labour and popular sector groups were virtually unanimous in their support for nationalist economic development strategies, business groups as a whole were not nearly as unanimous in their support for continentalist strategies as is often assumed.[2] A division is revealed with organized labour and the popular sector on one side, and most of business on the other. Clearly the differing weights of various interests are in evidence in contributing to political discourse and creating a transformative moment. A tension between the advocates of nationalist-style policies and those advocating continentalist ones emerges in these documents. Most significantly, this suggests that the breakdown in the post-war consensus concerning Canadian economic development strategies had not yet been replaced by a new conventional wisdom.

The Written Submissions to the Macdonald Commission

Which social actors influenced the commission to recommend a continentalist economic development strategy, that is, free trade? Did organized social actors simply confirm the commissioners' predetermined continentalist preferences? Or did they present a nationalist program which the commission chose to ignore? Were they really instrumental in influencing the commission? What contribution did social actors make to this exercise in legitimation, which has ultimately resulted in a renewed continental focus for Canada, especially economically? Did they tend to reinforce the nationalist direction that the Trudeau government had embarked upon? Or did they present the case for a continentalist stance, rejecting Keynesianism and nationalist economic development strategies?

The political economy view is expressed in Drache and Cameron's *The Other Macdonald Report*, a scathing criticism of the entire commission process.[3] They argue that the commission was simply captured by corporate Canada and that it completely ignored the 'alternative' discourse of the 'popular sector' – a wide-ranging grouping of social actors including churches, trade unions, women's groups, social agencies, Native peoples, farmers, and the disadvantaged: 'The popular sector groups contradict the urging of business that government reduce its role in the economy and give free rein to "market forces." The economy must serve human well-being rather than corporate balance sheets, the popular sector says, and for this end a fundamental break with the conventional value system of policy making is the only means available. They reject a view of economics that separates ends from means and is based on having people adjust, accommodate and lower their expectations to the short term profit considerations of business.'[4] Ultimately, Drache and Cameron assert that the Macdonald Commission was stacked in favour of the business community and that its recommendations were virtually foregone conclusions in spite of an 'alternative' economic development strategy presented by the popular sector. They argue that the commission's *Report* was 'crudely biased' in favour of corporate Canada. By focusing on the *discourse* of the submissions made to this royal commission, a fuller understanding of this process can be gained.

The commission asked for written briefs under the following conditions: 'It is the commission's intention to encourage debate and to develop public understanding of the issues involved in its inquiry. Unless otherwise agreed by the commission, briefs therefore will be treated as public documents as of the time they are received by the commission. They will be made available in the relevant communities and through the commission office approximately one week before the hearings at which they are to be presented. Participants in the hearing process will not be expected to read their briefs at the hearings. Rather, they should be prepared to present their submissions and to discuss them with the commission.'[5] In order to deal with the hearings organizationally, a division of labour was imposed wherein the commissioners did not sit as a panel of thirteen at every hearing, according to Macdonald: 'There was a conscious decision that, while in a number of cases, we did sit all together, and I would have to go back and look at the record, we soon divided up into panels. For example, one group of us went to Prince George and the other went to Whitehorse. So there was a division of labour. It was the only way it could be done. You could not go everywhere with thirteen people. And thirteen people would get bored with the thing because obviously some would have to yield all the time to be certain everyone was heard.'[6]

According to the commission terms of reference, 'the success of this process ... turns on the willing and active involvement of those who will live the economic and political future that is bearing down on us.'[7] If the public pronouncements of the commission chairperson are to be believed, the consultative process, and particularly the submissions received by the commission, were regarded as a key element in the process. On 6 December 1983, Donald Macdonald claimed:

Today, here in Vancouver, we begin *the most important phase of our inquiry*, and that is, the public search for the ideas that will shape a better future for

our country.... We are here to seek ideas, the advice, the views, but above
all, the assistance of Canadians ...

I think that as we proceed other Canadians will come to see what you
have already seen, *that the involvement of people in all regions and walks of life is
vital to the success of this inquiry,* and that the success of this inquiry is vital to
determining the future success of our country.[8]

Macdonald went on to suggest that 'the commission is truly dependent
on the participation of Canadians in its work. No goal that we recommend will make a bit of difference if Canadians decide they want to
achieve a different one.'[9]

While acknowledging the importance of the public consultations, Macdonald also noted the disdain with which they were held by the academics
of the commission. 'I will have to tell you that initially ... the research
directors were very sceptical about whether this process would produce
anything. They felt, if you are confident, and you have organized your discipline in your own mind, the notion that you would have to consult
seems extraneous.'[10] Still, it was Macdonald's view that the commission
could not very well proceed without broadly consulting Canadians:

I don't think it is possible to avoid doing that [talking to the public]. I
think it is essential that you go out and do that. We had an excellent orga-
nizer, Michel Rochon, who was something of a student of the broader question of public participation. But I think that on a question as broad as this,
it wasn't good enough just to talk to one or two specialists on a research
staff. You did have to put yourself out on the line. But in fact, I think that as
a public document, in order for it to have credibility, it is important to hear
from a wide range of people. And Rochon and his staff did an excellent job
of trying to get a balance in the presentations. If ... you find a kind of a neat
balance between Keynesians on one side, and Benthamites on the other,
then that is a tribute to Michel and his staff.[11]

That such a balance was found among the submissions is contested
below. But Rochon did develop an incredibly detailed guidebook to the
organization and process of the public hearings, and to the treatment
and codings of briefs with flow charts, timetables, coding instructions,
analysis of each brief, ranking of brief by order or quality and relevance,
computer processing, allocation of time per sector, instructions to
research analysts regarding sorting each brief into coded subject areas,
and the preparation of briefing books for the commissioners. His ana-

lysts were warned 'to keep extremely sensitive information for delivery to commissioners in the morning briefings, and are reminded that this document could become public. Watch your words!'[12]

The final *Report* of the commission refers in praiseworthy terms to the importance of the submissions it received: 'This Commission wishes to acknowledge that the submissions were received and the testimony we heard in the course of our hearings represents a contribution of inestimable value to [our] quest. Commissioners are deeply grateful to the many Canadians from all walks of life who took the time and, in many instances, made the effort to travel a great distance in order to contribute the information, the views and the proposals upon which our report is based. We wish to emphasize the great importance of this contribution to our task.'[13] Despite these pronouncements, it is hard to gauge the impact of the consultative process on the commissioners and the extent to which they could absorb the masses of data presented to them:

> In addition to assimilating the final reports of the research projects, they [the commissioners] had to absorb 59 days of testimony at which 700 representations were made and read, plus 1, 100 briefs that sometimes accompanied the testimony but were often submitted separately. As [research director Alan] Cairns notes, *the mass of documentation was beyond the capacity of the Commissioners to absorb* and several stratagems were used to integrate the material. These included the capacity to retrieve testimony from computerized records of hearings and, as research neared completion, a continuous programme of seminars in which Commissioners and members of the research groups debated findings and their implications. Even with these devices, *the Commissioners seem to have been unusually dependent on the research group for assistance in drafting the final report.*[14]

Ostensibly, the goal of a commission is to create a climate of legitimacy for a set of policies which it seeks to promote. This can be done through appearing to be consultative. Cairns's observations call into question the extent to which the commissioners actually listened to those whom they consulted.[15] Moreover, the appearance of consultation can be deceiving, since *who* speaks can have more impact than what is actually said.[16]

This question is all the more intriguing because Macdonald himself revealed his preference for free trade with the United States long before the consultations and studies had been completed. On 19 November 1984, Macdonald made his now well-known statement that Canada should take a 'leap of faith' into a comprehensive free trade agreement with the United States.[17] Somewhat ironically, he made this statement while in the United States:

> In Harriman, New York, Macdonald told a closed conference on Canada–United States relations (but repeated by a reporter) that he favoured a free trade arrangement with the United States as a long-term solution to Canada's economic difficulties. In his remarks he noted that some Canadians might be apprehensive about this development: 'Many Canadians are nervous about the prospect of putting in jeopardy that perhaps rather fragile structure of national sovereignty that was built in a country called Canada – a country started off, after all, with a plain defiance of the north-south economic pressures ... If we do get down to the point where it's going to be a leap of faith, then I think at some point some Canadians are going to have to be bold and say, yes, we will do that.'[18]

Wallace suggests, 'It is not clear whether Macdonald was deliberately setting out to provoke a public debate on the issue of free trade, but it did seem apparent that he was unwilling to wait until the Commission's final report before commenting on key economic questions.'[19] Macdonald's actions were derisively described by Drache and Cameron in the following terms: 'His action of publicly committing his commission to this option before it had even finished its fact-finding is without precedent – analogous to a judge commenting on the merits of a case before all the evidence is heard.'[20]

It should be noted, though, that Macdonald had earlier stated somewhat prophetically, 'I hope and my fellow commissioners hope that thoughtful Canadians representing every dimension of our country's life – *particularly those from the business community* – will help us to both define the problems we face and choose among the solutions.'[21] Thus Macdonald recognized that political viability was most likely to be supplied by business interests. This suggests that Drache and Cameron were fundamentally correct in asserting a pro-corporate bias on the part of the commission. So too does the observation that the commissions hearings were held at times which made it difficult for working-class people to present their ideas to the commission. One journalist noted this at the very first set of public hearings in Vancouver: 'There appeared to be few if any ordinary working class citizens who took the time to observe the commission in action during its first three days in Vancouver. But then they were probably working during the hours the commission sat... Asked why the inquiry didn't hold its hearings in Vancouver at night or on weekends so working people could attend, Mr. Macdonald says: '"That's a good idea ... I don't actually know why we didn't do it here."'[22]

Nonetheless, an extremely large and diverse number of social actors attempted to impress their views upon the Macdonald Commission, reflecting both the crisis in the political and economic life in Canada, and the growth in the role of the state in Canadian society in the last fifty years. It also reflects the concomitant growth in interest group activity over that time period. A broad array of organized interests now confronts the state, a fact amply demonstrated by comparing the submissions to the three royal commissions on the overall functioning of Canada's economy: the Royal Commission on Dominion-Provincial Relations, established in 1937 (the Rowell-Sirois Commission); the Royal Commission on Canada's Economic Prospects (the Gordon Commission, 1957); and the Macdonald Commission.[23] Allowing for the difficulty of comparing three commissions across so great a time span, the appearance of new collective identities in the latter commission reflects an image of crisis. Perhaps the most significant aspect of this is the mobilization of both *more* social actors, and *new* social actors by the period of the Macdonald Commission, as table 4.1 reveals.

In all but one category (provincial and territorial governments), the number of submissions to the Macdonald Commission is greater than the total made to the other two commissions combined. Indeed, 'there were [over] two and one-half times as many submissions to the Macdonald Commission, reflecting the changed conditions of the 1980s. Also there are many new types of groups participating. Some of these did not submit briefs in the earlier period; others did not even exist.'[24]

A closer look at the individual categories of participants further underlines these differences. For example, over eight times as many women's groups presented submissions to the Macdonald Commission as they did to the other two commissions combined. Similarly, submissions were made by over seven times as many voluntary and special interest groups; over six times as many social service and health groups; three times as many political parties; over three times as many labour groups; and over two times as many religious agencies.

The other picture which emerges from this comparison is the changed nature of the groups involved. Most striking is the fact that not a single Aboriginal organization made a submission to the first two commissions, while twenty-seven did to the Macdonald Commission.[25] As well, the overall increase in the number of popular sector groups is quite evident in comparing the numbers of Aboriginal groups, women's

Table 4.1
Submissions to three royal commissions on the economy: 1937, 1957, 1982[a]

	Rowell-Sirois 1937	Gordon 1957	Macdonald 1982[b]
Labour	2	17	61 [65]
Business associations and private companies	67	202	254 [373]
Professional associations	26	10	43
Federal government	24	3	34 [46]
Provincial and territorial governments	118	20	40 [46]
Municipal and regional organizations	45	23	67 [76]
Native People's groups	0	0	27
Women's organizations	4	1	34 [41]
Religious agencies	4	1	12
Social service and health groups	5	1	37
Political parties	3	1	12
Seniors' organizations	0	1	6
Educational and research institutions	4	11	36 [113]
Voluntary and special interest	29	6	234
Total	331	297	897 [1,513]

[a] Includes both written briefs and transcripts of public hearings
[b] Figures not final at time of research. Figures in brackets are final totals reported in Macdonald Commission *Report*, 3: 598.
Source: Thorburn, *Interest Groups*, 84.

groups, religious agencies, social service and health groups, and seniors' organizations that intervened in the three commissions. The most telling piece of evidence here is the increase in 'voluntary and special interest groups'[26] making submissions in 1982 compared to 1937 and 1957. A total of only 35 submissions from these groups were made to the Rowell-Sirois and Gordon Commissions, whereas 234 were made to the Macdonald Commission!

These numbers reflect the fact that as Canadian society evolved, the nature of the demands made on governments changed, and new and different social actors became important. In short, society in crisis sought to reconstitute itself through the social construction of new collective identities. However, the degree to which these interests could contribute political viability to the search for new policy prescriptions was limited by the relative lack of legitimacy they enjoyed compared to business groups.

Holding Up the Mirror

The reflection of Canadian ideology in the submissions to the Macdonald Commission can be compared to the image produced by a mirror in a fun house, which differs drastically depending upon the angle from which it is viewed. It is variously humorous, exaggerated, or complimentary, sometimes abhorrent, but never definitive. Much more than a single perspective needs to be contemplated in order to get an accurate picture of the whole.

Methodologically, as Thorburn points out, it must be noted that 'an analysis that focuses on the number of groups addressing a particular issue does not take into account the relative importance of the groups in society. *Who* says something is often more important than *how many* adopt one position as opposed to another. Any statistical analysis of the briefs must be treated cautiously.'[27] It should be noted, too, that several important business groups declined to present briefs to the Macdonald Commission, as did many multinational corporations, and that some briefs were poorly written, ambiguous, and ill-thought out.[28] Nonetheless, as a mirror of Canadian society, the entire corpus cannot be lightly dismissed. It represents an articulate and 'real' view of the world on the part of a large and broad cross-section of the Canadian people and a clear representation of paradigmatic views.

In order to evaluate the submissions to the commission, a set of five categories was devised to represent economic development strategies debated by nationalist and continentalists over the past few decades. They were selected because each can be related directly to the ideological positions of nationalism and continentalism, and there is a clear disagreement between the two sides over them. The categories are: government intervention in the economy; foreign direct investment; industrial strategy; regional economic development; and trade policy. A summary of nationalist and continentalist views on these five economic development strategies is provided in table 4.2.

The next step was to scan the 'Schedule of Written Submissions' provided in volume 3 of the commission *Report.*[29] Contained in Appendix B are 1,513 entries listing all written briefs and transcripts of public meetings (see table 4.3). The sheer number of briefs precluded the possibility of analysing all of them. Selecting a representative sample of submissions to the commission for this study led to a focus on the *written* submissions of *organized social actors;* in particular, business organizations, labour groups, and the popular sector.[30] The discourse of business and labour is

Table 4.2
Summary of nationalist and continentalist views

Categories	Nationalist view	Continentalist view
Government intervention	– favours activist role for government in economy, up to and including nationalization – supports welfare state, regulation of economy	– opposes role for state in economy except to create positive 'environment' for business – opposes welfare state, supports deregulation and privatization
Foreign direct investment	– sees nationality of capital as significant – opposes high levels of American FDI – supports Canadianization of industdry – advocates continued and strengthened role for FIRA	– nationality of capital regarded as irrelevant – welcomes America FDI – opposes attempts to regulate FDI – seeks elimination or restrictions on FIRA as with Investment Canada
Industrial strategy	– supports long-term economic planning – advocates government role in picking winners and losers in economy, e.g., in high-tech sectors	– believes task of picking winners and losers best left to free market – sees government as incapable, inefficient in this role
Regional economic development	– sees role for government in providing special programs, e.g., equalization grants for regions – activist role for federal government in regional economies	– believes market should be allowed to function without government interference in regions – little or no role for federal government in regional economies
Trade policy	– believes in multilateral negotiations through GATT – advocates protectionism, e.g. tariffs, marketing boards, – opposes comprehensive bilateral free trade with U.S.	– seeks bilateral negotiations with U.S. – opposes protectionism of any kind – advocates comprehensive bilateral free trade with U.S.

fundamental to revealing the ideological face of Canadian society, but inclusion of popular sector groups presents a broader, more representative cross-section of Canadian society than would be provided in a simple labour-capital dichotomy.[31]

The struggle to supply political viability is conditioned by differing levels of legitimacy accorded to different interests. Jane Jenson, in iden-

Table 4.3
Written submissions to the Macdonald Commission

Intervenors	No. of submissions
Private sector	373
Federal government	46
Provincial and territorial governments	46
Municipalities and regional development	76
Labour	65
Voluntary sector	231
Women's groups	41
Aboriginal organizations	26
Educational and research institutions	113
Individuals	496
Total	1,513

Source: Macdonald Commission, *Report*, vol. 3, 598.

tifying the universe of political discourse as the 'space in which socially-constructed identities emerge in discursive struggle,' suggests: 'As actors with a variety of collective identities co-exist in the universe of political discourse, their practices and meaning systems jostle with each other for social attention and legitimacy. At issue are conflicts over the representation and reproduction of power relations based on differences. In any social formation a multitude of relationships of difference exist. Age, sex, race, property ownership, workplace activities and language are but a few of the differences which might take on social meaning.'[32] Inclusion of business, labour, and popular sector groups, then, is both important and necessary to gain a more representative and comprehensive sample of the discourse presented to the Macdonald Commission.[33]

Once it was determined which categories of social actor were to be examined, a strategy was needed to select those groups that actually commented on Canada's economic development strategies. A content analysis of the submissions undertaken by the Macdonald Commission staff was consulted. As Hugh Thorburn reports:

In order to cope with the substantial value of submissions ... the staff of the Commission first created a subject classification for the briefs. This simple classification had to be elaborate in order to permit an analysis of the content of the briefs; therefore a content methodology was constructed. Every

Table 4.4
Total number of written briefs submitted to the Macdonald Commission by business,
labour, and popular sector group briefs surveyed (identified by content analysis as
related to categories), and number relevant to this study's categories

	Business groups	Labour groups	Popular sector	Total
No. of briefs presented to Macdonald Commission	373	65	298	736
No. of briefs surveyed	181	40	81	302
No. of briefs relevant to this study's categories	158	37	59	254

text (brief or transcript) was read and the main ideas extracted; then the data was classified by topic ...

The topics were divided into seven major categories, which in turn were subdivided into 52 subject areas; these were further subdivided into 300 topics.[34]

By using this content analysis, it was a relatively simple matter to determine which briefs contained comments relevant to the five economic developments strategies used as the categories in this study. This was done by first extracting those topics from the list of three hundred which related directly to five categories. A list of seventy-four topics resulted (see Appendix B). Then, the written briefs containing comment related to those seventy-four topics were identified. This produced a list of 302 briefs which were carefull assessed (see Appendix A).

Table 4.4 summarizes the total number of written briefs submitted to the Macdonald Commission by business, labour, and popular sector groups, the number of briefs identified by the commission content analysis as containing statements related to the five categories and therefore surveyed for this study, and the number of briefs which were actually relevant to the categories.[35]

Of the 736 written briefs submitted by business, labour, and popular sector groups to the Macdonald Commission, 302, or 41 per cent, contained reference to one or more of government intervention, FDI, industrial strategy, regional economic development, or trade policy, according to the commission content analysis, and therefore were potential subjects for this study. Of these, 254 (or just over 84 per cent of the 302), were found to actually contain statements relevant to the categories.

The tables below help to reveal the crisis and struggle for representa-

Table 4.5
Total number of briefs by each sector containing nationalist and continentalist references to all five categories.

	Business		Labour		Popular sector		Total	
	No.	%	No.	%	No.	%	No.	%
Nationalist	52	33	36	97	53	90	141	56
Continentalist	74	47	0	0	3	5	77	30
Both positions	32	20	1	3	3	5	36	14
Total	158	100	37	100	59	100	254	100

tion among collective identities by summarizing the discourse of organized social actors. As each written brief was read, a record was made of nationalist or continentalist statements within the five categories. Only one reference to each was recorded per brief, even if a brief contained several references to that category.[36] The goal was to identify statements about each of the five categories by business, labour, and popular sector groups and to classify each brief according to whether it could be said to represent a nationalist or continentalist orientation towards that particular category.

Cracks in the Mirror: Divisions within Canadian Society

The total number of briefs by sector containing nationalist, continentalist, or both kinds of statements is shown in table 4.5: 141 contained nationalist statements, while 77 contained continentalist statements. Thirty-six briefs contained both kinds of statements. Thus 56 per cent contained nationalist statements, while 30 per cent contained continentalist ones, and 14 per cent contained both types. While it is clear that the labour and popular sector groups overwhelmingly adopted nationalist positions (97 per cent and 90 per cent, respectively), business groups were much more divided, with 47 per cent adopting continentalist positions, 33 per cent adopting nationalist ones, and 20 per cent containing both kinds of statements.

Thus a pattern emerges suggesting two splits in Canadian society around the issue of nationalist and continentalist economic development strategies. First, the date suggest a split along class lines, with much

Table 4.6
Total number of nationalist and continentalist statements about each category contained in Macdonald Commission written briefs by all three sectors

	Government intervention		Foreign direct investment		Industrial strategy		Regional economic development		Trade policy	
	No.	%	No.	%	No.	%	No.	%	No.	%
Nationalist	125	58	18	28	49	54	38	73	28	40
Continentalist	89	42	47	72	42	46	14	27	42	60
Total	214	100	65	100	91	100	52	100	70	100

of the business class adopting a continentalist perspective, while the organized working class and popular sector overwhelmingly adopted a nationalist position. Second, it suggests that the business class is not as monolithic in its stand as are the organized working-class and popular sector groups, since over half of the business groups (53 per cent) made either nationalist or both types of statements in their written briefs.[37] The data also suggest that Canadian discourse was in a state of disharmony and had not reformed under a new conventional wisdom since the crisis of the 1970s shattered the post-war consensus in Canadian society.

Table 4.6 shows the total number of briefs by category which contained nationalist or continentalist statements. On the issue of government intervention, 58 per cent of all statements were nationalist and 42 per cent were continentalist. On FDI, 28 per cent took a nationalist stance, while 72 per cent took a continentalist one. Where industrial strategy is concerned, 54 per cent of the statements were nationalist, while 46 per cent were continentalist. Fully 73 per cent of the references favoured a nationalist orientation towards regional economic development, while only 27 per cent were continentalist. And on the issue of trade policy, 40 per cent favoured nationalist policies, while 60 per cent favoured continentalist ones.

On the basis of these data alone, the conclusion might be drawn that Canadian social actors sent the Macdonald Commission a message indicating a preference for nationalist economic development strategies. But a more nuanced analysis of these numbers is achieved by looking at which kind of statement (nationalist or continentalist) specific social actors made to each category. This will reveal the extent to which each

Table 4.7

Number and percentage of business group briefs containing nationalist and continentalist statements about each of the five categories (*n* = 158)

	Government intervention		Foreign direct investment		Industrial strategy		Regional economic development		Trade policy	
	No.	%	No.	%	No.	%	No.	%	No.	%
Nationalist	46	34	8	15	25	38	22	55	18	28
Continentalist	85	62	46	85	41	62	14	35	42	67
Both positions	6	4	0	0	0	0	4	10	3	5
Total	137	100	54	100	66	100	40	100	63	100

group is nationalist or continentalist in relation to specific economic development strategies. Table 4.7 breaks down the data to show the total number of business group briefs which contained nationalist or continentalist statements, table 4.8 does the same for labour groups, and table 4.9 for popular sector groups. These three tables also indicate the number of briefs which were ambiguous in their presentations by assuming both nationalist and continentalist positions.

Business Groups

Taken as a whole, business groups appear to have a preference for continentalist economic development strategies, though slightly less than half of the business groups surveyed adopted this position. As noted above, 47 per cent of their briefs indicated support for continentalism, while 33 per cent took nationalist positions, and 20 per cent took both (table 4.5). In four out of five categories, continentalist positions were preferred among the 158 business groups. Only on the issue of regional economic development was a preference expressed for nationalist strategies.

Most business groups were not as explicit about their continentalism as the Retail Council of Canada, which stated in a brief: 'Our trade sector feels that the forces of economics will continue to encourage integration of the Canadian and U.S. economies. We think it is unproductive and illogical to attempt to reduce or redirect these natural forces.'[38] The Dartmouth Chamber of Commerce put it this way: 'There has been too much nationalistic navel-gazing and as a result the world is passing us by.'[39]

GOVERNMENT INTERVENTION

Typical of the 62 per cent of business group briefs (table 4.7) that offered a continentalist view of government intervention was this statement by Placer Development Ltd.: 'By reducing the burden of government on the economy, Canada may succeed in releasing the energy and initiative of its workers and managers, its investors and entrepreneurs, its thinkers and doers. They will make the decisions, in the market-place and in the work-place, which will drive and direct the economy. The base of the economy will be the natural forces of competition and free enterprise instead of the artificial prop of government subsidies and controls. Growth and stability over the long-term will only be possible if the economy is based on a firm foundation of natural economic forces.'[40] Perhaps more direct was this statement by the Halifax Board of Trade: 'The operation of free market forces is better able to provide for our economic well being than all of the [government] intervention we can muster.'[41] Or, as the New Brunswick Telephone Company expressed it, 'it is our hope that the Commission's work will result in a thunderous, deafening outcry for a reduced level of government involvement [in the economy].'[42]

Notwithstanding these clarion calls for free enterprise, it is worth noting that regarding government intervention, 30 per cent of the business group briefs contained nationalist statements while 8 per cent contained statements which supported *both* nationalist and continentalist strategies.

FOREIGN DIRECT INVESTMENT

An overwhelming 85 per cent (forty-six out of fifty-four) of the business group briefs which referred to FDI were continentalist, easily the largest single percentages by business groups. For example, the Whitehorse Chamber of Commerce asserted that it 'does not believe that foreign investment constitutes a major threat to national sovereignty but rather believes that Canadian political institutions are strong enough to retain their identity and effectiveness despite such investment.'[43] The Calgary Chamber of Commerce argued that 'to expand our economic base, policies and attitudes must be restructured so as to encourage foreign investment in Canada.'[44] Several direct references to the Foreign Investment Review Agency (FIRA) are found in the briefs. For example, the Canadian Electrical Distributors Association said: 'If we are to encourage the process toward global mandates (presuming they can be made to work in our favour), then we must take steps to make foreign investors feel both welcome and wanted in Canada. Implicit in such action would be a reappraisal of the Foreign Investment Review Agency and its effects upon foreign investors.'[45] INCO, the giant mining multinational based in Sudbury, said 'foreign capital should be made welcome in the development of the mining process. The constraints (real or imagined) in the Foreign Investment Review Agency (FIRA) should be clarified.'[46] The Canadian Manufacturers Association appeared to be trying to strike a balance between the need for *some* controls on foreign investment as against no controls, but in the end came down in favour of liberalizing FIRA:

> Foreign capital has contributed significantly to Canada's economic development, and given a more supportive environment it could add to economic growth in the years ahead. This means that the Canadianization policies of the NEP [National Energy Program] should not be extended into other sectors, and that FIRA should continue to be administered more liberally ... We recognize that high foreign ownership in certain industrial sectors justifies FIRA and other legislative controls in certain key sectors. But the balance between encouraging desirable foreign investment and encouraging Canadian ownership and control is very delicate. Recent federal government policies and actions have disturbed this balance, we suggest to the detriment of Canada.[47]

INDUSTRIAL STRATEGY

Of the business group briefs which referred to industrial strategy, 62 per cent (41 out of 66) favoured a continentalist orientation. For example, the Mining Association of British Columbia, in a brief entitled 'The Benefits of Trade and the Dangers of Protectionism,' claimed that 'the pursuit of an "industrial policy," as the phrase has come to be understood, is almost certainly a snare and a delusion.'[48] Dominion Textile Corporation of Montreal revealed a confused understanding of industrial strategy when it claimed to reject the idea outright, while apparently arguing for a particular variant of industrial strategy. The corporation suggested that it should not be the role of the government to *pick* 'sunrise' high technology industries, but rather, echoing Stephen Cohen of the Berkeley Roundtable on the International Economy, said the solution is to *apply* high technology to existing sectors.[49] The Canadian Hardware and Housewares Manufacturing Association noted the constraints on pursuing an industrial strategy. 'While the changing dynamics of the world marketplace will probably prevent the devising or implementing of a national industrial strategy,' the association said, 'there is nevertheless a need to replace the industrial strategy of tariffs of the 1940s and 1950s with a new strategy ...' However, that new strategy must be initiated by the *private sector.*[50]

REGIONAL ECONOMIC DEVELOPMENT

While support for continentalist economic development strategies predominates in four areas, on the issue of regional economic development, 55 per cent of the business group briefs took a nationalist position, 35 per cent took a continentalist stand, and 10 per cent took *both* positions. Significantly, most calls for regional economic development programs came from the Atlantic provinces. For instance, the Greater Charlottetown Area Chamber of Commerce told the commission that Prince Edward Island needed the help of the federal government to develop new export markets and to help get the economy back on its feet: 'We do not want huge amounts of extra cash, we recognize that government spending has already reached its limit but a clear long term well-thought-out economic revitalization plan would be money well spent. The better we do on our own, the less dependent we will be on the federal government. It is wise for the federal government to help us get back on our feet.'[51]

TRADE POLICY

Finally, regarding trade policy, 67 per cent of business group briefs contained continentalist statements, 28 per cent took nationalist positions, and 5 per cent took *both*. Perhaps anticipating the arguments of the opponents to free trade, the Retail Council of Canada recommended that the Macdonald Commission 'should, in assessing Canada's future relationship with the United States, particularly explore the feasibility of the position that a closer commercial relationship with the United States is unlikely to jeopardize Canada's cultural sovereignty and independence.'[52] The Council goes on to suggest:

> In our belief, Canadians are more certain of their political, social and economic roots and in a better position to contemplate a fuller exchange of production, marketing and distribution between the two countries than many skeptics believe ...
>
> The problem as we see it, is that Canada does not really have a choice but to place its trade and economic performance more solidly in a North American setting.[53]

The Mining Association of British Columbia approvingly cited the work of economist John Young for the Gordon Commission, and regretted that his contributions there appeared to have been overlooked.[54] This association suggested that 'a policy of encouraging trade and avoiding protectionism is fundamental to the economic and political health of Canada.'[55] Striking the pose of concerned global citizen, another British Columbia group, the Employer's Council, contended that 'The argument against protectionism and for free trade is very simple and very strong. Free trade promotes a profitable regional and international division of labour. It greatly enhances the potential real national product of all nations and makes possible higher standards of living all over the globe. We must resist the present worldwide trend toward protectionism not only for ourselves but for the less fortunate peoples in less developed countries around the world.'[56] It is significant that the president of the Employer's Council of B.C., William Hamilton, was also a commissioner.

'Philosophically,' intoned the Canadian Electrical Distributors Association, 'the notion of free trade has a great appeal to free enterprise businessmen. Its connotation of freedom of choice in the marketplace is, on the surface, almost a motherhood issue.'[57] The Calgary Chamber of Commerce warned, 'if we are to expand and maintain our economic base we must recognize the importance of looking outward to foreign markets. In this regard, our closest, best and most stable market is the United States of America.'[58] The British Columbia Resources Investment Corporation pointed out in its brief that it is a Canadian-based natural resource company that is publicly owned exclusively by Canadians. It is also the most widely held public corporation in Canada, and had this to say about free trade:

> In order for this successful key sector of our economy to grow and prosper in the future, it must remain competitive on world markets and must be allowed access to world markets. A major challenge facing all resource based companies in Canada today is to sensitize the owners of the resource base (all Canadians) and the regulator of our activities in this sector (the Crown) to the harsh realities of competitive world markets.
>
> The trade off of free trade might be a dislocation of jobs in certain industries in Canada that are already unable to compete. However, it is our belief that a move towards freer world trade can only be a net long-term benefit to Canada and result in higher overall employment.[59]

It can be concluded on the basis of these data that the advice of *some* business groups advocating continentalist economic development strategies was heeded by the commission. But clearly the business community was not as singleminded in its opinions as were the other two sectors studied.

Further research into which *types* of groups proffered this kind of advice according to region, sector, nationality of ownership, and size has been done in part by Thorburn and by Rocher.[60] Thorburn points out, for instance, that 'very few of the groups that submitted briefs or appeared before the Commission are primarily territorial. Most represent an economic sector or special interest not defined in regional terms.'[61] Moreover, the most salient feature of the briefs related to nationality of ownership, for Thorburn, 'is the virtual absence of a key and leading element of the Canadian business community, namely the multinational corporations.' He posits that this was likely a reaction to 'their perception of the nationalism of a Liberal government that had enacted FIRA and the National Energy Program, and then promised to strengthen the former and implement an industrial strategy for Canada.'[62] Thorburn also contends that the positions of domestic firms were far less homogeneous than those of foreign multinationals, while few noteworthy differences between small and big business were evident in the briefs.[63]

Rocher's study of Canadian business during this same period also revealed divisions. He found that, with regard to the process of continentalization, analysing Canadian Business on the basis of the structural divide between monopoly and non-monopoly, or comprador and domestic fractions of capital, was inadequate.[64] Rather, orientation towards markets is a more useful explanatory variable. Thus, businesses that were already quite strong within the continental market supported free trade, whereas those oriented mainly towards the domestic market were less well disposed to bilateral economic relations. Indeed, in some cases, they feared free trade for the enhanced competition from American exporters it might inflict. Similarly, branch plants of American companies feared relocation of their production and distribution facilities to the United States. Rocher further concluded that

> support for free trade and a greater openness of the Canadian market to US competition is globally unrelated to the structure of ownership or the size of enterprise ... Generally, both foreign and Canadian corporations see the strategy of continental integration in a positive light. In their view, increased access to the continental market can only promote the process of industrial concentration and specialization to the detriment of firms that are mainly oriented toward the domestic market. The new class alliance to emerge within the Canadian bourgeoisie brings together elements of the business community that emphasize exports that depend on the continen-

tal market. Continental integration in fact is part and parcel of the coming of age of the Canadian bourgeoisie.[65]

Labour Groups

Despite their historical continental links[66] labour groups reveal a significantly different orientation towards these issues than business groups. Overall, thirty-six of thirty-seven, or 97 per cent, of the briefs by labour groups contained nationalist statements, none took an exclusively continentalist position, and one took *both* positions (table 4.5). Indeed, the number is actually 100 per cent in four of the five issues surveyed; only on trade policy was a single dissenting opinion expressed, and it is an ambiguous stance seemingly advocating both kinds of development strategies. Thus while business groups tended on balance to favour continentalist economic development strategies, labour groups overwhelmingly and almost unanimously favoured nationalist ones.

The brief by the International Union of Operating Engineers (Local 115) illustrates the problems some social actors have – even those with a long history in Canadian society – in establishing legitimacy for themselves as collective identities. That they experience difficulties in establishing their bona fides is evident in the statement, 'the labour movement as a whole is fundamentally committed to the preservation of our democratic system. It is change we want not destruction.'[67] It would be hard to imagine a business group having to begin its brief with such an apologia: 'Yet this government and its predecessors persist in regarding the labour movement and trade unionists as a disruptive annoyance. There is not yet in this country any recognition of the reality that trade unions represent, legitimately, a large number of working people in this country, people who speak through the labour movement and its leaders because we are their leaders and because without the labour movement they have no voice.'[68] In other words, the struggle to establish and sustain political viability has been, for the labour movement in Canada, historically an uphill battle.

GOVERNMENT INTERVENTION
On the issue of government intervention labour groups were most emphatic, with 100 per cent of the thirty-two briefs that commented on this topic adopting a nationalist stance (table 4.8). For example, the United Steelworkers of America noted how Canada could use the lessons of the Great Depression and war-time planning to greater benefit:

Table 4.8
Number and percentage of labour group briefs containing nationalist and continentalist statements about each of the five categories (n = 37)

	Government intervention		Foreign direct investment		Industrial strategy		Regional economic development		Trade policy	
	No.	%	No.	%	No.	%	No.	%	No.	%
Nationalist	32	100	7	100	17	100	7	100	4	80
Continentalist	0	0	0	0	0	0	0	0	0	0
Both positions	0	0	0	0	0	0	0	0	1	20
Total	32	100	7	100	17	100	7	100	5	100

As the 1930s advance, governments in Canada, the United States and elsewhere embarked on a series of what were, for the times, radical and imaginative experiments in economic and social policy, in an attempt to offset some of the worst effects of the depression. These experiments had not all the success that was hoped for and the process was interrupted by the war. However, it was infused by the learning process in the war effort of what planned, collective action executed by government could in fact accomplish. The post-war years saw the culmination of this in the assumption by government of responsibility for macro-economic management, in the formal commitment of national economic policy to full employment and in a host of new legislation, institutions and programs to give this effect.[69]

Furthermore, this brief emphasized the importance of tying government intervention to democratic decision making: 'The spirit which animated that change was the affirmation that collective action, exercised through the democratic institutions of government, can handle and *solve* the collective economic problem. This affirmation, to be sure, was not always made voluntarily by governments. It had often to be forced on government by the ballot box and other public pressures. Free trade unions were at the forefront of the pressures for change. It was a matter of the mass of the people making it clear to government that no other alternative but such an affirmation was acceptable.'[70] The major difference between the experiences of the 1930s and the 1980s, according to the Steelworkers, was that:

Effectively, a substantial measure of responsibility for moving the economy out of this depression, and for preventing the next one, is being abrogated to the corporate sector ... the corporate sector has the ability to move an economy into depression, it does not have the ability to manage an economy out of one.

Many of us in the labour movement had thought that the key lesson of the last depression had been ineradicably learned: that in a democratic political system *only* government can have the power, and *only* government can be entrusted with the responsibility to maintain economic stability and employment, and secure a fair distribution of income. Many of us now fear our society may have to go through a long and devastating process to relearn this, and that while we are re-learning our social and political system will be at risk.[71]

FOREIGN DIRECT INVESTMENT

While only seven labour groups commented on foreign direct investment, all of them took a nationalist position. Drawing a link between the issues of government intervention and the issue of FDI, the British Columbia and Yukon Territory Building and Trades Council claimed:

The most important single factor about the Canadian economy is that it is not controlled in Canada. Given the incredibly high degree of foreign ownership of most of our key industries, any meaningful domestic control of our economy can only be brought about through a major increase in government intervention. Most key economic decisions are being made by and in the interests of external corporate ownership. Unless governments in Canada are prepared to exercise significant and effective controls over the operations of transnational corporations in Canada, or are prepared to institute very substantial degrees of public ownership in Canada, there is no hope of meaningful direction of the Canadian economy.[72]

The Nova Scotia Federation of Labour (CLC) favoured broadening the mandate of FIRA to include regulations concerning where in Canada foreign companies could locate.[73] The Windsor and District Labour Council drew a connection between unemployment and foreign ownership of the Canadian economy. 'For many years, despite its wealth and natural resources, Canada has suffered the highest per capita jobless rate in the industrialized West,' their brief asserted, 'a condition that cannot be separated from the fact that Canada's industry and resources are foreign (US) owned and foreign (US) controlled to an extent unmatched by any other industrialized nation.'[74] The branch plant economy was responsible for a number of structural and policy problems in Canada, and wage controls, cuts in social services, and give-aways to corporations and the wealthy only exacerbated the situation, according to the Winnipeg Labour Council.[75]

INDUSTRIAL STRATEGY

Seventeen labour groups commented on the need for a nationalist industrial strategy in Canada, and in so doing revealed a variety of understandings of this concept. Many focused on the need for a policy that included full employment as a goal. The Nova Scotia Teachers' Union, for example, said 'an industrial strategy should be developed to create permanent and meaningful jobs.'[76] The Thunder Bay and District Labour Council approvingly quoted nationalist Walter Gordon's argument that unemployment and not inflation was the number one problem facing the country which governments should be focusing on, and called for an industrial strategy to do just that.[77] The United Steelworkers of America noted that the Macdonald Commission's terms of reference contained no mention of full employment as a topic of study, and that its mid-term report, *Challenges and Choices*, also ignored full employment.[78] 'As the ultimate of any industrial strategy full employment must be embodied in legislation' said the New Brunswick Federation of Labour.[79] This group was explicit about what it felt were the key elements of a national industrial strategy: a commitment to full employment; investment controls; manpower policies; increased processing of resources; tax reform; government purchasing policies; trade policies; transportation policies; industrial development initiatives; inventory support measures; increased research and development; and monetary and fiscal policies. 'If we are to resolve Canada's economic problems and deal effectively with regional disparities, particularly unemployment and income distribution, it is imperative that government first develop a comprehensive national industrial strategy,' said the federation.[80]

Another group from eastern Canada, the Association of University of New Brunswick Teachers (AUBNT), argued that: 'The AUNBT firmly believes that the key to eventual economic self-reliance in New Brunswick and reduction of dependence on the federal purse lies in the direction that our forefathers practiced so well – the use and development of applied technology complementary to our natural resource base. These goals necessitate a concerted effort by the Commission to develop an industrial strategy which, as far as we can ascertain, does not exist at any level in Canada.'[81]

REGIONAL ECONOMIC DEVELOPMENT

Of the seven labour organizations that wrote to the commission about regional economic development, all took a nationalist perspective. Some groups linked the issue to an industrial strategy. 'Without a national industrial strategy including a national transportation policy which encompasses shipping and shipbuilding,' said the Marine Workers Federation (CLC), 'the economic disparity of the Atlantic region will widen to the point that nationhood will soon lose its allure and prospects for a large number of citizens.'[82] This union joined the Nova Scotia Federation of Labour and the New Brunswick Federation of Labour in commenting on the continued need for regional economic development programs. The latter group, in tying several themes together, suggested: 'If we are to solve Canada's economic problems and deal effectively with regional disparities, particularly unemployment and income distribution, it is imperative that government first develop a comprehensive national industrial strategy. Incorporating economic development plans for each of the four Atlantic provinces together with a general plan of action for the Atlantic region, this industrial strategy must have as a central goal the achievement of full employment.'[83]

TRADE POLICY

Finally, on the issue of trade policy, four nationalist briefs were presented,[84] and one ambiguous brief attempted to straddle the nationalist-continentalist divide. The International Woodworkers of America suggested that tariff protection for the British Columbia coastal plywood industry had permitted inefficient industries which had failed to modernize or specialize, or even be competitive, to continue in business. While blaming tariffs and protectionism for some of the problems of their industry, they did not advocate abolishing the tariff structure, and indeed looked to further government intervention as a possible solution.[85]

In general, the labour group briefs echoed several of the themes articulated by the Winnipeg Labour Council – that the power of multinational capital had to be curtailed and primacy restored to governments. Thus, it advocated an 'alternative economic strategy': 'This strategy must constitute a clear break with the past and present economic policies ... and it must challenge directly the prevailing argument propounded by business interests that the only way to resolve the crisis is to give private investors a completely free hand to restructure the economy according to their priorities.'[86] The Labour Council went on to suggest that this strategy must satisfy the basic social and economic needs of Canadians rather than only maximizing the profits of wealthy investors; create jobs rather than use unemployment to deflate wages; promote socially useful investments rather than speculation; focus on raising wages and living standards; and improve public services.[87] Finally, it argued: 'The basic problem with government decision-making has been its subordination to the needs and priorities of the private sector ... Therefore, fundamental to the implementation of an alternative economic strategy is the recognition that it is a mistake to give more say over economic decision-making to private investors. What we need is to establish a genuine public control over economic policy. This will entail new forms of involvement – and accountability – for ordinary citizens.'[88] The specifics of such a democratizing strategy would include stimulating the economy; stopping cuts in public services; lowering interest rates; implementing exchange controls; nationalizing the banks; cutting defence spending; introducing price controls; expanding public ownership; extending public services; and reforming government finances[89] – all of which are anathema to the business groups surveyed. The term 'two solitudes,' coined by Hugh MacLennan, clearly describes more in Canada than just French-English relations.

Popular Sector Groups

A pattern similar to that found in the analysis of labour groups emerges with the popular sector. Of the fifty-nine popular sector briefs surveyed that commented on one or more of the five categories, fifty-three or 90 per cent, adopted nationalist positions, while three (5 per cent) adopted continentalist positions and three took both positions (table 4.5).

The tone of the brief by the Canadian Crafts Council towards Canadian-American relations is not representative of all of the popular sector group briefs. But it certainly spoke to a recurrent theme in many of them when it claimed: '"America First" means exactly what it says. At any date in the past when Canada has attempted to protect its own interests we have been threatened – and threatened is the correct word – by the United States, whether the matter is small or large. If multinationals and the dumping of industrial and cultural products won't achieve US dominance then there are dozens of politicians ready to bring forward legislation in Congress to do the job instead.'[90] This statement reflects nationalist fears of the strength and presence of the American hegemon in Canadian society, at the same time noting the problem of increasing American protectionism for Canadian producers and exporters in the 1980s.

GOVERNMENT INTERVENTION

Analysing the data by category (table 4.9) shows that 89 per cent of the popular sector group briefs favoured a nationalist orientation towards government intervention. Indeed, government intervention was by far

Table 4.9
Number and percentage of popular sector group briefs containing nationalist and continentalist statements about each of the five categories (*n* = 59)

	Government intervention		Foreign direct investment		Industrial strategy		Regional economic development		Trade policy	
	No.	%	No.	%	No.	%	No.	%	No.	%
Nationalist	47	89	3	75	7	88	9	100	6	100
Continentalist	4	7	1	25	1	12	0	0	0	0
Both positions	2	4	0	0	0	0	0	0	0	0
Total	53	100	4	100	8	100	9	100	6	100

the most commented upon of the five categories by these groups, indicating the extent to which they rely on government for assistance and even survival. It is interesting to note that many popular sector groups quoted from the 1983 New Year's Day statement by the Canadian Conference of Catholic Bishops, *Ethical Reflections on the Economic Crisis*.[91] This document was an articulate and thoughtful critique of the worst excesses of Canadian capitalism. It served to focus the debate in Canada over the depression of 1981–2 around such issues as the role of government in the economy, and it had an electrifying effect in so doing.

On the proper role of government, the Pacific Group for Policy Alternatives decried reliance on the 'invisible hand of the marketplace' and railed against the neoconservatism coming into vogue. 'The favour currently shown for monetarism and "supply side" economics,' said the Pacific Group, 'stems more from the inability of Keynesianism to offer a quick fix to inflation than to any proven success for those theories.' It warned against the commission blindly adopting monetarism and its attendant theories as 'common wisdom,' and asserted that the 'basic liberal values' of Canadians, including concern for human development, general well-being, and social justice, were worth preserving in Canadian politics and society. As well, it argued that 'government intervention is going to be absolutely necessary in order to achieve a broader distribution of available jobs, and to create additional employment ...'[92]

The Lambton County Board of Education said, 'we see the best prospects for full productive employment and resulting growth by interventionist policies of government designed to stimulate small and medium-sized businesses.'[93] The First United Church of Vancouver advocated greater government intervention through such policy instruments as a guaranteed annual income and a redistributive tax system. As well, it argued, 'our role as the Church is not to do the work of the government, but to challenge government bodies to serve its people justly and ensure that all basic human rights are met by the system.'[94]

New Dawn Enterprises of Sydney, Nova Scotia, a not-for-profit community development corporation, argued against a relianace on free enterprise capitalism. Arguing for broader thinking to overcome what they called the 'rigidities of the industrial revolution,' it cited the need to get away from: 'the simplistic ideological cry for a return to earlier days of a "pure" laissez faire capitalism untouched by government interference. Such a move is an invitation to long run disaster, a reinforcement of the rigidities that have to be overcome. We need a mixed economy, and the more mixed and innovative it is the better. We need a planned economy in one sense: more input of employees and citizens is needed in the economy.'[95] The British Columbia group Women United for a Non-Exploitive New Age adopted a similar theme: 'The government, elected to represent the needs of all Canadians is ultimately accountable for the management of our resources and our economy and in seeing that free enterprise capitalism, or any other monetary system, does not adversely affect the needs of the larger community, by making sure it operates within a responsible social structure.'[96] It too advocated the creation of a guaranteed annual income in its brief.[97]

The Social Action Commission of the Roman Catholic Diocese of Charlottetown presented a critique of capitalism as a system organized to benefit the few at the expense of the many. It contended that the problems inherent in Canadian society were the results of a lack of political will. 'This lack of will, coupled with political acceptance of business interests which place profits before people,' argued the committee, 'is at the root of the problems experienced by the vast majority of Canadians.' What is needed, then, is a 'socio-political ethos which is beyond profit.'[98]

The environmental group Ecology Action Centre of Halifax brought a somewhat different perspective to the issue of government intervention. It focused on the implications of the 'limits to growth' environmental view which sought: '... a larger and more effective role for government in environmental regulation, conservation, monitoring and enforcement; and the development of mechanisms for better design and environmental planning and the internalization of real environmental costs in business and industry. If these are perceived as deterrents to economic growth, then so be it: *only under these conditions is economic growth acceptable.*'[99] The Windsor Women's Incentive Centre advocated greater government intervention in the area of mandatory affirmative action programs, equal pay for work of equal value, and other 'socio-economic interventions' by governments.[100] Similarly, the Women's Information and Referral Centre of Montreal called for 'the direct and committed involvement of the federal government' in redressing the position of women in Canadian society. They urged that 'the federal government should offer direct support and/or incentives for development of progressive employment practices such as affirmative action programs ...'[101] Clearly the popular sector groups were sending a message to the commission that government intervention was not only desirable, but also needed if these kinds of groups could expect to continue to play a role in the Canadian social and economic fabric.

FOREIGN DIRECT INVESTMENT

Of the four briefs that offered some observations on the topic of foreign direct investment, three took a nationalist stance. While few comments emerged from the briefs by popular sector groups on this issue, the Social Action Commission of the Roman Catholic Diocese of Charlottetown did argue that 'what we are saying in this paper is that we do not want a Brascan model of development for Canada ... There are unlimited possibilities for Canadians to create our own future and to rid ourselves of multinationals which have no loyalty to Canada.' It went on to argue: 'The Social Action Commission calls for a self-reliant Canada which is politically and economically free. We oppose suggestions that Canada cultivate stronger economic ties with the United States. This close association with the United States has increased Canadian dependency, robbed us of our resource base, drawn us into United States exploitation of the Third World, and left us with a false and inflated notion of our prosperity.'[102] In saying this, the Social Action Commission is identifying the problems of the branch plant economy and dependence which have been Canada's lot, and explicitly rejecting this option for future Canadian development.

INDUSTRIAL STRATEGY

The concept of an industrial strategy received attention from eight popular sector group briefs; seven of these took a nationalist position. For example, Women Against the Budget claimed: 'It is also clear, from watching economic initiatives in this country, that Canada does not have an industrial strategy; economic decisions are not based on the needs of the people of Canada but rather they are based on what benefits the multi-national apparatus which is largely American dominated. Operating in the absence of an industrial strategy, with ad hoc responses based on expediency has proved to be profitable for *some* Canadians. The vested interests of corporations and, in turn, of governments are served well by these practices. It is those of us who are governed – who are outside the corporate and government worlds – who suffer.'[103] The Canadian School Trustees Association reiterated its 1980 resolution to 'urge the federal government to establish a national industrial strategy.'[104] And the Winnipeg Coordinating Committee for Disarmament said that, in the economic realm, it: 'recommends that the federal government develop an industrial strategy to meet the technological and economic challenges of the eighties. A key element of this industrial strategy must be industrial conversion from military to civilian-related research and development and manufacturing. An element of the conversion would be the gradual termination of the Defense Production Sharing Arrangement, the Defense Industry Productivity Program, the military middleman operation of the Canadian Commercial Corporation (CCC), and similar military programs.'[105]

REGIONAL ECONOMIC DEVELOPMENT

On the issue of regional economic development, nationalist prescriptions emerged from all nine of the popular sector groups which wrote about the topic. The Assembly of British Columbia Arts Councils made a plea to the commission to both upgrade the status of the arts in Canada while paying attention to regional sensitivities: 'We submit that the time has come for the federal government to accord the arts and culture status as a *major industry* on a par with other national industries, and at the same time recognize the validity of supporting, as they do other economic sector, [the arts] on a regional basis and for regional endeavours.'[106] The Nuu-Chah-Nulth Tribal Council, while regretting that the commission did not contain any 'ordinary citizens' and was 'heavily weighted with degrees,' also told the Commission that the federal government needed to create regional development policies that were more sensitive to regional needs.[107] The Makivik Corporation, representing the Inuit of Northern Quebec, argued that 'in order to create a stronger economic union within Canada, the economic problems of the North must be addressed by devising a comprehensive and coherent development strategy in collaboration with Inuit and other Aboriginal peoples in Northern regions.'[108] Furthermore, they suggested,

In order to take into account in a cohesive and coordinated fashion the multitude of issues which we have covered in our brief, we would propose the elaboration of a national Northern policy. Such a policy must not be restricted to the Territories but must also include sub-Arctic areas such as Northern Quebec ...

It is our view that such a new national perspective can be vital in strengthening the economic union within Canada of the North and its Aboriginal peoples in particular are viewed as equal partners. The vision we advocate would follow the spirit of Canada's constitution, providing for equal opportunities and reducing regional disparities.[109]

The Northern Flood Committee, representing five Indian bands in Manitoba, presented a working model of regional economic development to the commission: 'The Northern Flood Committee ... is attempting to deal with the problem of "mass poverty and mass unemployment." [We are] attempting to provide a mechanism whereby the resources of both governments, Manitoba Hydro, and the reserve communities are coordinated so that they reinforce each other and are not counter productive. It is a system of comprehensive community development planning whereby the gaps in the total matrix of physical, financial, socio-economic and community resources can be identified, examined, and utilized in a coordinated, realistic, and meaningful way.'[110] Thus 100 per cent of the popular sector groups which commented on the idea of regional economic development took a nationalist view towards it, supported the need for it, and generally regarded it as vital to the success and growth of the Canadian nation.

TRADE POLICY

On the question of trade policy, all of the six popular sector groups that said anything about it took a nationalist perspective. The Asia Pacific Foundation of Canada, a government-funded organization that promotes greater knowledge, understanding, and respect between Canada and the Pacific rim countries, took an approach to the question of trade policy which took ideology to task:

The question of free trade must also be examined ... We are sometimes very doctrinaire about such issues and are prone to talk about 'free market' versus 'government planning' approaches as two irreconcilable ways of economic progress. This is not necessarily so. We are primaily a trading nation. If it takes free trade to be successful, we should resort to free trade. If it takes government to government trading, we should resort to such trading. If it takes planned and organized trading we should do it also. Whatever is conductive to successful trade should be pursued. We should stop arguing about relative merits of two highly dogmatic concepts – one being 'free market,' the other being 'national planning.' The real choice is to do that which is successful in the circumstances.[111]

Recognizing the decline of the American hegemon, the foundation called for a shift to a multilateral approach which took into consideration the new importance of the Pacific countries as trading partners.

'Canada should aim for self-sufficiency in a milieu of mutually supportive world trade,' argued the Lambton County Board of Education.[112] The Windsor Coalition for Development and the Third World Resource Centre saw American economic control and the profit motive 'as the root problems causing hardships on the Canadian people.' It further argued that 'legislation on content restrictions on imports and fair trade with the international market, especially Third World countries, is a necessary step in developing the Canadian economy.'[113]

The data show that nationalist prescriptions were clearly favoured in all categories by popular sector groups that wrote briefs for the commission. The same is true for labour groups. Business groups, though tending to favour continental solutions to Canada's economic woes, were divided.

Conclusion

The content of the written submissions analysed suggest a polarization of Canadian society along class lines, with the organized working class and popular sector adopting a state-centred nationalist position, and a significant segment of the business class adopting a market-oriented continentalist one. This foreshadows the divisions that crystallized around the free trade debate in the 1988 federal election.

The data reveal disharmony in the discourse of Canadian society as represented by organized interests. It confirms that the post-war Keynesian consensus, shattered by a series of successive crises in the 1970s, had not been reconstructed and was in a state of disarray in the early 1980s. There is evidence among labour and popular sector groups, and among many of the business groups, of a certain longing for the nationalist economic development strategies of the past that shaped that consensus. But there is tension between the advocacy of that nationalist view and business groups groping for a new set of more continentalist strategies. The Macdonald Commission thus served as the site of a struggle between advocates of the crumbling nationalist mode and proponents of a more continentalist regime. This struggle is reflected in the disharmony among the written briefs.

Despite that disharmony, however, two paradigmatic views were clearly presented to the Macdonald Commission. These two views were animated by neoconservative and social democratic discourse, and they had obvious links to the ideologies of continentalism and nationalism. The next chapter will elaborate the two paradigms of social democratic nationalism and neoconservative continentalism. It will also show the extent to which sufficient political viability was garnered from the support of business groups to embolden Macdonald to take his leap of faith.

CHAPTER 5

The Battle of the Paradigms

We then collected evidence, but carefully dismissed
The opinion of anyone who actually kissed.[1]

Close examination of the arguments over ideas presented to the Macdonald Commission sheds light on the choices before the commissioners. Though it consulted with more Canadians than any other inquiry,
no comprehensive study exists of the contributions of social actors to
the Macdonald Commission.[2] Still, a conventional wisdom has emerged
centring on two broad views. Some argue that this inquiry was virtually
predetermined in its outcome, and that it was 'captured' by corporate
Canada. Others suggest that there was only one model on the table for
the commissioners to choose from in their deliberations – the mainstream liberal economics model. But as we saw in the previous chapter,
the Macdonald Commission was in fact presented with two contending
paradigms, as revealed through the ideological pronouncements of
social actors concerning economic development strategies. The discourse of social actors who presented briefs to the commission reveals
that the outcome was neither predetermined nor the result of a lack of
alternatives. Each of the two ideological camps struggled to impose itself
on the commissioners and thereby to persuade the Canadian state to
adopt a particular political stance backed up by a particular set of economic development policies.[3]

The written briefs presented to the commission indicate that an
attempt was made to reformulate the once-hegemonic Keynesianism in
the face of a challenge from a new paradigm based on neoconservatism.
As we have seen, they also reveal an explicit link between continentalism
and neoconservatism on the one hand, and nationalism and social

democracy on the other. The political discourse of these documents over-whelmingly favoured the social democratic paradigm rooted in Keynesi-anism. But the Macdonald Commission ignored this advice and opted for the minority approach outlined in the neoconservative paradigm. Despite its reputation as a legitimator of the status quo and corporate Canada's agenda, the Macdonald Commission adopted free trade and the ideolog-ical world-view accompanying it. The commission was thus actually radi-cal, in that these were not the views of the mainstream in Canada.

This chapter begins with a discussion of the contradiction within royal commissions which strikes at the debate about the legitimating role these bodies play in transformative change. It then turns to the Macdonald Commission itself and traces conflicting views about the extent to which it was either predetermined in its outcome or presented with only one viable set of policy prescriptions. The subsequent section analyses the dis-course of social actors which presented briefs to the commission, sketch-ing both the social democratic and the neoconservative paradigms.

Hegemonic paradigms, as discussed in the Introduction, within which collective identities are represented, are created through any number of institutions – political parties, trade unions and other social movements, churches, and scientific establishments – not to mention state institu-tions such as royal commissions. Such a process was ongoing in the 1980s and can clearly be seen through the agency of the Macdonald Commission. The briefs presented to the commission are the written testament to this process, as the old Keynesian paradigm was assaulted by a new paradigm in the struggle for hegemony. Broadly speaking, organized labour and the popular sector spoke almost unanimously from a social democratic nationalist ideology. This approach was rooted in a Keynesian interpretation of economics and politics, which involved an important role for the state in the market. They were joined by some business groups. Many business groups, however, spoke from a different ideology, a neoconservative continentalist one which deified the free market, sought to discredit Keynesianism, argued for a greatly dimin-ished role for the state in the economy, and sought greater integration with the United States. Assessing the briefs anticipates the question of which groups are able to supply the political viability requisite for policy change, an issue explored in more detail in following chapters.

Analysing the Macdonald Commission

According to Richard Simeon, the debate in the literature on the Mac-donald Commission is between those who focus on a pluralistic process as the shaper of decisions, and those who focus on structural determinants.[4] Political economists argue that the conclusion was foregone where the Macdonald Commission was concerned: the commission was 'stacked' with the backers of corporate Canada; the alternatives were not seriously canvassed; and large sectors of Canadian society were ignored. Political scientists suggest that the outcome of this commission was less the product of some conspiratorial process engineered by the business class in Canada, and more the result of an inductive process in which a lack of alternatives led the commission to an inescapable conclusion.[5]

To argue that the commission was simply captured by the corporate elite and put forward the business agenda ignores a fundamental reality – business interests were not monolithic, but were actually sharply divided over the issue of economic development strategies for Canada. The popular sector and organized labour were strongly united in their prescriptions, it is true, but nearly half of the business groups rejected neoconservative prescriptions, as chapter 4 demonstrated. This suggests that discourse and ideology were in a state of crisis in which a new conventional wisdom had not yet emerged.

Furthermore, several factors militated against the commission adopting a foregone conclusion. These included its unwieldy size (thirteen commissioners); its massive and unfocused mandate; the differing ideological predispositions of those who initiated the commission (the Trudeau Liberal government) compared to those who received its recommendations (the Mulroney Conservative government); and its ill-conceived structure for receiving and reviewing evidence and writing the *Report*. Some other explanation needs to be found for its adoption of a neoconservative, continentalist ideological vision.

However, the political science hypothesis, that the commission was presented with only one set of policy prescriptions, is not totally compelling either, even though the *Report's* analysis of economic matters reflected in virtually every respect the conventional wisdom of contemporary mainstream neoclassical economics.[6] The economists, it is suggested, were the only ones with a coherent programmatic set of policy prescriptions for the commission. According to the political science view, 'given their definition of the problems to be addressed, *there was no credible alternative before the Commissioners*. Their choice, ultimately, was between the economics model, or no model at all.'[7] Thus, an economic vacuum saw neoclassical theory become 'common sense.'

Furthermore, the commissioners, while perhaps intuitively sympathetic to the concerns of the popular sector, labour, and similarly minded business groups, felt these groups were off the mark in talking the language of social justice instead of economic growth. Arguments focusing on the weak and marginalized were well received, but Canada was no longer in an age of affluence when programs to alleviate disparities could easily be cooked up by money-spending bureaucrats. 'In the end, [these arguments] failed because they did not address the question of economic growth and efficiency; they simply talked to a different agenda.'[8] To the extent that alternatives were presented to the commission, 'it was for a more or less fundamental reorientation of Canadian capitalism that fell outside of the range which a reformist Commission would be likely to adopt.'[9] Ultimately, according to the political science view, only the market model was on the table, so 'there was only one set of alternatives which appeared credible to the Commissioners. They did not so much cynically ignore the views of the "popular sector" as conclude that it did not address what they had come to believe was the central question. They thus became captives of a set of ideas which are close to hegemonic.'[10]

But an analysis of the briefs presented to the Macdonald Commission shows that, in fact, another model of economic development strategies presented *was*. It was an amalgam of state interventionism, traditional Keynesian prescriptions, economic nationalism, and a new emphasis on economic democracy focusing largely on community-based control and local decision making. Moreover, this view addressed the issue of economic growth, linking it to the concept of social justice. It was advocated in varying degrees by virtually *all* of the labour groups appearing before the commission, virtually *all* of the popular sector groups, and nearly half of the business groups. And it was certainly no more 'radical' than many of the ideas presented in the neoconservative vein, such as comprehensive free trade with the United States. Along with the neoconservative world-view of the other business groups, these two paradigms were clearly presented for the consideration of the Macdonald Commission.

The Social Democratic Nationalist Paradigm

Since the Second World War, Western democratic societies have evolved within the ideological context of a social democratic consensus.[11] This does not imply, of course, that social democratic or socialist parties have monopolized power. In some countries like Canada they have actually been shut out of government nationally. But it alludes to 'the virtually unqualified acceptance, throughout the political spectrum, of the Keynesian idea that the market economy is not self-regulating and periodically generates turmoil.'[12] While the specific features of Canadian-style Keynesianism can be debated, it is generally conceded 'that Canada has adopted the fundamental tenets of the social democratic consensus, and generally – if loosely – complied with a Keynesian-inspired model of policy-making and state intervention.'[13]

In the 1980s, the voice and focus of this paradigm found expression largely through a radicalized and nationalistic union movement and in the crucible of new rights-based groups which emerged in response to several important factors, including the decline of the representativeness of political parties in Canada, and the politics of the Charter of Rights and Freedoms. It coalesced through the agency of the Macdonald Commission, but received its early articulation in the important Catholic Bishops' statement, *Ethical Reflections on the Economic Crisis*, released in 1982, which was quoted to the commission more often than any other document. The adherents of this ideology, apart from churches and unionists, included the women's movement, environmentalists, seniors organizations, the cultural community, and Native groups, among others in the popular sector, as well as certain segments of the business community.

The Keynesian paradigm underwent an evolution such that the ideas expressed to the Macdonald Commission looked backward and tried to save as much of the old model as possible, while also looking ahead by redefining it in light of the new realities of the 1980s. For example, as argued above, the United Steelworkers of America looked back to the experiences of the Second World War and the post-war era for evidence of what a planned collective effort organized by government could accomplish. It noted the assumption of macro-economic management by the state and the commitment to full employment and recalled that 'the spirit which animated that change was the affirmation that collective action, exercised through the democratic institutions of government, can handle and solve the collective economic problem.'[14] The tenor of significant parts of this brief was almost sentimental in its ideological defence of the status quo as it argued that a key lesson of the 1930s seemed to have been lost on the present generation of policy makers. There were also echoes of traditional social democratic critiques of capitalism in the commission briefs,[15] often linked to the idea that 'American control of our economy and the profit motive are seen as the root problems causing hardships on the Canadian people.'[16]

This paradigm also took from Keynesianism such well-known characteristics as a faith in technocratic responses to societal ills employing the power and resources of the state, and suspicion of free market solutions.

Repeated calls for government intervention in the economy were made. Women's groups, for example, recognized their reliance on government intervention for such programs as pay and employment equity, affirmative action, and day care.[17]

In one of its variants, the paradigm called for nationalization of key sectors of the economy. In its more moderate guise, Crown corporations were advocated along with a mixed economy of public and private control. At the very least, the trend towards deregulation, favoured by neo-conservatives, had to be resisted, according to the Canadian Airline Employees' Association. Arguing that transportation is a key element in determining regional and national development patterns, it suggested that 'regulation has the goal of serving the public interest through the integration of a national and regional transportation network designed to meet economic and social needs. Deregulation will undermine these goals to the benefit of increasing corporate concentration and to the detriment of the public at large and airline workers in particular.'[18]

The social demoncratic paradigm advocated controls on foreign direct investment and increased Canadian ownership of the economy. One group asserted that lack of Canadian ownership was the single most important fact about the Canadian economy, and meaningful domestic control of the economy could only be brought about by government intervention. 'Unless governments in Canada are prepared to exercise significant and effective controls over the operations of transnational corporations in Canada, or are prepared to institute very substantial degrees of public ownership in Canada,' it was argued, 'there is no hope for meaningful direction of the Canadian economy.'[19] The Windsor and District Labour Council suggested that persistent unemployment could be tied directly to the branch-plant nature of the Canadian economy and to the fact that 'Canada's industry and resources are foreign (U.S.) owned and foreign (U.S.) controlled to an extent unmatched by any other industrialized nation.'[20]

Calls were also made for state-sponsored regional economic development policies and an industrial strategy, and the theme of multinational control of the economy frequently surfaced in this regard. The B.C. group Women Against the Budget argued that in the absence of an industrial strategy, economic decisions benefit multinational corporations, which are mostly American-based, at the expense of ordinary Canadians.[21] Other groups tried to show how military spending prevents the development of an industrial strategy. The Winnipeg Coordinating Committee for Disarmament recommended that the federal government develop an industrial strategy based on industrial conversion from military to civilian-related research and development and manufacturing. Tying this to American domination of the Canadian economy, the group went on to propose that 'an element of the conversion would be the gradual termination of the Defence Production Sharing Agreement, the Defence Industry Productivity Program, the military middleman operation of the Canadian Commercial Corporation, and similar military programs.'[22]

Advocates of the social demoncratic paradigm also rejected the view which cites deficits as the root cause of Canada's economic problems, arguing that they can be used as tools of fiscal policy to pick up the slack in slumping economies. They also advocated full employment policies, which were frequently tied to the issue of regional development. The New Brunswick Federation of Labour argued that Canada's economic problems and regional disparities could only be solved if the government developed a comprehensive national industrial strategy, the central goal of which would be full employment. It suggested the key elements of this strategy included a commitment to full employment; controls on foreign investment; manpower policies; increased processing of resources; reform of the tax system; government procurement policies; diversified trade policies; transportation regulation and policies; industrial development initiatives; inventory support measures; and increased research and development.[23]

The Canadian Union of Public Employees foresaw an alternative economic strategy predicated on the belief that it is a mistake to give more say over economic decision making to private investors. 'What we need is genuine public control over economic policy,' it argued, and 'a commitment to use the public sector as the engine of economic development which makes it possible to formulate a coherent industrial strategy.' But this organization recognized that while more public ownership is necessary to rebuild the economy, the solution was not simply more Crown corporations of the type Canada had already. 'Crown corporations need to be organized in a fundamentally different manner. They can – and should – be models of open public decision making, responsive to the needs of local communities and supportive of a much greater role for workers in decision-making.'[24]

The Ecology Action Centre explored the implications of the 'limits to growth' environmental perspective and concluded that a larger and more effective role for government in environmental regulation, conservation, monitoring, and enforcement was needed. As well, new mechanisms were needed for the design and assessment of real environmental costs in business and industry. 'If these are perceived as deterrents to economic growth, then so be it,' it argued, '*Only under these conditions is economic growth acceptable.*'[25]

All of these kinds of arguments are representative of the 'puzzle-solving' theoretician Thomas Kuhn referred to. They represent a paradigm and ideology under strain in a period of crisis. As with any ideology, attempts are made to link the goals of these groups to positive values (like democracy and social justice), and arguments are premised on the unexamined contention that a group's interests and those of the general public are synonymous. Further, the ideas, values, and beliefs underlying these positions are animated by the defence of a decaying status quo. But for any ideology to persist, it must be dynamic, and so defenders must innovate and improvise new ideas within the boundaries of the old order. This was done by some groups, which developed new ideas on economic democracy, local decision making and community-based control (for example through the agency of the cooperative movement), and the impact of environmentalism on economic thinking. The social democrats tried to link, for example, the idea of an industrial strategy and economic democracy. An industrial strategy should include public participation in local economic development, according to the Manitoba Federation of Labour. 'Economic planning, contrary to popular image, does not mean handing over the economy to government agencies. It means, rather, drawing all elements of society into a joint development project in which individuals, small business, corporations, co-operatives, and the public sector each have a role to play.'[26] Another group argued that 'our resources, natural, technological, monetary and above all human should be used towards building community owned and controlled industries – economic investment should be dependent not on monetary judgements but on the needs of the people.'[27] Native groups, such as the Makivik Corporation representing the Inuit of Northern Quebec, sought changes in Canada's economic and political systems in order to provide for greater participation so that economic decision making would be more responsive to local community needs. It suggested that 'in order to create a stronger economic union within Canada, the economic problems of the North must be addressed by devising a comprehensive and coherent development strategy ...'[28]

One not-for-profit community development corporation in Nova Scotia argued that the coming communications revolution could bring economic decentralization, enabling more local economic decision making and control. It favoured a broad participatory approach to economic development, using community development corporations that belonged to the '"third sector" – neither government nor private enterprise, but an attempt to combine the virtues of both.'[29]

The Social Planning and Research Council of Hamilton and District argued for comprehensive community-based planning:

> We recommend that the federal government develop and implement a program for the creation of community development corporations at the local level, and to this end: seek an adequate mechanism for the provision of risk capital to community development corporations; develop a mechanism for ensuring the negotiated development and monitoring of performance standards for community development corporations; develop a mechanism for ensuring the community development corporations have access to and employ technical expertise commensurate with proposed activities; develop a mechanism for ensuring that local unemployed individuals are targeted for the employment creation efforts of local community development corporations, and ensure local communities are made aware of the community development corporation program.[30]

Noting the bureaucratization of government, its inefficiency, and its insensitivity, the Social Planning Council of Metro Toronto argued that the solution was not to reduce public provision of services and reinforce private decision making, but rather 'to pursue democratic decentralization in all aspects of policy making and service delivery.'[31] It went on to argue: 'The role of government in economic decision making must be much more instrumental in the achievement of socially desirable and democratically determined investment and production goals. Private profitability should not be the sole criteria for measuring contributions to social need. The alternative is a system where community based initiatives and entrepreneurship form the basis of a rational economic policy for full employment. Planning to meet human/social needs become the function of economic policy.'[32] Thus within this ideological perspective it is clear that an unqualified faith in the benevolence of government is conspicuous by its absence. It is replaced by a wariness of the 'big state' coupled with a recognition that a return to Adam Smith liberalism is untenable.

Most significantly, the social democrats articulated and developed a nationalist perspective. This was expressed partly through its call for multilateral trading relationships through GATT, as opposed to free trade with the United States. The seniors' organization Help the Aged argued that Canada's economy is closely linked to that of the United States, which has been and remains our major trading partner. Nevertheless, trade with other countries has been growing, signalling growing global interdependence. It suggested that protectionist policies may be self-defeating, but that at the same time, over-reliance on trade with the United States was not an answer either. Therefore it was incumbent upon the Canadian government to diversify its trading relationships, particularly with Third World countries, 'not only in our moral obligation to our fellow human beings, but also in self-interest for both political and economic reasons.'[33] Similarly, the Lambton County (Ontario) Board of Education argued that 'Canada should aim for self-sufficiency in a milieu of mutually supportive world trade.'[34] A trenchant critique was made of continental integration from a variety of perspectives – economic, political, and cultural – which were to resurface in the subsequent free trade debate. For example, one group called for 'a self-reliant Canada which is politically and economically free. We oppose suggestions that Canada cultivate stronger economic ties with the United States,' which would create a situation of increased dependency, rob Canada of its resource base, and leave it with a false and inflated sense of prosperity.[35]

Finally, the social democrats were quite clear about who the 'enemy' was in the battle of the paradigms. As one group put it, 'our governments have, in the vernacular, been swindled by some snake-oil salesmen – that group of economists, labelled monetarists, who have promised miracle cures for various economic problems ...'[36] The battle was cogently summarized:

> We suggest that the claims and promises put forward by the monetarist economists are merely a smokescreen to hide their real objectives which are ideological in nature. We suggest that those ideological objectives are two-fold: first to counter-act the tendency of the economic liberalism which has been prominent in Western countries since World War II to reduce income differentials between various sectors of society; second, to restore completely the non-interventionist concept of government ... We believe that monetarists want to see ... that commitment replaced by the 19th century view that every person gets what he or she can in the economic jungle. This also requires restoration of the principle that government should stay out of economic matters and not interfere in the struggle in the jungle.'[37]

The Winnipeg Labour Council argued for an 'alternative economic strategy' which struck at the root of the neoconservative paradigm. 'This strategy must ... challenge directly the prevailing argument propounded by business interests that the only way to resolve the crisis is to give private investors a completely free hand to restructure the economy according to *their* priorities.'[38] It called for concrete steps to be taken to implement this alternative economic strategy, including stimulating the economy; lowering interest rates; stopping cuts in social services; implementing exchange controls; nationalizing the banks; cutting defence spending; introducing price controls; expanding public ownership; and reforming government finances.[39]

In summary, then, the social democratic nationalist paradigm drew on the old Keynesian model, added new ideas on economic democracy, and foresaw dangers of increased integration with the United States Notwithstanding the assertion that the commissioners only had one model presented to them, it presented some concrete economic prescriptions to the Macdonald Commission. It contained a shared set of interconnected premises, an implicit view of human nature, and a definition of the proper forms of social relations and relations among societal institutions. But it was presented in a period of crisis, and confronted with an ascending paradigm in direct contrast to itself which also contained these features.

The Neoconservative Continentalist Paradigm

The shift towards neoconservatism, most pronounced in the United States under Reagan and in Britain under Thatcher, has touched many Western industrialized countries, including Canada.[40] Wherever it has arisen, it has raised fundamental questions about the role of the state in the economy and society. But neoconservatism, like many ideologies, is notoriously difficult to pin down. It is an expandable ideological package which includes a wide and contentious array of social and political attitudes which may vary from country to country.[41]

Some have argued that 'there is no single, widely acknowledged Canadian neoconservative manifesto ... and no systematic evidence which lays out the attitudinal structure of Canadian neoconservatism.'[42] But there is a rough consensus that, at a minimum, a core set of values and beliefs can be identified,[43] and in the early 1980s there *was* 'systematic evidence' that laid out the attitudinal structure of Canadian neoconservatism among the briefs submitted to the Macdonald Commission. This

Table 5.1

Number of neoconservative and social democratic business group briefs commenting on economic development strategies for Canada submitted to the Macdonald Royal Commission by sector of activity

Sector	Neoconservative	Social Democratic	Both	Total
Chambers of Commerce	11	3	8	22
Professional Association	7	13	1	21
Trade Associations	27	14	9	50
Consulting Firms	2	4	0	6
Communications Firms	2	1	2	5
Financial Institutions	6	3	0	9
Transportation	0	1	0	1
Manufacturing	7	2	3	12
Agriculture	0	6	4	10
Mining	3	0	2	5
Forestry	2	1	1	4
Oil and Gas	1	1	2	4
Natural Resources	1	3	0	4
Retail	2	1	0	3
Business Research Groups	3	0	0	3
Private Sector	3	0	0	3
Total	75	53	32	160

paradigm can be summarized as containing the following attitudes: it deifies the free market, discredits Keynesianism, and argues for a greatly diminished role for the state in the economy. A pronounced aversion to government intervention manifests itself in calls for privatization, deregulation, and the selling of Crown corporations. It seeks the elimination of controls on foreign direct investment, and opposes the idea of an industrial strategy. As well, it advocates terminating regional economic development programs in Canada, and reining in public spending on social programs. Moreover, there is a particularly Canadian variant of neoconservatism, characterized by an orientation not only toward free markets, but towards economic integration with the United States.[44]

The business groups analysed were divided into sector of activity, as shown in table 5.1.[45] Chambers of Commerce in particular frequently demonstrated a strongly held ethos rooted in the tenets of the neoconservative ideology. The Greater Summerside (P.E.I.) Chamber of Commerce set the tone: 'The Chamber views the ever increasing presence of government in the day to day operations of business, and in the day to day lives of the members of the community, as a catastrophic disincentive to the citizenry of our country ...': 'It would appear that politicians and civil servants have less confidence in the ultimate efficiency of the market place than do we who represent the private sector. The fact remains, however, that the displacement of great pieces of the private sector by public corporations cannot continue indefinitely without Canada becoming at some point in time, a state run enterprise where both the entrepreneur and the citizen at large becomes the servant of government rather than the government being the servant of the people.'[46]

The Halifax Board of Trade echoed these sentiments. It argued that 'by accepting government assistance, we open the door for increasing government intervention,'[47] the implication being that this was a negative development.

The Calgary Chamber of Commerce submission was premised on the belief that 'the private enterprise system ... provides for freedom of private business to organize and operate for profit in a competitive system without interference by government beyond regulation necessary to protect the public interest and keep the national economy in balance.'[48] This equation of the positive values of 'protecting the public interest' with 'freedom from government interference' makes the ideology attractive and the argument compelling while avoiding the need for critical scrutiny.

Of the big five banks, only the Bank of Montreal presented a brief to the Macdonald Commission.[49] 'We do favour policies,' said the bank, 'that place greater reliance on market forces to determine the allocation of the bulk of Canada's resources in order to promote greater efficiency and productivity.'[50] The bank focused on the idea that market forces must prevail, even over political decision making. 'If greater efficiency and productivity are to be promoted in the private sector, policy must be directed toward promoting greater market discipline,' the bank claimed, 'let the marketplace, not economic planners, mete out the rewards and punishments; let the conduct of business be compelled by the forces of competition, not by those who possess political power.'[51]

The New Brunswick Telephone Company adopted the tenets of Adam Smith and warned against the threat of socialism in Canada. The choice was a stark one, but the path to freedom was clear: 'Canada faces a choice of continuing down the path to socialism or rekindling the spirit of private enterprise. It is this latter course we recommended with all the enthusiasm and conviction we can muster. The nation has been far too long obsessed with the redistribution of wealth rather than the creation of wealth. Only by turning our attention to those factors which will make Canadian goods and services more competitive in domestic and international markets will we have any hope of fulfilling the aspirations of individual Canadians.'[52] However, several impediments stood in Canada's way. These included 'the crushing weight of government overhead at all levels,' the 'over-regulation of the private sector,' and a social welfare system 'which provides few incentives to work.' This corporation pulled no punches in its assessment of what ailed Canada. 'We believe the first step toward an exciting, prosperous future is a recognition,' said its brief, 'of the stifling effects of the growing burden and encroachment of big government on the national economy.'[53]

The express purpose of the brief by Placer Development Limited, a mining firm, was 'to convince the Royal Commission that the transfer during the past three decades of economic decision making and initiative from the private sector to the government must be reversed if the Canadian economy is to achieve renewed vitality over the long term.'[54] Furthermore, in a succinct statement of the neoconservative perspective, it said: 'Canada cannot support a governmental burden of the present dimension. The large deficits developing both federally and provincially indicate the extent to which government now exceeds the carrying power of society ... During the coming decades, the focus of government must shift away from the redistribution of wealth towards the creation of wealth. The focus of government policy must be enhancing and sustaining Canada's global competitive position. Government must contract so that the economy can expand.'[55]

To the Canadian Electrical Distributors Association, Orwell's 1984 was all too close. Canada had been heading down the path of socialism since the Second World War, and the trend had to be reversed. 'We believe that a responsible, free enterprise capitalist society can best look after the needs of our citizens ...' it argued in a brief in which the anti-government message was paramount. 'If Canada is to resume growth in any meaningful way, then the intrusions of government into business must be curtailed.'[56]

The Canadian Petroleum Association implied that economic considerations alone should determine Canada's energy policies, a position repeatedly articulated by holders of the neoconservative view. 'To realize the full potential [of the oil and gas industry],' argued the brief, 'will require a stable policy framework guided principally by economic factors.' Government involvement in the oil industry throughout the 1970s and early 1980s did nothing but increase uncertainty, according to this group, particularly regarding investment decisions. Among its recommendations were 'the lessening of government control and regulation and increasing reliance on market forces to provide the proper signals to investors and to consumers.' In short, 'government market management should be replaced with market freedom.'[57]

The Saskatchewan Mining Association took a hard line against government intervention in the economy, noting that 'the Association makes no apologies for stressing its belief, repeating as it may the theme of briefs presented by other groups, that the main problem facing the mining industry is "too much government."'[58] The association went on to point out the susceptibility of the mining industry to government intervention at every step in the process, from exploration to development to production and marketing. It argued that 'it is vital to reduce the man-induced [sic] risks of ill-conceived regulations, inequitable taxes, and instability that contribute to reducing the opportunities to be competitive in world markets.'[59]

The Western Stock Growers' Association at least found some humour in an otherwise dreary economy. 'Inflation has become so bad,' it said, 'it has hit the price of feathers. Down is up.' Apart from this bit of corn, so to speak, the group took an earnest neoconservative approach in its brief. Its long-term perspective on Canadian agricultural policy 'emphasizes vigorous movement toward less government intervention and more free enterprise market orientation to make full use of commercial agriculture's entrepreneurial skills.'[60]

This theme of limiting government involvement in the economy was repeated over and over again in the briefs, and was the most prominent common message among the neoconservative missives sent to the commission. Implicit in many presentations was a plea for the supremacy of economic principles over political or cultural considerations, reflecting the neoconservative view that economics is separate and detached from the political and cultural spheres.

Like many business groups, for the Employers' Council of British Columbia the value of *competition* lay at the core of the neoconservative view. 'Our ability to compete internationally,' it argued, 'must be the criterion by which we make decisions about trade, about labour-management relations, about unemployment, about productivity, about technology, about business-government relations, about federal-provincial relations and about national institutional reform.'[61] This assertion crowds out any possibility that other traditional Canadian values such as cooperation might have a role to play in determining the solutions to these problems. 'Only by adopting realistic policies,' it went on, 'can we deal with increasing global competition to improve our standard of living.'[62] By implication, then, any other policy would be 'unrealistic.' Realism, in this case, seems to be in the eye of the beholder, and so 'realistic' policies are those which are rooted in an ethos of competition.

Related to the issue of the role of the state is the issue of Crown corporations. 'The creation of crown corporations to compete head-to-head with the private sector is totally inconsistent with the private enterprise philosophy,' according to the Calgary Chamber of Commerce.[63] It recognized that there is a role for Crown corporations in Canada where there is a real need for an industry or an activity nationally and where there are insurmountable obstacles to private sector initiative. But 'the Chambers have a real concern with the proliferation of crown corporations under the guise of economic expansion. It simply does not work.'[64] Crown corporations also attracted the ire of the Canadian Hardware and Housewares Manufacturers Association. 'Crown corporations sometimes provide a useful forum for the implementation of government policy,' it conceded. 'But we see no need for any further crown corporations which in any case should not be used for the underhanded manipulation of the economy or direct competition with efficient private sector operations.'[65]

Oil and gas companies were experiencing the roller coaster ride of massive price fluctuations and government intervention in the form of the National Energy Program at the time that the Macdonald Commission came calling to get their views. The enmity and distrust between Ottawa and this segment of business has become the stuff of legend in the intervening years. So it is not surprising to find representatives of this sector adopting a neoconservative, anti-government discourse.[66] Dome Petroleum counselled against excessive use of Crown corporations. It recognized that they had been an important part of Canada's historical development, but argued that their future role should be limited.[67]

The politics of the deficit, in which a bloated public service and spending on social services are blamed for the government's indebtedness, also featured prominently in these briefs. Claiming its own views to be synonymous with those of 'all Canadians,' the Calgary Chamber of Commerce argued that the public service is a major contributor to deficits and must be cut back. 'Canadians in general perceive that the major problems facing Canada's economy today is [sic] the size of the federal deficit and government spending at all levels.'[68] The Winnipeg Chamber of Commerce argued for an end to universality and the imposition of user fees for social services,[69] while the Western Stock Growers' Association advocated an all-out attack on social programs. 'Canada needs to move in the direction of a market-oriented economy for agriculture,' it wrote, 'and toward termination of many existing social welfare programs which are currently adding to our deficit.'[70]

Government regulation is a frequent concern of the neoconservative. Thus the Canadian Hardware and Housewares Manufacturers Association decried the fact that Canadian business had to compete with Third World countries whose unregulated industries operated with substantially lower wage rates. 'It is our view that the policy of deregulation should be both reinforced and speeded up so, enabling a more competitive climate where unnecessary regulations impede the economic effectiveness of Canadian manufacturers.'[71] It went on to suggest that 'deregulation of transportation, airlines, railways and shipping would foster greater competition, increased efficiencies, and lower prices generally for the benefit of Canada's economy and population.'[72]

Perhaps the most stridently neoconservative private sector brief was from the real estate firm Campeau Corporation, headed by the self-proclaimed 'citizen of North America,' Robert Campeau.[73] This brief, relying partly on the research of the Economic Council of Canada, focused on the need for deregulation, stating that 'we concur with the final report of the Economic Council of Canada and recommend substantial deregulation of the Canadian economy.'[74] It also noted that 'we concur fully with the Economic Council's claims that deregulation or less restrictive regulation of a number of sectors of the Canadian economy would lead to improved economic efficiency and hence to higher growth rates.'[75]

Another prominent, though vague, argument made in these briefs was that, while government should not interfere with the market, it should nonetheless provide the appropriate 'environment' for profit making. The Halifax Board of Trade, for example, sought to enlighten the commission as to the proper places of the private and public sectors. 'The role of the private sector should be simply to do business. The role of government should be to provide overall coordination of the development of the nation.'[76] The Board of Trade of Metropolitan Toronto weighed in with this assessment of the role of governments:'Governments should take steps to reduce their involvement in the economy, both as owners and regulators. It should be recognized that economic prosperity can be achieved primarily through the private sector operating within the discipline of the market system. Each government program and each piece of legislation, present or proposed, should be subjected to a critical cost-benefit analysis. Governments can make their best contribution to economic achievement by providing the best possible infrastructure and creating a favourable economic environment for private enterprise.'[77] The Retail Council of Canada presented one of the longest briefs to the commission, and it stands as one of the clearest calls for a neoconservative approach. It argued that 'it is important that governments – all governments – play more of a role as facilitators of change, rather than as architects of the change. Governments do not have an enviable record in choosing winners or cushioning losers in the marketplace, or managing essentially private sector investments and operations.'[78] 'In the final analysis,' it also argued, 'clearly the best course is to create an atmosphere in which the generation of necessary capital from within the private sector is possible.'[79] But as David Yudelman points out in his examination of the mining industry briefs, no definition or explanation of this idea of creating the appropriate 'environment' was forthcoming.[80]

Ironically, its stand against government intervention did not prevent the Winnipeg Chamber of Commerce from arguing that 'substantial government assistance, including financial support, is required for small and medium businesses to gain a foothold in the foreign marketplace.'[81] Furthermore, of the six main recommendations in the brief by the Western Stock Growers' Association proposed to the commission, three involved calls for government assistance and intervention. Nonetheless, the overall tone of the brief, and many of the specific points in it, was clearly neoconservative.[82] Canadian Hunter Exploration Limited argued for a 'realistic Canadian energy policy' which would see the attainment of its objectives by market forces 'blended with government encouragement.'[83] But this call for government intervention was accompanied by the statement, 'we should rely as much as possible on free market discipline to dictate the orderly development of energy supplies.'[84]

Consolidated Bathurst also appealed to the commission not to become captured by 'special interest groups,' apparently failing to recognize itself as being just that. This attitude among briefs from both sides of the battle was pervasive. Each assumes that their interests and those of the country as a whole are synonymous and fails to see themselves as having particular self-interested concerns. The extreme manifestation of this view leads to an appeal for special treatment. The Canadian Soft Drink Association went so far as to argue that democracy was not an adequate forum in which to effect change. 'Under our present Parliamentary procedure there is no appeal against government decisions,' it asserted. 'The only route open is the political one, which is cumbersome, costly and not very effective.'[85] These scarcely disguised calls for special treatment are all the more astounding for the fact that the tone in which they are made suggests a total lack of self-consciousness. Like many other neoconservative groups, however, this association was 'looking for government to assist ... in preserving a free, competitive marketplace.'[86]

Finally, a distinguishing feature of Canadian neoconservatism is its continentalist perspective. While one aspect of continentalism is an overt desire for integration with the United States, another is an antipathy towards nationalism within Canada, or anti-nationalism.[87] Linking the themes of government intervention and nationalism, the Halifax Board of Trade said, 'Governments must realize that they cannot engineer prosperity on their own. That only a strong and growing private sector can assure economic prosperity and that current goals of Canadianization of industry are simply not workable.'[88] The Saskatoon Board of Trade cited excessive nationalism as the problem where regulation of the economy was concerned:

> To what extent, we speculate, was the economic unity of Canada aided by a National Energy Policy that pointed the way to the U.S. border for drilling rigs from Alberta, and that helped in the crystallization of separatist thought and the election of separatist representatives, not in the East, where the basis would be historical, cultural and linguistic alienation, but in the West, on grounds of economic alienation? What abundant benefit was brought to Canada by economic nationalism and the Foreign Investment Review Agency which, as we see it reported, is now given a secondary importance? We wonder, too, at the wisdom of a policy, now abandoned after ten years, that emphasized the 'Third Option' of trade with Europe, ignoring the reality of our prime trading partner south of the border, and the closeness of social, cultural, and even familial ties across that border.[89]

Another hallmark of the neoconservative view is to appeal to the 'natural forces of economics.' So, for example, North-South trade between Canada and the United States is seen as natural and any interference with this as unnatural. It expresses faith that economic wealth generated by the market will look after the political and cultural spheres in turn. Thus the Retail Council could argue with equanimity that closer economic integration with the United States through the establishment of greater North-South ties should be the goal of the Canadian government. 'The distributive trades sector feels that the forces of economics will continue to encourage integration of the two economies.'[90]

The link between continentalism and neoconservatism is also evident in the following statement by retail giant Burns Foods Limited: 'The company intends to expand all its activities into the United States, where there are no marketing boards, labour conditions are more favourable, the market is much larger, and sources of supply are greater.' The brief continued, 'our only recommendation is that governments do not interfere in the changes taking place. Let the marketplace make the rationalization decisions and for the most part leave the industry alone to develop export markets in its own way.'[91]

Interestingly, the self-described 'mini-multinational' Consolidated Bathurst focused in part on the declining significance of the nation state, a concept which bolsters the position of the MNC: 'It is a fallacy for governments to think that there is some magical closed circle in which they have the essential levers at hand. External competition, world trade, international movements of capital, exchange rates are effectively beyond the scope of their power. The reality is that government is mainly a collection of specialized interest groups in our society with the drawback of reasonably short-term horizons.'[92]

Various ideological techniques are readily apparent in the neoconservative briefs (as in the social democratic briefs), for example, linking 'natural forces' and 'inevitabilities' while pandering to a people's belief in themselves. But what is striking is the absence of detailed and carefully thought-out economic prescriptions.[93] The language of the neoconservative briefs was, on the whole, much more general and overtly ideological than the social democratic briefs. One observer, commenting on business briefs favouring free trade with the United States, complained that: 'it is apparent that there are problems of definition, absence of adequate data, and lack of knowledge of the U.S. political system and trade legislation ... As a general observation, many of the [business] associations do not have a clear understanding of what constitutes a free trade agreement, more specifically the general economic, political and legal parameters of such an agreement ... Consequently, certain of the submissions lack focus, do not come to grips with the key issues and therefore have little to offer in the way of concrete and realistic suggestions.'[94] Yet, the neoconservative continentalist vision for Canadian economic development was preferred by the Macdonald Commission and formed the basis of its signature recommendation. As with any ideology, it ultimately matters very little whether there is any hard evidence systematically organized and presented to support its claims. Repeated often enough, ideological pronouncements become the 'truth.'

Conclusion

Many of the groups that presented briefs to the Macdonald Commission revealed a strong understanding of the battle of the paradigms. 'The weakness of economic theory must be stressed since much of current public policy seems to be based on a blind faith in that theory,' argued the Pacific Group for Policy Alternatives. 'Our purpose is to remind you of the weakness of economic theory, so you will not reject our goals and choices out of blind faith for today's common wisdom.'[95] The Canadian Mental Health Association drew a very clear picture of the struggle between the values a society chooses to live by and the imposition of ideological orthodoxies by vested interests. It rejected the concept of an 'invisible hand' and asserted that economies are human artifacts. It also drew a connection between freedom and government intervention in direct contrast to neoconservative musings on this topic. 'The sense of freedom and restriction comes not only, nor even primarily, from freedom from government restrictions. It requires freedom of opportunity, not only in the sense of having no governmental barriers to reasonable aspirations, but of being able to avail oneself of opportunities. A person boxed in by debilitating circumstances will not be free, even if government does not intervene. In fact that person will be unfree because of government inaction.'[96] This group cleverly took one of the core values of the neoconservative paradigm, freedom of the individual, and turned it around to show that freedom is impossible in certain circumstances *without* government intervention.

On the neoconservative side of the battle, the Winnipeg Chamber of Commerce presented a critique of Keynesianism as applied by Canadian governments. 'Keynesian theory did not anticipate that Keynesian principles would become justifiable for running deficits in good economic times also,' it argued, 'nor did it foresee the potential financing problems looming beyond this development.'[97] It went on to point out that 'A look at the Canadian experience over the past ten years shows that our government has only half understood Keynesian principles. In ten out of ten years the government has operated with a deficit ... The numbers speak very clearly. We do not have a system of fine tuning the economy, smoothing out the peaks and valleys. When the economy is weak, the deficits are high; when it is strong, deficits are merely lower. We have a chronic, structural deficit.'[98] But while recognizing this apparent misapplication of Keynesianism, the chamber did not advocate a corrective to it. Rather, it argued that Keynesianism *cannot* work because governments cannot be trusted to apply its principles properly. Thus, the baby must be thrown out with the bath water. This attempt to discredit the use of Keynesianism was quite common among the neoconservative briefs, and formed one of the main interconnected premises of the neoconservative.

The Macdonald Commission was unique for two reasons. First, the rapid adoption of its key recommendation distinguishes it from the hundreds of other inquiries whose reports languish on the shelves of the government archives. Second, this commission was unlike typical reformist inquiries, which seek to maintain an orientation towards limited and pragmatic policy goals. It was radical if we define this term to mean advocacy of a minority viewpoint. The lines from 'The Royal Commission on Kissing' quoted at the outset of this chapter are appropriate in this regard:

We then collected evidence, but carefully dismissed
The opinion of anyone who actually kissed.[99]

The signature recommendation of the Macdonald Commission called for a fundamental reorientation of over one hundred years of Canadian economic development strategies. This radical prescription emerged out of the battle between the old hegemonic social democratic nationalist paradigm and the neoconservative continentalist one. The evidence shows that this royal commission was not predetermined in its outcome, because the business community which was supposed to have 'captured' it was divided. And it was not presented with only one model for economic development strategies. Indeed, a furious battle ensued between those who sought to modify the Keynesian model in light of changed conditions by emphasizing economic democracy and local control, and to link it with nationalism, and those who worked to discredit that model, drawing on the economic crises to propose an alternative premised on less state intervention, freer markets, and continentalism.

The site of this battle, however, was not limited to the public consultation process. It could also be found within the research program, though it was a much more one-sided fight. And it was evident in the intra-bureaucratic struggles within the commission, which gave rise to the policy group that oversaw the drafting of the final *Report.* These other agents of ideology within the commission are considered in the following chapters.

CHAPTER 6

(Mis-)Using Social Science Knowledge: The Research Program of the Macdonald Commission

The ideas of economists and political philosophers, both when they are right and when they are wrong, are more powerful than is commonly understood. Indeed the world is ruled by little else. Practical men, who believe themselves to be quite exempt from any intellectual influences, are usually the slaves of some defunct economist. Madmen in authority, who hear voices in the air, are distilling their frenzy from some academic scribbler of a few years back.[1]

It was noted in chapter 1 that the struggle over political discourse and the delineation of legitimate identities and ideas in a royal commission plays itself out largely through public consultation. But it also occurs within the research programs of royal commissions, as scholars draw upon symbols and concepts that provide shared definitions of reality and circulate them through the instrument of the inquiry. A dominant academic discourse is established that typically favours the interests of particular social actors; state and societal institutions then articulate that discourse. Those intellectuals who seek to achieve significant reform or radical change are forced to challenge the dominant discourse and attempt to gain legitimacy for an alternative one partly through the research program. But in many cases, those seeking reform or radical change will not even be engaged by the commission.

This chapter examines the research component of the Macdonald Commission. A review of each of the seventy-two volumes of research studies, important though they may be as academic literature, is outside the scope of this study. In any event, this has been undertaken in other places.[2] But factors other than the printed output of the research program merit consideration in any study of the politics and legacy of the commission. Analysis of the research program must begin with the question of who was picked to work on it, as well as how they were chosen. Such inquiring can provide important insights into the ideological slant of the work produced. Little effort was made to recruit left-wing academics to the Macdonald Commission, for example, and thus alternative conceptions of economic development for Canada were not explored. The commission, moreover recruited few women scholars, and was later charged with being insensitive to issues concerning women. In these cases and others, voices raised in the public consultation process had little resonance within the research program, and therefore less impact on the commissioners' deliberations. Most significantly, economists sharing a particular ideological perspective dominated the research program where economic development strategies for Canada were concerned and were able to impose their own discourse on the commission, as they had in the earlier Rowell-Sirois Commission.[3]

This chapter looks at how the research program was initiated; the assembling of research teams; the workings of the 'old boys network' therein; the problem of part-time researchers; the autonomy of the program; conflicts between researchers and the commission bureaucrats; the issue of original versus received knowledge; and the commission's own assessment of its research program. The theoretical literature on knowledge utilization – the relationship between the ideas of social scientists and their influence on state policy – will also be briefly outlined, as will the relationship between social science and ideology and the special relationship of economists to the state in Canada.

Social Science, Knowledge Utilization, and the State

The manifestations of ideology in the work of intellectuals has been hotly debated and is part of a broader debate about the role of intellectuals in politics and their impact on society.[4] But it is only recently that the social sciences as they now appear have played a part in this debate.[5] The demand for, and use of, social scientific knowledge has grown rapidly with the emergence of the welfare state, which has taken on a whole range of socio-economic functions previously left to the private sector.[6] This fact was acknowledged by the Macdonald Commission. Its 1984 progress report on the research program stated that scholars 'bring to the collective research enterprise of the Commission the specialized knowledge built up by the massive expansion of research in Canada and elsewhere in recent decades.'[7] As Jenson notes: 'One of the first actions of a royal commission is to appoint a research director and to organize a substantial staff. In doing so, it is carrying on the heritage of the Royal Commission on Dominion-Provincial Relations (the Rowell-Sirois Commission), which reported in 1940 and is usually identified as the turning point in the conversion to social science research. The Commissioners' increasing emphasis on research is a reflection of the growing legitimacy that the social sciences had acquired in the inter-war years. To be convincing, arguments about social, economic and political phenomena could not proceed simply from first principles or legal discourse. They required the support of "facts."'[8]

According to Gagnon, the growing role of the social sciences in contemporary life is based on: 'a modernist definition of technocratic rationality in its notions of policy, and the development of separate and discrete social scientific disciplines out of social and political philosophy and the development of sub-fields within them centred on the public policy process. Social science, then, as well as being an intellectual activity dedicated to the understanding of society, is also a mode of discourse that empowers and legitimates the political-economic practices of the modern state.'[9] Jenson argues that essential aspects of any royal commission's normal activity are that 'the primary criterion for any research is that it be "scientific" and that its credibility depends on its quality. An additional assumption is that the research will be published in order to fulfil the "educational mandate" of the royal commission.' She goes on to argue that:

> While such guidelines might be useful, they do presume an overly straight-forward relationship between royal commissions and their research, which renders invisible issues about the politics involved. Royal commissions, as institutions, are involved in both providing and shaping representation – of Canadians, of research and of certain ideas. For example, at least some recent discussions have pointed to the biases that may infuse research – no matter how scholarly – for royal commissions following from the choice of whom to consult. Putting it another way, only some research is represented in the commission's political process.
>
> The issue is, however, even more complicated than one of presence. In his reflections on the Macdonald Commission, Richard Simeon argued that the research of some disciplines may be more powerful than that of others. A system of representation of both ideas and actors may be based on differential power positions.[10]

The increasing influence of the social sciences on the state poses some interesting questions, particularly regarding the evolution of political discourse. The use of social science knowledge by the state is conditioned by two things. First, in the social sciences there is a division of labour. Only certain disciplines can claim discrete kinds of knowledge with which to influence policy making. This tends to institutionalize and compartmentalize the generation of policy recommendations. Second, particular political discourses are created and reinforced, which are then used to legitimize the actions of the state. Political discourse relies on social science to provide analyses and prescriptions, as well as to identify and define important ideas and societal values, which are adopted in turn by the state as part of the legitimation process.

Social Science, Knowledge Utilization, and Ideology

Stephen Brooks and Alain Gagnon, examining the role played by intellectuals in Canada in policy formation, including their role in royal commissions,[11] note the centrality of the debate within Canadian social science about the Americanization of Canada in the post-1945 era: 'The nationalist critique of Canada's dependent relationship with the U.S., and of the "Americanization" of Canadian universities as a microcosm of this colonized status, claimed an increasing number of followers among sociologists and political scientists, and found public expression in such journals of contemporary opinion as *Canadian Forum, Canadian Dimension, Our Generation,* and *This Magazine.*'[12] The nationalist position was also articulated in such state-sponsored studies as the Gordon Commission, the Watkins Report, the Wahn Report, and the Gray Report, as well as through the Science Council of Canada,[13] all of which commissioned social science research on the Americanization of Canada.

The left-nationalist position was given considerable intellectual momentum in the 1960s and 1970s, but it lacked an effective political vehicle to carry its ideas into the political arena. The New Democratic Party was offered the opportunity to become that vehicle, but rejected its chance when it expelled the most forceful proponents of the nationalist critique from the party, the so-called Waffle.[14] In the 1970s and early 1980s, the Trudeau government adopted parts of this critique in shaping state policy but failed to sustain it, as noted above in chapter 1.[15] In contrast, in the 1980s, the neoconservative continentalist position found an effective political vehicle in the Progressive Conservative Party under Brian Mulroney.[16]

Ultimately, left-wing intellectuals in English Canada were unable to articulate an analysis of Canadian society that found acceptance outside of marginalized social groups and regions.[17] According to Brooks and Gagnon, 'the mobilization of subordinate groups in support of a dependency analysis of Canadian society was impeded by the disorganizing effect of non-class cleavages and a dominant liberal ideology that stressed individual mobility rather than structural inequality.'[18] Despite its apparent lack of political success, the left nationalist critique of Canada as a dependent society locked into a subordinate relationship with the United States did not die. Instead, it underwent what Brooks and Gagnon call: 'a sort of involution, developing within the universities and in leftist periodicals such as *This Magazine* as a new version of political economy. While linking itself to the tradition of such figures as Innis, Fowke and Mackintosh, the new political economy made extensive use of Marxist concepts, welding to metropolitanism the dependency theory developed by André Gunder Frank in his study of Latin America.'[19] Evidence of the vigour of this intellectual movement can be found in the formation of a Canadian Political Economy section within the Canadian Political Science Association in 1976, and in the founding of the journal *Studies in Political Economy* in 1978.[20] But beyond intellectual circles, this movement has had little impact, despite its claims to be linked to subordinate social movements of a dozen different types.[21] 'Its logically supportive constituencies – marginal socioeconomic groups and peripheral regions – are not easily mobilized, and the critical ideology of the social scientists working within this framework precludes an expert relationship to the state.'[22] Thus, while a well-developed trend towards the integration of social science research into the policy-making process has occurred over the past several decades,[23] this trend has decidedly not included dissentient academics.

In any event, by the 1980s, a continentalist backlash had arisen within the academy. The growing influence of neoconservatism in America was spilling over the border and infecting, in particular, the economics departments of Canadian universities, as well as some important think-tanks.[24] A concerted and thorough ideological campaign was undertaken, using as its main ammunition the theoretical premises of the creed of free markets, free trade, and a greatly diminished role for the state.[25] This development, combined with the traditionally hegemonic position of economics within state-sponsored research programs, meant that, in some ways, the recommendations of the Macdonald Commission research were at least predictable, if not foregone.

Royal Commissions and the Role of Economists

The one group of academics whose influence has never waned in the application of social science research to state policy making has been the economists. While rational policy making models have gone in and out of fashion in Ottawa, and while the use of political scientists, historians, sociologists, anthropologists, and social psychologists ebbed and flowed throughout the post-1945 era, the influence of economists continued in one direction – upward. 'There can be little doubt,' according to Brooks and Gagnon, 'that economists remain pre-eminent among social scientists in their integration with the policy process.'[26] Their influence is particularly evident in the proliferation of policy research institutes which have sprung up in the past forty years, which mostly publish the work of economists.[27] Indeed, most of these organizations: 'take the economy, and whatever affects its performance, as their principal object of study, publishing mainly the analyses of professional economists. Their activities have thus reinforced the belief that these matters fall only within the expert purview of professional economists, thereby reinforcing the special relationship of economics to the policy process.'[28] The economics profession has enjoyed a privileged relationship to public policy at least since the application of Keynesianism in Canada and most of the capitalist democracies. Indeed, as Margaret Weir reports, Keynesiainism 'catapult[ed] economists into positions of unprecedented influence over policy making in most of the Western industrial world.'[29] As the governing of society has increased in complexity, and as state intervention has expanded, the use of econometric modelling, rational decision making, cost-benefit analysis, forecasting, and other tools of scientific analysis lent a credibility to economics denied other social science disciplines.[30] Economists became, in the words of the Canadian historian Frank Underhill, the 'intellectual garage mechanics of Canadian capitalism.'[31]

Royal commissions, or at least the larger, broader-ranging ones on Canadian society, are forums in which other social scientists can participate as policy experts, but only to a limited extent. The near hegemony of economists within royal commissions has been reduced in recent years, but Brooks and Gagnon assert that 'close inspection of the studies undertaken for ... later royal commissions reveals that economists, by the proportion of research they account for, continue to dominate.'[32] Table 6.1 shows the different disciplines which have been engaged by selected royal commissions since 1970. What is noteworthy is the presence of economists in every single one. Only the lawyers come close in terms of

Table 6.1
Special studies for selected royal commissions, 1967–1985

Royal Commission	Number of studies	Contributing disciplines
Status of Women, 1970	34	Economics, Law, Anthropology, History, Psychology, Sociology
Corporate Concentration, 1978	33	Economics, Law, Industrial Relations, Sociology, Political Science
Newspapers, 1981	32	Economics, Journalism, Law, Political Science
Economic Union and Development Prospects, 1985	72	Economics, Law, Political Science
Equality in Employment, 1985	29	Economics, Law, Sociology

Source: Stephen Brooks and Alain G. Gagnon, *Social Scientists and Politics in Canada: Between Clerisy and Vanguard*, (Kingston: McGill-Queen's University Press, 1988), 111.

presence.[33] But clearly economists are overrepresented. This, added to the presence of economists within other parts of the state apparatus, suggests that their influence is disproportionate.[34]

Some critics claim the economics discipline is characterized by a rigid orthodoxy and homogeneity within which there is little room for consideration of alternative conceptions, and that it enjoys intellectual hegemony over economic matters.[35] This affords economists a cachet which prevents others from being heard, and effectively ensures that the social science research that economists produce will be preferred by the state. An examination of the Macdonald Commission research program supports these assertions.

The Structure and Organization of the Macdonald Commission Research Program

Getting Started: Stacking the (Continentalist) Deck

In the fall of 1982, Macdonald and Godsoe decided that the research component would be divided into three streams – economics, political science, and law. As to why the three areas were chosen, Cairns simply suggested that 'political science and economics were fairly logical, given the Commissioner's mandate.'[36] Breton recalled that law and political science were chosen because the original mandate of the commission was heavily oriented towards constitutional issues.[37] The genesis of the inquiry, after all, originated around the time of the patriation of the constitution, a pet project of the prime minister's. Smith, too, felt that it followed from the nature of the terms of reference: 'It was on the economic union and development prospects for Canada so that there was in the title clearly the economy, or the economic side. It had the economic union with the political and legal and constitutional issues, that were relevant there. And I think that, I had the feeling that so many of the issues that we would be tackling did have some overlap among economics, politics and law. One of the very interesting features of the work for the Commission was that drawing together of those three areas. Not exclusively those three areas – we had people from other areas, but the emphasis in trying to draw together those three areas was, I think, very relevant.'[38]

The ultimate decision to create three streams of research was made early on by Godsoe and Macdonald. Some consultation with a few of the academic-minded commissioners took place, and they did talk privately with others in the academic community.[39] But originally they wanted a single research director who could both command the respect of the academic community and lend the commission some legitimacy. Godsoe and Macdonald were acutely aware that the commission looked like some sort of smoke and mirrors Liberal boondoggle. To establish that it was an exercise of consequence required employing a respected academic to head up the research, which would show the academic community that this was an opportunity not to be missed. Moreover, it would signal that the commission would have an impact on the public policy debate by virtue of a body of published material that would be taken seriously and be distributed broadly. The problem for Godsoe and Macdonald, though, was who could command that degree of credibility; where on the Canadian academic scene could they find such an academic giant?

As the two of them discussed various potential candidates, they continuously ran into the problem associated with modern social science of its lack of cross-disciplinarity. Some whom they considered were too specialized within their own disciplines. Others were towers of strength in the political science community but would likely not command the respect of the economists, and vice versa. It was clear that most research was going to have to come from economics and politics, and Macdonald

and Godsoe eventually realized that the one individual who could straddle these disciplines was dead. They were really looking for Harold
Adams Innis, that marvellous Canadian hybrid called a political economist.[40] An attempt was made to find one person who could encompass
the three research streams selected,[41] a modern-day Innis who could
bestride a wide array of disciplines and integrate them into a cohesive
whole.[42] Alas, they concluded, perhaps erroneously, such a figure no
longer exists in Canadian social science.[43]

In the absence of a single research director in the mould of Innis, the
decision was taken to have three (although having as many as five directors was considered).[44] At this stage, Godsoe and Macdonald entered
into extensive consultations on who they would be. Michael Kirby was
asked for his input:

> In many of those cases, entirely independent of my official position, I was
> asked for opinions. Ivan [Bernier] and I had run the Institute for Research
> on Public Policy for years before that. So I knew the research community in
> Canada up one side and down the other. So it was true that Godsoe and
> Macdonald would call and say, what did I think of so-and-so? But that
> wasn't because of the spot I held in the federal government, that was more
> because of my background. I was an academic for fifteen or sixteen years, I
> had run IRPP. I knew all these players. So it was in that context that I was
> asked. I wasn't asked officially, I was asked in the same way that Macdonald
> probably asked eight other guys who the researchers should be.[45]

The first research director chosen was Alan Cairns. Former head of
the Department of Political Science at the University of British Columbia
(but at the time William Lyon Mackenzie King Visiting Professor of
Canadian Studies at Harvard University), Cairns led the political science
stream. He recalled being surprised at the way in which he was
approached to join the commission: 'Over the [1982] Christmas holidays
I was at home and I remember we got a phone call from Donald Macdonald, which sort of surprised me. I'm still surprised when you get long-
distance phone calls, and the person at the other end of the line is someone you don't know, and I didn't know Macdonald except by name. He
said 'this is Donald Macdonald' and pauses and waits for you to respond.
So I felt really stupid and said 'I recognize your name.' I didn't know
whether he was in the next room.'[46] After this inauspicious introduction,
the two agreed to meet at the Montreal airport, where Macdonald outlined his plans and invited Cairns to become research director. Mac-

donald recalled that Cairns proved to be an invaluable selection: 'I forget where the nomination came from, and I have to say it was stroke of genius from somebody, because among the range of disciplines, I found the political scientists had a broader perspective, and were less inclined to get lost in the details of their own discipline. And he made a remarkable contribution in helping to pull the thing together. And I cannot remember who recommended Alan, or where I first heard about him. But it was one of our red-letter days.'[47]

David C. Smith, former head of the Department of Economics at Queen's University, was selected to head the economics stream, although halfway through the commission he was named principal of Queen's, a position he undertook on 1 September 1984, and thereafter his participation diminished significantly. Economists Kenneth Norrie and John Sargent assumed Smith's role and acted as co-directors of research for the concluding phase of the economics program. Macdonald sought the advice of the economist commissioners Breton and Barber on the choice of Smith. Smith recalled, 'Donald Macdonald asked to meet with me, and I was asked to be Director of Research for economics. Gerry Godsoe of course played an important role as the next in line to Donald Macdonald, but it was Macdonald who made the direct approach.'[48] Notwithstanding his commitment to Queen's, 'it was agreed that I would still help. I would try to do a few things in the Fall of 1984, though my time would be limited as I had to take on the administrative duties at Queen's, and the chairman Donald Macdonald had agreed that I would contribute what I could, but he understood that I would not be able to do it full time.'[49]

The third stream was almost as an afterthought, but it reflected the disciplinary and professional biases held by Godsoe and Macdonald, both of whom were lawyers. Several prominent legal academics within Godsoe and Macdonald's circle of professional friends went strongly to bat for a legal research stream, including Prichard and Commissioner Michel Robert.[50] In discussing the commission mandate with Smith and Cairns, it was determined that there should be a third, but considerably more modest and smaller, section on legal studies. So they selected the dean of the Faculty of Law at Laval University, Ivan Bernier, who was known to Macdonald through mutual acquaintances and colleagues in their respective law schools.

Another consideration in establishing the third stream was the need for access to the considerable Francophone literature which existed in the social sciences. It was regarded as important that the commission have a pipeline into the world of Francophone and Quebec scholarship, and that to tap into the best work of Quebec's scholars writing in French would require an inside voice who had weight in that community. Bernier's background perfectly suited him to the position, in the opinions of Macdonald, Godsoe, Cairns, and Smith. In addition, Bernier had a solid grounding in both trade issues and in political-constitutional issues, and was able to attract some prominent Quebec scholars to the project.

The selection of the troika of Cairns, Smith, and Bernier would have deep significance for the ideological shape of the research program. Certainly none of the three could be considered nationalists. Smith, in fact, as a mainstream economist, was a known anti-nationalist, while Cairns was regarded in academic circles as a 'reluctant nationalist' at best.[51] While Bernier's position was more ambivalent, it mattered less. The other two were the key directors, thus the research teams assembled were in many ways mirror images of their own intellectual biases. The two 'heavyweight' research directors were not about to chart a nationalist research path, or, as the evidence below demonstrates, one which balanced the nationalist-continentalist perspectives.

Meanwhile, one of the first actions undertaken by the fledgling commission was to authorize a small group of academics to scrutinize and comment upon the commission's terms of reference.[52] They submitted their reviews in writing in January 1983. Prichard was included in this group, hand-picked by Macdonald, as were the following: Albert Breton; Bernard Bonin of the École nationale d'administration publique; Kenneth Waldie, a consulting labour economist from Kingston and former staff member at the Canadian Labour Congress; Anthony Scott, an economist; John Grant of Wood Gundy; Michael Spence, a professor of economics at Harvard; and David Husband, an economist whose graduate thesis adviser at the London School of Economics was Albert Breton. In addition, Clarence Barber wrote a short piece on 'Economic Policies for Canada.'

Prichard approached the assignment by imagining what the table of contents of the final report would look like.[53] Quoting J.S. Mill, Prichard wrote 'no great improvements in the lot of mankind are possible until a great change takes place in their mode of thought.'[54] Waldie, whose name had been put forward by Docquier, took a more critical approach, asking why a royal commission was necessary in the first place, given the volumes of social science research and expertise already available to governments:

More than 2,000 people are employed by the federal government in the 'economist/statistician' category. The Finance Department alone employs some 140 economists. Other departments such as Industry, Trade and Commerce, Energy Mines and Resources, Regional and Economic Expansion, Labour, and Agriculture employ hundreds of policy analysts who devote their entire careers to the analysis of the very problems mentioned in the Commission's Terms of Reference. The Bank of Canada also has a substantial research capability. The Economic Council of Canada was created as a consensus-building body which would provide more independent and long-term advice ... Additional and even more independent advice is available from the universities. There are also several other research agencies in the private sector carrying out continuing studies of economic and public policy issues.[55]

Notwithstanding this early scepticism, Waldie went on to write a study for the commission anyway. He also lamented the absence of any reference to 'Canada's extreme dependence on economic conditions in the U.S., or the use of non-tariff barriers to trade,' and recommended that the commission add both subjects to its working program.[56]

Significantly, though, none of the eight contributors mentioned free trade with the United States as a potential area of inquiry, or as a desirable option for the commission to consider. There were, however, calls to investigate full employment, industrial policy, regional economic development, the effect of protectionist Canadian policies on the Third World, barriers to inter-provincial trade, GATT, and so on. Husband did raise the issue of trade policy in general, in a cautious manner. 'Are we willing to endorse a free trade policy,' he asked, 'with all that may follow for the textile industry and other such industries?' Without answering this question, he prophesied that 'a much tougher international trading climate is emerging that poses particular challenges for Canada,' and his prescription for the commission was to adopt econometric models to answer its many questions.[57] Husband went on to become a policy coordinator for the commission, and he had an important role as a member of the small but influential policy group which pushed for free trade with the United States.[58]

The Hart House Symposium

As the commissioners were digesting these commentaries, an important academic symposium was held at Hart House at the University of Toronto. Organized by Prichard in February 1983 at the request of Macdonald, its purpose was twofold. First, it was intended as an introduction to the plans of the commission, and an invitation to some of the best academics in the country to participate in it. One scholar enthusiastically remarked at the end of the symposium that 'this could well be our generation's Rowell-Sirois.'[59] Second, the academics were asked to suggest research topics on the basis of the commission's broad-ranging terms of reference.

This discussion was entangled with a secondary matter, namely, which disciplines should be chosen to conduct the research studies. The historians present, for example, argued that a royal commission of such magnitude would have to contain a history of Canada. But they were rebuffed by those who asked the only partly rhetorical question 'whose history would it be, exactly?'[60] Alan Cairns recalls that 'there were criticisms. I know Lorna Marsden was quite critical there wasn't a sociological stream, and some of the historians thought you should have an historical stream.'[61] Not surprisingly, Godsoe and Macdonald were subject to considerable lobbying, particularly by sociologists, who did not want to be cast in with politics or, worse still, ignored altogether. Sociology was aggressive in arguing that it should have been the third stream of research needed by the commission. But Godsoe and Macdonald were unsympathetic and felt sociology could not be comfortably incorporated into the existing research framework. The historians, sociologists, political economists, geographers, and others lost this battle and were formally excluded from the research program, although a few individuals from these disciplines were commissioned to write articles on specific issues.[62] Arguments that these disciplines should share in what some pejoratively referred to as the greatest SSHRC grant ever offered in Canadian history fell largely on deaf ears.

Interestingly, it was at Hart House that the nationalist versus continentalist debate emerged for the first time among the academics. Godsoe recalled that some left-nationalist scholars present mounted Keynesian-rooted arguments about what ought to be studied, and how the commission ought to go about its work. A clear, strong clash of nationalist and continentalist statements was made at Hart House, according to Godsoe, and this was one of the first major issues to arise. The clash between the Canadian nationalists and the free marketers stood out in his mind, with nationalist academics Abe Rotstein and Mel Watkins arguing vociferously that the commission was falling into the trap of mainstream economics, buying into a bunch of assumptions rooted in right-wing market dogma. But they were rebuffed. Moreover, Cairns did not rush to the defence of a more ideologically pluralistic academic exercise, in part because of his own continentalist intellectual background. The climate at Hart House proved to be a chilly one for the left-nationalists, and as a result few were invited to work with the commission thereafter.[63] Thus an opportunity was missed to create a genuinely broad-based approach to the study of the Canadian conundrum. Ideally, the three research streams were expected to provide a cross-section of studies which could produce a comprehensive, integrated analysis of the Canadian political economy. In fact, a narrow, discipline-based perspective was institutionalized wherein little cross-fertilization of ideas occurred. Moreover, the continentalist perspective was institutionalized within the research stream almost from this moment. The Hart House symposium proved to be important, for it helped establish the ideological boundaries and parameters of the areas to be studied.

Assembling the Research Teams

Macdonald and Godsoe, although possessing some limited academic background, were really corporate professionals, and they were more used to the way research is done outside universities, on contract with quasi-academic think-tanks whose method of operation is rather different from that of academe. So they sought the counsel of Prichard about staffing the research program. Prichard pitched a traditional research format to them, one which was very much university based and subscribed to the conventions of scholarly peer review, which is the way most Canadian royal commissions have operated.

They decided they wanted to recruit 'the best and the brightest' from the academic world. To do so would eradicate the political taint of the commission, as well as offering the possibility of publication. 'Clearly we thought if we were to draw the very best people who could synthesize the problems for us,' Smith recalled, 'that their reputation would depend upon their written piece being published if it met appropriate standards and that it not be used for political purposes per se. And so we did have a very strong emphasis on peer adjudication and the autonomy to publish provided quality standards were met.'[64] In addition, the research program was discussed in terms of developing a network of reasonably young people at the cutting edge of their careers. Rather than seeking older, established academics they wanted to find younger ones who had finished their PhDs fairly recently, who would get to know one another, get to know the process of government, how public policy is formed, who the players are, and so forth. Idealistically, this network of scholars was regarded as potentially important a legacy as the commission *Report* itself.

Once the research directors were in place, and some sense was gained of the projects to be undertaken, research teams began to be assembled. The directors worked out subjects within each of their own specialties and with each other, and suggested to the commissioners what studies ought to be undertaken. Smith recalled that he and the other two directors carefully consulted as to how this might best be handled. They sought ideas from the commissioners, the chair, and Godsoe. They then devised a proposal which was presented to a meeting of the commission in Victoria in early 1983. 'Our basic approach,' Smith remembered, 'was that given the enormous range of issues that the mandate covered, how best could we help bring the present state of knowledge on those issues to the awareness of the commissioners and more generally to be made available publicly?'[65]

Macdonald recalled that the commissioners were, on the whole, inclined to accept the directors' recommendations for establishing the research program.[66] Moreover, he credited them with helping to formulate the work of the commission more clearly. 'It was much easier once they spent some time working on it, and we had some fierce debates about what we should do and what we shouldn't do, but their focus on shaping the research program had a lot to do with the ultimate confines, the ultimate parameters of the commission.'[67] Macdonald was leery of traditional royal commission research exercises. 'So there the commission gets created and we set up a research program,' Breton recalled, 'We discuss at length what kind of research program. Initially, Macdonald doesn't want to do what has been done historically, which is to bring in an Ottawa bunch of economists like Gordon has done.'[68]

According to Cairns, 'the task in trying to figure out how to carve up the research, who to involve, was just paralysing,' and proceeded very slowly.[69] Notwithstanding the goal of developing a network of young academics, recruitment was largely an informal process whereby old friends and colleagues were called on and asked to work for the commission, or to suggest others who should be recruited. As a preliminary step, the directors selected over twenty research coordinators and charged them with commissioning studies. For instance, Smith set out the topics which seemed to him most relevant on the economics side for the commission's work. The breadth of the mandate meant that the commission could wander quite far, making this task difficult. He then tried to get listings of the very best people who had done research in each of the areas. As head of the economics department at Queen's for thirteen years, he felt he had a certain knowledge of who had been doing what in economics in Canada. But he also appointed advisory groups for each of the areas to help him select researchers, as well as to hear the research being presented in preliminary form in seminars, and who could give some guidance and direction as to where a project might be a bit off base. 'So it wasn't purely idiosyncratic to me. I wasn't the one who insisted that my choice as to who was a good economist in each of these areas would prevail, but rather I had small groups of others who advised on that too.'[70]

There was relatively little input from the commissioners themselves at this stage (a pattern which was to repeat itself throughout the commission, leadership came from elsewhere). As Keith Banting recalled, they 'could not get from the commissioners a precise definition of what they wanted to highlight, what their priorities were,' partly because the commission mandate was so broad. As a result, the coordinators had a fair amount of liberty to design their own research programs, which they did in consultation with one another: 'We had regular meetings with the research coordinators, they would be two day meetings, and they would be long meetings. And each of us presented our ideas for what we should commission in our sectors. There were long discussions about those. So it wasn't a privatized activity by individual coordinators, it was a collective process, and we commented on each others' choices of topics.'[71] It was decided to divide the research studies into five categories: economics; politics and institutions of government; law and constitutional issues; federalism and the economic union; and the North.[72] Scholars were hired, and contracts for the seventy-two commissioned volumes of research were drawn up for over three hundred academics, mainly from the three chosen disciplines.

The coordinators, in consultation with the director for their area, recruited academics to produce research in vaguely defined areas. Because the commission mandate was so broad almost any proposal could be accepted. Many coordinators simply contacted people they knew who had an expertise in a given field, asked them what they were currently working on, and if they would like to turn it into a commission study. They would then report on and defend these studies as they developed to the directors. The usual process of peer review and critical assessment was followed. But since many of the academics were colleagues, professionally or personally, it is questionable as to whether this was not more or less a case of having the foxes watch the chicken coop. Research Coordinator Jack Quinn's selection to work on the commission was perhaps typical of the closed world of Canadian academia. He recalled:

The reason that I got involved in the commission's work was that at the time I was teaching law at Osgoode Hall Law school, and I knew Donald Macdonald through a mutual friend, Rob Prichard. I knew Rob from when we were students together at Yale. And I knew Donald because Rob and I had done some work with Donald when there was some prospect that he would run for the leadership of the Liberal Party in the late 1970s ... So Macdonald decided to appoint me the research coordinator in charge of international economic issues. And the way the commission was organized, there was an overall legal research director, who was a friend of mine, Ivan Bernier ... So I think that probably Bernier's friendship also had something to do with my being picked.[73]

The effect of this selection process was that any biases carried within this closed world were reinforced. Not surprisingly, then, a continentalist bias was pronounced among significant numbers of the researchers chosen.

Throughout the development of the research program, there was a real lack of direction from the commissioners, and a feeling among research staff that they were aboard a rudderless ship. Banting recalled, 'My strongest impression of the definition of the research agenda was that the scope of the research agenda was driven by the lack of specificity about the agenda of the commission itself. The breadth of the agenda and the terms of reference, and the size of the commission, the number of commissioners, its internal complexity, the fact that it wasn't in the first instance going to be a chairman-dominated commission in the way some smaller, earlier commissions had been, meant that no one could provide the research directors at the outset with very specific terms of reference, saying "these are the things we want you to work on."'[74] Peter Aucoin felt that one of the major organizational deficiencies of the commission was that 'the research agenda was not tight at all.'[75] It was decided, for instance, to commission far more research than was realistically needed in order to be sure that every conceivable area of interest could be canvassed. And if half of it later got thrown out, at least the remaining 50 per cent would be relevant to the commissioners. This approach proved ineffective, as new topics continuously arose which required research in areas undreamed of by the directors and coordinators. For instance, Winham recalled that he and Stairs were recruited by Cairns to be co-chairs in the area of international political economy: 'We were brought in, and the reason we were brought in late first of all is that nobody thought that an internal examination of Canada's economy would deal with international relations, so therefore international relations was not included on the political institutions section. It was only after they got working that so many of the kinds of things that they had to deal with internally also dealt with issues externally, that they perceived that they had a shortcoming in that area, in fact that they had to open a new section on international political economy.'[76]

The emergence of free trade as an issue within the commission demonstrates the 'fly-by-the-seat-of-your-pants' approach to the research, and left Winham with the impression that 'we were taking our marching orders from the *Globe and Mail.*'[77] This was a reference to Macdonald's public pronouncement that he favoured a 'leap of faith' into free trade with the United States, a decision that had neither been communicated internally to the researchers nor agreed to by the other commissioners, but which was revealed through the media. Thus, the academics had to scramble to produce studies focusing on free trade after Macdonald went public.

When Macdonald revealed his position on free trade, one coordinator determined that no one had commissioned a study on sectoral free trade. After also discovering that no government department would admit to having looked at this question in any depth, and being refused access to any internal government studies which might have been done, he urged that some original research be undertaken, and quickly, for the commissioners.[78] But when he brought this proposal forward he was stonewalled by his research director, who pointed out that the research program was not set up to do original research. A minor imbroglio ensued, with the coordinator going to Nymark to convince him of the need for this research. Nymark agreed, and overruled the director. The coordinator got some money from the commission, employed four graduate students, and proceeded to conduct original research into the topic. This explains the anomalous research paper on sectoral free trade housed separately from the seventy-two volumes of studies,[79] and reveals the extent to which the research program, and the commission itself, was a 'disorganized organization.'

The Old Boys' Network

One liability of the casual approach to recruitment for the commission was that it resulted in research teams and a commission staff that were 'old-boy' in nature and composition.[80] The executive director, director of policy, the three directors of research, the commission secretary, the four senior advisers, and the two co-directors of research were all men.

The director of administration was the only senior staff person who was a woman. Further down the organizational ladder, four of the five policy coordinators were men, as were twenty-one of the twenty-four research coordinators and executive assistants. Of those staff members listed as secretariat officers, seven of eleven were men.

The authorship of the research studies shows a similar gender imbalance. In the 141 essays commissioned in the economics program, 155 men are cited as authors, whereas only 15 women are cited.[81] In the politics and institutions program, sixty-four essays were commissioned. Seventy-two men and six women are cited as authors.[82] Of the forty essays commissioned in the law and constitutional issues program, thirty-eight men and six women are listed.[83] In the program on federalism and the economic union, thirty-four essays were commissioned. Forty-one men and four women are named as authors.[84] Finally, in the program on the North, all eight essays commissioned are written by men. Thus, at virtually every level, the commission suffered from a severe gender imbalance. Not surprisingly, much subsequent criticism of the commission focused on the adverse impacts many of the commission's recommendations would have on women.[85]

The Part-Time Problem

Another factor which affected the research program was that most of the researchers, including many coordinators, worked part-time on the commission since most had full-time teaching jobs in universities. As well, they were dispersed across the country, convening only for the occasional meeting in Ottawa. Banting's experience as research coordinator was not untypical. 'I got on the plane Sunday, flew to Ottawa, did two days at the Commission, flew home [to Vancouver] and taught Wednesday to Friday. Saturday I collapsed, and Sunday I got back on the plane. And I made that trip eight times in the first term.'[86] Thus, apart from little overall direction, there was insufficient opportunity for interaction and consultation between the researchers as well. Aucoin cited this issue as one of the major organizational deficiencies impeding the work of the commission.[87] Macdonald found this particularly frustrating: 'I found that it is one thing to have a qualified person [doing research], but it is another thing to have him available to work for you, because if you start off in the Winter of 1982–1983, that person is involved in academic duties up until May, 1983. If they are any good, they probably have been committed for the summer to something or other. So chances are you probably wouldn't be able to get a real stretch of time from them until

the summer of 1984.'[88] Almost every academic and commissioner interviewed for this study emphasized the 'part-time problem.'

Research Autonomy

The directors were adamant that the research program should be
autonomous, and free from interference by the commission bureaucrats, as well as by meddlesome commissioners. The directors also
wanted to ensure that the research was not simply responding to issues
arising out of the hearings process. As Cairns recalled:

> Not that we felt that we could do anything we wanted. We had to get the
> agreement [of the commissioners] and it was also clearly understood that if
> individual commissioners felt that particular kinds of research that were
> doable should be done, then we would do it. We were their servants. We
> weren't just on the biggest SSHRC grant in the world. But we did everything
> possible to magnify the autonomy of the research, and that is one of the rea-
> sons why, for example, we had everything assessed as if it were a journal arti-
> cle ... The reason was that the research directors wanted to be able to say if
> someone on the commission didn't like a particular piece of research, we
> could say look, this has been assessed by a normal academic process.[89]

The directors engaged in some 'quite heated battles' with the commissioners and the bureaucrats over this issue, but won every one of them.
Cairns attributed victory in part to the fact that 'Macdonald himself is
academically inclined. He appreciates that.'[90] Strikingly, Cairns
remarked that this was a less significant factor for the economics
research team than for the other two. 'I think the economics stream ...
had a much more unified sense of what its task was all about, and
brought a much more explicit ideology to the task.'[91] The chorus of
economists, then, singing with a single voice, were less concerned about
interference with their work than the more heterogeneous political scientists or lawyers.

The insistence on autonomy was also expressed through the wishes of
the directors that the research would be published separately from the
Report. Cairns argued:

> Right from the very beginning the research directors pressed, very much,
> for the agreement that the product of the Macdonald Commission, in
> terms of physical output, was going to be double. The commission was not
> just producing a report. The commission was producing a separate body of

research, which might be critical of whatever direction the report went in, and we were consistently reminding the commissioners, because not all of them were academically attuned that the long-run academic output of the commission could well be as important as particular recommendations. And then we talked of the other great commissions in the past like Rowell-Sirois and Tremblay, etc., as an indication that these can become intellectually seminal in the subsequent understanding of the country, and indicated that the research, the separately published research, was often very important to that task.[92]

But this insistence on autonomy fed into another problem experienced by the commission – the rivalry between the academics and the bureaucrats.

Conflicting Cultures: Academics versus Bureaucrats

In contrast to the 'part-timers' in the research program, most of the over 180 staff members of the commission were full-time. While there was a considerable amount of turnover within this component of the commission, they were able to be far more effective as a unified organizational body than the researchers.

At the outset of the commission, it was made quite clear that the researchers and the bureaucrats were separate entities, and that there would be little cross-fertilization between them. This of course created the conditions for suspicion and intrigue, as jockeying for influence proceeded apace. The relationship between the two deteriorated as the commission evolved. Conflicts became common, probably because the culture of academia is quite different from that of bureaucracy.

The bureaucrats and the researchers were kept separate from each other, within 'two solitudes,' both physically and symbolically. Thus several participants commented on the deliberate decision to leave the 'suits and ties' to themselves on the twelveth floor, while the researchers in their more casual attire were sequestered in the 'country club' on the eleventh floor of the commission's Sparks Street offices.[93] The informality of this 'country club' atmosphere riled the bureaucrats, who were used to a more formal approach to conducting business. Cairns recalled:

I think we were on the 11th floor, most of our offices, and they were, well the commissioners, most of them weren't in town most of the time, but the sort of ongoing staff of the commission, the Nymarks and the Rochons and the David Abletts and others, and the sort of 12th floor staff, the real commission staff – I mean important people, I don't mean people who handle messages – they all came pretty well dressed. They were in business suits and ties, and the academics, many of them, came in shorts. It was very deliberate of them. I mean it was sending a message, you know, 'we're not you.' And so there was almost an exaggerated attempt to adopt a clothing style, which is quite easy for me to do – I have to ransack something to find a bloody tie – but it was a very different clothing style. Again, it was kind of an interesting, bureaucratic culture way of making a point. And we often talked about it. You know, they would kind of imply that coming down to the 11th floor they were coming down to a goddam country club or something. But it was very deliberate.[94]

Relations deteriorated so much at one point that Godsoe stopped talking to Cairns. 'I had just been very candidly saying certain things, not meaning to be offensive,' recalled Cairns. 'Whatever it was I said, he took really big offense to, and I remember him saying "I'm just never meeting with those Research Directors again."'[95] Seemingly minor disputes reflected more profound differences in the academic and bureaucratic cultures of the two groups. As a result of this poisoned atmosphere, a mediator had to be called in at one point to bring both sides back to the same table.[96]

Professional rivalries between the academics and those in charge of the public consultations also emerged. For instance, Rochon, who engineered the public consultation process, felt that this should be the most significant input into the commission's deliberations. The researchers, naturally, disagreed, and regarded their own work as more significant. The strains which emerged over this dispute resulted in some very difficult working relationships within the commission, and Macdonald was left with the impression that the directors were disdainful of the public consultation process. 'The research directors were very sceptical about whether this process would produce anything,' he recalled. 'They felt, if you are confident, and you have organized your discipline in your own mind, the notion that you would have to consult the public seems extraneous.'[97] In any event, the fact that the consultations had by and large wrapped up before the main body of research started to come in meant there was little opportunity to integrate the two, even if the main protagonists had desired it.

Original Research versus Received Knowledge

From the very start, the research directors decided that the studies commissioned would not be intended to produce new, original, or ground-breaking work, but rather summations of the state of the discipline in which scholars were writing. The goal was to collect all of the accumulated knowledge to date on particular and general subjects relevant to the commissioners' inquiries. The researchers were not to provide the commissioners with policy-relevant guidance through prescriptive recommendations linking the research directly to specific ends sought by the commissioners; they were to produce a body of research that could stand alone and apart from the final report of the commission and which would provide guidance to future generations of scholars. In comparing the Rowell-Sirois to the Macdonald Commission, Aucoin made the point that the latter 'had a large body of literature on which to draw, and that the primary thing which the Macdonald Commission had to do was to bring together the knowledge that had been developed essentially since the Rowell-Sirois Commission, and that, as a consequence, it wasn't necessary to commission a lot of original research, but rather to produce state-of-the-art reviews of what had been done.'[98] Cairns in particular argued very strongly that this was the only way that this work could be undertaken. He was especially concerned about the historical legacy of the research rather than its immediate utility to the commission.[99] Macdonald concurred with Directors over this issue: 'The two predecessors of the commission were the Gordon Commission and Rowell-Sirois. And the argument was put that there were a number of things that a commission is valuable for. Policy prescriptions are one thing, but that it is important from time to time to capture the current best thinking of the Canadian academic community on these kinds of questions. And this was an opportunity to do that. It seemed to me it was a legitimate thing, and judging by the comments I have had since then, I have been complimented for that choice.'[100]

Another motivation behind proceeding in this manner was simply that the commissioners did not know what direction they were headed in, according to Winham. 'I don't think the commissioners knew where they were going in terms of recommendations. And you have to know that in order to determine what you are going to be researching.'[101] In any event, the three-year lifespan of the commission, it was argued, mitigated against original research. Researcher Gerry Helleiner raised the issue of the time frame: 'Those who wrote papers typically wrote on things they were already engaged in anyway, that is what they were asked. There was really no fresh research commissioned as far as I know anywhere in the commission, there wasn't time for that. I can seem to recall our making that point, that you could not expect in the time frame they had that any serious fresh research could be undertaken.

The only way they could proceed was to build upon work that had already been done or was under way, and to piggy back on that. That was clear. So in a sense it was not research at all. It was an organizational effort to improve the utilization of what was available.'[102]

Practically speaking, the commission's approach resulted in two liabilities for the research program. It meant, first, that a fair amount of the research was largely irrelevant to the immediate needs of the commissioners. Not surprisingly, not everyone agreed with this plan. One coordinator, Gil Winham, said he argued long and hard with Cairns that the purpose of the research should be to produce original, policy-relevant prescriptions for the commission. While he lost that war, he managed to win a significant battle in that he was allowed to produce a special study related to sectoral free trade which was based on original research.[103]

Secondly, it meant that the commission had to scramble for research in areas which the commissioners focused on late in the process. Ironically, despite authorizing over one thousand studies, the commission found itself without research in some significant areas quite late in the process, and had to engage researchers to produce work on certain aspects of social policy, sectoral free trade, the North, international political economy, and other areas on very short notice.

The Progress Report

Many of the problems alluded to above were flagged in a so-called progress report on the research program published in 1984.[104] It complained about the difficulties associated with producing research on the basis of so broad a mandate. It also made ex post facto excuses for the interim report *Challenges and Choices*, commonly seen as disastrous,[105] while simultaneously distancing itself from that fiasco by suggesting that 'it is important to note that the studies being prepared in the Commission's research program have not been available to Commissioners during the preparation of their discussion document, *Challenges and Choices*.'[106] Although the progress report suggests that the research program was 'jointly worked out by the Commissioners and senior research staff,'[107] in fact, this is a generous description of the commissioners' role, which was reactive rather than proactive. Nonetheless, the progress report contended that the research studies were intended to do several things. First, they were expected to cast a look at the past to provide retrospective views of the economic, political, legal, institutional, and constitutional developments since the Second World War. This historical orientation was intended to 'help us understand the sources of our present discontents and to assess our future possibilities against our past performance.'[108] This perspective, it was expected, would enhance the quality of policy recommendations the commission would make. The research studies were also charged with a second task, interrelated with the first: that of 'identifying the factors that are likely to have a critical influence on developments over the next several decades.'[109]

The rationale for selecting researchers from only three disciplines was provided in this manner: 'The realities to which this Commission must respond are interdependent. Its mandate and the general theme of an adaptive political economy to which it leads give research priority to economic, political, legal and constitutional concerns. Accordingly, the researchers are primarily, but not exclusively, drawn from among those who specialize in the study of economics, political science, and law.'[110] But the directors revealed an acute sense of the difficulty of doing cross-disciplinary research given the rigid division of intellectual labour in the social sciences. They asserted that 'it is not as easy for researchers in the 1980s as it was for the scholarly generation of the 1930s, which produced the landmark Rowell-Sirois Report, to move comfortably back and forth across the boundaries of knowledge.'[111] They further recognized that 'the contemporary requirements for mastering a sub-field and for keeping up with burgeoning literature and abreast of new research tools do not, in the first instance, readily contribute to the broad overarching perspective appropriate to the sweeping mandate confronting this Commission.'[112] In other words, the research for this commission would have little policy relevance because the questions being asked were too many and too broad, and in any event, it would be impossible to integrate the work of the three disciplines.

The research plan involved trying to overcome these structural barriers – but only to an extent. The directors tried to rationalize their approach with some good old-fashioned academic doublespeak: 'the strategy for transforming increasingly specialized knowledge into an integrated analysis for the Commission is intended to maximize the unquestioned benefits from specialization and simultaneously to transcend specialization within and across disciplinary boundaries.'[113] The initial plan was to study issues individually. The research findings would then be brought together and integrated, 'drawing out of their connections across the range of interdependencies and linking them around the overriding themes emerging from the mandate.'[114] In hindsight, this was a wildly unrealistic goal.

The organization of the research into three streams was also justified as reflecting the institutional structuring of scholarship in the universities, from which most of the researchers were drawn. Within each of the three research areas, coordinators were responsible for organizing separate projects, and for drawing together the more specialized papers into an integrated overview paper, published along with the supporting studies. Subjects were assigned with the deliberate intent of creating some overlap on the issues and problems analysed. Furthermore, special arrangements were made to integrate the research on common problems under way in the three areas. For example, research on Canada's role in the international political economy was brought together in seminars and conferences in the summer of 1984. Different orientations to the state of the economic union in Canada, the development of the North, studies on federalism, work on industrial strategy and other areas were also so treated.

This was all to be followed by a process leading up to the final report which would ensure that 'the findings of the separate research projects dealing with various big issues and basic concerns that pervade the overall research effort will be brought to bear on the task of writing the final report.'[115] Perhaps over-optimistically, the progress report stated that: 'the simultaneous preparation and subsequent publication of so much analysis across such a broad range of subjects can scarcely avoid generating creative linkages between hitherto separately studied phenomena. Much integration and many leaps of understanding will develop from the unpredictable interactions between researchers and from the extensive exposure to unfamiliar disciplinary perspectives that will develop from our common intellectual task.'[116] In fact, what this exercise served to demonstrate was just how entrenched the separate disciplines are in their own intellectual worlds, with separate paradigms, methodologies, premises, goals, and so on.[117] Very little 'integration,' and fewer 'leaps of understanding' emerged. Instead, one major result was a lack of cross-disciplinarity. Another was a lack of relevance to what the commissioners were doing. Some research studies did not even appear until *after* release of the final report.[118]

Conclusion

The struggle to define and shape political discourse and the delineation of legitimate identities occurs in part through the research program of royal commissions. It is here that theoretical underpinnings are formed for the values, attitudes, and beliefs that constitute ideological world-views. A commission should provide for the establishment of a dominant academic discourse through the research program, as well as a contending or alternative discourse. The extent to which these develop is shaped in part by the organizational and structural imperatives imposed upon the commission.

As this chapter has revealed, *who* is picked to work on a commission, and *how* they are picked, have important implications for the outcome for the exercise. Two issues remain: first, how significant was the research in helping the commissioners make up their minds about what recommendations with which to proceed? And second, how did ideology impact upon the advice meted out through the research program?

As noted in chapter 1, the possibilities of modification of political discourse are not always equal. That discourse changes in response to social change, political action, and struggles by organizations and individuals seeking to modify restrictive boundaries of political imagination. To illuminate this point, the importance of the research in relation to the other parts of the commission must be established. As well, the weight of the various research streams relative to one another must be determined, and the impact of the research program on the drafting of the *Report* must be assessed. Finally, the role of ideology within the research program must be elucidated. These are the concerns of the next chapters.

CHAPTER 7

The Rout Is On:
The Influence of the Research Program

It is significant that much of the history of Canada could be interpreted through the work of commissions of inquiry.[1]

As the Macdonald Commission research studies began pouring in throughout 1984 and into 1985, the commissioners started to formulate their conclusions. Presented with conflicting and contradictory positions both within the research itself, and between the research and the public submissions, they had somehow to distil the data and arrive at a consensus position. Ultimately, this process involved rejecting some arguments and favouring others. The question arises: What research impressed and influenced the commissioners?

The manner in which the creative intellectual output of academic, research, and policy "experts" is acquired, assessed, and accepted (or rejected) is a key element of transformative change. This chapter establishes that the research as represented by the seventy-two volumes of studies commissioned by the inquiry had relatively little influence, except in one regard. Why was this so? A vast majority of participants within the commission played down the utility of the research program for the commissioners.[2] Four related themes emerged from interviews which explain the lack of utility of the research exercise. First, it suffered from poor organization, owing in part to the massive size of the undertaking. It was simply too large and too overwhelming to have the desired impact, and it lacked direction. Thus, while the research was relevant in a few select areas, it was largely irrelevant in many others. Second, there was resistance from certain anti-intellectual commissioners, who refused to pay it much heed. Some commissioners simply viewed the advice of the academics as the ranting of ivory-tower scribblers who had never had to meet a payroll. Third, there was a lack of integration between the research and the other parts of the commission, as well as between the three research streams. And fourth, the 'iron law of oligarchy' imposed itself on the process, as a small band of staff and researchers took control of the final stages of the commission. This process was fed by professional rivalry between the researchers and the bureaucrats, which resulted in the latter monopolizing the report-writing stages of the commission, inviting a small group of like-minded academics to assist them in this process and shutting out the rest. These first three explanations are considered in this chapter, while the fourth is examined in detail in chapter 9.

While the research had little direct influence on the commissioners, it did have *some* noteworthy influence in select areas. In particular, the economists impressed their views on the commission where free trade as an economic development strategy for Canada was concerned, couching their recommendations in the discourse of neoconservative continentalism. The economists were able to overcome the organizational deficiencies of the commission, and they impressed the commissioners as the only group that had concrete policy prescription at the ready.

Before turning to the influence of the economists, however, this chapter first establishes the influence of the research overall compared with the other sections of the commission by tabulating the number of footnote references to the research studies found in the final *Report*. It also canvasses the views of the commissioners and other key players for their assessment of the role and influence of the research program. Finally, it details the deficiencies of the research program. Overall, in assessing the influence of that program, it is safe to say (with apologies to Churchill) that never had so much been produced by so many for so little purpose.

References to the Research Studies

One crude comparative measure of the influence of various sources of information can be had by simply totalling the number of footnote references to them in the commission's *Report*. By counting the footnotes it may be possible to see which component of the commission exerted more influence than the others.[3] Table 7.1 categorizes the footnotes in the *Report* into four areas: references to testimony in the commission transcripts; references to the written briefs received by the commission; references to the research studies prepared for the commission; and references to a broad category referred to here as academic literature.

Table 7.1
Classification of all citations found in the Macdonald Commission *Report*

	References to transcripts	References to briefs	References to research studies	References to academic literature
Volume 1	8	24	37	141
Volume 2	45	69	84	387
Volume 3	7	12	52	148
Total	60	105	173	676

This last heading includes articles from learned journals, academic monographs, and various government publications (Canadian, foreign, and from the United Nations), almost all of which were prepared by professional academics. The results are interesting, though they must be interpreted cautiously. Since the commission studies were primarily summations of the received academic literature on various topics, the authors of the *Report* might well have been inclined to quote from original sources rather than the research studies. As well, not all of the research studies were read by either the commissioners or those charged with writing the *Report*. Indeed, as mentioned above several studies were not even finished by the time the *Report* was published. Nonetheless, a crude picture of the extent to which different components of the Commission process were used by the *Report's* authors can be established, (see Table 7.1).

The results are quite revealing. While it might be expected that the *Report* writers would rely primarily upon the commission research studies and the transcripts and briefs from the public consultations, in fact these three categories together contain fewer than the total number of references to academic literature. The *Report* refers to the research studies twice as many times as to the transcripts and briefs combined. But it refers to the academic literature twice as many times as the other three categories combined! If there is a correlation between citations and influence, then the transcripts were least influential, and the briefs were the next least influential. The research studies were twice as influential as the briefs and transcripts, but other academic literature proved most influential of all.

It is clear from these data that the authors of the *Report* relied most heavily on the existing academic literature to support their contentions, and relied least on the public consultation process for sources of information and guidance.[4] But what is surprising is that so little reliance was placed on what was, after all, the largest single research project in the

Table 7.2
Number of footnote references to research studies by type in Macdonald Commission *Report*.

	Economics	Politics and the Institutions of Government	Law and Constitutional Issues	Federalism and the Economic Union	The North
Volume 1	14	7	8	0	0
Volume 2	63	11	2	5	0
Volume 3	2	20	4	15	2
Total	79	38	14	20	2

history of Canada. Explanations for this finding need to be considered. But to the extent that the commission's own research was employed, there was a distinct bias towards the work of economists. This can be discerned by noting that the commission requisitioned twenty-seven volumes of studies on economics compared to only eighteen volumes of studies on politics and the institutions of government; twelve volumes of studies on law and constitutional issues; twelve volumes of studies on federalism and the economic union; and one volume of study on Canada's North.[5] It can also be seen by comparing the number of footnote references to each of the five different types of studies commissioned by this inquiry as cited in its *Report* (see table 7.2).

These data suggest that where the *Report* paid any attention to the commission's own research, it did so overwhelmingly to the economics research, whose citations outnumber the citations of the other four types combined by more than two-to-one.[6]

The View from Within

The observations and perceptions of commission participants must be considered in order to explain the relative lack of influence of the research program overall. The following factors will be considered below: the size of the research program; the anti-intellectualism of certain commissioners; and the lack of integration of the research.

The Size of the Research Program

Many commission researchers and staff suggested that the size of the research project militated against it being fully integrated into the

Report. There was just too much for the commissioners to read, and they were not all interested in the diverse topics canvassed. Academically inclined commissioners like Breton, Barber, Shoyama, and Macdonald enjoyed perusing the material, but others, like Seaman and Hamilton, found it tedious, boring, and irrelevant. Others still, like Wadds, drew more inspiration from the public hearings. But all were confronted with the feeling of being overwhelmed by paper. The photo accompanying a *Saturday Night* magazine article by Robert Fulford on the commission reflected this impression. It showed a bemused Macdonald with paper flying through the air around him. Fulford noted disdainfully: 'There was not one person there [on the commission] who read all of them [the research studies] nor will there ever likely be any single human who can claim to have read all the research. Certainly no Commissioner had the time to read all the papers; the Commissioners read summaries, as did most of the research staff. Yet all of the studies were designed not only for the university libraries of the future ... but to contribute to the final report itself.'[7] Nymark contended that the Fulford article was a little unfair, but it did make a valid point. For instance, the policy group gave the commissioners five complete drafts of the *Report*, totalling over 3,500 pages, on top of the research.[8]

Timing also played a role in determining the impact of the research. The commissioners were fatigued by the amount of reading, listening, and travelling they had done during the consultation process. And as Cairns noted, 'Some of them weren't young, Jean Wadds was not young, Tommy Shoyama had health problems, and Barber was retired, and Catherine Wallace. So there were some older people, and it was very fatiguing.'[9] By the time the research started to cross their desks, many barely had the energy to deal with it effectively. Draft after draft after draft, totalling thousands of pages, was at best cursorily examined, at worst ignored. Macdonald recalled, 'I guess I read all that stuff in drafts, and again, just because of sheer volume, not always meaningfully. I may have covered it, but I didn't necessarily get it all neatly stowed away.'[10] But even accomplishing this much was more than many of the commissioners were able to do. Barber recalled, 'Ideally, all commissioners would have read all research reports, attended all meetings of the research advisory groups and insisted on further research in areas where gaps were evident. But this was impossible. For commissioners who had heavy responsibilities in their regular jobs, even a careful reading of the successive drafts of the final *Report* was something of a burden.'[11]

Cairns viewed this problem as a result of the size of the mandate. It seemed to have no boundaries. 'There was this terrifying feeling that one had to try to tackle the whole bloody world,' Cairns recollected. 'And that was what was so, so disabling early on; finding what kind of focus we are going to get.'[12] The commissioners were little help in this regard, as they themselves did not know what could be safely excluded. Moreover, many were part-timers lacking professional disciplinary backgrounds. Towards the end they were receiving literally cartons of research. 'Thirty different pieces of research from three different disciplines, and some of them are the third version of a paper because they've been assessed and sent back,' Cairns recalled. 'And then in another week there would be another thirty pieces. Well, obviously, most of this wasn't read and it couldn't have been read. They would have had to say this is a full time job and they would have needed a young academic post-doc to get through it.'[13]

But Cairns also noted that it was important to keep the research flowing to the commissioners, even if dealing with it all was beyond their human capabilities. 'We were very adamant that all the research had to keep flowing to the Commissioners,' Cairns recalled. 'But in some ways, I think, this was ritual behaviour. It was to give them the feeling that they were being fully informed and to allow us to say "Look we sent drafts of some things to you."'[14]

One significant consequence of this was a state of siege mentality. The commissioners became desperate to find a peg on which they could hang their collective hats and say 'this is what this Commission stands for.' Free trade became the symbolic issue for the commission – one which it could use to justify the massive amounts of unheeded research safe in the knowledge that no one – apart from the odd, slightly demented graduate student writing a thesis – was going to look at all that research anyway.

The lack of direction offered by the commissioners to the research program alluded to in chapter 6 had real consequences for the program. It meant that practically any proposal could be accepted, whether it related to the commissioners' interests or not. As a result, for many commissioners, it was hard to see the relevance of much of the research. As well, since the original research strategy involved doing far more research than was necessary, given the broad mandate of the commission, it is not surprising that much material fell by the way-side. As Cairns recalled, 'The overall agenda was just staggering. So it was hard to know what was excluded and the Commissioners, themselves, it took them a long time to get a grip on the issues. And so one of the pressures that led to the research program being so big was the feeling that well, we didn't quite know where we were going to be asked to have appropriate analysis available and so we had to cover just a lot of territory, just as sort of a safety device.'[15] In effect, the directors decided to do 50 per cent more research than they had to, just to cover all the bases, since they were not getting any direction from the commissioners.

Anti-Intellectualism among Certain Commissioners

The commissioners were not initially very happy when they were informed of the research plans that had been drawn up by Godsoe and Macdonald in conjunction with Cairns, Smith, and Bernier. Those with academic backgrounds – Barber, Breton, Picard, Robert, Shoyama, and Wallace – were at ease with the proposed plan. But several were from outside the world of academe, and when they heard that the vast majority of the commission's research dollars would be spent in contract research with academics, that the program would be steered by people drawn from the universities, and that very little contract research would be done by outside think-tanks, research houses, or businesses, they were suspicious and dismayed. Assured that some research work would be done by organizations like the CMA and BCNI, several business-oriented commissioners nonetheless remained very anxious and opposed to the research program presented to them; they did not know these academics, and some regarded academics in general as 'fuzzy thinkers.' They did not share the values of the academics, nor perhaps understand the utility of careful analysis and research.[16] Thus, there was a real onus on Macdonald, Godsoe, and the research directors to prove that their approach could work.

Moreover, some commissioners felt the public consultations should carry more weight than the research. Wadds felt this way, for instance:

> I'm pretty sure that some of the commissioners who were very academic had such enormous respect for the books being pulled together in the research that they thought that that was god-given wisdom, whereas I and some of the others I know, we got to know one another pretty well, and so decided that we wanted to form our opinions directly from the public. I suppose partly liking politics and liking the job of being an MP I thought the whole work of politics was communication where people were involved, with the people of your riding. And maybe it's because I am not academic by nature, I don't know, I like books well enough, but I would never put an opinion I'd read in a book above what I was hearing on the street.[17]

There was a gap between the commissioners and the research early on, but it cut both ways and was difficult to overcome because the researchers, too, were a little stand-offish. Wadds recalled that 'there was a great deal of disdain amongst the researchers for some of the commissioners. I ran full tilt into that. Because people who think you haven't read a particular book think you're very stupid. There are lots of people like that.'[18] Moreover, many researchers felt that the commission was simply the last political gasp of the dying Trudeau administration, that it was a worthless smoke-and-mirrors exercise in obfuscation, that it would not go anywhere, and nobody would listen to it anyway. In other words, it suffered from the typical maladies of many royal commissions, and there was a lot of scepticism from both sides of the two solitudes. Recognizing that this might be a problem, Godsoe and Macdonald recruited directors of research who could give the research function sufficient credibility with the academic community, and held out the promise of publication, such that it did not really matter what the academics thought of the commissioners themselves. Complete academic freedom, granted after considerable debate, helped to assure that the academics would feel the exercise was a legitimate one. But the gap between researchers and certain commissioners was difficult to bridge in the first year.

To bring the two solitudes together, the researchers were required to put on symposia for the commissioners, where they would discuss drafts of their papers, talk about their research, and offer ideas, options, and analysis. The researchers initially resented this process intensely, since it was distracting and derailing. However, when they did it, they found it was a lot of fun because several of the commissioners could ask penetrating questions. They became excited about what was going on and the ideas that were coming forward. Thus, according to Godsoe, an intellectual bonding process gradually took hold through a process of dialogue and discussion.[19]

By the fall of 1984, the research had developed some credibility with the commissioners, and the researchers were less sceptical about the commission itself. But in the early days, the suspicion and scepticism were difficult to handle and the pressure and the stress were tremendous. Every member of Godsoe's senior staff resigned at least once due to stress. A very competitive air prevailed as researchers' ideas were held up to scrutiny and compared to alternatives, which put a lot of pressure on people who were not used to those kinds of conditions. Most academics were not used to having to fight for their status in the way bureaucrats routinely did, and that made them uneasy. They also, according to Godsoe, became a little paranoid when they found someone else would be doing a paper and they would say, 'Well, nobody told me about that. I was supposed to be "in charge."'[20] This competitive pressure cooker played itself out very clearly in the development of the free trade option, discussed in chapter 9.

Certain commissioners – mainly those whose background was in business – felt that the academics were largely out of touch with the real world. Hamilton, Seaman, and Peters in particular were representative of the anti-intellectualism which existed among the commissioners. Docquier, coming from the world of labour, was not as overtly suspicious of academe but had some reservations about the research nonetheless. Some fairly heated discussions among the commissioners as to the utility of the research took place on a number of occasions. Cairns recalled, 'I think most of the commissioners were really quite delighted with the research. But there were some meetings early on, extremely tense meetings, in which there was a conflict between the Bill Hamilton view, who had been Postmaster General of the Diefenbaker government, and I think at that time he was head of the Employer's Council of British Columbia. And he, of course, was kind of anti-intellectual, and some of the commissioners wanted what they would call more hands-on people who knew the real world of business. And we just argued back. But it was very tense.'[21] Cairns recalled that these debates and differences of opinion were especially prominent at the start of the commission, when the research staff was presenting its initial proposals to the commissioners. But they remained an undercurrent throughout the whole process, 'This was quite early when we would be presenting. See, we would have to present our big outlines of what we were doing with descriptive statements of the thrust of the research and its utility. Sometimes it would be a twenty-five- or thirty-page document. But we would go to weekend retreats and discuss this and sometimes there would be a lot of criticism from some commissioners that this is a lot of egghead stuff: "have you ever met a payroll" kind of thing.'[22] Cairns placed these considerations in the context of differing cultural outlooks, and emphasized the tensions which resulted. In particular, he recalled an incident in which Smith was badly criticized for the abstract research proposals that he suggested. Cairns responded to the criticisms by saying, 'Look, we've all got to realize that we've got very different worlds coming together here. You are of the world of business – there were academics on the commission, Barber, Breton and to a limited extent Shoyama – but you come from the world of business, the world of politics, you're in the world of organizations, and we come from the world of universities and the world of ideas.' This meant that each sees the world through different lenses. 'And you think there is a way of understanding the world that is just not the same as how we think the world should be interpreted,' he concluded.[23]

There were other, related difficulties and tensions that had to be articulated and overcome, according to Cairns. In particular, he felt it was vital that everyone be clear on the chain of command within the commission, but at the same time also realize that the research was an autonomous project. Most of the commissioners were used to ordering people around and telling them what to do. But, Cairns maintained, academics are not, and cannot be treated in that manner. He pleaded with the commissioners to understand that academics are autonomous and make up their own minds. While he acknowledged that the commissioners would be dictating the subjects, and enjoyed the power of veto, they still had to be made to understand the academic way of doing things. In meetings with the research directors, the commissioners, and some senior staff, Cairns tried to explain, 'we researchers have to understand that in the last analysis, it's your commission. This is going to be known by your names. And everything we do has to serve ultimately your purposes. That includes a big separate research output. But you have got to understand, although we serve your purposes, we're not servants, we're not civil servants. And so you can't treat us that way. It simply will not work.' He recalled these meetings getting quite animated. 'I didn't sleep the whole night before because I knew I was going to make this speech the next morning. Who the hell knew what was going to happen? But, anyway, these were just necessary meeting points of separate worlds and ultimately, you know, I think we did come to that kind of rapprochement. So it was all sort of very interesting intellectual developments as the researchers and the commissioners developed a working relationship.'[24]

A certain air of anti-intellectualism persisted nonetheless, and informed the commissioners' deliberations. But ultimately they were convinced of the desirability of protecting the autonomy of the research in the interest of its longer term utility. To illustrate this point the researchers talked of great commissions of the past, such as Rowell-Sirois and Tremblay, as evidence that such inquiries can become intellectually significant in the subsequent understanding of the country. And they indicated that the separately published research was often very important to that task.[25]

But Cairns was walking a fine line here, for attaining intellectual freedom might make the research irrelevant to the 'real-world' concerns of the non-academic commissioners. That the research should have some concrete utility for these people smacked of common sense. To the business-oriented commissioners, Cairns seemed like someone arguing for the freedom to be irrelevant.

Smith also sensed a decided reluctance on the part of certain commissioners to give much credence to the research project. He recalled, 'I think the commissioners initially were a little surprised by the approach we proposed in that they had not seen as substantial a research program, perhaps, at least some of them, and more advising on particular issues that came up in the commissioners' minds so that I did have the impression when we first presented it that they thought it was rather broader and more ambitious than they had in mind.'[26] As the researchers explained their suggestions, most commissioners gradually came around: 'But as we talked it out, the recognition that here was a contribution that the commission could make as a drawing together of the state of knowledge in these areas, and that would be very important, in that it was not always entirely clear where the hearings would take the commission, and so one did need to have people drawn together who represented expertise in the state of knowledge in quite a wide variety of areas. And they did seem to become very positive about it then.'[27] Since the commissioners were a rather diverse group, however, the impact of the research was watered down considerably by those who refused or neglected to take it very seriously.

Just what were the research directors' suggestions? A synopsis was published in early 1984 for three main reasons. One was the prosaic need to demonstrate that the research effort was coordinated, functioning, and running smoothly. Second, there was the need to distance the research from the disastrous *Challenges and Choices* episode.[28] And third, there were internal political reasons. It became important for the research to justify itself and to show that it had gone at least part-way down the road demanded by the anti-intellectual commissioners. It had to be able to demonstrate some practical value while still maintaining the integrity of the 'freedom to be irrelevant' desired by Cairns. Some of the observations in the booklet must be read as admissions of culpability, coming some sixteen months after the commission had started. They represent a bit of back-peddling on the part of the research directors who had been burned by the cool reception initially given to their ideas by many of the commissioners. Thus the booklet must be read for the political document it is as much as for the outline of research it purports to be.

The booklet, entitled *Research for the Commission on Canada's Future*, indicated an ambitious, wide-ranging attempt was under way to bridge traditional disciplines and to avoid duplication of work already done by the academic community and former commissions.[29] Out of a thorough examination of the political and economic research extant in the land, coupled with the widest examination ever undertaken by the Canadian legal community, the expectation was for 'creative linkages' and 'new insights' to arise out of the collective enterprise.

The booklet argued that the royal commission was an important exercise because government was so caught up in the daily pressures of governing it found it hard to take a longer view. Moreover, the shifting world had thrown into question policies designed for yesterday's problems and past understanding, and knowledge was no longer relevant for generating new policies. It also acknowledged the challenges of the unwieldy mandate with which the commission was saddled, and the implications of this mandate for the research. It meant that the commissioners and senior research staff had to wrestle (or 'jointly work out,' in the booklet's more gentle phrasing) a research program that could somehow capture the mandate in a manageable form.

The studies undertaken, it was determined, were meant to fulfil several requirements in the terms of reference. They were meant to look at the past for retrospective views on economic, political, legal, institutional, and constitutional developments in Canada since the Second World War. A historical orientation would foster an understanding of the sources of present discontents (even though the commission had earlier decided on eschewing a history component in the research) and assess the future against the past. Moreover, it would provide a frame of reference in which the interplay of social forces and institutional arrangements could be fulfilled over time.[30]

In addition, the booklet claimed that the studies undertaken were intended to identify factors likely to have a critical influence on developments over the coming decades. The research sought to examine possible institutional changes and policy options that offered prospects of improved economic performance, of a more sensitive and responsive political system, and of a more legitimate constitutional order.[31]

According to the booklet, the public hearings had revealed that Canadians were concerned about their social contract with each other and with their governments. The fear had developed that without improving the social contract Canadians would occupy the same space, but would lack the widespread acceptance of a common citizenship that is essential to respond to interrelated economic, political, and constitutional problems. In looking at the domestic context, the research was influenced by a pervasive sense of malaise about the functioning of the economy and about the political, legal and constitutional systems, and relations between them. The booklet argued that anxiety, concern, and worry were pervasive due to the recession, high unemployment, slow productivity growth, high inflation, weakening industrial structure, labour-management relations, and the uneven distribution of wealth.[32] The research was to provide perspectives on these pessimistic assessments by examining the evidence of and explanations for previous longer term successes in the capacity of the economy to adapt, to foster high employment and low inflation, and to generate economic growth.[33]

In addition, the booklet noted that the political system had become increasingly conflict-riven and displayed a diminished capacity for effective policy making on economic issues. The political system was viewed by Canadians as less stable and less secure than in the earlier post-war years. Indications of this malaise included the ongoing debate about Quebec in Confederation; western alienation; the decline of the party system as an instrument of national integration; the coexistence of competing and contradictory definitions of Canada; aggressive and hostile rhetoric in intergovernmental relations; and the recent constitutional struggle.[34]

The legal system, according to the booklet, was not immune to criticism. It had become overregulated, expensive, and closed to minorities, the disadvantaged, and the unorganized. It had become overly complex and tended to foster conflict and rivalry rather than collaboration and compromise. 'Extensive government regulation in particular,' claimed the booklet, 'with the attendant high costs of compliance, is said to impede businesses' ability to respond quickly to changing market conditions.'[35] Noting that problems are numerous, the booklet offered that 'as in the past, Canadians undoubtedly will respond to the demands for adaptability posed by future conditions not by repudiating our past but by working within our economic, political, and constitutional heritage.'[36]

The booklet also looked at the global and comparative context. Inflation, unemployment, low growth rates, the technological revolution, international competition, the burgeoning world population, regional assertiveness and ethnic and nationalist challenges to authority, the women's movement, Aboriginal concerns, and environmental movements all reflected fundamental changes in the consciousness, identity, and values that transcended national boundaries. Moreover, the contemporary democratic state had become subject to these same economic trends and social forces. The internationalization of economic activity through multinational corporations, the movement of capital, and the new international division of labour and global economic interdependence as well as international institutions such as GATT and the IMF illustrated the increasingly international dimension to which economic managers in modern states must respond. The booklet suggested the commission must recognize both the uniquely Canadian and universal characteristics that shape and constrain opportunities.

It went on to detail the goal of an adaptive political economy. At its most general level, the focus of the research was to examine how the Canadian political economy could better adapt to change. This meant that the research must search for flexibility in political and economic institutions so that Canada is not left with institutional arrangements and policies designed for yesterday. The expectation was that the theme of an adaptive political economy would necessarily lead to interdisciplinary research. For instance, the theme linked the pursuit of a more representative political system with the search for more effective economic policy-making structures. It was also linked to the need for more relevant international economic policies and the pursuit of more harmonious federal-provincial relations in economic matters.[37]

Ironically, the booklet argued that the goal of a more adaptive political economy does not presuppose a clean slate. It preferred to move in directions that were consistent with those of the past, rather than advocating a 'convulsive transformation' employing a completely new set of economic and political arrangements, which it argued was both undesirable and unattainable. In effect, the document was foreclosing any radical alternatives. The irony lies in the fact that free trade was a radical alteration of the Canadian political economy.

Lack of Integration

Godsoe characterized as perhaps his biggest disappointment the relative failure of the disciplines to collaborate. He attributed that failure in part to the failure to find a modern-day Innis, although he conceded that such a person does not exist. He regretted this, believing that a political economist who understood both economics and politics could understand what a market economy in an institutional setting requires. But it was not to be. Instead, what Godsoe got was turf wars between academics, some of which he had to resolve personally, as the disciplinary walls proved difficult to breach.[38] Projects were established to break them down, such as having co-authors from different disciplines producing or editing studies, and writing and research responsibilities with linkages between politics and economics or law and politics or economics and law were created. On the free trade issue, Stairs and Winham debated with the economists and presented papers at seminars along with papers presented by economists. The debate was thus joined in a small way, but overall, the attempt at instituting interdisciplinary research was a failure.[39]

Virtually the only people who did not believe that the research was not well integrated were the director of the economics research program, David Smith, and the policy group member responsible for the free trade argument in the *Report*, Michael Hart. Smith recalled being pleased with the level of integration across the research streams. He started with the assumption that integration was extremely difficult to achieve, especially where one is bringing people from across Canada for particular meetings rather than having a small group working together side by side in offices. The problem of drawing together people with geographically dispersed bases of operation, as well as quite different disciplinary bases, he thought would be very difficult. 'But I was really very impressed with the way in which people did interact. And I thought that, for some of us in economics and politics, we had not had as much interaction with people from law schools often. And that was a very positive dividend to have some very active law profs involved.'[40] But Smith left the commission after only about a year, and his impressions are thus based on a limited time frame.

Hart argued that, where the free trade question was concerned, there was extensive integration:

> The section [of the *Report*] dealing with the international dimension, particularly the trade question, Whalley was the senior researcher from the economics perspective, and he had a group of people working for him: Gil [Winham] and Denis [Stairs] were the principal ones from the political science group, and they had some people working with them; and Ivan Bernier and Jack Quinn and so on from the legal side; and on a number of occasions we sat down and discussed these things together. I talked to all three of them. And Alan Nymark's role was to ensure that there was this kind of coordination. And so to say that there was not coordination on what I think was the most important recommendation made by the commission is just not true.[41]

But what Hart was actually witnessing were one-way interactions, not integration. The economists may have talked to Hart; and the political scientists may have talked to Hart; and the lawyers may have talked to Hart, but the three groups of academics did not talk to each other. Thus, Hart's view of widespread integration simply was not shared by others. Indeed, the weight of evidence very clearly suggests that it did not occur.

The lack of integration problem cut across the commission in two ways. First, the research was not well integrated with the public consultations and the information received therein. Indeed, the directors were sceptical of the utility of the public consultation process. Although they had all of the information generated from that process at their fingertips through the elaborate computer content analysis constructed by Rochon and his staff, the researchers seldom made use of it. They only rarely went to the consultations, preferring to oversee the research program from Ottawa. In any event, Smith noted that such attendance was difficult because of the time constraints and the wide ranging nature of the public hearings: 'But we used to, on the research side, try to get to the hearings. Now, that was not always possible if we were to get some of our own work done. But we would get immediately a record of the hearings. And we would meet and pore over what was being said, and to what extent did our research program correctly anticipate, or to what extent should it be modified to take into account some of the concerns that were coming up in the hearings. So the hearings, we listened to the discussion there and tried to take them into account in the research project.'[42] Again, though, Smith's sanguine view is out of step with the observations of most others on the commission.

Second, the research was not well integrated across the three research streams, with a couple of exceptions. One political science coordinator recalled meeting with his counterparts from economics and law only once or twice, and then only in social settings rather than structured, formal meetings designed to thrash out common areas of academic and scholarly interest.[43] Another political science coordinator recalled: 'There was relatively little interaction between us and the economists and the lawyers. More so with the economists, I think, and relatively less with the lawyers ... There were a few meetings, but what we would tend to do was present what we were doing, and there was some discussion back and forth. But it was more a show and tell session rather than a fundamental give and take, or lengthy discussion of what the subject was, of what the principles were, what the conclusions were or analysis about the veracity of the conclusions or whatever.'[44] Indeed, many commission researchers, from the directors on down, expressed their disappointment that greater integration did not occur. But, given the intellectual histories of the disciplines involved, this should not be too surprising. The tradition in the social sciences of discrete disciplinary walls proved impossible to breach.

A third reason for the lack of integration is simply the size and bureaucratic complexity of the exercise. Winham accepted that the lack of integration was a problem. 'But I think it was the bureaucratics of it as much as anything,' he argued. 'It's just a lot of people to get together. I mean scheduling meetings was tough, you know, everybody has their own schedule. So there is a limited number of opportunities you have to bring people together.'[45] When asked how the commission was able to integrate the work coming out of the research with the commission's developing ideas, Macdonald replied that an effort was made to systematically review and integrate the material. But this proved impossible:

> We thought that, initially in the hearing process, we would hear people, say, from 9 to 4 in the afternoon, and then for the last hour we would say, okay, what did we learn today, and how do we fit this in? Well, the volume was so enormous, that eventually everybody was just bushed, and they could not do anything. You would be well prepared, if you were going for a four day stint, from the previous weekend for perhaps the first day, or day and a half. But, you could be looking at more than 1,000 pages of reading, and eventually you reach days where you might not have anything unless you burn the midnight oil. So fatigue just tired people out. So in answer to that part of the question, it wasn't as though we systematically put things into place and said 'now we've decided this.'[46]

Nymark concurred. He saw the research department as an attempt to be multidisciplinary, but this only worked in part. The ability to integrate the legal, political science, institutional, and economic streams was circumscribed by the lack of any tradition of working together, he thought, and he concluded that some areas worked better than other areas.[47]

Notwithstanding the failure to integrate across the three research streams, there was a certain noteworthy congruity of outlooks between the economists and lawyers. The legal research was the least significant of the three streams. It had the smallest budget, and its research director referred to the other two directors as the 'big guys.'[48] But while the legal research played a rather inconspicuous role overall, it was important in one particular regard where the free trade recommendation was concerned. According to Stairs, the economics position was strengthened by the nature of the legal discipline as much as by its substantive positions regarding the free trade issue:

> It was, I think, buttressed – and this is a complicated phenomenon – but I think it was buttressed by the lawyers. Not because the lawyers were thinking

necessarily in economics terms, but because the lawyers, like the economists
– now there are all kinds of problems with what I am about to say, I understand that – but they were in a way epistemological rationalists. So the lawyers were tending to argue in favour of institutionalization of the Canada-
U.S. relationship. And that fit in quite well with what the economists were
concerned about, which was to remove the free operation of the continental
economy from the vagaries of Congressional politics for example. So therefore, the rational thing to do was to let continental economic forces operate
in a free environment in which protectionist influences, which always represent narrow vested interests as opposed to the economic aggregate and so
on, get these under control. And that required a certain kind of regime,
which was ultimately what the FTA was about. Well that fit in well with the
lawyers' view of how you deal with politics, which is essentially to make it subject to legal norms abjudicated by institutionalized processes.[49]

Stairs saw a natural meeting of premises there. He observed, at the risk
of oversimplifying, 'I never sensed any incompatibility, for example,
with what the lawyers were saying and what the economists were saying.
There was a mating there.'[50] Although the lawyers overall played a less
significant role than the other two sides of the research, to the extent
that their work was important, the nature of their research tended to
reinforce the economists' position. Stairs further explained: 'I would
argue that it did [reinforce the economists' position] in a sense that the
absence of discourse can be as significant as an alliance of argument, if
you see what I mean. In other words, the lawyers had the disposition to
think about politics as a problem to be gotten rid of and controlled and
so on, which one did by institutionalizing processes and norms, and,
well, that put them in the same tent in their conception of politics as the
economists were. Whereas with the political scientists, there is the possibility that politics is a perpetual inevitability, and it raises other issues
that are outside both the legal and economic paradigm.'[51] Epistemolog-
ically and methodologically, the lawyers and economists were allies.

This did not mean that all the legal researchers were free traders. It
simply meant that the lawyers' preference for rationalistic and legalistic
solutions meshed with the empiricism and methodological rigour of the
economists, and gave the free trade option a boost.[52] It should be noted,
however, that some researchers, like Jack Quinn, the ardent free trade
proponent from the legal side of the research, recognized the narrow-
ness of the economists' position. Achieving free trade, then, according to
Quinn:

wasn't just this magic thing that went 'poof,' like the mathematical economists were saying. But what it really meant was that it mattered very much
how the trade treaty operated to legally remove these barriers. And what we
see, in my view, is a system where most of the barriers that were of concern
to the U.S. were taken down, but most of the barriers that were of principal
concern to guys like me who were looking at this from a Canadian perspective have been left up. So that, in most ways, the mathematical economists
can say 'now well, in our frictionless, perfect model of the political process
and legal system, we just assumed that all these things would vanish over-
night, and we would get this big increase in income.' We [the lawyers] said,
'well why the hell did you assume that? Didn't you read our part of the
research program? Didn't you read the part about free trade that said if
you don't get rid of the anti-dumping, countervail, if you don't get legally
binding ways to limit the Americans administrative discretion that it is not
going to be meaningful free trade?' And they would say 'well, no we really
don't read law, we read economics.'[53]

Quinn argued that a legal regime needed to be negotiated in which
American countervail and anti-dumping could be avoided, but that the
economists overlooked this point: 'If your industries become heavily
dependent upon U.S. sales, and they become vulnerable to anti-dumping suits in the U.S., people will not want to invest here, they will invest in
the U.S. So the U.S. will use all these policies to get all the good investment to go South. So what we have to do is have an arrangement that
would avoid this. I was one of the authors of those kind of dynamic arguments. Donald Macdonald, I think, as a lawyer who is interested in con-
stitutions and institutions and, you know, big ideas about how we should
organize inter-government relations, was more of a proponent of that
view.'[54] Thus the economists, in Quinn's view, lacked the breadth of
vision to appreciate the legal and political barriers to free trade.

Conclusion

The evidence presented in this chapter shows that the research as represented by the seventy-two volumes of studies commissioned by the
inquiry had little influence on the commission's ultimate recommendations. Participants within the commission differed in their assessments
of the utility of the research program to the commissioners, but the vast
majority cited organizational deficiencies as major impediments to the
impact the research might have been expected to have on their deliber-

ations. In the result, only the economists managed to impress their views on the commission where economic development strategies for Canada were concerned.

In explaining the way in which the free trade recommendation emerged, one more piece of the puzzle needs to be elucidated: the role that ideology played, that is, the successful imposition of an economic and political discourse by certain social agents from both the academic and bureaucratic realms. Given the prominent position historically enjoyed by economists in royal commissions in Canada, it should not be too surprising that they were able to prevail. Perhaps more surprising was the lack of effective opposition to their views about economic development strategies for Canada.

CHAPTER 8

Ideological Homogeneity in the Research Program

In this day and age, espousal of economic nationalism fares in the same category as membership in the Flat Earth Society.[1]

Both the division of labour within the social sciences and the creation and reinforcement of particular political discourses by social scientists had an impact on the Macdonald Commission. The lack of cross-fertilization between the three research streams, coupled with institutionalized claims to discrete forms of knowledge, afforded the economists an influential position within the commission research program, and were important factors shaping the output of this process. The economists enjoyed a near monopoly on economic policy prescriptions. The empiricism of the discipline, based on methods of so-called scientific inquiry, left it in an influential position. The ideological homogeneity of the mainstream of the discipline reinforced its claims to expertise and exclusive knowledge, thereby conferring the economic viability necessary for acceptance and the resultant transformative change. Of the three research streams, the economics research was most readily accepted and adopted by the commissioners. This was generally true in regard to strategies for economic development and particularly true with respect to the free trade recommendation.[2]

Ideological Homogeneity and the Dominance of the Neoconservative Continentalist View

The history of the social sciences reveals an increasing concern with establishing the scientific rigour, credibility, and legitimacy of its disciplines.

Historically, the social scientists most successful in establishing these criteria: 'were those who managed to establish some paradigmatic consensus over the fundamental objects of their study and the methods to be used to study them. Economics and sociology were perhaps the most successful disciplines in establishing their claim to scientific legitimacy both internally and in the eyes of the outside world. Armed with agreement over fundamentals, they could turn more easily to applied problems of policy and persuade prospective consumers of social research of their expertise in the field.'[3] In addition, discrete disciplines added to their claims to paradigmatic exclusivity by developing a scientific language, technical concepts, and research techniques not easily understood by those outside that particular scientific community.[4] As Gagnon suggests, this further buttressed claims to professionalism. Thus, 'the hegemony of a particular paradigm within the discipline, and the successfully enforced claim that only those trained in it by the profession should be accounted "experts," were important components in the differential influence of the various social scientific disciplines.'[5]

The perceived legitimacy of the economics profession in Canada had serious repercussions in terms of the influence of the economists on the commission. It was largely taken as a given that the economists were best able to supply advice about the economy.[6] Hence, the work of political scientists which explored economic questions, for instance André Blais's work on industrial policy and public aid to industry, was largely marginalized or ignored.[7] Macdonald found the economics research produced by the commission useful in clarifying and supporting his convictions regarding free trade. And he credited Smith and his team of economists: 'David Smith had to leave us early in the game, happily because he became the principal of Queen's, but he did, I thought, a particularly good job in getting good economic advice for us on the research side. John Whalley in particular, but also the Wonnacott brothers and others were included in that regard. And when one began to spend some time with them, one eventually began to find their arguments, particularly in light of what we heard, irreversible, that we really had to seek a broader vocation for Canada.'[8] This reflects the view that the economists are the recognized disciplinary 'experts.' Furthermore, the hegemony of classical liberalism within the economics profession meant that the economists assumed that markets must prevail and that politics has no place in the consideration of economic analyses. For instance, according to Cairns, 'David Smith thought that, first of all, the mandate was going to focus on matters where market analysis was most signifi-

cant, and I guess he just thought that is where the heart of the economics discipline was. So he put his team together. My assumption would be
that he put it together with much less concern for what might be the
diversity within the discipline than was true in political science and
law.'[9] The recruitment of economists thus reinforced ideological homogeneity. Barber felt that Smith was firmly rooted within the dominant
neoconservative paradigm of the economics profession, and furthermore 'it was common knowledge around the commission that economists held more conservative, that is, more market-oriented views than
the lawyers and political scientists, and these economists were distinctly
to the right of the dominant view among the commissioners.' As evidence of this assertion, he offered that 'by way of example, in one draft
[of the *Report*] commissioners were asked to recommend elimination of
minimum wage laws. There was little enthusiasm for this recommendation and it was deleted, although parts of the report still carry overtones
of the original recommendation.'[10]

But Smith argued that ideological homogeneity was avoided through
the recruitment process, which simply sought out the 'best minds' in the
discipline, rather than trying to find representatives of the whole ideological spectrum. He explained: 'I guess the general approach we took
was that if you asked who might be the leading thinkers in say an area
like industrial organization or international trade, it is not long before
you would get quite a consensus on who would be the top ten or twelve
people in Canada. And you wanted to have that quite openly determined, not only in the sense of only asking a small group to identify that
set, but to genuinely try and get the names of those who are regarded as
being thinkers in that area. And given that, then from there to try to get
the people who would do various parts of that area.'[11] Furthermore,
Smith felt that it was not preferable to approach the selection of academics from the point of view of covering the ideological spectrum. He
claimed to be trying to secure scholars who, through general peer evaluation, were regarded as the leading thinkers in the area. 'So yes, there
would be some areas of the spectrum some people would say were not
well covered.'[12] The point was not necessarily to recruit researchers
from both mainstream and alternative perspectives, according to Smith.
'We did not want homogeneity. We wanted people who would have different ideas,' he recalled. 'But we wanted first-rate people. First-rate not
simply because they had an unusual position on a spectrum, but first-
rate no matter where they are on the spectrum.'[13] Of course, the claim
that 'the best and the brightest' were sought out is a convenient means

of diverting attention from the fact the process of peer review tends to promote those with ideologically convergent views. For instance, peer review involves the selection of academics who publish in the same journals, a process which subtly reinforces dominant ideas as aspiring academics (particularly younger ones seeking career advancement) try to conform to mainstream expectations.

As suggested in chapter 6, the left-nationalist view was raised before the commission at the Hart House meeting in February 1983, but rebuffed. While a handful of commission papers and seminars included representatives of this perspective, they were massively outnumbered by the holders of contrary views. Winham argued that 'if you were to try to take just academics, and represent academics fairly, in terms of a left-right continuum, you probably could argue that the left was not adequately represented given their strength in the academy across the country. And that would probably be the case, especially in political science.'[14]

Nonetheless, several commissioners were very sympathetic towards the left-nationalist message, and a good deal of scepticism was expressed within the commission about the discipline of economics. There were two major sources of suspicion about the academic work. Some commissioners asked, 'why do all of the economists agree and what if they are all wrong?' The second was rooted in methodological scepticism. Mainstream economics had, by the 1980s, become so obsessed with mathematical modelling that it had become a dominant value within the profession.[15] Economics had largely ceased to debate its assumptions with anything near as much attention as it did forty years earlier.[16] Moreover, the assumptions of the discipline exhibit an avowed faith in methodological infallibility. This view is reflected in the aphorism that an economist is someone who crosses a deep ravine by assuming a bridge.[17] But given the dominance of the Chicago school in the early 1980s, it was very difficult for dissenters to inject objections into economic debate. To the extent that first principles and assumptions were subject to questioning, according to Godsoe, the fight was virtually fixed. 'The economists said, "Oh, you want a debate, okay, we'll get so and so. He's pretty radical." And so-and-so was coming in and these guys sliced poor old so-and-so up and sent him back to the showers. And you say, "Hmm, we're not too sure about this." But that was a major debate.'[18] Godsoe also concurred that the commission was plagued with the problem of ideological homogeneity among the researchers. He claimed the commission was able to offset it somewhat with a variety of techniques and methods, but conceded that it was not an unfair criticism to say it was a concern both throughout the commission, and for himself personally.[19]

In considering the extent to which there was a debate within the economics profession as to appropriate trade strategies for Canada, or whether there was a fairly homogeneous view about what was appropriate for Canada within the economics profession, Smith claimed:

> You always get differences among economists. There wasn't any fixed unanimous view. I think that some of the more interesting discussions took place among the researchers as we would get together and talk. Some of the more interesting discussions took place with respect to the political scientists and the economists. On balance I would say there were more economists in favour of a free trade approach than political scientists. That was by no means universally true. But that led to some very interesting discussions as to why that should be so, and were there fears about political independence that could be better handled through certain types of economic arrangements. Those were some of the more interesting discussions that I was in. I thought they were excellent. And of course the lawyers got in on it on the question of whether there were certain kinds of legal arrangements under freer trade that would reduce the worries that some political scientists had about loss of sovereignty.[20]

But, again, Smith's view constituted a minority position among the commission participants.

Hart, the other dissenter from the majority view, also rejected the notion that the economics section managed to impose its own homogeneous ideological view on the commission.[21] But perhaps most significantly, Macdonald came to believe that the economics research team was widely representative of the spectrum of ideological views. He had some observations on the infighting within the economics profession, while citing particular economists such as Whalley and Smith as being particularly helpful:

> David Smith put together a hell of a good team, though he of course could not continue. But he put together as good a representative group of Canadian economists as you could get. Orange and Green in Ireland are no fiercer in their antagonisms than different schools of economists. Albert Breton used to say to me, you know, tenure in universities was put in really to protect university professors from the outside community. The way it works now is to protect some members of the economics faculty from other members ... And he said you know it's an interesting reflection on the university as a free place of ideas that there was a kind of intellectual totalitarianism. And so in a sense that David – you know Khrushchev said there are

neutral governments but no neutral men, none of us is neutral on these questions – but I thought he did a remarkably good job, in terms of trying to get a balanced representation of economists.[22]

But in fact, the ideological homogeneity of the economist researchers was one of the most striking features of the team, according to the vast majority of commission participants, as well as outside observers.[23] The range of ideological thought of mainstream economics is reminiscent of Dorothy Parker's description of Katharine Hepburn's acting in a play she reviewed as having run 'the whole gamut of human emotions from A to B.' While the economists themselves may have felt the issues were fully debated, to dissentient economists or other social scientists, the striking feature of the debate is the congruity of ideological premises and approaches of the economics research.

Apart from a few 'token' left-wing academics, most of the economists came from the mainstream of their professions,[24] and when 'established' economists departed in the least from orthodoxy, as was the case with Richard Harris's views on the relationship between industrial policy and trade,[25] they were greeted with a chilling dismissiveness. While cautious about labelling academics from other disciplines, Stairs felt that all of the economists he had anything to do with were pro–free traders 'for the usual liberal economics reasons. That was a very powerful influence on the research operation generally, but also to some extent on the commissioners because it coincided with what they were hearing from the business community people and so on.'[26]

Gerry Helleiner, a member of the Research Advisory Group on International Trade, recalled that the economists in his group 'had made up their mind before they started, and nothing was going to change their minds.' They were, in his view, adherents of the mainstream liberal economic school, and trapped inside that paradigm. Moreover, they occupied important positions within the hierarchy of the commission:

We did have some public debate between Mel Watkins and the orthodox types [of economists], and a couple of other people from the labour movement and so on did appear at public meetings, and they wrote papers for it, but they were not part of the organizing group. The organizing group was overwhelmingly mainstream ... I thought that the organizers, John Whalley in particular, and certainly Rick Harris, had their minds pretty firmly set on what they thought of the principal issues. John had already in the very first meeting expressed the view, and I think it was in writing in the background paper, that you could not expect too much from the GATT, and that there were major risks in U.S. protectionist policy, and that a major option was going for free trade with the U.S. Ron Wonnacott was a member of the group, and he has been advocating this for thirty or forty years ... So I had the feeling that our group was somewhat stacked.[27]

This does not imply that there were no disagreements among the researchers on various issues. It does suggest, however, that the realm of inquiry and prescriptive policy suggestions were severely circumscribed. Another coordinator put it this way: 'I did have the sense that on the economic side, that the economic nationalist advocates, if you like, sort of fell away. There were one or two of them. I don't know if Abe [Rotstein] was one of them, and Mel Watkins. But they kind of dropped away because they felt it was an exercise from their point of view in futility and that they weren't being taken seriously by the mainstream economics crowd. But in general, economists who had doubts about the free trade option found that it was an environment that was not very congenial.'[28] But Winham argued that the left in Canadian political science 'is way out from the public view in Canada. And I think therefore to have chosen a group of academics of the sort that Duncan Cameron's views represent would have been a great mistake for a commission that was intended to serve a public function as opposed to an academic function. Sorry, I just think the middle is a reality and that Duncan Cameron is not here.'[29]

The notion that the distinct disciplines within the social sciences enjoy monopolies on certain types of knowledge was another factor at work within the Macdonald Commission. When questioned on the influence of the economists within the commission compared to that of the other researchers, many participants felt that the economists were most able to produce policy-relevant prescriptions due to the nature of their discipline. They were the 'experts' where economic development strategies for Canada were concerned. Cairns felt that: 'It was partly that economists – maybe misguidedly – had a much more confident sense of their disciplinary selves. They seem to have a discipline which actually provided answers. I mean, we assume we have a discipline which could provide some helpful answers and the plausible scenarios that might follow, but we couldn't talk of 4 per cent increases in something that we were responsible for the way they could talk about the allegedly big increases in GNP.'[30] Shoyama recalled that in his experience as a senior mandarin in the Finance Department, 'the economic analysis was always straightforward and came to a conclusion. There was always theory that lent itself to quantitative measurement. This is not true in the case of political science where you are dealing with intangibles, or law where you are dealing with interpretation.'[31]

In modern academic life social scientists have been successful in establishing themselves and creating a use for their work.[32] However, their success "relied on more than the internal development and refinement of their disciplines and their academic institutionalization,' according to Brooks and Gagnon. 'Their ability to align themselves with and speak for political forces and movements pressing for societal reform was also of key importance ...'[33] Notwithstanding the fact that academics are traditionally thought of as independent of class interests and somehow above the hurly-burly of political life, social scientists' work is rooted in their role as social agents within society. But they offer their knowledge on a neutral basis as 'experts.' The positivist view of social science suggests that academics are generators of objective social knowledge which can be used to improve public policy, a view which is also helpful in improving the social status and reward structure of social scientific and professional occupations: 'Social scientists offer their expertise in problem solving to the state or other important organizations and receive funding and research grants to pursue their problem-solving research. In other cases, they are employed in semi-independent commissions of inquiry (the Macdonald Commission ...), and task forces to study issues of concern to these organizations ...'[34] To consolidate their positions and status, social scientists often directly serve the state as policy makers, applying their expertise to the decision-making process within government and then returning to academe. Thus, they maximize their utility in a self-interested manner, consciously or not, employing a strategy that advances their own interests and political influence. The success of the economics profession in this area is most pronounced. However: 'Critics of this process essentially see much of this work as the intellectual legitimation of dominant ideologies and the various power elites within the social structure. These types of social scientists are essentially seen as a conservative clerisy engaged in aiding the dominant interests in the state and society through the ideological reproduction of modern capitalist social relations. The key to their success and influence revolves around making themselves useful to dominant political and social interests.'[35] Thus, the commissioners found a reflection within the economics research of the minority message generated within the public hearings by neoconservative, continentalist business interests.

It is, however, an oversimplification to assert that *all* economists are ideologically homogeneous. Moreover, not all of them are inexorably tied to the reward system, or endlessly seeking privileged status from the state. As Brooks and Gagnon point out:

> not all social scientists, even those who are comfortably ensconced in the disciplinary reward structures, are legitimators of the social organization and values they see around them. Indeed, some are vociferous and radical critics of the underlying structures of society. While the intellectual freedom and relative autonomy of academic institutions in Western democracies allow for the tolerance of virulent criticism, as long as it conforms to the norms of respectable social science research, there are times when the intellectual and political influence of the vanguard of critics becomes much more significant. In these periods, critical social scientists align themselves with and articulate alternative political projects, often challenging the existing order. In other words, the dominant thrust of social thought in these periods shifts from justifications of society – or at most its piecemeal reform – to radical criticism and fundamental restructuring projects.[36]

If there are dissentient academics, even within the economics profession, where were they in the Macdonald Commission? To answer this question, it must be recalled that the critical ideology of the left-nationalist critique precludes an expert relationship to the state. This is particularly relevant to the Macdonald Commission, for one of the inquiry's major weaknesses was its failure to employ social scientists from across the ideological spectrum. One director admitted making but a single (failed) attempt to attract a left political economist to the commission as a research coordinator.[37]

Despite a flourishing alternative academic community under the rubric of the new Canadian political economy, little effort was made to draw its conceptions of Canadian society into the research component of the commission. Moreover, economic nationalists, neo-Marxists, left political economists, Innisian economic historians, and others were almost completely shut out, resulting in a stilted and narrow review of economic options for Canada. Winham observed

> You might choose someone like [left political economist] Duncan Cameron to be part of the exercise. Although, in fairness to us, we did have some articles that were representative of left thinking. But we never went out to try and garner Duncan Cameron's views in the research. Quite

frankly, Duncan is a real ideologue. If he and I were sitting down to try and do up a program of research, we would disagree enormously on the ideology. We might have some agreement in terms of what subjects need to be considered. We had a paper from Robert Boardman on the foreign service and what not. I am not sure Duncan would disagree with doing that, he might disagree with who we chose to do that. He might say, you know if you pick Boardman, you are going to get a middle of the road thing, take Leo Panitch or someone like that. But I understand where he is coming from.[38]

Within the antinationalist countermovement in economics, the hegemony of the liberal school meant that most dissentient scholars were not even considered for work by the Macdonald Commission. One coordinator put it this way: 'In the context of the economic policy side ... a particular school of thought within the [economics] profession captured the commission, and I don't think there is any doubt about that. It was clearly the particular school of thought that was emerging at the time, which had emerged internationally at that time ... It was dominant and it was dominant in the commission.'[39] One commission economist went so far as to deny that anyone practising outside this paradigm was really an economist at all. He argued, 'it is certainly true that they [dissentient economists] would have gotten a very hostile audience, in the sense that most economists do not regard these people as economists in the sense that they do not practice methods of scientific inquiry to the standards that we would usually require.'[40] So, although the nationalist social democratic critique was presented to the commissioners through the public consultation process, it was not presented in any systematic way within the research studies, except in a few 'token' instances.

Given this reality, social science knowledge utilization by the commission was stunted and narrow in scope. Within the debate between nationalists and continentalists, this meant that the former's arguments were largely omitted from the research program, while those of the latter were prominently presented.[41] The commissioners were effectively limited in their perusal of economic development strategies for Canada by the imposition of a dominant paradigm on the research program and a failure to canvass alternative views. This reflected a trend that has predominated in most inquiries in which social science knowledge has been sought. More specifically, it reflects the hegemony of the economics profession within state-sponsored research exercises.

Within the Macdonald Commission, it was clear that the primary role of knowledge utilization by the economics profession was as a source of legitimation for the neoconservative continentalist ideology in Canadian society. This can be made clearer by examining the absence of critical social democratic nationalist discourse within the research program and the attempt to manufacture counterarguments to the dominant discourse.

Manufacturing Dissent: Whither the Social Democratic Nationalist View?

Three researchers, one each from economics, political science, and law, played key roles in mounting the free trade case before the commission. Of the three, economist Whalley, a British expatriate educated in England, was the key. According to Hart:

> One of the staff economists at the Commission was John Whalley, an economics professor at the University of Western Ontario in London. His expertise lay in general equilibrium models ... He was asked to take the lead in preparing research and background papers on trade policy. It did not take him long to decide that the only issue of any consequence was Canada-U.S. free trade and he began to devote his considerable energy to organizing seminars and research projects that would examine the issue from every angle ... By the time his assignment with the Commission came to an end, he had written, edited, or encouraged the production of seven volumes of research related to this theme. More than any other person on the Commission staff, he ensured that the free trade option gained a full hearing.[42]

The other two were political scientist Winham, and Osgoode Hall law professor Jack Quinn, both American expatriates.[43] Together the three of them coordinated an effort over the summer and fall of 1984 to produce a free trade proposal for the commissioners.

Their argument, in brief, was that economic considerations were of paramount importance.[44] Canadian economists had long studied the possible effects of bilateral free trade with the United States, some suggesting that it could increase Canadian GNP by as much as 10 per cent.[45] As Quinn, the University of Chicago–trained lawyer, put it: 'Basically, the idea was that you could achieve a fairly substantial increase in per capita GNP or GDP, however you want to measure it, by eliminating existing barriers to investment and trade between the two countries. There was a kind of static-dynamic model, that is, it is a global equilibrium model of the economy that these mathematicians dreamed up. The guys from

Queens – Harris was the principal guy who did this work – wanted to demonstrate that making what appeared to be some fairly modest assumptions about the structure and the framework within which these restrictions are removed, then you could see as much as an 8 per cent gain in national product over a period of seven or eight years.'[46] Moreover, 'the increase in GNP would result in part because free trade would eliminate some distortion in relative prices,' according to Hart. 'When consumers are given prices that more accurately reflect costs, they maximize their consumption in a way that minimizes the cost of the nation's resources and labour. This is the so-called classical economic argument for free trade.'[47]

In addition, a significant part of the rise in GNP would be the result of increased economies of scale among firms. Well-meaning governments that intervene in the market through the use of tariffs, taxes, quotas, and subsidies to support industries are only compounding the weaknesses of the Canadian economy, according to this view. Tariff removal would have a dramatic effect on Canadian competitiveness and the economy overall, increasing production runs for a market ten times larger than the Canadian market. While there would be some dislocation as free trade was ushered in, the overall expectation was for a significant net gain in output and employment and that adjustment would be manageable. Ultimately, 'the purpose of trade negotiations with the United States was to expand opportunities in such a way as to benefit strong firms and encourage weaker firms to strengthen their competitive position.'[48] Quinn and the others concluded that the non-economic arguments against free trade were simply overwhelmed by the economic rationale: 'Let's forget about all this stuff about nationalism, and protecting professional elites from competition, and this argument from the left and the right about what kind of country to make. It wasn't sort of a conservative agenda to deregulate Canada. The argument was look – this is Donald Macdonald after all, and Tommy Shoyama and all these guys, these Liberal guys, this is not a bunch of Chicago economists sitting down and saying whatever – the message was, the average person is going to be better off if we take these restrictions off.'[49] And they advised the commissioners accordingly. Moreover, the argument that the Americans were becoming dangerously protectionist was linked to the notion that government policies that restrict trade and investment negatively influence the flow of investment funds into Canada. Quinn argued, 'if your industries become heavily dependent upon U.S. sales, and they become vulnerable to anti-dumping suits in the U.S., people will not want to invest here, they will invest in the

U.S.'[50] Thus a legal regime negotiated between the two countries was needed both to overcome American protectionism and guarantee continued investment in Canada.

The basis of much of the economists' theorizing was the so-called Harris-Cox general equilibrium model, a summary of which was presented to the commissioners in the research studies and in seminars.[51] This work, based on a data set from 1976,[52] alleged huge increases in Canadian productivity under conditions of bilateral free trade, and was cited repeatedly by Whalley and the other economists in their arguments for free trade.[53] Concerns over the adjustment costs of free trade were shown conclusively to be misplaced, as econometric modelling purportedly showed that gains from trade liberalization outweighed adjustment costs by a factor of 62 to 1.[54] Moreover, Harris-Cox predicted real income would rise by about 9 per cent and employment by over 5 per cent. But economist Bruce Wilkinson argued that the estimates of net real income gains were much too high and that the employment gains in large-scale models such as Harris-Cox are suspect at best.[55] Noting the diverse results that appear in comparing various econometric models predicting the effects of free trade, Wilkinson argued, 'we should not rely too heavily on the results from these macromodels in estimating the net benefits from BFT [bilateral free trade] or in devising policies for negotiating free trade.'[56] Yet this is precisely what Whalley and the commissioners did. Wilkinson concluded about the role of the economic arguments that: 'much more than narrow economic analysis is involved in BFT. Economists have tended to shy away from or assume aside a number of the most difficult issues in making their economic assessment of the net gains from free trade. When these are introduced, the outcome is not nearly so evident and neither is the exact magnitude of the net gains. There may well be a significant loss of Canadian sovereignty in the process.'[57] Similarly, Ricardo Grinspun argued that the proponents of free trade 'place many of their cards on the economic front, emphasizing the aggregate efficiency gains expected ... In so doing, they have used technical tools, such as computable general equilibrium models, to make their point.'[58] But, Grinspun suggested, these models are predicated on erroneous assumptions such that the aggregate economic gains are actually smaller than proclaimed. Yet the economists felt no need to engage an internal critique of their methodology.

It took another political scientist to recognize the inherent dangers of the limited view set out by the dominant neoconservative, continentalist discourse within the emerging research for the commission. When

Cairns discerned that the commission seemed to be leaning towards making a recommendation for Canada-U.S. free trade, he realized that no one within the commission was making any counterarguments. In particular, he worried that not only were there no economists putting forward the counterarguments to the free trade position, no one was pointing out the political, social, or cultural consequences of free trade. For instance the argument that Canadian sovereignty might be threatened was not considered by the economists because it was not an economic concern, strictly speaking. Whalley argued that the national sovereignty position was 'exceptionally difficult to quantify or even formulate in analytical terms,' and therefore of little value in the debate. Taking this view a step further, he argued that 'the possible impacts on sovereignty are so speculative that it can even be argued that Canada's sovereignty (defined as the freedom to take independent action) would be enhanced under a free trade arrangement.'[59] But in any event, it was not being forcefully raised by any of the other academics on the commission.

If the economists were presenting the arguments for free trade so effectively, who was presenting the counterarguments? Macdonald felt that no one was: 'I think it's a good point because there really wasn't an argument made. Abe [Rotstein] came and gave testimony as a witness and put the arguments I expected to hear from him, and I can't remember whether Bruce Wilkinson from Edmonton appeared. I subsequently appeared with him later on platforms about the free trade agreement itself. I'm trying to identify someone among the research staff who was saying 'no.' I can't remember anyone saying that.'[60]

When asked if he recalled the position taken by leading nationalist political economist Mel Watkins, Macdonald replied that he could not remember Watkins making any presentation to the commission. 'I don't think Mel appeared. He might have been in some of the peer groups,' Macdonald recalled. When reminded that both Watkins and Wilkinson participated in an important round table discussion on free trade which was published as part of the commission's research,[61] Macdonald expressed surprise, and suggested that there was really no one constantly present on the commission making the nationalist argument. 'So the [nationalist] voice was heard occasionally, but I can't identify someone who was working there [on the commission] week after week.'[62]

Because no one appeared to be championing the nationalist position, Cairns became concerned. A flurry of memos passed between Macdonald and Cairns in which Cairns made the case that someone ought to stand up for Canada in this discussion, and resist the economics-inspired juggernaut. Cairns recalled that 'there was much more apprehension about free trade coming from the political scientists, but they were not coming for market reasons, they were coming for the reasons that they were scared about the political consequences.' He and Stairs in particular raised these non-economic concerns. Tapping into the anxieties of some commissioners, they said 'let's try to play out the political consequences of a free trade regime with the United States and let's remember this is an historic decision.'[63] Strongly argued but speculative arguments were made about declining autonomy that would flow from free trade with Washington. The fear was raised that the U.S. capital would become a new centre of power within which Canadians enjoyed no political power. Congress would be making decisions, it was feared, and Canadians, with no votes in the American system, would have no way to overturn decisions taken there. As well, psychologically, it would integrate Canadians into a North American definition of self. 'I argued that that was one plausible scenario, and that Canadian business would spend more time lobbying in Washington than they would in Ottawa,' Cairns recalled. 'So this was a very big change. And the commissioners listened. The economists didn't agree with this but we did present these alternative arguments.'[64]

But the free trade argument was made by the economists because it was initially defined as an economic issue. And the overwhelming bulk of the research on it was done by the economists. Thus, it was quite difficult for Cairns to persuade Stairs or Winham to research the political implications of free trade for Canada. With some persistence, Cairns did manage to get some research done. For instance, he commissioned a historical overview of the idea of Canada-U.S. free trade by J.L. Granatstein, and an essay by Charles Pentland focusing on the lessons of Europe for Canada.[65]

The problem was that the economists were dealing in 'hard facts,' including allegedly measurable gains in per capita GNP that Canada would obtain from free trade. They also backed up their empirical arguments with vague premonitions about 'globalization' and the 'changing world' full of constraints and implications for economic development in which Canada had fewer and fewer free choices. This contrasted with the political scientists' arguments, which were couched more in terms of 'maybe there are some political and constitutional aspects of it which we, as Canadians, better be clear we understand as best we can before proceeding.' But the political scientists' arguments did not contain alternative economic strategies.[66] For instance, there was some research by Keith Banting and Leo Panitch on tripartism,[67] but they concluded that for a variety of societal, cultural, and institutional reasons, Canada could not operate a tripartite regime. There was no real consensus among government, business, and labour, as some European countries had. Moreover, virtually no one was arguing for an industrial strategy. Cairns remembered someone said, 'Well, maybe the commissioners should be paying much more attention to the possibility of an industrial strategy,' implying that the state could play a very effective dirigiste role:

> And as I recall, a number of commissioners who had been in government including Macdonald, just said 'You guys are dreaming. Have you ever seen government in action? The idea of government fine-tuning,' and I am sure there was this kind of statement from Macdonald, 'it can't be done. Government is a big bumbling mastodon. It can't fine-tune. It bumbles much more than it pushes the right button.' So, the objection, and this was more of a speculative suggestion at some meeting was, 'Well look, we've been there, we've seen government, we know the complexity of this society. We don't think that there is some sort of social reconstruction for Canada kind of policy – like the League for Social Reconstruction – which can be applied. That might look fine in a university seminar but we just don't believe you.' Period. This was coming out. I'm sure Macdonald said something, not quite vehemently as that, but 'look, it makes no sense, you're dreaming. You've never been in the real world.'[68]

Cairns also linked these developments to ideological shifts in the same period. 'But, of course, the whole thing was occurring at a time when neoconservatism and the whole intellectual climate was pushing in that direction,' he recalled, 'and there were not a lot of powerful believers in dirigisme anywhere. Maybe a few more than there are now, but that wasn't a kind of basic current of opinion and certainly not amongst the economists.'[69] There was much more sympathy for state intervention among the political scientists, who by training are generally much more state-oriented than economists, and who could see the possibility of the state playing a role as a policy instrument in itself. But in the absence of convincing models, and without any standard-bearers, the political science view was muted.

One researcher, who worked under a special arrangement for Docquier, confirmed that no one within the commission was making the nationalist argument among the research teams:

> I don't think there was anyone. You have to take into account that neoconservative economics was just on a roll. So the whole profession, whatever

people's individual intellectual biographies were, the whole economics profession [had moved to the right]. You have to cast your mind back to that time, I mean, you literally had guys from Western ... advocating a return to the gold standard. So one doesn't have to be an enthusiast of conspiracy theories to say, well, gee, where was the other view? Well, the whole profession had moved to the right in dramatic fashion from really 1978 onwards with the Carter administration. There is no other argument being made in the whole profession, let alone, who is going to be duking it out with any career-limiting impacts in a royal commission?[70]

The economics profession was completely unself-conscious about the fact that it expressed a limited ideological world-view. Thus, economists within the commission would argue that of course there was a great deal of debate about free trade within the commission, and that the issue was thrashed out from top to bottom, not really cognizant of the fact that that debate took place only within the parameters of their ideological world-view. To the extent to which a debate occurred, it was not over 'free trade – yes or no?,' but 'free trade yes, but in what manner?' Picking up on this notion, Warrian argued that by the mid-1980s, the economics profession had almost uniformly adopted a neoconservative perspective. 'The whole profession had moved to that spot. You don't get any goal-line stands of divergent views in the profession across the country,' he argued. 'If Mel Watkins or a few other people, or Jack Weldon got up and said something, they would just be viewed as some quaint left remnant of the Empire of the St Lawrence or something, not anything that had any credibility or standing with the commission.'[71]

When it became apparent that there was no one to present the nationalist position within the commission, Cairns suggested that Denis Stairs ought to assume this role. Stairs remembered that Cairns rang the alarm bells about the non-economic consequences of free trade, and asked him to write something on it, since Stairs had been the only one among the commission researchers who had even remotely considered the question. Stairs recalled: 'Now, on my side, I was hit by this somewhat by surprise. We were getting studies going, but what happened was that Alan Cairns came to me one time, if I recall, and I think it was just during some discussions when the research coordinating group was together, and during the break he said "Denis, you know, we have a bit of a problem. This free trade thing is becoming a very major part of the commission's interest, and it is becoming a major part of our inquiries, and hence the studies we are asking you and Gil to organize. But the fact is that there is nobody around here to make the anti-free trade case."'[72] Cairns was alarmed that the image of the commission would suffer if it presented a case for free trade without having canvassed alternate views. Winham was also alerted to the lack of an anti-free trade position within the commission. 'And so Alan Cairns put out a little internal memo on free trade. He essentially panned the idea from a number of perspectives, and that came out around September [1984], so I wrote an alternative view to that. I tried to pan Alan Cairns's view,' Winham recalled. 'And so these two memos circulated, and we had some internal debates on that kind of thing. And then we made presentations to the commissioners too.'[73] As one of the full-time researchers on the Commission, Winham enjoyed a distinct advantage over his colleagues. With the luxury of time, he was able to construct a powerful countercase to the nationalist position. Moreover, Stairs remembered Cairns saying, 'I don't know what I think about this one way or the other. That is not the point. The point is essentially, that Gil [Winham] is pro–free trade, all the economists are pro–free trade, most of the evidence coming in from the hearings is pro–free trade,' the chair is pro–free trade.' Cairns was concerned as a political scientist that this was occurring without reference to political implications, or to the counterarguments. And Cairns said to Stairs, 'You know, this matter has come up many times in the course of Canadian history, and in fact it has usually been thrown back, and it has always been surrounded by discussions having as much to do with political implications as with economic gain. Somebody has got to remind people that there may be other issues at stake here, and that has got to be you, because there ain't no one else!'[74]

Stairs then set out to raise the non-economic consequences of free trade, and discovered that there really was no debate among the commission researchers on this issue. This was several years before the great free trade debate which shook the country and, according to Stairs, the arguments against the free trade deal had not yet been publicly articulated. He was very much on his own: 'So I got asked to raise, or to draw attention to, the non-economic ingredients of the debate – not so much of the debate, because at that point there wasn't any economic debate. The stuff that came out later in the free trade debate among the general public, you know, 'If You Love This Country" and all that sort of stuff, and the sort of thing [Duncan] Cameron came out with, that all came out later in Ottawa – you know, he sort of edited things and waged a sort of one person campaign against it. But all of that was later. There really wasn't any public debate about the political aspects of this in the earlier phase at all. And so it was just a blank.'[75] But in commissioning Stairs to undertake this job, Cairns was effectively asking him to put some water in his wine. 'Since I was the one who basically had issued the warnings about potential non-economic consequences, Alan was saying, you know, could you do that, but draft it in a way that won't tear apart the foundation for the recommendation.'[76] This suggestion rankled Stairs a little, and his reaction to it is reflective of the differences between the bureaucratic and academic worlds. He had difficulty taking on this assignment because he regarded it more as the type of assignment that civil servants take on, 'but I am an academic, and I had not thought of myself in quite this kind of civil service staffer role. And I had a little difficulty adjusting to that.'[77] Still, Stairs accepted the challenge:

> So I told Alan Cairns, I don't know how far I can go with this, but I will give it a whirl. So I did, and I guess they liked the drafting, but they kept coming back and saying, well look, can you state this argument a little more strongly, and down play that, and so on and so forth. And I think I did one or two drafts, and finally I said 'look Alan, that is the best I can do. If you want to say that, you go ahead and say it, but I can't, I don't feel very comfortable.' Now, that was probably being a bit precious under the circumstances. But I didn't feel that I was a staffer in the same sense that Alan Nymark and his colleagues were. I mean I was an academic asked to express some personal views at various stages and to organize a research enterprise. But I am a little uncomfortable writing an argument that I felt quite strongly about, but then being instructed to write it weakly. It was kind of an odd assignment![78]

So Stairs proceeded to draft arguments against the free trade recommendation – but not too strongly. Macdonald agreed to let Stairs undertake this task for strategic reasons. Macdonald calculated that if the commission simply came out and said, 'let's have free trade for all these reasons' without exploring the counterarguments, it would be accused of presenting a simple-minded and one-sided case. But if it was able to present the arguments against free trade alongside of those in favour, and effectively shoot the former down, it could cloak its arguments in a garb of balance, sophistication, and respectability it might otherwise be denied. Stairs argued that, from a political point of view, it was far more effective to admit cognizance of these concerns, to have thought about them carefully, and to recognize there is an element of risk. 'After all, Donald Macdonald himself was talking about this as a leap of faith and all of that,' Stairs recalled. But if they could say that on balance, having looked at all of the other concerns, and considering the potential economic pay-off that we foresee, it is something that the country should do. 'Well, that is a much more powerful argument than simply coming out and ignoring all that,' Stairs concluded, 'because you in a sense pre-empt your critics.'[79] Stairs recalled the discussions of how the *Report* should present the case for free trade:

> It was difficult because they wanted me to [construct the arguments against free trade] because I was the only one who addressed those issues. And they apparently made a decision – Alan Nymark could talk about this, although I am not sure that he supported the idea – because there was one school of thought that said, look, we just come out and make the argument for free trade – period! And I think Nymark was initially in favour of that view. But there was another view which was, no, if we are going to make the argument, we must recognize that there are counter-arguments, that there is going to be opposition, it is going to be controversial, and if we are going to be persuasive, we have to acknowledge those counter-arguments.[80]

Even having put this water in the wine, Stairs's perspective was diluted further when it got into the hands of Hart: 'Denis was a passionate spokesman for the sovereignty, Canadian identity, and so on dimension of it, and because of that there is about a thirty-page section in [volume 1 of] the *Report* which discusses that, largely written by Denis. And I was told that I had to incorporate his set of arguments even though I was not comfortable with them, because this was not my report, it was the commission's report. But I put a couple of paragraphs in there which I think kind of toned the argument down. They agreed that I could do that.'[81] Ultimately, the watered-down arguments suffered a further set of revisions, this time by the explicitly pro–free trade Hart.

Stairs, as de facto chief spokesperson for the nationalist position within the research program of the commission, was asked to present his arguments to his academic colleagues in a series of seminars and presentations. Winham also participated in these to offer the pro–free trade side. 'Stairs argued against it, so we had a kind of "dog and pony show" where Denis would be asked to speak against and I would be asked to speak for,' Winham recalled. 'We did that a number of times in the commission as I recollect.'[82] Stairs recalled that he was asked to write a memorandum on the political implications, both pro and con, of free trade. Cairns did not ask him specifically to write an argument against it, but rather simply to illustrate some of the political issues and concerns that might be raised by this issue. In any event, Stairs recalled, 'I wasn't religiously against it, and I didn't necessarily accept a lot of the arguments that were being made by those who were opposed to it.'[83] Indeed, Stairs is not considered a nationalist within the Canadian academic community, and does not self-identify as such. Intellectually, he is known as an international relations specialist originally from the John Holmes school. Thus even the 'champion' of the anti–free trade forces within the commission was ambivalent about his own position. Stairs, like Cairns, can only be considered a 'reluctant nationalist' at best. Effectively, the nationalist position was without a bona fide spokesperson.

Stairs also explained that while he was placing himself far too centrally in the drama, he 'was very concerned that people just weren't thinking about the political implications. So that is how I got saddled with that role,' he recalled. He also noted the hegemony of the economics arguments, based as they were on apparently 'scientific' method and rigour: 'There was a kind of persuasiveness about economic argumentation that could not be evident in a political argument about whether there would be forced policy harmonization as a result of political forces that would be unleashed in the wake of a free trade regime being established and so forth. Those kind of questions, those predictions or judgement calls – you know, you draw attention to political processes that may be let loose, and you know, some people can look at that kind of argument and say, well, it doesn't matter. So what were you to say to them? You either bought them, or you didn't. So I think it wasn't an environment in which those kind of arguments mounted well.[84] But Cairns and Stairs nonetheless felt it was important that the non-economic arguments be brought forward for the consideration of the commissioners. In so doing, however, they recognized that the free trade arguments were being made within an ideological framework which had at its heart the larger project of reducing the role of government in Canadian society:

> The premise underlying most of this was that there should be free movement of factors of production including labour. And that the basic premise underlying all of this was, therefore – and this is buttressed by a lot of other things, this came up over and over again – the government cannot pick winners, the government cannot develop the regions, we cannot afford it, we don't know how to do it, it is always money down the drain, and so forth. It is not that we are natural right wingers, it is just that we do not know any other way of doing it, so the market is best, and the continental

market is necessary because it requires economies of scale, and keeping Congress out of our lumber industry, and so on. All of that was premised, of course, on the proposition that people should in fact move if you could not artificially create jobs in their own community.[85]

Moreover, the changes being sought by the neoconservative continentalist position were, in Stairs's view, contrary to the political culture and traditions of Canadian society. He made the argument that Canada was premised on the assumption that it is basically a grouping of economically diversified and differently rewarded communities. Moreover, he argued, 'it is the job essentially of the government to maintain some commonality of standard in public service in the various sectors of the country, and to try to sustain communities where they are, not because that is economically efficient, but because the whole concept of the Canadian state, the purposes of federalism and everything else, rests on the premise that the purposes of the state are to make people happy in their communities. That is the job of the state.'[86] That is a different premise from the one that underlies the American position, where, 'at the ideological level,' according to Stairs, 'the premise is that if you want to live in Maine, you can live in Maine, but you will be a bit poorer, and don't whine. If you want to get rich, you go to Arizona or some place.' In Canada, on the other hand, there has always been the assumption that, by and large, there is an obligation on the part of the state to sustain Canadians in whatever part of the country they chose to live, according to Stairs. He regarded this as quite a fundamental change in the premises of Canadian politics. Moreover, in discussions with Whalley and other economists, and with the commissioners, Stairs became convinced that he was witnessing a fundamental reconfiguration of elite opinion in Canada:

I became convinced that there had been a kind of a sea-change, and I use the term quite deliberately, because I think it was quite profound. There had been a sea-change in the attitudes among Canadian elites, because I can remember on one occasion, and I used to say this over and over, as Gil would probably testify, that expressing political, or even raising, political questions in these discussions was a bit like in the old days a gentleman talking about women or religion in his club – there was a kind of deathly silence. Now, why? Well, it might well be that I expressed myself so badly and in such primitive and emotional fashion that everybody was appalled. That is one explanation and there might be something in it – you would have to ask someone else. But I don't think that was it. It had to do partly with the fact that that wasn't the prevailing consensus.[87]

But it was more than this. It had to do with the emergence in Canada of a new discourse as articulated by the economists:

But it also had to do with another aspect of the kind of epistemological argument ... A lot of the advantage went to the orthodox economists, because the ones who were doing studies were, by and large, orthodox economists, number one; and number two, they were able to advance their argument with what appeared to be irrefutable supporting quantitative evidence – that is, they had models, and they had a clear set of premises. Then they could run numbers through these models, and come up with predictions about 'if ... then.' If we do this, then these things will happen. If we don't do it, then these other things much more horrible will happen. So their studies had the look of scientific truth. They looked as though they were producing engineering, and the rest of us were producing, or at least I was producing, prejudices.[88]

Stairs recalled that, in discussing his ideas with the economists like Whalley, 'he would listen to this, apparently attentively, and say that is very interesting, and it is an argument that should be heard, but it is not an argument that economics can accommodate.' Moreover, the economists 'dominated the epistemology. They dominated the conception of what constituted a sound argument. And that helped them win the day.'[89]

Meanwhile, whereas only one academic could be found to make the anti–free trade case out of the approximately three hundred hired by the commission, there was no shortage of proponents on the other side. Ultimately the task fell to Stairs's Dalhousie colleague, Gil Winham. The choice of Winham, an international relations political science expert, rather than one of the economists, was calculated to give the exercise a stamp of legitimacy it might otherwise have lacked. Here was a non-economist, after all, refuting the political concerns of the meagre anti–free trade forces within the commission. Stairs recalled that Winham was a free trader right from the start, with academic training in economics. 'And he is an American-educated and reared liberal. That is what he is. And I think he simply agreed with the economists. And those would be his priorities.'[90]

Winham is an American expatriate who came to Canada to study and teach at the height of the nationalist-inspired anti-American backlash within Canadian universities. As Stairs noted, Winham developed a very strong distaste for things nationalistic within Canada as a result of his early, negative experiences as an American at McMaster University, where he taught just as the wave of economic and other forms of nationalism ran through Canadian academia, from the mid-1960s to the early 1970s: 'McMaster became a particularly notorious case; and within the university the political science department was a prominent case; and the upshot was that a lot of the Americans working on the staff came under heavy fire from Canadian academic nationalists who were there. And Gil felt the sting of that quite strongly. My sense from many discussions with him was that this left Gil with a pretty unpleasant taste in his mouth about Canadian nationalism.'[91] But it was not just his experience as an American expatriate in a hostile environment that left Winham with this predisposition, Stairs recalled. 'I don't think that made him a free trader, because I think *that* came from his economics training, and from his acceptance of the premises of liberal economics as defined in the neo-Keynesian world,' Stairs recalled. 'So in that he would think like John Whalley, although not as an expert economist in quite the same way, but as a very well educated economist just the same.' But having said that, Stairs conceded that Winham would have less sympathy with anti–free trade positions if he thought they were rooted in Canadian nationalism.[92]

Winham argued that he supported free trade more for reasons of realpolitik than anything else. Canada had tried to adopt other policies, and Winham agreed with the intent of these efforts. 'I always argued, frankly, that the desideratum of the Third Option was the correct desideratum. I would like to see a balanced, diversified export portfolio,' he recalled. 'But from analysis you conclude that is really impossible. We did some analysis on that, and so therefore, events were taking us toward a bilateralized situation with the United States. There was nothing we could do.'[93]

Winham also noted the extent to which the lack of internal direction from the commissioners shaped this debate. 'I mean, this was an era in which, as I say, we got our marching orders from the *Globe and Mail*, and we were seeing in the *Globe and Mail* all these references to free trade, and the Commission is going to recommend free trade and so on, and you have to realize it was in the air.'[94]

Thus the free trade 'debate,' to the extent it was engaged within the commission research program at all, was characterized by a nationalist position presented by a non-nationalist political scientist and subsequently watered down by an expressly continentalist editor. The continentalist position, on the other hand, had the full weight of the economics profession and paradigm behind it. By handing presentation of the pro–free trade position to a political scientist, the appearance of intellectual pluralism was created. In this way, some sense of legitimacy was garnered for this 'debate' before the commissioners though, in reality, it was but a façade.

Conclusion

Both the division of labour within the social sciences, and the creation and reinforcement of particular discourses by social scientists had an impact on the Macdonald Commission. The lack of cross-fertilization between the three research streams, coupled with institutionalized claims to discrete forms of knowledge, afforded the economists an influential position within the commission research program, and were important factors shaping the outcome of this process. This chapter has revealed the success of the economists in imprinting their ideological vision on the commission, and the virtual absence of a credible anti–free trade position within its massive research component, despite the appearance of two important actors who ostensibly assumed the role of nationalist champions. The economists enjoyed a near-monopoly on economic policy prescriptions. The empiricism of the discipline, based on its methods of so-called scientific inquiry, enabled it to impose a discourse on the commission, and the ideological homogeneity of the mainstream of the discipline reinforced its claims to expertise and exclusive knowledge. One observer, however, also made the point that the ascendance of mainstream economics in fact owes a debt of gratitude to the Macdonald Commission: 'The notion that economists are in a perpetual rage of disagreement, that economics divides into "right-wing" and "left-wing" camps, is a popular fantasy. In point of fact, most economists agree most of the time. The real ideological divide of our times has not been between rival bands of economists but between the economic view of the world and the non-economic view, or indeed, as it has been put, the *pre*-economic. The partisan battles of recent years have not so much been about what was the right course to take, but between those parties that were prepared to act on economists' recommendations and those that were not.'[95]

CHAPTER 9

Royal Commission Politics: The Triumph of the Policy Group

Our consistent knowledge of the political life of the principal civilized nations of the world authorizes us to assert that the tendency toward oligarchy constitutes one of the historic necessities, one of the iron laws of history, from which the most democratic modern societies and, within these societies, the most advanced parties, have been unable to escape.[1]

Chapter 5 revealed the differing ideological roots of the economic development strategies suggested by the public for the commission as part of the search for viability for transformative change. It also showed that the majority of the public submissions went largely unheeded. Chapters 6, 7, and 8 uncovered the ideological contours of a research exercise of epic proportions. revealing that economic viability was derived from scholarly contributions emanating from those privileged academics within the social science pantheon, the economists, as well as the ideological homogeneity that overshadowed the work of the research teams. But a third factor in shaping the free trade recommendation, political and bureaucratic leadership, requires some scrutiny. This third factor, the so-called policy group assembled and headed by Alan Nymark, was also infused with the influence of ideological forces. Indeed, ideology played a vital role in guiding its work.

Ideology is a dynamic which includes a program for change. But it also requires adherents: the ideologues who carry the values, attitudes, and beliefs of the ideology with them; the agents who transmit the ideological messages and implement the program for change; the actors whose use of political discourse spreads the gospel of the believers. Within the commission, adherents of neoconservative continentalism could be found among the economics research team. But alone, they were not capable of imposing their views on the commission and causing transformative change. It required agents and structures closer to the organizational centre of the project to give shape to political discourse and carry to fruition the programmatic elements of the ideology. Typically, the most important adherents of an ideological position are the political and bureaucratic elite who possess the combination of commitment, resources, and opportunity necessary to forward their vision. This is where the small but influential policy group came into play. This chapter will examine the ideology of this puissant body which dominated the drafting of the commission's *Report.* The ideology of neoconservative continentalism is powerfully reflected in the final product of the inquiry largely because of the facilitative role played by this key group.

The Policy Group and the Iron Law of Oligarchy

In virtually any organizational enterprise, control devolves into the hands of a small group of activists, or 'oligarchy.' In a royal commission, it might be expected that this would be the commissioners themselves. But in the case of the Macdonald Commission, it was not. The massive size of the enterprise, the sheer number of Commissioners, and the fact that they were part-time ensured that they would not be 'holding the pen.' Partly because of these organizational handicaps, a concerted effort was made to centralize control over the commission. This was particularly true after the interim report, *Challenges and Choices,* was released in April 1984, and met with universal derision. The media in particular savaged the report. For instance, the Toronto *Star* editorialized 'it is deeply disappointing that after 18 months and an expenditure of $21.8 million, all the Macdonald Commission on Canada's economy has been able to come up with is a list of questions that anyone familiar with economic policy could have posed after a few hours thought.'[2] Jeffrey Simpson offered, 'long awaited and much debated, the report represents what two graduate students, working at a leisurely pace, might have produced in a week.'[3] But other groups attacked the report as well. The president of the Canadian Federation of Independent Business called it 'a bucket of mush and said he could have written the same document by compiling a years'copies of financial newspapers.'[4] Ablett, the journalist with primary responsibility for this document, 'who had been rather prominent in the Commission to that point, went back to his office and the door was never opened again.'[5] Vastel, the other journalist with a major hand in *Challenges and Choices*, resigned from the commission. Rochon and Godsoe engaged in a fierce struggle for control, eventually won by the latter. And Smith left shortly after *Challenges and Choices* was released (for unrelated reasons). Simeon remembered that 'there were amazing turf wars within that bureaucratic group between Godsoe and Rochon, and later between Nymark and Ablett. I had never seen a bureaucratic bloodletting before, but wow, this was no holds barred.'[6] Cairns referred to the struggle for power on the commission as 'kind of a Darwinian struggle.' The nature of the bureaucracy was such that no one knew who was going to be doing what in three months. 'So people rise, people fall, and a lot of people were destroyed on the commission. A lot of marriages broke up. Some people were totally just kind of done in. They didn't in a sense survive the competition.'[7] Cairns felt this was particularly true of people from government in various commission roles who were battling with each other for relative influence. In the end, Macdonald, Godsoe, and Nymark emerged holding the uppermost hand.

Godsoe's concern was an administrative one – to finish the *Report* by the government's deadline. Macdonald's concern was to have something substantial over which his signature would appear. And Nymark's concern was to produce a bold, clearly articulated policy statement that would overcome the lack of legitimacy afforded the commission, and the cynicism generated by *Challenges and Choices*, and not incidentally enhance his own career within the bureaucracy. What was needed was a high-profile, politically salient issue on which the commission could focus as a key economic recommendation.

To facilitate this process, Nymark assembled a team that assumed responsibility for various segments of the *Report*. This was the policy group that Nymark charged with developing a credible argument regarding economic development strategies for Canada which could stand as the commission's signature recommendation. But to do so, the group needed a clear directive.

Looking for an Issue

The policy group had no central role until after the *Challenges and Choices* episode in April 1984. More than any other development, this public relations disaster focused the attention of Macdonald and the senior staff on making certain that the commission achieved something noteworthy. Cairns recalled: 'The publication of *Challenges and Choices* had a very salutary effect on the commission. It shook them, and it undermined their morale very, very seriously. Because Macdonald had had this $800 a day tag attached to him and made the comment, "I would have made more money, had I stayed at my practice as a lawyer in Toronto." It's probably true, but wasn't helpful. So the commission was getting a lot of bad publicity, and *Challenges and Choices*, I guess, was a good trial run. It forced them to realize that you can't sit on the fence forever, you've gotta start coming down one way or the other.'[8] Smith recalled, 'in my memory, one of the low periods was that *Challenges and Choices*, which had to come out to show what the commission was hearing, didn't go over terribly well, and was viewed publicly as a bit superficial.' It raised questions as to whether the commission was going to respond substantively to the important issues it was considering, according to Smith: 'But I think on the research side, we always had a quiet confidence that "oh no, just hang on, we are coming." That, in a sense, *Challenges and Choices* was perhaps unwise, but it was politically probably necessary to show that the Commissioners were hearing and were listening to some very important matters. So I think that is where there was some concern as to whether, if that was the shape of the final *Report*, it wasn't going to be very well accepted. But I think with the knowledge that there was a very strong research output coming along that would underpin a very much more substantive final report, most of us were not nearly as concerned.'[9] Still, *Challenges and Choices* underlined just how disorganized and out of focus the commission was. It heightened the sense of urgency which, combined with the commission's looming deadline and the arrival of a new government in November 1984, motivated the search for an issue that would galvanize the commission and serve as the signature-piece of its vast corpus of recommendations.

This concern was foreshadowed in an internal commission memo from Victor Clarke to Nymark. Clarke was a senior executive seconded to the commission from Canadian General Electric, and he was particularly concerned that the reflections on trade policy in *Challenges and Choices* were too 'soft.' In March 1984 he wrote to Nymark: 'Regarding trade orientation, the statements of the "Choice" recognizes that there are risks to the USA option. I would like to see a clear challenge here to those who do not favour this approach [free trade]. I think the Commission badly needs a well-researched contrary view for two reasons – first we have to understand the real alternatives – and second, we have to keep in mind that whoever does the negotiating with the USA needs a strong hand – and we do not want to weaken their position by suggesting an open and shut case.'[10]

For Nymark, the wishy-washiness of the interim report, and the damage it did to the commission's already suspect reputation, were appalling. In the aftermath of *Challenges and Choices*, Nymark saw the necessity of 'taking control' to ensure the commission would have something to show for its work. Simeon recalled 'Nymark emerged as the critical person. If the *Report* was going to contain anything of importance, Nymark was going to make it happen.'[11] This was the point at which Nymark assumed a stronger hand in the commission. Previously, responsibilities were rather diffuse, he recalled, with some people having the commissioner's ear at one time, other people at another. While he did not draft the interim report, Nymark did think there was deep disappointment about it, and so engineered some major changes right after that. And this, according to Nymark, was when the policy group really came into its own in terms of attempting to add some substance to the commission's work.[12] Following this incident, and particularly from the moment that Macdonald uttered his famous pronouncement in November 1984, the focus of the commission became clear to Nymark. Once his political boss identified free trade as the key issue, Nymark moved into bureaucratic high gear. The 'leap of faith' was his directive, and he carefully assembled a team that could and would pursue it within the commission and quietly promote it without.

As noted in previous chapters, it was not at all clear that free trade would even be considered by the commission. But once Macdonald, Godsoe, and Nymark latched on to the idea, it slowly spread. Stairs felt that the genesis of the free trade issue could be found in what Nymark's staff reported as coming out of the public submissions. The issue emerged slowly, promoted quietly by commission staff, and gradually took on momentum: 'Well, it happened by degrees. We began to get rumours coming mainly through the staff people, not the research personnel initially, but the staff people who were following the commission around. And it started to come out of a lot of the testimony they received. And I think they were quite surprised by the amount of consensus, not a lot of dissent at all, a lot of consensus around the notion that one dramatic economic management lever that might be pulled would be the trade one. So we began to hear rumours, and people would sort of say, I guess we had better do some work here because they are talking more and more about this. So it gradually developed that way.'[13] As Richard Van Loon put it, like any royal commission, this one began with a mandate, descended into chaos, and then rose from the ashes. And it rose from the ashes by virtue of a change in staff roles that saw Nymark take charge.[14]

Careful management created the impression that free trade was an issue emerging spontaneously from the public. To consolidate this impression, Nymark arranged a series of specialized consultations which the policy group put on for the commissioners' edification.[15] Most importantly, this included private meetings with business groups coming around to free trade. Among these groups, most significant were the Canadian Manufacturers Association (CMA) and the Business Council on National Issues (BCNI), which had publicly endorsed free trade by 1984.[16] In addition, arrangements were made for Macdonald to meet privately with the American ambassador to discuss the progress of the commission as it related to Canadian-American relations.[17] While observing protocol and the usual diplomatic niceties about not meddling in the internal affairs of their neighbours, Ronald Reagan's representative nonetheless expressed a strong interest in the outcome of the commission.

Macdonald admitted that the impetus for free trade came from *within* the commission, not from the public consultations, or even the research. Indeed, he did not hear much on the subject from the public at all: 'The initiative on trade really came from the commission itself, within the commission. Myself, obviously, but back and forth with others who were like-minded within the commission. And in a certain sense, this was an issue not addressed first time around when we went to the public, but addressed subsequently, *when it became clear where we were going.* We then set out in a less formal fact finding way to try to get some kind of reaction.'[18] This marked an important shift, for now Macdonald was no longer soliciting views; rather, he was seeking support for his already decided position. Macdonald also acknowledged that the trade issue was initiated by the inquiry staff despite being absent from the commission's mandate. 'I think you would find it difficult in the terms of reference to find whether there is any specific mandate on that subject,' he recalled. 'I don't think that there was. This is something that really developed out of the exchanges within the commission.'[19] Cairns remembered the internal search for an issue upon which the commission could focus: 'It seems to me that its [free trade] emergence in the process is something that is internal to the commissioners, and probably it's driven by Macdonald's developing perception that this was the only way to go because, for a long time the commission really didn't have a coherent sense of direction. You notice that in the little interim paper they put out, *Challenges and Choices,* which just devastated the commission's public image. But it was an honest reflection of the fact that they had not made up their mind. They didn't know what to do.'[20]

From the publication of *Challenges and Choices* and the completion of the public consultations to the commission deadline, there was just over a year to produce something coherent and meaningful. Nymark and his team assumed responsibility for guiding the ship into port. He admitted that 'on free trade there was relatively little in the initial research programs. It was not identified early on in the research process as being a driving force in the *Report*.'[21] But he realized that it could admirably fill the sails if it were 'managed' correctly. Banting argued that: 'When it came to the drafting of the final *Report*, Nymark was *the* person. And there was the sense in which the real question was whether any report would have emerged because it was so vast, and there was no direction, there was no coherence, there was no process, and there was a struggle over who was going to write it. And the impression I had was that Alan Nymark was probably important in the fact that a report emerged. Our impression was that he did not really care what was in it very much, as long as a report emerged, and that under his watch it could not be said that the commission collapsed into chaos.'[22] Nymark determined the best way to achieve this goal was by asserting centralized control over the report-writing stage of the commission.

Drafting the Final Report

The policy group is particularly important in the key question of authorship of the *Report*. Surprisingly, Cairns recalled, the vital issue of who would write the *Report* was not settled until late in the commission's life: 'Well, you know, I remember quite late on we kept saying, "Who the hell is going to write this damn thing?" And you didn't get clear answers. And I think you didn't get clear answers because nobody knew. It wasn't clear who was going to write it. No one knew, because we would have debates about what kind of report is it going to be? Is it going to be kind of a consciousness-raising report, or is it going to be a tough analytical report? Is it going to be a big report, or is it going to be a short report? None of these questions were answered, I guess, until one's into the final year.'[23]

As noted earlier, differences in the way bureaucrats and academics perceive and organize their worlds created tensions within the commission. These tensions extended into the planning of the *Report*. For instance, it was the desire – indeed, the expectation – of the senior researchers that they would have a prominent role in drafting it. However, it was the expectation of the senior bureaucrats that the researchers would not. Cairns recalled: 'I think the researchers always assumed that at minimum they would be key players in the writing of the report. They probably would do quite a bit of writing, but that was never definitively worked out ahead of time. Then what happened is that different sections, as we got towards the deadline, that different sections ended being parcelled out to different people. So the question of who would hold the pen in the report-writing stage was subject to some internal dispute. If the researchers were left out, then conceivably, so would much of their research. This type of concern emerged more and more forcefully as the project moved into its final stages.'[24]

Who was *not* going to take on this important job was clearly settled early on. Journalists like Ablett and Vastel were blamed by the commission bureaucrats and academics for the embarrassment caused by *Challenges and Choices*. and henceforth marginalized within the commission. Moreover, there was conflict between Rochon and the research directors because Rochon was in charge of the hearings process and argued that the hearings should be the key input. The research directors naturally thought the research should be more important. 'So there was a sort of a battle being waged there as to which body of information coming forth should be more significant,' Cairns recalled.[25] But if the research directors thought they and their academic teams were going to have the major input into the *Report*, they were soon disabused of that notion. This was far too important a task to be left to a crew of flighty eggheads. Nymark, the quintessential bureaucrat, moved to take tight control of the process.

By eagerly agreeing with Macdonald that free trade was to be the centrepiece of the *Report*, Nymark was able to arrange for his own hand-picked team to oversee its drafting. Nymark divided the work of the policy group into five sections, each of which was led by a policy coordinator. He assigned federal government bureaucrat Richard Van Loon to take the lead on social issues; economist David Husband became head of the section on economic issues; University of Ottawa law professor Jamie Benedickson steered the institutional side; and Anne Martin worked on international and environmental issues, and also on the area of technology. But Nymark, besides overseeing the group as a whole, personally assumed leadership of the free trade issue.[26] The most prominent members of Nymark's free trade team included Whalley, Winham, Sargent, and Hart.[27]

This arrangement was not without its detractors. For instance, Aucoin argued that the establishment of the policy group at the centre of this process was a major strategic mistake. 'It was much like using line departments to do the work of government and then having central agencies, instead of just coordinating, actually doing the policy for those departments.'[28] The analogy is telling, considering Nymark's professional background in the PCO. Moreover, Macdonald recalled that Nymark's mere presence in a senior position on the commission caused some tensions. 'A critical role was played by Alan Nymark,' recollected Macdonald, 'who I had known when he worked for the PCO. And initially there was kind of an inclination on the part of the research directors to reject this fellow who wasn't from the regular academic stream.'[29] Seeing Nymark had the confidence of 'the boss,' of course, helped allay some trepidation. Still, there were problems at the outset:'Initially, David Smith was very suspicious of him. He didn't like a guy coming from the bureaucracy. Alan [Cairns] and David kind of got the notion that we were going to have a federal government bureaucrat come in and try, just by being there, to twist opinions around into supporting government policy. But there's no doubt about the fact that in due course, he won people over. David had gone by then, so I don't know what his final view of the matter was. I remember when it started, and I'd had a very favourable experience with Nymark and wanted to bring him in, and then David, he can be very tough on this kind of thing, said "how did he relate to us, and what is he going to do?"'[30] But Macdonald thought Nymark would be an asset. Besides, he argued, 'I wasn't prepared to leave entirely to people who were outside government, the production of a piece which was going to have a high policy, process, and political orientation.'[31] Moreover, Macdonald could see that Nymark was the willing agent who could produce a pro–free trade final report, notwithstanding the objections of several commissioners.

As the consummate bureaucrat, Nymark cloaked his personal policy preferences and the belief system which shaped them. Indeed, Macdonald remembered that Nymark, as a senior bureaucrat in the PCO when Macdonald was a Cabinet minister, was a tough read. 'I had known him as a member of the Privy Council staff, and I can't remember from that time Alan's particular views on anything,' Macdonald recalled. 'And as a member of the Privy Council staff, it probably wasn't his role to express his views on things, except in dealing with the documents that were in front of him, as clerk of the Privy Council.' Nonetheless Macdonald developed an inkling that Nymark was pro–free trade. 'I think that intellectually, Alan probably was there with free trade before I was,' he recalled.[32] According to Winham, 'as I remember it – and I was working a level below the top – Alan Nymark was quite committed to the notion of free trade. He had decided.'[33] But as the consummate bureaucrat, Nymark recognized that his role was not to decide for his political masters. Rather, it was to guide them inexorably towards the rational, most persuasive, and beneficial policy conclusions. To this end, Nymark did his job extraordinarily well, for years after the fact, Macdonald professed not to know what Nymark's position was regarding free trade:

> I don't recall him specifically on the trade question in a broader sense. He made an important contribution by achieving a sense of synthesis. And I can't remember now, you would have to go and ask him, whether he said at a certain point, 'okay, the chairman wants to go this way, therefore, unless this ship's going to go on the rocks, we better make it possible for this to happen.' Alan lives intellectually as an agnostic, I think. You have to ask, 'is this a passionate, committed person on issues to the exclusion of all others?' Not at all. I think that there is a quality of agnosticism to his mind that causes him to look at all sides of an agenda. The consummate bureaucrat? Well, the consummate bureaucrat, maybe. It just didn't seem to me, anyway, that he favoured, or suppressed, or anything like that. But he's entitled to be remembered to his credit for the contribution he made.[34]

The issue of Nymark the bureaucrat versus Nymark the ideologue is important, for it is in the former role that he shone, even while acting out the interests of the latter role. Both he and Macdonald, of course, claimed that Nymark was simply a value-neutral servant of the commission. But Nymark's own interpretation of the predominant economic issues facing the commission and the country reveal that he carried his own ideological baggage. Having been part of the bureaucracy which was increasingly investigating free trade, Nymark had a sense that this issue could be cultivated. Aware of the changing ideological winds within the PCO, DEA, and ITC (see chapter 1), and, later, sensitive to new political masters in Ottawa, he foresaw that free trade would logically emerge from his interpretation of Canadian economic development, and that the commission could identify it as both a panacea for the country and its signature recommendation.

Nymark brought these perceptions to the commission, and they coloured his interpretation of the public consultation and research processes. Later, he argued that the public consultations were fundamental to the recommendations in the *Report*. He interpreted the public mood as suggesting that there was a sense of malaise arising out of the fact that Canada was just emerging from the deepest recession since the 1930s, and was at the end of a sixteen-year prime ministership. Nymark and the commission staff were concerned that the inquiry would become the lightning rod for the discontent rampant in the land. It was hard to see how the commissioners could go out and talk to Canadians without being stoned. 'Why would they want to listen to us? And would we get creative thinking? Was the country in the mood for creative, positive, forward-looking thinking in those circumstances, or were we going to simply put our Commissioners out to suffer all the bad feeling that we supposed was in the country?' wondered Nymark.[35]

But both the commissioners and their staff were surprised by what they found, according to Nymark. It was generally assumed that confidence in Canada had been severely shaken after a decade of high inflation and unemployment, and a deep recession. But the country was looking outward, people appeared to understand the pressures going on in the world, and to understand the need to be competitive. Nymark claimed this was not what the commission expected to find in the public consultation process.[36]

In addition, Nymark thought the changing structure of the Canadian economy appeared to be better recognized than expected. First, the Canadian economy had become more service oriented. Second, the manufacturing sector had undergone some decline and had to be sharpened up significantly. And third, the resource sector was undergoing severe challenges from abroad and might no longer sustain the Canadian standard of living as in the past. That sense of the changing structure of the economy and changing comparative advantage emerged forcefully in the consultation process, according to Nymark, more so even than it did in the research. Moreover, where free trade was concerned, the research teams had to be prodded in some cases to produce viable research. According to Nymark, in the area of constitutional and institutional reform and fiscal federalism, research teams actually came forward with more coherent interdisciplinary views than was the case with trade.[37]

Having formed his opinions based on his reading of the public consultations and research exercise, Nymark determined that the single issue which would galvanize the commission was absent. Some muttering about free trade had reached the commissioner's ears, but not very forcefully. When Macdonald dictated his 'leap of faith' as his preferred imprimatur, Nymark had a policy goal that dovetailed neatly with the emerging ideological position of the senior bureaucracy within the government,[38] and which was consistent with his own views. Now all he had to do was fit the facts to the evidence, and devise the vehicle through which the 'boss's' desires could be realized.

Target Identified: Full Steam Ahead

To consolidate and centralize control over the commission. Macdonald, Godsoe, and Nymark had to exploit the weaknesses of the inquiry. Fortunately for them, this was not difficult. All three were cognizant of the problem of bringing the research and public and private consultations together into a coherent whole. To try to synthesize these inputs into a report that the commissioners would agree to was a complex process. For instance, the troika recognized the research program's inability to integrate across its three streams. It was also aware of the difficulty of combining the public submissions, the research, and the commissioners' own views into a coherent whole. But Nymark saw a role for his policy group in overcoming these liabilities. He saw the policy group drawing together the consultations, three research streams, and commissioners' deliberations by centralizing control over the drafting of the *Report*.[39]

Nymark acknowledged that the commissioners were inundated by paper, including a draft *Report* of over 3,500 pages.[40] How they could intelligibly absorb that much data over a few months is not clear. Macdonald himself ruefully noted, 'we had a long series of meetings where we would have to consider issue after issue, and agree on what we were going to say and the directions we might go, and of course that had to be captured in the written word.' But while he tried to read all of the material in preparation for those meetings, at least in draft, he admitted to not absorbing it all due to the sheer volume.[41] Indeed, the commissioners were effectively being kept in the dark by the policy group's management of 'information overload.'

The role of the policy group was to devise a process that would bring together the major inputs into the commission. The dynamics and organization of this were devised by Nymark and Godsoe. They established a writing process in which each member of the policy group took a lead role in a particular field, and conscripted a handful of individuals to assist in drafting chapters for the *Report*. An attempt was made to get at least one senior individual who had worked on the consultations and two or three who had worked on the research to draft chapters under the direction of the policy group leaders, according to Nymark. Outlines of each chapter were set out, contributions from each policy group area were solicited, and attempts at drafting were initiated. Sometimes the pen was held by the policy group leader, sometimes by one of the researchers. Commissioners gave their input in either long papers or hours and hours of meetings. Eventually, the policy group came up with chapters it felt represented the commissioners' views.[42]

Nymark personally oversaw the group drafting the free trade chapter. But it initially lacked sufficient theoretical ammunition, even from the economics research, to support its case. Thus, according to Nymark, his group had to scramble to get research done on the issue. The lead research person on free trade was Whalley, whose program of research consisted mainly of holding seminars, and not particularly with a view of publishing a great deal of research on free trade. When it became clear to Nymark that the commissioners were moving in this direction, he commissioned more research, and asked Whalley to upgrade his approach.[43] The result was a lack of congruity between the published research program and the proposed contents of the *Report*. Nymark acknowledged this disjuncture, and had Whalley and his research group significantly alter its approach on free trade. In the end, he felt Whalley did a superb job with fairly limited resources.[44]

The research group changed its approach to free trade largely because Nymark kept sending Whalley and the others back to rewrite the relevant sections over and over. Breton recalled the way the policy group operated:

So, essentially what happened is that you had staff meetings with the chairman, Donald Macdonald with Gerry Godsoe and one guy, at the beginning, David Ablett or the journalist from Montreal, Michel Vastel ... and Nymark. These guys would sit there and they would talk about the content of the report. And so I think that it is fair to say that the basic decision to go for what I call bilateral free trade with the United States originated in that group. This led to preparation of a document, essentially written by John Whalley. A big fat document written by John Whalley, which was not accepted by the commission, not on the grounds of rejecting at that stage the idea of free trade, although some commissioners did remain against it, I think as you can see from the minority reports. But essentially on the grounds that the case was too weak. It is very hard to make a strong case. And there was not a very strong case.[45]

Winham was intimately involved in the efforts to pull together all the available information on free trade for the policy group. As one of the few researchers who worked full-time on the commission, he was in a unique position as a participant in, and observer of, the process. 'I got quite involved in the early period of the final report in addition to carrying on my research duties,' he recalled. 'And of course I had the time because I was full-time at the commission.'[46] The drafting of the free trade argument was surrounded by an air of uncertainty, according to Winham:

> We had had a couple of meetings. I remember John Whalley pulled together a bunch of stuff for an early draft of the report in the area of bilateral trade especially, and let me tell you that this was a difficult thing to do, because at that time it was not clear how the commissioners were going to go. And so we didn't know whether to lead or to follow, we didn't know what we were leading or following. It was extreme uncertainty ... There would be statements made by Macdonald or the other commissioners, and we would say 'aha!, that is what they are thinking of now, and so we had better be going in that direction!' Because we had the feeling that there wasn't much direction being given internally, and I suspect that was because the Commissioners hadn't really made up their minds.[47]

Winham was never sure whether free trade would be accepted by the commissioners, but pushed ahead on it anyway. 'It was always a struggle, and the outcome of it was never really particularly certain. I had developed convictions that it was the correct thing to do, but I never really knew whether or not the commission was going to end up recommending that. It was uncertain. It was always an uncertainty.'[48] What was clear was that the policy group was determined to pursue free trade: 'And I'm not sure what the chemistry was in [the commissioners] making up their minds, particularly on free trade, but we did determine that there would be an effort to try and push along the free trade issue. John Whalley was instrumental in this at a very early period because he commissioned a whole series of studies and he of course had a strong position in favour of free trade.'[49]

But attempts at a rough draft of a chapter recommending free trade were not immediately successful. Whalley's vast preliminary report did not seem to work very well, and several other proposals were made internally as to how to proceed. A series of meetings were convened at which Winham put forward a proposal, as did Whalley. Neither meshed with the other, though. 'These are meetings with Alan Nymark, as I recall, as chair,' Winham noted.[50] In the fall of 1984, Winham and Whalley put together a third draft after Nymark had rejected the first two. But Winham and Whalley were having basic disagreements about how best to make the free trade argument. Winham recalled: 'This would have been about September or October 1984. Things were moving fast at that point. We were having to pull together drafts. And then I remember working on a third draft which, as I recollect I was much more involved with on a kind of co-chairing basis with John Whalley, and that was put forward towards December, I guess. And that got criticized, scrapped and refurbished as I recall.'[51] Their inability to agree on the content of the free trade section led Nymark to farm out the work to another trusted bureaucrat and confirmed free trade advocate, Michael Hart. As Winham recalled, 'in the end I believe it was Mike Hart that wrote, or pulled together, what was out there in terms of our bits and pieces of the documentation.'[52] This process unfolded gradually, with the main protagonists conscious of the necessity of coming up with something acceptable to Nymark, and through him, to Macdonald. Hart's role in this stage was key. Hart was deeply, ideologically in favour of free trade, free markets, and greater economic integration with the United States, and against state intervention. It was Hart who had organized a series of seminars on sectoral free trade as part of the DEA's review of Canadian trade policy in 1982.[53] He was a key proponent of the neoconservative continentalist view.

Hart's first involvement with the commission came when he was approached by Bernier to produce a study on trade safeguards. He declined because he was not interested in this question. Hart then proposed writing a paper on the domestic economy and the international trading system, which was published as a commission research study.[54] That led him into contact with various academics on the commission, and he was next asked by Nymark to join the research advisory group on international trade along with Stairs, Winham, and others. Hart's self-described role involved reviewing papers written by this group. As well, he participated in Whalley's economics seminars on free trade.

Nymark had approached Hart, then a bureaucrat in the Department of Transportation, in the summer of 1984 and tried to have him seconded to the commission. Nymark had gone to External Affairs to Marcel Massé, who was the undersecretary of state, and told him that the commission was moving towards free trade. He suggested that Massé might find it helpful if they were to second somebody to the commission; it would then be easier to adapt the commission's recommendation to External Affairs and International Trade. But Massé could not spare anyone. So, Nymark recalled, 'I knew Michael Hart, and I went to Michael, and he was from External Affairs, but was on a secondment at Transport. I brought him in. He's a great drafter. So he did a lot of the drafting.'[55] Hart worked with

Whalley, Winham, Stairs, and Jack Quinn from the legal side, and others on the international trade dimension, giving them background material and helping them draft position papers.

Drafts of the free trade chapter were discussed by the commissioners on two important occasions, in November of 1984, and in January 1985. Hart recalled that it was after these meetings that the commissioners proceeded with the free trade recommendation. Hart prepared memos for them on the background to the issue, and practical advice on negotiating with the United States. He was disdainful of members of the commission who had academic backgrounds and no practical experience. 'So I was there to give the practical dimension to the question,' he suggested. In addition, Hart felt that 'Donald Macdonald's own personal views were very influential in shaping the final recommendation.' Hart had several private meetings with Macdonald, over lunch, for instance, at which free trade was discussed.[56] But contrary to the recollection of most others on the commission, Hart remembered that 'the discussion in the commission, both at the staff level, and amongst the commissioners, was very lively on this. There were pros and cons. The kind of debate that we saw in the country at large was very much reflected within the commission. There were several senior staff members who had very different views. There were senior staff who were very supportive of it.'[57] Hart further argued that the research studies also reflected the deeper debate he alleged was going on in Canadian society at that time about free trade:

What they [the research studies] did is they kind of gave an intellectual legitimacy to a debate that was going on, and the commission in many ways captured the debate that was going on in the country already. I mean it was not just taking place in the commission. There were a lot of conferences sponsored by industries, academic seminars, and so on. Free trade was in the air in 1983–1984, and the commission became the focus, because here was a major royal commission looking at the future of Canada from an economic perspective and so on, and that was the place to do it. You know, they hired 250 researchers and so on to do every Tom, Dick and Harry piece of work you can think of, and there are 72 volumes of research. The question was fully examined intellectually, and emotionally in that process.[58]

But others did not share Hart's expansive view of the free trade debate, either within the commission or nationally. Stairs's recollection is that the issues which emerged during the great free trade debate of 1986–8 were absent from the discussions among the commissioners.[59] They would not emerge until after the commission galvanized public opinion with its radical recommendation. And Barber recalled that, rather than setting up any real debate within the commission, the 'commissioners received a "hard sell" from the staff on the merits of a Canada-U.S. free trade area.'[60]

Notwithstanding ideological homogeneity among the writers working under Nymark, the process of developing an argument for free trade was not a smooth one. For instance, conflict emerged between Winham, Hart, and Whalley as to how to present the free trade case in the *Report*. According to Winham:

> There was an argument that I had with Mike Hart and John Whalley about all these pronouncements by the economists. Of course Whalley wanted them in, because to his profession it was essential, but I said, for crying out loud, don't put that stuff in because those economists are all over the map! One would say that there was going to be a 5 per cent GNP advantage, another will say 1 per cent, and another will say 10 per cent, or whatever. And I said, you know, this is only going to be embarrassing. I said it's best to just leave them all out, you know, you're just going to confound the thing. Well, anyway, in the end they felt it was best to put it in. I mean, these are the kind of debates that you have that go all the way through as to what should be in the final draft and what should not be in the final draft.[61]

To overcome these conflicts, Hart was given the task of writing the section of the final draft dealing with free trade. According to Winham, 'Mike Hart had been commissioned by Alan Nymark to pull the free trade drafting together; now at that point he had lots of bits and pieces. I had written a fair bit, and he had the sectoral study, which was cited a couple of times in the write up, and he had the stuff that John Whalley had brought in.'[62] Since most of the academic researchers for the commission had returned to their universities, Hart was left with a vital task: 'So Alan Nymark asked if I had the time, if I could take all the various pieces that had been forged by that time on this question, and rewrite it and recast it into the report. And so in the winter and early spring of 1985, I took the various materials that had been prepared by Whalley, by Winham, by Quinn, by Stairs, and so on, and massaged it, rewrote it, edited it and so on, into the draft report that dealt with that ... and it was integrated into the final report.'[63] After receiving Hart's revisions, Nymark took hold of the pen and put the final touches on the free trade argument, and this is what appears in the *Report* as the second half of volume I. Nymark's views reflected those of the other neoconservative continentalists working within the policy group. As Winham recalled, 'I suspect it was Alan Nymark's writing, and I suspect that what Alan Nymark took from a number of people, and I think including myself, was the notion that free trade represented an easing up of government interventionism in a trade dependent country.' Winham noted that several key players among Nymark's group shared these ideological views, including Nymark, Whalley, Sargent, most of the economists, and himself. 'I got quite wound up with it, I must confess.'[64]

There was little doubt that free trade was linked ideologically to the desire to reduce the role of the state. That was an explicit rationale for free trade, according to Winham:

> I tried to generalize and generate reasons why I thought Canada had gone for free trade. In a nutshell, I think that what you had at that period of time was economic reform that was being considered by a number of countries. You had the Reagan revolution, with deregulation in the United States. You had Mitterrand doing roughly the same thing. You had Thatcher doing roughly the same thing. The Germans were always deregulated, and so were the Japanese more or less, but also thinking along the same line. And I concluded that for a trade-dependent country like Canada, because Canada had a much higher trade to GNP ratio than any of these other countries, certainly the United States, that you couldn't deregulate the economy without free trade, and so therefore free trade becomes a natural sort of notion for deregulating the economy and moving, tilting let us say, because it is always overplayed in the press, but tilting more towards the private market and less towards government interventionism.[65]

Looking back, Warrian argued that in the policy group, there was strong ideological homogeneity. 'The fact is, the right had all of the staff positions,' he suggested. 'There were no people with broader social policy or political views. Conservative economics was in charge of the commission top to bottom. And that is reflected in the *Report*.'[66]

Conclusion

The organizational decision to consolidate control in the policy group helps to explain why the commission adopted free trade as a key recommendation. While it made use of the research produced by the commission, the group used it selectively and with an eye towards establishing the free trade case, following both its own ideological predispositions and particularly the preferences of the group leader.

Supporters of free trade among the economics research team alone, were not capable of imposing their views on the commission; agents and structures closer to the organizational centre of the project were required to carry to fruition the programmatic elements of the ideology. Nymark's influential policy group played this role. Nymark ensured that the key people charged with drafting the section of the *Report* on economic development strategies would be sympathetic fellow travellers. It was the task of these agents to shape the universe of political discourse into an acceptable form for presentation to the commissioners who, besieged with paper inputs and prodded by Macdonald, Godsoe, and Nymark, ultimately approved the free trade recommendation. The role of the policy group is vital, as is the personal conversion of Donald Macdonald. Together they provided the political and bureaucratic leadership necessary for transformative change.

CHAPTER 10

Leap of Faith:
Ideology in the Chair

I never would have suspected that at the end of it that I would come
through with strong support for free trade.[1]

The central role played by the policy group in drafting the *Report* begs
the question: what influence did the commissioners have at this important stage of the inquiry? Surprisingly, the answer is relatively little.
Chapter 11 will examine the limited capacity of the titular heads of the
commission to shape its decisions concerning economic development
strategies. The present chapter will first explain the role of the chairperson, focusing on Donald Macdonald's leadership in driving the free
trade agenda to further illustrate the role of political and bureaucratic
leadership in this story. It will also reveal the evolution of Macdonald's
thinking. Macdonald's transformation from a Walter Gordon nationalist to a Mulroney continentalist was the product of several interrelated
factors. Most prominent were the failure, in his perception, of several
Trudeau-era government interventions and the unrealized nationalist
impulse of those times, and his post-political life in the world of continental corporate power. As a cautionary note, the reflections upon
which these observations are based came some ten years after the commission, are limited by the capacities of human memory, and necessarily
contain an element of historical revisionism. Nonetheless, they provide
some measurement of the ideological position of the key commissioner
and reveal the extent to which he had absorbed and reflected the neoconservative continentalist paradigm.

The Power in the Chair

Assessments of Macdonald's leadership of the commission generally fell into one of two camps. A minority of observers felt the lack of direction plaguing the commission was a sign of weakness. They suggested that Macdonald was ineffective, and cite the apparent floundering and indecisiveness of the commission as evidence. But the majority consensus regarded this lack of direction as a shrewd manoeuvre on Macdonald's part to ensure that irreconcilable divisions did not surface among the commissioners, and that he was, in fact, a strong and able leader. Underlying both views was the issue of the unmanageable scope of the commission's mandate.

Thomas Shoyama, Macdonald's former deputy minister, believed that he was a strong chair, but one who did not try to dominate. 'I think that he was very skilled and quite able to provide the kind of leadership that was essential in that kind of exercise where you are dealing with such a diversity of people, interests and personalities,' Shoyama recalled.[2] Alan Cairns also subscribed to the thesis that Macdonald was, in fact, a strong leader: 'I would say I would lean towards the strong side. I think he is strong in the sense that he did view it as very important and threw a lot of his effort into it and he is intellectually in all kind of ways, very, very knowledgable. But not strong in the sense that he tried to take charge and impose his will on the commission. I think he realized "goddamn this is a big commission and we do not want it to fall apart." So, in that sense, I think he worked hard in keeping relations good amongst the commissioners. But I don't view that as weakness, I view that as just good political management.'[3] However, notwithstanding this view, Cairns felt that when the commission got to the actual *Report*, Macdonald was the important player. 'So I would say he was strong. In fact, if it had been without a strong chair, a commission with twelve diverse people and a mandate like that would have totally floundered. So it just seems to me to be impossible to assume that he was weak.'[4]

Gerrard Docquier's view on Macdonald's role as chair was that 'he was good at trying to bring people together. Of course Macdonald had strong views as the leader – but I don't think he ever abused that leadership. He was really running a good show.'[5] David Smith saw Macdonald's leadership in light of the difficulty of dealing with so diverse a group of people. 'Well they [the commissioners] were an enormously disparate group. But I was very impressed with how Donald Macdonald handled them, because you could have had such a disparate group really not come together,' Smith recalled. 'But he had a good skill in making sure they had their say, but also converged and supported, by and large supported, the final *Report*.'[6]

Alan Nymark was convinced that the personal reputation of the chair was the decisive factor in the free trade issue. He argued that the commission turned out to be very much led by Macdonald, and the other commissioners quickly sensed this. To support this contention, Nymark noted that while the *Report* was signed by all thirteen, if a straw vote had been taken even two-thirds of the way through, there would have been less emphasis on free trade. Nymark felt that it was Macdonald's persistence that this was an issue Canada had to face. Moreover, Nymark recalled, these were the early Reagan years, and there was a certain antipathy to the political and social culture in the United States. This implied that there was some reticence about moving in the direction of greater integration. But the commissioners developed immense respect for Macdonald, according to Nymark. Macdonald's expertise in the area of trade was greater than any of the other commissioners, except perhaps Shoyama, so he could carry it politically and substantively. And he did.[7]

Gil Winham generally concurred with this argument, suggesting that Macdonald was forceful in promoting the free trade agenda, and that his ultimate position reflected deeper underlying ideological sensibilities about how life ought to be organized and run. 'I think Macdonald probably, like all good chairmen, I don't want to say railroaded, although I might say it if I was being flip, but I think he was a strong chairman, and he, in the operations of the commission, I think he, somewhere along that fall [1984], or maybe even earlier, philosophically convinced himself that free trade was the correct way to go.'[8]

Macdonald's developing perception of the issues undoubtedly was important. The first indication that he was seriously considering free trade for which there is a written record came at a private meeting with the Employers' Council of British Columbia on 20 June 20 1983: 'We have to consider where we are going on tariff and trade policy. We are the only country at the GATT summit with a market of less than 100 million people. [Senator] George Van Roggen recommended that we move towards free trade with the U.S. There is an alternative. We could drop all of our protective barriers on the theory that those Canadian industries which survive would be competitive. In the further alternative, we could go back to a highly protective tariff system and take the drop in the standard of living which that involves.'[9] While he was already sketching the alternatives to free trade in a negative light, Macdonald knew that if he attempted to force his will upon the commissioners too soon, they might fracture into numerous cliques, and no overall agreement would be possible. 'If he had tried to overlord it, that could have led to severe strain within the commission,' Shoyama felt.[10] Macdonald was constantly walking a tight-rope between lack of direction and hesitancy in imposing direction, according to Cairns: 'But, to put it another way, to put it more kindly, it could well be that they realized that when they – "they" would mean Mac-donald and whoever were thought of as his key advisors, Nymark, and maybe the executive director, Gerry Godsoe – that once you started coming down on issues, within the commissioners themselves, then of course you generate minorities and factions and it is possible that the reason for the delay in the commission making up its mind on some of these issues was a desire to keep it united as long as they could.'[11] Ultimately, though, Cairns rejected this explanation. 'But I don't think that's the case. I think the mandate was construed as overwhelming and they had great difficulty deciding, and they knew that they were conceivably about to make an historic recommendation.'[12]

Clarence Barber found Macdonald to be fair to all commissioners. 'He did a good job because he really went out of his way to let everyone have a say. He didn't try to dominate the discussion at all.'[13] Nymark saw Macdonald's role as akin to that of a chairperson of the board, or a prime minister. But he also suggested that Macdonald went to extraordinary lengths to be just one of the commissioners. While he chaired and led the commission, he also tried very hard to give all thirteen at the table as much say as they wanted.[14] Moreover, Nymark regarded Macdonald as eminently fair in the chair. While ostensibly a positive characteristic, this in fact created some problems for the commission. Some found him too democratic. With the mandate as broad as it was, at different times in the commission there was a strong desire to try.to provide a greater clarity in the major objectives, and to focus on a narrower set of issues. But, Nymark claimed, Macdonald was ultimately true to the mandate.[15]

Macdonald was pivotal in setting the free trade recommendation in motion. But to enforce his authority as chairperson of the commission, he held in his hands a secret weapon. It is one of the more obscure facts about royal commissions that, as a matter of law, all that has to be produced is a report with one signature: the chairperson's. There is no requirement in law for the commissioners to write anything, issue a report, or sign anything. It is essentially the chairperson's report. Theoretically, Macdonald could have used this stick to entice his colleagues to concur with his position. The preferable situation, however, was to have all thirteen signatures on the page, which is what Macdonald got, much to his own amazement as well as Godsoe's. It was not easy, especially given the disagreements over the free trade issue. And in this one vital area, of course, Macdonald acted unilaterally, displaying tactical leadership skills that were both shrewd and divisive. His 'leap of faith' statement caught both supporters and detractors off guard, forced free trade onto the agenda as the predominant issue, and suddenly imposed direction on a heretofore rudderless ship. The underlying reasoning behind Macdonald's conversion to this position, as well as the tactical decision to pre-empt the commission with this stunning pronouncement, are treated below. But first, a brief examination of Macdonald's ideological roots is needed to indicate the depth of his later conversion.

Macdonald's Nationalist Roots

Macdonald, as already mentioned, started his political career as a Walter Gordon nationalist. Indeed, he regarded Gordon as a mentor. 'I had been in my earlier political career much associated with Walter Gordon. He was certainly one of my political patrons,' Macdonald admitted,[16] and he consulted with Gordon twice before deciding to work on the commission. 'I talked to Walter in this office, and just over the way in Commerce Court West, about doing it [chairing the commission], and he said "sure, go ahead and do it."'[17] Macdonald's early ideological leanings led him to support nationalist principles underlying a number of policy initiatives, such as controls on foreign investment. 'And in party debates in the 1966 Liberal convention, I strongly supported the views that Walter Gordon had put forward at that time. He was actively involved in the debates at that time on behalf of controls on foreign investment.'[18] Ironically, Gordon was perhaps the first intervenor to raise the issue of free trade before the commission. On 13 April 1983, as part of a delegation from the Canadian Institute for Economic Policy that included Abe Rotstein, Gordon said: 'I think you will have to have some discussion of the question of free trade in economic union with the U.S. John Crosbie thinks that that is what we should do. I hope we do not do that and I hope your commission has something to say about it. I cannot see how free trade with the U.S. would create more employment. I think there would be less employment. Expansion would take place south of the border because plants would be closer to markets there.'[19]

Nymark remarked that while Macdonald was not a protectionist, he realized there was enough of a reputation behind him that people were surprised when he advocated free trade with the United States, especially as the principal recommendation of the commission.[20] Yet, by 1983, Macdonald had undergone a personal transformation in his views. Indicative of the totality of Macdonald's conversion was his contention, a quarter-century after the fact, that anti-nationalist classical liberal economist Harry Johnson had been right: 'I have to tell you that just within the last year I read a monograph that I had not read for years – since I was a member of Parliament – a speech given by Harry Johnson in 1961 or 1962, in which he argued for Canada opening up its markets and taking a chance with the competition, which I'm sure I intellectually rejected at the time. But it seems to me now, twenty-three years on, that Harry Johnson, I thought, was proven right in the end. But I would not have agreed with him much of the time when I was younger.'[21]

Macdonald's membership in Pearson's government and Trudeau's Cabinet allowed him a ring-side seat in the development of policy at a time when Canada was evolving in social democratic and nationalist directions. For instance, in social policy, there was the extension of the welfare state. In foreign and trade policy, there was the 'Third Option' of diversification away from continental ties. In the cultural realm, there was the expansion of state protection for the Canadian arts community through a beefed-up CRTC and Canadian content regulations. In the area of investment, FIRA was empowered to review and restrict foreign takeovers of Canadian firms. But for Macdonald, apart from social and cultural policy, these became abject lessons in the limitations of nationalism. For instance, where FIRA was concerned, he said, 'it was a gradual disillusionment with the success or non-success of the FIRA that caused me to move away from it.'[22]

Moreover, as Macdonald's biography in the commission terms of reference points out, after he left politics 'he returned to his law practice at the firm McCarthy and McCarthy in Toronto in 1978. Aside from the practice of law, he conducts a class at the University of Toronto Law School and *serves on the boards of a number of corporations* and of charitable organizations ...'[23] The corporate boards Macdonald sat on represented a mix of domestic and foreign (i.e., American-owned) interests, making him simultaneously comprador and national bourgeoisie, fully implicated in the continental corporate structure. These companies spanned the financial, natural resource, chemical, and manufacturing sectors of the economy. The domestically owned Canadian companies included the Bank of Nova Scotia and the Alberta Energy Corporation; the foreign-owned subsidiaries included Shell Canada Limited, Dupont Canada Limited and McDonnell Douglas Canada Limited. All were major corporate players.[24] For instance, in 1984 the Bank of Nova Scotia ranked 124th overall in the *Report on Business* top 1,000 corporations in Canada.[25] It was the fourth largest by assets (worth over $59 billion) and sixteenth most profitable company in the country. The Alberta Energy Corporation ranked 176th overall with a cash flow of over $222 million and was the 54th most profitable company in Canada. The foreign-owned subsidiaries were significant corporate actors as well. With a cash flow in excess of $619 million Shell Canada was the third largest by cash flow, twenty-fourth largest by assets, and twenty-sixth most profitable company in Canada. Dupont Canada Incorporated ranked 250th overall, with pre-tax profits of over $63 million, making it the second most profitable company in the chemical field in Canada. It also was the fourth largest by assets and seventy-sixth most profitable company overall in the country. Macdonald sat on the boards of several American multinationals as well. These included Fortune 500 members McDonnell Douglas (St Louis, Missouri), Boise Cascade (Boise, Idaho) and Manufacturers Life Insurance Company. Moreover, he was a member of the Trilateral commission (Canadian Group), the Niagara Institute, the C.D. Howe Research Institute, and, strangely enough, the Harold Innis Foundation. He was also a member of the Canadian American Committee, director of the Institute of Research on Public Policy, chair of the International Development Research Centre, and member of the Law Society of Upper Canada. In addition, he belonged to the exclusive Toronto Cricket, Skating and Curling Club, and the Jovial Fish and Game Club of Buckingham, Quebec. This rarefied atmosphere provided the air which he breathed in the years between 1978 and 1985. Macdonald's immersion in the world of continental corporate power in his professional, academic, and social life undoubtedly had an effect on his thinking, and contributed to the ideological conversion that surprised even himself. As Shoyama put it, 'he had gone back to private life, had been on the board of directors of several multinational corporations, and he was very much in the business world. So I think he had very much developed this conviction. Where do we go? Free trade.'[26]

In addition, Macdonald was generally more interested in economic matters than other areas investigated by the commission. In Albert Breton's view, 'I think that's it's fair for me to say that once Macdonald accepted the job, he is not, and I don't think has ever been, really interested in constitutional matters. Consequently, he emphasizes the economics.'[27] Not surprisingly, then, the focus of Macdonald's attention was on economic development strategies.

Macdonald's Conversion

A variety of influences external to the commission shaped Macdonald's thinking. Not all of them can be catalogued here, but prominent among them were the impact of continental corporate power backed up by the academic arguments of the economics profession. For instance, Macdonald took several trips to Harvard to talk to economists he knew. They included Michael Porter, whose views on the fundamentals of Canadian growth affected Macdonald's thinking. Indeed Porter, a Canadian who made his career teaching at Harvard, was perhaps one of the most important influences on Macdonald's thinking, according to Godsoe.[28] Happily, these trips sometimes coincided with Macdonald's work as a board member on several American corporations. For instance, Simeon recalled flying to Boston with Macdonald and another commissioner one evening to have dinner with some Harvard academics. 'The next morning the two of us flew back to Ottawa, and Donald Macdonald flew on to Idaho for a board meeting of Boise Cascade, the big multinational timber company. So, you know, he was certainly of that world.'[29] As well, returning to his Bay Street law office, Macdonald served the interests of many corporate clients. While searching for solutions to Canada's economic problems, Macdonald was immersed in an ideological milieu which heavily influenced his thinking.

Internal to the commission, the public consultations and the research program also contributed to Macdonald's thinking. Notwithstanding that he was already immersed in corporate culture, Macdonald claimed that he 'saw' what the broader public and the academic community reflected in the commission. In fact, Macdonald's remembrances border on the myopic.

The View from the Chair: The Public Consultations

For the purposes of discerning the impact of the public testimony on Macdonald, it must be divided into two parts. The first is the public consultations, analysed in Chapters 4 and 5, for which a public record exists, the second is a series of 'private public consultations.' This was a round of closed-door meetings with representatives of corporate Canada which Macdonald and others credit with being an important influence.

Macdonald was driven by the public hearings to the conclusion that Canada's economic vocation, which had worked so well for the forty years since the war, was not going to be as promising in the future, particularly in the resource sector. The staples industries, the cornerstone of Canadian growth, were going to decline for a number of reasons, and he felt the testimony was prescient in this regard.[30] It became clear to Macdonald that the staples basis of the Canadian economy was no longer sufficient to support expectations of unlimited growth: 'For example, the mining industry was very explicit about this. They had limited expectations of growth. The grain trade came in, and they were hurting badly then, and it became clear that they were going to hurt in the future. And that therefore the old concept that we had of a country with substantial comparative advantage in a number of resource products which we could sell with little competition on the world market, and then protect the domestic market for manufacturers – that was something that wasn't going to persist, and we had better try to find another vocation for Canada.'[31] Macdonald summarized the impressions he received from the resource sector, noting the similarity in the message across different industries:

> The one area that the testimony brought home to me, and I think it's been borne out of the last decade, is the fact that, for a variety of reasons, the resource industries are not going to be powerful producers for us in the future as they have been in the past. And that miners came and gave testimony to that effect, and they are inclined to say tax policies were wrong and they could be changed to be more favourable. It was clear that the grain trade already was in trouble. The forest product industry, it was not so clear that they were running into the same problems as say with the environment that has appeared in the decade since then. But there was also a recognition that in terms of the forest product industry, the amount of fibre that we could harvest was limited, and we were right about there. So it was going to continue to be an important building block but it couldn't be the source of continuing growth. That was a message that came through almost from industry to industry.[32]

Strikingly, free trade did not suggest itself as the solution to these problems.

As for the manufacturing sector, Macdonald was not pressured extensively to promote free trade. Rather, he was struck by a certain ambiguity in the manufacturers' position overall. 'They certainly weren't pessimistic about the trade possibility. I can't recall a specific fragment that said "Yes sir, boy can we ever do well in a free trade agreement. Why don't you negotiate one of those?" But whereas in 1911 or even in 1946, Canadian manufacturers probably would have been insisting that the protective system remain, I can't recall intensive lobbying that we shouldn't change it.'[33] And notwithstanding the worst recession since the 1930s, Macdonald did not sense a mood of pessimism among Canadian manufacturers. 'Some of them, I think, felt quite confident about themselves. I don't recall them as having feelings of doom and gloom.'[34] He recalled in particular interventions from a bicycle manufacturing firm and a farm implement maker in St Georges de Beauce, south of Quebec City. 'Now these are guys from a small rural community. So there were some people who would have success stories and have done very well, and they made an impression.'[35] On the other hand, certain sectors did express concern about the consequences of free trade with the United States. 'It became quite clear to us then that in the [furniture] industry, that the furniture manufacturers said to us, you know, "you put us down there in equal markets with those guys from Appalachia, they'll eat us for lunch." And they did. It happened. What they had to say then was perfectly justified.'[36] These anecdotal reminiscences confirm the existence of splits in the business community on economic development strategies for Canada. But why did Macdonald privilege one view over the other in his thinking?

Nymark witnessed the transition in Macdonald's thinking and argued that the consultation process contained confident, forward-looking messages.[37] The realism of the global pressures and the need to recognize once and for all that Canada's basic economic relationships were not with Europe, but with the United States, had an impact on Macdonald. Moreover, Nymark argued, Macdonald saw that Canada had been transformed from the 1960s and 1970s to the point where it could no longer deny geography. Given that Canada relied for three-quarters of its trade on the United States, it needed to secure that relationship in a context of multilateral negotiations while not denying the need to be a global participant. Only by safeguarding Canada against American protectionism, using free trade to address productivity problems, and enhancing Canada's ability to compete globally, could Canada in the longer term hope to diversify its business relationships away from the United States. Nymark noted that Macdonald had been a part of the government which had looked for alternatives to Canada's trade relationship with the United States, and had failed. Canada could not, as a third option, deem or dictate diversification in the economic relationships, as it tried to do in the early 1970s. Canadian industry had the capacity to survive on a more diversified basis, but to achieve the productivity levels in growth necessary to be competitive with Europe and Asia, it was necessary to be competitive in the North American continent, Nymark contended.

The set of arguments that Macdonald claimed to hear in the public submissions indicated that access to a larger market was the key. Canada had a declining economy from a manufacturing productivity point of view and, more importantly, from a commodities point of view. And natural resources, the historical basis of much of this country's wealth, had a questionable future at best due to overseas competition and price instability. The answer with respect to services, manufacturing, and technology, was that Canada had to have larger markets to sell to. As the internal market in Canada could not support the level of activity needed to maintain Canada's standard of living, the question became, which large market should Canada focus on? Europe? Japan? The United States? The answer seemed easy and obvious, given that over 70 per cent of Canada's trade was with one of those markets already. Moreover, Macdonald had very strong views about Europe. He felt that it was Canada's natural competitor, as opposed to the United States, and that it would never 'do a deal' with Canada. The memory of the Third Option was still lingering in Macdonald's mind, since he had been a part of the government which had initiated that failed policy of trade diversification to Europe in the 1970s. Thus he tuned out when people started talking about a free trade arrangement with the European Community, claiming that it just was not going to happen.

Macdonald's thinking was also influenced, he reported, by various messages received from business backed up by economists in the hearings: 'Yes, we got some strong messages about the unemployment insurance program, as it existed. Some rather obvious ones from the Canadian Chamber of Commerce, but also some thoughtful ones from professional economists saying, 'Hey, you know we're, to a degree, subsidizing unemployment. That is encouraging it rather than the other way around." So that is an important contributor.'[38] But Macdonald's views were already developed in some cases. For instance, where foreign investment was concerned, Macdonald had already begun to see FIRA as a failure. 'I think I brought that from being in [law] practice here. And my experience in actually dealing with some of those situations,' he suggested.[39] In addition to the public consultations, a flurry of private meetings with corporate interests helped consolidate Macdonald's thinking.

For instance, in the winter and spring of 1983, the commissioners made a series of speeches to select groups in order to interest them in the work of the commission, as well as to solicit their advice. Twenty speaking engagements were scheduled between 12 January and 6 July 1983. Curiously, no notes were taken during these engagements, even though they contained opportunities for questions and answers.[40] Later, a series of meetings was held with the CMA as it became apparent that not only was the CMA going to treat free trade very seriously, but that they might well come out in favour of it. The CMA had long been regarded as one of the most protectionist bodies in Canada. When it began to look like it was going to favour free trade with the United States, Macdonald, Nymark, and Godsoe started talking about this possibility, and Macdonald himself started rethinking his own position. The CMA had not actually come out in favour of free trade, but the fact that it was even prepared to countenance it was a wake-up call to Macdonald. As well, the BCNI was suggesting, by September 1984, that free trade be considered in a new light, arguing that perhaps there was a lot more support in Canada for free trade with the United States than had been previously suspected.[41] On this basis, Macdonald also concluded that there was much less opposition to it. This belief proved to be mistaken, of course, as the evidence in chapters 4 and 5 revealed, and as the great free trade debate during the 1988 election indicated. Still, with the CMA and the BCNI leaning towards the free trade option, Macdonald was swayed to look at the issue more carefully.[42] Macdonald's claim that a number of issues came out of the public hearings not considered initially in the terms of reference, including free trade, refers primarily to these 'private public consultations.'

Warrian argued that a sharp division existed between the views of the chairperson and several commissioners regarding the message from the testimony about free trade. He asserted that a minority of the commissioners argued that there was no support in the country for the free trade option. According to this position, pro–free trade arguments did not accurately reflect the majority mood in the country and, at the end of the day, neither did they represent the majority view of the commissioners themselves.[43] Still, the outcome of the debate was very much shaped by the fact that a few influential business groups were privately coming around to the concept. Nymark acknowledged the role these groups played in the process. He saw in the briefs and the discussions held with the major business groups in Canada that the latter were moving in the direction of free trade. They told the commission that, for the largest firms, a process of substantial restructuring was under way, that the Tokyo

GATT round had been the penny that dropped for them, and that eventually they were going to have to rationalize since Canada could not remain a high tariff–protected economy. The message from big business, according to Nymark, was that manufacturing was going to have to adapt; the faster it did so, the easier it would be in the long run. Nymark felt there was a real sense from the big business community that it had seen the writing on the wall at the end of the 1970s and, by the time the commission consulted with it in 1983–4, it was very much on side.[44]

Nymark also noted the importance of the policy group in helping facilitate business's new-found faith before the commissioners. It worked extensively with the business community to help articulate key demands, Nymark recalled. The policy group went through all kinds of debates with the business community and with the commissioners as to whether it should be 'freer trade' or 'free trade' or a series of sectoral agreements, or whatever. They went through the whole debate, according to Nymark, bringing in a variety of business people and groups and others for intense discussions.[45] These influences shaped the view from the chair, and the relative influence of the public consultations must be weighed against that of the 'private public consultations.' The latter were more significant, and they were backed up by the chair's perception of the research program.

The View from the Chair: The Research Program

Nymark attributed to Macdonald a prescience that he saw as lacking in the research group. He argued that Macdonald had almost to drag the research to his point of view on several issues, including free trade. For example, he kept pressing his research directors to look at the changing structure of the economy and to recognize that the manufacturing sector had to be much more competitive and productive because of the shift in comparative advantage away from the resource sector. The research department reluctantly participated in those discussions because it was not able to find the dramatic evidence of that shifting structure in the way Macdonald saw it, according to Nymark, or, indeed, in the way that he seemed to perceive it in the public consultations.[46] For Nymark, it was largely a case of Macdonald leading the process, and the others coming round to his point of view. The evidence in the consultations led Macdonald to prod the researchers, with whom he maintained constant personal contact. Similarly, he argued, the research group did not see the efficiency gained from the freer trade initiative in comparison to other initiatives. Macdonald saw the need for a more dynamic shock to the attitudes of Canadians to make them understand how to be players in the wider world, a process that began in the United States.[47] Initially reluctant to commission much research in this area, it was only after the leap of faith, the 'shock' Nymark referred to, that reluctant research directors engaged work in this area. Macdonald recalled: 'Then there was the feeling that more work should be done, and this was one of the problems – a lot of theoretical work had been done by Ron and Paul Wonnacott, for example, or by John Whalley, but we suddenly, pressed by time and a shortage of funds, did some of the additional work to try and support the argument that instinctively and politically I had already chosen.'[48]

Nymark felt the research only revealed part of the greater picture that Macdonald saw where the benefits of free trade were concerned. Macdonald, according to Nymark, had an insight into the broader dynamic that a radical move like free trade would force upon the country to shake it out of its doldrums. The kind of traditional static gains from free trade which economists talk about were part of the equation. But there were more dynamic implications. If Canada became competitive and established a new basis for wealth, it could continue to support generous social programs, as well as play a larger role in world markets. In Nymark's view, this was the philosophical idea that Macdonald held, surprising though it may sound, given his ideological roots.[49]

As Macdonald reflected on what he had heard and read, and struggled to arrive at conclusions regarding future economic development strategies for Canada, he travelled a long way from where he had begun his political life.

Assessing Macdonald's Views

GOVERNMENT INTERVENTION
Macdonald was a member of the federal government from 1963 to 1977, and his political career coincided with one of the most dirigiste regimes in Canadian history. Thus, the concept of government intervention was well known to him. The main lesson he drew from this experience was that, apart from certain aspects of industrial policy and regional economic expansion, only intervention in the cultural realm and social policy was warranted, or even desirable:

> I think that in the area of cultural policy it was essential. It was often difficult, and even our allies never really thanked us very much for it. But it was

essential, not so much for the job creating measure in Canada, but as a clinical instrument. Unless Canadians had some means of talking to each other through the daily press, magazines, communicating through music and through other kinds of art, unless we kept a place in the sun for Canadian producers, we would be drowned out. It would be 'U.S.A. Today' every day in Canada, and I think it was important intervention. As I say, it was not done to preserve jobs at the CBC or Macleans, it was done for a purely political motive to keep their Canadian voice.[50]

During the 1960s and 1970s, much government action was animated by the ideological belief that intervention was appropriate in many sectors of the economy. Macdonald acknowledged that the view prevailed that there were many problems that could be solved by government. 'Some of them worked and some of them didn't. In industrial policy terms, it was said that very few of them worked. I think that government intervention in social policy, on the whole was beneficial, and that it will continue to be seen so.'[51] He cited the unemployment insurance system as an intervention that had worked well initially when it functioned as important protection for people who were genuinely displaced from work. But, in later years, it became a kind of a transfer payment policy as well, which Macdonald did not regard as a success. 'In the Royal commission *Report*, we concluded that it probably contributes to Canada running more of a higher level of unemployment than other countries because it's just more generous than in most other OECD countries,' Macdonald recalled. 'In one sense, it was a good intervention. Later on, some of the changes made were malignant rather than benign.'[52]

The recession of 1981–2, of course, figured prominently in the commission's life. It invariably got tied into the question of the appropriate level of government intervention in the economy as the commission went about its work. But while Macdonald recalled a certain amount of debate, 'it wasn't, as I recall, so much in favour of a kind of a Keynesian type of reaction to it of running a fiscal deficit in order to kind of work your way out of it. It was more of a reflection on the kind of policy that you should take, like training and employment and adjustments assistance and that kind of thing.'[53] It was evident to Macdonald that some people were moving away from Keynesian prescriptions. This affected his thinking on job creation and training, for instance. 'It seemed to me that a more indirect kind of intervention by way of manpower policy was indicated. There was a feeling that you didn't get the same leverage from the amount that you spent in public works that you might get if people in mid-career change their skills to something else.'[54] Certain problems with traditional employment policy, such as the fact that people sometimes receive training for jobs that are on the way out, led Macdonald to reassess the role of the government in this and other areas. He also acknowledged that there are all kinds of interventions in tax policy, some of which worked and some of which did not. But, he argued, it is hard to generalize about interventionist policy in this area. Allowing for the creation of RRSPs, for example, caused a lot of people to save for their retirement, which they might not have done in the absence of this policy, he suggested.[55]

On many occasions, Macdonald and the commissioners were confronted by business groups arguing vociferously against government intervention and, in the next breath, pleading for a continuation of their special status as recipients of various forms of government largesse. Macdonald cited the mining industry as a good example of this attitude. The posture, generally, was that the government ought not to intervene in the economy, except, of course, to supplicants from the business community, who ought to get special treatment: 'The mining guys were good examples. As you know there had been a much more benign taxation regime for mining prior to when the Carter commission changes were adopted. I think they were inclined to say "let's return it to that favourable environment. We run up some big costs finding and developing mines, and we should get some kind of additional help so that we can shelter the income that those investments produce in the early years, just so we can get back, not just 100 cents on the dollar, but 125." So that was the kind of thing that we got.'[56] This apparent contradiction did not seem to bother those who adopted this position. But Macdonald recalled that the 'gentlemanly' Thomas Shoyama was particularly adept at handling these groups. 'Actually, one of the great stars, in his gentle but very incisive way, at pointing out these contradictions was Tommy Shoyama, former deputy minister. He had a light touch in bringing the contradiction to light,' Macdonald recalled. 'And Tommy has a personal characteristic that I think is natural rather than cultivated, but when he gets interested in pressing home a point, he kind of smiled. And it's probably not a smile, it's the grimace of a man concentrating. But he looks benign when he's asking the questions. And in fact it's very difficult to answer.'[57]

INDUSTRIAL POLICY

After twenty years of hands-on experience with a variety of industrial policies, Macdonald regarded only two as having any lasting or significant success:

The most successful governmental policy that I can think of about inter-vening in industrial policy would be the Auto Pact, the policy of Walter Gordon and Bud Drury in 1963–4. And the most single successful policy I was involved in, and I was involved in a few of them, was the Syncrude development, the oil sands development in western Canada, where the crit-ical moment in time was the lead of the federal government and compli-ance of Alberta and the participation of Ontario. And you had government coming in with a slug of money that enabled that development to proceed and now it's important for major contributors to the Canadian petroleum supply. So those two worked.[58]

By self-confession, Macdonald was closely associated in a ministerial sense with a number of losers. Atomic Energy of Canada's policy of expanding foreign sales of the Candu nuclear reactor failed to generate a return on investment, according to Macdonald, who was minister of energy, mines and resources during many of AEC's foreign forays. The result was a sur-plus of heavy water plants and a series of money-losing contracts agreed to out of desperation to win business abroad. 'We took a bath on the Argentine contract in particular. We did it successfully with the one in Korea. The one in Korea was successful. The sale of a research reactor to Taiwan was successful. But on the whole, this was an intervention in which you put a lot of public money and got a poor result from it.'[59]

A more successful industrial initiative involved the government's inter-vention in the aircraft industry. In particular, its dealings with DeHavil-land Canada produced significant benefits. 'It was honestly a brilliant piece of work because it produced a set of aircraft that was uniquely suit-able to Canadian needs and flying conditions,' Macdonald asserted. 'And I think if one could argue in a broader sense that by having the Beaver, the Otter and the Twin Otter available, in that sense, you would have much more effective communication out to the Canadian Arctic at the time when oil refining and other resource industries were evolving.'[60] But even this silver lining had a cloud for Macdonald. When the govern-ment backed DeHavilland in its development of small commuter aircraft, it lost its momentum. 'You're running into foreign competition where you had no particular "shtick," you know, where there was no particular Canadian twist that gave us an advantage, and at that point, a lot of the money that was put in the aircraft industry was hard to justify.'[61]

The great difficulty with industrial policy was that no particular pat-tern could be seen in determining which policies were going to produce winners and which were going to be losers: 'One of the particular conclusions that I came to from being around the cabinet table and being concerned about these things was over a period of time, and I had seen some of what seemed like really hot ideas become losers, was the feeling of just what makes us believe that a bunch of bureaucrats sitting here in Ottawa can put forward a policy for a bunch of ministers sitting here in Ottawa that determine what are going to be winners and losers in the market? They thought they had good analysis but on the whole, the notion of defining a policy from the centre, over a period of time to me became theoretically unsupportable. There was a lot of practical evidence that it hadn't worked.'[62] But Macdonald was at a loss to explain the success of the winners. 'I guess that it would be remarkable to have a zero, zero, zero, zero batting average. Even the laws of chance would produce something right. And I never stopped to go into deeper analysis but I just know that the Auto Pact was one hell of a success.'[63] He drew interesting parallels between the Canadian labour movement's opposition to the Auto Pact in the 1960s and its opposition to free trade in the 1980s. 'I used to be amused at the interventions of Bob White against the Free Trade Agreement. I thought, you know, this is exactly the same thing. You know, the old fellow, George Burton, who was in charge of the Auto Workers in Canada at the time the Auto Pact came in was opposed to the Auto Pact. These guys, really, they're not dumb, they're just limited in their objectives.'[64] Within the commission, Macdonald was hearing mixed messages about industrial policy. 'I think we were still hearing some of the clichés from business organizations that the government should get out of the way. But then inevitably hearing from individual firms and industries that continuation of this or that support program should be assured.'[65] To deal with this apparent contradiction, Macdonald was inclined to suggest that it was time that the government tried to get out of some of these kinds of things. He expressed concern about firms becoming so dependent on government policy that it was no longer justified. Enabling an industry to adjust and assist is one thing, he argued. But it should not expect to continue indefinitely as a ward of the state. More importantly, Macdonald drew a link between industrial policy and trade policy. He came to believe that the former was inconsistent with the latter, particularly if your trade policy was based on free trade. 'You say you want to open your market up to competition and you should stop subsidizing firms. So there you go.'[66]

FOREIGN DIRECT INVESTMENT

Where foreign direct investment was concerned, an important exogenous development affected both the commission and Macdonald's thinking. As the commission was preparing its *Report*, the Conservative government was dismantling the foreign investment review process, replacing FIRA with Investment Canada.[67] Thus, 'it seemed clear that this, at least, was a policy decision that had been taken, and if you have to pick and choose among the ones that are still open and under which guidance is necessary, it didn't seem to be useful to try and revise the debates on that one.'[68] In Macdonald's mind, the government of the day effectively foreclosed one option, notwithstanding the fact that the commission was expected to make recommendations for the longer term.

In any event, Macdonald's view had been influenced by his years of practice in a major corporate law firm. He felt that the principal result of FIRA was to concentrate control of Canadian business in fewer and fewer Canadian hands: 'You had about ten or a dozen big groups like CPR, Bell Canada Enterprises, two Bronfman families, the Thomson interests, the Desmarais interests and so on, who were always, at any point in time when competition arose over the ownership of a corporation or acquiring it and so on, they had a distinct, in some case, almost a prohibitive advantage over foreign purchasers, just because of FIRA. So that on the one hand, setting out to try and prevent a greater concentration of Canadian industry in foreign hands, we were resulting in a competition policy problem of concentrating too much control in too few hands in Canada.'[69] After ten years of FIRA, and in Macdonald's case, nearly twenty years of pursuing that particular issue, it was not notoriously successful. In Macdonald's view, major Canadian multinationals had not developed where they had not already existed, despite the policy. Moreover, Macdonald did not subscribe to the view that it was possible to attribute rising levels of Canadian investment in the United States in the 1980s to FIRA. He did not support one thesis about the maturation of the Canadian capitalist class: that once Canadian capital got its own 'backyard' in order, partly through programs like FIRA which allowed it to expand and grow, it looked abroad and headed to the United States.[70]

Moreover, by the time the commission began its work, Macdonald felt that the foreign ownership debate in Canada had really run its course. As evidence, he offered the fact that neither arch-nationalist Mel Hurtig nor other long-standing advocates of foreign investment limitations appeared as witnesses before the commission. 'So, it kind of ran out of gas at that point, so we didn't hear very much about it. The issue just wasn't strongly before us.'[71] While this contention is contradicted by the evidence presented in chapters 4 and 5, it is conceivable that Macdonald did not 'hear' much about it because ideologically he had already come to his own conclusions.

REGIONAL ECONOMIC DEVELOPMENT

Regional economic development was a beguiling issue for Macdonald, both as politician and as commissioner. The basic conundrum was that regional economic development was frequently a political necessity, but an economic boondoggle. The focus of much of this policy is Atlantic Canada, and Macdonald knew there were economically unjustifiable projects there. But he was also cognizant of the storm of protest that had greeted an earlier royal commission when it suggested that residents ought to move out of their region in search of opportunities. Macdonald argued, 'it is very difficult in a confederation to say, "well, nothing much can be done about those guys. Just let them move." As a matter of fact, Walter Gordon really didn't say that, but the preliminary report, as I recall, for the Gordon commission left that impression. And of course, it was a political disaster. Atlantic premiers and Atlantic newspapers and so on dropped on him and on the government.'[72] More often than not, as this example revealed, the political outweighed the economic in calculations of regional economic development. But while the reasons for providing financial assistance were valid ones in a federation, Macdonald argued, governments are not very good at picking winners.

There were exceptions, of course. Macdonald cited the Michelin tire plant as an example of successful regional development, notwithstanding the flak it received from the Americans over unfair subsidies. Macdonald acknowledged that the Candu reactor was not a great success in foreign sales, but it was a great success in New Brunswick. But, he concluded, there were a lot of losers. The main problem was how, as a politician, one squared the circle of rejecting industrial policy and yet applying it to a particular region in the guise of regional economic development. 'That's why it's not easy. The answer is yes, it's a lousy way to do things, but can you simply do nothing?' Macdonald argued. 'Critically, I don't think you can do nothing. You struggle to try and do something to help you through that situation.'[73]

While the commissioners heard about the importance of regional economic development primarily from the Atlantic provinces, it also surfaced as an issue in other locales. Macdonald remembered in particular the moving testimony of workers in communities like Windsor, Ontario in the wake of the 1981–2 recession. 'Now Windsor was a good example of a community which took a beating. Windsor was probably on my mind because of the eloquence of the statements made there. In communities like Windsor a number of people turned up to talk about the dislocation of people's lives that that particular event had caused.' He claimed that

this: 'certainly had an important impact on the commission and its recommendations. And not just because of changes in tariff policy, but
because of other changes that occur in the economy from time to time,
it is important to have adjustment assistance provisions. It's not only
important for the individuals to have adjustment assistance so they can
move to work. It's important for the rest of the economy that they can
move to work because otherwise they'll become dependent. And certainly the 1981–2 recession had, because it had left such scars on a community which pretty well, since the end of the war, had avoided this kind
of experience, that certainly had an impact on it.'[74] In particular, the testimony caused the commissioners to consider adjustment assistance for
workers and communities dislocated by economic upheaval due to
changes in government policy. According to Macdonald, it made the
commission think that 'government really shouldn't just sit back and say
"Okay, people are out of work and that's too bad, but Adam Smith will
take over and they'll all wind up working again." The period of time in
which that happened is such that most of the main economic aims of people are destroyed and so too is their self-confidence.'[75] Nonetheless, the
impulse to restrict the role of the state combined with the perceived legacy of failed industrial policies. This outweighed the desire to develop a
coherent and comprehensive industrial policy which might alleviate
cases like Windsor or Atlantic Canada. Instead the political defence of
disjointed regional economic development prevailed, despite its lack of
economic logic.

TRADE POLICY

Macdonald, of course, had some academic background in the area of
international trade. For instance, shortly before he took on the commission job, he taught a course at the University of Toronto Law School
called 'Public Policy Formation,' in which 'we tried to use almost a business school technique of having four major cases that we would talk
about. And one of those was the Tokyo round of trade negotiations.
And I had done some work in the field in the past. A thesis I did for a
diploma at Cambridge was on GATT. So this was an area with which in a
textbook sense I was familiar. So I did have some background.'[76]

Macdonald's views on trade policy had a long genesis. Although initially a Gordon Liberal, as minister of finance in the late 1970s he moved
to the right.[77] Direct exposure to the growing continentalist neoconservative views among the senior mandarins in Finance had its impact on his
thinking. The power of this group to reprogram its ministers is enor-

mous.[78] By the early 1980s their influence, coupled with Macdonald's reading of Canadian history and relations with the United States, suggested that Canada could simply not afford to stand still any longer: 'We couldn't remain with the type of commercial policy that we had since the National Policy, since 1878. We had it for about 110 years, and we just couldn't stay in that particular position. We had to keep moving. If we wanted to grow, then Canada had to accept the fact that it was no longer a colony, it was no longer simply a resource supplier, it had to be prepared to break out of that kind of thing. And really the only way that you were going to increase your access to a market that would make it possible for you to become competitive on a world scale was to be prepared to open up to the market of our biggest customer.[79] In addition, Macdonald had admired the contribution to internationalism of the Pearson years as Canada played an important role in the construction of post-war multilateral institutions, partly to balance the disproportionate weight of the United States in Canadian-American relations. Moreover, he was a member of a government in the mid-1970s whose commitment to counterbalancing the influence of the United States found expression in the Third Option policy and other initiatives. But by the 1980s, he had seen the poverty of multilateralism, and on this point he was unequivocal. He had been deeply involved, first as a minister, and then as a practitioner, in following the multilateral trade process. He felt he knew the limitations of Canada's involvement therein, and he determined that this was no longer the preferred route. For instance, he developed a scepticism about the GATT. 'The Uruguay Round had not been announced, but I knew there was another round coming. And given the length of time it took to achieve what was achieved in the Tokyo Round, I knew that we were not going to be able to make the progress that I thought was necessary.'[80] Hence, Macdonald converted from multilateralism to bilateralism. In addition, his years spent in the continental corporate world had a profound impact on Macdonald's thinking in this area. Unremitting exposure to continentalist ideas from his colleagues on corporate boards and from clients in his law practice contributed to his reconceptualization of the Canadian-American relationship.

As Macdonald crystallized the free trade notion in his own mind, he was also conscious of other imperatives that could be served by advocating so radical a step. It could potentially focus the commission on a noteworthy policy recommendation, prevent the commissioners from fragmenting into cliques, and salvage the reputation of his commission. This was all realized through the political machinations of his 'leap of faith' statement, the impact of which is the subject of the next section.

The Impact of the 'Leap of Faith'

The 'leap of faith' statement had a dramatic effect on the internal dynamics of the commission, and on the free trade debate in particular. Macdonald admitted at the time that he made the remark that 'these were his own words and that the thirteen members of the commission have not yet reached a consensus with respect to trade policy.'[81] The reactions of the commissioners varied according to their own ideological predispositions. Those not persuaded of free trade thought Macdonald was wrong to go public, while those who supported free trade welcomed his bold pronouncement. It was a risky strategy, as it introduced a side issue into the commission's already overloaded agenda, which was, 'why was the chairperson talking publicly without consulting with the other commissioners?' As Macdonald explained:

> I, at a certain point, got a head of steam of my own on it. It was not as though I had to be talked into it. At a certain point I arrived at my own conclusion, by November 1984. There was a meeting down at Harriman, New York, and I went public with Bill Johnson of the Globe and Mail on that. And, I have to recognize afterwards, rather unfairly to Gerry Docquier. But we had a very full discussion down there, and Bill said, 'you know, what you said is a substantial departure from where the world expects the commission to be.' So I decided rather than him writing a story and attributing things, I might as well give a story. But I agree, it did circumscribe the choices that the others had available. I would also add that, having done that, I could have lost it altogether. There was a chance of that.[82]

Macdonald rolled the dice and gambled, even though such a precipitous move might irrevocably split the commission. 'It was just something that occurred. But I think it had begun to become apparent by late 1984 that I was moving in this direction, and apparent that I was not alone.'[83]

Shoyama felt that Macdonald's arbitrary initiative was meant to galvanize the commission while giving it more of a public profile.[84] Macdonald and Godsoe had discussed how the commission could be galvanized around a particular issue. But even Godsoe was surprised, not so much that Macdonald said something in public, but by what came out in the public pronouncement.[85] Cairns felt that the pronouncement carried considerable weight for the commission, considering the source. His speech 'was kind of a combination of "this is my personal view, but I am the chairperson of this commission, so what I am saying carries some weight." So this was the direction we had to go.'[86]

Winham argued that Macdonald's developing perceptions of the Canadian economic condition led him inexorably down a particular ideological path:

> And I think that is the reason he came up with the statement 'leap of faith,' which I think was an analytically correct and politically inappropriate thing to say, because it was panned, as you know – I mean everyone should jump into the abyss with Donald Macdonald? But I do think ultimately that issues of liberalism or protectionism or something like that are based on beliefs and values of how life is best run. And I think ultimately ... that democracy, which is freedom of politics, and free trade and liberalism, which is freedom of economics, are bound up together in a peaceful, orderly international system. And I think some of those philosophical ideas came to Macdonald over that year and culminated in that fall of 1984.[87]

The debate within the commission at that point had barely been engaged and was far from settled. In meetings subsequent to the statement,commissioners like Messer, Docquier, and Barber continued to oppose the idea while others, like Breton and Shoyama, were lukewarm or held their counsel. But all eventually realized the political utility for Macdonald of having gone public, and the futility of opposing the powerful chair, who was supported by the policy group and the economics researchers. But at no point was there ever unanimous support expressed for the chair's position, Macdonald recalled: 'It never was unanimous. Jack Messer and Gerry opposed it. And I think that Clarence, though a good economist, still had some reservations about it. Well, they took their position, I thought, with great good grace. But they were quite explicit. Gerry was vice-president of the CLC and said "look, there is no way I can support this," and he got some assistance from the Congress and worked out his position. I'm not sure if Jack got some assistance from the Saskatchewan NDP. He knew that he then had to put a case from a minority position, and he did that.'[88] Notwithstanding the risks associated with taking this position, Macdonald was firmly convinced of its correctness. As for the impact of his statement on the other components of the commission, for example, the Research directors, or Nymark and his staff, Macdonald professed not to be sure. 'I think that I can't be quite sure, you know. If they didn't like the boss's position they kept their own counsel. I think some of them, at least, were glad to have the direction.'[89]

Dennis Stairs recalled the free trade issue being given tremendous momentum by Macdonald's 'leap of faith' statement. 'That caused a considerable flurry of discussion around the shop, because it was known that this had not been a decision of the full commission,' Stairs said.[90] He was at the conference at which Macdonald uttered the fateful words, and unsure of the extent to which it was a calculated strategic ploy. Nonetheless it was given considerable attention because many thought Macdonald was trying to pre-empt the commission. Stairs regarded the statement as a reflection of the need to impose some direction on what was, to that point, a rudderless commission by engaging in some creative, albeit risky, 'people management.' The question of timing was crucial. When Macdonald made his pronouncement, frustration among the research staff and others with the lack of direction from the commissioners was running pretty deep, according to Stairs. He also allowed that Macdonald had long since come to the realization that he was dealing with a pretty eclectic bunch. 'One of the reasons we got very little direction from him at the beginning, I think, was that he was very conscious of the fact that he had somehow to get as much consensus out of this eclectic gang as he could,' Stairs argued. 'If he jumped too soon, he ran the risk of generating cleavages which then could not be closed later on.'[91] Macdonald was initially very cautious, but by the fall of 1984 he realized that he was going to have to push the commission towards consensus. 'And as it turned out, his decision to go then was about right, I think, looking at it from his point of view,' Stairs maintained, 'if that is what you want to do, and you want to get the commission behind you, I think by then, the uncertainty and lack of decision had gone on long enough that people were about ready to be led, even though some of them might have protested.'[92] The move caused a kind of 'temporary irritation,' according to Stairs. But it had the desired long-term effect from Macdonald's point of view.

Breton recalled the surprise with which the other commissioners greeted this development. 'We were taken aback. We knew nothing about it,' Breton remembered. 'The announcement came through the media that the commission decided to go for bilateral free trade.'[93] Breton was unclear as to Macdonald's motives, but he knew that several commissioners were upset with his actions. 'However unhappy some of us might have been – learning through the media this was it – I do not know if it was intentional. Macdonald is crafty enough that I think it must have been. He has been in that game all his life, you know.' But in the end, 'there would be no big debates. Clearly he could not have persuaded, he did not in fact sway guys like Docquier. People like Shoyama and Barber, who have all converted to free trade since, at that time were so-so.'[94] But Macdonald did not need to sway his opponents, since they occupied relatively powerless positions. 'So the decision on free trade was discussed and debated, but it had been announced in public. It would have been a tremendous business for the commission to reverse that. It would have just put the chairman on one side, and the commissioners on the other.'[95] Shoyama recalled that 'there might have been some private conversations about it, because it didn't come up in commission meetings as far as I can remember.'[96] For Breton, this signalled very clearly the circumscribed role that the commissioners were expected to play. 'At that time, it became very clear that we were not in a decision making body, we were there more or less to say 'this could be improved or "this should be changed that way" and I think that throughout, at the end, that process was reinforced.'[97] Moreover, the November 1984 announcement was timed such that it left little opportunity for opponents of free trade to mount an effective opposition. In any event, such a move would have fractured the commission, Breton recalled. 'The government was saying you better bring this thing to an end by September 1985, I think. Which meant that we had to finish by April. We stopped meeting, I stopped going to Ottawa in April 1985 for the commission.'[98]

Macdonald's motives were not as obvious to Breton as was the effect of the pronouncement, but it was not enough to cause a revolt among the commissioners. After the public hearings process ended, the commissioners met rarely as a group, except to discuss the drafts of the *Report*. In those meetings, time was at a premium, as the commissioners had mostly returned to their real working lives. In the absence of an organizational focus, or a champion to lead them, any dissenting commissioners found themselves isolated and marginalized not by stealth and planning, but by ennui. 'There was no revolt or anything like that. I think we were too numerous to revolt,' Breton believed. 'To have a revolt, it would have been a long, drawn-out type of thing. Because we were so numerous, we did not meet that often.'[99]

Perhaps the only agent who might have led opposition to free trade was Docquier. Given his labour background, it was obvious that he was in a position to do so. But his position was a two-edged sword. As the 'labour representative,' he was expected to oppose the proposals of corporate Canada; but for the same reason, his opinion carried little relative weight.

Docquier was very surprised by the leap of faith statement, and felt it had an immediate impact on the thinking of most of the other commissioners. 'I think a lot of the others, their mind switched from 'free trade, well maybe, to free trade – we cannot reject forthright anything that is submitted to us,'" he recalled.[100] Yet very little subsequent discussion ensued about Macdonald's statement, according to Docquier. In part, this was because Docquier intuitively recognized that Macdonald's position was linked to some of the broader ideological trends becoming apparent in Canadian society: 'There was this move to the right, and the last kick at the cat was when the Conservative government was elected. There was obviously right there an indication that the country was in a different mood, and that the more right thinking was to prevail. And it did for nine years, let's not kid ourselves. I think everything changed in these years from a more liberal kind of thinking, and a more nationalist kind of thinking, to a more international, free trade, market-oriented way.'[101] Thus Macdonald adopted and reflected the ideological views of neoconservative continentalism, and made a substantial contribution to a new policy regime rooted in the discourse of free trade.

Conclusion

When it became apparent that Macdonald – Walter Gordon's protégé and friend, the left-Liberal from the nationalist wing of the party, the elite spokesperson for traditionally protectionist Ontario business interests – was prepared to consider free trade with the United States, it caught the commissioners by surprise. When Macdonald went public with his position, those commissioners who felt free trade was not something they wanted to see happen were suddenly left trying to figure out who was going to defend against this juggernaut. But by then it was already too late.

Most commission participants felt that Macdonald played an integral role in driving the agenda towards free trade. Nymark certainly felt the outcome was the result of the chairperson's own will. 'Now I think a lot of where it ended up has to do with the chairman,' he recalled. 'And my own interpretation of how it evolved, and this is my own interpretation, and it might not jibe totally with Donald Macdonald or any of the other commissioners, but I think it was very much him.'[102]

Perhaps the great irony of the entire process is that Macdonald maintained, 'I never would have suspected that at the end of it that I would come through with strong support for free trade.'[103] Notwithstanding this admission, the phrase 'leap of faith' has entered the Canadian lexicon. As a choice of words, it proved rather unsettling in the great free trade debate of the late 1980s, suggesting as it does a potential plunge into a void. Nonetheless it had resonance for both sides of the debate, and graphically symbolized the choice Canada would soon be asked to make. Macdonald had made the choice, partly as a result of his immersion in continental corporate life, and partly as a result of his disillusionment with Walter Gordon nationalism, and with Trudeau's nationalist proclivities. According to Rod McQueen, 'The real leap of faith was Macdonald's. As Emerson has said, "an institution is the lengthened shadow of one man." Never was it more true than with the Macdonald Commission.'[104]

The Commissioners' Role and the Final Report

> Commissioners believe that in some important areas we Canadians must significantly increase our reliance on market forces. Our proposals to increase our openness to the international economy and, specifically, to enter into a free trade arrangement with the United States reflect our general preference for market forces over state intervention as the appropriate means through which to generate incentives in the economy, from which growth will follow.[1]

The role of the chairperson of a royal commission can only be understood in the context of the working relationship of the commissioners as a whole. As noted in chapter 2, royal commissions are granted considerable leeway in their design and execution. The chair and his or her chief advisers often enjoy broad discretion in translating the imprecise terms of reference into action. This chapter examines the role of the other commissioners. It looks at the drafting of the commission's *Report* from the perspective of those commissioners, and shows that debate over Macdonald's free trade declaration was muted and controlled. The role of the commissioners was limited, and therefore no credible and sustained opposition to Macdonald, or to the policy group, would come from this group. If the march of neoconservative continentalism was going to be stopped, it would not happen here.

The Commissioners' Role

The design of the Macdonald Commission posed some unique problems, due in particular to its size and diverse make-up. As a result, opinions differed as to the appropriate analogy to describe the role played by the commissioners. Some thought they functioned collectively as a 'board of directors,' others thought they were more like a 'Cabinet.'

Cairns preferred the analogy of a board of governors. 'The commissioners conducted themselves as a board of governors, sort of, or a board of directors. That is, they sat and received things,' Cairns recalled. This rather surprised Cairns: 'I guess I had thought that they would be more kind of in charge and hands on and decisive and working more closely with us or with the rest of the commission and staff and so on, but that was not the case.'[2] Cairns was unhappy with the characterization of the commissioners as forming a Cabinet, because they did not have portfolios and specific responsibilities, nor were they responsible for separate jurisdictions. 'I would not say a Cabinet is a good analogy as compared to a board of directors,' he argued. 'But while it's a board of directors that ultimately is sort of making the decisions, they were not sort of operationally in charge. In that sense, things kept flowing to them. They would have meetings and discuss things and the direction of events, but it was all the staff, including research, which was really doing all the work.'[3] If this analogy is correct, it implies that important policy development functions existed elsewhere within the commission.

Several commissioners assumed an advocacy role for particular interests, as Cabinet ministers do with specific responsibilities and jurisdictions. Most obviously, Docquier brought a trade union interest; Seaman, an energy producers' interest; Messer, a western Canada and agricultural perspective; and several commissioners, including the chair, brought a business perspective. Shoyoma saw some limited parallels between the way a Cabinet operates and the way the commission functioned. 'There are parallels, but of course a Cabinet is composed of full-time ministers with their own axes to grind, concerns to push, particular constituencies or interests to serve.' The analogy was further limited by the differences in the decision-making process, according to Shoyoma. 'In Cabinet you make a decision, and it is very specific and concrete. You bring in mandatory wage and price controls – bang! Whereas in this case, what is the decision? We are going to recommend this, that or the other thing?' But, he concluded, 'There are parallels there in terms of having politicians you have to look to to make the decisions, and you have a bureaucracy.'[4]

Breton supported the view that the commissioners' role was like that of a Cabinet, but an odd one in which ministers lacked the decision-making prerogative: 'the commissioners in a commission like this play a very strange role, because on the one hand, we were not there to do the decision making process ... I'm not blaming anyone because don't forget we were thirteen, an enormous Commission. So we were not part of any of decision-making process except probably as ministers are in cabinet, to a degree. I don't know how they work, but I would imagine that some ministers follow some particular dossiers, but all the rest, their officials say yes, no, I like it, etc. So we were more or less like this.'[5] Breton preferred this analogy because Macdonald had been a minister. 'You have to remember, to understand how the Royal Commission works, that Macdonald was the commission's chairman, and had been for years and years and years a minister in the government,' Breton recalled. 'Therefore, he learned to work the way ministers work. So the commission really worked the way the government worked.'[6]

In both analogies, it is noteworthy that the commissioners largely played a reactive rather than a proactive role, receiving information rather than initiating actions. This was particularly true where drafting the *Report* was concerned. As Jenson points out: 'People sometimes point to the "part-time commissioners" as a factor contributing to commissioners' difficulties in coming to grip with the issues ... Discussions of the Macdonald Commission stress that its size and diversity hindered this kind of focus within the commission. One result was that little sense "of the whole" ever took hold in that commission. Decisions were dealt with seriatim and the final report lacked the coherence and vision that it might have had. Moreover, the final product was controlled more by the actual "holders of the pen" than by the commissioners themselves.'[7] This led to some dissent, as commissioners discovered that their roles were more prescribed than they had presumed. An examination of commissioner involvement in the writing stage will explain why this was so.

The Process

How did the commissioners assimilate information and arrive at recommendations for the report? The process essentially reinforced the idea that they were rubber stampers rather than decision makers. The commissioners, for instance, did not write the *Report* themselves. Draft material came up to them 'through the kind of senior team, Cairns, Nymark, Godsoe, who put in long hours themselves debating as to how this should be dealt with,' according to Macdonald.[8] On occasion a commissioner would be asked to draft something if he or she had special qualifications, or a strong viewpoint on a given issue. But this was the exception to the rule.

The design of the *Report* was determined by the controlling oligarchy from the policy group, including Godsoe, Nymark, and Macdonald. Godsoe came up with the structure, which he talked about with Macdonald, and he negotiated with the commissioners over the topics to be addressed, the order, and the logic, all on the understanding that the *Report* would be drafted without recommendations. This was because, Godsoe recalled, the commissioners refused to make decisions. Those were postponed up until the last minute because there was insufficient agreement among the commissioners on several issues, including free trade. Needless to say, this proved to be a very frustrating process.[9]

The policy group then came up with a model of how each chapter would look by pulling the various threads of the commission together to form a coherent set of statements about what the commissioners felt about various issues. These in turn were transformed into recommendations. The idea of having the policy group do this, according to Godsoe, was to try and pull the statements and the recommendations together. Rochon and his staff on the hearings side produced a series of quotations on various topics which the policy group took to the commissioners and which found their way into various places in the *Report*. They were also used to inform the academics of positions taken in the public consultation process. The policy group was seen as the glue in the system. Policy group members would write a paper in collaboration with Nymark, and the result would become a section of a chapter of a hypothetical *Report*.

Godsoe organized the process into blocks divided into monthly cycles. For instance, during the first week of the month the commissioners would consider macroeconomic issues, the second week might be microeconomic issues, the third week might be social policy, and the fourth week might be institutional reform. Then the cycle would begin again with a slightly different emphasis, because different information would have become available. Typically the commissioners would receive a document the Friday before week number one began and read it over the weekend. They would then meet as a group (or however many were available) on Monday or Tuesday for a one- or two-day meeting in which they would comment on the document. The commissioners would be joined in this work by the policy group and its writers, and any researchers who had an interest in the topic under discussion. They would all breeze through the draft and send instructions back to the writers, who would turn it around, and thirty days later they would have a completely new draft incorporating the changes.[10] According to Cairns: 'As these things were being written, the commissioners would come down and we would have maybe a couple of days in which we would be going through drafts of the *Report* and the chairman would sit there and would say "okay, we're on Chapter 27, anybody got any problems with page one, two, and three?" One of the researchers would say, "look you had better look at page five. There's some quite important things that are controversial. Do you understand what you're agreeing with?" Sometimes that would produce a change.'[11] In the meantime, of course, Godsoe and Nymark were working to make sure that the writers understood what their instructions were and that there was a clear channel of communication. Godsoe argued that he and Nymark had been living with the commission much more closely than the writers, so they could fill in a lot of blanks, and say, 'well, look, what the commission really meant was.'[12] This process went on for about six months.

The drafts of the *Report* began with a historical-descriptive section, then proceeded with a status report, an analysis, and a selection of options. These were all produced by writing teams put together by the policy group. But in many cases the commissioners would review the drafts and complain that they did not contain what they understood to have agreed on. According to Godsoe, this provoked fierce debates, particularly over the historical sections, mainly because a number of the commissioners took a personal interest in some of the events described. By this time, the commissioners had attended a series of seminars staged by the policy group aimed at educating them about the options and the analysis. But few seminars on the historical picture were painted in the drafts. Several battles on the descriptive parts of the drafts they ensued.[13]

Once these were resolved, the staff role theoretically ended, and the commissioners were expected to fill in the rest with their recommendations. But Godsoe found that they would stall and stall. In the fall of 1984, Macdonald and Godsoe 'were sort of doing some table pounding' to get the commissioners to agree on various issues, including free trade.[14] Deadlines were looming, and Macdonald had to get the commissioners to sign off if the final product were to be ready for translation and publication. Godsoe, as the chief administrative officer, was following a critical path, with dates by which the commissioners simply had to make decisions and move on. He recalled that there was a lot of bullying to get them to meet those dates so that the commission could stay on schedule, and within its budget.[15]

Once they got to the formal drafts of the final version of the *Report*, the process started to close down very quickly. Overall, this was a period of exhausting work because of the sheer amount of material. As Godsoe recalled, the commissioners were complaining that they had to build additions on their houses to hold all the paper:

> They worked their butts off! They argued fiercely and passionately and then they accepted their lumps. It was difficult because they had all agreed to accept these appointments on the basis that they wouldn't have to spend humongous amounts of time. Well, of course, that was a big lie. I mean this thing derailed all of them. They had no idea what they were getting into, not one of them, not even the most sophisticated. Even Shoyama didn't really know what kind of a train he was getting on. He probably knew a little more about what was coming down than the rest of them. And, quite frankly, I didn't either. I had no idea that it would be quite as monstrous as it turned out to be.[16]

But the commissioners clearly played purely reactive roles, and sometimes even had to be coaxed to see the full significance of the issues they were considering. Cairns recalled that 'the commissioners had to be told sometimes "look, you're just about to approve something that's significant. I don't mean free trade or no free trade, but within those boundaries. Something that matters. You've got to realize that you're saying yes or no to this." And then something like that would produce a debate.'[17]

Breton was dismayed by this process. He had fully expected that the commissioners would do the writing. Instead, he said, 'what we have is a staff, and essentially what we do as a commission is get documents from the staff, which we read and we approve or disapprove. For a number of commissioners that is okay. I found that very hard. I think other people like Barber and other people possibly Shoyama also [found that hard]. But I don't know, because I thought that I would be involved in writing parts of the *Report*. I don't mind writing.'[18] But the commission functioned like a cabinet in his view, and 'ministers don't write. So consequently, we didn't write.' Breton wrote some memos for commissioners on certain issues, but the only significant piece he did 'was a so-called supplementary report, which I understand is still much more read nowadays than the *Report* itself. The *Report* can't be read. Its just too big.'[19] To Cairns, the commissioners enjoyed symbolic positions rather than ones of real power. 'I mean they controlled the direction, they decided, or at least they gave the formal ultimate decisions, on the direction in which we should go,' he argued, 'but in actual writing, the actual wording and the actual substance of particular recommendations would in the first draft be produced by those who were writing the *Report*, which over-whelmingly was the team that Nymark brought together.'[20] As a result, commissioners were constantly reading other people's work, and being shaped by discourse rather than giving shape to discourse.

This critical view of the design of the commission emerged in a paper delivered by Barber to the Learned Societies Conference in Winnipeg in 1986. He noted that 'because of the extremely broad scope of the Commission's mandate, Commissioners constantly found themselves in the position of making recommendations and approving text for which they felt inadequately prepared.'[21] But as Nymark recalled, many commissioners were 'disengaged' from the process. Discussions between commissioners and key members of the staff were held in which the policy group would present the commissioners with reams of data and a handful of carefully chosen recommendations. But several commissioners could not devote much time to the proceedings at this stage, particularly those who were running their own businesses, and those who were elderly or ill. They had all been dragged across the country on three different occasions, and had travelled to the Arctic, and this proved to be a little more than they thought they were getting into. Thus Nymark argued, some commissioners necessarily played a more minor role, while Macdonald encouraged others to play a larger role than they appeared to be able to play.[22]

Guiding this process were the key members of the oligarchy, especially Godsoe and Nymark. Cairns assisted them when it became apparent that they needed to tone down some of the more extreme discourse working its way into the drafts. 'Gerry Godsoe was not only the man who looked after the over-all structure and made sure the thing functioned, but he has an active interest in policy questions,' according to Macdonald. 'And so he was a witness to a lot of the work that went on in these discussions, and he made a contribution too. So the three of them together were responsible for taking great batches of text and helping them develop.'[23] While certain efficiencies could be gained by this approach, it circumscribed the role of the commissioners, and casts doubt on the question of whether free trade was given a thorough hearing.

Debating the Options?

Notwithstanding the relatively passive role played by most commissioners in the drafting of the *Report*, several did offer forceful arguments about the free trade recommendation as it emerged. Godsoe noted that at the outset the commissioners, with one or two exceptions, did not warm to free trade particularly. This meant the oligarchy feared a significant debate on free trade at the commissioner level, and it was not clear how that debate was going to go because of the diverse interests of various commissioners. Some were very concerned with the integrity of social programs; others were concerned about the survival of Canada as a nation state; still others were concerned about the ability to utilize industrial policy, and how that would be consistent with free trade, Godsoe recalled. Alternative trade strategies for Canada were mooted. The fear that Canada was going to tie its hands behind its back by constraining the actions of the state in the economy was raised. And, of course, the labour movement as presented by Docquier was clearly opposed to free trade from the beginning, and retained that position throughout.[24]

As the debate was engaged across the whole range of issues considered by the commission, the commissioners struggled with their workload, and with the imposition of control by the policy group. The strain was tremendous. But Macdonald maintained that overall, the commissioners were a collegial group, notwithstanding their very different backgrounds and interests. 'On the whole it worked quite well. There were no shouting matches that I can remember. And I don't think that was just because we had the biggest chairman in the history of royal commissions! No, it was conducted with some civility. Heat sometimes, but always civility.'[25] In this regard, Macdonald was very appreciative of the restraint demonstrated by Docquier, who was under pressure from his labour colleagues to vigorously oppose free trade. 'I really appreciated the restraint that Gerry Docquier showed, because he was being associated with something that his labour colleagues were bound to be opposed to,' Macdonald said.[26]

To the extent that the free trade issue was debated by the commissioners, it emerged within their deliberations and discussions after the 'leap of faith' statement. By late 1984, it was the subject of ongoing discussions, according to Warrian, who received his view of the commission from Docquier. He recalled: 'There were very intense discussions from late the previous fall [1984], as I recall, in terms of the nuts and bolts of the thing. So free trade was an issue that was "up there" in discussions throughout, but it was the fall of 1984 that the issue came up as increasingly important. There was several major meetings of the commission dealing with this as the overriding issue. But fall was when things really started to heat up. There were intense discussions among the commissioners.'[27] Although not present himself, Warrian received both pre- and post-meeting briefings from Docquier. 'Certainly it was my impression that the free trade issue was very hotly debated,' Warrian recalled. And Docquier clearly identified to Warrian the key players pushing the free trade option. 'There was the overt, explicit advocacy of free trade that emanated in particular from Macdonald and the staff of the commission, more than from a majority of the Commissioners,' Warrian remembered. However, the outcome was not immediately obvious. 'The chair, Macdonald, on at least one occasion was losing that argument in the late fall.' But, Warrian argued, 'the chair ultimately simply stated that he was going to write a report in support of free trade, and that people could adjust themselves within that framework. Because there certainly was not a uniform support for it.'[28] Alternative trade strategies, such as sectoral free trade, were considered but rejected. According to Warrian, 'I think the appropriate notion of – whatever the appropriate word or the phraseology would be – "sectorized" trade liberalization with adjustment and productivity sharing, you know, managed trade, that didn't bite at the time because we hadn't been through the trauma of the 1980s.'[29]

In the context of the early 1980s and the Macdonald Commission, the choices were the GATT or managed, sectoral, or free trade. The GATT, for Macdonald, appeared to have lost its cachet, as shown in chapter 10, despite Docquier's attempts to revive and shore up arguments for it: 'The labour movement has historically had a position in favour of the GATT, and that has remained so. A trajectory of the negotiated reduction of tariffs over time on a multilateral basis was certainly supported then, and throughout. We argued for the need to supplement that with active adjustments measures and also change the dumping codes to deal with so-called social dumping, which was castigated and laughed at then. But those side deals in NAFTA on the environment and labour standards are exactly to deal with those issues. So that is as far as we pushed it.'[30] Others argued for the GATT, since it was a multilateral forum in which a moderate power like Canada could seek out partners with similar kinds of concerns to act in concert against a hegemonic power. But the slowness of the GATT process and the inability of the Uruguay Round to make much progress diminished its viability. It was also difficult for the commissioners to resist the logic of the argument that the GATT was too slow and cumbersome, whereas Canada's economic development problems were pressing and had to be dealt with immediately. Cairns recalled that among the commissioners in general, there was support for the idea that the GATT would be better, but it was not attainable. There was a perception that Canada does not have a choice of markets, and that even if it diversified, 'this does not mean that the diversity is going to suddenly reinstate Great Britain or make the United States a minor trading partner. We are tied into the American market,' according to Cairns.[31] Given this reality, the next consideration was: 'what kind of institutional/legal nexus does one wish to have this tie-in of these two economies regulated by? And, to repeat, I think the first preference would have been GATT, but the choice was also dictated by what was doable. And it was thought Canada-U.S. free trade could be doable much more easily than GATT. And, also, the premise was that these, in some sense, were not competing, but the fact that one might go Canada-U.S. did not necessarily mean that you could not put this under some kind of GATT umbrella in the future.'[32]

Godsoe's view was that virtually every commissioner became involved in the free trade issue to a greater or lesser degree. It became central to all of them eventually, despite its original absence in the mandate. Arguably, it was an implied topic within the commission's title, since almost anything dealing with economic policy in Canada entails the continental relationship, and, by extension, trade. As well, any examination of the economic union involves looking at internal trade too. But the radical nature of what the commission recommended did not become apparent until about halfway through the commission's life. It was a course of action which was of interest academically, as all sorts of propositions were examined academically. But it did not really begin to look like a possible recommendation until after Macdonald's statement, and after the economics research had pushed it as a realistic objective to which the commissioners could respond that it was a theoretical choice.[33]

Nymark recalled that the issue presented to the commissioners was not, 'here is the case for free trade. What do you think?' Rather, it was presented as 'here is the debate about free trade.' He remembered that Macdonald promoted the free trade option cautiously at first. Indeed, there are some cautionary notes in the *Report* that the 'r' in freer was only dropped in the final draft. The nature of the debate thus involved nuance, as well as substance. Moreover, according to Nymark, the *Report* went to great lengths to say that the multilateral system is still the fundamental pulse of trade in Canada, and that if that appeared to be faltering, it should move on to freer trade. There were a number of cautionary notes, and there was still hesitancy, Nymark recalled. But the free trade agenda came.[34]

By the time that decision making about free trade was under way, some of the economics research had come in. But the commissioners themselves, even those with economics training, background, or competence, were much less enthusiastic about free trade than the economists on the research staff. Barber, Breton, Shoyama, and others were sceptical and raised pointed questions. But when the economists talked about free trade, they had the methodological and empirical authority of impressive-sounding statistics: 80 per cent of Canadian exports were now going to the United States; about 80 per cent of our imports came from there; Great Britain was a very significant trading partner at one time, but it now accounted for only about 2 per cent of our trade, much less than Japan. There was a powerful, inexorable necessity to talk about free trade in the context of a discussion that did not ask, 'is our main trading partner going to be the United States?' because Canada's main trading partner was already the United States. None of the economists assumed there was any alternative to that, notwithstanding the scepticism of the commissioners. Thus, towards the end, the commissioners came more and more to accept the relentless arguments of the economists, Macdonald, and the policy group, whose opinions, moreover, were buttressed by certain fractions of the business community. This left Barber with the distinct impression that 'There may have been vigorous debates among Macdonald's advisory staff, but debates among the commissioners weren't, I think, that vigorous.' He further recalled, 'I remember going to some meetings, and there was considerable debate, but very few commissioners ever attended.'[35]

As noted in chapter 10, several private hearings with various corporations, individuals, and think-tanks influenced the debate among the commissioners. Godsoe specifically cited, for example, a series of conferences organized by the Niagara Institute (of which Macdonald was a member) quite early on, before the public hearings. In some of these it became apparent that the CMA was going to take the Macdonald Commission quite seriously and present a piece of its own research into free trade.[36] Breton argued that the changing views of some important business associations played an important role. 'I think that it was interesting that the BCNI and the CMA, strongly in the person of Laurent Thibault, who was secretary-general at that time, were very strongly for free trade, which was new. And I think that if all these sectors have been against it, I don't know if Donald's political instinct would have gone with it.'[37] Breton found that a few major engineering firms in Montreal which, in the past, had stressed the importance of government procurement for their engineering, claimed that they did not need this any more, and that they were otherwise willing to have free trade. 'They thought that they would be able to do okay in the U.S., They didn't see that they would have any problems.'[38] He further argued, 'I think that it's fair to say that the fact that the big organizations were in favour, the BCNI and the CMA, which we saw quite a few times, and there was no opposition really from the Chambers of Commerce,' was persuasive. On the other hand, 'the labour unions stayed away from us, on the whole. They could have voiced an opinion, but they did not.[39] Considering the presence of Docquier on the commission, and his widely known opposition to free trade, this is a rather odd observation.

Timing was also important. For not only were the commissioners confronted with the ideological front put forward by the policy group, the economists, and the business groups, they were also sensitive to the shifting political winds in the country at large, according to Docquier: 'Generally speaking the commissioners were quite influenced by the research that was in front of them, and I think by the evolution in the political arena. Because there was definitely a switch. When you look at the results of the election in 1984, Mulroney was not elected with 30 per cent. He was elected with a majority of the votes. And this was an indication that Canadians were not very much divided on who should run the country. I have the sense that people who worked on the commission really wanted their work to be listened to. And if you want to be listened to, at least you have to say things that the government in power will take seriously, and not just say, well they are a bunch of Liberals.'[40] But having raised this issue, Docquier also declaimed, 'I think the commissioners were a very honest bunch, and highly intelligent people. I think they produced a document that they believed in.'[41]

Two Key Debates

A pair of meetings devoted exclusively to the topic of free trade were particularly important in the process leading to the free trade recommendation. Hart recalled the sessions as being vital in the free trade debate, but also noted the absence of a key player: 'I am sure that the commissioners talked privately among themselves. But there were two sessions that were set up to discuss this, and I have them vividly in mind in the room there on Sparks Street, with Don sitting at the table, and standing up and leading the discussion, and Albert Breton there, and all the others. All the commissioners were there except Gerard Docquier. He was not at either one of the sessions, which is why I thought it was kind of strange that he wrote the most passionate dissent, when he was not party to the discussions. All the others were there.'[42]

Each of the sessions, held in the fall of 1984 and the winter of 1985, were two days long and involved a thorough discussion. Both commissioners and staff participated and they produced a consensus on a recommendation for free trade, according to Hart: 'It was like a Cabinet session. A lot of words are spoken and a lot of anxieties are expressed, and concerns and so on. But it was my professional judgment, as it was Alan Nymark's at the end of that discussion, that they had reached a consensus. That is where they wanted to go. Now it was not, you know, that Don had them all hold hands and do that. I mean, that is not how things are done. It was our judgment that we should proceed to write it up on the basis that they had formed a consensus, and then the drafts, as they emerged, were given to the commissioners to comment on.'[43] Some of the commissioners commented more critically than others on the recommendation. For instance, Breton commented quite extensively on various drafts because he had stronger views than some of the others, according to Hart. As to which commissioners were intellectually engaged in the free trade debate, Hart had his own hierarchy of who was important: 'Breton was very active in the discussion, Shoyoma was. I am casting my mind back around the room. Clarence Barber did not say much. I mean he was there and he contributed. In fact he had written an important article that we used many years ago, but he did not say much in the discussion. Albert did. Gerard Docquier was not there. William Hamilton did not say much. Nor did the farmer from Saskatchewan [Messer]. Mrs Peters asked some interesting housewife kind of questions, you know. The kind of things that someone not versed in this would ask. They are not bad questions. Laurent Picard was all over the place. It was very hard for me to tell where in the end he stood. Michael Robert was very actively involved and had quite a lot to say. It was interesting, the kinds of things he said. Seaman said virtually nothing. Tommy Shoyama had very good questions, as did Jean Wadds, as did Catherine Wallace.'[44] Nonetheless, the policy group 'made a judgment' that the commissioners had reached a consensus concerning free trade.[45]

But it was more than just the commissioners who participated in the conversation. Hart recalled that the three research directors were very active (although Smith had left by then, to be replaced by Norrie and Sargent). 'And there were other members of the staff who were not critical to this particular thing, but who were there and who raised questions or put forward points of view,' Hart recalled. 'It was a two-day discussion, a wonderful seminar, the first one. That kind of shaped it, and on the basis of that we did the first draft, which was discussed at the second seminar.'[46]

Cairns's memo cautioning the commissioners about the political and social consequences of free trade, and Winham's memo in favour of free trade served as the basis of part of the debate among the commissioners, Cairns remembered. Although this was not his 'intellectual territory,' Cairns felt the need to wade into the debate to provide a corrective to the prevailing arguments. 'And my recollection is that I was saying to myself, "look, I think there's another set of issues that are not being adequately explored so I'm just going to write down a little think piece and it may be somewhat incoherent, I don't know, but these are sort of concerns one might have, or ways one might think about this."' Cairns wrote a memo, which he sent to Winham and several others, and said, 'you know, "I want the commissioners to see this," and maybe Gil said "I would like to reply" or something.'[47] Cairns thought that his memo plus Winham's reply probably occasioned the most significant debate amongst the commissioners about free trade: 'It was very emotional ... There was a very passionate presentation. Some of the commissioners got – as I recall, one commissioner got so emotional he was crying ... So it was about what this might do to Canadian identity and integrity and capacity to retain an autonomous capacity to generate social policy, all those sorts of things. So it really was a good debate. I remember when we had left, saying well we do not really care, in one sense, what they decide. We have done our duty.'[48]

Macdonald's own reading of the positions of the various commissioners is instructive. He was worried about the level of opposition that might emerge from the group: 'The opposition I was concerned about, of course, was on the panel itself, among the commissioners. As I said, Messer, Docquier and Barber. Clarence Barber was really more skeptical than he was hostile. But Hamilton, Seaman, Peters, Jean Casselman-Wadds all were in favour. I can't remember where Catherine Wallace was. She was very much focused on the social policy side. Those were the ones I think who were most in favour of the trade position.'[49] But Warrian recalled these meetings somewhat differently. He and Docquier felt that the decision to move on free trade was taken by the policy group and foisted on the commissioners by Macdonald. 'There was a fairly dramatic meeting,' Warrian remembered, 'in the fall of 1984, that is the fall before the final draft.' He recalled that the way Macdonald was going had become obvious. Docquier had talked to some of the other commissioners, and it was absolutely clear that an overwhelming majority were adamantly opposed to Macdonald making an explicit advocacy of free trade the dominant feature and direction of the *Report*. 'And they all opposed it,' Warrian recalled, 'and Docquier said Macdonald was going to go ahead and do it anyway.'[50] Warrian also recalled that Macdonald had virtually to force some of the commissioners to see his viewpoint: 'My recollection is that it is around November of 1984, and it was apparently clear and explicit in an executive meeting of the Commission that they were adamantly opposed to this direction. And Macdonald simply went into brinkmanship and said that was the way it would come out and they could like it or lump it. From that time on, we were operating on a train that led to a minority report.'[51] The two meetings in the fall of 1984 were the turning point. From this stage onward, the commissioners knew that the *Report* would contain some sort of recommendation regarding free trade. With the stage set for the drafting of the *Report*, several commissioners began contemplating writing dissenting statements.

The Commissioners and Drafting the Report

The process of drafting the *Report*, as reported in chapter 10, was tightly controlled by the policy group; the commissioners' role was largely passive and reactive. Nymark recalled that the policy group fed the commissioners information and, as director of policy, Nymark personally took drafts to them.[52] Nymark asked Whalley to turn the seminars on trade policy he had organized for the commission into drafts of the *Report*, and on the basis of commissioners' discussions, buttress the free trade case. Nymark also brought in a variety of people to discuss the issues with the commissioners.[53]

Docquier recalled, 'I am not a writer, personally. The staff was preparing documents, and we would go through the documents at meetings, and make suggestions for re-writes or additions or eliminations. That was a process that was done. But commissioners were not writing per se.'[54] The commissioners received other people's material and commented on it. Docquier found this to be a satisfactory process, given that he had so much material to deal with, and so little time, but others did not.

Breton recalled that the early drafts of the *Report* were ideologically one-sided and needed some balance. He helped convince Macdonald that Cairns ought to be conscripted to add some balance and moderation to the *Report*: 'A lot of the final draft of the *Report*, the beginning of the *Report*, was written by Alan Cairns. Alan writes, and if you know his style, you can recognize it, but you know at one point Alan said to the commissioners the way this document is going to appear in the world you will be known as extreme right-wingers. It's just terrible. There is no sense of relationship with anything. It's just a bunch of – and that struck Macdonald as correct. In fact, Macdonald told me after that he was unbelievably grateful to Cairns for having written the beginning and putting things in a broad context. It made us look better than if we had not.'[55] Breton was by this time writing his own dissent, and knew it would be difficult at this late stage to get anyone to write something to balance the extreme views in the drafts of the *Report.* He was therefore relieved when Cairns agreed to do it on relatively short notice. 'I could not see anyone around that would do it. And you could not ask anyone to do it; it was very late in the game when Alan was asked to do this. If he had not been the kind of writing machine as he is, you know writing extremely well, with no need of revisions, practically, I don't think it ever would have been done.'[56]

Docquier argued that the combination of the economics research and the timing of the drafting of the *Report* were fortuitous for those interested in promoting the free trade option. By 1984–5, economic conditions in the country were far improved over the period when the commission started, and this had an important impact on the commissioners' view of the proposed recommendations. Docquier recalled:

I think the research had a great deal of influence. And it happened because the economy was picking up, and everybody had the hope that the forces of the market would create the jobs that were necessary. And that in order to create more jobs, it was important to open up the U.S. market. So it was a combination of the research, that was of course good quality research, and the economic situation that was picking up. So the mood of people was different in 1985 than it was at the end of 1982. So everything is fine when you are drafting the Report, and the drafting took place in the last year, in 1984–5. And that had a great deal of influence. And the projections made by the researchers were – well, the pick-up in the industry was giving credence to that. So the commissioners said well, maybe after all we are back on the right track, and this is the way of the future. Basically I think people had the word of Macdonald we should make this leap of faith. Well, they had faith.[57]

In February 1985, Macdonald solicited the assistance of writer Rod McQueen to help cope with the 3,500-page draft confronting the commissioners. By April, McQueen had produced a 3,500-word synopsis, but found himself pulled in several different directions when he presented his work to the commission: 'Every writer needs a good editor; never have I had so many. For two long days, Macdonald occupied one end of a conference table, I the other, with ten more Commissioners ranged between us and a myriad of senior researchers ringing the room. Debate was still heated in several key policy areas. My manuscript offered a last vehicle to argue those differing views. To my left, former deputy finance minister Thomas Shoyama talked economics; to my right, retired educator Catherine Wallace whispered punctuation corrections. My offering proved to be too small a bed for everyone to lie on at a time when there were threats of minority reports. The document was shelved.'[58] Nonetheless, McQueen's efforts were not totally in vain. His synopsis was later published as the official abridged version of the *Report* with a foreword by Macdonald.[59]

The Supplementary Statements

When material was brought to the commissioners for their deliberation, Macdonald claimed he always sought a consensus. 'I wanted people to agree. I had the notion that if we had a seven to six decision, the commission was not exactly giving a clear guide to the community. So I wanted to get as much consensus as possible. And we got quite a bit.'[60] But it was obvious in some circumstances that consensus was not going to be achievable, and eventually it was decided that differences would be noted. Resources were provided to commissioners who wished to indicate dissenting opinions and a remarkable six out of twelve did so in the form of dissenting statements: Commissioners Barber, Breton, Docquier, Messer, Picard, and Wadds.[61] Each found that some aspects of the *Report* were less than acceptable. But curiously, their 'dissents' were cited as 'supplementary statements' in the final *Report*, as if to imply afterthoughts rather than disagreement. Breton recalled writing a 'dissent' and not being informed that it would be published as a 'supplementary statement': 'In the period preceding [the publication of the *Report*,] in the months preceding this, I think, Macdonald was worried that a number of us would not sign, so I think that the idea of the minority reports came up. The Godsoe group decided – once we got the Report we saw that we had written supplementary reports and not minority reports, and essentially what seems throughout as our work was seen as – I think I'm being fair, we were never told this – supplementaries.'[62]

It is indicative of just how contentious the issues raised by this commission were that almost half of the commissioners felt compelled to write dissents. Warrian expressed astonishment at this number: 'It is an odd wind-up to this whole thing, because, at the end of the day, I think you had a situation with a commission report with about six dissents in it. I can't recall another commission that has had six or seven dissents! I mean, a three-person commission and two agreed and one didn't, that happens in labour-management relations all the time. There may be larger commissions where, you know, four of them went over here and three of them went over there. You don't have a situation where a chairman and six went over here, and six went over somewhere else! But on the other hand, the diversity and the failure to get any consensus – I mean the six didn't come out with one view either.'[63]

Notably, the dissenting statements had little to say about the free trade recommendation. Breton, a professional economist, toyed with writing something against the free trade proposal, but eventually decided that what was being recommended was hard for him to be against, so he did not critique it in his dissent.[64] This lack of commentary reflects the muted debate about free trade among the commissioners. Warrian, who wrote Docquier's dissent for him, felt there was no real debate in the economics profession about free trade, which was surprising enough. But he also noted that 'at the end of the day, there was no real fight from the other commissioners. No one was going to go to the wall with this.'[65] He attributed this in part to the absence of coalition politics which, since the free trade debate, has become a more significant factor in Canadian political life: 'The politics of participation was changing through the decade. Coalition politics was changing. And the same thing wouldn't replicate itself today. Macdonald, I don't think, today would get away with his unilateral imposition that he got away with then, in part because there would be coalition politics. Either they wouldn't be there at all, or they would be there in a way that would affect the outcome.'[66] Warrian suggested that there would still be a report, and it might still say what the Macdonald Commission *Report* said. But today, there would also be a greater chance of a different report, or an alternate report, 'not just me sitting at a word processor by myself saying, okay, how can we take pokes at this for the outside world?'[67]

Docquier's decision to write a dissent came late in the life of the commission, and he was struck by how forcefully some of the other commissioners resented this gesture. 'I have to say that my decision to write a dissent was made in the last couple of months of the commission. I think some were really taken aback by my view; they really disliked it, and did not appreciate it.'[68] Docquier was motivated not only by the free trade issue but also by the fact that, in his judgment, the *Report* was an attack on the unemployment insurance system, and an attack on the unemployed. It lacked vision in terms of the need to have government involvement in job creation, or in the economy. 'We were really moving in the Reagan kind of thinking, and that was troublesome to me. So my criticism and my dissent really focused on these two issues – the unemployed, and free trade and what it would do to the unemployed.'[69]

Given the timing of his dissent, there was little opportunity to debate his opinions with the other commissioners, several of whom had largely disengaged from active work for the commission. As well, according to Docquier, the government was anxious to end the commission, particularly since it was not a creature of its making. A full-scale debate on the issues in Docquier's dissent, then, was simply not on the table.

The Two Tiers of Commissioners

There were clearly two tiers within the commission where the free trade issue was concerned: there were those Commissioners with a strong interest, some background, and the intellectual tools to consider the issue in some depth, and there were the rest. The first group consisted of Macdonald, Barber, Breton, and Shoyoma. The second tier consisted of commissioners with limited interest, little or no background, and considerable intellectual tools, who were attuned to other issues. These included Messer, Picard, Robert, Seaman, Wadds, Wallace, Hamilton, and Peters. Docquier stands somewhat apart from both groups. He clearly maintained an abiding interest in the free trade issue, and as the sole spokesperson for labour, his views merit particular attention. While such broad classification of the interests, abilities, and roles of particular commissioners is fraught with some danger in terms of generalization and lack of attention to the nuances of each individual's views, role, and ability, it is useful nonetheless in arriving at an understanding of the debate within the commission at this level of its organization.

Cairns's assessment of the relative interests and strengths of particular commissioners in debating various issues is relevant to the free trade debate within the commission:

> There would be three or four commissioners who were really on top of all the issues. I would speculate that that would include Breton, Barber, Shoyoma. Well I would really say Barber, Breton, Shoyoma, and Laurent Picard sometimes. But the others, well I think there were clearly two tiers on the commission. I would identify those as the first tier. Michel Robert was quite

important since he had important links in Quebec, and it was felt that he could speak about federalism, and he was a very good constitutional lawyer, so he brought a lot of legal knowledge and expertise, and Docquier represented a kind of labour and trade union interest and in that sense, when he spoke, it was always important. But in terms of being intellectually in charge of the issues, those are the ones that I would cite.[70]

Barber was very sceptical about free trade. One of the major issues he was concerned about was grain subsidies. Once assured by Macdonald that agriculture would be exempted from any free trade deal, Barber became a reluctant proponent.[71] Barber was also concerned about investments. 'When the report was finished, I don't think Clarence was very much in favour of free trade, I think he was still opposed to it,' Breton recalled. 'He was worried about investments. That the investments will move to the U.S. But in terms of the movement of goods and services, it was okay. But over time, he thought, capital would be invested abroad.'[72]

Macdonald was very interested and concerned to know what this economist felt about the issue: 'The thoughtful voice that was in the middle and I used to watch, and it kind of troubled me, was Clarence Barber, because there was an economist of very considerable standing, well-liked by his colleagues across the country, and a marvelous personable man. A very non-didactic, gentle person. And he was obviously having intellectual agony, having come from Manitoba and a kind of liberal environment where the general feeling was that protection had not served it well. So he was contesting the position of free trade, but he did so with a troubled conscience. He was in an intellectual dilemma there. He was very honest about it. He would almost reason out loud on it.'[73] But even as an economist Barber was sceptical of the capabilities of his profession to forecast the future. 'Most striking of all is the willingness of economists to draw conclusions on a very flimsy basis of evidence,' Barber wrote subsequent to the commission. 'Milton Friedman once claimed that a majority of economists had shifted from a belief in the quantity theory of money to a Keynesian viewpoint essentially on the basis of no evidence whatever. I would suggest that many have now changed back again, once more on the basis of little solid evidence.'[74]

Barber wrote his dissent in the last few weeks of the drafting of the *Report*. He was uncomfortable with the views of Whalley and the other economists, and felt that some issues he was interested in had not been adequately addressed. But he did not inform Macdonald in advance of his decision to write a dissent, nor did he consult with other commissioners. Barber later opposed the particular free trade deal negotiated by the Mulroney government.[75]

Albert Breton was very 'prickly' about free trade, according to Godsoe, and it was difficult to pin him down on the issue. Godsoe regarded him as probably the brightest of the commissioners. Breton viewed himself as kind of a leader of the opposition on the commission, but it was never clear exactly what his thinking was. He was a good debater and could argue virtually any side of any economic issue. But until the final accounting around the table, Godsoe was not sure which way Breton was going to go. Eventually he did favour free trade.[76]

Breton recalled, 'I think it's fair to say that outside of the economists nobody was very keen on free trade. I think that is quite true. Among the three economists as commissioners – Shoyoma and Barber and myself – we weren't too keen.' In his supplementary statement, Breton decried the ascendance of markets over governments: 'there are, not one, but two broad arenas in which people seek to obtain the things which increase their well-being: markets and governments. Markets, when they are well structured and competitive, do a good job over the longer term in allocating resources in ways that maximize the well-being of the population. That is a generally accepted proposition and one in which I strongly believe. What is less accepted, but an idea in which I nonetheless believe just as strongly, is that governments, when they are well structured and competitive, do as good a job as markets, and like them over the longer term, allocate resources in ways that maximize the well-being of people.'[77] Thus, Breton criticized the commission for its wholesale adoption of the neoconservative view of the primacy of economics over politics, and he rejected the argument that government intervention always represented a 'distortion' of the marketplace.

Breton was in any case annoyed that the issue of free trade had been pushed on the commission by Macdonald through the media. For Breton, it was clear that 'the momentum came from Macdonald, Godsoe and that group.'[78] Then, once a decision had been made, Whalley and others in the policy group tried to make a stronger and stronger case for free trade. As for Breton's own personal opinion on trade, he considered himself a multilateralist: 'I was, and I remain, and I defend it in public talks, I have always been a multilateralist. I would proceed through the GATT. I don't believe in these bilateral games, and I still don't believe in them. I still think that the small teeny weeny country like us dealing with the United States is just bound to get fixed up by the Americans whenever they need something. And we're naive. We think they are nice guys. They are in a way, when we meet them out there. People see that if you go to the U.S., they're the nicest people in the world. But don't touch their interests, otherwise you know what!'[79]

Breton also emphasized the importance of a mission to Sweden that he and Macdonald took in April 1984. Macdonald invited Breton to a conference, and after it was over, they met a number of government officials, ministers, and deputy ministers over four or five days. The Canadian embassy in Stockholm organized their itinerary and ferried them around. Breton recalled that Macdonald was very impressed that the Swedes essentially had unilateral free trade with other nations, even though many of those same nations had tariffs against them. And the prosperity of Swedish society was attributed by several officials to its free trade position. 'And I remember the last night we went to dinner together and we flew back together,' Breton recalled, 'and Donald talked at that point. He was toying with the idea of unilateral free trade.'[80]

Macdonald also recalled the impact this trip had on his thinking about free trade. He was struck rather strongly by the position of Sweden vis-à-vis Germany and Western Europe in particular, and Canada vis-à-vis the United States. Both Canada and Sweden started off as staples-based economies. But Macdonald discovered that:

> Sweden, by a process which I haven't quite understood, had developed a number of very successful multinational companies like Electrolux, Alphalaval, Volvo, and had made some penetration of the European market. And the Swedes we talked to at that time had no doubt about the fact that the kind of carefully structured and protected economy that they then lived in was not going to last for them. The decision had been taken in the last year [to enter the EEC], I think, and was something that they had already decided to proceed with. So I was certainly influenced by talking with these people, who, as I say, were in a comparable position to Canada's. Of course most of the comparisons to Sweden by Ed Broadbent and others were to their social programs. But it struck me that there was an analogy here that had meaning for us.[81]

While the trip influenced Macdonald's thinking, Breton recalled, 'When he came back to Ottawa, that was shot down immediately by what we called the Godsoe group. It was chaired by Donald. And I had never heard Donald talk about the Swedish model again.'[82]

Thomas Shoyama, the twelfth commissioner chosen by Macdonald, was another important member of the first tier of commissioners. Macdonald noted that Shoyama had some reservations about free trade, 'but we had such a close relationship in the past that I think he decided that if I wanted to do this, then he wouldn't make it more difficult for me.' Macdonald was cognizant of the fact that Shoyama had come from a different political orientation. 'He had worked for the CCF government in Saskatchewan, and we were associated in Ottawa in a Government that was certainly left of centre. I think he may have decided, "well all right, if the chairman wants to do this," just as he would have said "if the premier wants to do this, then we'll do the best job we can for him."'[83]

Godsoe regarded Shoyama as incredibly thoughtful, and thus felt that when Shoyama came around to free trade, it was not a precipitate decision. Like Macdonald, his public policy ethos was rooted in the Gordon era, so the conversion to free trade was difficult for him. But, Godsoe argued, as a thoughtful and analytical person, Shoyoma was perhaps one of the most influential persons on Macdonald's thinking. The fact that Shoyama accepted the free trade argument was of great importance to Macdonald.[84]

Shoyama recalled that he was convinced by Macdonald that there was nothing inconsistent between support for free trade and continued reliance on the GATT. Coupled with the recognition that the GATT was floundering, Shoyama gradually softened in his opposition to free trade. Moreover, he recalled, 'I had been impressed by the international trade people in the Finance Department, who said that if you do not keep going the thing will collapse. That was a strongly held view.'[85] In addition, Shoyama was influenced by the public submissions, arguing that 'It wasn't easy to be persuaded by the nationalist point of view. Or get a sense that the unions weren't justifying a position in their own interest, in the same way, of course, that big business was. But I think there seemed to be more logic in the position of the business community. They were rather more persuasive.'[86]

Shoyama was also persuaded by the research studies which argued that, while there were costs to free trade, they were clearly outweighed by the benefits. 'Studies suggested, for example, that we won't be able to compete in household furniture, but we can be strongly competitive in office furniture. It was that kind of argument that was persuasive,' Shoyama maintained. The other telling argument for him was 'if you are going to go multilateral, that means you have to be able to compete on a global basis. Well if you can't compete in the U.S.,' Shoyama wondered, 'how can you compete globally? That was, as far as I was concerned, a rather convincing argument. If you can't market it in the U.S., how can you market it in Japan or Europe or anywhere else?'[87]

The second tier of commissioners, as indentified above, included

Messer, Picard, Robert, Seaman, Wadds, Wallace, Hamilton and Peters.
Messer, a former Saskatchewan NDP Cabinet minister turned resource
industry businessperson, was initially unhappy with the free trade recommendation, but eventually accepted it. Docquier argued that Messer had
adopted a business perspective. 'He was in business. So I would say, even
with a good social mind, a good social orientation, he was thinking more
in terms of business. And he was in a business where international trade
was important. He was selling potash.'[88] Picard was particularly interested
in industrial strategy, and terribly concerned that free trade would wipe
that out. Thus he was an unhappy and reluctant convert. Robert was concerned largely with other kinds of issues, but eventually supported free
trade. Seaman was, of course, a proponent of free trade in its purest form
from day one. Coming from an oil and gas perspective, and as an Alber-
tan, he felt that free trade was vital to the economic success of his industry, his region, and ultimately his country. Indeed, he was constantly
pushing Macdonald towards this end, coaxing him away from the academics and into the business community to find out what really worked
and why free trade would create jobs, wealth, and a better economy.

Wadds, a self-described right-wing Conservative, was well connected
to the business community. Her contacts there told her that free trade
was good, and that was good enough for her. She held the view that to
support free trade was to be a Canadian nationalist. 'I don't think it follows that people who felt very nationalistic and anxious to promote
Canadianism or Canadiana would not give a hearing to free trade. I
don't think that follows at all.' Moreover, she trusted Macdonald's judgment and was not the least bit perturbed by his leap of faith. 'That was
part of the pleasure and satisfaction of working under Don Macdonald
because I had complete trust in his integrity and I knew nothing was
decided ahead of time by him.'[89] As former high commissioner to
England, Wadds was well aware of trade as a key issue: 'Having just been
in London, it was particularly in the forefront of my mind. Trade is the
lifeblood of our economy and I've always been very aware of it. I was
always aware of this being a basic part of politics. I always thought politics was basically a business thing. I mean you had to make the income
to suit what you wanted to spend and that kind of thing. A business.
Therefore, I think I was always attuned to the business points we heard,
particularly. So that was my foremost interest and I guess I was watching
a bit for ideas on the free trade idea.'[90]

Wallace, an American-born educator, was perhaps one of the more
sceptical commissioners about free trade. But ultimately she supported it

principally because she too came to trust Macdonald. Both Hamilton and Peters were very ill towards the end of the commission's life, and so did not play a prominent role in the debates concerning free trade or in the drafting of the *Report*. But as former president of the B.C. Employer's Council, Hamilton was very much a free trader.

As the most important anti–free trade commissioner, Docquier's position is deserving of some greater consideration. He was regarded by Godsoe as a sophisticated and interesting person, and Godsoe thought the commission was very lucky to have him. He felt that he understood why Docquier did certain things politically, for example, going public with the *Report* before it was published.[91] Godsoe also understood that Docquier would write a dissent. In fact, Docquier was given research money in order to do that.[92] Docquier gradually accepted a version of the free trade proposal, but not the one adopted by the Canadian government. In Docquier's view, the approach that he endorsed throughout was not to support free trade as a one-time unilateral proposition. He supported trade liberalization in return for major new assistance for adjustment, including a Guaranteed Annual Income (G.A.I.). His endorsement, such as it was, was limited to trade liberalization in support for a G.A.I. and greater adjustment assistance for workers. The latter two elements were conveniently forgotten by the government, the media, and apparently by everybody else, according to Warrian.[93]

Docquier also took the position that a policy of full employment was the tonic for what ailed Canada. He argued:

> In my dissent I said that we have been in a vicious circle. You reduce unemployment insurance because it is too costly, and by doing that, you reduce the purchasing power of people and you are putting more people out of work, instead of addressing the issue of creating work. But at one point in time, there will not even be enough money to have unemployment insurance if we go along that route ... We need people with good paying jobs if we want to sustain our system. I used a phrase in my report that there will always be somebody somewhere that will work hard enough through oppression and repression to beat us on the wage level – on the way down. There will always be somebody that will pay less than we are. That is the process that drives us towards the lowest common denominator. And this is why I opposed that part of the *Report*.[94]

In making the case against free trade, Docquier argued that Canada could not hope to escape from the political pressures of the American

Congress, wherein it has no representatives: 'My experience as a steel-worker was that even if we were to sign a treaty with the U.S. on free trade, we would never avoid the political pressure that the American people would put on their politicians to curb the penetration of Canadian goods on their market. And that was true with the steel industry. And you can go to the steel makers today, and look at the trouble they have been in since free trade, while they were trying to gain access to the U. S. market. So the political pressures in the U.S. and the ability of the Congress to pass legislation that is favourable to them and not to us will never be changed. We have to live with that. Free trade or not, we still have to live with the same problem.'[95] It is only through managed trade that Canada stands a chance in competition with the American behemoth, according to Docquier. 'It is only agreements like the Auto Pact or the multi-fiber agreement – which they have just destroyed in the last round of negotiations – it is through that kind of mechanism that we would have true access to the U.S. market,' he contended. 'I believe in trade, but I believe in managed trade. And some people now say that is protectionism.'[96]

Docquier was cognizant of the rapid transformations of the world economy in making these arguments. Indeed, he argued that managed trade might have cushioned some of the blows of the recession of the early 1990s had Canada opted for managed trade instead of free trade:

> I am not saying, by the way, that we would not have, because of globalization, because of changes and the new technologies, the speed of communication, would not have a lot of the same problems – but maybe not to the same extent. Because, what we see today, in Ontario after the Free Trade Agreement when we entered the recession of 1991, the American subsidiaries were moving back to the U.S. They had no reason to be here. Globalization called for concentration of production means. They would not have a small plant here to serve our market, and they would not give them world mandates. So we have lost not only jobs, but we have lost, and I am talking for the steel industry, we have lost business that was using steel or material of great importance for a resource-based country like we were.[97]

Given his particular perspectives on the labour community and the steel industry, free trade was simply untenable for Docquier.

But interestingly enough, from Docquier's perspective, the labour movement was preoccupied with other matters, and did not really engage the business community over the issue of free trade through the commission. 'Their preoccupation was much more with unemployment and jobs,' according to Docquier. 'To be honest with you, it is in the last year the discussion on free trade really took shape. And I would say that the *Report* was as much driven by the research that was made during the process than by what we heard and by the various communities that submitted their views.'[98]

Docquier felt the thirteen commissioners worked well together as a group, notwithstanding their different perspectives. 'They worked well as a group. Honestly there was an attempt in the group, although there was a lot of discussion and, when I say disagreements, let us say arguments around the issues. And I took part in these discussions of course, but we had some very healthy discussions.'[99] And the fact that he was from a labour background, with its participatory democratic elements, meant that the idea of thirteen (or more) people sitting around making decisions was not foreign to Docquier. 'I didn't find that particularly difficult,' recalled Docquier. But it had a positive effect: 'I don't think anybody, apart perhaps from Macdonald, was able to impose something that others would not like. It was by consensus.' But he also felt that the commission make-up was slanted in favour of business. 'But of course there were not thirteen labour people there. I was the lone soldier. It was not always easy, I must say.'[100] Macdonald said this about Docquier's position: 'Gerry Docquier was entirely consistent with his affiliation and Gerry was entirely candid about it. He said "You know there's some debates here, but as a vice president of the Canadian Labour Congress, I really can't agree to this policy." He put the consequences forward for his membership, for some of his membership. It was an important part of the discussion.'[101]

Conclusion

As this chapter has revealed, the commissioners had relatively limited input in the writing of the *Report*. Their role was more reactive and passive. Material was brought to them for approval, and its volume made the exercise largely pro forma. I have also idenftied two tiers among the commissioners: some were free traders, most were not, and where support was given, it was often given grudgingly. In any event, the chair and his senior advisers had charted the course in advance of consultation with the commissioners. To speak of a 'debate' about free trade within the commission at this level is thus to overstate what actually occurred.

CHAPTER 12

Continentalizing Canada: The Politics and Legacy of the Macdonald Commission

It be resolved, that this House is of the opinion that the welfare of Canada requires the adoption of a national policy, which, by a judicious readjustment of the tariff, will benefit and foster the agricultural, the mining, the manufacturing and other interests of the Dominion; that such a policy will retain in Canada thousands of our fellow countrymen, now obliged to expatriate themselves in search of employment denied them at home, will restore prosperity to our struggling industries, now so sadly depressed, will prevent Canada from being made a sacrifice market, will encourage and develop an active interprovincial trade, and moving (as it ought to do) in the direction of a reciprocity of tariffs with our neighbours, so far as the varied interests of Canada may demand, will greatly tend to procure for this country, eventually, a reciprocity of trade ...[1]

An editorial cartoon in the *Ottawa Citizen*[2] depicted the Macdonald Commission as a massive elephant with a $20 million price tag on its side. Around the elephant were four blind men representing a New Democrat, a Liberal, a Conservative, and a taxpayer, each trying to discern what the creature was by touching it. The New Democrat suggested it was a 'big business hobbyhorse'; the Liberal called it a 'paper tiger'; the Conservative felt it was 'a gift horse, perhaps'; while the taxpayer proclaimed 'It is an elephant! And I'm pretty damn sure it's *white!*'

The analogy of an elephant was quite appropriate, since everything about the Macdonald Commission was so *big*. As noted in this study, its mandate, budget, size, public consultations, research program, and final *Report* all exceeded any previous exercise of this nature. Even its chairperson, Donald Macdonald, boasted that, at over 190cm tall, he was the biggest chair of any royal commission in Canadian history! As to whether it was a *white* elephant, history will judge, but the swift adoption of its signature recommendation suggests not.

In reality, the biggest thing about the Macdonald Commission was not its resemblance to an elephant, white or otherwise, but the change in economic development strategies for Canada which it legitimized. As a result, a new politics rooted in anti-statism and a new economics which fully integrated the Canadian economy into the American economy was accorded a level of credence heretofore denied.

By way of conclusion, the following pages will reflect on the Macdonald Commission as a temporary institutional site which managed to bring together the ideas, interests, and institutions containing the main requisites for transformative change. To do so necessitates revisiting the *politics* of the commission by highlighting the power of ideas and the role of ideology in contributing to the profound political and economic changes promoted when this commission held up a mirror to the face of Canadian society. But I will preface these considerations by briefly examining post–Macdonald Commission developments in Canada in order to establish more fully the *legacy* of the commission to date.

The Aftermath of the Macdonald Commission

The Historical Record

From mid-summer 1985 onward, a dizzying series of events transpired. With the ideological arguments and legitimacy supplied by the Macdonald Commission, the ideologues who supported its central thrust towards free trade redoubled their efforts. Similarly, free trade opponents began organizing themselves with a level of intensity perhaps not seen since the 1911 free trade election. Both sides were gearing up for a struggle which had been foreshadowed in the work and findings of the commission.

In March 1985, Prime Minister Brian Mulroney called for negotiations which led to the Free Trade Agreement with the United States three years later. As noted in chapter 1, Mulroney had the commission's *Report* in his hands in the summer of 1985, before it was released to the public. It resonated very strongly with the prime minister's evolving ideological views. The Macdonald Commission *Report* was released on 5 September 1985. On 9 September Mulroney announced to the House of Commons his decision to adopt the commissions' recommendation, and on 26 September he telephoned President Ronald Reagan to announce formally that his government wanted to negotiate 'the broadest possible package of mutually beneficial reductions in tariff and nontariff barriers between our two countries.'[3] When Mulroney made his famous speech to New York bankers in 1984 proclaiming Canada 'open for business,' he revealed his antipathy towards the state and nationalism. 'The North Shore was not built by federal civil servants or people preaching economic nationalism from the safety of downtown Toronto,' he said.[4] The anti-state continentalist vision encapsulated in the Macdonald Commission free trade recommendation thus fit perfectly with the prime minister's ideological predilections.

But free trade opponents also had advance notice of the contents of the *Report*. For instance, political economists Daniel Drache and Duncan Cameron surreptitiously received a preliminary draft of the *Report* from Peter Warrian. They used this information to publish their critique of the commission before the public release of the *Report*. Both sides geared up for battle having advance knowledge of the pro–free trade blueprint propounded by the commission.

The Nationalist Response

Several observers have noted the catalysing effect of the release of the Macdonald Commission *Report* on forging a new coalition of anti–free trade forces.[5] Bleyer suggests, 'the increasingly clear continentalist orientation of the Mulroney government and its corporate allies was revising some of the nationalist sentiment more or less demobilized by the Liberal government's own initially nationalist response to the economic crises.'[6] Indeed, Canadian nationalists had begun mobilizing even in advance of the summer of 1985. For instance, the Council of Canadians was created by Edmonton publisher Mel Hurtig in January of that year. Later, the pro–free trade position of the Mulroney government inspired the formation of the nationalist Pro-Canada Network in April 1987. It was comprised of about thirty-five member groups, including the Council of Canadians, trade unions, church groups, environmentalists, feminists, social welfare organizations, Aboriginals, and cultural and farm groups. They were joined by a modest number of businesses. Strikingly, this represented a mirror image of the popular sector and labour interests which presented social democratic nationalist prescriptions and analyses to the Macdonald Commission. Together, they spent just under $1 million opposing free trade during the period leading up to the 1988 federal election – an election which many viewed as a plebiscite on the issue.

Their main expense was $650,000 for the production of 2.2 million copies of a twenty-four-page pamphlet by *Montreal Star* cartoonist Aislin (Terry Mosher) and Toronto writer Rick Salutin entitled 'What's the Big Deal?'[7] By the early 1990s, the Pro-Canada Network evolved into the Action Canada Network, through which more than fifty groups continued the fight against continental corporate power.

The Continentalist Response

The pro–free trade interests also organized themselves beyond the usual lobbying activities engaged in by the business community in Canada. The main actor was the Canadian Alliance for Trade and Job Opportunities, also formed in April 1987. Its membership included about thirty-five business associations which contributed roughly $5,250,000 between April 1987 and March 1989 to the free trade cause. It spent about $2.9 million during the period prior to the fall 1988 election, of which more than $2.3 million was devoted to advertising and consultants. Another $2 million was devoted to promoting free trade during the seven-week election campaign period. Other estimates suggest this group's spending was even higher. Its members included the Business Council on National Issues, the Canadian Manufacturers' Association, the Canadian Chamber of Commerce, the Canadian Federation of Independent Business, and the Pharmaceutical Manufacturers' Association. Support also came from the National Citizens' Coalition, the National Association of Manufacturers, the Canadian Exporters Association, and the Council of Forest Industries of British Columbia.[8] Again, it is noteworthy that these were many of the same groups whose neoconservative continentalist views found expression in the mirror of the Macdonald Commission.

But the most striking thing about the coalition was its leadership. It was co-chaired by none other than Donald Macdonald himself, along with his old nemesis, former Alberta Premier Peter Lougheed. Macdonald's role as co-captain of the corporate continentalists graphically signalled the distance he had travelled ideologically. In Michael Hart's view, Macdonald epitomized the broader changes under way in Canadian society. 'As a newly elected MP in the 1960s, he had prided himself on being labelled an economic nationalist. As a senior government minister in the 1970s, he had seen himself as a pragmatist in the mold of Lester Pearson, Mitchell Sharp, and Bud Drury. As chair of the commission in the 1980s, he accepted the new realities and saw a need to return to the discipline of market-driven economics.'[9]

The Debate Engaged

A furious national debate over the pros and cons of free trade ensued. Macdonald himself played a very prominent role, making speeches and engaging in nationally televised debates as well as local town hall meetings. He enthusiastically trumpeted the benefits of free trade as propounded by his supposedly authoritative and non-partisan commission, notwithstanding important differences between his recommendations and the actual deal put forward by the Mulroney government (discussed below). Macdonald recalled the response of his own party to the recommendation for free trade: 'And indeed, the Liberals, as you know, were baffled as to how to deal with it. Initially, they were inclined to congratulate me. But gradually their opinion hardened against the recommendation, and by 1987 we were shouting at each other.'[10]

The academic community divided along predictable lines, with economists and most mainstream political scientists favouring the deal, while political economists opposed it.[11] In addition, Manitoba, Ontario, and P.E.I. formally opposed the FTA. Public opinion initially appeared to favour the concept of free trade, according to various polls. But between December 1987 and October 1988, polling results showed a majority of Canadians *against* the free trade deal for the first time since April 1984.[12] While the Liberal and New Democratic Parties both opposed the FTA, the election was won by the Conservatives.[13] But the popular vote showed nearly 60 per cent of Canadians had voted *against* the Mulroney government, again reflecting the Macdonald Commission public submissions in which a majority opposed neoconservative continentalism.

Nonetheless, it appeared that many of the requisites for transformative change were in place. *Political viability* was present in the existence of significant actors who could help deliver electoral success to the policy's political supporters. *Economic viability* was derived from an articulated economic development strategy with the imprimatur of an important part of the research community. And *political and bureaucratic leadership* was present in that the legal and political authority of state officials and their resulting institutional capacity to sway decision makers to accept their preferred course of action was engaged. These requisites were either absent or only partially present in the anti–free trade forces. Indeed, Denis Stairs argued that once the debate over free trade was joined by the broader society, it was too late to prevent the free trade deal from happening:

Most of the establishment testimony, business community testimony anyway, was for it. Very powerful forces in the bureaucracy were for it. Donald

Macdonald, reputed to have been one of the Liberal nationalists in the Trudeau government, was for it. Mulroney, in the end, gratefully seized on this to sustain his own view, as it developed. So, you know, where are the enemies? Well, the enemies of the free trade initiative came in very late – they didn't see this coming, I don't think until it was essentially a fait accompli, and who were they? Well, they were a sort of a handful of intellectuals associated with the CBC, with some political science departments, with literary people, with artists, and with the labour movement. They were late, and they were ineffectual.[14]

Moreover, the arguments the opponents mounted, while ideological, differed qualitatively from those mounted by the proponents of free trade. According to Stairs, 'if you looked at what they wrote, it was, as you might expect, emotional exhortation very largely. And that was not the sort of thing that would stand up to the kinds of arguments the John Whalleys of the world were making.'[15] He went on to say: 'I really think that Canadian elites threw in the towel – that is an expression I have often used – on the Canadian experiment as traditionally understood. If you thought of the Canadian political enterprise as an enterprise very distinct from that of the United States and incorporating more ascriptive values as opposed to more achievement values, less individualist, more community-oriented, all that kind of thing that people like George Grant talk about, and also people like Seymour Martin Lipset or Pierre Berton in their various ways. That kind of view of Canada is quite different from the United States and needs a certain kind of public policy to protect it.'[16] In any event, according to Bashevkin, 'as the experiences of [Mel] Watkins and others suggested, by the late 1980s the economic views of the business community were often considered to be more legitimate than those advanced by critics of free trade.'[17]

The FTA was signed into law in 1988 and came into effect on 1 January 1989 after a bitterly wrought negotiation process.[18] But the story does not end there. Despite widespread opposition in Canada, Mexico and, to a lesser extent the United States, and with widespread support from the business community in all three countries, the FTA was expanded. In 1990 the United States indicated a desire to enter into free trade with Mexico. Canada, fearing the development of a hub-and-spoke arrangement with the United States dominating from the centre, quickly jumped on the bandwagon. As a result, the trade ministers of Canada, Mexico, and the United States met in Toronto on 12 June 1991 to open negotiations for a North American Free Trade Agreement (NAFTA). An agreement was concluded on 12 August 1992, and it came into force on

1 January 1994.[19] The same sets of actors which had mobilized in defence of and against the FTA now turned their attentions to NAFTA. In the end, the ideological arguments articulated by the Macdonald Commission found concrete expression through the public policy actions of the three North American governments.

Reality Check: The Macdonald Commission Report and the Free Trade Deals

In fairness to Macdonald and his commission, it must be pointed out that the FTA and NAFTA differ significantly from the recommendations made by the Macdonald Commission, although often in ways its detractors had predicted during the commission's study. Godsoe critically referred to the FTA as 'only half a trade agreement,' and argued that 'Mr Mulroney's negotiators failed to fulfill the key criteria for a successful agreement as spelled out in the [Macdonald] report – a strong initiative in multilateral trade negotiations under the General Agreement on Tariffs and Trade, not a deal with the United States.'[20] Moreover, the theoretical notion of bilateral free trade in principle, as argued by economists from their models, and articulated in the Macdonald Commission research program, bore little resemblance to the deal actually struck by the Mulroney, Reagan, and Salinas governments. For instance, the fundamental goal articulated by the commission of eliminating all non-tariff barriers to trade has not been realized. American countervailing and other punitive measures against Canadian businesses still occur. No agreement was reached on a subsidies code, notwithstanding the importance accorded to this measure both in the commission research and subsequent pronouncements by pro–free trade spokespersons. The Auto Pact was ostensibly exempted from the trade deals as per Macdonald's recommendation, at least initially, yet a new North American content rule of 62.5 per cent and other provisions for autos and major components appeared in NAFTA. Despite the recommendation by the commission that agriculture be exempted from any deal, the FTA and NAFTA both contained important conditions in this area. Moreover, the FTA and NAFTA went far beyond trade to incorporate a variety of measures designed to restrict the state from taking action in several non–trade related areas. They ensured, for instance that in the field of energy no government in Canada could enact any public policy resembling the National Energy Program. In the area of investment, barriers to foreign ownership were significantly reduced. And cultural industries in Canada were made the potential targets of countervailing actions by the United States Congress for perceived trade transgressions in other areas, despite the recommendation by the Macdonald Commission that culture be left out of the deal.

The Macdonald Commission research neglected to incorporate consideration of the trade agenda of the American Congress into its projections for bilateral free trade. This rather striking oversight occurred despite a proposal submitted to the commission by a political economist to conduct a study of how the position of the Congress regarding its trade and investment agenda with Canada might affect the outcome of negotiations over Canadian proposals for a free trade agreement with the United States – a proposal rejected on the basis that its author was 'too nationalistic.'[21] As the protracted and difficult negotiations over the FTA reveal, Canadian policy makers blithely assumed that the American interest was substantially synonymous with the Canadian one, despite Breton and Docquier's warnings to the contrary. But the Reagan administration was eager to reverse declining American global hegemony, and the highly protectionist Congress was in no mood to concede even an inch of American sovereignty over its trade relations with other countries. Rather, the American approach was to 'extract every possible concession that could benefit American interests, and then to demand even more.'[22] The Canadians, on the other hand, were negotiating from a position of weakness, according to Clarkson: 'An inherently unequal match made more asymmetrical by the urgency with which the [Prime Minister's Office] defined the need for an agreement and the inflated claims that the government made about the gains expected from "free" trade meant that it was negotiating on its knees with the world's most powerful nation.'[23] Thus, according to critics and even some pro–free traders, the Canadian negotiators had to sacrifice much more in their zeal to consummate a deal than the Macdonald Commission had recommended.

Canadian negotiators mistakenly and naively assumed the Americans placed as high a priority on signing a deal as the Canadian government did. Fired up with ideological passions after a stirring electoral victory interpreted as a mandate for free trade, the Canadian proponents of the FTA assumed a relatively clear path lay ahead. They were soon disabused of this notion when they sat down to negotiate with the Americans. After handing the Canadian file to über-bureaucrat Simon Reisman, the Mulroney Tories were stunned to learn of the low priority attached to the negotiations by the Americans, who assigned a relatively inexperienced and junior official to head up their team.[24] As Ritchie recalled: 'In Canada, Prime Minister Mulroney had staked his government's future on the success of these negotiations and put our best team on the field under the leadership of a significant public figure in Simon Reisman. In the United States, President Reagan had replaced the leading promoter of the negotiations, Bill Brock, with a light-weight who had in turn named a relative non-entity to head a non-existent negotiating team.'[25] None of the commission economists who promoted free trade foresaw these aspects of realpolitik, which coloured the attainment of a free trade regime.

But perhaps the most glaring disjuncture between the Macdonald Commission recommendations and the actual free trade deals was the total absence of any adjustment assistance programs for workers and communities adversely affected by the changes brought about by free trade. This is an idea with a long pedigree, appearing in writings on free trade as early as the eighteenth century. Adam Smith himself noted the problem of introducing free trade too quickly. He argued that if free trade threatened to dislocate domestic labour or capital, it should be introduced 'only by small gradations, with a good deal of reserve and circumspection.'[26] The Macdonald Commission *Report*, on Docquier's insistence, advocated a Transitional Adjustment Assistance Program (TAAP) for workers displaced by the new economic realities of the eighties.[27] And, notwithstanding the ascendance of the neoconservative continentalist view, Donald Macdonald himself expressed some regret that it was not in the end tempered, ironically enough, by a latent role for the state in cushioning the blow of adjustment to the new, harsher world. Asked if he were able to project what the major legacy of his commission would be in a generation or two, Macdonald replied:

Well I hope one of the major legacies is going to be in terms of the adjustment assistance, and not just for the trade policies, but the recognition that outside economic events will occur which have an adverse impact on people's occupations and their ability to use their skills. And it's not good enough to say 'Well, let them work it out in the market.' But in the old days when the skills were not quite so highly specialized as they are now, a fellow was used to using a shovel and a pick, and could move around and get work, but in this modern age it's quite different. I hope that the outcome of the current experience in terms of the Canadian economy is that all parties will agree that this [adjustment assistance] should be a priority. I think the serious mistake the Conservatives made was not recognizing it and putting it up front of the economic policy.[28]

But Macdonald claimed that he was unable to make this argument to Mulroney, 'because by then I was in London [as high commissioner]. I was out of the game, so to speak. I thought that they would articulate the policy this time. I kept waiting for it, but it never came.'[29] Whether this represents ex post facto rationalization or a genuine change of view is irrelevant. The reality is that this very significant recommendation was overlooked by the Mulroney government. The result was widespread popular displeasure with the ongoing economic dislocations and recession in the wake of the free trade deal. Crane points out that between 1980 and 1988, Canada's exports grew at almost 11 per cent a year, but in the first four years of the FTA they grew at just 4.5 per cent. In 1985, Canada had a $20.4 billion trade surplus with the United States; in 1992, the surplus was $16.8 billion. And after the FTA came into effect, large numbers of plant closings in Canada contributed to a rise in the unemployment rate from 7.5 per cent in 1988 to 11.3 per cent by 1992.[30]

After NAFTA replaced the FTA, the economic prognosis continued to be problematic. According to the U.S.- based Economic Policy Institute, an evaluation of NAFTA in 2001 showed a 'continent-wide pattern of stagnant worker incomes, lost job opportunities, increased insecurity and rising inequality.'[31] In Canada, trade has become more concentrated with the United States – rising from 74 per cent in 1989 to 85 per cent by 2000; growth performance in the 1990s was worse than in any decade of the twentieth century except the 1930s; average per capita income fell steadily between 1990 and 1998 and only reached 1989 levels by the end of the decade; real income declined for the majority of Canadians in the 1990s (although it increased for the top one-fifth); and the overall productivity gap with the United States widened.[32]

Moreover, in the Canadian context, as Stritch argues, there are some particular difficulties associated with the nature of the free trade deals this country signed: 'Locking ourselves into a North American free trade arrangement has been portrayed as the abandonment of narrow nationalism, and as something in line with the inevitable march of globalization in the world economy. In reality, we have increasingly turned away from the rest of the world and have retreated into a continental trading bloc dominated by the United States. The proportion of Canada's trade with countries other than the United States has diminished over the past ten years, with exports to the rest of the world falling from 27.1 percent of the total in 1983 to 22.7 percent in 1992. Such bloc formation is not globalism; it is actually a process of deglobalization and regional parochialism.'[33] Thus Stritch concludes we have gone through an important watershed in Canadian history. 'We have turned away from defensive expansionism and economic nationalism, and have embraced continentalism and closer integration with the United States.'[34]

The Legacy of the Macdonald Commission

While the Rowell-Sirois recommendations concerning federal-provincial fiscal relations were not acted upon for about a generation after their release, responses to the main ideological thrust of the Macdonald Commission have been strikingly rapid. The speed with which the Mulroney government moved on free trade surprised almost everyone, including the commission chair: 'I was delighted at the time, and I guess I shouldn't have been surprised because in fairness to the Mulroney government, they had, when they were leading up to the 1984 election – they did not say so much after they got elected – but leading up to the election they were very much in favour. I suspect that you may find that they may have been debating internally what is so good about this particular aspect of the program [free trade] when out of the mill comes this document done by that notorious Liberal Macdonald and his associates, appointed by Trudeau, who say "this is what we better do." And remember they had the essence of the findings about two months before [the *Report* was publicly released].'[35]

One assessment of the legacy of the commission by Andrew Coyne suggests that 'our national ideology is Macdonaldism,'[36] by virtue of the influence of the commission in a variety of areas.[37] Not only have governments moved on free trade, but a number of the commission's other recommendations have been slowly but surely influencing the public agenda, according to Coyne: the commission's stand against an industrial policy targeting specific firms has by and large been accepted; a major reworking of regional development programs has come to fruition; the privatization of Crown corporations and deregulation of many sectors of the economy have proceeded apace; the commission's suggestions for loosening regulations on foreign investment, first realized by Mulroney's transformation of FIRA into Investment Canada, have been retained; conditions have been established to prevent the introduction of any successor to the National Energy Program; and movement towards breaking down interprovincial barriers to trade has been initiated.[38] Coyne suggests these developments are mainly attributable to the ascendence of mainstream economics given legitimacy by the commission: 'As a summary of the present state of economic thought in Canada and abroad, the report and its 72 volumes of supporting research served, and serves, not only as a reference library for experts. It also gave mainstream political legitimacy to the ideas of neoclassical economics – ideas that strike many laymen as strange or controversial but are accepted commonplaces within the profession.'[39] Coyne may be paying exaggerated homage to the Macdonald Commission, but there is no doubt that several Canadian governments have increasingly adopted the creed of neoconservative continentalism articulated by this inquiry.[40]

Bradford summarizes the broader impact of the Macdonald Commission in this way:

> The commission closed ranks around a neo-liberal agenda that had mobilized considerable support in the business community and economics profession since the mid-1970s. The commission integrated policy reforms in numerous fields in a coherent discourse of market liberalization and social adjustment that would substantially retrench the federal government's role in the economy and society. With an abiding commitment to market values and incentives, the commission emphasized the modest administrative-political demands of its package. Politically attractive to a floundering new government seeking to confirm support in the multinational business community and free trade provinces, the Macdonald Commission's neo-liberal discourse became the blueprint for two terms of Progressive Conservative government. And since 1993, the Liberals have practiced 'Macdonaldism' with a vengeance.[41]

By advocating free trade with the United States, the Macdonald Commission was not simply selecting one among a number of economic development alternatives, it was fundamentally reshaping and redefining Canada. What the Macdonald Commission did, in short, was significantly alter the *lineaments*, that is, the distinctive features or characteristics, of ideology in Canada by promoting and legitimating a neoconservative continentalist perspective previously found only among a small number of senior government bureaucrats, a fraction of the business community, and mainstream economists. The depth of the change in the wake of the commission can be discerned by comparing the broad political and economic frameworks prevalent in Canada in the pre– and post–Macdonald Commission worlds (see Figure 12.1).

Changes in the political framework created the conditions for limiting the role of the state; changes in the economic framework fostered and promoted greater economic integration between Canada and the United

	Political framework	Economic framework
Pre–Macdonald Commission	Keynesian social demo- cratic consensus in crisis ideologically pluralistic (liberalism, socialism, conservatism) positive role for the state nationalism ascendant	mixed economy of public and private enterprise Fordism prevails, but in crisis mild liberal continentalism tempered by nationalism expressed through state intervention
Post–Macdonald Commission	neoconservatism ideological polarization, liberal centre squeezed out reduction of role of state continentalism ascendant	free market principles prevail intensified economic integration with U.S. privatization, deregulation, decentralization, globaliza- tion

Figure 12.1   Summary of pre– and post–Macdonald Commission political and economic frameworks

States. These closely linked goals were accomplished after ideological struggles to reformulate political discourse. The Macdonald Commission's hearings revealed broad ideological conflict over the turf of Canadian politics, as expressed through economic development strategies. Organized labour and the popular sector spoke almost unanimously from a social democratic nationalist paradigm rooted in a Keynesian interpretation of economics and politics that revolved around an important role for the state in the market. They were joined by some business groups, but many others adopted a different ideological paradigm, a neoconservative continentalist one which deified the free market, sought to discredit Keynesianism, and argued for a greatly diminished role for the state in the economy. Buttressed by a major academic exercise in legitimation, pushed by a powerful oligarchy, championed by a puissant chairperson, and resisted only weakly by an enfeebled gaggle of commissioners, the neoconservative continentalist option prevailed.

But judging from the deleterious results of the FTA and NAFTA, the direction signalled by the Macdonald Commission and subsequently followed by Canadian governments has not been acceptable to large numbers of Canadians.[42] The commission attempted to design a new 'grand compromise,' but its signature recommendation, acted on as a 'leap of faith,' fostered ongoing conflict. Ayres argues that an important legacy of the Macdonald Commission was that it played a catalysing role in the consolidation of the Canadian anti–free trade movement:

> For many in the popular sector, the report drew a clear public line between a neo-conservative corporate vision of Canada and a popular-sector perspective. The commission's recommendation ignored the many dozens of briefs presented by popular-sector groups, which reinforced the sense of marginalization from the policy process felt by many popular-sector groups that had begun with the Tory election. It also signalled, in their view, a definitive closure of the polity to their concerns. Yet, most importantly the commission unwittingly presented the popular sector with the glue it needed to cement alliances. The commission's strong embrace of the free trade option provided a common point of concern; it represented a threat that would hasten efforts to unite despite remaining areas of disagreement.[43]

Bradford noted that this consequence of the Macdonald Commission was quite different from the mobilizing effects it had on political and bureaucratic elites: 'By disregarding critics of corporate neo-liberalism in their report, after hearing from them during public consultations, the commissioners galvanized a "popular sector" reflecting the concerns of previously disparate social movements. In this way, the process of supplying a governing paradigm had the unintended effect of crystallizing an alignment of oppositional social forces that have mounted a campaign of resistance ever since, even as the brokerage parties embrace the Macdonald Report.'[44] Until a more broadly based compromise around a modified political discourse can be achieved, ongoing conflict between nationalist and continentalist ideologies would seem to be the real legacy of the 'age of Macdonaldism.'

An interesting hypothetical question is, would Canada and the United States (and Mexico) have entered into free trade without the Macdonald Commission? It is beyond the scope of this study to speculate on the American or Mexican positions, of course. But it is possible to argue that the momentum for free trade in Canada was building among certain traditional interests and institutions. Nonetheless, it would appear that without the imprimatur of the Macdonald Commission, progress towards free trade would have been unlikely. For instance, the business community which represented the coalition of interests with sufficient electoral influence to assist the governing party in any free trade initiative was still strikingly divided. Without the forum of the Macdonald Commission, the

BCNI and CMA may have lacked the requisite weight to convince the government of the way ahead. And certainly there was no great outcry from civil society for such an initiative. In addition, those economists who advocated free trade throughout the 1960s, 1970s, and 1980s were voices in the wilderness, as preoccupations with applying Keynesian principles within the framework of a National Policy that sought to protect and nourish a staples-based branch-plant economy prevailed. Finally, the requisite political and bureaucratic leadership was largely absent. The Liberal Party under Trudeau was preoccupied with constitutional politics. To the extent that continental trade policy was considered at all, it was in the context of diversifying trade to other parts of the world through the Third Option and other initiatives. Free trade with the United States was so far down the list of priorities as to be almost invisible. The Conservative Party under Brian Mulroney was divided as to economic development strategies prior to the publication of Macdonald's *Report.* Mulroney himself was of two minds about free trade, as revealed in his pre-election statements during the leadership convention he won. The upper echelons of the bureaucracy were by no means wholly convinced of the merits of free trade, busy as they were adjusting to restructuring. And while certain free trade advocates had emerged within the Department of Foreign Affairs and International Trade, their ideas had yet to achieve the level of viability they subsequently received with the Macdonald Commission's stamp of authority.

Overall, the importance of the Macdonald Commission lies not in the *particulars* of its recommendations for free trade, nor in the extent to which the actual free trade deals signed in its wake have been good or bad for Canada. Rather, the importance of the commission lies in its role as the institutional embodiment of the requisites for transformative change which facilitated the legitimation of the concept of free trade. The commission crystallized the set of ideas, interests, and institutions necessary to allow the dramatic break from an old but not-yet dead paradigm and condition Canadian society to accept the idea of free trade in the abstract. As McBride and Shields note, 'the Macdonald Commission helped to foster an elite consensus around free trade and to confer considerable public legitimacy on the continentalist option as well.'[45]

The ideological battle between two paradigms waged in the institution of the Macdonald Commission (and elsewhere) was fundamentally about legitimizing a new politics and market-driven economic development strategies. Why was the Macdonald Commission so prominent a site for this struggle? Politicians must sometimes employ apparently 'objective' policy instruments to lend legitimacy to their efforts. The royal commission is one such tool. A royal commission is itself a transitory object ostensibly free of the baggage of traditional institutions. It is a temporary institutional site for the intense coalescence of ideas, interests, and institutions in a potentially opportunistic setting. The royal commission can be deftly employed to assist in the complex process of deciding what should be discussed, how issues are defined, whose views are to be taken seriously, and what sorts of solutions are possible. Royal commissions can be used to lend credence to and provide an affirmation of the importance of a problem, and of the values and conflicts associated with it. The words and symbols attached to issues give them shape and meaning. Thus the idea of free trade with the United States emerged after a period of dormancy as various societal actors used the institution of the Macdonald Commission to reintroduce the political discourse of bilateral trade liberalization onto the political agenda.

The commission enabled them to exert influence on the direction and tenor of public discourse and, ultimately, on the policy choices of the state. In the words of Brodie and Jenson, 'a powerful coalition of conservative think-tanks, provincial and federal politicians and business leaders adopted [neoconservatism], tacking on to it support for continental free trade.'[46] These groups used the Macdonald Commission to great advantage in promoting their ideological views.

Indeed, the issue of free trade has spawned a new ideological polarization of Canadian society, one in which the traditional liberal middle has been squeezed out by the neoconservative and social democratic alternatives,[47] and in which nationalism and continentalism have been propelled to the forefront of Canadian consciousness. Bradford argues that 'the Macdonald Commission generated a public philosophy and programmatic ideas that redefined the official policy agenda and crystallized a new alignment of class forces in the political system mobilized to contest its legitimacy.'[48] 'The definition of a system of regulation,' according to Jenson, 'is that it regulates – i.e. stabilizes – social relations even though these relations are contradictory.'[49] Not even the most ardent supporters of the FTA and NAFTA would admit that that goal has been realized. Canada, once an ideological milque-toast by world standards, has became a more overtly ideological battleground in the wake of the Macdonald Commission. The great free trade debate in the 1988 election, as well as the subsequent debate over NAFTA, revealed ongoing contestation over appropriate polices for Canada's economic development and heightened ideological conflict in Canada.[50] For instance, opposition to political union with the United States is higher now than in the 1960s while at the same time a majority of Canadians profess to support the concept of free trade agreements.[51] The issue of privatization of the health care system in Canada has forcefully emerged in recent years, yet 87 per cent of Canadians maintain the Canadian and American health care systems should not be harmonized.[52] The ongoing debate about cultural policy continues to raise issues of national sovereignty. Sixty-seven per cent of Canadians disagree that Canada and the United States basically have the same values,[53] giving rise to serious questions about North American policy convergence.[54] All of these issues are reflective of the ideological conflict that persists. So too is the mobilization by social movements to kill the Multilateral Agreement on Investment (MAI) and challenges to globalization in the streets of Seattle, Genoa, Quebec City, and elsewhere. The nature of that conflict, rooted in nationalist and continentalist positions as they have evolved historically from the era of one Macdonald to another, suggests that Canadian social scientists ought to pay more attention to the role of what Napoleon called that 'shadowy metaphysics which subtly searches for first causes on which to base the legislation of the people,' ideology.

Transformative Moments and Royal Commissions

The introductory chapter of this book asked: How do we explain those transformative moments when new ideas seek to supplant old ones in promoting innovative public policy choices? The transition to neoconservative continentalism as reflected in the FTA and NAFTA is clearly one of those moments wherein conflict concerning strategies for economic development came to a head. In this moment a new policy approach emerged and attempts were made to constitute a new dominant paradigm, complete with a widely recognized theory (free trade) that defined the problem and its solutions. Some problems were acknowledged and received attention, while others were relegated to the margins of public policy concern or rejected.[55] The new paradigm resulted in profound and far-reaching policy choices and changes, including a radical departure from 'conventional' practice. How long this new approach will prevail remains to be seen, but eventually its limitations will be revealed, another alternative conceptual framework will begin to emerge, and the process will repeat itself.

A dynamic relationship among ideas, interests, and institutions drives policy change and lies behind many transformative moments in public policy.[56] Paradigm shift occurs when the inadequacy of an existing policy frame or theory is revealed through unsustainable disruptions that affect the political and social order. Under these conditions, ideational challenges are more likely to successfully assail governments and the major ideas underlying their policies.[57] Thus Keynesianism became the dominant theory in the post-war years, supplanting the set of ideas which failed to cope with the upheaval of the Great Depression. As the prevailing orthodoxy, though, eventually Keynesianism too fell into disrepute for failing to provide policy prescriptions for the crises in capitalism which arose in the 1970s.[58]

So long as Keynesianism was hegemonic, other ideational paradigms languished on the margins of legitimacy. But the inability of a hegemonic paradigm to explain and deal with growing numbers of contradictions undermines its sustainability, and interests and institutions then turn to alternative theories, models, and systems to make better sense of the new reality. Thus when crises emerged in the 1970s (and especially the depression of 1981–2), and the Keynesian formula failed to provide solutions, a new set of ideas was proposed to challenge and ultimately to replace it. This occurred as conflict emerged between interests and institutions seeking to preserve and promote, or to challenge and replace, the prevailing paradigmatic views and practices in the political and economic system. Such struggles can be protracted, for although 'in the long run we may all be dead, it may take a very long time to kill a powerful set of ideas.'[59] Ideological conflict is the driving force as proponents of the new, and defenders of the old, pose their arguments. Each seeks to employ discourse which unifies society around a common vision or, as Thompson calls it, a 'representation of its unity.'[60] Transformative moments arise out of this cauldron of conflict between ideas, presuming the existence of interests and an institutional site where the requisites of transformative change can successfully coalesce.

Traditional interests and institutions (prime ministers and Cabinets, the bureaucracy, Parliament, courts, political parties, etc.) might be able to provide such a site.[61] But the Canadian experience has witnessed another location where this can take place – the royal commission. This was clearly reflected in the Macdonald Royal Commission: 'The Macdonald Commission became the "switch-point mechanism" in shifting the terms of economic policy debate and practice. Like earlier era-defining royal commission inquiries, it intervened as partisan channels of political representation and bureaucratic networks of policy formation were each unable to devise or implement solutions to protracted economic problems. The commission constructed a policy discourse of corporate neo-liberalism that galvanized the business community and the economics profession, at the same time that it provided a governing agenda for a PC administration in serious political difficulty.'[62] All these conditions pertained in Canada in the 1970s and 1980s and found expression through the various components of the Macdonald Commission. Political viability was achieved through selective use of the public submissions which created the perception that widespread support for free trade was 'in the air.' Important business groups like the BCNI, the CMA, and the Chambers of Commerce were repeatedly cited as supporters for this new course of action, supplying the requisite electoral support to the policy's political supporters. This support for a program for change found intellectual sustenance in the work of neoclassical economists who were given place of prominence in the commission in the consideration of economic development strategies for Canada. In the absence of strong, vocal social science research refuting the views of the economists, free trade was made to appear as the only economic option available.[63] Thus, economic viability was supplied through the economists' ability to deliver the requisite of addressing serious economic problems better than existing policies were able. Political and bureaucratic leadership was the third requisite, and as we saw, the policy group ensured free trade was the key focus and recommendation of volume I of the *Report*. The lead commissioner, ensconced in the world of corporate continental power, manipulated the process with public pronouncements (most notably the 'leap of faith' statement) and force of character to ensure the outcome he desired. The result was the legitimation of free trade, an ideological concept which historically had been regarded with distrust by most Canadians since the 1878 National Policy of that other Macdonald.

The requisites supporting the neoconservative continentalist ideology did not go unopposed, of course. However, to the extent that there was opposition, it was successfully marginalized. Political viability, therefore, was achieved notwithstanding the objections of organized labour and the popular sector to free trade who, in any event, could not easily muster the resources to unite an electoral coalition. Economic viability was achieved partly because the opposition could only garner intellectual sustenance for its arguments from a handful of dissentient academics within the economics profession, mainly from those in political economy who were frozen out of meaningful participation within the commission research program. Thus, the nationalist social democratic arguments were handed over to two mainstream political scientists whose ambivalence towards the position they were supposedly defending was well known. In the end the research program, dominated by pro–free trade economists and laden with its 'freedom to be irrelevant,' massaged economic arguments in favour of free trade, while largely excluding contrary positions. The political and bureaucratic leadership which might have formed in opposition to free trade was isolated or effectively marginalized as well. In the face of Macdonald's command of the commission, other commissioners were left relatively mute and impotent, while the internecine battles within the bureaucracy of the commission resulted in the ascendance of Nymark, Godsoe, Hart, and other supporters of the free trade position.

Ideology and the Role of the Macdonald Commission

Ideology, as a set of values, attitudes, and beliefs, needs three things to distinguish it from other thought systems or philosophies. It needs at its origin to have a program for change (or maintenance of the status quo); to have agents willing to take action to initiate or defend that program; and, in order to be functional, it must be tied to groups or classes with concrete material interests. Once these conditions are satisfied, ideology works to legitimize political discourse.

The FTA (and NAFTA) were clearly about much more than trade, just as the political economists had been saying all along, and notwithstanding the protestations of the economists to the contrary. As Stritch argues, 'underlying this whole movement toward continental free trade has been a resurgent faith in the virtues of laissez-faire economics over industrial planning, which has been a feature of the rightward swing in North American politics in the 1980s.'[64] Gary Teeple argues that the virtue of the free market is invoked because 'it is the philosophical rationale for the advancement of the interests of private property and for undoing much of the postwar [Keynesian Welfare State]. It is the rationale for privatizing public corporations and for deregulating the operation of the economy, for relieving the state of any functions that restrict private accumulation.'[65] As Brodie and Jenson explain: 'The Macdonald Commission and the Mulroney government have presented free trade as if it is governed by the neutral mechanisms of the market, but it is anything but neutral. It harmonizes perfectly with the neoconservative political agenda and strategy for industrial restructuring which entails a market-driven approach to economic growth, continental rationalization, government cut-backs in social services, reduced rights for workers, and a lesser role for the state in the economy.'[66] Thus the ideology behind free trade has an intellectual pedigree, and must be recognized for what it is: a set of values, attitudes, and beliefs animated by a critique of the status quo and a programme for change. That program is promulgated in the interests of particular societal and state actors. And it is this ideology that the Macdonald Commission officially endorsed.

However, the contradictions of the system in crisis have not been transcended. The new paradigm and political discourse has not been totally embraced because it has been unable to completely erase the disjuncture between ideology and economic reality. Ideological conflict continues.[67] Neoconservative continentalism has made vast changes to the ideological complexion of Canada; indeed, it could be argued that the old left-centre-right ideological spectrum has shifted significantly as a result. But this has not been without serious ongoing contestation and protest. A new paradigm has been constructed and erected, but it stands on feeble supports, lacking the broad-based social consensus enjoyed by the edifice it replaced, the Keynesian paradigm.

Theories of ideology in Canada have been inadequate to explain the dynamic nature of Canadian ideologies. Premised as they are on a static view of ideology, and one which largely neglects to incorporate the notions of nationalism and continentalism, traditional scholarship in this area needs to be rethought. The approach taken in this study has been to view ideology as dynamic and to accord a place of prominence to nationalism and continentalism as a key point of division in Canadian society and policy making. In addition, this study has shown the malleability and flexibility of ideology by revealing how nationalism and continentalism can be linked to other ideologies, such as social democracy and neoconservatism. Moreover, it has also shown how ideologies require attachment to social groups and actors to be realized. Transformative moments in public policy are dependent upon the power of ideas in alignment with interests and institutions. Together these constitute the requisites which lend viability to alterations in the political economy of a society.

Political discourse finds expression through the ideological pronouncements of political and societal actors, a point illustrated in a 1985 article by journalist Tom Walkom. He described the emergence of neoconservative discourse in Canada under the leadership of Brian Mulroney's Tories as a crusade to make Canada safe for capital by manipulating the language of politics.[68] Walkom cited many of the holy nostrums of this discourse, such as: 'Canadians must start facing up to economic reality' and 'get the government off our backs' in order to 'create confidence' which will allow us to 'compete in the global economy.' But while the purpose of these phrases is to fortify the representation of unity, Walkom pointed out that underlying these statements are a whole set of unexamined assumptions, and that the words used leave no room for questions:

> The metaphors of the new conservatism are systematic and shameless. The late Karl Marx once pointed out that the genius of bourgeois political economy was its ability to cloak a specific historical economic system (the way things are) in the guise of nature (the way things must be).
>
> He would be glad to know that the old magic still holds. The 'economic realities' which the assemblage of politicians, experts and pundits insist we must face because we have no choice are, in fact, questions. And they are questions about which we do, or should have, a great deal of choice.[69]

This discourse originated in the ideologies of Thatcherism and Reaganism, and in the work of economists like Friedman, Hayek, and others, the latter ostensibly 'neutral' and therefore authoritative social scientists. Walkom also laid part of the blame on the Trudeau government, when the former prime minister lectured the nation on television in 1982 and 1983 using such phrases as 'international competitiveness' and 'belt-tightening.'[70] But of course it went deeper than that, as Trudeau was only popularizing a language and way of talking which had originated elsewhere:

> Rather, this language is the pure product of elites. It contains no earthy 'chicken in every pot' or 'Bennett buggy' metaphors like those which characterized earlier economic crises. Instead, phrases like 'international competitiveness' and 'disincentive to job search' were obviously cooked in university economics departments by the Milton Friedmans and George Stiglers of the world. Then the phrases were processed and moulded – first through so-called think tanks, such as the Fraser Institute; secondly, through a legion of analysts and business economists working for stock brokers, investment dealers and banks. At this latter stage, the language was peppered with what passes as common sense among businessmen – phrases such as 'living beyond our means' or 'belt tightening' or 'business confidence.' These analysts, in turn, were the experts whom financial journalists could interview. Here the real word smithery was done: phrases such as 'repairing the corporate balance sheets' were hammered out on word processors across the country by finely skilled artisans.[71]

Walkom also suggests that bureaucrats in Ottawa picked up on the new discourse under the Tories for fear that failure to do so would cost them their jobs.[72] Thus, several influential segments of society were soon speaking the new discourse, or were being exposed to a relentless barrage of it, in a concerted effort to reshape political discourse. And as the experience of the Macdonald Commission reveals, when powerful interests like the BCNI, the CMA, and the Chamber of Commerce mobilize ideology and launch an assault on the prevailing political discourse, the outcome can be dramatic.

Ideology depends crucially on dissemination through various media to implicitly and invisibly foster social consensus. Royal commissions can play this function. The process of widespread public debate and discussion dealing with all aspects of life creates the impression that social relations are fully reciprocal and that speech circulates without internal obstacles or constraints. The 'expert' emerges (e.g., the disinterested social scientist, or the authoritative royal commissioner), appearing as anonymous and neutral while expressing and diffusing so-called objective knowledge. No matter how banal (e.g., 'leap of faith'), intimate words providing constant assurance of a social bond are used to erase the intolerable fact of social division.[73]

Once ensconced, ideology tries to preclude questions concerning the established order or the possible. It creates a closed universe which is repetitive and pre-arranged. But it makes this closure invisible by the very essence of a totalizing discourse. This does not mean that all contradictions are easily resolved. On the contrary, the more the ideology seeks to coincide with the social itself, that is, the more 'invisible' it seeks to become, the more it runs the risk of losing the function which ideology has assumed – legitimation of established order.[74] Indeed, the construction of a compromise that might bring the system back into regulation is by its nature a process of representing power relations based on differences, according to Jenson, in which collective identities develop: 'Not all identities are possible, however; there are limits which arise from the weight of the past, as well as from the balance of the forces in the present. Imagining a new way of living or being – imagining a new collective identity, in other words – is not simple. The new will often arise out of the old, because it is, after all, experience which is usually the best guide to the future. Yet there is always the possibility of taking a leap of faith, of simply dreaming of a new situation in which the wrongs of the present disappear.'[75]

These theoretical points are illustrated by the disjuncture between the ideological promise of free trade and the economic reality of its effects in Canada. The promotion of a political discourse whose main features are a pronounced anti-statism and greater integration into the continental economy has been contentious. The ongoing crisis in capitalism it seeks to explain away has not abated. The emergence of the anti-globalization movement speaks to this reality. In concrete terms, the promise of the ideology of free trade has not been realized; the 'leap of faith' has so far revealed an abyss without a safety net, notwithstanding the ideological invocation of prosperity and 'jobs, jobs, jobs.'

Capitalist society is in a perpetual state of struggle and conflict, dynamism and evolution. We need to understand the transition in capitalism from long periods of relative stability to periods of crisis, and back to stability again. A consideration of the role of ideology assists in this endeavour. The changes undergone by Canada in the period from the 1970s onward, politically and economically, are reflective of a society undergoing profound, even cathartic reordering. The ideologically driven prescriptions articulated by the Macdonald Commission to deal with those changes reflect this. Changes to the capitalist system invoked a crisis which was marked by a variety of trends and phenomena rocking the Western industrialized world since the 1970s, leading to severe questioning of the post-war Keynesian consensus.

The transition from Keynesianism has not been a smooth one, and it has engendered much debate and soul searching among Canadians.[76] Despite its turbulent history, punctuated by periods of crisis, capitalism is remarkable for its propensity for long periods of relative stability. As Alain Lipietz points out: 'Even in times of conflict and recession, its overall framework, its aims and rules are by and large accepted by almost everyone. This framework and these aims and rules have been thrown into turmoil three times in the course of history: at the end of the nineteenth century, in the 1930s–50s and since the end of the 1960s. But in the intervals between these major crises, there was a "grand compromise" between social groups, the basis of which was a 'development model' consisting of a definition, adopted for the time being, of what humanity can best expect from economic activity: the organizing principles of the labour process, the aims of production and the ground rules for resolving tensions.'[77] While relative prosperity prevails, a broad world-view is inculcated in most citizens in society, including a definition of the benefits of living in that society. The model prevails as a practical ideal of the good life, and while critics of the actual process of realizing the model may offer 'utopian' alternatives, in general the overall design of the model itself is not challenged.

On the other hand, in periods of crisis the model comes to make little sense, according to Lipietz: 'On these occasions, the model and its aims, rules and promises seem out of date; unworkable economically and rejected politically and socially. These periods are the crossroads of history, when initiatives for change override the dead weight of routine; they are open periods, where the outcome remains uncertain for well over a decade – periods when blueprints or 'projects' are redefined, and social forces realigned.'[78] Lipietz argues that this situation prevailed in the 1970s and 1980s, when we were in 'one of those open periods when what is in contention is not the fairest and most efficient way to apply an agreed model, but the actual definition of a new development model, a new grand compromise.'[79] The crisis persists as long as societal elites and social groups fail to devise a world-view and development model acceptable to society as a whole. The Macdonald Commission stands as a bold attempt to choose a new direction at the crossroads and to develop a new 'grand compromise.'

Jenson argues that 'as the crisis of fordism arrived in Canada the economic contradictions which it exposed were those of a permeable regime of accumulation, while politics took the form of ideological debate over competing national identities ...'[80] The search for solutions and answers to the crisis involved both casting backwards to traditional Keynesian solutions, as well as seeking to supplant the old with something new. Inevitably, the Canadian rejoinder involved observing and copying the British and American responses. Thus, one ideologically rooted answer to these problems was to adopt a version of the Thatcher-Reagan–inspired neoconservative vision and append it to the continentalist imperative inherent in the Canadian-American relationship. Hence, a market-driven model struggles to implant itself. The Macdonald Commission is testament to a 'period of efflorescence,'[81] as the old Keynesian paradigm was assaulted by a new one. The success of that new paradigm is reflected in the altered political and economic conditions which emerged in the wake of the Macdonald Commission's work. At the root of these changes is a fervent belief in free markets and free trade. But to legitimate this view requires altering thinking in a way that makes minimizing the role of the state broadly acceptable. This is no easy task, since it stands in sharp contrast to over a hundred years of Canadian experience. But this option was chosen by the Mulroney government after it was given the imprimatur of the most significant exercise in legitimation in a generation. The ideological appeal of free trade was used to achieve its broader goals of downsizing the Canadian state. The Macdonald Commission played an important role in providing the rationale for the ideological masking of this process by couching it in the discourse of free trade, economic growth, and development which only partially hid a patently pro-market, anti-state, neoconservative world-view.

In the Canadian setting, there is a direct link between a pro–free market and anti-state political perspective and continentalist economic development strategies. Writing shortly after the Macdonald Commission, Peter Leslie observed that the continentalist option, which called for minimal government interference in the market as the mechanism for allocating economic resources, had triumphed: 'This option holds pride of place in Canada today, in the sense that much political rhetoric voices it, some policies are clearly inspired by it, most business opinion is ranged in its favour, and intellectually it is supported by an overwhelming majority of the economics profession. It has received comprehensive formulation, and qualified endorsement in the report of the Macdonald Commission: the report, while making some gestures toward the interventionist provincialist opposition, adopts mainly a liberal-continentalist line.'[82] Free trade fosters greater economic integration between Canada and the United States. It reorients the traditional East-West economic foundation upon which Canada was built and aims it North-South. It creates the conditions for fostering greater integration into the American economy.[83] But it depends for its existence on a fundamentally anti-state orientation.

Free trade with the United States is not a new concept.[84] But it had always been resisted and rejected on the basis that the Canadian economy was fundamentally national in orientation, with overtones of continentalism. The Macdonald Commission reversed that pattern by legitimating development strategies that were continentalist in orientation and which subsumed traces of the national perspective.

Where economic development strategies for Canada are concerned, the nationalist perspective has always suffered from a fundamental dilemma: determining the appropriate level of state involvement in the economy. In order to thrive as a capitalist economy, Canada has been forced to be cognizant of the American manner of doing business. Carolyn Tuohy suggests that this has resulted in an ambivalence in Canada about the appropriate roles of the state and the market: 'The integration of the Canadian and U.S. economies constrains the extent to which Canada can deviate from the state-market mix adopted in the United States. Closer integration, indeed, implies increased access for Canadian products to the larger U.S. market. But the Canadian desire to preserve its distinctiveness from the United States argues for the counterposing of state to market pressure.'[85] The Canadian state historically has attempted to temper the worst excesses of unbridled American-style capitalism through a political and social ethos of compassion and caring. Whatever the sociological roots of these differences between America and Canada,[86] the fact remains that the main instrument for the social and political development of Canada has been the state. Tuohy underscores the essential dilemma this provokes for a country tied so closely to the United States in terms of providing social and other forms of adjustment assistance to citizens broadsided by changes to the economy: 'The ability to develop and implement adjustment policies has been constrained by the significance of U.S. trade and investment in the Canadian economy, and by the fact that economic performance, and the costs and benefits of economic policies, vary widely across regions. Because it entails these fundamental tensions of Canadian political life, the challenge of economic adjustment is as much a political as an economic problem.'[87] The counterposing of state to market has been severely compromised by the institutionalization of continentalist policies in the form of the FTA and NAFTA, or the new 'economic constitution of North America,' as Ronald Reagan called it.[88]

The reality is that the final image reflected by the mirror of the commission Macdonald headed is a distorted one. Reflecting the interests and beliefs of some Canadians, but failing to reflect those of most others, the Macdonald Commission legitimized continentalist accumulation for Canada, signalling the ascendance of market principles and a loss of concern for preserving the distinctiveness Tuohy refers to. But it remains a contested legitimation, since the emerging political discourse has not completely supplanted the old one. Antipathy towards embracing the free market model in total is evidenced in the vibrant ongoing debate in Canada over health care, the provision of other public services, and culture, for instance, as well as the vocal and growing anti-globalization movement. The politics of the Macdonald Commission produced a legacy within which crisis persists.

Written Briefs Examined for This Study

Following is a list of the written briefs examined for this study. The numbers in the left hand column are those assigned to each brief by the Macdonald Commission.

Business Groups

Total number surveyed – 181

BRIEF	NAME OF ORGANIZATION
0006	Family Farm Foundation of Canada
0007	Grocery Products Manufacturers of Canada
0012	Retail Council of Canada
0021	H.N. Halvorson Consultants Ltd.
0026	Diament Knitting Mills Ltd.
0030	Cartier Circle
0062	Federated Co-operatives Ltd.
0079	Canadian Manufacturers Association
0080	B.C. Central Credit Union
0086	Association of British Columbia Professional Foresters
0092	Mainland Dairyman's Association
0103	Council of Forest Industries of British Columbia
0105	Vancouver Board of Trade
0107	Mining Association of British Columbia
0110	Registered Nurses Association of British Columbia
0113	Placer Development Ltd.
0114	British Columbia Association of Social Workers
0145	Canadian Federation of Agriculture

0147	Software Industry Development Association
0158	St. John's Board of Trade
0163	Greater Victoria Chamber of Commerce
0165	Atlantic Provinces Chamber of Commerce
0173	Greater Charlottetown Area Chamber of Commerce
0181	Canadian Manufacturers Association (P.E.I. Branch)
0186	Employer's Council of British Columbia
0193	St. John Board of Trade
0207	Fredericton Chamber of Commerce
0228	New Brunswick Telephone Company Ltd.
0231	Fisheries Council of Canada
0239	Maritime Lumber Bureau
0241	Maritime Electric Company Ltd. (Charlottetown)
0242	Greater Summerside Chamber of Commerce
0251	Newfoundland Light and Power Company Ltd.
0259	Industrial Cape Breton Board of Trade (Sydney)
0266	Yukon Visitors Association
0268	Whitehorse Chamber of Commerce
0287	Prince George Chamber of Commerce
0289	Nashwaak Consulting
0305	North West Territories Chamber of Commerce
0319	Canadian Forestry Association
0334	Halifax Board of Trade
0335	Prince Edward Island Federation of Agriculture
0345	Jim Lotz Associates
0352	Dartmouth Chamber of Commerce
0355	Film Factory Ltd.
0368	Canadian Pulp and Paper Ltd.
0385	Falconbridge Ltd.
0392	Winnipeg Commodity Exchange
0393	Canadian Hardware and Housewares Manufacturing Assoc.
0394	Motor Vehicle Manufacturers Association
0395	Canadian Council of Furniture Manufacturers
0396	Canadian Electrical Distributors Association
0397	Tourism Industry Association of Canada
0412	Association of Canadian Advertisers Inc.
0415	Canadian Direct Marketing Association
0416	Electrical and Electronic Manufacturers Association
0420	Novatron Information Corporation
0424	Chamber of Commerce Northwest Inc.

0657	Housing and Urban Development Association of Canada
0661	London Life Insurance Company
0665	Saskatoon Board of Trade
0667	Pratt and Whitney Canada Inc.
0668	Canadian Cattleman's Association
0679	Lethbridge Chamber of Commerce
0691	Management Council for Responsible Employee Relations
0697	Canadian Association for Professional Engineers
0701	Canadian Food Processors Association
0703	Canadian Institute of Forestry
0708	Canadian Soft Drink Association
0710	Canadian Council of Professional Engineers
0722	Ottawa – Carleton Board of Trade
0723	Canadian Agricultural Chemicals Association
0728	Association of Professional Engineers of Saskatchewan
0736	Bell Canada Enterprises Incorporated
0737	Canadian Life and Health Insurance Association
0738	Canadian Business and Industry International Advisory Council
0744	Ontario Secondary School Teachers Federation
0745	Canadian Teachers Federation
0746	Board of Trade of Metro Toronto
0750	SNC Group
0754	Control Data Canada Ltd.
0760	Northern Telecom Ltd.
0761	Ontario Federation of Agriculture
0762	Cooperative Trust Company of Canada
0783	CNCP Telecommunications
0784	Dow Chemical Canada Ltd.
0786	Canadian Organic Producers Marketing Cooperative Ltd.
0790	Society of AECL Professional Employees (WNRE)
0792	Canadian Hospital Association
0795	Association of Deans of Pharmacy of Canada
0808	Prairie Implement Manufacturers Association
0810	Foreign Bank Section of the Canadian Bankers Association
0813	George Weston Ltd.
0823	Canadian Business Equipment Manufacturers Association
0858	Smith International Canada Ltd.
0862	Association of Canadian Financial Corporations
0864	Canadian Nurses Association
0874	Machinery and Equipment Manufacturers Association of Canada

1074	BP Selco Incorporated
1085	Ontario Teachers Federation
1103	Canadian Chamber of Commerce (Montreal)
1138	Corner Brook Chamber of Commerce
1148	Michael Jarvis Consultants Ltd.

Labour Groups

Total number surveyed – 40

BRIEF	NAME OF ORGANIZATION
0117	British Columbia and Yukon Building and Construction Trades Council
0126	International Union of Operating Engineers (Local 115)
0166	Nova Scotia Federation of Labour (CLC)
0169	Marine Workers Federation
0185	International Woodworkers of America
0191	Newfoundland and Labrador Federation of Labour
0200	National Farmers Union (P.E.I.)
0208	United Steelworkers of America (Local 1064, Sydney)
0250	United Mine Workers of America (District 26, Sydney)
0255	New Brunswick Public Employees Association
0257	New Brunswick Federation of Labour
0261	North West Territories Public Service Association
0280	Association of New Brunswick Teachers
0356	United Steelworkers of America (Local 6500, Sudbury)
0373	Nova Scotia Teachers Union
0380	United Steelworkers of America (Local 6166, Thompson)
0408	Nova Scotia Nurses Union
0456	Windsor and District Labour Council
0488	Thunder Bay and District Labour Council
0573	Winnipeg Labour Council
0613	Non-Organized Workers of Thunder Bay
0633	United Steelworkers of America
0687	Canadian Airline Pilots Association
0689	Alliance of Canadian Television and Radio Actors
0720	International Association of Machinists and Aerospace Workers
0740	Labour Council of Metro Toronto
0747	Communications Workers of Canada
0755	National Union of Provincial Government Employees

0819   United Mine Workers of America District 18 (Alberta)
0842   Manitoba Federation of Labour
0903   Canadian Air Line Employees Association
0909   Professional Institute of the Public Service of Canada
0913   Ontario Public Service Employees Union
0934   United Auto Workers of Canada
0946   Hamilton and District Labour Council (CLC)
0990   Saskatchewan Federation of Labour (CLC)
0991   National Farmers Union
1042   Canadian Labour Congress
1048   Canadian Union of Public Employees
1049   Canadian Federation of Labour

Popular Sector

Total number surveyed – 81

BRIEF   NAME OF ORGANIZATION
0036   Pacific Group for Policy Alternatives
0100   Assembly of British Columbia Arts Councils
0109   Canadian Council on Social Development
0115   Lambton County Board of Education
0123   Capital Families
0170   Federation of New Brunswick Faculty Associations
0174   Status of Women Action Group of British Columbia
0197   First United Church (Vancouver)
0198   Asia Pacific Foundation of Canada
0210   Federation of Community Development Corporation of
       Canada
0217   Social Planning and Review Council of British Columbia
0240   New Dawn Enterprises Ltd.
0263   Storefront for Voluntary Agencies (Yellowknife)
0269   Women Against the Budget
0285   Nuu-Chah-Nulth Tribal Council
0294   Human Resources Development Association
0295   Women United for a Non-Exploitive New Age
0307   Nunavut Constitutional Forum
0336   Social Action Commission of the Roman Catholic Diocese of
       Charlottetown
0344   Northwestern Ontario Women's Centre

0347   Thunder Bay and District Council of Clergy
0349   Canadian Pensioners Concerned Incorporated
0350   Ecology Action Centre
0375   Lakehead Social Planning Council
0378   Family Service Association of Metro Toronto
0381   Nishnawbe-Aski Nation
0382   Women and Economic Development Committee of the
       Northwestern Ontario Women's Decade Council
0400   Thunder Bay Multicultural Association
0401   Windsor Women's Incentive Centre
0405   Canadian School Trustees Association
0423   Windsor Coalition for Development and the Third World
       Resource Centre
0428   United Way of Thompson
0432   Sudbury 2001
0471   Women's Information and Referral Centre of Montreal
0501   Makivik Corporation
0588   Winnipeg Coordinating Committee for Disarmament
0591   Northern Flood Committee (Winnipeg)
0595   Paradigm Health
0634   Canadian Crafts Council
0652   St Patrick's Social Justice Committee
0654   Lethbridge Interagency Committee
0658   Canadian Baha'i Community
0666   Canadian Mental Health Association
0677   Midas Reform Movement of Alberta
0684   Help the Aged
0686   Coalition for National Voluntary Organizations
0690   Young Women's Christian Association of Canada
0693   Citizens for Public Justice
0698   National Council of Women of Canada
0699   Canadian Red Cross Society
0714   Council of National Ethnocultural Organizations
0741   Canadian Rehabilitation Council for the Disabled
0742   Association of Universities and Colleges of Canada
0767   Social Planning Council of Winnipeg
0787   Community Forum on Shared Responsibility
0789   National Action Committee on the Status of Women
0798   Catholic Social Services
0806   Churches of Edmonton

Categorization of Topics from Macdonald Commission Content Analysis

In its content analysis, the Macdonald Commission categorized the briefs according to the issues and topics each brief dealt with. It is on the basis of this categorization that the written briefs were chosen for this study.

Following is the list of topics from the Macdonald Commission content analysis which was used to categorize each brief and as the basis for selecting briefs for this study.

The Canadian Economy
The Canadian Economy
Economic Performance
Statistics
Canadian Historic Trends
Canadian Future Projections
International Trends, Patterns and Projections
International Comparisons
Goals and Objectives
Economics: Theory and Society
Economic Competitiveness
Productivity
Wages and Incomes
Comparative Advantages
Adaptability
Economic Union
Canadian Common Market
Mobility of Labour
Mobility of Goods
Mobility of Capital

Government Intervention in the Economy
Federal Industrial Development Policies
Provincial Industrial Development Policies
Federal-Provincial Industrial Development Policies
Research and Development Assistance
Government Intervention (continued)
Competition Policy, Combines and Monopolies
Foreign Investment and FIRA
National Energy Policy

Sectors of the Economy
Industrial Structure
The Small Business Sector
Canadian Multinationals
Foreign Ownership
Competition
Profitability
International Comparisons
Economic Adjustment and Long Term Restructuring
Research and Development
Labour-Management Relations
Canadian Management
Markets
Proposals
Economic Diversification

Commerce, Finance, and Public Revenue
Public Debt
Government Spending
Financial Management and Accountability

International Trade and Foreign Policy
International Trade and Foreign Policy
Trade
Open Economy Versus Protectionism
Statistics
International Comparisons
International Treaties and Agreements
Impact of International Trade on the Canadian Economy
Canada-United States Relations

People Interviewed

Following is a list of people interviewed for this study. Interviews were conducted between 1992 and 1994 with over thirty-five individuals involved in the Macdonald Commission, as well as with government officials. A complete list of the staff of the Macdonald Commission can be found in Appendix E of the Macdonald Commission *Report*, vol. 3, 691–4.

Commissioners
Donald Macdonald (Toronto, 18 August, 13 September 1993)
Clarence Barber (Victoria, 23 August 1994)
Albert Breton (Toronto, 4 October 1993)
Jean Casselman-Wadds (Prescott, ON, 16 September 1994)
Gerard Docquier (Ottawa, 21 February 1994)
Thomas Shoyama (Toronto, 4 August 1993)

Directors of Research
Ivan Bernier (Quebec City, 24 August 1994)
Alan Cairns (Ottawa, 8 June 1993)
David C. Smith (Toronto, 6 June 1994)

Co-Directors of Research
John Sargent (Ottawa, 8 June 1993)

Director of Policy
Alan Nymark (Ottawa, 2 June 1993)

Senior Advisers
David Ablett (Ottawa, 21 June 1993)

Policy Coordinators
Jamie Benedickson (Ottawa, 22 November 1992)
Michael Hart (Ottawa, 27 November 1992)
David Husband (Ottawa, 30 May 1994)
Richard Van Loon (Ottawa, 16 June 1993)

Special Adviser
Michel Vastel (Ottawa, 23 February 1994)

Researcher Coordinators
Peter Aucoin (Toronto, 8 January 1993)
Keith Banting (Ottawa, 6 June 1993)
Bruce Doern (Ottawa, 6 June 1993)
Karen Jackson (Ottawa, 8 June 1993)
John Quinn (Toronto, 23 June 1993)
Richard Simeon (Toronto, 18 November 1992)
Denis Stairs (Halifax, 18 May 1994)
John Whalley (London, ON, 18 January 1993)
Cynthia Williams (Ottawa, 21 June 1993)
Gilbert Winham (Ottawa, 7 June 1993)

Researchers
Marsha Chandler (Toronto, 15 June 1993)
Richard Harris (Toronto, 13 July 1992)
Gerry Helleiner (Toronto, 4 June 1993)
Peggy Ann Wall (Ottawa, 22 June 1993)

Government Officials
Michael Kirby (Ottawa, 8 June 1993)
Arthur Kroeger (Toronto, 18 November 1992)
Ian Stewart (Ottawa, 22 June 1993)

Others
Robert Prichard (Toronto, 13 May 1993)
Peter Warrian (Toronto, 20 September 1993)

Commissioners' Biographies

The following biographical material was distributed by the Macdonald Commission in Canada, *A Commission on Canada's Future: Be a Part of It,* (Ottawa: 1982), 1–15.

Donald Macdonald

A Member of Parliament for 16 years, Donald Macdonald was appointed as President of the Privy Council and Government House Leader in 1968, and served as Minister of National Defense, Energy, Mines and Resources, and Finance. He returned to his law practice at the firm of McCarthy and McCarthy in Toronto in 1978. Aside from the practice of law, he conducts a class at the University of Toronto Law School and serves on the boards of a number of corporations and charitable organizations. As well as being chairman of this Royal Commission on the Economic Union and Development Prospects for Canada, he is also chairman of the International Development Research Centre.

Dr. Clarence Barber

Dr. Barber is a professor of economics at the University of Manitoba. His publications include articles and books on unemployment, tariffs, trade and fiscal policy. He is past president of the Canadian Economics Association and a Fellow of the Royal Society of Canada. He was Commissioner on Welfare for the province of Manitoba, a federal one-man Commission on Farm Machinery (1966–1970) and a United Nations Advisor on National Income in the Phillipines [sic]. He was Director of Research for the Royal Commission on Flood Cost Benefit for the province of Manitoba.

Dr. Albert Breton

A graduate of the University of Manitoba and Columbia University, Dr. Breton is an author and professor of economics at the University of Toronto. He has focused his writing in areas related to problems of theory and policy in economics and to matters of social and institutional concern. He has received several scholarships and awards for his work from the Social Sciences and Humanities Research Council of Canada and the Canada Council. He is a member of the Canadian Economic Policy Committee C.D. Howe Research Institute. Dr. Breton was Vice-Chairman of the Federal Cultural Policy Review (Applebaum-Hebert) Committee from 1979–82.

Gerard Docquier

Gerard Docquier, now serving his second term as National Director of the United Steelworkers of America, is a Vice-President of the Canadian Labour Congress representing both the CLC and the Steelworkers at the International Conference of Free Trade Unions and the International Labour Organization. He is also the Canadian Steelworkers representative on the Central Committee of the International Metalworkers Federation and is a member of the General Council of the Quebec Federation of Labour. Founding president of the St. Jean Credit Union and Housing Co-op, Mr. Docquier is active in the co-op movement. Born in Belgium, he settled in Quebec after the Second World War.

Honourable William Hamilton

Mr. Hamilton was the President and Chief Executive Officer of the Employers' Council of B.C. from 1972–83. He was elected to Parliament in 1952 and served as Post-Master General for five years in the Diefenbaker government prior to his business career in Vancouver. The recipient of many honours and awards, he is Chairman of Fidelity Life Assurance Company and Century Insurance Company of Canada as well a Director of, among other organizations, the Institute for Research on Public Policy and the Investment Dealers Association of Canada.

John Messer

Mr. Messer has been both a farmer and businessman, but is perhaps best known as a former member of the Government of Saskatchewan. Before his resignation in 1980, he held the cabinet portfolios of Agriculture, Industry and Commerce, and Energy and Resources. As well he was Chairman of a number of Saskatchewan resource and public utility corporations and a member of the Crown Investment Corporation and the Saskatchewan Treasury Board. Mr. Messer serves on the boards of a number of Canadian companies and is a principal in a western Canadian investment and resource development company.

Angela Cantwell Peters

Born and raised in Newfoundland, Angela Peters is Chairman of Bowring Brothers Ltd., St. John's. She is a Director of Central Trust and a member of the Prime Minister's Committee on Public Sector Compensation. She studied advanced business management at Harvard University, served as a member of Memorial University's Board of Regents for five years and was Chairman of the Finance Committee for three of the five years. She is a past Director of the St. John's Board of Trade.

Laurent Picard

Born in Quebec City, Mr. Picard holds degrees in philosophy, applied science (physics) and business administration. He began his career in the academic world as Director of the Business Administration Department, and as Associate Dean as L'Ecole des Hautes Etudes Commerciales at the University of Montreal, returning to it in 1978 as Dean of the Faculty of Management of McGill University, Montreal. At present a director of several companies, he was President and Chief Executive Officer of the Canadian Broadcasting Corporation, the first President of the Commonwealth Broadcasting Association, a Commissioner on the Industrial Inquiry Commission on St. Lawrence Ports and President of the Research Commission on the Shoe Industry of Quebec. Most recently he served as a Commissioner of the Royal Commission on Newspapers.

Michel Robert

The founding partner of his own law firm in Montreal, Michel Robert has been a member of the Legislation and Law Reform Committee of the Canadian Bar Association. As one of Canada's senior constitutional lawyers, he represented the Canadian government as counsel on the patriation of the constitution. He also represented the government of Canada before the Jean F. Keable Commission which inquired into police operations in the province of Quebec and earlier the Commission of Inquiry into Certain Activities of the Royal Canadian Mounted Police. A past president of the Professional Training Committee for the Quebec Bar and past president of the Federation of Law Societies of Canada, Mr. Robert was Batonnier for Quebec in 1976.

Daryl Kenneth Seaman
Born and raised in Saskatchewan, 'Doc' Seaman is Chairman of the Board and Director of Bow Valley Industries, a worldwide explorer and developer of energy resources. He is also a director of several other resource companies. An enthusiastic sportsman, he is a former Governor of the Hockey Canada Foundation and is one of the owners of the Calgary Flames Hockey Club. A graduate of mechanical engineering, Mr. Seaman was awarded an Honourary Doctor of Laws degree from the University of Saskatchewan in 1982. Mr. Seaman owns and operates a working ranch in the foothills of Alberta.

Thomas Shoyama
Born in Kamloops, B.C., Mr. Shoyama began his career as a journalist before joining the Canadian Army Intelligence Corps. A long and distinguished career in the public services of Saskatchewan and Canada included appointments with the Economic Council, as Deputy Minister of Energy, Mines and Resources and Deputy Minister of Finance. Honoured with the Outstanding Achievement Award of the Public Service of Canada, Mr. Shoyama retired from the service in 1978. In 1979 he became Chairman of Atomic Energy of Canada, and served as constitutional advisor to the Privy Council Office. Currently he is Visiting Professor, University of Victoria, a Trustee of the Donner Canadian Foundation, and a director of several companies including Petro-Canada and Hawker-Siddeley Canada Inc.

Jean Wadds
Mrs. Wadds has recently returned from a distinguished term as Canada's High Commissioner in London, England. In 1958, she was elected to the House of Commons. She served as a member of Canada's Delegation to the United Nations, as Parliamentary Secretary to the Minister of Health and Welfare, as a member of the Commons Committees on Agriculture, Broadcasting, Civil Service and External Affairs. From 1975–79 she was a member of the Ontario Municipal Board. She holds several honourary degrees and received the Freedom of the City of London, England in 1981 and was invested with the Order of Canada in 1982.

Dr. Catherine T. Wallace
A Masters and Ph.D. graduate in literary criticism, Dr. Wallace became the first Principal of Notre Dame High School in Vancouver in 1953 and went on to join the faculty of Mount St. Vincent University if Halifax as a

professor of English. Six years later, in 1965, she was appointed that university's President. From 1974–82 she was the Chairman of the Maritimes Provinces Higher Education Commission in Fredericton. At present she is a member of the Steering committee of the Canadian Conference on Higher Education. Dr. Wallace's Directorships include those of the Canadian Bank of Commerce and Maritime Telegraph and Telephone. She was awarded the Order of Canada's Medal of Service in 1972, the Canadian Silver Jubilee Medal in 1977, and holds 11 honourary degrees from Canadian universities.

Notes

Introduction

1 G. Bruce Doern and Brian W. Tomlin, *Faith and Fear: The Free Trade Story* (Toronto: Stoddart, 1991), 45.

2 See Nicholas d'Ombrain, 'Public Inquiries in Canada,' *Canadian Public Administration* 40, 1 (Spring, 1997): 86–107; and Neil Bradford, 'Innovation by Commission: Policy Paradigms and the Canadian Political System,' *Canadian Politics*, 3rd ed., ed. James P. Bickerton and Alain G. Gagnon, 541–60 (Peterborough, ON: Broadview Press, 1999).

3 Canada. Royal Commission on the Economic Union and Development Prospects for Canada (the Macdonald Commission), *Report*, 3 vols. (Ottawa: Minister of Supply and Services, 1985).

4 See Canada, Department of External Affairs, *The Canada-U.S. Free Trade Agreement* (Ottawa: Supply and Services, 1987). Numerous partisan volumes analysing the FTA were produced during the great national debate leading up to the 1988 federal election. For the pro–free trade position, see John Crispo, ed., *Free Trade: The Real Story* (Toronto: Gage, 1988). For the anti–free trade side, see Duncan Cameron, ed., *The Free Trade Deal* (Toronto: James Lorimer, 1988). A more balanced collection of analyses is found in Marc Gold and David Leyton-Brown, eds., *Trade-Offs on Free Trade: The Canada-U.S. Free Trade Agreement* (Toronto: Carswell, 1988). On the negotiation of the FTA, see Gordon Ritchie, *Wrestling with the Elephant: The Inside Story of the Canada-U.S. Trade Wars* (Toronto: Macfarlane, Walter and Ross, 1997).

5 See Maxwell A. Cameron and Brian W. Tomlin, *The Making of NAFTA: How the Deal Was Done* (Ithaca and London: Cornell University Press, 2000); and Maryse Robert, *Negotiating NAFTA: Explaining the Outcome in Culture, Textiles, Autos, and Pharmaceuticals* (Toronto: University of Toronto Press, 2000).

6 The Macdonald Commission was arguably the most significant factor in influencing the Canadian government to seek a free trade agreement with the United States. See, for example, Doern and Tomlin, *Faith and Fear*, 24 ff.

7 This approach thus avoids the limitiations of relying on unidimensional explanations for public policy change such as those found in pluralism (groups as the explanatory variable), public choice (individuals as the explanatory variable), neo-Marxism (class as the explanatory variable), political culture (attitudes, values, and beliefs as the explanatory variable), or statist theories (government organizations as the explanatory variable). See Neil Bradford, *Commissioning Ideas: Canadian National Policy Innovation in Comparative Perspective* (Toronto: Oxford University Press, 1998), 8–12.

8 Bradford, *Commissioning Ideas*, 2.

9 Reo Christenson et al., *Ideologies and Modern Politics* (New York: Dodd, Mead and Company, 1971), 2. See also Neil Bradford, 'The Policy Influence of Economic Ideas,' in *Restructuring and Resistance: Canadian Public Policy in an Age of Global Capitalism*, ed. Mike Burke, Colin Mooers, and John Shields, 50–79 (Halifax: Fernwood, 2000). For a consideration of the role of ideology in the political party system, see William Cross and Lisa Young, 'Policy Attitudes of Party Members in Canada: Evidence of Ideological Politics,' *Canadian Journal of Political Science* 35, 4 (December 2002): 859–80.

10 See David R. Cameron, 'Not Spicer and Not the B & B: Reflections of an Insider on the Workings of the Pepin-Robarts Task Force on Canadian Unity,' *International Journal of Canadian Studies* 7, 8 (Spring-Fall 1993): 333–45; and d'Ombrain, 'Public Inquiries in Canada.'

11 See Michael Howlett and M. Ramesh, *Studying Public Policy: Policy Cycles and Policy Subsystems,* 2nd ed. (Toronto: Oxford University Press, 2003); Leslie A. Pal, *Beyond Policy Analysis: Public Issue Management in Turbulent Times* (Scarborough, ON: Nelson, 2001); and Sylvia Bashevkin, *Welfare Hot Buttons: Women's Work and Social Policy Reform* (Toronto: University of Toronto Press, 2002).

12 No attempt is made here to critically examine the *output* of the research program as a whole, which would be the subject of another entire book.

13 See Thomas Kuhn, *The Structure of Scientific Revolutions* (Chicago: University of Chicago, 1962), 74; and Peter A. Hall, 'Policy Paradigms, Social Learning, and the State: The Case of Economic Policymaking in Britain,' *Comparative Politics* (April 1993): 275–96.

14 Peter A. Hall, 'Introduction,' in *The Political Power of Economic Ideas*, ed. Peter A. Hall, 4 (Princeton, NJ: Princeton University Press, 1989).

15 Ibid., 15.

16 Cy Gonick, *The Great Economic Debate: Failed Economics and a Future for Canada*

(Toronto: Lorimer, 1987), 45. See also Peter A. Hall, 'Keynes in Political Science,' *History of Political Economy* 26, 1 (1994): 137–53.

17 John B. Thompson, *Studies in the Theory of Ideology* (Berkeley: University of California Press, 1984), 25. To study ideology, then, is not to analyse a particular type of discourse to be found in a particular society, but primarily to examine the ways in which meaning serves to sustain relations of domination, according to Thompson.

18 On the outlines of these two positions, particularly with regard to contending visions of the role of the marketplace and the role of the state, see Jeanne Kirk Laux, 'Shaping or Serving Markets? Public Ownership and Privatization,' in *The New Era of Global Competition: State Policy and Market Policy*, ed. Daniel Drache and Meric S. Gertler, 288–315 (Montreal: McGill-Queen's University Press, 1991).

19 These terms are similar to those employed by Neil Bradford, who talks about economic viability, administrative viability, and political viability. See Bradford, *Commissioning Ideas*, 19–20. Bradford, in turn, is influenced by Peter A. Hall's use of these categories. See Hall, 'Conclusion,' in *The Political Power of Economic Ideas*, ed. Hall, 370–5. See also Geoffrey E. Hale, 'Reintegrating Federal Economic and Social Policies in the 1990s: Implementing Macdonald's Ideas by Trial and Error,' paper presented to the Annual Meeting of the Canadian Political Science Association, Laval University, 30 May 2001.

20 Jane Jenson, '"Different" but Not "Exceptional": Canada's Permeable Fordism,' *Canadian Review of Sociology and Anthropology* 26, 1 (1989): 73–4. See also Jane Jenson, 'Commissioning Ideas: Representation and Royal Commissions,' in *How Ottawa Spends 1994–95: Making Change*, ed. Susan D. Phillips, 39–69 (Ottawa: Carleton University Press, 1994); and Jane Jenson, 'Paradigms and Political Discourse: Protective Legislation in France and the United States before 1914,' *Canadian Journal of Political Science* 22, 2 (June 1989): 235–58.

21 Jane Jenson, 'Changing Discourse, Changing Agendas: Political Rights and Reproductive Policies in France,' in *The Women's Movement of the United States and Western Europe*, ed. Mary Fainsod Katzenstein and Carol McClurg Meuller (Philadelphia: Temple University Press, 1987), 66. See also Stephen Clarkson, 'Anti-Nationalism in Canada: The Ideology of Mainstream Economics,' *Canadian Review of Studies in Nationalism* 5, 1 (Spring 1978): 45–65. In the 1980s Brian Mulroney's Conservatives and his corporate supporters successfully displaced the Keynesian discourse of the governing Liberals with a neo-conservative discourse of deregulation, privatization, and free markets, in part through the agency of organized social actors. One commentator argued that 'the Tories have captured the ideological high ground virtually

unopposed. The reason is quite simple: the Conservatives have taken control of the language of political discourse.' See Tom Walkom, 'Tory Talk: How the Conservatives Captured the English Language,' *This Magazine* 18, 6 (February 1985): 5–8. See also David V.J. Bell, 'Political Culture in Canada,' in *Canadian Politics in the 1990s*, 3rd ed., ed. Michael S. Whittington and Glen Williams (Scarborough, ON: Nelson, 1990), 139; M. Janine Brodie and Jane Jenson, *Crisis, Challenge and Change: Party and Class in Canada Revisited* (Ottawa: Carleton University Press, 1988), chap. 10; and John W. Warnock, *Free Trade and the New Right Agenda* (Vancouver: New Star Books, 1988).

22 An example of a successful challenge to a dominant discourse was the Berger Commission. This commission issued a landmark report which recommended against building a pipeline across the northern Yukon and argued for a ten-year moratorium on pipeline construction in the Mackenzie Valley to permit prior settlement of Native land claims. See Thomas Berger, *Northern Frontier, Northern Homeland: The Report of the Mackenzie Valley Pipeline Inquiry* (Ottawa: Supply and Services Canada, 1977). Berger's reflections on his experience can be found in Thomas Berger, 'Canadian Commissions of Inquiry: An Insider's Perspective,' in *Commissions of Inquiry: Praise or Reappraise?* ed. Allan Manson and David Mullan, 13–28 (Toronto: Irwin Law, 2003).

23 See Jenson, 'Changing Discourse, Changing Agendas,' 66; Hugh G. Thorburn, *Interest Groups in the Canadian Federal System. Macdonald Royal Commission Research Study, Volume 69* (Toronto: University of Toronto Press, 1985); Patricia O'Reilly, *Health Care Practitioners: An Ontario Case Study in Policy Making* (Toronto: University of Toronto Press, 2000).

24 The 1988 free trade election lends credence to this supposition. In this election, many of the business interests that argued for free trade before the Macdonald Commission mobilized themselves in opposition to labour and popular sector groups which opposed free trade. The outcome was that the Mulroney Conservatives were elected with about 40 per cent of the vote, while 60 per cent of the electorate split their vote between the two parties that opposed free trade. For an analysis of the mobilization of interests around this election, see Jeffrey M. Ayres, *Defying Conventional Wisdom: Political Movements and Popular Contention against North American Free Trade* (Toronto: University of Toronto Press, 1998), chap. 5.

25 See Peter Gourevitch, 'Breaking with Orthodoxy: The Politics of Economic Policy Responses to the Great Depression of the 1930s,' *International Organization* 38 (Winter 1984): 95–130. A related point is that while ideological arguments are constructed and disseminated throughout the broader society, invariably, some groups and individuals are better endowed with the

resources to achieve this goal, which assists in establishing the dominance of their values, attitudes, and beliefs. Moreover, the manner in which ideology is used may in fact disguise quite different purposes. Thus ideological arguments are constructed which at their core reflect the material interests of particular actors, but which are cloaked in the political discourse of broader societal interests or goals. For instance, arguments for reforming trade policy may cloak the deeper purpose of restricting the role of the state in economic matters.

26 This was the 'argument' frequently used by economists defending the free trade proposal before the Macdonald Commission. See chapter 8.

27 Terry Eagleton, *Ideology: An Introduction* (London: Verso, 1991), 129. According to Eagleton, 'In the case of a "successful" ideology, it is not as though one body of ideas is perceived to be more powerful, legitimate or persuasive than another, but that the very grounds for choosing rationally between them have been deftly removed, so that it becomes impossible to think or desire outside the terms of the system itself. Such an ideological formation curves back upon itself like cosmic space, denying the possibility of any "outside," forestalling the generation of new desires as well as frustrating those we already have. If a "universe of discourse" is truly a *universe* then there is no standpoint beyond it where we might find a point of leverage for critique. Or if other universes are acknowledged to exist, then they are simply defined as incommensurable with one's own.' A powerful example of this process is the debate over the importance and role of government deficits. For an alternative analysis to the dominant discourse in this area, see Linda McQuaig, *Shooting the Hippo: Death by Deficit and Other Canadian Myths* (Toronto: Viking, 1995).

28 On the spread of neoconservative ideas in Canada, see Walkom, 'Tory Talk,' 5–8.

29 See Cameron, 'Not Spicer and Not the B & B,' 334–5.

30 Margaret Weir, 'Ideas and Politics: The Acceptance of Keynesianism in Britain and the United States,' in *The Political Power of Economic Ideas*, ed. Hall, 59. See also Margaret Weir and Theda Skocpol, 'State Structures and the Possibilities for "Keynesian" Responses to the Great Depression in Sweden, Britain and the United States,' in *Bringing the State Back In*, ed. Peter Evans, Dietrich Rueschemeyer, and Theda Skocpol, 107–63 (Cambridge: Cambridge University Press, 1985).

31 Ayres, *Defying Conventional Wisdom*, 41.

32 Peter Bleyer, 'Coalitions of Social Movements as Agencies for Social Change: The Action Canada Network,' in *Organizing Dissent: Contemporary Social Movements in Theory and Practice*, ed. William K. Carroll (Toronto: Garamond Press, 1991), 105.

33 Geoffrey Hale argues that the Macdonald Commission introduced a set of neoconservative continentalist ideas which were consonant with the desire by federal officials to forge a new economic model that could adapt to this crisis-ridden, rapidly changing environment. See Hale, 'Reintegrating Federal Economic and Social Policies in the 1990s.'

34 Bradford, *Commissioning Ideas*, 8–9.

35 See A. Paul Pross, Christie Innis, and John A. Yogis, eds., *Commissions of Inquiry* (Toronto: Carswell, 1990); Bradford, *Commissioning Ideas*, 62; d'Ombrain, 'Public Inquiries in Canada'; and Manson and Mullan, *Commissions of Inquiry.*

Chapter 1

1 Karl Marx, 'Address on the Question of Free Trade, 1848,' *The Poverty of Philosophy* (New York: International Press, 1963), 223.

2 See Stephen Clarkson, 'Disjunctions: Free Trade and the Paradox of Canadian Development,' in *The New Era of Global Competition: State Policy and Market Power*, ed. Daniel Drache and Meric S. Gertler, 104–9 (Montreal: McGill-Queen's University Press, 1991).

3 Elie Kedourie, *Nationalism* (London: Hutchinson, 1966), 9. Anthony Birch suggests that: 'The first of Kedourie's three propositions, while accurate as a summation of the logical foundation of nationalist theory, is at complete variance with historical truth.' Anthony Birch, *Nationalism and National Integration* (London: Unwin Hyman, 1989), 7. David Chennells talks about 'exclusive nationalism' as 'a kind that seeks to privilege one recognizable way of life over others, in the sense of imposing it and intentionally altering the balance present among adherents of various real communities of religion, language, or culture.' David Chennells, *The Politics of Nationalism in Canada: Cultural Conflict Since 1760* (Toronto: University of Toronto Press, 2001), 7.

4 William Christian and Colin Campbell, *Political Parties and Ideologies in Canada*, 3rd ed. (Toronto: McGraw-Hill Ryerson, 1990), 243.

5 Ibid., 244.

6 This type of nationalism has, however, been taken up from time to time by those who would have all Canadians assimilate into a single linguistic (usually English) and cultural (usually Anglo-Saxon and Protestant) community. It has also been advocated by some Québécois who have sought independence for Quebec. It is this strain of nationalism that Pierre Trudeau credited with promoting 'the most devastating wars, the worst atrocities, and the most degrading collective hatred the world has ever seen ...' See Pierre

Elliott Trudeau, 'New Treason of the Intellectuals,' in *Federalism and the French Canadians* (Toronto: Macmillan, 1968), 151–81.

7 Craig Brown, 'The Nationalism of the National Policy,' in *Nationalism in Canada*, ed. Peter Russell (Toronto: McGraw-Hill Ryerson, 1966), 155.

8 See Christian and Campbell, *Political Parties and Ideologies in Canada*, chap. 6. The application of the concept of nationalism to Canada is doubly difficult due to the existence of French-Canadian nationalism, in all its various manifestations, alongside English-Canadian nationalism.

9 David Chennells, *The Politics of Nationalism in Canada: Cultural Conflict since 1760* (Toronto: University of Toronto Press, 2001), 5. Chennells provides a brief review of taxonomies of nationalism.

10 Sylvia Bashevkin, *True Patriot Love: The Politics of Canadian Nationalism* (Toronto: Oxford University Press, 1991), 2–3. See also Stephen Clarkson, 'Anti-Nationalism in Canada: The Ideology of Mainstream Economics,' *Canadian Review of Studies in Nationalism* 5, 1 (Spring 1978): 45–65; and Denis Stairs, 'North American Continentalism: Perspectives and Policies in Canada,' in *Regionalism and Supranationalism*, ed. David M. Cameron, 83–109 (Montreal: Institute for Research on Public Policy, 1981).

11 Bashevkin, *True Patriot Love*, 3.

12 Exceptions include Glen Williams, 'Regions within Region: Continentalism Ascendant,' in *Canadian Politics in the 1990s*, 4th ed., ed. Michael S. Whittington and Glen Williams, 19–39 (Toronto: Nelson, 1995); Stephen Clarkson, 'Continentalism: The Conceptual Challenge for Canadian Social Science,' unpublished paper presented to the Canadian Sociology and Anthropology Association, Université de Montréal, June 1985; and Stephen Clarkson, 'Continentalism,' in *The Canadian Encyclopedia* (Edmonton: Hurtig, 1985), 420–1.

13 Strikingly, this same source omits the term nationalism. See John McMenemy, *The Language of Canadian Politics: A Guide to Important Terms and Concepts*. Rev. ed. (Waterloo: Wilfrid Laurier University Press, 1995), 67.

14 G. Bruce Doern and Richard W. Phidd, *Canadian Public Policy: Ideas, Structure, Process*, 2nd ed. (Scarborough, ON: Nelson, 1992), 237. The problem of establishing the validity of respondents' values, attitudes, and beliefs is compounded by the fact that, while it is relatively easy to find individuals and groups who self-identify as nationalists, it is not so easy to find those who publicly call themselves continentalists. The term has pejorative connotations for many, and it has frequently been used as a political epithet in the polemical sense of ideology. Those who advocate what may be described as continentalist policies in public generally do so only in the realm of economics under the guise of free trade, the unfettered market, and so forth, and

are reluctant to draw the obvious political conclusions from increased economic integration with the United States. See Clarkson, 'Continentalism.'

15 See, for example, Edelgard Mahant and Graeme S. Mount, *Invisible and Inaudible in Washington: American Policies toward Canada* (Vancouver: UBC Press, 1999); John Holmes, *The Better Part of Valour: Essays on Canadian Diplomacy* (Toronto: McClelland and Stewart, 1970), and *Life with Uncle: The Canadian-American Relationship* (Toronto: University of Toronto Press, 1981); Livingston T. Merchant and A.D.P. Heeney, 'Canada and the United States: Principles for Partnership,' *Department of State Bulletin* (2 August 1965); Isaiah A. Litvak and Christopher J. Maule, 'Canadian-United States Corporate Interface and Transnational Relations,' in *Canada and the United States: Transnational and Transgovernmental Relations*, ed. Annette Baker Fox, Alfred O. Hero, and Joseph S. Nye, 140–61 (New York: Columbia University Press, 1974); Paul Phillips, 'National Policy, Continental Economics and National Disintegration,' in *Canada and the Burden of Unity*, ed. David Jay Bercuson, 19–43 (Toronto: Macmillan, 1977); Garth Stevenson, 'Continental Integration and Canadian Unity,' in *Continental Community? Independence and Integration in North America*, ed. W. Andrew Axline et al., 194–217 (Toronto: McClelland and Stewart, 1974); Charles Pentland, 'Political Integration: A Multidimensional Perspective,' in Axline, *Continental Community*, 42–66; Naomi Black, 'Absorptive Systems Are Impossible: The Canadian-American Relationship as a Disparate Dyad,' in Axline, *Continental Community*, 92–108; John H. Redekop, 'Continentalism: The Key to Canadian Politics,' in *Approaches to Canadian Politics*, ed. John H. Redekop, 28–57 (Scarborough, ON: Prentice-Hall, 1978); and Michael B. Dolan, Brian W. Tomlin, and Harald von Riekhoff, 'Integration and Autonomy in Canada-United States Relations, 1963–1972,' *Canadian Journal of Political Science* 15, 2 (June 1982): 331–63.

16 See Stairs, 'North American Continentalism,' 83–109.

17 Carl Berger, *The Writing of Canadian History: Aspects of English-Canadian Historical Writing: 1900–1970* (Toronto: Oxford University Press, 1976), 259.

18 See J.L. Granatstein, *How Britain's Weakness Forced Canada into the Arms of the United States* (Toronto: University of Toronto Press, 1989).

19 Goldwin Smith identified union with the United States as the only option for Canadian survival over a hundred years ago. See Goldwin Smith, *Canada and the Canadian Question* (Toronto: University of Toronto Press, 1971).

20 Cited in Ted Magder, 'A Political Economy of Communications,' in *The New Canadian Political Economy*, ed. Wallace Clement and Glen Williams (Kingston: McGill-Queen's University Press, 1989), 288.

21 See Paul Litt, 'The Massey Commission, Americanization and Canadian Cultural Nationalism,' *Queen's Quarterly* 98, 2 (Summer 1991): 375–87.

22 On the recent mobilization of nationalist interests, see Jeffrey M. Ayres, *Defying Conventional Wisdom: Political Movements and Popular Contention against North American Free Trade* (Toronto: University of Toronto Press, 1998).

23 On the mobilization of continentalist interests, see John W. Warnock, *Free Trade and the New Right Agenda* (Vancouver: New Star Books, 1988); and G. Bruce Doern and Brian W. Tomlin, *Faith and Fear: The Free Trade Story* (Toronto: Stoddart, 1991).

24 Redekop, 'Continentalism,' 31.

25 See Kari Levitt, *Silent Surrender: The Multinational Corporation in Canada* (Toronto: Macmillan, 1970).

26 A more recent exception can be found in the following statement made at the University of Alberta by Canadian-born global press baron, Conrad Black a week before the October 1995 referendum on sovereignty in Quebec. In the event of a 'yes' vote, 'no longer having to squander an inordinate amount of our national energy in unrequited passion for our parting compatriots, our choices would be enviable ... We could also draw officially closer to the United States, with whom, if we chose, we could make a much more rewarding arrangement than we have had with an unappreciative Quebec.

'Canada could negotiate arrangements with the United States that would preserve our regional distinctiveness as Texas and New England have preserved theirs, would raise our standard of living, lower taxes, reduce our debt burden and doubtless involve a translation into U.S. from Canadian dollars that would be very advantageous to us. Just 220 years after its founding, the most conceptually and materially powerful country would be virtually born again geopolitically by gaining access to Canadian resources and population.

'Any U.S. president consummating such an arrangement would be the greatest builder of the American Republic since Jefferson bought much of the south and midwest from Napoleon. There would be ample incentive for the United States to be generous and the president of the day could achieve a great deal more for a good deal less than the federal German Chancellor Helmut Kohl accomplished for the East German mark when Germany was reunified.' Quoted in Scott Disher, 'Conrad Black, Press Lord Redux: Contravallating His Biographers,' *Books in Canada* 5, 25 (Summer 1996): 37.

27 Harry G. Johnson, 'Problems of Canadian Nationalism,' *The Canadian Quandary* (Toronto: McClelland and Stewart, 1977), 13.

28 See, for example, Redekop, 'Continentalism,' 28–57. More recent concerns have emerged over the extent to which economic integration is leading to policy convergence between Canada, the United States, and Mexico. See George Hoberg, ed., *Capacity for Choice: Canada in a New North America* (Toronto: University of Toronto Press, 2002).

29 Cited in Ramsay Cook, *The Maple Leaf Forever: Essays on Nationalism and Politics in Canada* (Toronto: Macmillan, 1971), 46.

30 Allan Smith, *Canada: An American Nation? Essays on Continentalism, Identity, and the Canadian Frame of Mind* (Montreal: McGill-Queen's University Press, 1994), 6.

31 See Alan Ernst, 'From Liberal Continentalism to Neoconservatism: North American Free Trade and the Politics of the C.D. Howe Institute,' *Studies in Political Economy* 39 (Autumn 1992): 109–40.

32 Doern and Phidd, *Canadian Public Policy*, 239.

33 Ibid., 240. See also Anthony Westell, 'The Case for Greater Economic Integration with the United States,' in *Friends So Different: Essays on Canada and the United States in the 1980s*, ed. Lansing Lamont and J. Duncan Edmonds, 60–7 (Ottawa: University of Ottawa Press, 1989).

34 The literature on American hegemony is quite large. For a regulation analysis, see Michel Aglietta, *A Theory of Capitalist Regulation: The U.S. Experience* (London: New Left Books, 1979); and Michel Aglietta, 'World Capitalism in the Eighties,' *New Left Review* 136 (November-December 1982): 6–16. See also Paul Kennedy, *The Rise and Fall of the Great Powers: Economic Change and Military Conflict from 1500 to 2000* (New York: Random House, 1987); Stephen Gill, *American Hegemony and the Trilateral Commission* (Cambridge: Cambridge University Press, 1990); John J. Kirton, 'America's Hegemonic Decline and the Reagan Revival,' in *Southern Exposure: Canadian Perspectives on the United States*, ed. D.H. Flaherty and W.R. McKercher, 42–6 (Toronto: McGraw-Hill Ryerson, 1986); and Robert O. Keohane, *After Hegemony: Cooperation and Discord in the World Political Economy* (Princeton: Princeton University Press, 1984).

35 Philip Resnick, *The Land of Cain: Class and Nationalism in English Canada, 1945–1975* (Vancouver: New Star Books, 1977), 19. Various segments of Canadian society adopted nationalist positions vis-à-vis the declining American hegemon, including important segments of the intelligentsia, students, middle class professionals, trade unions, political parties, artists, and some fragments of capital.

36 See M. Janine Brodie and Jane Jenson, *Crisis, Challenge and Change: Party and Class in Canada Revisited* (Ottawa: Carleton University Press, 1988); and David A. Wolfe, 'The Rise and Demise of the Keynesian Era in Canada: Economic Policy, 1930–1982,' in *Modern Canada 1930–1980s*, ed. Michael S. Cross and Gregory S. Kealey, 46–78 (Toronto: McClelland and Stewart, 1984). A corrective to the commonplace assumption that pure Keynesianism was applied to the Canadian experience can be found in Robert M. Campbell, *Grand Illusions: The Politics of the Keynesian Experience in Canada, 1945–1975* (Peterborough, ON: Broadview Press, 1987).

37 Gary Teeple, *Globalization and the Decline of Social Reform* (Toronto: Gara-mond Press, 1995), 17.

38 Wolfe, 'The Rise and Demise of the Keynesian Era,' 48.

39 Fordism 'is generally seen as a system of mass production employing semi-automated assembly lines and giving rise to rapidly expanding domestic and external markets for "cheapened" consumer goods – that is, mass consumption. These developments are associated with large production units, complex work hierarchies, and national labour markets.' Teeple, *Globalization*, 18. See also Alain Lipietz, 'Towards Global Fordism?' *New Left Review* 132 (March-April 1982): 34–5, who suggests Fordism 'refers to a *mode of capital accumulation*: one based upon radical and constant change in the labour process, such that the workers' "know-how" is incorporated in the form of machinery ... Secondly, Fordism refers to *the continual adjustment of mass consumption* to the historically unprecedented rise in productivity generated by intensive accumulation' (emphasis in original). Jane Jenson refers to the unique continental regime of accumulation in Canada as 'permeable Fordism.' See Jane Jenson, '"Different," but Not "Exceptional": Canada's Permeable Fordism,' *Canadian Review of Sociology and Anthropology* 26, 1 (1989): 69–94.

40 See Granatstein, *Britain's Weakness*.

41 See Glen Williams, *Not for Export: The International Competitiveness of Canadian Manufacturing*, 3rd. ed. (Toronto: McClelland and Stewart, 1994).

42 John Myles, 'Introduction. Understanding Canada: Comparative Political Economy Perspectives,' *Canadian Review of Sociology and Anthropology* 26, 1 (1989): 5.

43 See Duncan Cameron, 'Political Discourse in the Eighties,' in *Canadian Parties in Transition: Discourse, Organization, Representation*, ed. Alain G. Gagnon and A. Brian Tanguay, 66–73 (Scarborough, ON: Nelson, 1989).

44 See, for example, George Grant, *Lament for a Nation: The Defeat of Canadian Nationalism* (Toronto: McClelland and Stewart, 1965); and *Technology and Empire*, (Toronto: Anansi, 1968). W.L. Morton was Canada's leading historian of western Canada. See *The Progressive Party in Canada* (Toronto: University of Toronto Press, 1950); and *Manitoba: A History* (Toronto: University of Toronto Press, 1957). Donald Creighton's main contributions in this vein include *Canada's First Century 1867–1967* (Toronto: Macmillan, 1970), *The Forked Road* (Toronto: McClelland and Stewart, 1976), and *The Passionate Observer: Selected Writings* (Toronto: McClelland and Stewart, 1980).

45 Sylvia Bashevkin points out that, 'from the Nationalist perspective, Howe was a key villain in the [continental integration] process, functioning as the willing and anxious comprador suitor to US direct investment.' See *True Patriot Love*, 19.

46 See the Royal Commission on Canada's Economic Prospects, *Final Report* (The Gordon Commission) (Ottawa: Queen's Printer, 1957); *Troubled Canada: The Need for New Domestic Policies* (Toronto: McClelland and Stewart, 1961); *A Choice for Canada: Independence or Colonial Status* (Toronto: McClelland and Stewart, 1966); *Storm Signals: New Economic Policies for Canada* (Toronto: McClelland and Stewart, 1975); and *A Political Memoir* (Toronto: McClelland and Stewart, 1978).

47 On the nationalism of the Waffle, see the collection of essays on the twentieth anniversary of the movement in Reg Whitaker et al., 'The Waffle: 20th Anniversary Reflections,' *Studies in Political Economy: A Socialist Review* 32 (Summer 1990): 167–201, especially the contribution by Mel Watkins, 'The Waffle and the National Question,' 173–6.

48 The left nationalist literature is immense. A representative sampling includes: *Foreign Ownership and the Structure of Canadian Industry: Report of the Task Force on the Structure of Canadian Industry* (The Watkins Report) (Ottawa: Queen's Printer, 1968); Levitt, *Silent Surrender*, Ian Lumsden, ed., *Close the 49th Parallel, etc.: The Americanization of Canada* (Toronto: University of Toronto Press, 1970); Resnick, *The Land of Cain*; and Williams, *Not for Export.*

49 See William Coleman, *The Independence Movement in Quebec, 1945–1980* (Toronto: University of Toronto Press, 1984).

50 See Paul Phillips and Stephen Watson, 'From Mobilization to Continentalism: The Canadian Economy in the Post-Depression Period,' in *Modern Canada 1930–1980s*, ed. Michael S. Cross and Gregory S. Kealey, 20–45 (Toronto: McClelland and Stewart, 1984).

51 Resnick, *The Land of Cain*, 18.

52 See Clarkson, 'Disjunctions,' 105.

53 See Bertrand Bellon and Jorge Niosi, *The Decline of the American Economy* (Montreal: Black Rose Books, 1988).

54 Joel Krieger, *Reagan, Thatcher and the Politics of Decline* (New York: Oxford University Press, 1986), 12. Krieger details the factors contributing to America's decline in chapter 1, 17–35.

55 William C. Berman, *America's Right Turn: From Nixon to Bush* (Baltimore: Johns Hopkins University Press, 1994), 14. Berman also notes 'the trade deficit, which stood at $9.5 billion in 1976, expanded to $31.1 billion in 1977 and jumped again in 1978 to over $34 billion. More specifically, from 1975 to 1977 the amount of imported steel increased from 13.5 percent to 17.8 percent of domestic consumption; and foreign auto producers, who had captured about 8% of the U.S. home market in 1970, now controlled nearly 22 percent by 1979. In 1970, 8.3 percent of the GNP was tied to exports and imports; by 1980 that figure had jumped to 17.4 percent, indicating the

growing extent of America's economic integration into the larger international system' (39).

56 See James O'Connor, *The Fiscal Crisis of the State* (New York: St Martin's Press, 1973). Both right and left interpretations of the decline of the American hegemon are summarized in Krieger, *Reagan, Thatcher*, 17–35.

57 Krieger, *Reagan, Thatcher*, 133 Emphasis in original.

58 *Hansard*, 14 April 1972: 1328. Cited in Clarkson, 'Disjunctions,' 106.

59 See Jenson, '"Different" but Not "Exceptional,"' 69–94.

60 Wolfe, 'The Rise and Demise of the Keynesian Era,' 48–9. See also Timothy Lewis, *In the Long Run We're All Dead: The Canadian Turn to Fiscal Restraint* (Vancouver: UBC Press, 2003), chap. 3.

61 See Richard D. French, *How Ottawa Decides: Planning and Industrial Policy Making, 1968–1984* (Toronto: James Lorimer, 1984).

62 For instance, productivity growth in Canada averaged 2.5 per cent from 1966 to 1973, while it was zero between 1974 and 1982.

63 As Denis Smith has pointed out, it is a paradox of Canadian nationalism that 'the postwar Prime Minister most committed in rhetoric to the defense of national interests, John Diefenbaker, was probably the least effective in that defense; the Prime Minister most ardently opposed in principle to nationalism, Pierre Elliott Trudeau, zealously defended a nationalist energy policy.' Denis Smith, 'Nationalism,' *Canadian Encyclopedia* (Edmonton: Hurtig, 1985), 2: 1200.

64 These differences found popular expression in bumper-stickers in western Canada which read 'let the Eastern bastards freeze in the dark.'

65 See Stephen McBride and John Shields, *Dismantling a Nation: Canada and the New World Order*, 2nd ed. (Halifax: Fernwood Publishing, 1997), 146–7.

66 See Donald V. Smiley, *The Federal Condition in Canada* (Toronto: McGraw-Hill Ryerson, 1987), chap. 4; and Kathy L. Brock, 'The End of Executive Federalism?' in *New Trends in Canadian Federalism*, ed. François Rocher and Miriam Smith, 91–108 (Peterborough, ON: Broadview Press, 1995).

67 Jane Jenson, 'Naming Nations: Making Nationalist Claims in Canadian Public Discourse,' *Canadian Review of Sociology and Anthropology* 30, 3 (1993): 337–58.

68 See Alan Cairns and Cynthia Williams, eds., *The Politics of Gender, Ethnicity and Language in Canada: Macdonald Royal Commission Study Volume 34* (Toronto: University of Toronto Press, 1985); and Cairns and Williams, eds., *Constitutionalism, Citizenship and Society in Canada: Macdonald Royal Commission Study Volume 33* (Toronto: University of Toronto Press, 1985).

69 Cameron, 'Political Discourse in the Eighties,' 74.

70 On the rise of new social movements, see, for example, William K. Carroll, ed., *Organizing Dissent: Contemporary Social Movements in Theory and Practice*

(Toronto: Garamond, 1992), 102–17. On the difficult relationship between new social movements and political parties in Canada, see Peter Bleyer, 'Coalitions of Social Movements as Agencies for Social Change: The Action Canada Network,' in Carroll, ed., *Organizing Dissent*, 114.

71 See Berman, *America's Right Turn*, chaps. 4–5.

72 The Reagan era led some social scientists to proclaim the reassertion of American hegemony, or to deny that the United States had seriously declined relative to other nations. See, for example, Kirton, 'America's Hegemonic Decline and the Reagan Revival,' 42–61.

73 See Stephen Clarkson, *Canada and the Reagan Challenge: Crisis and Adjustment, 1981–1985*, Updated ed. (Toronto: Lorimer, 1985), chap. 3.

74 See, for example, François Rocher, 'Canadian Business, Free Trade and the Rhetoric of Economic Continentalization,' *Studies in Political Economy* 35 (Summer 1991): 135–54; and Robert J. Brym, ed., *The Structure of the Canadian Capitalist Class* (Toronto: Garamond Press, 1985).

75 The BCNI is composed of the chief executive officers of the 150 largest multinational corporations in Canada. See David Langille, 'The Business Council on National Interests and the State,' *Studies in Political Economy* 24 (Fall 1987): 64–70. In 2001, the BCNI changed its name to the Canadian Council of Chief Executives. In 2002, the companies in the council administered in excess of $2.1 trillion in assets, had annual revenues of more than $500 billion and accounted for a significant majority of Canada's private sector investment, exports, training, and research and development.

76 'In 1975, Canada itself became a net capital exporter. In terms of direct investment or ownership capital, Canadian firms were acquiring more assets abroad than foreigners were acquiring in Canada.' Cameron, 'Political Discourse in the Eighties,' 69.

77 See Christian and Campbell, *Political Parties and Ideologies in Canada*. Duncan Cameron argues that there was a major split in Canadian liberalism, with business and welfare liberals forced to choose sides, due to the trajectory of the world economy. He also argues that inflation was the main cause of the downfall of the post-war Keynesian consensus and the ascendance of business liberalism under the guise of neoconservatism, first in Britain under Thatcher and later in the United States under Reagan. See Cameron, 'Political Discourse in the Eighties,' 67–71.

78 The positions taken by the major political parties in Canada in the 1988 election reflected these developments. This election polarized the parties around the issue of free trade, with the Progressive Conservatives supporting it and the Liberals and New Democrats opposing it. This is not to argue that liberalism simply disappeared from the Canadian political land-

scape. It clearly persists. But in the period under question liberalism underwent a metamorphosis whereby it was forced to choose between greater or lesser state intervention and the concomitant set of public policies which derive from each of these two positions. On the centrality of liberalism to the post-war policy debate in Canada, see Ronald Manzer, *Public Policies and Political Development in Canada* (Toronto: University of Toronto Press, 1985).

79 Cameron, 'Political Discourse in the Eighties,' 73.

80 On the history of the free trade question in Canadian politics see Edelgard Mahant, *Free Trade in American-Canadian Relations* (Malabar, FL: Krieger Publishing, 1993); and Jack Granatstein, 'Free Trade: The History of an Issue,' in *The Future on the Table: Canada and the Free Trade Issue*, ed. Michael Henderson, 1–34 (North York: Masterpress, 1987).

81 Cited in Graham Fraser, *Playing for Keeps: The Making of the Prime Minister, 1988* (Toronto: McClelland and Stewart, 1989), 344.

82 *Globe and Mail*, 23 June 1983. Cited in Jeffrey M. Ayres, *Defying Conventional Wisdom: Political Movements and Popular Contention against North American Free Trade* (Toronto: University of Toronto Press, 1998), 25. Interestingly, President Salinas of Mexico initially expressed similar reservations about free trade with the United States. In 1988 he said 'I am not in favour of such a proposal. I believe that through the GATT we have a multilateral way to deal with our neighbours. There is such a different economic level between the United States and Mexico that I don't believe such a common market would provide an advantage to either country.' Cited in Maxwell A. Cameron and Brian W. Tomlin, *The Making of NAFTA: How the Deal Was Done* (Ithaca, NY: Cornell University Press, 2000), 59.

83 Fraser, *Playing for Keeps*, 345. Emphasis added.

84 G. Bruce Doern and Brian Tomlin, *Faith and Fear: The Free Trade Story* (Toronto: Stoddart, 1991), 15. Doern and Tomlin provide the most comprehensive overview of the genesis of the free trade issue within the Canadian state. See also Robert M. Campbell and Leslie A. Pal, 'A Big Deal? The Canada-US Free Trade Agreement,' in *The Real Worlds of Canadian Politics: Cases in Process and Policy*, 2nd ed., ed. Robert M. Campbell and Leslie A. Pal, 187–266 (Peterborough, ON: Broadview Press, 1991).

85 Alan Gotlieb and J. Kinsman, 'Reviving the Third Option,' *International Perspectives*, (January/February 1981): 2–5. Gotlieb argued that the Third Option policy was the route for Canada in the 1980s.

86 Michael Hart interview (Ottawa, 27 November 1992). For a list of published reports favourable to sectoral or comprehensive free trade between 1975 and 1988, see Bashevkin, *True Patriot Love*, 106.

87 Michael Hart interview.

88 Ibid. For a profoundly ideological analysis of the move towards free trade and the actual negotiations over the FTA with the United States, see Michael Hart with Bill Dymond and Colin Robertson, *Decision at Midnight: Inside the Canada-U.S. Free Trade Negotiations* (Vancouver: UBC Press, 1994).

89 Doern and Tomlin, *Faith and Fear*, 16–17.

90 The theme of 'western alienation' as a result of the Trudeau government's national mode has been documented in many sources on western Canada. See, for example, Roger Gibbins, 'The Prairie Provinces,' in *Canadian Politics in the 1990s*, 3rd ed., ed. Michael S. Whittington and Glen Williams, 60–75 (Scarborough, ON: Nelson, 1990).

91 See Clarkson, *Canada and the Reagan Challenge*, chap. 3.

92 Doern and Tomlin, *Faith and Fear*, 17.

93 Ibid. See also Alan Frizell and Anthony Westell, *The Canadian General Election of 1984: Politicians, Parties, Press and Polls* (Ottawa: Carleton University Press, 1985), 7–9.

94 Denis Stairs interview (Halifax, 18 May 1994).

95 Doern and Tomlin, *Faith and Fear*, 18.

96 Ibid., 19.

97 Ibid., 20.

98 Ibid., 19.

99 Government of Canada, *Canadian Trade Policy for the 1980s: A Discussion Paper* (Ottawa: Department of External Affairs, 1983).

100 Doern and Tomlin, *Faith and Fear*, 21.

101 Ibid. See also James Rusk, 'Ottawa to Expand Trade Links With U.S. "Partner,"' *Globe and Mail*, 1 September 1983, A1–2.

102 See Michael Smith, 'Sectoral Free Trade with Canada,' *International Perspectives* (May/June 1984): 17–18 and David Leyton-Brown, 'The Canada-U.S. Free Trade Agreement,' in *Canada Under Mulroney: An End-of-Term Report*, ed. Andrew B. Gollner and Daniel Salée (Montreal: Véhicule Press, 1988), 104–5.

103 The areas initially considered for sectoral free trade included steel, urban transit equipment, and computer services. Canada also raised the issues of petrochemicals, textiles and clothing, and beef and red meat, while the United States was interested in forest products, cosmetics, alcoholic beverages and furniture. See Leyton-Brown, 'The Canada U.S. Free Trade Agreement,' 104–5.

104 Ibid., 103.

105 Michael Hawes, 'The National Economy,' in *Canadian Annual Review of Politics and Public Affairs, 1984*, ed. R.B. Byers (Toronto: University of Toronto Press, 1987), 139.

106 Ibid., 140.
107 Mulroney also said in the same speech, 'The maturity and self-confidence of our country make it possible for us now to confront issues in a realistic manner, and to examine options that a few years ago produced emotional reflexes that made rational discussion difficult. Nowhere is this more true than the subject of our bilateral relations with the United States.' Brian Mulroney, 'Address to the Economic Club of New York,' 10 December 1984.
108 See Canada, Department of Finance, *Agenda for Renewal* (Ottawa: Supply and Services, 1984).
109 Arthur Kroeger interview (Toronto, 18 November 1992).
110 James Kelleher, 'Notes for a Speech to the 55th Annual Meeting of the Canadian Chamber of Commerce' Toronto, September, 1984. Cited in Doern and Tomlin, *Faith and Free Trade*, 22.
111 Gordon Ritchie later detailed Burney's role in the bureaucratic machinations behind the negotiation of the Canada-United States Free Trade Agreement, where Burney was second and Ritchie was third in command on the Canadian negotiating team. See Gordon Ritchie, *Wrestling with the Elephant: The Inside Story of the Canada-U.S. Trade Wars* (Toronto: Macfarlane, Walter and Ross, 1997).
112 Doern and Tomlin, *Faith and Fear*, 24.
113 Ibid. The full significance of this development will be considered below.
114 Canada, Department of External Affairs, *How to Secure and Enhance Access to Export Markets* (Ottawa: Supply and Services, 1985).
115 Doern and Tomlin, *Faith and Fear*, 24–5.
116 Hawes, 'The National Economy,' 140.
117 Doern and Tomlin, *Faith and Fear*, 26.
118 Richard Lipsey and Michael Smith, *Canada's Trade Policy Options* (Toronto: C.D. Howe Institute, 1985).
119 See, in particular, John Whalley, *Canadian Trade Policies and the World Economy: Macdonald Royal Commission Study, Volume 9* (Toronto: University of Toronto Press, 1985); John Whalley, ed., *Canada and the Multilateral Trading System: Macdonald Royal Commission Study, Volume 10* (Toronto: University of Toronto Press, 1985); Roderick Hill and John Whalley, eds., *Canada–United States Free Trade: Macdonald Royal Commission Study, Volume 11* (Toronto: University of Toronto Press, 1985); Richard G. Harris, *Trade, Industrial Policy and International Competition: Macdonald Royal Commission Study, Volume 13* (Toronto: University of Toronto Press, 1985). The impact of the commission's research is analysed in detail in chapters 6, 7, and 8.
120 Doern and Tomlin, *Faith and Fear*, 27.
121 Canada, Department of External Affairs, *Competitiveness and Security: Direc-*

tions for Canada's International Relations (Ottawa: Supply and Services, 1985).

122 Doern and Tomlin, *Faith and Fear*, 27.

123 Ibid., 28. See Government of Canada, *Minutes of Proceedings and Evidence of the Special Joint Committee of the Senate and of the House of Commons on Canada's International Relations* (Ottawa: Queen's Printer, 1985).

124 Doern and Tomlin, *Faith and Fear*, 29.

125 Clarkson, 'Disjunctions,' 115.

126 Michael Hawes, 'The National Economy,' in *Canadian Annual Review of Politics and Public Affairs, 1985*, ed. R.B. Byers (Toronto: University of Toronto Press, 1988), 139–40.

Chapter 2

1 Sir Allen Herbert, 'Pageant of Parliament,' *Punch* 186 (27 June 1934), 708. Cited in Frank Iacobucci, 'Commissions of Inquiry and Public Policy in Canada,' in *Commissions of Inquiry*, ed. Paul Pross et al. (Toronto: Carswell, 1990), 21.

2 Thomas Berger, 'Canadian Commissions of Inquiry: An Insider's Perspectives,' in *Commissions of Inquiry: Praise or Reappraise?* ed. Allan Manson and David Mullan (Toronto: Irwin Law, 2003), 14.

3 The following summary is derived from Canada, Law Reform Commission of Canada, *Commissions of Inquiry: A New Act. Working Paper 17* (Ottawa: Supply and Services Canada, 1977), 7–11. See also Canada, Privy Council Office, *Commissions of Inquiry* www.pco-bcp.gc.ca/ (2003); and Peter Desbarats, 'Public Inquiries: A Case Study,' in *Public Administration and Policy: Governing in Challenging Times*, ed. Martin W. Westmacott and Hugh P. Mellon (Scarborough, ON: Prentice Hall, 1999), 108–9.

4 Law Reform Commission of Canada, 'Commissions of Inquiry,' 10.

5 Canada, Royal Commission on the Economic Union and Development Prospects for Canada, *Report* (Ottawa: Supply and Services Canada, 1985), 3: 562. The entire order-in-council authorizing the creation of the Macdonald Commission is reprinted in volume 3 of the *Report* as Appendix A.

6 An important exception which places the role of ideas generated by royal commissions in a comparative perspective is Neil Bradford, *Commissioning Ideas: Canadian National Policy Innovation in Comparative Perspective* (Toronto: Oxford University Press, 1999). For a comparison of the policy impact of five major Canadian royal commissions across time, see Neil Bradford, 'Innovation by Commission: Policy Paradigms and the Canadian Political

System,' in *Canadian Politics*, 3rd ed., ed. James P. Bickerton and Alain-G. Gagnon, 541–60 (Peterborough, ON: Broadview Press, 1999).

7 Peter Stursburg, 'Canada and Its Royal Commissions,' *Saturday Night* 21 (January 1961). Cited in Barry L. Anderson, *Royal Commissions, Economists and Policy: A Study of the Economic Advisory Process in Post-War Canada* (Ann Arbor, MI: University Microfilms International, 1983), 7. For a summary of the average number of public inquiries instituted annually by each prime minister since Confederation, see Nicholas d'Ombrain, 'Public Inquiries in Canada,' *Canadian Public Administration* 40, 1 (Spring 1997): 88.

8 Paul Litt, 'The Care and Feeding of Canadian Culture,' *Globe and Mail*, 31 May 1991, A15. Cited in Ontario Law Reform Commission, *Report on Public Inquiries* (Toronto: 30 March 1992), 19–20.

9 David R. Cameron, 'Not Spicer and Not the B & B: Reflections of an Insider on the Workings of the Pepin-Roberts Task Force on Canadian Unity,' *International Journal of Canadian Studies* 7, 8 (Spring-Fall 1993): 343.

10 See, for example, Allan Manson and David Mullan, eds., *Commissions of Inquiry: Praise or Reappraise?* (Toronto: Irwin Law, 2003); Cameron, 'Not Spicer,' 333–45; Sylvia B. Bashevkin, 'Does Public Opinion Matter? The Adoption of Federal Royal Commission and Task Force Recommendations on the National Question, 1951–1987,' *Canadian Public Administration* 31, 1 (Fall 1988): 390–407; Jane Jenson, 'Commissioning Ideas: Representation and Royal Commissions,' in *How Ottawa Spends 1994–95: Making Change*, ed. Susan D. Phillips, 39–69 (Ottawa: Carleton University Press, 1994); Jane Jenson, 'Learning by Doing: Decision-Making in Royal Commissions,' unpublished paper presented for discussion by the Royal Commission on Aboriginal Peoples, 13 August 1992; Pross, *Commissions of Inquiry*, V. Seymour Wilson, 'The Role of Royal Commissions and Task Forces,' in *The Structures of Policy Making in Canada*, ed. Peter Aucoin and G. Bruce Doern, 113–29 (Toronto: Macmillan, 1971); John C. Courtney, 'In Defense of Royal Commissions,' *Canadian Public Administration* 12 (Fall 1969): 198–212; J.E. Hodgetts, 'The Role of Royal Commissions in Canadian Government,' in *Proceedings of the Third Annual Conference of the Institute of Public Administration of Canada, 1951* (Toronto: 1952), 351–76; J.E. Hodgetts, 'Should Canada Be De-Commissioned? A Commoner's View of Royal Commissions,' *Queen's Quarterly* 70 (Winter 1964): 457–90; J.E. Hodgetts, 'Royal Commission on Government Administration,' *Canadian Journal of Economics* 32 (November 1966): 528–31; Hugh R. Hanson, 'Inside Royal Commissions,' *Canadian Public Administration* 12 (Fall 1969): 356–64; C.E.S. Walls, 'Royal Commissions: Their Influence on Public Policy,' *Canadian Public Administration* 12 (Fall 1969): 365–71. A useful longer study is Anderson, *Royal Commissions*.

11 Tongue-in-cheek, one observer claims the study of public inquiries 'lies in the borderland between "law," "political science" and "practical politics," with the result that few have ventured to explore it, it being too high for the lawyers, too low for the political scientists, and too arduous for the practical politicians.' J. Willis, 'Comment: The Role of the Public Inquiry in Our Constitutional System,' in *Law and Social Change*, ed. J.S. Ziegel (Scarborough, ON: Carswell, 1973), 98. In legal terms, no real distinction exists between a public inquiry and a royal commission, but in practical terms the latter title is generally reserved for matters of national significance. See A. Wayne Mackay, 'Mandates, Legal Foundations, Powers and Conduct of Commissions of Inquiry,' in Pross, *Commissions of Inquiry*, 31.

12 George J. Bedard, 'Constructing Knowledge: Realist and Radical Learning Within a Canadian Royal Commission,' *Educational Policy* 13, 1 (January and March 1999): 153.

13 Cameron, 'Not Spicer,' (Spring-Fall 1993): 333.

14 M.J. Trebilcock et al., *The Choice of Governing Instruments* (Ottawa: the Economic Council of Canada, 1982), 39.

15 Iacobucci, 'Commissions of Inquiry,' 22. These have included, for example: the Rowell-Sirois Commission on Dominion-Provincial Relations, 1937; the Massey Commission on National Development in the Arts, Letters and Sciences, 1951; the Gordon Commission on the Economic Prospects for Canada, 1957; the Dunton-Laurendeau Commission on Bilingualism and Biculturalism, 1967; the Royal Commission on the Status of Women, 1970; the Citizens' Forum on Canada's Future (the Spicer Commission), 1991; the Royal Commission on Aboriginal Peoples, 1993; and others.

16 On the history of the use of royal commissions, which dates back in the British parliamentary tradition to 1517, see Iacobucci, 'Commissions of Inquiry,' 22; and 'Royal Commissions,' in *The Canadian Encyclopedia* (Edmonton: Hurtig, 1985), 1603. Anderson notes that 'Miss Agnes Macphail, M.P., alleged that on April 9th, 1934, at Kingston Penitentiary two men used "abusive and profane language concerning her." A royal commission was appointed to look into the matter.' Anderson, *Royal Commissions*, 8. See also J.E. Hodgetts, 'Public Power and Ivory Power,' in *Agenda 1970: Proposals for a Creative Politics*, ed. T. Lloyd and J.T. McLeod, 271 ff. (Toronto: University of Toronto Press, 1968).

17 An indication of the difficulty of producing a taxonomy is indicated by Anderson, who, finding a twofold classification of royal commissions by Hodgetts as inadequate, expanded it into a twelvefold one! See Anderson, *Royal Commissions*, 10. Indeed, even locating a comprehensive listing of royal commissions in Canadian history is nearly impossible given the ambiguity

surrounding their definition. One attempt to do so can be found in George Fletcher Henderson, *Federal Royal Commissions in Canada, 1867–1966: A Checklist* (Toronto: University of Toronto Press, 1967). This has been updated twice. See Denise Ledoux, *Commissions of Inquiry under the Inquiries Act, Part I, 1967 to Date* (Ottawa: Library of Parliament, Information and References Branch, February 1980); and Anna Bombak, 'Canadian Federal Royal Commissions, 1978–1988: An Update,' *Input* 10, 2 (March 1989): 1–12.

18 These numbers were compiled from Henderson, 'Federal Royal Commissions' Bombak, 'Canadian Federal Royal Commissions' and Ledoux, 'Commissions of Inquiry.' See also Canada, National Library of Canada. *Index to Royal Commissions*, www.nlc-bnc.ca/indexcommissions/index-e.html.

19 Liora Salter, 'The Two Contradictions in Public Inquiries,' in Pross, *Commissions of Inquiry*, 174. See also Jenson, 'Commissioning Ideas,' 39–69. See also Liora Salter, 'The Complex Relationship between Inquiries and Public Controversy,' in *Commissions of Inquiry: Praise or Reappraise?* ed. Allan Manson and David Mullan, 185–209 (Toronto: Irwin Law, 2003). Salter makes the important point that while conventional wisdom suggests inquiries are intended to defuse policy controversies, in fact they often stir them up.

20 Berger, 'Canadian Commissions of Inquiry,' 14.

21 Salter, 'The Two Contradictions in Public Inquiries,' 174.

22 Ibid.

23 Ibid., 177.

24 Richard Simeon, 'Inside the Macdonald Commission,' *Studies in Political Economy* 22 (Spring 1987): 169–70. Simeon is reacting in this article to the Drache and Cameron critique of the Macdonald Commission, *The Other Macdonald Report: The Consensus on Canada's Future that the Macdonald Commission Left Out* (Toronto: James Lorimer, 1985). A spirited rebuttal to Simeon's position can be found in Duncan Cameron and Daniel Drache, 'Outside the Macdonald Commission: Reply to Richard Simeon,' *Studies in Political Economy* 26 (Summer 1988): 173–80.

25 See Thomas Berger, *Northern Frontier, Northern Homeland: The Report of the Mackenzie Valley Pipeline Inquiry* (Ottawa: Supply and Services Canada, 1977). Two critics lament the fact that the Berger Commission was not used as a model for the Macdonald Commission: 'the Macdonald Commission had an admirable model, in the Berger Commission ... for carrying through the true spirit of public inquiry. The Berger Commission financed research by Native groups that, unlike the oil companies, did not have the means to make themselves heard in a sophisticated way. Berger's empowering of these groups was undoubtedly an influence on the commission's landmark decision to slow down resource development in the North ... the Macdonald

Commission did not find the Berger model worthy of emulation.' Drache and Cameron, *The Other Macdonald Report*, xi. See also Peter Puxley, 'A Model of Engagement: Reflections on the 25th Anniversary of the Berger Report,' *Canadian Policy Research Networks* (August 2002): 1–14.

26   Salter, 'The Two Contradictions in Public Inquiries,' 182. Emphasis added.

27   Drache and Cameron, *The Other Macdonald Report*, xi.

28   Ibid., xiii.

29   See Michael Hawes, 'The National Economy,' in *The Canadian Annual Review of Politics and Public Affairs, 1985*, ed. R.B. Byers (Toronto: University of Toronto Press, 1988), 140.

30   See, for example, Drache and Cameron, *The Other Macdonald Report*; Simeon, 'Inside the Macdonald Commission,' 167–79; Cameron and Drache, 'Comment: Outside the Macdonald Commission,' 173–80; and Marjorie Cohen, 'The Macdonald Report and Its Implications for Women,' *Feminist Action Feministe* 1 (December 1985): 13–15. A very useful study that places the Macdonald Commission in a comparative political economy perspective is Neil Bradford, *Commissioning Ideas: Canadian National Policy Innovation in Comparative Perspective* (Toronto: Oxford University Press, 1998).

Collections of essays reviewing the Commission *Report* from a leftist perspective are found in 'The Right Stuff: A Critique of the Macdonald Commission Report,' *Atkinson Review of Canadian Studies* 3, 1 (Spring 1986); and 'Rebutting the Macdonald Report,' *The Facts* 8, 2 (March-April 1986). 'Mainstream' reviews of the *Report* can be found in 'The Macdonald Report: Twelve Reviews,' *Canadian Public Policy* 12, supplement (February 1986).

There is no book-length study of the Macdonald Commission. But the following provide limited views of it: Pross, *Commissions of Inquiry*; Jenson, 'Commissioning Ideas,' 39–69. G. Bruce Doern and Brian W. Tomlin, *Faith and Fear: The Free Trade Story* (Toronto: Stoddart, 1991); John W. Warnock, *Free Trade and the New Right Agenda* (Vancouver: New Star Books, 1988); and James Laxer, *Leap of Faith: Free Trade and the Future of Canada* (Edmonton: Hurtig Publishers, 1986).

31   d'Ombrain, 'Public Inquiries in Canada,' 92.

32   Michael Kirby interview (Ottawa, June 8 1993).

33   Ibid.

34   Ibid. Kirby et al. were prescient in at least one regard here: the commission succeeded in freeing itself of the 'narrow ideology of the left.' It was, however, dominated by the 'narrow ideology of the right,' as the following chapters will show.

35   Donald Macdonald interview (Toronto, 18 August 1993).

36   Ibid.

37 Ibid.
38 Gerry Godsoe interview (Halifax, 26 July 1994).
39 Alan Nymark Interview (Ottawa, 22 June 1993).
40 Ibid.
41 Ibid.
42 Ibid.
43 Ibid.
44 Donald Macdonald interview (Toronto, 13 September 1993).
45 Michael Kirby interview.
46 Donald Macdonald interview (Toronto, 18 August 1993).
47 Canada, Macdonald Commission, 'Dinner with the Prime Minister: Confidential,' National Archives of Canada, RG 33/137, Volume 12, 28 February 1983, n.p.
48 Donald Macdonald interview (Toronto, 18 August 1993).
49 Ibid.
50 Doern and Tomlin, *Faith and Fear*, 52–3. This statement must be qualified by the fact that, as minister of finance, Macdonald had begun to move away from some of his earlier nationalist positions, particularly in terms of industrial strategy.
51 Michael Kirby interview.
52 Ibid.
53 Ibid.
54 Gerry Godsoe interview.
55 Cited in Christina McCall and Stephen Clarkson, *Trudeau and Our Times*, Vol. 2, *The Heroic Delusion* (Toronto: McClelland and Stewart, 1994), 283.
56 In any event, a very unflattering portrait of Pitfield was published just a month before the commission was announced which may have compromised his selection as chairperson. See Christina McCall-Newman, 'Michael Pitfield and the Politics of Mismanagement,' *Saturday Night* 97, 10 (October 1982): 24–44. See also McCall and Clarkson, *Trudeau and Our Times*, 2: 282–3.
57 Michael Kirby interview. Kirby's 'Maritime mafia' was his network of Liberal partisans in that part of the country. He also characterized Godsoe as a civic-minded individual. 'Take a guy like Godsoe. Godsoe had always been on the fringe of politics all his life, loved the idea of finding out how Ottawa really works, was a Rhodes Scholar, led his class at Dalhousie law school, likes living in Halifax and all that. But all of a sudden here was an opportunity for him to get out of the mundane into the truly intellectually stimulating. And yes he had a practice, and he couldn't give up his practice, and so on, yet he winds up doing it anyway. The thing is, there is a lot of idealism with which these people approach these jobs, like the royal commission jobs. People

think you do it for the money. The really good guys, the money is not the issue. But they really genuinely have a sense of commitment, and a sense of intellectual curiosity about what it is that needs to be done and how to do it. When they do that, when they pull that off, that is pretty sensational.'

58 Ibid.
59 Ibid.
60 Ibid.
61 Ibid.
62 Ibid.
63 Ibid.
64 Godsoe detailed these provisions in 'Comment on Inquiry Management,' in Pross, *Commissions of Inquiry*, 71–3.
65 Gerry Godsoe interview.
66 Ibid.
67 Godsoe, 'Comment on Inquiry Management,' in Pross, *Commissions of Inquiry*, 72.
68 Donald Macdonald interview (Toronto, 18 August 1993).
69 Alan Nymark interview.
70 For a somewhat embittered account of the secretive process by which Prime Minister Trudeau and a few trusted advisers decided on staging this royal commission, see Donald Johnston, *Up the Hill* (Montreal: Optimum Publishing International, 1986), 71–3.
71 Michael Kirby interview.
72 Gerry Godsoe interview.
73 Canada, *House of Commons Debates* (5 November 1982), 20444–445.
74 Johnston, *Up the Hill*, 72.
75 Ibid.
76 Gerry Godsoe interview.
77 Alan Nymark interview.
78 Johnston, *Up the Hill*, 73.
79 Canada, Macdonald Commission, 'Information Package on Royal Commissions: Briefing Notes for Commissioners: Confidential,' National Archives of Canada, RG 33\137, Volume 2 November 1982, n.p.
80 See Canada, Royal Commission on the Economic Union and Development Prospects for Canada, *A Commission on Canada's Future: Be Part of It* (Ottawa: Minister of Supply and Services, 1982). The commission terms of reference are contained in this document.
81 Ian Mulgrew, 'Stumbling Out of the Starting Gate: Macdonald Commission Strives for Credibility,' *Globe and Mail*, 10 September 1983.
82 Michael Kirby interview.
83 Ibid.

84 Alan Nymark interview.
85 Michael Kirby interview.
86 Alan Nymark interview.
87 Canada, Macdonald Commission, *A Commission on Canada's Future*, 14.
88 Ibid., 15.
89 Ibid.
90 Ibid., 13.
91 Ibid. Emphasis in original.
92 Ibid. Emphasis in original.
93 Ibid. Emphasis in original.
94 Ibid., 10. Emphasis in original.
95 Ibid., 9. Emphasis in original.
96 Ibid., 10. Emphasis in original.
97 Ibid. Emphasis in original.
98 Ibid., 6. Emphasis in original.
99 Ibid. Emphasis in original.
100 Peter Warrian interview (Toronto, 20 September 1993).
101 Canada, Macdonald Commission, *A Commission on Canada's Future*, 9.

Chapter 3

1 Alan Cairns interview (Ottawa, 8 June 1993).
2 By way of comparison, J.E. Hodgetts expressed outrage that between 1958 and 1968, the total cost of *seven* major royal commissions to the Canadian taxpayer was 'close to $20 million.' J.E. Hodgetts, 'Public Power and Ivory Power,' in *Agenda 1970: Proposals for a Creative Politics*, ed. T. Lloyd and J.T. McLeod (Toronto: University of Toronto Press, 1968), 277. The Rowell-Sirois Commission (1937) cost $533,600; the Gordon Commission (1957) cost $1,303,819. See Robert M. Folwer, 'The Role of Royal Commissions,' in *Economic Policy Advising in Canada: Essays in Honour of John Deutsch*, ed. David C. Smith, 93–104 (Montreal: C.D. Howe Institute, 1981). A comparison of the costs of various public inquires can be found in Nicholas d'Ombrain, 'Public Inquiries in Canada,' *Canadian Public Administration* 40, 1 (Spring 1997): 86–107.
3 Donald C. Wallace, 'Ottawa and the Provinces,' in *Canadian Annual Review of Politics and Public Affairs, 1983*, ed. R.B. Byers, (Toronto: University of Toronto Press, 1985), 96.
4 R.J. Drummond, 'Parliament and Politics,' in *Canadian Annual Review of Politics and Public Affairs, 1983*, ed. Byers, 14.
5 Ibid., 26.

6 Donald Macdonald interview (Toronto, 18 August 1993).
7 Drummond, 'Parliament and Politics,' 26.
8 Albert Breton interview (Toronto, 4 October 1993).
9 See for example, Ian Mulgrew, 'Stumbling Out of the Starting Gate: Macdonald Commission Strives for Credibility,' *Globe and Mail*, 10 September 1983.
10 Donald Macdonald interview (Toronto, 18 August 1993).
11 Ibid.
12 Robert Prichard interview (Toronto, 13 May 1993).
13 Michael Kirby interview (Ottawa, 8 June 1993).
14 Ibid.
15 Gerry Godsoe interview (Halifax, 26 July 1994).
16 Michael Kirby interview.
17 Alan Nymark interview (Ottawa, 22 June 1993).
18 Michael Kirby interview.
19 Gerry Godsoe interview.
20 Ibid.
21 Ibid.
22 Alan Nymark interview.
23 The biographies of the commissioners can be found in Canada, Macdonald Report, *A Commission on Canada's Future: Be a Part of It* (Ottawa: Minister of Supply and Services, 1982). They are reprinted here as Appendix D.
24 Donald Macdonald interview (Toronto, 18 August 1993).
25 Michael Kirby interview.
26 Canada, Macdonald Commission, 'Information Package on Royal Commissions: Briefing Notes for Commissioners: Confidential,' National Archives of Canada (NAC), RG 33\137, volume 2 November 1982, n.p.
27 Michael Kirby interview.
28 Donald Macdonald interview (Toronto, 18 August 1993).
29 Daniel Drache and Duncon Cameron, *The Other Macdonald Report: The Consensus on Canada's Future that the Macdonald Commission Left Out* (Toronto: James Lorimer, 1985).
30 Donald Macdonald interview (Toronto, 13 September 1993).
31 Docquier had a unique arrangement with the commission that permitted him to employ his own research staff in recognition of the position he held as the labour representative. Docquier recalled that 'Peter was our [the Steelworkers] research director at that time. Now the arrangement that I had with the commission was that Ken Waldie would help me, and he was paid by the commission. What kind of arrangement he had, I don't know. But he was paid by the commission to work with me, and of course with

others who might need his help. Warrian was there because of his relationship with me. I would naturally go to him as well. But he had no role in the commission. None whatsoever.' Nonetheless, while formally remaining outside the commission, Warrian played a major role in assisting Docquier to analyse the voluminous materials received from the commission. He also 'held the pen' for Docquier's supplementary statement in the commission's *Report*. Gerard Docquier interview (Ottawa, 21 February 1994).

32 Peter Warrian interview (Toronto, 20 September 1993).
33 Ibid.
34 Ibid.
35 Ibid.
36 Gerard Docquier interview.
37 Ibid.
38 Ibid.
39 Canada, Macdonald Commission, *A Commission on Canada's Future*, 2.
40 Canada, Macdonald Commission, 'Memo from Michel Rochon, Commission Secretary,' NAC RG 33\137, volume 1, 1983, n.p.
41 These 'private public consultations' are considered in the context of writing the final *Report* in chapters 9 and 11.
42 Alan Nymark interview.
43 Gerry Godsoe interview.
44 Alan Nymark interview.
45 Canada, Macdonald Commission, 'Hawkins Report, Volume 1: Letter From R.E. Hawkins, Lawyer to Commission,' NAC RG 33\137, Volume 1, 1982.
46 Gerry Godsoe interview, (Halifax, 26 July 1994).
47 Ibid.
48 Ibid.
49 Ibid.
50 Ibid.
51 Jane Jenson notes the Canadian state's response to an earlier crisis – the depression of the 1930s – was also to create a royal commission. See 'Representations in Crisis: The Roots of Canada's Permeable Fordism,' *Canadian Journal of Political Science* 23, 4 (December 1990): 681.
52 Macdonald Commission, *Report*, 1: 305–7.
53 Ibid., 374–5.
54 Ibid., 381.
55 Ibid., 382.
56 Ibid.
57 Ibid., 383.
58 Ibid.

59 Canada, Department of External Affairs, *Canadian Trade Policy for the 1980s: A Discussion Paper* (Ottawa: Supply and Services, 1983).
60 Macdonald Commission, *Report*, 1: 269.
61 Ibid., 270. Rotstein's brief was contained in the presentation by the Canadian Institute for Economic Policy, later published as Abraham Rotstein, *Rebuilding from Within: Remedies for Canada's Ailing Economy* (Ottawa: Canadian Institute for Economic Policy, 1984).

Chapter 4

1 St. John's Board of Trade, *Brief 0158 to the Royal Commission on the Economic Union and Development Prospects for Canada* (1983), 2–3.
2 An exploration of this theme is presented in François Rocher, 'Canadian Business, Free Trade and the Rhetoric of Economic Continentalism,' *Studies in Political Economy* 35 (Summer 1991): 135–54.
3 For the political economy view, see Daniel Drache and Duncan Cameron, eds., *The Other Macdonald Report: The Consensus on Canada's Future that the Macdonald Commission Left Out* (Toronto: James Lorimer, 1985); and Duncan Cameron and Daniel Drache, 'Comment. Outside the Macdonald Commission: Reply to Richard Simeon,' *Studies in Political Economy* 26 (Summer 1988): 173–80. For the political science view, see Richard Simeon, 'Inside the Macdonald Commission,' *Studies in Political Economy* 22 (Spring 1987): 167–79; and A. Paul Pross et al., *Commissions of Inquiry* (Toronto: Carswell, 1990).
4 Drache and Cameron, *The Other Macdonald Report*, ix.
5 Canada, Royal Commission on the Economic Union and Development Prospects for Canada (the Macdonald Commission), *A Commission on Canada's Future: Be Part of It* (Ottawa: Supply and Services, 1983), 3.
6 Donald Macdonald interview (Toronto, 18 August 1993).
7 Canada, Macdonald Commission, *A Commission on Canada's Future*, 2.
8 *Royal Commission on the Economic Union and Development Prospects for Canada*, Hearings at Vancouver, British Columbia (6 September 1983) 1: 1–2. Emphasis added.
9 Ibid., 4.
10 Donald Macdonald interview (Toronto, 13 September 1993).
11 Ibid.
12 See Canada, Macdonald Commission, 'Guide Book for Analysis,' National Archives of Canada (NAC), RG 33\137, Volume 1, 15 August 1983, 3.
13 Macdonald Commission *Report*, vol. 1: xix.

14 Pross, *Commissions of Inquiry*, 11–12. Emphasis added.
15 Cairns also argued that the hearings do not simply legitimate an inquiry and build a consensus that will ultimately support the commissioners' recommendations. 'In his view, the hearings are learning mechanism for the commissioners and a means of testing the feasibility of potential recommendations.' Pross *Commissions of Inquiry*, 12.
16 Harold Adams Innis recognized this problem in regard to the Rowell-Sirois Commission. Commenting on the public consultations before that inquiry, he said 'the Commission followed the unfortunate precedent of other commissions in not admitting evidence from individual Canadians and confining it to that presented by a representative of organizations ... These restrictions may not have been serious as individual Canadians exercised considerable ingenuity in donning the necessary apparel of various organizations, political and otherwise, which had clothing to spare. The practice may have reduced the work of the Commission by excluding individual Canadians with peculiar tastes in clothes, but the varied livery of innumerable organizations can scarcely have been less hideous. It should be possible for Canadians to appear before royal commissions in their own clothes.' Harold Adams Innis, 'The Rowell-Sirois Commission,' *Canadian Journal of Economics and Political Science* 6 (1940): 563.
17 See William Johnson, '"Leap of Faith": Canada Must Act on Free Trade, Macdonald Says,' *Globe and Mail* (19 November 1984), 1, 11. The statement was made during a closed, three-day conference sponsored by the Council on Foreign Relations and Columbia University's The American Assembly. Macdonald's remarks to the conference closely mirror the free trade recommendation found in the commission *Report* in regard to a number of specific areas.
18 Donald C. Wallace, 'Ottawa and the Provinces,' in *Canadian Annual Review of Politics and Public Affairs, 1983*, ed. R.B. Byers (Toronto: University of Toronto Press, 1987), 82. See also G. Bruce Doern and Brian W. Tomlin, *Faith and Fear: The Free Trade Story* (Toronto: Stoddart, 1991); Michael Hawes, 'The National Economy,' *Canadian Annual Review of Politics and Public Affairs, 1984* (Toronto: University of Toronto Press, 1987), 140.
19 Wallace, 'Ottawa and the Provinces,' 82.
20 Drache and Cameron, *The Other Macdonald Report*, xx–xxi. This issue is considered in more detail in chapter 10.
21 Donald Macdonald, 'Preparing for the 21st Century,' *Chimo Magazine* (Summer 1983): 8. Emphasis added.
22 Ian Mulgrew, 'Stumbling Out of the Starting Gate: Macdonald Commission Strives for Credibility,' *Globe and Mail*, 10 September 1983.

23　Hugh G. Thorburn, *Interest Groups in the Canadian Federal System* (Toronto: University of Toronto Press, 1985), 83.

24　Ibid.

25　This fact presages the creation of a royal commission dealing specifically with Aboriginal issues. See Canada, *Report of the Royal Commission on Aboriginal Peoples* (Ottawa: Indian and Northern Affairs Canada, 1996).

26　The term 'special interest group' carries pejorative connotations, but is the term employed by the Macdonald Commission in its categorization of submissions it received.

27　Thorburn, *Interest Groups,* 86. For a similar argument see Patricia L. O'Reilly, *Health Care Practitioners: An Ontario Case Study in Policy Making* (Toronto: University of Toronto Press, 1999).

28　For example, some businesses simply submitted their annual shareholder reports rather than a brief addressing the questions raised by the commission.

29　Macdonald Commission, *Report,* 3: 575–98.

30　Consequently, transcripts of public meetings are not analysed in this study. Neither are written submissions from individuals, from governments, or from educational and research institutions as defined by the Macdonald Commission categorization.

31　The emergence of several new rights-based entitlements has given rise to a variety of social groups who have organized and mobilized themselves throughout the last thirty or more years, and particularly since the 1982 Charter of Rights and Freedoms. The emergence of new rights-based groups in Canadian society was analysed in two Macdonald Commission background studies. See Alan Cairns and Cynthia Williams, 'Constitutionalism, Citizenship and Society in Canada: an Overview,' in *Constitutionalism, Citizenship and Society in Canada,* ed. Alan Cairns and Cynthia Williams, 1–50 (Toronto: University of Toronto Press, 1985); and Alan Cairns and Cynthia Williams, eds., *The Politics of Gender, Ethnicity and Language in Canada* (Toronto: University of Toronto Press, 1985). See also Alan Cairns, 'Political Science, Ethnicity, and the Canadian Constitution,' in *Federalism and Political Community: Essays in Honour of Donald Smiley,* ed. David P. Shugarman and Reg Whitaker (Peterborough, ON: Broadview Press, 1989), 119.

32　Jane Jenson, 'Paradigms and Political Discourse: Protective Legislation in France and the United States Before 1919,' *Canadian Journal of Political Science* 12, 2 (June 1989): 238.

33　Indeed, Drache and Cameron considered the contributions of these popular sector groups so important to an understanding of the discourse presented to the Macdonald Commission that they reproduced several of their submissions in *The Other Macdonald Report.*

34 Thorburn, *Interest Groups*, 85. See Macdonald Commission, *Content Analysis of Briefs and Transcripts by Organization Type (1st Round)* Five Volumes (Ottawa: 1985). The seven major categories devised for the content analysis were: the Canadian Economy; Sectors of the Economy; Commerce, Finance and Public Revenue; Government and Politics; International Trade and Foreign Policy; Law and the Constitution; and Canadian Society, Social Policy and Conditions. See Appendix B.

35 Forty-eight briefs identified by the commission content analysis as relevant to the five categories actually were not relevant (twenty-three business group briefs, three labour groups briefs, and twenty-two popular sector group briefs).

36 The frequency with which a category is mentioned, then, is not what is being measured. Thus, for example, even if the brief from Group X referred to government intervention fifteen times, it was only recorded once as either a nationalist or continentalist statement. If a particular brief contained a nationalist statement about government intervention, and subsequently a continentalist statement, then both were recorded. But multiple nationalist or continentalist references to a particular category were not recorded. Since a few briefs were not consistent in their positions and made references to both nationalist and continentalist strategies, a single brief could theoretically have been recorded with one nationalist and one continentalist statement about each of the five categories, for a total of ten references. (In reality, the most statements recorded in a single brief was six, by the Electrical and Electronic manufacturer's Association of Canada (Brief 0416)).

37 François Rocher analyses the various factions of the bourgeoisie in more detail to determine which ones actually supported increased continentalization. See Rocher, 'Canadian Business, Free Trade and the Rhetoric of Economic Continentalization,' 135–54.

38 Retail Council of Canada, *Brief 0012* (October 1983), viii.

39 Dartmouth Chamber of Commerce, *Brief 0352* (September 1983), 2.

40 Placer Development Ltd., *Brief 0113* (1983), 5.

41 Halifax Board of Trade, *Brief 0334* (1983), 16.

42 New Brunswick Telephone Company Ltd., *Brief 0228* (1983), 2.

43 The Whitehorse Chamber of Commerce, *Brief 0268* (September 1983), 8.

44 Calgary Chamber of Commerce, *Brief 0558* (19 October 1983), 10.

45 Canadian Electrical Distributors Association, *Brief 0396* (1983), 10.

46 Inco Ltd. (Sudbury), *Brief 0457* (19 October 1983), 3.

47 Canadian Manufacturers Association, *Brief 0079* (6 September 1983), 29–30.

48 Mining Association of British Columbia, *Brief 0107* (1983), 8.

49 Dominion Textiles Inc. (Montreal), *Brief 0478* (14 October 1983), 55–7.

50 Canadian Hardware and Housewares Manufacturers Association, *Brief 0390* (1983), 7.

51 Greater Charlottetown Area Chamber of Commerce, *Brief 0173* (1 September 1983), 6.

52 Retail Council of Canada, *Brief 0012* (October 1983), 44.

53 Ibid., 77.

54 See John Young, *Canadian Commercial Policy* (Ottawa: Gordon Commission, 1957). Interestingly, the Macdonald Commission did cite Young's work approvingly in its final *Report*. In 1957, Young wrote 'The principal result of this analysis can be summarized in a sentence. In general and over the long run, increases in protection can be expected to lead to economic losses and decreases in protection to economic gains for the country as a whole. This follows not only from the direct effect the Canadian tariff has on the Canadian economy, but also from the effect Canadian commercial policy has on the treatment accorded this country's exports.' See Macdonald Commission, *Report* vol. 1, 328.

55 Mining Association of British Columbia, *Brief 0107* (1983), executive summary.

56 Employers' Council of Canada, *Brief 0186* (7 September 1983), 11.

57 Canadian Electrical Distributors Association, *Brief 0396* (1983), 8.

58 Calgary Chamber of Commerce, *Brief 0558* (19 October 1983), 13.

59 British Columbia Resources Investment Corporation, *Brief 0624* (9 November 1983), 8–9.

60 See Thorburn, *Interest Groups*; and Rocher, 'Canadian Business.' A limited view focusing on one sector of the Canadian economy can be found in David Yudelman, *Mining and the Macdonald Commission: The State of the Industry in the Mid-1980s* (Kingston: Centre for Resource Studies, 1985).

61 Thorburn, *Interest Groups*, 111. Thus the briefs from Quebec, for instance, did not demonstrate a regional consciousness or homogeneity of view rooted in a common geography. This is not to deny that there are, of course, certain issues that elicit responses along regional lines, especially related to regional economic development.

62 Ibid., 113–14.

63 Ibid., 111–12. A sectoral analysis of the business briefs is presented below in chapter 5.

64 Rocher, 'Canadian Business,' 150. Besides the Macdonald Commission, Rocher also looked at briefs and memoranda presented by representatives of business to the 1978 and 1982 reports of the Senate Standing Committee on Foreign Affairs and the 1985 Special Joint Committee of the Senate and the House of Commons on External Affairs.

65 Rocher, 'Canadian Business,' 151.

66 In 1902, 95 per cent of Canadian union members were affiliated with inter-national (American) unions. By 1967, the number has dropped to 64 per cent. By 1978, only 37 per cent of organized Canadian workers belonged to international unions, and in 1990 this figure had been reduced to 32 per cent. See Alton W.J. Craig, *The System of Industrial Relations* (Scarborough, ON: Prentice-Hall, 1990), 63; Ed Finn, 'The Struggle for Canadian Labour Autonomy,' *Labour Gazette* 70 (November 1970): 768; and Virginia Galt, 'Workers Changing Loyalties,' *Globe and Mail,* 19 January 1991, B18. On the evolution of Canada's largest labour organization, see Miriam Smith, 'The Canadian Labour Congress: From Continentalism to Economic National-ism,' *Studies in Political Economy* 38 (Summer 1992): 35–60.

67 International Union of Operating Engineers (Local 115), *Brief 0126* (6 September 1983), 5.

68 Ibid.

69 United Steelworkers of America, *Brief 0633* (31 October 1983), 7–8.

70 Ibid.

71 Ibid., 7–11.

72 British Columbia and Yukon Territory Building and Trades Council, *Brief 0117* (1983), 5.

73 Nova Scotia Federation of Labour (CLC), *Brief 0166* (1983), 15.

74 Windsor and District Labour Council, *Brief 0456* (13 October 1983), 3.

75 Winnipeg Labour Council, *Brief 0573* (21 October 1983), 1.

76 Nova Scotia Teachers Federation, *Brief 0373* (September 1983), 15.

77 Thunder Bay and District Labour Council, *Brief 0488* (1983), n.p.

78 United Steelworkers of America, *Brief 0633* (31 October 1983), 12.

79 New Brunswick Federation of Labour, *Brief 0257* (22 September 1983), 6.

80 Ibid., 9.

81 Association of University of New Brunswick Teachers, *Brief 0280* (12 September 1983), n.p.

82 Marine Workers Federation (CLC), *Brief 0169* (6 September 1983), 6.

83 New Brunswick Federation of Labour, *Brief 0257* (22 September 1983), 9.

84 See the Winnipeg Labour Council, *Brief 0573* (21 October 1983); Windsor and District Labour Council, *Brief 0456* (13 October 1983); The United Steel-workers of America, Local 1064, Sydney, Nova Scotia, *Brief 0208* (September 1983); and the United Auto Workers of Canada, *Brief 0934* (1983).

85 International Woodworkers of America, *Brief 0185* (1983), 2.

86 Winnipeg Labour Council, *Brief 0573* (21 October 1983), 9.

87 Ibid.

88 Ibid.

89 Ibid., 10–13.
90 Canadian Crafts Council, *Brief 0634* (26 October 1983), 40.
91 Canadian Conference of Catholic Bishops, *Ethical Reflections on the Economic Crisis* (Ottawa: Corca can Inc., 1983). Drache and Cameron argue that no other source was as widely cited before the Macdonald Commission. See Drache and Cameron, *The Other Macdonald Report,* 208.
92 Pacific Group for Policy Alternatives, *Brief 0036* (1983), 6, 9.
93 Lambton County Board of Education, *Brief 0115* (1983), 2.
94 First United Church, Vancouver, *Brief 0197* (6 September 1983), 2.
95 New Dawn Enterprises Ltd., *Brief 0240* (22 September 1983), 9–10.
96 Women United for a Non-Exploitive New Age, *Brief 0295* (1983), 1.
97 Ibid., 6.
98 The Social Action Commission of the Roman Catholic Diocese of Charlottetown, *Brief 0336* (19 September 1983), 7–8.
99 Ecology Action Centre (Halifax), *Brief 0350* (3 October 1983), 7. Emphasis in original.
100 Windsor Women's Incentive Centre, *Brief 0401* (1983), 6.
101 Women's Information and Referral Centre, Montreal, *Brief 0471* (October 1983), 10.
102 Social Action Commission of the Roman Catholic Diocese of Charlottetown, *Brief 0336* (19 September 1983), 9.
103 Women Against the Budget, *Brief 0269* (September 1983), 9.
104 Canadian School Trustees Association, *Brief 0405* (3 October 1983), 4.
105 Winnipeg Coordinating Committee for Disarmament, *Brief 0588* (October 1983), 11.
106 Assembly of British Columbia Arts Councils, *Brief 0100* (23 August 1983), 5.
107 Nuu-Chah-Nulth Tribal Council, *Brief 0285* (7 September 1983), 1, 3.
108 Makivik Corporation, *Brief 0501* (14 October 1983), 24.
109 Ibid., 84–5.
110 Northern Flood Committee, *Brief 0591* (1983), 4.
111 Asia Pacific Foundation of Canada, *Brief 0198* (9 September 1983), 11.
112 Lambton County Board of Education, *Brief 0115* (1983), 2.
113 Windsor Coalition for Development and the Third World Resource Centre, *Brief 0423* (1983), 3.

Chapter 5

1 From 'The Royal Commission on Kissing,' in Sir Allen Herbert, 'The Pageant of Parliament,' *Punch* 176 (27 June 1934): 708. Cited in Frank

Iacobucci, 'Commissions of Inquiry and Public Policy in Canada,' in *Commissions of Inquiry*, ed. A. Paul Pross et al. (Toronto: Carswell, 1990), 21

2 A quantitative study of the groups which presented briefs to the Macdonald Commission can be found in Hugh Thorburn, *Interest Groups in the Canadian Federal System* (Toronto: University of Toronto Press, 1985). One of the only qualitative studies can be found in an analysis of the briefs contributed by the mining industry in Canada. See David Yudelman, *Mining and the Macdonald Commission: The State of the Industry in the Mid-1980s* (Kingston: Centre for Resource Studies Working Paper No. 34, 1985). There is also a very short analysis of the briefs from business groups that commented on free trade. See Isaiah A. Litvak, 'Freer Trade With the U.S.: Conflicting Views of Canadian Business,' *Business Quarterly* 51, 1 (Spring 1986): 30–1.

3 Jane Jenson has suggested that the crises in global capitalism arising in the 1970s and 1980s prompted scholars to look beyond 'an exclusive focus on the state and its apparatuses towards the representation of interests and the mobilization of political actors in different economic circumstances.' See '"Different," but Not Exceptional: Canada's Permeable Fordism,' *Canadian Review of Sociology and Anthropology* 26, 1 (1989): 70.

4 Richard Simeon, 'Inside the Macdonald Commission,' *Studies in Political Economy* 22 (Spring 1987): 169–70. Simeon is responding in this article to the Drache and Cameron critique of the Macdonald Commission. See Daniel Drache and Duncan Cameron, *The Other Macdonald Report: The Consensus on Canada's Future the Macdonald Commission Left Out* (Toronto: Lorimer, 1985).

5 See chapter 4 note 3.

6 Simeon, 'Inside the Macdonald Commission,' 168.

7 Ibid., 173. Emphasis in original.

8 Ibid., 174.

9 Ibid., 177. Ironically, the effects of the Macdonald Commission's main recommendation was to more or less fundamentally reorient Canadian capitalism.

10 Ibid., 178.

11 The United States is the outstanding exception to this statement. For the Canadian case, see David A. Wolfe, 'The Rise and Demise of the Keynesian Era in Canada: Economic Policy, 1930–1982,' in *Modern Canada 1930-1980s: Readings in Canadian Social History*, vol. 5, ed. Michael S. Cross and Gregory S. Kealey, 46–78 (Toronto: McClelland and Stewart, 1984).

12 Andrew B. Gollner and Daniel Salée, 'A Turn to the Right? Canada in the Post-Trudeau Era,' in *Canada under Mulroney: An End-of-Term Report*, ed. Andrew B. Gollner and Daniel Salée (Montreal: Véhicule Press, 1988), 12.

13 Gollner and Salée, 'A Turn to the Right?' 12. See also Timothy Lewis, *In the*

Long Run We're All Dead: The Canadian Turn to Fiscal Restraint (Vancouver: UBC Press, 2003).

14 United Steelworkers of America, *Brief 0633* (31 October 1983), 7–8. It is noteworthy that this brief was presented to the Macdonald Commission by Gerard Docquier who, besides being the national director of the Canadian arm of this union, was also one of the commissioners.

15 See, for example, the Social Action Commission of the Roman Catholic Diocese of Charlottetown, *Brief 0336* (19 September 1983), 7–8.

16 Windsor Coalition for Development and the Third World Resource Centre, *Brief 0423* (1983), executive summary.

17 Women's Information and Referral Centre, *Brief 0471* (October 1983), 6–10.

18 Canadian Airline Employees' Association, *Brief 0903* (1983), 15.

19 British Columbia and Yukon Territory Building and Construction Trades Council, *Brief 0117* (1983), 5.

20 Windsor and District Labour Council, *Brief 0456* (13 October 1983), 3.

21 Women Against the Budget, *Brief 0269* (September 1983), 9.

22 Winnipeg Coordinating Committee for Disarmament, *Brief 0588* (October 1983), 11. Similar kinds of arguments were put forward by the St Patrick's Social Justice Committee, *Brief 0652* (1983).

23 New Brunswick Federation of Labour, *Brief 0257* (22 September 1983), 9.

24 Canadian Union of Public Employees, *Brief 1048* (1983), 49.

25 Ecology Action Centre, *Brief 0350* (3 October 1983), 7. Emphasis in original.

26 Manitoba Federation of Labour, *Brief 0842* (1983), 11.

27 Windsor Coalition for Development and the Third World Resource Centre, *Brief 0423* (1983), 3.

28 Makivik Corporation, *Brief 0501* (14 October 1983), 24.

29 New Dawn Enterprises Ltd., *Brief 0240* (22 September 1983), 11–12.

30 Social Planning and Research Council of Hamilton and District, *Brief 0828* (1983), ii.

31 Social Planning Council of Metro Toronto, *Brief 0857* (1983), 74.

32 Ibid., 79.

33 Help the Aged, *Brief 0684* (31 October 1983), 4.

34 Lambton County Board of Education, *Brief 0115* (1983), executive summary.

35 Social Action Commission of the Roman Catholic Diocese of Charlottetown, *Brief 0336* (September 1983), 9.

36 British Columbia and Yukon Territory Building and Construction Trades Council, *Brief 0117* (1983), 3.

37 Ibid., 4.

38 Winnipeg Labour Council, *Brief 0573* (21 October 1983), 9.

39 Ibid., 10–13.

40 See, for example, Peter Aucoin, *The New Public Management: Canada in Comparative Perspective* (Montreal: Institute for Research on Public Policy, 1995).

41 'Moreover, public debate does little to clarify the dimensions of neoconservatism; its opponents link it to a variety of noxious social attitudes while its proponents defend it in the language of cherished, though often ambiguous, democratic values such as "freedom."' Neil Nevitte and Roger Gibbins, 'Neoconservatism: Canadian Variations on an Ideological Theme?' *Canadian Public Policy* 10, 4 (December 1984): 385.

42 Ibid.

43 See, for example, Irving Kristol, 'What Is a "Neo-conservative?"' *Newsweek* (19 January 1976): 17.

44 Confusing the issue, though, is the reluctance of continentalists to identify themselves as such. For example, in a truly Orwellian twist, many of the supporters of the FTA self-identify as nationalists, defining that term to mean anyone who seeks economic development strategies that will enhance Canadian prosperity. Michael Hart, for instance, who wrote much of the section of the Macdonald Commission *Report* calling for free trade, asserts that the enhanced prosperity resulting from the FTA will mean a stronger, more vibrant and more independent nation, and therefore calls himself a Canadian nationalist. Michael Hart, interview (Ottawa: 27 November 1992).

45 See Appendix A. The sectors were chambers of commerce, professional associations, trade associations, consulting firms, communications firms, financial institutions, transportation, manufacturing, agriculture, mining, forestry, oil and gas, natural resources, retail, business research groups, and private sector groups. As William Coleman points out, the business community in Canada is poorly integrated and lacks a peak association which speaks for the whole community. See *Business and Politics in Canada: A Study of Collective Action* (Kingston: McGill-Queen's University Press, 1988).

46 Greater Summerside Chamber of Commerce, *Brief 0242* (19 September 1983), 1–2.

47 Halifax Board of Trade, *Brief 0334* (1983), 16.

48 Calgary Chamber of Commerce, *Brief 0558* (19 October 1983), 1.

49 However, the Canadian Bankers Association, to which the big five banks belong, presented a brief to the commission.

50 Bank of Montreal, *Brief 0933* (1983), 15.

51 Ibid., 16.

52 New Brunswick Telephone Company, *Brief 0228* (1983), executive summary.

53 Ibid.

54 Placer Development, *Brief 0113* (1983), executive summary.

55 Ibid., 2.

56 Canadian Electrical Distributors Association, *Brief 0396* (1983), 2.

57 Canadian Petroleum Association, *Brief 0552* (7 November 1983), 8.

58 Saskatchewan Mining Association, *Brief 0590* (1983), 2.

59 Ibid., 5. It also went on to suggest that the processing of minerals into manufactured or finished products before export was undesirable, arguing that 'it would be detrimental to Canada's economy to defer a mining venture operation until such time as domestic and foreign markets would warrant such a development. There is no shame in being hewers of wood and drawers of water, and there is certainly no economic disadvantage at this time.'

60 Western Stock Growers' Association, *Brief 0644* (November 1983), 16, 4.

61 Employers Council of British Columbia, *Brief 0186* (7 September 1983), 2.

62 Ibid., 3.

63 Calgary Chamber of Commerce, *Brief 0558* (19 October 1983), 19.

64 Ibid.

65 Canadian Hardware and Housewares Manufacturers Association, *Brief 0393* (1983), 5.

66 It is noteworthy that Commissioner Daryl Seaman was a Calgary oil executive.

67 Dome Petroleum, *Brief 0584* (November 1983), 1.

68 Calgary Chamber of Commerce, *Brief 0558* (19 October 1983), 15.

69 Winnipeg Chamber of Commerce, *Brief 0577* (1983), 23.

70 Western Stock Growers' Association, *Brief 0644* (November 1983), 20.

71 Canadian Hardware and Housewares Manufacturers Association, *Brief 0393* (1983), 2.

72 Ibid., 5. Curiously, this group held up Singapore as a model for Canadian society: 'one of the world's most successful democracies – where there is virtually no poverty, no unemployment, no unemployment pay and no welfare.'

73 'Robert Campeau, the grade 8 drop-out who is the newest United States retail king, has grown too big for Canada. "I consider myself a North American," the 63 year-old chairman of Campeau Corporation told a news conference yesterday.' *Toronto Star*, 6 April 1988, A1. Campeau declared bankruptcy within three years of making this statement.

74 Campeau Corporation, *Brief 0983* (1983), 3.

75 Ibid., 24.

76 Halifax Board of Trade, *Brief 0334* (1983), 17.

77 Metropolitan Toronto Board of Trade, *Brief 0746* (1983), 1.

78 Retail Council of Canada, *Brief 0012* (October 1983), 60.

79 Ibid., 39.

80 See Yudelman, *Mining and the Macdonald Commission*.

81 Winnipeg Chamber of Commerce, *Brief 0577* (1983), 18.
82 Much of this brief was based on a speech by D. Gale Johnson, the chair of the Department of Economics at the University of Chicago, home of much of the neoclassical economic theorizing that spawned neoconservatism.
83 Canadian Hunter Exploration Limited, *Brief 0592* (24 October 1983), 4.
84 Ibid., 16.
85 Canadian Soft Drink Association, *Brief 0708* (1983), 5.
86 Ibid., 8.
87 See Stephen Clarkson, 'Anti-Nationalism in Canada: The Ideology of Mainstream Economics,' *Canadian Review of Studies in Nationalism* 5, 1 (Spring 1978): 45–65.
88 Halifax Board of Trade, *Brief 0334* (1983), 19.
89 Saskatoon Board of Trade, *Brief 0665* (1983), 11.
90 Retail Council of Canada, *Brief 0012* (October 1983), 77. The language of this brief is striking for the way in which it anticipates the arguments used in the free trade debate.
91 Burns Foods Limited, *Brief 0589* (23 October 1983), 4.
92 Consolidated Bathurst, *Brief 0529* (3 November 1983), 6.
93 Richard Simeon calls the business briefs 'vague, undefined and unspecific.' Simeon, 'Inside the Macdonald Report,' 170. See also Thorburn, *Interest Groups*, chap. 5.
94 Litvak, 'Freer Trade with the U.S.,' 30–1.
95 Pacific Group for Policy Alternatives, *Brief 0036* (1983), 9.
96 Canadian Mental Health Association, *Brief 0666* (24 October 1983), 8–9.
97 Winnipeg Chamber of Commerce, *Brief 0577* (1983), 24.
98 Ibid.
99 Herbert, 'The Pageant of Parliament,' 708. Cited in Iacobucci, 'Commissions of Inquiry,' 21.

Chapter 6

1 John Maynard Keynes, *The General Theory of Employment, Interest and Money* (London: Macmillan, 1936), 383.
2 Academic journal reviews of the individual volumes abound, and are too numerous to list here. But no comprehensive analysis of the research program as a whole has been done, either internally by the commission or externally.
3 In this regard the experience of the Macdonald Commission mirrors that of the Rowell-Sirois Commission. Some fifty-five years ago, Harold Adams Innis

lamented the domination of economists evident in the Rowell-Sirois report. 'Has the sovereignty of economists been finally established in Canada? Is this a further indication of the menace of the economists in the decline of political alertness? Unable to meet the political horn of the dilemma has the Commission become impaled on the economic horn?' Harold Adams Innis, 'The Rowell-Sirois Report,' *Canadian Journal of Economics and Political Science* 6 (1940): 565.

4 On the role of 'truth-seeking' through science in public inquiries, see Liora Salter, 'The Complex Relationship between Inquiries and Public Controversy,' in *Commissions of Inquiry: Praise or Reappraise?*, ed. Allan Manson and David Mullan (Toronto: Irwin Law, 2003), 190 ff.

5 'The social sciences, as a set of disciplines self-consciously claiming discrete and specialized knowledge of social reality, are relatively new historical phenomena dating from no later than the mid-nineteenth century.' Alain-G. Gagnon, 'The Influence of Social Scientists on Public Policy,' in *Social Scientists, Policy, and the State*, ed. Stephen Brooks and Alain-G. Gagnon (New York: Praeger, 1990), 1. See also Carol H. Weiss, ed., *Using Social Research in Public Policy Making* (Toronto: Lexington Books, 1977).

6 See, for example, Nicole Morgan, *Implosion: An Analysis of the Federal Public Service in Canada (1945–1985)* (Montreal: Institute for Research on Public Policy, 1986), chap. 2. Jenson notes the reciprocal relationship that has developed between the state and social science researchers. 'Mandated to inquire into a policy issue (more or less specifically defined), royal commissions have traditionally used public hearings and legal expertise as the basis for developing their policy recommendations. In the middle of the twentieth century, however, royal commissions began to turn to "research," especially social science research, to obtain relevant information about the policy realm under investigation. As such, they have become major supporters and funders of research.' Jane Jenson, 'Commissioning Ideas: Representation and Royal Commissions,' in *How Ottawa Spends 1994–95: Making Change*, ed. Susan D. Phillips (Ottawa: Carleton University Press, 1994), 43–4.

7 Macdonald Commission, *Research for the Commission on Canada's Future: A Progress Report* (Ottawa: Supply and Services, 1984), 7. The Rowell-Sirois Commission was the first major exercise of its kind to draw extensively on the work of social scientists, establishing a model emulated by successive inquiries, including the Macdonald Commission.

8 Jenson, 'Commissioning Ideas,' 41–2.

9 Gagnon, 'The Influence of Social Scientists,' 2.

10 Jenson, 'Commissioning Ideas,' 43–4.

11 See Stephen Brooks and Alain Gagnon, *Social Scientists and Politics in Canada:*

Between Clerisy and Vanguard (Kingston: McGill-Queen's University Press, 1988).

12 Brooks and Gagnon, *Social Scientists and Politics in Canada*, 107. It is noteworthy that most economists reject this nationalist critique. See Stephen Clarkson, 'Anti-Nationalism in Canada: The Ideology of Mainstream Economics,' *Canadian Review of Studies in Nationalism* 5, 1 (Spring 1978): 45–65.

13 See Canada, Royal Commission on Canada's Economic Prospects (the Gordon Commission), *Final Report* (Ottawa: Queen's Printer, 1958); Canada, Privy Council Office, *Foreign Ownership and the Structure of Canadian Industry: Report of the Task Force on the Structure of Canadian Industry* (the Watkins Report) (Ottawa: Queen's Printer, 1968); Canada, Standing Committee on External Affairs and National Defense, *Report (11th) of the Committee Respecting Canada-U.S. Relations* (the Wahn Report) (Ottawa: Queen's Printer, 1970); Canada, *Foreign Direct Investment in Canada* (the Gray Report) (Ottawa: Information Canada, 1972); and John N.H. Britton and James M. Gilmour, *The Weakest Leak: A Technological Perspective on Canadian Industrial Underdevelopment. Background Study no. 43* (Ottawa: Science Council of Canada, 1978).

14 The Waffle was led by nationalist intellectuals Mel Watkins and Jim Laxer. On the Waffle, see Reg Whitaker et al., 'The Waffle: 20th Anniversary Reflections,' *Studies in Political Economy* 32 (Summer 1990): 167–201. On the relationship between social democracy, nationalism and intellectuals in Canada, see Neil Bradford, 'Ideas, Intellectuals, and Social Democracy in Canada,' in *Canadian Parties in Transition: Discourse, Organization, and Representation*, ed. Alain G. Gagnon and A. Brian Tanguay, 83–110 (Scarborough, ON: Nelson, 1989).

15 See also Stephen Clarkson, 'Constitutionalizing the Canadian-American Relationship,' in *Canada Under Free Trade*, ed. Duncan Cameron and Mel Watkins (Toronto: Lorimer, 1993), 9.

16 See Stephen McBride and John Shields, *Dismantling a Nation: Canada and the New World Order* (Halifax: Fernwood Publishing, 1993); and Andrew B. Gollner and Daniel Salée, 'Introduction: A Turn to the Right? Canada in the Post-Trudeau Era,' in *Canada Under Mulroney: An End of Term Report*, ed. Andrew B. Gollner and Daniel Salée (Montreal: Véhicule Press, 1988), 12 ff.

17 Social scientists in Quebec, by comparison, 'succeeded in defining Quebec as a distinct national society, a conceptualization that supported province-building activities which expanded the career activities of a growing francophone middle class, and that was successful precisely for this reason.' Brooks and Gagnon, *Social Scientists and Politics*, 108.

18 Ibid.

19 Ibid. On the new Canadian political economy, see Wallace Clement and

Glen Williams, eds., *The New Canadian Political Economy* (Kingston: McGill-Queen's University Press, 1989).

20 See Clement and Williams, 'Introduction,' in ibid., 3.

21 An important exception to this statement was the mobilization of a variety of social movements against the FTA during the 1988 election. See Rick Salutin, *Waiting for Democracy: A Citizen's Journal* (Markham, ON: Viking, 1989).

22 Brooks and Gagnon, *Social Scientists and Politics*, 108–9.

23 See Richard French, *How Ottawa Decides: Planning and Industrial Policy Making, 1968–1980* (Toronto: Lorimer, 1983).

24 See, for example, Alan Ernst, 'From Liberal Continentalism to Neoconservatism: North American Free Trade and the Politics of the C.D. Howe Institute,' *Studies in Political Economy* 39 (Autumn 1992): 109–40; and the scathing critique of the C.D. Howe Institute in Linda McQuaig, *Shooting the Hippo: Death by Deficit and Other Canadian Myths* (Toronto: Viking, 1995).

25 See Shields and McBride, *Dismantling a Nation*, chap. 1; John W. Warnock, *Free Trade and the Right Agenda* (Vancouver: New Star Books, 1988); and Tom Walkom, 'Tory Talk: How the Conservatives Captured the English Language,' *This Magazine* 18, 6 (February 1985): 5–8.

26 Brooks and Gagnon, *Social Scientists and Politics*, 109. Neil Bradford notes that economists had even become dominant within left analysis in the NDP in the 1970s and 1980s, displacing an earlier reliance on political scientists and political sociologists. See Bradford, 'Ideas, Intellectuals, and Social Democracy in Canada,' 108.

27 These have included: the Vancouver-based Fraser Institute; the C.D. Howe Institute established in 1973 from the merger of the C.D. Howe Memorial Foundation and the Private Planning Association of Canada; the Institute for Research on Public Policy, an independent organization established in 1972 and supported by public and private sector contributions; the Canadian Institute for Economic Policy (disbanded in 1984); the Canadian Council on Social Development; and the Conference Board, based in New York and supported by corporate contributions, which provided quarterly economic reports on Canada.

28 Brooks and Gagnon, *Social Scientists and Politics*, 110.

29 Margaret Weir, 'Ideas and Politics: The Acceptance of Keynesianism in Britain and the United States,' in *The Political Power of Economic Ideas: Keynesianism Across Nations*, ed. Peter A. Hall (Princeton, NJ: Princeton University Press, 1989), 53.

30 The importance of 'scientifically based' models in economics research is evident in many of the Macdonald Commission economics studies. For example, one analysis of the regional impact of various policy elements within

Confederation utilizes 'quantitative general equilibrium modelling.' See John Whalley and Irene Trela, *Regional Aspects of Confederation: Macdonald Royal Commission Research Study, Volume 68* (Toronto: University of Toronto Press, 1986). See also Richard Harris, *Trade, Industrial Policy and International Competition: Macdonald Royal Commission Research Study, Volume 13* (Toronto: University of Toronto Press, 1985).

31 Frank Underhill, *In Search of Canadian Liberalism* (Toronto: Macmillan, 1961), 180.

32 Brooks and Gagnon, *Social Scientists and Politics*, 111.

33 It should not be surprising that the legal profession would be represented in virtually all royal commissions; these things are, after all, quasi-judicial bodies empowered with the ability to subpoena witnesses, and they are frequently carried out as semi-judicial inquiries. See A. Paul Pross et al., eds., *Commissions of Inquiry* (Toronto: Carswell, 1990).

34 For example, about half of those classified under the Economics, Sociology and Statistics Group in 1975 by the Public Service Commission were professional economists. See R.B. Bryce, 'Public Servants as Economic Advisers,' in *Economic Policy Advising in Canada: Essays in Honour of John Deutsch*, ed. David C. Smith (Montreal: C.D. Howe Institute, 1981), 55.

35 See Mel Watkins, 'The Economics of Nationalism and the Nationality of Economics: A Critique of Neoclassical Theorizing,' *Canadian Journal of Economics* 11 (November 1978): 87–120; and Stephen Clarkson, 'Continentalism: The Conceptual Challenge for Canadian Social Science,' unpublished paper presented to the Canadian Sociology and Anthropology Association, University of Montreal (30 May 1985), 22 ff.

36 Alan Cairns interview (Ottawa, 8 June 1993).

37 Albert Breton interview (Toronto, 4 October 1993).

38 David Smith interview (Toronto, 6 June 1994).

39 Macdonald also consulted with some of his old personal friends and colleagues, like Robert Prichard at the University of Toronto law school. While insisting that his influence was minimal, Prichard described his role in the following terms: 'Don Macdonald and I used to teach a course together at the Faculty of Law, and as I was the junior member of the faculty, I was assigned to co-teach with him. That led to a course called Public Policy Formation, how to think about the process of policy formation ... Hughie Segal joined us as a third member. And through that, I became good friends with Macdonald and we built a serious bond. I gave the eulogy at his first wife's funeral, for example. Just to exaggerate, I was the son he never had. He had four wonderful daughters. And we became very close friends. He, in that context, told me about his being asked to do the royal commission and

sought some input.' Prichard's input included suggesting potential candidates for the positions of research director. Robert Prichard interview (Toronto, 13 May 1993).

40 It is one of the great ironies of this commission that Innisan political economy was held in disrepute by the mainstream neoconservative economists by the time Godsoe and Macdonald launched their search. Indeed, even Innis's former academic home, the University of Toronto, had ceased to have a department of political economy, dividing itself into separate departments of political science and economics.

41 David Husband interview (Ottawa, 29 May 1994).

42 Gerry Godsoe interview (Halifax, 26 July 1994).

43 It is a further irony that political economists like Mel Watkins, a disciple of Innis, and others of the same intellectual bent were all but excluded from the research program of the commission.

44 Alan Cairns interview (Ottawa, 8 June 1993).

45 Michael Kirby interview (Ottawa, 8 June 1993).

46 Alan Cairns interview.

47 Donald Macdonald interview (Toronto, 18 August 1993).

48 David Smith interview.

49 Ibid.

50 Donald Macdonald interview (Toronto, 18 August 1993).

51 See David P. Shugarman, 'The Problems of the Reluctant Nationalist: A Comment on Alan Cairns's "Political Science in Canada and the Americanization Issue,"' *Canadian Journal of Political Science* 9, 1 (March 1976): 122–6; and Alan Cairns, 'Political Science and the Americanization Issue,' *Canadian Journal of Political Science* 8, 2 (June 1975): 191–234.

52 See Canada, Macdonald Commission, 'Information Package on Royal Commissions: Briefing Notes for Commissioners: Confidential,' National Archives of Canada (NAC), RG 33/137, volume 2, n.d. [1982].

53 Robert Prichard interview (Toronto, 13 May 1993).

54 Robert Prichard, [no title] (7 January 1983), NAC 'Information Package on Royal Commissions,' RG 33/137, volume 2 n.d. [1982], 2.

55 Kenneth G. Waldie, 'An Interpretation of the Terms of Reference' (Kingston, January 1983), NAC 'Information Package on Royal Commissions,' RG 33/137, volume 2, n.d. [1982], 2–3.

56 Ibid., 7.

57 David Husband, 'Terms of Reference of the Royal Commission on the Economic Union and Development Prospects for Canada' (19 January 1983), NAC 'Information Package on Royal Commissions,' RG 33/137, volume 2 n.d., [1982], 6, 10.

58 The other members of the group were Alan Nymark, Michael Hart, Anne Martin, and Richard Van Loon. It is explored in detail in chapter 10.

59 Richard Simeon interview (Toronto, 18 November 1992).

60 Robert Prichard interview.

61 Alan Cairns interview.

62 Later, Breton argued with Smith that an historian should be engaged to write a history along the lines of that produced by J.W. DeFoe for the Rowell-Sirois Commission. Eventually a compromise of sorts emerged – a journalist was hired to write a history of federal-provincial relations up to 1980. But in the end, this work was never published. Albert Breton interview (Toronto, 4 October 1993).

63 Gerry Godsoe interview.

64 David Smith interview.

65 Ibid.

66 Donald Macdonald interview (Toronto, 18 August 1993).

67 Ibid., 13 September 1993.

68 Albert Breton interview.

69 Alan Cairns interview.

70 David Smith interview.

71 Keith Banting interview (Ottawa, 6 June 1993).

72 The latter category was added quite late in the process, after the commissioners had journeyed to that region of the country and come to see the need for an analysis of it. This was one of the few research areas where the commissioners actively intervened in the selection of topics. For a list of titles produced in each of the five research categories, see Macdonald Commission, 'Appendix D: The Collected Research Studies,' *Report*, 3: 677–90. An index of the commission research volumes is also available. See Jeff Moon and John Offenbeck, eds., *Index to the 72 Studies of the Macdonald Commission on the Economic Union and Development Prospects for Canada* (Kingston: Queen's University Documents Library, 1988).

73 Jack Quinn interview (Toronto: 23 June 1993). One liability of the cosy, closed little world of Canadian academe is that most established scholars in particular fields know each other both professionally and personally. This reality was underlined graphically in one review of the Macdonald Commission research studies on Canada and the international political economy. David Haglund wrote: 'of 14 authors who had a hand in the writing of these three volumes, all but one is a personal acquaintance; some are current of former colleagues, many are close friends. To the diplomatic problem of rendering frank criticism to such an assemblage in a way that close friends do not become ex-friends is added the credibility problem that would attach

to any review that heaped too much praise on the project.' David G. Haglund, 'Unbridled Constraint: The Macdonald Commission Volumes on Canada and the International Political Economy,' *Canadian Journal of Political Science* 20, 3 (September 1987): 600.

74 Keith Banting interview.

75 Peter Aucoin interview (Toronto, 8 January 1993).

76 Gil Winham interview (Ottawa, 7 June 1993).

77 Ibid.

78 It is striking that the Canadian government had actually initiated sectoral free trade negotiations with the United States in 1984 at the recommendation of the Department of External Affairs (see chapter 1, part III above), but that neither this department nor others would provide the commission with any relevant analyses of the issue.

79 Gil Winham interview. See Gilbert Winham, *Canada-U.S. Sectoral Trade Study: The Impact of Free Trade* (Halifax: Centre for Foreign Policy Studies, Dalhousie University, 1986). The preface to this document, published by the Centre for Foreign Policy Studies at Dalhousie University, states that it was not published by the Macdonald Commission, although some copies were released in September 1985 to accompany publication of the commission *Report*. The original preface from 1985, over the signature of Alan Nymark, was also reprinted in the Centre's version, and said in part, 'This study under the direction of Professor Gilbert R. Winham ... served as background to the Commission's deliberations on the sectoral impact of freer trade. Although not formally part of the published research program of the Commission, we are making it available to the public as a resource tool in the ongoing discussion on Canada's trade options.'

80 See Macdonald Commission, *Report*, 3: Appendix D.

81 Some essays were co-authored, and some authors wrote more than one essay. As well, sixteen authors were identified by first initials only, and so were not categorized.

82 Some essays were co-authored, and some authors wrote more than one essay.

83 Some essays were co-authored, and some authors produced more than one essay; five authors were identified by first initials only and could not be categorized.

84 Some essays were co-authored and some writers produced more than one essay; three authors were identified by first initials only, and therefore were not categorized.

85 As Drache and Cameron point out, three women were recruited as commissioners, but none of them could be said to represent the women's movement in Canada. Drache and Cameron, *The Other Macdonald Report*, xii. Feminist

critiques of the commission can be found in Marjorie Cohen, 'The Macdonald Report and its Implication for Women,' *Feminist Action Feministe* 1 (December 1985): 13–15; and Margot Trevelyan, 'Women's Equality,' *The Facts* 8, 2 (March-April 1986): 31–6.

86 Keith Banting interview.

87 Peter Aucoin interview.

88 Donald Macdonald interview (Toronto, 18 August 1993).

89 Alan Cairns interview.

90 Ibid.

91 Ibid.

92 Ibid.

93 The 'suits and ties' and 'country club' analogies were used by both commission staff and researchers in several separate interviews. All were males.

94 Alan Cairns interview.

95 Alan Cairns interview.

96 Richard Simeon interview.

97 Donald Macdonald interview (Toronto, 18 August 1993).

98 Peter Aucoin interview.

99 Alan Cairns interview.

100 Donald Macdonald interview (Toronto, 18 August 1993).

101 Gil Winham interview.

102 Gerry Helleiner interview (Toronto, 4 June 1993).

103 Gil Winham interview.

104 See Canada, Macdonald Commission, *Research for the Commission on Canada's Future: A Progress Report* (Ottawa: Supply and Services, 1984).

105 Virtually everyone interviewed for this study concurred that *Challenges and Choices* was a disaster. It is considered in more detail in chapter 9.

106 Macdonald Commission, *Research for the Commission on Canada's Future*, i.

107 Ibid., 2.

108 Ibid., 3.

109 Ibid.

110 Ibid., 6–7.

111 Ibid., 7.

112 Ibid.

113 Ibid.

114 Ibid.

115 Ibid., 7–8.

116 Ibid., 8.

117 This was likely exacerbated by the relative homogeneity *within* each discipline produced through a selection process circumscribed by fairly tight

circles of academic friends and colleagues. Even the few younger academic participants were usually strongly linked to one or two of the 'old boys' or leading academics involved in the process. I am indebted to Patricia O'Reilly for bringing this point to my attention.

118 The last Macdonald Commission research study was not published until 1990. See Richard Simeon and Ian Robinson, *State, Society, and the Development of Canadian Federalism: Macdonald Commission Research Study, Volume 71* (Toronto: University of Toronto Press, 1990).

Chapter 7

1 Canada, Law Reform Commission of Canada, *Commissions of Inquiry: A New Act. Working Paper 17* (Ottawa: Supply and Services), 11.

2 It must be borne in mind that influencing the thinking of the commissioners was but one of two main goals of the research program. The other, to produce a state of the art body of research to stand outside of the commission, is beyond the scope of this analysis.

3 This technique was used to determine that professional economists had a disproportionate amount of influence over the Gordon Commission. See Barry Anderson, 'Royal Commissions, Economists and Policy: A Study of the Economic Advisory Process in Post-War Canada' (PhD dissertation, Duke University, 1978), 157–8.

4 This may in part account for the discrepancy between the message sent by organized interests to the commission, and the recommendations of the commission, particulary where free trade is concerned. That is, the commission chose to largely ignore the briefs and transcripts.

5 The seventy-two volumes of Commission research were divided into the following headings: Economics (volumes 1–27); Politics and Institutions of Government (volumes 28–45); Law and Constitutional Issues (volumes 46–58); Federalism and the Economic Union (volumes 59–71); and the North (volume 72). See Canada, Royal Commission on the Economic Union and Development Prospects for Canada (the Macdonald Commission), *Report* (Ottawa: Minister of Supply and Services, 1985), vol. 3, 679–90.

6 It must be acknowledged that this is a crude form of measurement since not all of the economists' work was confined to volumes 1–27 of the studies.

7 Robert Fulford, 'Mission Impossible,' *Saturday Night* 100, 3 (March 1985): 41.

8 Alan Nymark interview (Ottawa, 22 June 1993).

9 Alan Cairns interview (Ottawa, 8 June 1993).

10 Donald Macdonald interview (Toronto, 18 August 1993).
11 Clarence L. Barber, 'The Macdonald Report in Retrospect,' unpublished paper delivered to the Learned Societies Conference (Winnipeg, 1986), 1. This is one of the only post-commission evaluations by a former commissioner. Dr Barber kindly sent this author a copy.
12 Alan Cairns interview.
13 Ibid.
14 Ibid.
15 Ibid.
16 As Jane Jenson notes, 'because only a minority of commissioners are professional academics – although a much higher percentage have advanced degrees – they are often less familiar with and not necessarily enamoured of academics' enthusiasm for detail, caveat, and intellectual one-upmanship.' Jane Jenson, 'Learning by Doing: Decision-Making in Royal Commissions,' unpublished paper prepared for discussion by the Royal Commission on Aboriginal Peoples (13 August 1992), 8.
17 Jean Wadds interview (Prescott, 16 September 1994).
18 Ibid.
19 Gerry Godsoe interview (Halifax, 21 July 1994).
20 Ibid.
21 Alan Cairns interview.
22 Ibid.
23 Ibid.
24 Ibid.
25 Ibid.
26 David Smith interview (Toronto, 6 June 1994).
27 Ibid.
28 Discussed in chapter 9.
29 Canada, Royal Commission on the Economic Union and Development Prospects for Canada, *Research for the Commission on Canada's Future* (Ottawa, 1984). This document was released just after *Challenges and Choices*.
30 Ibid., 2–3.
31 Ibid., 3.
32 It is striking how these claims stand in such sharp contrast to what Nymark and Macdonald claim they heard in the hearings, both of whom claimed to be pleasantly surprised at the confidence demonstrated by Canadians. See chapters 10 and 11.
33 Canada, Macdonald Commission, *Research for the Commission on Canada's Future*, 4.
34 Ibid., 5.

35 Ibid.
36 Ibid.
37 Ibid., 6.
38 Gerry Godsoe interview.
39 Ibid.
40 David Smith interview (Kingston, 6 June 1994).
41 Michael Hart interview (Ottawa, 27 November 1993).
42 David Smith interview.
43 Denis Stairs interview (Halifax, 18 May 1994).
44 Gil Winham interview (Ottawa, 7 June 1993).
45 Ibid.
46 Donald Macdonald interview (Toronto, 18 August 1993).
47 Alan Nymark interview (Ottawa, 22 June 1993).
48 Gerry Godsoe interview.
49 Denis Stairs interview.
50 Ibid.
51 Ibid.
52 See, for example, John J. Quinn, ed., *The International Legal Environment: Macdonald Royal Commission Study, Volume 52* (Toronto: University of Toronto Press, 1986).
53 Jack Quinn interview (Toronto, 23 June 1993).
54 Ibid.

Chapter 8

1 William Mulholland, chairman of the Bank of Montreal, to a panel of international journalists during the 1982 Annual Meeting of the International Monetary Fund in Toronto, 8 September 1982. Cited in Michael M. Hart, *Canadian Economic Development and the International Trading System: Macdonald Royal Commission Research Study, Volume 53* (Toronto: University of Toronto Press, 1985), 2.
2 It should be noted that, while this chapter focuses on the ideological homogeneity of the economics research, this was also a factor in some of the other research too. For instance, in his review of the three volumes on Canada and the international political economy, David Haglund found 'the perhaps inevitable skewing of the research findings as a result of the rather remarkable "paradigmatic" congeniality of most of the authors ... it does seem odd that the 'ideological diversity' remarked by the Commission's three research directors ... should have been so lacking in at least three of the volumes of

research output ...' David Haglund, 'Unbridled Constraint: The Macdonald Commission Volumes on Canada and the International Political Economy,' *Canadian Journal of Political Science* 20, 3 (September 1987): 600.

3 Alain-G. Gagnon, 'The Influence of Social Scientists on Public Policy,' in *Social Scientists, Policy, and the State*, ed. Stephen Brooks and Alain-G. Gagnon (New York: Praeger, 1990), 8.

4 See Thomas Kuhn, *The Structure of Scientific Revolutions* (Chicago: University of Chicago Press, 1962).

5 Gagnon, 'The Influence of Social Scientists on Public Policy,' 8.

6 See Richard Simeon, 'Inside the Macdonald Commission,' *Studies in Political Economy* 22 (Spring 1987): 167–79.

7 See André Blais, *Industrial Policy: Macdonald Royal Commission Research Study, Volume 44* (Toronto: University of Toronto Press, 1986) and *A Political Sociology of Public Aid to Industry: Macdonald Royal Commission Research Study, Volume 45* (Toronto: University of Toronto Press, 1986). The economic argument against industrial policy can be found in Donald G. McFeteridge, 'The Economics of Industrial Policy: An Overview,' in *Canadian Industrial Policy in Action: Macdonald Royal Commission Study, Volume 4*, ed. Donald G. McFeteridge, 1–47 (Toronto: University of Toronto Press, 1985).

8 Donald Macdonald interview (Toronto, 18 August 1993).

9 Alan Cairns interview (Ottawa, 8 June 1993).

10 Clarence L. Barber, 'The Macdonald Report in Retrospect,' unpublished paper delivered to the Learned Societies Conference, Winnipeg, 1986, 1–2.

11 David Smith interview (Toronto, 6 June 1994).

12 Ibid.

13 Ibid.

14 Gil Winham interview (Ottawa, 7 June 1993).

15 See Stephen Clarkson, 'Economics: The New Hemispheric Fundamentalism,' in *The Political Economy of North American Free Trade*, ed. Ricardo Grinspun and Maxwell A. Cameron (Montreal: McGill-Queen's University Press, 1993), 62–3.

16 For a review of the Chicago school see Melvin W. Reder, 'Chicago Economics: Permanence and Change,' *Journal of Economic Literature* 20 (March 1982): 1–38.

17 See J.O. Stanford, 'Continental Economic Integration: Modelling the Impact on Labour,' *Annals of the American Academy of Political and Social Science* (March 1993). Cited in Bruce Campbell, 'Continental Corporate Economics,' in *Canada under Free Trade*, ed. Duncan Cameron and Mel Watkins, 21–40 (Toronto: Lorimer, 1993).

18 Gerry Godsoe interview (Halifax, 26 July 1994). This attitude is reflected in

one economist's dismissive attitude towards the literature on industrial policy, which he claimed was 'too inconclusive, argues form vague philosophical positions and often uses incorrect economic argument. Some of my impatience with this literature stems, no doubt, from my view of these matters as an economist.' Richard Harris, *Trade, Industrial Policy and International Competition: Macdonald Royal Commission Research Study, Volume 13* (Toronto: University of Toronto Press, 1985), 111.

19 Gerry Godsoe interview (Halifax, 26 July 1994).

20 David Smith interview.

21 Michael Hart interview (Ottawa, 27 November 1993). Hart's views are considered in more detail in chapter 9. Hart wrote in 1994 that 'Nationalists on the staff [of the Commission] and at seminars lamented that the Commission had been captured by neoclassical economists. They complained that the Commission was responding to the views of the scions of Canadian business ...' Michael Hart with Bill Dymond and Colin Roberts, *Decision at Midnight: Inside the Canada-U.S. Free Trade Negotiations* (Vancouver: UBC Press, 1994), 29.

22 Donald Macdonald interview (Toronto, 18 August 1993).

23 See Daniel Drache and Duncan Cameron, eds., *The Other Macdonald Report: The Consensus on Canada's Future That the Macdonald Commission Left Out* (Toronto: Lorimer, 1985).

24 For instance, the only academic study of the contentious issue of foreign direct investment was by a mainstream economist. See A.E. Safarian, 'Government Control of Foreign Business Investment,' in *Domestic Policies and the International Economic Environment: Macdonald Royal Commission Research Study, Volume 12*, ed. John Whalley, 7–55 (Toronto: University of Toronto Press, 1985).

25 See Richard G. Harris, *Trade, Industrial Policy and International Competition: Macdonald Royal Commission Research Study, Volume 13* (Toronto: University of Toronto Press, 1985). A critical assessment of Harris's views can be found in John Whalley with Colleen Hamilton and Roderick Hill, *Canadian Trade Policies and the World Economy: Macdonald Royal Commission Research Study, Volume 9* (Toronto: University of Toronto Press, 1985), 89–93.

26 Denis Stairs interview (Halifax, 18 May 1994).

27 Gerry Helleiner interview (Toronto, 4 June 1993). This view is considered in more detail in chapter 10.

28 Denis Stairs interview (Halifax, 18 May 1994).

29 Gil Winham interview.

30 Alan Cairns interview.

31 Thomas Shoyama interview (Toronto, 4 August 1993).

32 The growth of professionalism in the social sciences has important conse-
    quences, according to Paquet, including 'the growth of a population of full-
    time mental workers operating in discipline-bound fields. There, narrow dis-
    ciplinarian leaders rule through their control on the instruments of publica-
    tion and dissemination of ideas but also on the mechanisms of research
    funding. In such a world, being normal translates into a higher probability
    of being hired and promoted, i.e., into a probability of survival in academe.
       This enforced balkanization of the social sciences into fragmented disci-
    plines has had important consequences for their usefulness. There has been
    a tendency toward a high degree of hyper-specialization, toward the concen-
    tration of effort of full-time mental workers on the solution of real or imagi-
    nary problems defined by the leadership of the disciplinary professions, and
    toward a proliferation of publications for the sake of publications, i.e., much
    printed material with comparatively little addition to knowledge.' Gilles
    Paquet, 'Elegant but Not Helpful to Negotiation: Social Sciences Research
    and the Free Trade Debate,' in *Knocking on the Back Door: Canadian Perspec-
    tives on the Political Economy of Freer Trade with the United States*, ed. Alan M.
    Maslowe and Stanley L. Winner (Halifax: Institute for Research on Public
    Policy, 1987), 168.
33 The following paragraph is based on Stephen Brooks and Alain-G. Gagnon,
    Social Scientists and Politics in Canada: Between Clerisy and Vanguard (Kingston:
    McGill-Queen's University Press, 1988), 9–10.
34 Ibid.
35 Ibid., 10. See also Clarkson, 'Economics: The New Hemispheric Fundamen-
    talism,' 62–7.
36 Brooks and Gagnon, *Social Scientists and Politics in Canada*, 10.
37 Alan Cairns interview. Cairns asked political economist Jean Laux to be a
    research coordinator: 'She certainly is somewhere on the left. You know, a
    political economist. She didn't think she could do it, ultimately. I think she
    just had other things on her plate. But she may have had other private rea-
    sons for not doing it.' Walter Gordon suggested a prominent nationalist
    political economist as a research director to Macdonald, but the individual
    was never asked to participate in the commission in any manner.
38 Gil Winham interview. There were exceptions to the contention that politi-
    cal economists were shut out of the process, of course. These would include
    Leo Panitch, David Wolfe, Leon Muszynski, Mel Watkins, and Liora Salter.
39 Peter Aucoin interview (Toronto, 8 January 1993).
40 Richard Harris interview (Toronto, 14 July 1992). He also argued that 'there
    are almost no Marxists in Canadian economics departments, or economics
    departments in North America.'

41 This is evident in the Macdonald Commission study, which purports to be an overview of the pro and con arguments about free trade, but which actually lionizes the work and views of the Wonnacott's and other mainstream economists while giving short shrift to those holding contrary views. See Whalley et al., *Canadian Trade Policies and the World Economy*.

42 Hart, *Decision at Midnight*, 29–30. See volumes 9–14 and 68 of the commission research studies.

43 Shortly after his appointment to the commission, Quinn was also given the job of rewriting the Foreign Investment Review Act for the Mulroney government, turning it into the Investment Canada Act. Jack Quinn interview (Toronto, 23 June 1993).

44 The views of various economists are summed up in John Whalley, ed., *Canada–United States Free Trade: Macdonald Commission Research Study, Volume 11* (Toronto: University of Toronto Press, 1985). A brief summary of the arguments for and against free trade from an economics point of view can be found in Whalley et al., *Canadian Trade Policies*, 54–61.

45 For useful critiques of the methodology, assumptions and conclusions of these arguments, see Paquet, 'Elegant but Not Helpful,' 165–98.

46 Jack Quinn interview.

47 Hart, *Decision at Midnight*, 30.

48 Ibid., 32.

49 Jack Quinn interview.

50 Ibid.

51 See Richard G. Harris, 'Summary of a Project on the General Equilibrium Evaluation of Canadian Trade Policy,' in *Canada–United States Free Trade*, ed. Whalley, 157–77.

52 The original study based on this data set appeared as Richard G. Harris with David Cox, *Trade, Industrial Policy, and Canadian Manufacturing* (Toronto: Ontario Economic Council, 1983).

53 An internal commission memo to Godsoe from Victor Clarke commenting on a free trade symposium organized by Whalley had this to say about Harris's work: 'It is obvious that Harris has the respect of his colleagues, including those on the other side of the argument.' In the same memo, he dismissed the critics of free trade: 'Mel Watkins and Fred Lazar spoke forcefully against free trade but were criticized for not providing at least some definition and dimensioning of whatever the alternative was they were recommending.' Canada, Macdonald Commission, 'Royal Commission Internal Documents Volume 2: Memo to G. Godsoe from V. Clarke October 24/83 on Free Trade Symposium, October 6/83,' National Archives of Canada, RG 33/137 volume 15, (24 October 1983), 1.

54 Whalley, *Canadian Trade Policies*, 60.

55 Wilkinson was one of the only economists on the commission to take an anti-free trade position. See Bruce Wilkinson, 'Some Comments on Canada-U.S. Free Trade,' in *Canada–United States Free Trade: Macdonald Royal Commission Research Study, Volume 13*, ed. Roderick Hill and John Whalley, 91–102 (Toronto: University of Toronto Press, 1985).

56 Bruce W. Wilkinson, 'Canada-United States Free Trade: Setting the Dimensions,' in *Knocking on the Back Door: Canadian Perspectives on the Political Economy of Freer Trade with the United States*, ed. Alan M. Maslowe and Stanley L. Winner (Halifax: Institute for Research on Public Policy, 1987), 15.

57 Ibid., 24.

58 Ricardo Grinspun, *North American Free Trade Area: A Critical Economic Perspective* (Ottawa: Canadian Centre for Policy Alternatives, 1991), 1.

59 Whalley, *Canadian Trade Policies and the World Economy*, 58, 60.

60 Donald Macdonald interview (Toronto, 18 August 1993).

61 See Mel Watkins, 'Reservations Concerning a Free Trade Area,' and Bruce W. Wilkinson, 'Some Comments on Canada-U.S. Free Trade,' in *Canada and the Multilateral Trading System*, ed. John Whalley.

62 Donald Macdonald interview (Toronto, 18 August 1993).

63 Alan Cairns interview.

64 Ibid.

65 See J.L. Granatstein, 'The Issue That Will Not Go Away: Free Trade between Canada and the United States,' in *The Politics of Canada's Economic Relationship With the United States: Macdonald Royal Commission Research Study, Volume 29*, ed. Denis Stairs and Gil Winham, (Toronto: University of Toronto Press, 1985), 11–54; and Charles Pentland, 'North American Integration and the Canadian Political System,' in ibid., 95–126.

66 Richard Simeon made this argument in his reply to commission critics Drache and Cameron. See Richard Simeon, 'Inside the Macdonald Commission,' *Studies in Political Economy* 22 (Spring 1987): 167–79.

67 See Keith Banting, 'The State and Economic Interests: An Introduction,' in *The State and Economic Interests: Macdonald Royal Commission Research Study, Volume 32*, ed. Keith Banting, 1–33 (Toronto: University of Toronto Press, 1985); and Leo Panitch, 'The Tripartite Experience,' in *The State and Economic Interests*, ed. Banting, 37–119.

68 Alan Cairns interview. It is striking that the arguments linking free trade to industrial strategy by mainstream economist Richard Harris were rejected by the commission. See Harris, *Trade, Industrial Policy and International Competition*.

69 Alan Cairns interview.

70 Peter Warrian interview (Toronto, 20 September 1993). The contention that 'there is no other argument being made in the whole profession' is an exag-

geration, though not by much. But the subsequent point concerning career limitations is worth considering in light of the literature on knowledge utilization in the social sciences. Once a new approach gains hold of a discipline, it tends to replicate itself in subtle and insidious ways. Graduate students apprenticing in the discipline pick up the teachings of their mentors, and, when embarking upon a career, may surreptitiously seek to satisfy dominant paradigms by conforming in their methodological and epistemological approaches to that dominant paradigm. See Gagnon, 'The Influence of Social Scientists on Public Policy,' 1–18.

71 Peter Warrian interview.
72 Denis Stairs interview.
73 Gil Winham interview.
74 Denis Stairs interview. It must be noted that Stairs's contention that 'most of the evidence coming in from the hearings is pro-free trade' is factually incorrect, as revealed by the evidence in chapters 4 and 5. Nonetheless this statement underlines the *perception* which developed within the commission that there was an overwhelming call for free trade from the majority of Canadians during the consultation process.
75 Denis Stairs interview.
76 Ibid.
77 Ibid.
78 Ibid.
79 Ibid.
80 Ibid.
81 Michael Hart interview (Ottawa, 27 November 1993).
82 Gil Winham interview. It is noteworthy that these arguments do not appear in print in the seventy-two volumes of research studies. The closest they come to presenting these views is in the three volumes (28, 19, and 30) co-edited by Stairs and Winham. See Denis Stairs and Gilbert R. Winham, eds., *Canada and the International Political/Economic Environment: Macdonald Royal Commission Research Study, Volume 28* (Toronto: University of Toronto Press, 1985); Denis Stairs and Gilbert R. Winham, eds., *The Politics of Canada's Economic Relationship with the United States: Macdonald Royal Commission Research Study, Volume 29* (Toronto: University of Toronto Press, 1985); and Denis Stairs and Gilbert R. Winham, eds., *Selected Problems in Formulating Foreign Economic Policy: Macdonald Royal Commission Research Study, Volume 30* (Toronto: University of Toronto Press, 1985).
83 Denis Stairs interview.
84 Ibid.
85 Ibid.
86 Ibid.

87 Ibid.
88 Ibid.
89 Ibid.
90 Ibid.
91 Ibid.
92 Ibid.
93 Gil Winham interview.
94 Ibid.
95 Andrew Coyne, 'A Decade of Macdonaldism,' *Globe and Mail,* 9 September 1995, D3.

Chapter 9

1 Roberto Michels, *First Lectures in Political Sociology* (1927; repr. Minneapolis: University of Minnesota Press, 1949), 141–2.
2 'Debate Choices on Economy,' *Toronto Star,* 17 April 1984, A16.
3 Jeffrey Simpson, 'An Irrelevant Report,' *Globe and Mail,* 17 April 1984, A6.
4 'Debate Choices on Economy,' *Toronto Star.*
5 Peter Aucoin interview (Toronto, 8 January 1993). While it is true that, prior to working for the commission, Ablett had been a press secretary in the PMO, and a functionary in the PCO, he was a journalist by training, and planned to return to journalism once the commission completed its work. David Ablett interview (Ottawa, 21 June 1993).
6 Richard Simeon interview (Toronto, 18 November 1992).
7 Alan Cairns interview (Ottawa, 8 June 1993).
8 Ibid.
9 David Smith interview (Toronto, 6 June 1994).
10 Canada, Macdonald Commission, 'Registry Correspondence Files, # 100, Private Sector Volume 2, 1984: Memo to Alan Nymark from Victor L. Clarke Re: Business Sector Perspectives on "Challenges and Choice,"' National Archives of Canada (NAC), RG 33/137, Volume 5, 13 March 1984, 2. Clarke was also deeply concerned about how the business community would respond to *Challenges and Choices.* He wrote to Godsoe, arguing 'as you know there is still some cynicism among the business community and this interim report will be studied carefully for signs of bias or political idealogy [sic] ... Just before the report comes out we should call the heads of associations and others to tell them what to expect and ask for their support, etc.' Memo to J.G. Godsoe from Victor Clarke Re: 'Challenges and Choices' – Business Sector Reaction, ibid., 16 March 1984, 1.
11 Richard Simeon interview (Toronto, 18 November 1992).

12 Alan Nymark interview (Ottawa, 22 June 1993).
13 Denis Stairs interview (Halifax, 18 May 1994). Again, Stairs's perception of the emergence of the free trade issue is at odds with the evidence presented in chapter 5. The strength of this perception is testament to the adage that *who* says something is often more important than *how many* say it, since it was influential organizations like the BCNI, the CMA, and the Chamber of Commerce which were voicing the free trade position to the commission.
14 Richard Van Loon interview (Ottawa, 16 June 1993).
15 Alan Nymark interview.
16 These developments are discussed further in chapters 11 and 12. See also G. Bruce Doern and Brian Tomlin, *Faith and Fear: The Free Trade Story* (Toronto: Stoddart, 1991), 46–48.
17 Gerry Godsoe interview (Halifax, 25 August 1994). The ambassador was Paul H. Robinson Jr, well known for pushing his belief in free trade. Indeed, he took credit for convincing Thomas D'Aquino, head of the BCNI, to support it. See Mel Hurtig, *The Betrayal of Canada* (Toronto: Stoddart, 1991), 178.
18 Donald Macdonald interview (Toronto, 13 September 1993). Emphasis added.
19 Ibid.
20 Alan Cairns interview.
21 Alan Nymark interview.
22 Keith Banting interview (Ottawa, 6 June 1993).
23 Alan Cairns interview.
24 Ibid.
25 Ibid.
26 Alan Nymark interview.
27 Hart is also listed as a Policy Co-ordinator in Appendix E of the commission *Report* out of deference to the prominent role he came to play as Nymark's right-hand man during the actual drafting of the sections of the *Report* on free trade. An asterisk beside Hart's name indicates that he was a 'voluntary consultant.'
28 Peter Aucoin interview.
29 Donald Macdonald interview (Toronto, 13 September 1993).
30 Ibid.
31 Ibid.
32 Ibid.
33 Gil Winham interview (Ottawa, 7 June 1993).
34 Donald Macdonald interview (Toronto, 13 September 1993).
35 Alan Nymark interview.
36 Ibid.

37 Ibid.
38 See Doern and Tomlin, *Faith and Fear*, and chapter 1 above.
39 Alan Nymark interview.
40 Ibid.
41 Donald Macdonald interview (Toronto, 13 September 1993).
42 Alan Nymark interview.
43 Ibid.
44 Ibid.
45 Albert Breton interview (Toronto, 4 October 1993).
46 Gil Winham interview.
47 Ibid.
48 Gil Winham interview.
49 Gil Winham interview.
50 Ibid.
51 Ibid.
52 Ibid.
53 See chapter 1.
54 M.M. Hart, *Canadian Economic Development and the International Trading System: Macdonald Royal Commission Studies, Volume 53* (Toronto: University of Toronto Press, 1985).
55 Alan Nymark interview.
56 Michael Hart interview (Ottawa, 27 November 1993).
57 Ibid.
58 Ibid.
59 Denis Stairs interview.
60 Clarence L. Barber, 'The Macdonald Report in Retrospect,' unpublished paper delivered to the Learned Societies Conference, Winnipeg, 1986, 2.
61 Gil Winham interview.
62 Ibid.
63 Michael Hart interview.
64 Gil Winham interview.
65 Ibid.
66 Peter Warrian interview (Toronto, 20 September 1993).

Chapter 10

1 Donald Macdonald interview (Toronto, 13 September 1993).
2 Thomas Shoyama interview (Toronto, 4 August 1993).
3 Alan Cairns interview (Ottawa, 8 June 1993).

4 Ibid. One of the sources of Macdonald's strength was his intellectual capabilities, according to Cairns. 'I mean the kind of thing that really struck me once is I was arguing something and he said "That's not what you wrote in 1975." It turned out he had been teaching a course in law with Rob Prichard in which I gather a handful of my articles had been on the reading list. But that was the point. I mean, he operated in the intellectual community, both in law and political science. Probably not so much in economics, but then he had been Minister of Finance.'

5 Gerard Docquier interview (Ottawa, 21 February 1994).

6 David Smith interview (Toronto, 6 June 1994).

7 Alan Nymark interview (Ottawa, 22 June 1993).

8 Gil Winham interview (Ottawa, 7 June 1993).

9 Canada, Macdonald Commission, 'Minutes of a Meeting with Employers' Council of B.C., June 20/83,' National Archives of Canada (NAC), RG 33/137 Volume 1, 20 June 1983, 2.

10 Thomas Shoyama interview.

11 Alan Cairns interview. Cairns discusses this factor in 'Reflections on Commission Research,' in A. Paul Pross et al., *Commissions of Inquiry* (Toronto: Carswell, 1990), 92–3.

12 Alan Cairns interview.

13 Clarence Barber interview (Victoria, 24 August 1994).

14 Alan Nymark interview.

15 Ibid.

16 Donald Macdonald interview (Toronto, 13 September 1993). On Gordon's important contributions as the leading nationalist in the Liberal Party of Canada, see Denis Smith, *Gentle Patriot: A Political Biography of Walter Gordon* (Edmonton: Hurtig Publishers, 1973); Walter Gordon, *A Political Memoir* (Toronto: McClelland and Stewart, 1977); and Christina McCall-Newman, *Grits: An Intimate Portrait of the Liberal Party* (Toronto: Macmillan, 1982).

17 Donald Macdonald interview (Toronto, 13 September 1993).

18 Ibid.

19 Canada, Macdonald Commission, 'Hawkins Report, Volume I-II,' NAC, RG 33\137, Volume 1, 13 April 1983, 231–2.

20 Alan Nymark interview.

21 Donald Macdonald interview (Toronto, 13 September 1993). Johnson was the dean of Canadian mainstream economics and the bane of nationalists. See Harry G. Johnson, *The Canadian Quandary: Economic Problems and Policies* (Toronto: McGraw Hill, 1963).

22 Donald Macdonald interview (Toronto, 13 September 1993).

23 Canada, Macdonald Royal Commission, *A Commission on Canada's Future*, 1. Emphasis added.

24 The possibility that Macdonald and other commissioners might be accused of conflict of interest was dealt with by the commission in a booklet advising the commissioners on how to deal with the media. It read in part, 'all Commissioners have other responsibilities, and the breadth of experience and insight gained through that experience are necessary to the success of the Commission. The "insider knowledge" criterion has no application here at all. The major royal commissions of recent years dealing with economic topics (Bryce Commission on Corporate Concentration; Commission on Banking and Finance; Carter Commission on Taxation; Gordon Commission) have all involved commissioners with other duties and corporate/social directorships.' Canada, Macdonald Commission, 'Information Package on Royal Commissions: A Framework for Responses to Public and Media Enquiries,' NAC, RG 33/137, Volume 2, 1982, n.p.

25 All figures are for 1984 and are from 'Ranking Corporate Performance in Canada: The Top 1,000,' *Report on Business Magazine* (June 1985): 31 ff.

26 Thomas Shoyama interview.

27 Albert Breton interview (Toronto, 4 October 1993).

28 Porter later wrote an influential study for the Mulroney government. See Michael Porter, *Canada at the Crossroads: The Reality of the New Competitive Environment* (Ottawa: Business Council on National Issues, 1991). Godsoe claimed that Porter was 'absolutely world class, and he was one of the guys that we talked to, and Don even tried to hire him but he was just booked. We talked to him actually several times.' Gerry Godsoe interview (Halifax, 25 August 1994).

29 Richard Simeon interview (Toronto, 18 November 1992).

30 Donald Macdonald interview (Toronto, 18 August 1993).

31 Ibid. (13 September 1993).

32 Ibid. (18 August 1993).

33 Ibid. (18 September 1993).

34 Ibid. (18 August 1993).

35 Ibid.

36 Ibid.

37 Alan Nymark interview. These two paragraphs are based on Nymark's interpretation of the impact of the public hearings on Macdonald.

38 Donald Macdonald interview (Toronto, 18 August 1993).

39 Ibid.

40 See 'List of Private Sector Meetings Where no Notes Were Taken,' NAC, RG 33/137, volume 1, Hawkins Report, volume 1, 15 July 1983, 1. The groups included: the Business Council on National Issues; the Canadian Energy Research Institute; the Canadian Foundation for Economic Education; the Canadian Tax Foundation; the C.D. Howe Institute; the Conference Board

of Canada; the Institute for Policy Analysis; the John Deutsch Memorial Society for the Study of Economic Policy; the Niagara Institute; and the North-South Institute. The commissioners also met with four other groups: the Canadian Federation of Independent Business; the North-West Territories Association of Municipalities; the St John's Board of Trade; and the Governor of the Bank of Canada.

41 See David Langille, 'The Business Council on National Issues and the Canadian State,' *Studies in Political Economy* 24 (Autumn 1987): 68.

42 This underscores Hugh Thorburn's contention that *who* says something is often more important than *how many* say it. See Hugh Thorburn, *Interest Groups in the Canadian Federal System: Macdonald Commission Studies, Volume 69* (Toronto: University of Toronto Press, 1985), 86. See also A. Paul Williams, 'Access and Accommodation in the Canadian Welfare State: The Political Significance of Contacts Between State, Labour and Business Leaders,' *Canadian Review of Sociology and Anthropology* 26, 2 (1989): 217–39.

43 Peter Warrian interview (Toronto, 20 September 1993).

44 Alan Nymark interview.

45 Ibid.

46 Ibid.

47 Ibid.

48 Donald Macdonald interview (Toronto, 13 September 1993).

49 Alan Nymark interview.

50 Donald Macdonald interview (Toronto, 13 September 1993).

51 Ibid.

52 Ibid.

53 Ibid.

54 Ibid.

55 Ibid.

56 Ibid. (18 August 1993).

57 Ibid. (13 September 1993).

58 Ibid.

59 Ibid.

60 Ibid.

61 Ibid.

62 Ibid.

63 Ibid.

64 Ibid.

65 Ibid.

66 Ibid. Macdonald's position stands in contrast to that expressed in Richard Harris's study for the commission. See Richard Harris, *Trade, Industrial Policy*

and International Competition. Macdonald Commission Studies, Volume 13 (Toronto: University of Toronto Press, 1985).

67 Notably, Alan Nymark went from the commission to a senior position with Investment Canada.

68 Donald Macdonald interview (Toronto, 13 September 1993).

69 Ibid.

70 On the maturation of the Canadian capitalist class, see Jorge Niosi, 'Continental Nationalism: The Strategy of the Canadian Capitalist Class,' in *The Structure of the Canadian Capitalist Class*, ed. Robert J. Brym, 53–65 (Toronto: Garamond Press, 1985).

71 Donald Macdonald interview (Toronto, 13 September 1993).

72 Ibid. The Gordon Commission incident is recalled in Gordon, *A Political Memoir*, 64–6.

73 Donald Macdonald interview (Toronto, 13 September 1993).

74 Ibid.

75 Ibid.

76 Ibid.

77 Macdonald was the finance minister who introduced wage and price controls, for instance.

78 See Donald J. Savoie, *Governing From the Centre: The Concentration of Power in Canadian Politics* (Toronto: University of Toronto Press, 1999), chap. 6.

79 Donald Macdonald interview (Toronto, 13 September 1993).

80 Ibid.

81 William Johnson, '"Leap of Faith:" Canada Must Act on Free Trade, Macdonald Says,' *Globe and Mail*, 19 November 1984, 1.

82 Donald Macdonald interview (Toronto, 13 September 1993).

83 Ibid.

84 Thomas Shoyama interview.

85 Gerry Godsoe interview.

86 Alan Cairns interview.

87 Gil Winham interview.

88 Donald Macdonald interview (Toronto, 13 September 1993).

89 Ibid. (18 August 1993).

90 Denis Stairs interview.

91 Ibid.

92 Ibid.

93 Albert Breton interview.

94 Ibid.

95 Ibid.

96 Thomas Shoyama interview.

97　Albert Breton interview.

98　Ibid.

99　Ibid.

100　Gerard Docquier interview (Ottawa, 21 February 1994).

101　Ibid.

102　Alan Nymark interview.

103　Donald Macdonald interview (Toronto, 13 September 1993).

104　Rod McQueen, 'The Macdonald Commission Then and Now,' *Financial Post*, 13 December 1989, 12.

Chapter 11

1　Canada, Royal Commission on the Economic Union and Development Prospects for Canada (the Macdonald Commission), *Report* (Ottawa: Minister of Supply and Services, 1985), 1: 66.

2　Alan Cairns interview (Ottawa, 8 June 1993).

3　Ibid.

4　Thomas Shoyama interview (Toronto, 4 August 1993).

5　Albert Breton interview (Toronto, 4 October 1993).

6　Ibid.

7　Jane Jenson, 'Learning by Doing: Decision-Making in Royal Commissions,' unpublished paper prepared for discussion by the Royal Commission on Aboriginal Peoples, 13 August 1992, 16, fn. 14. But Jenson also suggests it does not always have to be this way in royal commissions. In the Royal Commission on Electoral Reform and Party Financing, 'explicit efforts were made to keep the "big picture" in front of the commission, as a yard-stick against which decisions could be measured. The resulting coherence of its analysis testifies to the strengths of this way of managing process.'

8　Donald Macdonald interview (Toronto, 13 September 1993).

9　Gerry Godsoe interview (Halifax, 26 July 1994).

10　Ibid.

11　Alan Cairns interview.

12　Gerry Godsoe interview.

13　Ibid.

14　Ibid.

15　Ibid.

16　Ibid.

17　Alan Cairns interview.

18　Albert Breton interview.

19 Ibid.
20 Alan Cairns interview.
21 Clarence L. Barber, 'The Macdonald Report in Retrospect,' unpublished paper delivered to the Learned Societies Conference, Winnipeg, 1986, 1.
22 Alan Nymark interview (Ottawa, 22 June 1993).
23 Donald Macdonald interview (Toronto, 18 August 1993)
24 Gerry Godsoe interview.
25 Donald Macdonald interview (Toronto, 18 August 1993).
26 Ibid.
27 Warrian did research, advised, and talked to Docquier about the free trade issue 'all the time. That was the biggest single issue.' Peter Warrian interview (Toronto, 20 September 1993).
28 Ibid.
29 Ibid. The 'trauma of the 1980s' Warrian was referring to was the depression of 1981–2.
30 Ibid.
31 Alan Cairns interview.
32 Ibid.
33 Gerry Godsoe interview.
34 Alan Nymark interview.
35 Clarence Barber interview (Victoria, 24 August 1994).
36 Gerry Godsoe interview.
37 Albert Breton interview.
38 Ibid.
39 Ibid. According to Godsoe, the commission also assisted in the development of these ideas by proffering assistance to these groups. Resources generated by the commission's hearings, research, and policy group were presented to help them cut some of the time and effort that were required to put together a good submission. The commission provided both a forum and resources to help groups which could get information and help for free, and yet still control their own submission and agenda and what they were going to say to the commission. This process also helped the commission, according to Godsoe, because it received submissions much faster than if they were just left alone. 'This was done quite a bit. And it also helped the researchers understand where other people were coming from. Now that's not well known or well documented, but that's in fact what we did.' Gerry Godsoe interview.
40 Gerard Docquier interview.
41 Ibid.
42 Michael Hart interview (Ottawa, 27 November 1993).
43 Ibid.

44 Ibid.
45 Ibid.
46 Ibid.
47 Alan Cairns interview.
48 Ibid.
49 Donald Macdonald interview (Toronto, 13 September 1993).
50 Peter Warrian interview.
51 Ibid.
52 Alan Nymark interview.
53 Ibid.
54 Gerard Docquier interview.
55 Albert Breton interview.
56 Ibid.
57 Gerard Docquier interview.
58 Rod McQueen, 'The Macdonald Commission Then and Now,' *Financial Post*, 13 December 1989, 12.
59 See Rod McQueen, *Leap of Faith: The Macdonald Report: An Abridged Version of the Report of the Royal Commission on the Economic Union and Development Prospects for Canada* (Toronto: Cowan and Company, with assistance from Woods Gordon, Clarkson Gordon, 1985).
60 Donald Macdonald interview (Toronto, 18 August 1993).
61 Macdonald Commission, *Report*, 3: 483–555.
62 Albert Breton interview.
63 Peter Warrian interview.
64 Albert Breton interview.
65 Peter Warrian interview.
66 Ibid.
67 Ibid.
68 Gerard Docquier interview.
69 Ibid.
70 Alan Cairns interview.
71 Gerry Godsoe interview.
72 Albert Breton interview.
73 Donald Macdonald interview (Toronto, 13 September 1993).
74 Clarence Barber, 'The Macdonald Report in Retrospect,' unpublished paper presented to the Learned Societies Conference, Winnipeg, University of Manitoba, 1986, 5.
75 Clarence Barber interview. Barber briefly explained his evolving views in a newspaper article in 1989. See Clarence Barber, 'Research Aided Foreign Trade Pact,' *Financial Post*, 14 December 1989, 12.
76 Gerry Godsoe interview.

77 See Albert Breton, 'Supplementary Statement,' in Macdonald Commission, *Report*, 3: 522–3.

78 Albert Breton interview.

79 Ibid.

80 Ibid. A brief account of the impact of this trip on Macdonald's thinking is provided in G. Bruce Doern and Brian Tomlin, *Faith and Fear: The Free Trade Story* (Toronto: Stoddart, 1991), 54.

81 Donald Macdonald interview (Toronto, 13 September 1993).

82 Albert Breton interview.

83 Donald Macdonald interview (Toronto, 13 September 1993).

84 Gerry Godsoe interview.

85 Thomas Shoyama interview.

86 Ibid.

87 Ibid.

88 Gerard Docquier interview.

89 Jean Wadds interview (Prescott, 16 September 1994).

90 Ibid.

91 Docquier shared drafts of the *Report* with Drache and Cameron, among others. Hence they were able to publish their critique of the Macdonald Commission in advance of the publication of the *Report* itself.

92 Gerry Godsoe interview.

93 Peter Warrian interview.

94 Gerard Docquier interview.

95 Ibid.

96 Ibid.

97 Ibid.

98 Ibid.

99 Ibid.

100 Ibid.

101 Donald Macdonald interview (Toronto, 13 September 1993).

Chapter 12

1 *Journals of the House of Commons of the Dominion of Canada*, From the 7th February 1878 to the 10th May 1878 Being the 5th Session of the 3rd Parliament of Canada ([Ottawa]: House of Commons, [1878]), vol. 12, 78.

2 The cartoon is reprinted in Robert J. Jackson et al., *Politics in Canada: Culture, Institutions, Behaviour and Public Policy* (Scarborough, ON: Prentice-Hall, 1986), 70.

3 *Globe and Mail,* 27 September 1985. Cited in Jeffrey Ayres, *Defying Conventional Wisdom: Political Movements and Popular Contention against North American Free Trade* (Toronto: University of Toronto Press, 1998), 29.

4 Cited in Sylvia Bashevkin, *True Patriot Love: The Politics of Canadian Nationalism* (Toronto: Oxford University Press, 1991), 126.

5 See Ayres, *Defying Conventional Wisdom;* Bashevkin, *True Patriot Love;* and Peter Bleyer, 'Coalitions of Social Movements as Agencies for Social Change: The Action Canada Network,' in *Organizing Dissent: Contemporary Social Movements in Theory and Practice,* ed. William K. Carroll (Toronto: Garamond Press, 1992), 102–17.

6 Bleyer, 'Coalitions of Social Movements as Agencies for Social Change,' 106.

7 See Bashevkin, *True Patriot Love,* 110.

8 Ibid., 115.

9 Michael Hart with Bill Dymond and Colin Robertson, *Decision at Midnight: Inside the Canada-U.S. Free Trade Negotiations* (Vancouver: UBC Press, 1994), 34.

10 Donald Macdonald interview (Toronto, 13 September 1993). The question of Macdonald's personal role in the free trade debate and election is an intriguing one. Here was a life-long Liberal, former Cabinet member, one-time potential leadership candidate, and sworn enemy of the dreaded Tories supporting the main plank of his political enemies and turning his back on the leader of his own party, John Turner. Macdonald was confronted with a Hobson's choice in that crucial 1988 election: to vote for free trade and against his party and leader; or to vote against free trade and for his party and leader.

11 For the pro–free trade side see John Crispo, ed., *Free Trade: The Real Story* (Toronto: Gage, 1988); for the anti–free trade side see Duncan Cameron, ed., *The Free Trade Deal* (Toronto: Lorimer, 1988).

12 Bashevkin, *True Patriot Love,* 128.

13 See Richard Johnston et al., 'Free Trade and the Dynamics of the 1988 Canadian Election,' in *The Ballot and Its Message: Voting in Canada,* ed. Joseph Wearing, 315–39 (Toronto: Copp Clark-Pitman, 1991); and Richard Johnston et al., *Letting the People Decide: Dynamics of a Canadian Election* (Montreal: McGill-Queen's University Press, 1992).

14 Denis Stairs interview (Halifax, 18 May 1994).

15 Ibid.

16 Ibid.

17 Bashevkin, *True Patriot Love,* 114.

18 See Hart, *Decision at Midnight;* and Gordon Ritchie, *Wrestling with the Elephant: The Inside Story of the Canada-U.S. Trade Wars* (Toronto: Macfarlane, Walter and Ross, 1997).

19 See Maxwell A. Cameron and Brian W. Tomlin, *The Making of NAFTA: How the Deal Was Done* (Ithaca and London: Cornell University Press, 2000); and Maryse Robert, *Negotiating NAFTA: Explaining the Outcome in Culture, Textiles, Autos, and Pharmaceuticals* (Toronto: University of Toronto Press, 2000).

20 J.D. Godsoe, 'Only Half a Trade Agreement,' in *Partners Nevertheless: Canadian-American Relations in the Twentieth Century*, ed. Norman Hillmer (Toronto: Copp Clark Pitman, 1989), 312.

21 As Daniel Drache points out, in contrast, 'the Commission saw nothing wrong with hiring from the Business Council on National Issues a researcher to prepare a background paper on American attitudes. His political biases apparently did not trouble them.' Daniel Drache, 'The Macdonald Commission: The Politics of Neo-Conservatism,' *Atkinson Review of Canadian Studies* 3, 1 (Spring 1986): 24.

22 Ritchie, *Wrestling with the Elephant*, 183. Ritchie, who was third in command of the free-trade negotiations, is especially adamant that the Americans out-negotiated the Canadians.

23 Stephen Clarkson, *Uncle Sam and Us: Globalization, Neoconservatism, and the Canadian State* (Toronto: University of Toronto Press, 2002), 32.

24 One of the most thorough recounting of the Canadian-American negotiations is provided by Hart, who was part of the Canadian team. Hart provided some insight into how disappointed the Canadians were when they looked across the table and saw the face of Peter Murphy instead of a more senior member of the American administration. Hart also reveals how the deal was all but lost until last-minute intervention at the highest political level on both sides. See Hart, *Decision at Midnight*. A similar but more critical version of events is provided by Ritchie, *Wrestling with the Elephant*.

25 Ritchie, *Wrestling with the Elephant*, 69.

26 Cited in Douglas A. Irwin, *Against the Tide: An Intellectual History of Free Trade* (Princeton: Princeton University Press, 1996), 82.

27 See Randall Litchfield, 'The Macdonald Commission's Other Recommendation,' *Canadian Business*, 65, 5 (May 1992): 23.

28 Donald Macdonald interview (Toronto, September 1993).

29 Ibid. See also Donald Macdonald, 'Leap of Faith,' in *Free Trade: Risks and Rewards*, ed. L. Ian MacDonald, (Montreal: McGill-Queen's University Press, 2000), 53.

30 See David Crane, 'Trail of Broken Promises,' *Toronto Star*, 1 January 1994, D1, D5. The view that free trade has been good for Canada is presented in Gordon Ritchie, 'Deal "Part of the Solution to Unemployment,"' *Toronto Star*, 1 January 1994, D5.

31 Robert E. Scott et al., 'NAFTA at Seven: Its Impact on Workers in All Three

Nations,' *Briefing Paper* (Washington, DC: Economic Policy Institute, 2001), 2.

32 Bruce Campbell, 'False Promise: Canada in the Free Trade Era,' in Scott et al., 'NAFTA at Seven,' 21.

33 Andrew Stritch, 'The Costs of Free Trade,' in *Crosscurrents: Contemporary Political Issues*, 2nd ed., ed. Mark Charlton and Paul Barker (Scarborough, ON: Nelson, 1994), 526–7.

34 Ibid., 526.

35 Donald Macdonald interview (Toronto, 13 September 1993). It is also noteworthy that Macdonald went to see the new prime minister in November 1984 to discuss the possible termination of the commission. There is no public record of their discussion, but some commission insiders suggested that a deal was cut between the two: the commission would be allowed to finish its work in return for a *Report* that was sympathetic to the new Tory government's general ideological position – including recommending free trade. Other commission insiders vehemently denied such a deal was made or even proposed.

36 Andrew Coyne, 'A Decade of Macdonaldism,' *Globe and Mail*, 9 September 1995, D3.

37 See Geoffrey E. Hale, 'Reintegrating Federal Economic and Social Policies in the 1990s – Implementing Macdonald's Ideas by Trail and Error,' paper presented to the Annual Meeting of the Canadian Political Science Association, Laval University, 30 May 2001.

38 Coyne, 'A Decade of Macdonaldism,' D3. See also Neil Bradford, 'Innovation by Commission: Policy Paradigms and the Canadian Political System,' in *Canadian Politics*, 3rd ed., ed. James P. Bickerton and Alain-G. Gagnon (Peterborough, ON: Broadview Press, 1999), 557 ff.

39 Coyne, 'A Decade of Macdonaldism,' D3. Coyne argues 'if politicians of whatever stripe are today more inclined to listen to economists – if the economists have taken over the asylum – that is in part because economists' ideas are less foreign-sounding to the public at large. That is the enduring legacy of the Macdonald Commission's work.'

40 This of course includes the federal Liberal government of Jean Chrétien, which came to power as an opponent of NAFTA, and whose predecessor, John Turner, led his party's crusade against the FTA. On the impact of neo-conservatism in Canada see Brooke Jeffrey, *Hard Right Turn: The New Face of Neo-Conservatism in Canada* (Toronto: HarperCollins, 1999).

41 Neil Bradford, *Commissioning Ideas: Canadian National Policy Innovation in Comparative Perspective* (Toronto: Oxford University Press, 1998), 164–5.

42 The historically unprecedented, crushing defeat of the Conservatives in the

1993 federal election, which saw the party reduced to two seats in the House of Commons, while not wholly attributable to dissatisfaction over free trade, is at least partly so. Ironically, the Chrétien and Martin Liberals were accused of implementing the Mulroney neoconservative program. They certainly have not opposed the continued march of continentalism. Although Chrétien campaigned against NAFTA in 1993, he subsequently changed his position. But in any event, no election has hinged so directly on the free trade issue as the 1988 election.

43 Ayres, *Defying Conventional Wisdom*, 42.
44 Bradford, 'Innovation by Commission,' 558.
45 Stephen McBride and John Shields, *Dismantling a Nation: Canada and the New World Order*, 2nd ed. (Halifax: Fernwood Publishing, 1997), 163.
46 Janine Brodie and Jane Jenson, *Crisis, Challenge and Change: Party and Class Revisited* (Ottawa: Carleton University Press, 1988), 312.
47 Brodie and Jenson argue that in the 1980s there was an 'uncharacteristic, if incomplete, polarization in federal party politics. The Liberal and Conservatives, for the first time in many years disagreed over three fundamental orientations which had formed the basis of consensus for much of the postwar period.' These were the issues of decentralization of economic policy making; the proper role for government in the economy; and economic nationalism. Brodie and Jenson, *Crisis, Challenge and Change*, 313–14. Indeed, Brian Mulroney deliberately provoked partisan conflict rather than try to coopt the Liberal and New Democratic parties.
48 Bradford, *Commissioning Ideas*, 129.
49 Jenson, '"Different" but Not "Exceptional,"' 72.
50 Both the academic and non-academic literature on free trade and neoconservatism attest to this new ideological combativeness in Canada, as does the emergence of the Reform/Alliance Party nationally and various neoconservative parties in several provinces.
51 'Trade, Globalization and Canadian Values,' *The CRIC Papers* (Ottawa: Centre for Research and Information on Canada, 2001), 3. See also Matthew Mendelsohn, Robert Wolfe, and Andrew Parkin, 'Globalization, Trade Policy and the Permissive Consensus in Canada,' *Working Paper 27* (Kingston: Queen's University School of Policy Studies, November 2001).
52 'Canada and the United States: An Evolving Partnership,' *The CRIC Papers* (Ottawa: Centre for Research and Information on Canada, 2003), 4.
53 Ibid., 20.
54 See the collection of essays on North American integration in George Hoberg, ed., *Capacity for Choice: Canada in a New North America* (Toronto: University of Toronto Press, 2002).

55 See Thomas Kuhn, *The Structure of Scientific Revolutions* (Chicago: University of Chicago Press, 1962), 74; Peter A. Hall, 'Policy Paradigms, Social Learning, and the State: The Case of Economic Policymaking in Britain,' *Comparative Politics* (April 1993): 275–96; and Hugh Heclo, 'Ideas, Interests and Institutions,' in *The Dynamic of American Politics: Approaches and Institutions,* ed. Lawrence C. Dodd and Calvin Jillson, 363–93 (Boulder, CO: Westview Press, 1994).

56 Peter A. Hall, 'Introduction,' in *The Political Power of Economic Ideas,* ed. Peter A. Hall (Princeton: Princeton University Press, 1989), 4.

57 Hall, 'Introduction,' 15.

58 Cy Gonick notes that Keynesianism became the overwhelmingly dominant school of thought in the post-war years because the earlier brand of orthodox economic thought had no acceptable answers to the Great Depression: 'Whatever its actual practice, government policy was largely enunciated in terms of the Keynesian goals of economic stability and full employment. And whatever the merits of the claim, Keynesian economics took much of the credit for the long prosperity following the war, helping to legitimize the 'managed' capitalist economy.' Cy Gonick, *The Great Economic Debate: Failed Economics and a Future for Canada* (Toronto: Lorimer, 1987), 45. See also Peter A. Hall, 'Keynes in Political Science,' *History of Political Economy* 26, 1 (1994): 137–53.

59 Timothy Lewis *In the Long Run We're All Dead: The Canadian Turn to Fiscal Restraint* (Vancouver: UBC Press, 2003), 192.

60 John B. Thompson, *Studies in the Theory of Ideology* (Berkeley: University of California Press, 1984), 25.

61 Bradford, in conducting a comparative study of policy innovation, concludes that many major policy innovations in Canada have not 'featured the partisan political leadership and meaningful public debate accompanying such profound policy changes in other liberal democracies. Indeed, the particular economic ideas that have been viable in Canada are those that do not demand much from representative processes and democratic institutions.' Bradford, *Commissioning Ideas,* 165.

62 Ibid., 129.

63 This study has only tangentially implicated American interests in this process. For more detailed, though journalistic, accounts of the American role see Linda McQuaig, *The Quick and the Dead: Brian Mulroney, Big Business and the Seduction of Canada* (Toronto: Viking, 1991), chap. 6; and Lawrence Martin, *Pledge of Allegiance: The Americanization of Canada in the Mulroney Years* (Toronto: McClelland and Stewart, 1993).

64 Stritch, 'The Costs of Free Trade,' 526. Stritch goes on to suggest, 'in the

industrial development of North America the principles of laissez-faire have been more apparent in ideology than in practice. In both Canada and the United States, governments at all levels have been very active in shaping the course of national economic history through a variety of interventionist policies such as protective tariffs, government procurement, labour market regulation, business subsidies, market development policies, and the provision of a transportation infrastructure.'

65 Gary Teeple, *Globalization and the Decline of Social Reform: Into the Twenty-First Century* (Toronto: Garamond, 2000), 87.

66 Brodie and Jenson, *Crisis, Challenge and Change*, 323.

67 One striking manifestation of this ongoing conflict occurred in the 2003 Progressive Conservative leadership contest. Brian Mulroney made a speech touting free trade as among his most successful and outstanding accomplishments as prime minister. But the winner of that convention, Peter Mackay, was forced to sign a deal with one of his contenders, the anti–free trader David Orchard, to review NAFTA as a condition of Orchard's support. Mackay later reneged on this deal.

68 Tom Walkom, 'Tory Talk: How the Conservatives Captured the English Language,' *This Magazine* 18, 6 (February 1985): 5–8.

69 Ibid., 6. According to Gil Winham, 'The FTA is a magnet in Canada for those who oppose modern economic life, and for those who oppose the preponderant presence of the United States in Canadian life. Neither the effects of modern economic life nor American influence will be reduced by rejecting the FTA. In all nations today, people are facing the internationalization of the domestic economy, as well as increased competition on a world scale. These changes are painful, but they are not a result of the FTA or any other trade agreement. Instead, the FTA is an intelligent response to these pressures, because by removing trade protectionism it removes incentives to be inefficient.' Cited in Michael Hart, 'A history of Canada-U.S. Free Trade,' http://www.freetradeat10.com/hart.html (1999).

70 These speeches were drafted for the prime minister by none other than Alan Nymark.

71 Walkom, 'Tory Talk,' 7–8.

72 At a private seminar at the University of Toronto shortly after the Conservative victory in 1984, a former assistant deputy minister of finance argued that no matter which party had won the election, the government of the day had no choice but to adopt neoconservative policies.

73 John B. Thompson, *Studies in the Theory of Ideology* (Berkeley: University of California Press, 1984), 28.

74 See ibid., 28.

75 Jenson, '"Different" But Not "Exceptional,"' 75.
76 See Rick Salutin, *Waiting for Democracy: A Citizen's Journal* (Toronto: Viking, 1989); and Lewis, *In the Long Run We're All Dead.*
77 Alain Lipietz, *Towards a New Economic Order: Postfordism, Ecology and Democracy* (New York: Oxford University Press, 1992), x.
78 Lipietz, *Towards a New Economic Order,* xi.
79 Ibid.
80 Jenson, '"Different" but Not "Exceptional,"' 71.
81 See Jane Jenson, 'Paradigms and Political Discourse: Protective Legislation in France and the United States before 1914,' *Canadian Journal of Political Science* 22, 2 (1989): 239.
82 Peter Leslie, *Federal State and National Economy* (Toronto: University of Toronto Press, 1987), 165.
83 Indeed, the current manifestation of the debate is focussing on whether North America should share a single currency. It has also spawned a burgeoning literature on policy convergence within North America. See, for example, Hoberg, ed., *Capacity for Choice.*
84 For a detailed chronology of the evolution of trade policies in Canada up to 1985, see John Whalley, *Canadian Trade Policies and the World Economy: Macdonald Royal Commission Research Study, Volume 9* (Toronto: University of Toronto Press, 1985).
85 Carolyn Tuohy, *Policy and Politics in Canada: Institutionalized Ambivalence* (Philadelphia: Temple University Press, 1992), 213.
86 See Seymour Martin Lipset, *Continental Divide: The Values and Institutions of the United States and Canada* (New York: Routledge, 1990).
87 Tuohy, *Policy and Politics in Canada,* 213.
88 See Clarkson, *Uncle Sam and Us,* 71.

Select Bibliography

In addition to the sources and interviews listed below, the author spent time in the National Archives in Ottawa perusing official documents from the Macdonald Royal Commission.

Books and Articles in Books

Abbott, Michael G. *Labour Economics Research of the Macdonald Commission.* Kingston: Queen's University Industrial Relations Centre, 1986.

Aglietta, Michel. *A Theory of Capitalist Regulation: The U.S. Experience.* London: New Left Books, 1979.

Aucoin, Peter. *The New Public Management: Canada in Comparative Perspective.* Montreal: Institute for Research on Public Policy, 1995.

Axline, Andrew, et al., eds. *Continental Community? Independence and Integration in North America.* Toronto: McClelland and Stewart, 1974.

Ayres, Jeffrey M. *Defying Conventional Wisdom: Political Movements and Popular Contention Against North American Free Trade.* Toronto: University of Toronto Press, 1998.

Bashevkin, Sylvia. *True Patriot Love: The Politics of Canadian Nationalism.* Toronto: Oxford University Press, 1991.

Baum, Gregory, and Duncan Cameron. *Ethics and Economics: Canada's Catholic Bishops on the Economic Crisis.* Toronto: James Lorimer, 1984.

Bell, Daniel. *The End of Ideology: On the Exhaustion of Political Ideas in the Fifties.* Rev. ed. New York: Free Press, 1962.

Bell, David, and Lorne Tepperman. *The Roots of Disunity: A Look at Canadian Political Culture.* Toronto: McClelland and Stewart, 1979.

Bell, David V.J. 'Political Culture in Canada.' In *Canadian Politics in the 1990s.* 3rd ed., edited by Michael S. Whittington and Glen Williams, 137–57. Scarborough, ON: Nelson, 1990.

Bellon, Bertrand, and Jorge Niosi. *The Decline of the American Economy.* Montreal: Black Rose Books, 1988.

Berger, Carl. *The Sense of Power: Studies in the Ideas of Canadian Imperialism 1867–1914.* Toronto: University of Toronto Press, 1970.

– *The Writing of Canadian History: Aspects of English-Canadian Historical Writing 1900–1970.* Toronto: Oxford University Press, 1976.

Berger, Thomas. 'Canadian Commissions of Inquiry: An Insider's Perspectives.' In *Commissions of Inquiry: Praise or Reappraise?* edited by Allan Manson and David Mullan, 13–28. Toronto: Irwin Law, 2003.

Berkowitz, S.D., ed. *Models and Myths in Canadian Sociology.* Toronto: Butterworths, 1984.

Berman, William C. *America's Right Turn: From Nixon to Bush.* Baltimore: Johns Hopkins University Press, 1994.

Birch, Anthony H. *Nationalism and National Integration.* London: Unwin Hyman, 1989.

Black, Naomi. 'Absorptive Systems are Impossible: The Canadian-American Relationship as a Disparate Dyad.' In *Continental Community? Independence and Integration in North America,* edited by Andrew Axline, 92–104. Toronto: McClelland and Stewart, 1974.

Blackburn, Robin, ed. *Ideology in Social Science: Readings in Critical Social Theory.* New York: Random House, 1973.

Blais, André. *Industrial Policy. Macdonald Royal Commission Study, Volume 44.* Toronto: University of Toronto Press, 1986.

– *A Political Sociology of Public Aid to Industry. Macdonald Royal Commission Research Study, Volume 45.* Toronto: University of Toronto Press, 1986.

Blake, Donald. 'Division and Cohesion: The Major Parties.' In *Party Democracy in Canada,* edited by George Perlin, 32–53. Scarborough, ON: Prentice-Hall, 1988.

Bleyer, Peter. 'Coalitions of Social Movements as Agencies for Social Change: The Action Canada Network.' In *Organizing Dissent: Contemporary Social Movements in Theory and Practice,* edited by William K. Carroll, 102–17. Toronto: Garamond Press, 1991.

Bliss, Michael. 'Canadianizing American Business: The Roots of the Branch Plant.' In *Close the 49th Parallel etc.,* edited by Ian Lumsden, 27–42. Toronto: University of Toronto Press, 1970.

Boyer, Robert. *The Regulation School: A Critical Introduction.* Trans. Craig Charney. New York: Columbia University Press, 1990.

Bradford, Neil. *Commissioning Ideas: Canadian National Policy Innovation in Comparative Perspective.* Toronto: Oxford University Press, 1998.

– 'Innovation by Commission: Policy Paradigms and the Canadian Political System.' In *Canadian Politics*. 3rd ed. Edited by James P. Bickerton and Alain-G. Gagnon, 541–60. Peterborough, ON: Broadview Press, 1999.

– 'The Policy Influence of Economic Ideas.' In *Restructuring and Resistance: Canadian Public Policy in an Age of Global Capitalism*, edited by Mike Burke, Colin Mooers, and John Shields, 50–79. Halifax: Fernwood, 2000.

Brock, Kathy L. 'The End of Executive Federalism?' In *New Trends in Canadian Federalism*, edited by François Rocher and Miriam Smith, 91–108. Peterborough, ON: Broadview Press, 1995.

Brodie, M. Janine, and Jane Jenson. *Crisis, Challenge and Change: Party and Class in Canada*. Toronto: Methuen, 1980.

– *Crisis, Challenge and Change: Party and Class in Canada Revisited*. Ottawa: Carleton University Press, 1988.

– 'Piercing the Smokescreen: Brokerage Parties and Class Politics,' In *Canadian Parties in Transition: Discourse, Organization, Representation*, edited by Alain-G. Gagnon and A. Brian Tanguay, 24–44. Scarborough, ON: Nelson, 1989.

Brooks, Stephen. 'The Market for Social Scientific Knowledge: The Case of Free Trade in Canada.' In *Social Scientists, Policy, and the State*, edited by Stephen Brooks and Alain-G. Gagnon, 79–94. New York: Praeger, 1990.

– *Public Policy in Canada: An Introduction*. Toronto: McClelland and Stewart, 1990.

Brooks, Stephen, and Alain-G. Gagnon. *Social Scientists and Politics in Canada: Between Clerisy and Vanguard*. Kingston: McGill-Queen's University Press, 1988.

Bryce, R.B. 'Public Servants as Economic Advisers.' In *Economic Policy Advising in Canada: Essays in Honour of John Deutsch*, edited by David C. Smith, 51–68. Montreal: C.D. Howe Institute, 1981.

Brym, Robert J. 'The Canadian Capitalist Class, 1965-1985,' In *The Structure of the Canadian Capitalist Class*, edited by Robert J. Brym, 1–20. Toronto: Garamond Press, 1985.

Brym, Robert J., with Bonnie J. Fox. *From Culture to Power: The Sociology of English Canada*. Toronto: Oxford University Press, 1989.

Brzezinski, Zbigniew. *Ideology and Power in Soviet Politics*. New York: Frederick A. Praeger, 1962.

Cameron, Duncan, ed. *The Free Trade Deal*. Toronto: Lorimer, 1988.

– *The Free Trade Papers*. Toronto: Lorimer, 1986.

Cameron, Duncan, and François Houle. *Canada and the New International Division of Labour*. Ottawa: University of Ottawa Press, 1985.

Cameron, Duncan, and Mel Watkins, eds. *Canada under Free Trade*. Toronto: Lorimer, 1993.

Cameron, Duncan. 'Political Discourse in the Eighties.' In *Canadian Parties in*

Transition: Discourse, Organization, Representation, edited by Alain-G. Gagnon and A. Brian Tanguay, 64–82. Scarborough, ON: Nelson, 1989.

Cameron, Maxwell A., and Brian W. Tomlin. *The Making of NAFTA: How the Deal Was Done.* Ithaca and London: Cornell University Press, 2000.

Campbell, Bruce. 'Continental Corporate Economics.' In *Canada Under Free Trade*, edited by Duncan Cameron and Mel Watkins, 21–40. Toronto: Lorimer, 1993.

– 'False Promise: Canada in the Free Trade Era.' In Robert E. Scott et al., 'NAFTA at Seven: Its Impact on Workers in All Three Nations,' *Briefing Paper* (Washington, DC: Economic Policy Institute, 2001), 21–30.

Campbell, Robert M. *Grand Illusions: The Politics of the Keynesian Experience in Canada, 1945–1975.* Peterborough, ON: Broadview Press, 1987.

Campbell, Robert M., and Leslie A. Pal. 'A Big Deal? The Canada-US Free Trade Agreement.' In *The Real Worlds of Canadian Politics: Cases in Process and Policy.* 2nd ed., edited by Robert M. Campbell and Leslie A. Pal, 187–266. Peterborough, ON: Broadview Press, 1991.

Canadian Conference of Catholic Bishops. *Ethical Reflections on the Economic Crisis.* Ottawa: Concacan Inc., 1983.

Carney, Thomas F. *Content Analysis: A Technique for Systematic Inference from Communications.* Winnipeg: University of Manitoba Press, 1972.

Carnoy, Martin. *The State and Political Theory.* Princeton: Princeton University Press, 1984.

Carroll, William K. 'Introduction: Social Movements and Counter-Hegemony in a Canadian Context.' In *Organizing Dissent: Contemporary Social Movements in Theory and Practice*, edited by William K. Carroll, 1–19. Toronto: Garamond, 1992.

Cetron, Marvin and Owen Davies. *American Renaissance: Our Life at the Turn of the 21st Century.* New York: St Martin's Press, 1989.

Chandler, M.A. 'The State and Industrial Decline,' In *Industrial Policy. Macdonald Commission Study Volume 44*, edited by André Blais. Toronto: University of Toronto Press, 1986.

Chennells, David. *The Politics of Nationalism in Canada: Cultural Conflict Since 1760.* Toronto: University of Toronto Press, 2001.

Christenson, Reo M., et al. *Ideologies and Modern Politics.* New York: Dodd, Mead and Company, 1971.

Christian, William, and Colin Campbell. *Political Parties and Ideologies in Canada: Liberals, Conservatives, Socialists and Nationalists.* 3rd ed. Toronto: McGraw-Hill, 1990.

Clark-Jones, Melissa. *A Staple State: Canadian Industrial Resources in Cold War.* Toronto: University of Toronto Press, 1987.

Clarkson, Stephen. *Canada and the Reagan Challenge: Crisis and Adjustment, 1981–1985*. Updated ed. Toronto: Lorimer, 1985.

– 'Disjunctions: Free Trade and the Paradox of Canadian Development.' In *The New Era of Global Competition: State Policy and Market Power*, edited by Daniel Drache and Meric S. Gertler, 103–26. Montreal: McGill-Queen's University Press, 1991.

– 'Economics: The New Hemispheric Fundamentalism.' In *The Political Economy of North American Free Trade*, edited by Ricardo Grinspun and Maxwell A. Cameron, 61–9. Montreal: McGill-Queen's University Press, 1993.

Clarkson, Stephen. *Uncle Sam and U: Globalization, Neoconservatism, and the Canadian State*. Toronto: University of Toronto Press, 2002.

Clarkson, Stephen and Christina McCall. *Trudeau and Our Times: Volume 1: The Magnificent Obsession*. Toronto: McClelland and Stewart, 1990.

Clement, Norris C., et al. *North American Economic Integration: Theory and Practice*. Cheltenham, UK: Edward Elgar Publishers, 1999.

Clement, Wallace. 'The Canadian Bourgeoisie - Merely Comprador?' In *Imperialism and Canada*, edited by John Saul and Craig Moron, 71–84. Toronto: New Hogtown Press, 1977.

– *The Canadian Corporate Elite: An Analysis of Economic Power*. Toronto: McClelland and Stewart, 1975.

– 'Canadian Political Economy.' In *An Introduction to Sociology*. 2nd ed., edited by M. Rosenburg et al., 375–400. Toronto: Methuen, 1987.

– *Class, Power and Property: Essays on Canadian Society*. Toronto: Methuen, 1983.

– *Continental Corporate Power: Economic Elite Linkages between Canada and the United States*. Toronto: McClelland and Stewart, 1977.

Clement, Wallace, and Glen Williams, eds. *The New Canadian Political Economy*. Kingston: McGill-Queen's University Press, 1989.

Cohen, Marjorie. *Free Trade and the Future of Women's Work: Manufacturing and Service Industries*. Toronto: Garamond Press, 1987.

Coleman, William. *Business and Politics: A Study in Collective Action*. Kingston, ON: McGill-Queen's University Press, 1988.

– *The Independence Movement in Quebec 1945–1980*. Toronto: University of Toronto Press, 1984.

Connolly, William E. *Political Science and Ideology*. New York: Atherton Press, 1967.

Cook, Ramsay. *The Maple Leaf Forever: Essays on Nationalism and Politics in Canada*. Toronto: Macmillan, 1971.

Cox, Richard H., ed. *Ideology, Politics and Political Theory*. Belmont, CA: Wadsworth Publishing, 1969.

Cox, R.W., and S.M. Jamieson. 'Canadian Labour in a Continental Perspective.'

In *Canada and the United States,* edited by A.B. Fox et al., 210–33. New York: Columbia University Press, 1976.

Craig, Alton W.J. *The System of Industrial Relations.* Scarborough, ON: Prentice-Hall, 1990.

Crean, Susan, and Marcel Rioux. *Two Nations: An Essay on the Culture and Politics of Canada and Quebec in a World of American Pre-Eminence.* Toronto: Lorimer, 1983.

Creighton, Donald. *Canada's First Century, 1867–1967.* Toronto: Macmillan, 1970.

– *The Forked Road.* Toronto: McClelland and Stewart, 1976.

– *John A. Macdonald: The Young Politician.* Toronto: Macmillan, 1952.

– *The Passionate Observer: Selected Writings.* Toronto: McClelland and Stewart, 1980.

Crispo, John, ed. *Free Trade: The Real Story.* Toronto: Gage, 1988.

Cuneo, Carl J. 'A Class Perspective on Regionalism.' In *Modernization and the Canadian State,* edited by Daniel Glenday, et al., 132–5. Toronto: Macmillan, 1978.

– 'A Classical Marxist Perspective.' In *Introduction to Sociology: An Alternate Approach,* edited by J. Paul Grayson, 35–77. Toronto: Gage, 1983.

Dahl, Robert A. *A Preface to Democratic Theory.* Chicago: University of Chicago Press, 1956.

Dawson, R. MacGregor. *The Government of Canada.* 5th ed. Rev. Norman Ward. Toronto: University of Toronto Press, 1979.

Desbarats, Peter. 'Public Inquiries: A Case Study.' In *Public Administration and Policy: Governing in Challenging Times,* edited by Martin W. Westmacott and Hugh P. Mellon, 108–9. Scarborough, ON: Prentice Hall, 1999.

Dixon, Beverly R., Gary D. Bouma and G.B.J. Atkinson. *A Handbook of Social Science Research: A Comprehensive and Practical Guide for Students.* Oxford: Oxford University Press, 1987.

Doern, G. Bruce, and Richard W. Phidd. *Canadian Public Policy: Ideas, Structure, Process.* Toronto: Methuen, 1983.

Doern, G. Bruce, and Brian W. Tomlin, *Faith and Fear: The Free Trade Story.* Toronto: Stoddart, 1991.

Drache, Daniel. 'The Canadian Bourgeoisie and its National Consciousness.' In *Close the 49th Parallel etc.,* edited by Ian Lumsden, 3–25. Toronto: University of Toronto Press, 1970.

– 'English-Canadian Nationalism.' In *The New Practical Guide to Canadian Political Economy,* edited by Daniel Drache and Wallace Clement, 162–9. Toronto: Lorimer, 1985.

– 'Staple-ization: A Theory of Canadian Capitalist Development.' In *Imperialism,*

Nationalism and Canada: Essays from the Marxist Institute of Toronto, edited by Craig Heron, 15–33. Toronto: New Hogtown Press, 1977.

Drache, Daniel, and Duncan Cameron. *The Other Macdonald Report: The Consensus on Canada's Future the Macdonald Commission Left Out.* Toronto: Lorimer, 1985.

Drummond, R.J. 'Parliament and Politics.' In *Canadian Annual Review of Politics and Public Affairs, 1982*, edited by R.B. Byers, 5–49. Toronto: University of Toronto Press, 1984.

– 'Parliament and Politics.' In *Canadian Annual Review of Politics and Public Affairs, 1983*, edited by R.B. Byers, 5–45. Toronto: University of Toronto Press, 1985.

Dye, Thomas R. *Politics, Economics and the Public: Policy Outcomes in the American State.* Chicago: Rand McNally, 1966.

Eagleton, Terry. *Ideology: An Introduction.* London: Verso, 1991.

Easterbrook, W.T., and M.H. Watkins, eds. *Approaches to Canadian Economic History.* Toronto: McClelland and Stewart, 1967.

Festinger, L., and D. Katz, eds. *Research Methods in the Behavioral Sciences.* New York: Holt, Rinehart and Winston, 1953.

Feuer, Lewis S. *Ideology and Ideologists.* New York: Harper and Row, 1975.

Forcese, Dennis. 'Canada's Politics: Class, Region and Continentalism.' In *Models and Myths in Canadian Sociology*, edited by S.D. Berkowitz, 115–25. Toronto: Butterworths, 1984.

Forcese, Dennis. *The Canadian Class Structure.* Toronto: McGraw-Hill Ryerson, 1975.

Fowler, Robert M. 'The Role of Royal Commissions.' In *Economic Policy Advising in Canada: Essays in Honour of John Deutsch*, edited by David C. Smith, 93–104. Montreal: C.D. Howe Institute, 1981.

Francis, Diane. *Controlling Interest: Who Owns Canada?* Toronto: Macmillan, 1986.

Fraser, Graham. *Playing For Keeps: The Making of the Prime Minister, 1988.* Toronto: McClelland and Stewart, 1989.

French, Richard D. *How Ottawa Decides: Planning and Industrial Policy Making, 1968–1984.* 2nd ed. Toronto: Lorimer, 1984.

Friedrich, Carl J. *Man and His Government: An Empirical Theory of Politics.* New York: McGraw-Hill, 1963.

Frizell, Alan, and Anthony Westell. *The Canadian General Election of 1984: Politicians, Parties, Press and Polls.* Ottawa: Carleton University Press, 1985.

Gagnon, Alain-G. 'The Influence of Social Scientists on Public Policy.' In *Social Scientists, Policy, and the State*, edited by Stephen Brooks and Alain-G. Gagnon, 1–18. New York: Praeger, 1990.

Gerbner, George et al., eds. *The Analysis of Communication Content: Developments in*

Scientific Theories and Computer Techniques. New York: John Wiley and Sons, 1969.

Gill, Stephen. *American Hegemony and the Trilateral Commission.* Cambridge: Cambridge University Press, 1990.

Godsoe, J.G. 'Comment on Inquiry Management.' In *Commissions of Inquiry,* edited by A. Paul Pross et al., 71–3. Toronto: Carswell, 1990.

– "Only Half a Trade Agreement.' In *Partners Nonetheless: Canadian-American Relations in the Twentieth Century,* edited by Norman Hillmer, 311–14. Toronto: Copp Clark Pitman, 1989.

Gold, Mark, and David Leyton-Brown, eds. *Trade Offs on Free Trade: The Canada-U.S. Free Trade Agreement.* Toronto: Carswell, 1988.

Gollner, Andrew B., and Daniel Salée, eds. *Canada under Mulroney: An End-of-Term Report.* Montreal: Véhicule Press, 1988.

Gonick, Cy. *The Great Economic Debate: Failed Economics and a Future for Canada.* Toronto: Lorimer, 1987.

Gordon, Walter. *A Choice for Canada: Independence or Colonial Status.* Toronto: McClelland and Stewart, 1966.

– *A Political Memoir.* Toronto: McClelland and Stewart, 1978.

– *Storm Signals: New Economic Policies for Canada.* Toronto: McClelland and Stewart, 1975.

– *Troubled Canada: The Need for New Domestic Policies.* Toronto: McClelland and Stewart, 1961.

Gorecki, Paul K., and W.T. Stanbury, eds. *Perspectives on the Royal Commission on Corporate Concentration.* Toronto: Butterworths, 1979.

Granatstein, J.L. 'Free Trade: The History of an Issue.' In *The Future on the Table: Canada and the Free Trade Issue,* edited by Michael Henderson, 1–34. North York: Masterpress, 1987.

Granatstein, J.L. *How Britain's Weakness Forced Canada into the Arms of the United States.* Toronto: University of Toronto Press, 1989.

Grant, George. *Lament For A Nation: The Defeat of Canadian Nationalism.* Toronto: McClelland and Stewart, 1965.

– *Technology and Empire.* Toronto: Anansi, 1968.

Grayson, J. Paul. 'Culture, Ideology and Society.' In *Introduction to Sociology: An Alternate Approach,* edited by J. Paul Grason, 372–409. Toronto: Gage, 1983.

Grinspun, Ricardo. *North American Free Trade Area: A Critical Economic Perspective.* Ottawa: Canadian Centre for Policy Alternatives, 1991.

Grinspun, Ricardo, and Maxwell Walker, eds. *The Political Economy of North American Free Trade.* Montreal: McGill-Queen's University Press, 1993.

Hall, Peter A. 'Policy Paradigms, Experts, and the State: The Case of Macroeconomic Policy Making in Britain.' In *Social Scientists, Policy and the State*, edited by Stephen Brooks and Alain-G. Gagnon, 53–78. New York: Praeger, 1990.

– ed. *The Political Power of Economic Ideas: Keynesianism across Nations*. Princeton: Princeton University Press, 1989.

Harris, Richard G. *Trade, Industrial Policy and International Competition. Macdonald Royal Commission Study, Volume 13*. Toronto: University of Toronto Press, 1985.

Hart, Michael M. *Canadian Economic Development and the International Trading System: Macdonald Royal Commission Study, Volume 53*. Toronto: University of Toronto Press, 1985.

– *A Trading Nation: Canadian Trade Policy From Colonialism to Globalization*. Toronto: University of Toronto Press, 2002.

Hart, Michael, with Bill Dymond and Colin Robertson. *Decision at Midnight: Inside the Canada-U.S. Free Trade Negotiations*. Vancouver: UBC Press, 1994.

Hartz, Louis, ed. *The Founding of New Societies: Studies in the History of the United States, Latin America, South Africa, Canada and Australia*. New York: Harcourt, Brace and World, 1964.

– *The Liberal Tradition in America: An Investigation of American Political Thought Since the Revolution*. New York: Harcourt, Brace Jovanovich, 1955.

Hawes, Michael. 'The National Economy.' In *Canadian Annual Review of Politics and Public Affairs, 1984*, edited by R.B. Byers, 100–41. Toronto: University of Toronto Press, 1987.

Heclo, Hugh. 'Ideas, Interests and Institutions.' In *The Dynamic of American Politics: Approaches and Institutions*, edited by Lawrence C. Dodd and Calvin Jillson, 363–93. Boulder, CO: Westview Press, 1994.

Henderson, George Fletcher. *Federal Royal Commissions in Canada, 1867–1966: A Checklist*. Toronto: University of Toronto Press, 1967.

Hillmer, Norman, ed. *Partners Nonetheless: Canadian-American Relations in the Twentieth Century*. Toronto: Copp Clark Pitman, 1989.

Hoberg, George, ed. *Capacity for Choice: Canada in a New North America*. Toronto: University of Toronto Press, 2002.

Hodgetts, J.E. 'Public Power and Ivory Power.' In *Agenda 1970: Proposals for a Creative Politics*, edited by Tl. Lloyd and J.T. McLeod, 256–80. Toronto: University of Toronto Press, 1968.

Holmes, John. *The Better Part of Valour: Essays on Canadian Diplomacy*. Toronto: McClelland and Stewart, 1970.

– *Life with Uncle: The Canadian-American Relationship*. Toronto: University of Toronto Press, 1981.

Holsti, Ole. 'Content Analysis.' In *The Handbook of Social Psychology*. Volume 2. *Research Methods*. 2nd ed., edited by G. Lindzey and E. Aronson, 596–692. Reading, MA: Addison-Wesley, 1968.

Holsti, O.R. *Content Analysis for the Social Sciences and Humanities.* Reading, MA: Addison-Wesley, 1969.

Horowitz, Gad. *Canadian Labour in Politics.* Toronto: University of Toronto Press, 1968.

Howlett, Michael, and M. Ramesh. *The Political Economy of Canada: An Introduction.* Toronto: McClelland and Stewart, 1992.

– *Studying Public Policy: Policy Cycles and Policy Subsystems.* 2nd ed. Toronto: Oxford University Press, 2003.

Hurtig, Mel. *The Betrayal of Canada.* Toronto: Stoddart, 1991.

Iacobucci, Frank. 'Commissions of Inquiry and Public Policy in Canada.' In *Commissions of Inquiry*, edited by A. Paul Pross et al., 21–8. Toronto: Carswell, 1990.

Inwood, Gregory J. *Understanding Canadian Public Administration: An Introduction to Theory and Practice.* 2nd ed. Scarborough, ON: Pearson, 2004.

Irwin, Douglas A. *Against the Tide: An Intellectual History of Free Trade.* Princeton: Princeton University Press, 1996.

Jeffrey, Brooke. *Hard Right Turn: The New Face of Neo-Conservatism in Canada.* Toronto: Harper Collins, 1999.

Jenson, Jane. 'Changing Discourse, Changing Agendas: Political Rights and Reproductive Policies in France.' In *The Women's Movement of the United States and Western Europe*, edited by Mary Fainsod Katzenstein and Carol McClurg Meuller, 64–88. Philadelphia: Temple University Press, 1987.

– 'Commissioning Ideas: Representation and Royal Commissions.' In *How Ottawa Spends 1994–95: Making Change*, ed. Susan D. Phillips, 39–69. Ottawa: Carleton University Press, 1994.

Johnson, Harry G. 'Problems of Canadian Nationalism,' In *The Canadian Quandary*, 11–21. Toronto: McClelland and Stewart, 1977.

Johnson, Leo A. 'The Development of Class in Canada in the Twentieth Century.' In *Capitalism and the National Question in Canada*, edited by Gary Teeple, 141–84. Toronto: University of Toronto Press, 1972.

Johnston, Donald. *Up the Hill.* Montreal: Optimum Publishing International, 1986.

Johnston, Larry. *Ideologies: An Analytic and Contextual Approach.* Peterborough, ON: Broadview Press, 1996.

Johnston, Richard et al. 'Free Trade and the Dynamics of the 1988 Canadian Election.' In *The Ballot and its Message: Voting in Canada*, edited by Joseph Wearing, 315–39. Toronto: Copp Clark Pitman, 1991.

– *Letting the People Decide: Dynamics of a Canadian Election.* Montreal: McGill-Queen's University Press, 1992.

Kedourie, Elie. *Nationalism.* London: Hutchinson and Company, 1966.

Kennedy, Paul. *The Rise and Fall of the Great Powers: Economic Change and Military Conflict from 1500 to 2000*. New York: Random House, 1987.

Keohane, Robert O. *After Hegemony: Cooperation and Discord in the World Political Economy*. Princeton: Princeton University Press, 1984.

Kirton, John J. 'America's Hegemonic Decline and the Reagan Revival.' In *Southern Exposure: Canadian Perspectives on the United States*, edited by D.H. Flaherty and W.R. McKercher, 42–61. Toronto: McGraw-Hill Ryerson, 1986.

Krieger, Joel. *Reagan, Thatcher and the Politics of Decline*. New York: Oxford University Press, 1986.

Kuhn, Thomas. *The Structure of Scientific Revolutions*. Chicago: University of Chicago, 1962.

Laux, Jeanne Kirk. 'Shaping or Serving Markets? Public Ownership and Privatization.' In *The New Era of Global Competition: State and Market Policy*, edited by Daniel Drache and Meric S. Gertler, 288–315. Montreal: McGill-Queen's University Press, 1991.

Laxer, Gordon. *Open for Business: The Roots of Foreign Ownership in Canada*. Toronto: Oxford University Press, 1989.

– 'The Political Economy of Aborted Development: The Canadian Case,' In *The Structure of the Canadian Capitalist Class*, edited by Robert Brym, 67–102. Toronto: Garamond, 1985.

Laxer, James. 'Free Trade and Canada's Choice of an Economic Model.' In *The Future on the Table: Canada and the Free Trade Issue*, edited by Michael D. Henderson, 55–77. North York: Masterpress, 1987.

– *Leap of Faith: Free Trade and the Future of Canada*. Edmonton: Hurtig, 1986.

Laxer, James, and Robert Laxer. *The Liberal Idea of Canada*. Toronto: Lorimer, 1977.

Laxer, Robert, ed. *(Canada) Ltd. The Political Economy of Dependency*. Toronto: McClelland and Stewart, 1973.

LeDain, Gerald E. 'The Role of the Public Inquiry in Our Constitutional System.' In *Law and Social Change*, edited by Jacob S. Zeigel, 79–97. Toronto: Osgoode Hall and York University, 1972.

Leslie, Peter. *Federal State, National Economy*. Toronto: University of Toronto Press, 1987.

Levitt, Kari. *Silent Surrender: The Multinational Corporation in Canada*. Toronto: Gage, 1970.

Lewis, Timothy. *In the Long Run We're All Dead: The Canadian Turn to Fiscal Restraint*. Vancouver: UBC Press, 2003.

Leyton-Brown, David. 'The Canada-U.S. Free Trade Agreement.' In *Canada Under Mulroney: An End-of-Term Report*, edited by Andrew B. Gollner and Daniel Salée, 103–18. Montreal: Véhicule Press, 1988.

Lichtheim, George. *The Concept of Ideology and Other Essays*. New York: Random House, 1967.

Lindquist, Evert A. 'The Third Community, Policy Inquiry, and Social Scientists.' In *Social Scientists, Policy, and the State*, edited by Stephen Brooks and Alain-G. Gagnon, 21–51. New York: Praeger, 1990.

Lipietz, Alain. *The Enchanted World: Inflation, Credit and the World Crisis*. London: Verso, 1983.

– *Mirages and Miracles: The Crisis of Global Fordism*. Trans. David Macey. London: Verso, 1987.

– *Towards a New Economic Order: Postfordism, Ecology and Democracy*. Trans. Malcolm Slater. New York: Oxford University Press, 1992.

Lipset, Seymour Martin. *Continental Divide: The Values and Institutions of the United States and Canada*. New York: Routledge, 1990.

Litvak, Isaiah A., and Christopher J. Maule. 'Canadian-United States Corporate Interface and Transnational Relations.' In *Canada and the United States: Transnational and Transgovernmental Relations*, edited by Annette Baker Fox, Alfred O. Hero, and Joseph S. Nye. New York: Columbia University Press.

Lumsden, Ian, ed. *Close the 49th Parallel etc.: The Americanization of Canada*. Toronto: University of Toronto Press, 1970.

Macdonald, Donald S. 'Leap of Faith.' In *Free Trade: Risks and Rewards*, edited by L. Ian MacDonald, 48–54. Montreal: McGill-Queen's University Press, 2000.

MacDonald, L. Ian. *Free Trade: Risks and Rewards*. Montreal: McGill-Queen's University Press, 2000.

Mackay, A. Wayne, 'Mandates, Legal Foundations, Powers and Conduct of Commissions of Inquiry.' In *Commissions of Inquiry*, edited by A. Paul et al., 29–47. Toronto: Carswell, 1990.

Mahant, Edelgard. *Free Trade in American-Canadian Relations*. Malabar, FL: Krieger Publishing, 1993.

Mahant, Edelgard, and Graeme S. Mount. *Invisible and Inaudible in Washington: American Policies Toward Canada*. Vancouver: UBC Press, 1999.

Mahon, Rianne. 'Canadian Public Policy: The Unequal Structure of Representation.' In *The Canadian State: Political Economy and Political Power*, edited by Leo Panitch, 165–98. Toronto: University of Toronto Press, 1977.

– *The Politics of Industrial Restructuring: Canadian Textiles*. Toronto: University of Toronto Press, 1984.

Mallory, J.R. *The Structure of Canadian Government*. Toronto: Gage, 1971.

Mannheim, Karl. *Ideology and Utopia: An Introduction to the Sociology of Knowledge*. Trans. Louis Wirth and Edward Shils. New York: Harcourt, Brace and Company, 1936.

Manson, Allan and David Mullan, eds. *Commissions of Inquiry: Praise or Reappraise?* Toronto: Irwin Law, 2003.

Manzer, Ronald. *Public Policies and Political Development in Canada.* Toronto: University of Toronto Press, 1985.

Marchak, M. Patricia. *Ideological Perspectives on Canada.* 2nd ed. Toronto: McGraw-Hill Ryerson, 1981.

– *In Whose Interests: An Essay on Multinational Corporations in a Canadian Context.* Toronto: McClelland and Stewart, 1979.

Martin, Lawrence. *Pledge of Allegiance: The Americanization of Canada in the Mulroney Years.* Toronto: McClelland and Stewart, 1993.

Marx, Karl. 'Address on the Question of Free Trade, 1848 Delivered before the Democratic Association of Brussels, Belgium January 9, 1848. Appendix one section 5, 206–8.' In *The Poverty of Philosophy,* New York: International Press, 1963.

McBride, Stephen, and John Shields. *Dismantling a Nation: Canada and the New World Order.* 2nd ed. Halifax: Fernwood Publishing, 1997.

McCall, Christina and Stephen Clarkson. *Trudeau and Our Times.* Volume 2: *The Heroic Delusion.* Toronto: McClelland and Stewart, 1994.

McCready, John. *The Context for Canadian Social Policy: Values and Ideologies.* Toronto: University of Toronto Faculty of Social Work, 1981.

McFetridge, Donald G. *Canadian Industrial Policy in Action: Macdonald Royal Commission Study, Volume 4.* Toronto: University of Toronto Press, 1985.

McMenemy, John. *The Language of Canadian Politics: A Guide to Important Terms and Concepts.* Rev. ed. Waterloo: Wilfrid Laurier University Press, 1995.

McQuaig, Linda. *The Quick and the Dead: Brian Mulroney, Big Business and the Seduction of Canada.* Toronto: Viking, 1991.

– *Shooting the Hippo: Death by Deficit and Other Canadian Myths.* Toronto: Viking, 1995.

McQueen, Rod. *Leap of Faith: The Macdonald Report.* Toronto: Cowan and Company, 1985.

McRae, Kenneth D. 'The Structure of Canadian History.' In *The Founding of New Societies: Studies in the History of the United States, Latin America, South Africa, Canada and Australia,* edited by Louis Hartz, 219–74. New York: Harcourt, Brace and World, 1964.

Michels, Roberto. *First Lectures in Political Sociology.* Minneapolis: University of Minnesota Press, 1949.

Miliband, Ralph. *The State in Capitalist Society: The Analysis of the Western System of Power.* London: Quartet Books, 1973.

Minar, David W. *Ideas and Politics: The American Experience.* Homewood, IL: Dorsey, 1964.

Molot, Maureen Appel, and Glen Williams. 'The Political Economy of Continentalism.' In *Canadian Politics in the 1980s*. 2nd ed., edited by Michael S. Whittington and Glen Williams, 81–104. Toronto: Methuen, 1984.

Moore, Steve, and Debbi Wells. *Imperialism and the National Question in Canada.* Toronto: New Hogtown Press, 1975.

Morton, W.L. *Manitoba: A History.* Toronto: University of Toronto Press, 1957.

– *The Progressive Party in Canada.* Toronto: University of Toronto Press, 1950.

Naylor, R.T. 'Dominion of Capital: Canada and International Investment.' In *Domination*, edited by A. Kontos, 35–56. Toronto: University of Toronto Press, 1975.

– *Monetarism and Canadian Policy Alternatives.* Ottawa: Canadian Centre for Policy Alternatives, 1982.

Niosi, Jorge. *Canadian Capitalism: A Study of Power in the Canadian Business Establishment.* Toronto: Lorimer, 1981.

– 'Continental Nationalism: The Strategy of the Canadian Bourgeoisie.' In *The Structure of the Canadian Capitalist Class*, edited by Robert J. Brym, 53–65. Toronto: Garamond Press, 1985.

– *The Economy of Canada: A Study of Ownership and Control.* Montreal: Black Rose Books, 1978.

O'Reilly, Patricia L. *Health Care Practitioners: An Ontario Case Study in Policy Making.* Toronto: University of Toronto Press, 1999.

Ornstein, Michael D. 'Canadian Capital and the Canadian State: Ideology in an Era of Crisis.' In *The Structure of the Canadian Capitalist Class*, edited by Robert J. Brym, 129–66. Toronto: Garamond Press, 1985.

– *Political Cleavages in the Canadian Capitalist Class.* Toronto: Institute for Behaviourial Research, 1982.

Orren, Gary R. 'Beyond Self Interest,' In *The Power of Public Ideas*, edited by Robert B. Reich, 13–29. Cambridge, MA: Balinger Publishing, 1988.

Pal, Leslie A. *Beyond Policy Analysis: Public Issue Management in Turbulent Times.* Scarborough, ON: Nelson, 2001.

Panitch, Leo, ed. *The Canadian State: Political Economy and Political Power.* Toronto: University of Toronto Press, 1977.

Panitch, Leo, and Donald Swartz. *The Assault on Trade Union Freedoms: From Wage Controls to Social Contract.* Toronto: Garamond, 1993.

Paquet, Gilles. 'Elegant but Not Helpful to Negotiation: Social Sciences Research and the Free Trade Debate.' In *Knocking on the Back Door: Canadian Perspectives on the Political Economy of Freer Trade with the United States*, edited by Allan M. Maslowe and Stanley L. Winer, 165–98. Halifax: Institute for Research on Public Policy, 1987.

Pentland, Charles. 'Political Integration: A Multidimensional Perspective.' In *Continental Community? Independence and Integration in North America*, edited by W. Andrew Axline, 42–66. Toronto: McClelland and Stewart, 1974.

Perlin, George, ed. *Party Democracy in Canada*. Scarborough, ON: Prentice-Hall, 1988.

Phillips, Paul. 'National Policy, Continental Economics, and National Disintegration,' In *Canada and the Burden of Unity*, edited by David Jay Bercuson, 19–43. Toronto: Macmillan, 1977.

Phillips, Paul, and Erin Phillips. 'Class Formation.' In *The New Practical Guide to Canadian Political Economy*, edited by Daniel Drache and Wallace Clement, 16–24. Toronto: James Lorimer, 1985.

Phillips, P., and S. Watson. 'From Mobilization to Continentalism: The Canadian Economy in the Post-Depression Period,' In *Modern Canada, 1930–1980s*, edited by Michael S. Cross and Gregory S. Kealey, 20–45. Toronto: McClelland and Stewart, 1984.

Plamenatz, John. *Ideology*. New York: Praeger Publishing, 1970.

Pool, Ithiel de Sola, ed. *Trends in Content Analysis*. Urbana: University of Illinois, 1959.

Porter, John. *The Vertical Mosaic: An Analysis of Social Class and Power in Canada*. Toronto: University of Toronto Press, 1965.

Pross, A. Paul, Innis Christie, and John A. Yogis, eds. *Commissions of Inquiry*. Toronto: Carswell, 1990.

Quinn, John J. *The International Legal Environment: Macdonald Royal Commission Study, Volume 52*. Toronto: University of Toronto Press, 1986.

Rea, K.J., and J.T. McLeod. *Business and Government in Canada: Selected Readings*. 2nd ed. Toronto: Methuen, 1976.

Redekop, John H. 'Continentalism: The Key to Canadian Politics.' In *Approaches to Canadian Politics*, edited by John H. Redekop, 284–57. Scarborough: ON: Prentice-Hall, 1978.

Reich, Robert B., ed. *The Power of Public Ideas*. Cambridge, MA: Balinger Publishing, 1988.

Resnick, Philip. *The Land of Cain: Class and Nationalism in English Canada, 1945–1975*. Vancouver: New Star Books, 1977.

Richards, John, and Larry Pratt. *Prairie Capitalism: Power and Influence in the New West*. Toronto: McClelland and Stewart, 1979.

Ritchie, Gordon. *Wrestling with the Elephant: The Inside Story of the Canada-U.S. Trade Wars*. Toronto: Macfarlane, Walter and Ross, 1997.

Robert, Maryse. *Negotiating NAFTA: Explaining the Outcome in Culture, Textiles, Autos, and Pharmaceuticals*. Toronto: University of Toronto Press, 2000.

Rosengren, Karl Erik, ed. *Advances in Content Analysis*. London: Sage, 1981.

Rotstein, Abraham. *The Precarious Homestead: Essays on Economics, Technology and Nationalism*. Toronto: New Press, 1973.

– *Rebuilding From Within: Remedies for Canada's Ailing Economy*. Ottawa: Canadian Institute for Economic Policy, 1984.

Russell, Peter, ed. *Nationalism in Canada.* Toronto: McGraw-Hill Ryerson, 1966.

Salter, Liora. 'The Complex Relationship Between Inquiries and Public Controversy.' In *Commissions of Inquiry: Praise or Reappraise?*, edited by Allan Manson and David Mullan, 185–209. Toronto: Irwin Law, 2003.

– 'The Two Contradictions in Public Inquiries.' In *Commissions of Inquiry*, edited by A. Paul Pross et al., 173–95. Toronto: Carswell, 1990.

Salutin, Rick. *Waiting for Democracy: A Citizen's Guide.* Toronto: Viking, 1989.

Shields, John, and Stephen McBride. 'Dismantling a Nation: The Canadian Political Economy and Continental Free Trade.' In *Power and Resistance: Critical Thinking About Social Issues*, edited by Les Samuelson, 227–600. Halifax: Fernwood, 1994.

Smith, Allan. *Canada: An American Nation? Essays on Continentalism, Identity, and the Canadian Frame of Mind.* Montreal: McGill-Queen's University Press, 1994.

Smith, David C. *Economic Policy Advising in Canada: Essays in Honour of John Deutsch.* Montreal: C.D. Howe Institute, 1981.

Smith, Goldwin. *Canada and the Canadian Question.* Toronto: University of Toronto Press, 1971.

Smith, James A. *The Idea Brokers: Think Tanks and the Rise of the New Policy Elite.* New York: Free Press, 1991.

Soldatos, P. 'Free Trade Continentalization in Canada-U.S. Relations: Theorization on the Political Dimensions and Outlines of an Institutional Framework,' In *The International Legal Environment: Macdonald Royal Commission Study, Volume 52*, edited by John J. Quinn, 115–91. Toronto: University of Toronto Press, 1986.

Stairs, Denis. 'North American Continentalism: Perspectives and Policies in Canada.' In *Regionalism and Supra-Nationalism*, edited by Duncan Cameron, 83–109. Montreal: Institute for Research on Public Policy, 1981.

Stairs, Denis, and Gilbert R. Winham. *Canada and the International Political/Economic Environment. Macdonald Commission Study Volume 28.* Toronto: University of Toronto Press, 1986.

– *The Politics of Canada's Economic Relationship with the United States. Macdonald Commission Study Volume 29.* Toronto: University of Toronto Press, 1986.

Stevenson, Garth. 'Continental Integration and Canadian Unity.' In *Continental Community? Independence and Integration in North America.* edited by W. Andrew Axline et al., 194–217. Toronto: McClelland and Stewart, 1974.

Stone, P.J., et al. *The General Enquirer: A Computer Approach to Content Analysis.* Cambridge: MIT Press, 1966.

Stritch, Andrew. 'The Costs of Free Trade.' In *Crosscurrents: Contemporary Political Issues.* 2nd ed., edited by Mark Charlton and Paul Barker. Scarborough, ON: Nelson, 1994.

Taylor, Charles. *Radical Tories: The Conservative Tradition in Canada.* Toronto: Anansi, 1982.

Teeple, Gary. *Globalization and the Decline of Social Reform: Into the Twenty-First Century.* Toronto: Garamond Press, 2000.

– ed. *Capitalism and the National Question in Canada.* Toronto: University of Toronto Press, 1972.

Thompson, John B. *Studies in the Theory of Ideology.* Berkeley: University of California Press, 1984.

Thorburn, Hugh G. *Interest Groups in the Canadian Federal System. Macdonald Royal Commission Study Volume 69.* Toronto: University of Toronto Press, 1985.

– 'Interpretations of the Canadian Party System.' In *Party Politics in Canada.* 5th ed., edited by Hugh G. Thorburn, 20–40. Scarborough, ON: Prentice-Hall, 1985.

Timpson, Annis May. 'Challenging Policy Paradigms: Women, Royal Commissions, and the Public-Private Divide.' In *Commissions of Inquiry: Praise or Reappraise?*, edited by Allan Manson and David Mullan, 229–45. Toronto: Irwin Law, 2003.

'Trade, Globilization and Canadian Values.' *The CRIC Papers.* Ottawa: Centre for Research and Information on Canada, 2001.

Trebilcock, M.J., et al. *The Choice of Governing Instruments.* Ottawa: Economic Council of Canada, 1982.

Trudeau, Pierre Elliott. *Federalism and the French Canadians.* Toronto: Macmillan, 1968.

Tucker, Robert C., ed. *The Marx-Engels Reader.* 2nd ed. New York: W.W. Norton, 1978.

Underhill, Frank. *In Search of Canadian Liberalism.* Toronto: Macmillan, 1961.

Van Loon, Richard, and Michael S. Whittington. *The Canadian Political System: Environment, Structure and Process.* 4th ed. Toronto: McGraw-Hill Ryerson, 1987.

Wallace, Donald C. 'Ottawa and the Provinces,' In *Canadian Annual Review of Politics and Public Affairs, 1983,* edited by R.B. Byers, 46–115. Toronto: University of Toronto Press, 1985.

Warnock, John W. *Free Trade and the New Right Agenda.* Vancouver: New Star Books, 1988.

Watkins, Mel. *Madness and Ruin: Politics and the Economy in the Neoconservative Age.* Toronto: Between the Lines, 1992.

– 'The Political Economy of Growth.' In *The New Canadian Political Economy,* edited by Wallace Clement and Glen Williams, 16–35. Kingston: McGill-Queen's University Press, 1989.

– 'A Staple Theory of Economic Growth.' In *Approaches to Canadian Economic*

History: A Selection of Essays, edited by W.T. Easterbrook and Mel Watkins, 141–58. Toronto: McClelland and Stewart, 1967.

Weir, Margaret. 'Ideas and Politics: The Acceptance of Keynesianism in Britain and the United States." In *The Political Power of Economic Ideas: Keynesianism across Nations*, edited by Peter A. Hall, 53–86. Princeton: Princeton University Press, 1989.

Weir, Margaret, and Theda Skocpol. 'State Structures and the Possibilities for "Keynesian" Responses to the Great Depression in Sweden, Britain and the United States.' In *Bringing the State Back In*, edited by Peter Evans, Dietrich Rueschemeyer, and Theda Skocpol, 107–63. Cambridge: Cambridge University Press, 1985.

Westell, Anthony. 'The Case for Greater Economic Integration.' In *Friends So Different: Essays on Canada and the United States in the 1980s*, edited by Lansing Lamont and J. Duncan Edmonds, 60–7. Ottawa: University of Ottawa Press, 1989.

Whalley, John, ed. *Canada and the Multilateral Trading System: Macdonald Royal Commission Study, Volume 10*. Toronto: University of Toronto Press, 1985.

– *Canada–United States Free Trade. Macdonald Royal Commission Study, Volume 11*. Toronto: University of Toronto Press, 1985.

– *Domestic Policies and the International Economic Environment: Macdonald Royal Commission Study, Volume 12*. Toronto: University of Toronto Press, 1985.

Whalley, John, and Irene Trela. *Regional Aspects of Confederation: Macdonald Royal Commission Study, Volume 68*. Toronto: University of Toronto Press, 1986.

Whalley, John, with Colleen Hamilton and Roderick Hill. *Canadian Trade Policies and the World Economy: Macdonald Royal Commission Study, Volume 9*. Toronto: University of Toronto Press, 1985.

Whitaker, Reginald. 'Neo-Conservatism and the State.' In *The Socialist Register 1987*, edited by R. Miliband, L. Panitch, and J. Saville, 1–31. London: Merlin, 1987.

Whittington, Michael S., and Glen Williams, eds. *Canadian Politics in the 1980s*. 2nd ed. Toronto: Methuen, 1984.

Wilkinson, Bruce. 'Commercial Policy and Free Trade with the United States.' In *Canada among Nations, 1984: A Time of Transition*, edited by Brian W. Tomlin and Maureen Molot, 164–84. Toronto: Lorimer, 1985.

Williams, Glen. 'Afterword: The March to Continental Free Trade.' In Glen Williams, *Not For Export: Toward a Political Economy of Canada's Arrested Industrialization*. Updated ed., 173–86. Toronto: McClelland and Stewart, 1986.

– *Not For Export: The International Competitiveness of Canadian Manufacturing*. 3rd ed. Toronto: McClelland and Stewart, 1994.

– 'Regions within Region: Continentalism Ascendant.' In *Canadian Politics in the*

1990s. 4th ed., edited by Michael S. Whittington and Glen Williams, 19–39. Toronto: Nelson, 1995.

Willis, J. 'Comment: The Role of the Public Inquiry in Our Constitutional System.' In *Law and Social Change*, edited by J.S. Ziegel, 98–101. Toronto: Carswell, 1973.

Wilson, V. Seymour. 'The Role of Royal Commissions and Task Forces.' In *The Structures of Policy Making in Canada*, edited by Peter Aucoin and G. Bruce Doern, 113–29. Toronto: Macmillan, 1971.

Winham, Gilbert R. *Canada-US Sectoral Trade Study: The Impact of Free Trade.* Halifax: Centre for Foreign Policy Studies, Dalhousie University, 1986.

Wolfe, David A. 'The Rise and Demise of the Keynesian Era in Canada: Economic Policy 1930–1982.' In *Modern Canada 1930-1980s*, edited by Michael S. Cross and Gregory S. Kealey, 46–80. Toronto: McClelland and Stewart, 1984.

– 'The State and Economic Policy in Canada, 1968–1975,' In *The Canadian State: Political Economy and Political Power*, edited by Leo Panitch, 251–88. Toronto: University of Toronto Press, 1977.

Wooton, Ian. 'The Case for a More Liberal Trade Regime.' In *Crosscurrents: Contemporary Political Issues.* 2nd ed., edited by Mark Charlton and Paul Barker, 516–24. Scarborough, ON: Nelson, 1994. 516–24.

Young, John H. *Canadian Commercial Policy.* Ottawa: Queen's Printer, 1957.

Yudelman, David. *Mining and the Macdonald Commission: The State of the Industry in the Mid-1980s.* Kingston: Centre for Resource Studies, 1985.

Periodical Articles and Unpublished Papers

Abbott, M.G. 'Labour Economics Research of the Macdonald Commission: A Review of Volumes 17 and 18.' *Canadian Public Policy* 12, 4 (December 1986): 628–39.

Aglietta, Michel. 'World Capitalism in the Eighties,' *New Left Review* 136 (November-December 1982): 5–41.

Archer, Keith, and Alan Whitehorn. 'Opinion Structure among New Democratic Activists: A Comparison with Liberals and Conservatives.' *Canadian Journal of Political Science* 23, 1 (March 1990): 101–13.

Auld, Douglas. 'Human Resources and Social Support Policy in Canada.' *Canadian Public Policy* 12, supplement (February 1986): 84–91.

Averyt, William F. 'Canadian Development Priorities and U.S. Trade Policy: Recent Trends and a Changing Future?' *American Review of Canadian Studies* 21, 1 (Spring 1986): 59–72.

Barber, Clarence. 'Jobs, Jobs: Specific Proposals.' *Policy Options* (April 1986): 3–4.

– 'The Macdonald Commission in Retrospect.' Unpublished paper presented to the Learned Societies Conference, Winnipeg, University of Manitoba, 1986.
– 'Research Aided Foreign Trade Pact.' *Financial Post* (14 December 1989): 12.
Bashevkin, Sylvia. 'Does Public Opinion Matter? The Adoption of Federal Royal Commission and Task Force Recommendations on the National Question, 1951–1987.' *Canadian Public Administration* 31, 1 (Fall 1988): 390–407.
Bedard, George J. 'Constructing Knowledge: Realist and Radical Learning Within a Canadian Royal Commission.' *Educational Policy* 13, 1 (January and March 1999): 152–65.
Berger, Thomas. 'The Mackenzie Valley Pipeline Inquiry.' *Queen's Law Journal* 3 (1976): 639–54.
Bombak, Anna. 'Canadian Federal Royal Commissions, 1978–1988: An Update.' *Input* 10, 2 (March 1989): 1–12.
Brady, Alexander. 'The Meaning of Canadian Nationalism.' *International Journal* 19, 2 (Summer 1964): 348–63.
Brecher, Irving. 'Burying Industrial Strategy.' *Policy Options* 4 (September–October 1983): 19–21.
– 'Strengthening the Trade Case.' *Policy Options* 7, 1 (January 1986): 24–9.
Brenner, Robert, and Mark Glick. 'The Regulation Approach: Theory and History.' *New Left Review* 188 (July/August 1991): 45–119.
Breton, Albert. 'The Economics of Nationalism.' *Journal of Political Economy* 74, 4 (1964): 376–86.
Cairns, Alan. 'Political Science in Canada and the Americanization Issue.' *Canadian Journal of Political Science* 8, 2 (June 1975): 191–234.
Cameron, David R. 'Not Spicer and Not the B & B: Reflections of an Insider on the Workings of the Pepin-Robarts Task Force on Canadian Unity.' *International Journal of Canadian Studies* 7, 8 (Spring-Fall 1993): 333–45.
Cameron, Duncan, and Daniel Drache. 'Outside the Macdonald Commission: Reply to Richard Simeon.' *Studies in Political Economy* 26 (Summer 1988): 173–80.
Campbell, Robert Malcolm. 'Post-Keynesian Politics and the Post-Schumpeterian World.' *Canadian Journal of Political and Social Theory* 8 (Winter 1984): 72–91.
'Canada and the United States: An Evolving Partnership." *The CRIC Papers*. Ottawa: Centre for Research and Information on Canada, 2003.
'Canada-U.S. Trade and Policy Issues.' *Canadian Public Policy* 8 (October 1982): 405–514.
Canadian Review of Studies in Nationalism. Special Issue on Anglo-Canadian Nationalism, 1980.
Carmichael, Edward A., Wendy Dobson, and Richard G. Lipsey. 'The Mac-

donald Report: Signpost or Shopping Basket?' *Canadian Public Policy* 12, supplement (February 1986): 23–39.

Carroll, William K. 'The Canadian Corporate Elite: Financiers or Finance Capitalists?' *Studies in Political Economy* 8 (Summer 1982): 89–114.

Chernomas, Bob. 'Keynesian, Monetarist and Post-Keynesian Policy: A Marxist Analysis.' *Studies in Political Economy* 10 (Winter 1983): 123–42.

Christian, William. 'A Note on Rod Preece and Red Tories.' *Canadian Journal of Political and Social Theory* 2 (Spring-Summer 1978): 128–34.

Clarkson, Stephen. 'Anti-Nationalism in Canada: The Ideology of Mainstream Economics.' *Canadian Review of Studies in Nationalism* 5, 1 (Spring 1978): 45–65.

– 'Continentalism: The Conceptual Challenge for Canadian Social Science.' Unpublished paper presented to the Canadian Sociology and Anthropology Association, Montreal, June 1985.

Clement, Wallace. 'Inside "The Canadian Establishment": Trivia or Tempest?' *This Magazine* 10 (April-May 1976): 30–2.

Cohen, Marjorie. 'The Macdonald Report and Its Implications for Women.' *Feminist Action Feministe* 1 (December 1985): 13–15.

Coleman, William. 'The Capitalist Class and the State: Changing Roles of Business Interest Associations.' *Studies in Political Economy* 20 (1986): 135–59.

Conklin, David W., and Thomas J. Courchene. 'New Institutions for a Market Economy.' *Canadian Public Policy* 12, supplement (February 1986): 40–50.

Connelly, Patricia. 'Capital and the State in Canada: Critical Questions in Carroll's Finance Capitalists.' *Studies in Political Economy* 12 (Fall 1983): 163–8.

Courtney, John C. 'In Defense of Royal Commissions.' *Canadian Public Administration* 12 (Fall 1969): 198–212.

Coyne, Andrew. 'A Decade of Macdonaldism.' *Globe and Mail* (9 September 1995): D3.

Cross, William, and Lisa Young. 'Policy Attitudes of Party Members in Canada: Evidence of Ideological Politics.' *Canadian Journal of Political Science* 35, 4 (December 2002): 859–80.

Cuneo, Carl J. 'The Controlled Entry of Canadian Managers to the United States.' *International Journal of Comparative Sociology* 18 (March-June 1977): 81–101.

– 'The Social Basis of Political Continentalism in Canada.' *Canadian Review of Sociology and Anthropology* 13, 1 (1976): 55–70.

De Vroey, Michael. 'A Regulation Approach Interpretation of the Contemporary Crisis.' *Capital and Class* 23 (Summer 1984): 45–66.

Dolan, Michael B., Brian W. Tomlin, and Harald von Riekhoff. 'Integration and Autonomy in Canada–United States Relations, 1963–1972.' *Canadian Journal of Political Science* 15, 2 (June 1982): 331–63.

d'Ombrain, Nicholas. 'Public Inquiries in Canada." *Canadian Public Administration* 40, 1 (Spring 1997): 86–107.

Drache, Daniel. 'The Crisis of Canadian Political Economy: Dependency Theory versus the New Orthodoxy.' *Canadian Journal of Political and Social Theory* (Special Issue: 'Beyond Dependency') 7 (Fall 1983): 25–49.

– 'The Macdonald Commission: The Politics of Neo-Conservatism.' *Atkinson Review of Canadian Studies* 3, 1 (Spring 1986): 21–6.

– 'Reject Macdonald.' *Policy Options* (June 1986): 22–3.

– 'Whatever Happened to Canadian Nationalism?' *Canadian Dimension* 18 (October–November 1984): 15–20.

Drummond, Ian M. 'On Disbelieving the Commissioners' Free Trade Case.' *Canadian Public Policy* 12, supplement (February 1986): 59–67.

Ernst, Alan. 'From Liberal Continentalism to Neoconservatism: North American Free Trade and the Politics of the C.D. Howe Institute.' *Studies in Political Economy* 39 (Autumn 1992): 109–40.

Evans, Patricia M. 'Holes in the Social Safety Net: The Macdonald Commission and the Guaranteed Annual Income.' *Atkinson Review of Canadian Studies* 3, 1 (Spring 1986): 33–6.

Finn, Ed. 'The Struggle for Canadian Labour Autonomy.' *Labour Gazette* 70 (November 1970).

Forbes, H.D. 'Hartz-Horowitz at Twenty: Nationalism, Toryism and Socialism in Canada and the United States.' *Canadian Journal of Political Science* 20, 2 (June 1987): 287–315.

– 'Rejoinder to "A Note on "Hartz-Horowitz at Twenty"": The Case of French Canada.' *Canadian Journal of Political Science* 21, 4 (December 1988): 807–11.

Fulford, Robert. 'Mission Impossible.' *Saturday Night* 100, 3 (March 1985): 34–41.

Furlong, Kieran, and Douglas Moggach. 'Efficiency, Competition and Full Employment in Canadian Free Trade Literature.' *Studies in Political Economy* 33 (Autumn 1990): 135–59.

Gibbins, Roger, and Neal Nevitte. 'Canadian Political Ideology: A Comparative Analysis.' *Canadian Journal of Political Science* 18, 1 (March 1985): 577–98.

Glenday, Daniel. 'Canada, the Left and Free Trade,' *Queen's Quarterly* 95, 2 (Summer 1988): 251–84.

Goldstein, Judith. 'Ideas, Institutions, and American Trade Policy.' *International Organization* 42, 1 (Winter 1998): 179–217.

Gonick, Cy. 'Boom and Bust: State Policy and the Economics of Restructuring.' *Studies in Political Economy* 11 (Summer 1983): 27–47.

Gotlieb, Alan, and J. Kinsman. 'Reviving the Third Option,' *International Perspectives* (January/February 1981): 2–5.

Gourevitch, Peter. 'Breaking with Orthodoxy: The Politics of Economic Policy

Responses to the Great Depression of the 1930s.' *International Organization* 38 (Winter 1984): 95–130.

Grant, John. 'The Macdonald Commission on Stabilization Policy.' *Canadian Public Policy* 12 supplement (February 1986): 76–83.

Grayson, J. Paul. 'The Ignored Costs of the Macdonald Solution.' *Atkinson Review of Canadian Studies* 3, 1 (Spring 1986): 29–31.

Haglund, David G. 'Unbridled Constraint: The Macdonald Commission Volumes on Canada and the International Political Economy.' *Canadian Journal of Political Science* 20, 3 (September 1987): 598–624.

Hale, Geoffrey E. 'Reintegrating Federal Economic and Social Policies in the 1990s – Implementing Macdonald's Ideas by Trail and Error.' Paper presented to the annual meeting of the Canadian Political Science Association, Laval University, 30 May 2001.

Hall, Peter A. 'Keynes in Political Science.' *History of Political Economy* 26, 1 (1994): 137–53.

– 'Policy Paradigms, Social Learning, and the State: The Case of Economic Policymaking in Britain.' *Comparative Politics* (April 1993): 275–97.

– 'Political Science and the Three New Institutionalisms.' *Political Studies* 44 (1996): 936–57.

Hanson, Hugh R. 'Inside Royal Commissions.' *Canadian Public Administration* 12 (Fall 1969): 356–64.

Hart, Michael. 'A History of Canada-U.S. Free Trade.' http://www.freetradeat10.com/hart.html (1999).

– 'Almost but Not Quite: The 1947–1948 Bilateral Canada-U.S. Negotiations.' *American Review of Canadian Studies* 19, 1 (Spring 1989): 25–58.

Henderson, Michael D. 'The "Global Outlook": Through a Glass Darkly.' *Atkinson Review of Canadian Studies* 3, 1 (Spring 1986): 17–20.

Hodgetts, J.E. 'The Role of Royal Commissions in Canadian Government.' *Proceedings of the Third Annual Conference of the Institute of Public Administration of Canada, 1951* (1951): 351–76.

– 'Royal Commission on Government Administration.' *Canadian Journal of Economics* 32 (November 1966): 528–31.

– 'Should Canada Be De-Commissioned? A Commoner's View of Royal Commissions.' *Queen's Quarterly* 70 (Winter 1964): 457–90.

Horowitz, Gad. 'Conservatism, Liberalism and Socialism in Canada: An Interpretation.' *Canadian Journal of Economics and Political Science* 32, 2 (May 1966): 143–71.

Horsman, Mathew. 'Still Awaiting Commission's Brave New World.' *Financial Post*, 12 December 1989, 14.

Houle, François. 'Economic Strategy and the Restructuring of the Fordist Wage-

Labour Relationship in Canada.' *Studies in Political Economy* 11 (Summer 1983): 127–47.

Hum, Derek P.J. 'UISP and the Macdonald Commission: Reform and Restraint.' *Canadian Public Policy* 12, supplement (February 1986): 92–100.

Hurl, L.F., and D.J. Tucker. 'Limitations of an Act of Faith: An Analysis of the Macdonald Commission's Stance on Social Services.' *Canadian Public Policy* 12, 4 (December 1986): 606–21.

Innis, Harold Adams. 'The Rowell-Sirois Report.' *Canadian Journal of Economics and Political Science* 6 (1940): 562–71.

Jenson, Jane. '"Different" but Not "Exceptional": Canada's Permeable Fordism,' *Canadian Review of Sociology and Anthropology* 26, 1 (1989): 69–94.

'Gender and Reproduction: or, Babies and the State.' *Studies in Political Economy* 20 (Summer 1986): 9–46.

'Learning by Doing: Decision-Making in Royal Commissions.' Unpublished paper presented for discussion by the Royal Commission on Aboriginal Peoples, 13 August 1992.

'Naming Names: Making Nationalist Claims in Canadian Public Discourse' *Canadian Review of Sociology and Anthropology* 30, 3 (1993): 337–58.

'Paradigms and Political Discourse: Protective Legislation in France and the United States before 1914.' *Canadian Journal of Political Science* 22, 2 (June 1989): 235–58.

'Rebel Sons: The Regulation School. An Interview with Alain Lipietz.' *French Politics and Society* 5, 4 (September 1987): 17–26.

'Representations in Crisis: The Roots of Canada's Permeable Fordism.' *Canadian Journal of Political Science* 23, 4 (December 1990): 653–83.

Kellog, Paul. 'State, Capital and World Economy: Bukharin's Marxism and the "Dependency/Class" Controversy in Canadian Political Economy.' *Canadian Journal of Political Science* 22, 2 (June 1989): 337–62.

Kennedy, Emmet. '"Ideology" From Destutt de Tracy to Marx,' *Journal of the History of Ideas* 40, 3 (July-September 1979): 353–68.

Kesselman, Jonathan. 'The Royal Commission's Proposals for Income Security Reform.' *Canadian Public Policy* 12, supplement (February 1986): 101–12.

Kierans, Eric. 'Canada and the New U.S. Empire.' *Canadian Forum* 63 (January 1984): 5–6.

Kristol, Irving. 'What Is a "Neoconservative"?' *Newsweek*, 19 January 1976, 17.

Langille, David. 'The Business Council on National Issues and the Canadian State.' *Studies in Political Economy* 24 (Autumn 1987): 41–85.

Laxer, Gordon. 'Class, Nationality and the Roots of Canada's Branch Plant Economy.' *Studies in Political Economy* 21 (Autumn 1986): 7–56.

– 'Foreign Ownership and Myths about Canadian Development.' *Canadian Review of Sociology and Anthropology* 22, 3 (August 1985): 311–45.

Lazar, Fred. 'The Economics of the Macdonald Commission.' *Atkinson Review of Canadian Studies* 3, 1 (Spring 1986): 8–14.

Lindquist, Evert A. 'Think Tanks or Clubs? Assessing the Influence and Roles of Canadian Policy Institutes.' *Canadian Public Administration* 36, 4 (Winter 1993): 547–79.

Lipietz, Alain. 'Imperialism or the Beast of the Apocalypse.' *Capital and Class* 22 (Spring 1984): 81–109.

– 'Toward Global Fordism?' *New Left Review* 132 (March-April 1982): 33–47.

Litchfield, Randall. 'The Macdonald Commission's Other Recommendation.' *Canadian Business* 65, 5 (May 1992): 23.

Litt, Paul. 'The Massey Commission, Americanization and Canadian Cultural Nationalism.' *Queen's Quarterly* 98, 2 (Summer 1991): 375–87.

Litvak, Isaiah A. 'Freer Trade with the United States: Conflicting Views of Canadian Business.' *Business Quarterly* 51, 1 (Spring 1986): 30–1.

Macdonald, Donald S. 'Chapter 11 of NAFTA: What Are the Implications for Sovereignty?' *Canada-United States Law Journal* 24 (1998): 261–9.

Macdonald, L.R. 'Merchants against Industry: An Idea and Its Origins.' *Canadian Historical Review* 56 (September 1975): 263–81.

'The Macdonald Report: Twelve Reviews.' *Canadian Public Policy* 12, Supplement (February 1986).

Matkin, James. 'The Future of Industrial Relations in Canada.' *Canadian Public Policy* 12, supplement (February 1986): 127–32.

McCall-Newman, Christina. 'Michael Pitfield and the Politics of Mismanagement.' *Saturday Night* 97, 10 (October 1982): 24–44.

Mendelsohn, Matthew, Robert Wolfe and Andrew Parkin. 'Globalization, Trade Policy and the Permissive Consensus in Canada.' *Working Paper 27.* Kingston, ON: Queen's University School of Policy Studies (November 2001).

Mulgrew, Ian. 'Stumbling Out of the Starting Gate: Macdonald Commission Strives for Credibility.' *Globe and Mail,* 10 September 1983.

Murray, Robin. 'The Internationalization of Capital and the Nation State.' *New Left Review* 67 (May-June 1971): 84–109.

Myles, John. 'Introduction: Understanding Canada: Comparative Political Economy Perspectives,' *Canadian Review of Sociology and Anthropology* 26, 1 (1989): 1–9.

Nevitte, Neal, and Roger Gibbins. 'Neo-Conservatism: Canadian Variations on an Ideological Theme?' *Canadian Public Policy* 10, 4 (December 1984): 384–94.

Niosi, Jorge. 'The Canadian Bourgeoisie: Towards a Synthetical Approach.' *Canadian Journal of Political and Social Theory* (Special Issue: 'Beyond Dependency') 7 (Fall 1983): 128–49.

Nöel, Alain. 'Accumulation, Regulation and Social Change: An Essay on French Political Economy.' *International Organization* 41 (Spring 1987): 303–33.

Oliver, Michael. 'The Impact of the Royal Commission on Bilingualism and Biculturalism on Constitutional Thought and Practice in Canada.' *International Journal of Canadian Studies* 7, 8 (Spring-Fall 1993): 316–32.

Ornstein, Michael D., and H. Michael Stevenson. 'Ideology and Public Policy in Canada.' *British Journal of Political Science* 14 (1984): 313–44.

Panitch, Leo. 'Dependency and Class in Canadian Political Economy.' *Studies in Political Economy* 6 (Autumn 1981): 7–33.

Pratt, Cranford. 'Dominant Class Theory and Canadian Foreign Policy: The Case of the Counter-Consensus.' *International Journal* 39, 1 (1983–4): 99–117.

Pratt, Larry. 'Energy: The Roots of National Policy.' *Studies in Political Economy* 7 (Winter 1982): 27–59.

Preece, Rod. 'Liberal-Conservatism and Feudalism in Canadian Politics: A Response to Christian.' *Canadian Journal of Political and Social Theory* 2 (Spring-Summer 1978): 135–41.

– 'The Myth of the Red Tory.' *Canadian Journal of Political and Social Theory* 1 (Spring-Summer 1977): 3–28.

– 'Tory Myth and Conservative Reality: Horowitz Revisited.' *Canadian Journal of Political and Social Theory* 2 (Winter 1978): 175–8.

Proulx, Pierre-Paul. 'Free Trade Is Not Enough.' *Policy Options* 7, 1 (January 1986): 11–16.

Puxley, Peter. 'A Model of Engagement: Reflections on the 25th Anniversary of the Berger Report,' *Canadian Policy Research Networks* (August 2002): 1–14.

'Rebutting the Macdonald Report.' *The Facts.* (Canadian Union of Public Employees) 8, 2 (March-April 1986).

Reder, Melvin W. 'Chicago Economics: Permanence and Change.' *Journal of Economic Literature* 20 (March 1982): 1–38.

Redekop, John H. 'A Reinterpretation of the Canadian-American Relationship.' *Canadian Journal of Political Science* 9, 2 (June 1976): 227–43.

Resnick, Philip. 'The Maturing of Canadian Capitalism.' *Our Generation* 15 (Fall 1982): 11–24.

– 'State and Civil Society: The Limits of a Royal Commission.' *Canadian Journal of Political Science* 20, 2 (June 1987): 379–401.

'The Right Stuff: A Critique of the Macdonald Commission Report.' *Atkinson Review of Canadian Studies* 3 (Spring 1986).

Rocher, François. 'Canadian Business, Free Trade and the Rhetoric of Economic Continentalization.' *Studies in Political Economy* 35 (Summer 1991): 135–54.

Rotstein, Abraham. 'Is There an English Canadian Nationalism?' *Journal of Canadian Studies* 13 (Summer 1978): 109–18.

Rutland, Peter. 'The Flourishing Literature on Nationalism.' *Choice* (February 1995): 901–9.

Ryerson, Stanley. 'Who's Looking After Business? A Review.' *This Magazine* 10 (November–December 1976): 41–6.

Schmidt, Ray. 'Canadian Political Economy: A Critique.' *Studies in Political Economy* 6 (1981): 65–92.

Schwartz, Bryan. 'Public Inquiries.' *Canadian Public Administration* 40, 1 (Spring 1997): 72–85.

Scott, Robert E. et al. 'NAFTA at Seven: Its Impact on Workers in All Three Nations.' *Briefing Paper*. Washington, DC: Economic Policy Institute, 2001.

Seward, Shirley. 'More and Younger?' *Policy Options* 7, 1 (January 1986): 16–19.

Sexty, Robert W. 'The Ideology of Canadian Business.' *Canadian Issues / Themes Canadiens: Topics on Canadian Business* 10, 3 (1988): 23–46.

Sharp, Mitchell. 'Canada-U.S. Relations: Options For the Future.' *International Perspectives* (Autumn 1972): 1–24.

Shearer, Ronald A. 'The New Face of Canadian Mercantilism: The Macdonald Commission and the Case for Free Trade.' *Canadian Public Policy* 12, supplement (February 1986): 51–8.

Shugarman, David P. 'The Problems of the Reluctant Nationalist: A Comment on Alan Cairn's "Political Science in Canada and the Americanization Issue."' *Canadian Journal of Political Science* 9, 1 (March 1976): 121–6.

Simeon, Richard. 'Inside the Macdonald Commission.' *Studies in Political Economy* 22 (Spring 1987): 167–79.

Smiley, Donald. 'Canada and the Quest for a National Policy.' *Canadian Journal of Political Science* 8 (March 1975): 40–62.

– 'The Three Pillars of the Canadian Constitutional Order.' *Canadian Public Policy* 12, supplement (February 1986): 113–21.

Smith, Michael. 'Sectoral Free Trade With Canada.' *International Perspectives* (May/June 1984): 17–18.

Smith, Miriam. 'The Canadian Labour Congress: From Continentalism to Economic Nationalism,' *Studies in Political Economy* 38 (Summer 1992): 35–60.

Stevenson, Garth. 'Canadian Regionalism in Continental Perspective.' *Journal of Canadian Studies* 15, 2 (Summer 1980): 16–28.

– 'The Political Economy Tradition and Canadian Federalism.' *Studies in Political Economy* 6 (1981): 113–33.

Tillett, Anthony. 'Technology Needs a Framework.' *Policy Options* 7, 1 (January 1986): 19–23.

Truman, Tom. 'A Scale for Measuring a Tory Streak in Canada and the United States.' *Canadian Journal of Political Science* 10 (1977): 597–614.

Tupper, Allan. 'Think Tanks, Public Debt, and the Politics of Expertise in Canada.' *Canadian Public Administration* 36, 4 (Winter 1993): 530–46.

Walkom, Tom. 'Tory Talk: How the Conservatives Captured the English Language.' *This Magazine* 18, 6 (February 1985): 5–8.

Walls, C.E.S. 'Royal Commissions: Their Influence on Public Policy.' *Canadian Public Administration* 12 (Fall 1969): 365–71.

Warrack, Allan. 'Spurs to Resource Development.' *Policy Options* 7, 1 (January 1986): 29–32.

Watkins, Mel. 'The Economics of Nationalism and the Nationality of Economics: A Critique of Neoclassical Theorizing.' *Canadian Journal of Economics* 11 (November 1978): 87–120.

– 'The Innis Tradition in Canadian Political Economy.' *Canadian Journal of Political and Social Theory* 6 (Winter-Spring 1982): 12–34.

– 'The Waffle and the National Question.' *Studies in Political Economy* 32 (Summer 1990): 173–6.

Wherrett, Jill. 'The Research Agenda of the Royal Commission on Aboriginal Peoples.' *Canadian Public Administration* 38, 2 (Summer 1995): 272–82.

Whitaker, Reg, et al. 'The Waffle: 20th Anniversary Reflections.' *Studies in Political Economy* 32 (Summer 1990): 167–201.

Williams, A. Paul. 'Access and Accommodation in the Canadian Welfare State: The Political Significance of Contacts Between State, Labour and Business Leaders.' *Canadian Review of Sociology and Anthropology* 26, 2 (1989): 217–39.

Williams, Glen. 'On Determining Canada's Location within the International Political Economy.' *Studies in Political Economy* 25 (Spring 1988): 107–40.

Wiseman, Nelson. 'A Note on "Hartz-Horowitz at Twenty": The Case of French Canada,' *Canadian Journal of Political Science* 21, 4 (December 1988): 795–806.

– 'The Pattern of Prairie Politics.' *Queen's Quarterly* 88, 2 (Summer 1981): 298–315.

Wolfe, David A. 'The Canadian State in Comparative Perspective.' *Canadian Review of Sociology and Anthropology* 26, 1 (1989): 95–126.

– 'Economic Growth and Foreign Investment: A Perspective on Canadian Economic Policy.' *Journal of Canadian Studies* 13 (Spring 1978): 3–20.

Wolfson, Michael. 'A Guaranteed Income.' *Policy Options* 7, 1 (January 1986): 35–45.

Wonnacott, R.J. 'Trade Liberalization: Canadian contributions since the 1960s.' *Canadian Journal of Economics* 26, 1 (February 1993): 14–25.

Young, Robert A. 'Political Scientists, Economists and the Canada-U.S. Free Trade Agreement.' *Canadian Public Policy* 15 (1989): 49–56.

Yudelman, David. 'The Practice of Consensus.' *Policy Options* 6, 8 (October 1985): 6–7.

Government Publications

Berger, Thomas. *Northern Frontier, Northern Homeland: The Report of the Mackenzie Valley Pipeline Inquiry*. Ottawa: Supply and Services Canada, 1977.

Britton, John N.H., and James M. Gilmour. *The Weakest Link: A Technological Perspective on Canadian Industrial Underdevelopment*. Background Study no. 43. Ottawa: Science Council of Canada, 1978.

Brown, Douglas, and Julia Eastman. *The Limits of Consultation: A Debate among Ottawa, the Provinces and the Private Sector on Industrial Strategy*. Discussion Paper Prepared by the Institute of Intergovernmental Relations, Queen's University. Ottawa: Supply and Services, 1981.

Campbell, Robert M. *The Full Employment Objective in Canada, 1945–1985: Historical, Conceptual, and Comparative Perspectives. A Study Prepared for the Economic Council of Canada*. Ottawa: Supply and Services, 1991.

Canada. *Final Report of the Royal Commission on Canada's Economic Prospects* (The Gordon Commission). 1958.

– *Report of the Royal Commission on Aboriginal Peoples*. Ottawa: Indian and Northern Canada, 1996.

Canada. Department of External Affairs. *The Canada-U.S. Free Trade Agreement*. Ottawa: Supply and Services, 1987.

– *Canadian Trade Policy for the 1980's: A Discussion Paper*. Ottawa: Supply and Services, 1983.

– *Competitiveness and Security: Directions for Canada's International Relations*. Ottawa: Supply and Services, 1985.

– *How to Secure and Enhance Access to Export Markets*. Ottawa: Supply and Services, 1985.

– *A Review of Canadian Trade Policy: A Background Document to Canadian Trade Policy for the 1980s*. Ottawa: Supply and Services, 1983.

Canada. Department of Finance. *Agenda for Renewal*. Ottawa: Supply and Services, 1984.

Canada. Department of Trade and Commerce. *Foreign Direct Investment in Canada* (The Gray Report). 1972.

Canada. Economic Council of Canada. *The Bottom Line: Technology, Trade and Income Growth*. Ottawa: Economic Council of Canada, 1983.

– *Looking Outward: A New Trade Strategy for Canada*. Ottawa: Economic Council of Canada, 1975.

Canada. Law Reform Commission of Canada. *Commissions of Inquiry: A New Act. Working Paper 17*. Ottawa: Supply and Services, 1977.

Canada. National Library of Canada. *Index to Royal Commissions*. www.nlc-bnc.ca/indexcommissions/index-e.html

Canada. Parliament, Standing Committee on Foreign Affairs. *Canada-United States Relations*. Volume 11. *Canada's Trade Relations with the United States*. Ottawa: Supply and Services, 1982.

Canada. Privy Council Office. *Commissions of Inquiry*. www.pco-bcp.gc.ca

Canada. Royal Commission on Corporate Concentration. *Report*. Ottawa: Royal Commission on Corporate Concentration, 1978.

Canada. Royal Commission on the Economic Union and Development Prospects for Canada (Macdonald Commission). *A Commission on Canada's Future: Be Part of It*. Ottawa: Supply and Services, 1983.

– *A Commission on Canada's Future: Challenges and Choices*. Ottawa: Supply and Services, 1984.

– *Report*. 3 vols. Ottawa: Supply and Services, 1985.

– *Research for the Commission on Canada's Future: A Progress Report*. Ottawa: Supply and Services, 1984.

Canada. Science Council of Canada. *Hard Times, Hard Choices: Technology and the Balance of Payments*. A Statement by the Science Council Industrial Policies Committee. Ottawa: Science Council of Canada, 1981.

Canada. Task Force on the Structure of Canadian Industry. *Foreign Ownership and the Structure of Canadian Industry*. (The Watkins Report). 1968.

Government of Canada. *Minutes of Proceedings and Evidence of the Special Joint Committee of the Senate and the House of Commons on Canada's International Relations*. Ottawa: Queen's Printer, 1985.

Ledoux, Denise. *Commissions of Inquiry under the Inquiries Act, Part I, 1867 to Date*. Ottawa: Library of Parliament, Information and References Branch, February, 1980.

Ledoux, Denise, updated by C. Russo. *Commissions of Inquiry under the Inquiries Act, Part I, 1867 to Date*. Ottawa: Library of Parliament, Information and References Branch, February, 1997.

Merchant, Livingston P., and A.D.P. Heeney. 'Canada and the United States: Principles for Partnership.' *Department of State Bulletin*. 2 August 1965.

Ontario. Law Reform Commission. *Report on Public Inquiries*. Toronto: Ontario Law Reform Commission, 1992.

Steed, Guy P.F. *Threshold Firms: Backing Canada's Winners*. Background Study no. 48. Ottawa: Science Council of Canada, 1982.

Whalen, Murray. *Records of Federal Royal Commissions*. Ottawa: National Archives of Canada, 1990–19994.

Dissertations and Theses

Anderson, Barry L. 'Royal Commissions, Economists and Policy: A Study of the

Economic Advisory Process in Post-War Canada.' PhD dissertation, Duke University, 1978.

Clark, Melissa Helen. 'The Canadian State and Staples: An Ear to Washington.' PhD dissertation, McMaster University, 1980.

Cuneo, Carl J. 'Social Class, Language and the National Question in Canada: An Analysis of the Social Support for the Integration of Canada With the United States.' PhD dissertation, University of Waterloo, 1973.

Fransen, David. 'Unscrewing the Unscrutable: The Rowell-Sirois Commission, the Ottawa Bureaucracy and Public Finance Reform, 1935–1941.' PhD dissertation, University of Toronto, 1984.

Inwood, Gregory J. 'Nationalism versus Continentalism: Ideology in the Mirror of the Macdonald Royal Commission.' PhD dissertation, University of Toronto, 1997.

Litt, Paul R. 'The Donnish Inquisition: The Massey Commission and the Campaign for State-Sponsored Cultural Nationalism in Canada, 1949–1951.' PhD dissertation, University of Toronto, 1990.

McCready, John. 'Political Ideology and Social Policy: Expenditure and Revenue in Three Canadian Provinces, 1947–60.' PhD dissertation, University of Toronto, 1983.

Wolfe, David A. 'The Delicate Balance: The Changing Economic Role of the State in Canada.' PhD dissertation, University of Toronto, 1980.

Index

Breton, Albert, 77, 81, 159, 161–2,
  166, 183, 185, 187, 203, 236, 249–50,
  266–8 (*passim*), 272–3, 276, 281–92
  (*passim*), 305, 370n8, 387n37,
  389n62, n68, 405n27, 407nn93–5,
  408nn97–9, 408nn5–6, n18, 409n19,
  nn37–9, 410nn55–6, n62, n64, n72,
  411nn77–80, n82
Bretton Woods, 28
'Briefing Notes for Commissioners,'
  67, 83
Britain (or Great Britain), 9, 140, 280,
  281
British, 209, 322
British Columbia, 81, 82, 115, 121,
  124, 135, 187
British Columbia Employer's Coun-
  cil, 295
British Columbia Resources Invest-
  ment Corporation, 115
British Columbia and Yukon Territory
  Building and Trading Council, 119
British Empire, 26
Britishness, 20
Britton, John N.H., 385n13
Broadbent, Ed, 292
Brock, Bill, 306
Brock, Kathy L., 357n66
Brodie, M. Janine, 313, 317, 348n21,
  354n36, 415nn46–7, 417n66
Bronfman family, 261
Brooks, Stephen, 155–8 (*passim*), 206,
  207, 384n11, 385n12, nn17–19,
  386n22, n26, n28, 387n32, 397n33–6
Brown, Craig, 18, 351n7
Bryce, R.B., 387n34
Brym, Robert J., 358n74
Buckingham, Quebec, 249
Burke, Mike, 346n9
Burney report, 42–3

Burns, Tom, 43
Burns Foods Limited, 149
Business Council on National Issues
  (BCNI), 33, 37, 39, 40, 44, 185, 229,
  254, 281–2, 301, 312, 316, 320

CBC, 21, 81, 257, 303
CCF (Cooperative Commonwealth
  Federation), 293
CCF-NBCP government, 81
C.D. Howe Institute, 21, 43, 44, 249
Cabinet, Canadian, 40, 260
Cairns, Alan, 88, 101, 158–75 (*passim*),
  183–9 (*passim*), 200, 205, 212–19
  (*passim*), 226, 229–32 (*passim*), 244,
  246, 265, 272–3, 276–7, 280, 284–6
  (*passim*), 289, 357n68, 369n1,
  372n15, 374n31, 387n36, 388n44,
  n46, n51, 389n61, n69, 391nn89–92,
  nn94–5, n99, 392n9, 393nn12–15,
  nn21–5, 396n30, 397n37, 399nn63–
  4, nn68–9, 401nn7–8, 402n20,
  nn23–5, 403n3, 404n4, nn11–12,
  407n86, 408nn2–3, n11, n17,
  409n20, nn31–2, 410nn47–8, n70
Calgary, 81
Calgary Chamber of Commerce, 112,
  115, 142, 145
Cambridge, UK, 263
Cameron, David R., 346n10, 349n29,
  363n9, n10, 364n13
Cameron, Duncan, 32, 34, 52, 64, 83,
  84, 98, 99, 102, 205, 207–8, 216, 300,
  345n4, 355n43, 357n69, 358n76,
  359n79, 365n24, 366n25, n27, n28,
  n30, 370n29, 372n3, n4, 373n20,
  374n33, 378n91, 379n4, 390n85,
  396n23, 412n11
Cameron, Maxwell A., 345n5, 359n82,
  413n19

Studies in Comparative Political Economy and Public Policy